MW00810635

The Encyclopedia of LGBTQIA+ Portrayals in American Film

The Encyclopedia of LGBTQIA+ Portrayals in American Film

Erica Joan Dymond
Salvador Jiménez Murguía

ROWMAN & LITTLEFIELD
Lanham • Boulder • New York • London

Published by Rowman & Littlefield
An imprint of The Rowman & Littlefield Publishing Group, Inc.
4501 Forbes Boulevard, Suite 200, Lanham, Maryland 20706
www.rowman.com

86-90 Paul Street, London EC2A 4NE, United Kingdom

British Library Cataloguing in Publication Information Available

Library of Congress Cataloging-in-Publication Data

Names: Dymond, Erica Joan, editor. | Murguía, Salvador Jimenez, editor.
Title: The encyclopedia of LGBTQIA+ portrayals in American film / Erica Joan Dymond and Salvador Jiménez Murguía.
Description: Lanham : Rowman & Littlefield, 2022. | Includes index. | Summary: "This fascinating reference explores the depiction of the LGBTQIA+ community in over 200 works from the past fifty years of American film history. It will not only educate and inform, but also help guide readers to see injustice more clearly and to inspire art that is both inclusive and thoughtful"—Provided by publisher.
Identifiers: LCCN 2022020105 (print) | LCCN 2022020106 (ebook) | ISBN 9781538153901 (cloth) | ISBN 9781538153918 (epub)
Subjects: LCSH: Homosexuality in motion pictures—Encyclopedias. | Sexual minorities in motion pictures—Encyclopedias. | Gays in motion pictures—Encyclopedias. | Motion pictures—United States—History.
Classification: LCC PN1995.9.H55 D96 2022 (print) | LCC PN1995.9.H55 (ebook) | DDC 791.43/65303—dc23/eng/20220510
LC record available at https://lccn.loc.gov/2022020105
LC ebook record available at https://lccn.loc.gov/2022020106

Contents

Acknowledgments

We would like to acknowledge the help, guidance, and support of Christen Karni-ski, senior acquisitions editor at Rowman & Littlefield.

We extend our gratitude to our loved ones. They gently tolerated our sleep-less nights, our endless staring at computer screens, and our frequent consulta-tions. Thank you for your patience and support as we toiled over this important volume.

A special note of appreciation must be extended to Andrew Grossman for his tremendous investment in this volume. Thank you for entrusting your work to us.

Without a doubt, we are extremely grateful to all of the contributors. Their unflagging devotion to this volume has resulted in genuinely impressive work. We are both awed by and appreciative of their thoughtful work. This volume would not exist without their tireless efforts. A heartfelt thank-you to all who invested their time and efforts into these entries.

Introduction

At the conclusion of Barack Obama's presidency, the White House website entered an "archiving phase," which is customary and accompanies a shift in administration. However, this time LGBTQIA+ issues were removed from the site. When they did not return, news services took notice. The *Washington Post* reported, "While it's standard for the new administration to update the White House's official website with its agenda as part of the transition, it is notable that the Trump administration did not choose to include anything about the LGBT community" (Itkowitz 2017). This sparked great concern that the new administration was silently erasing the rights afforded to the LGBTQIA+ community under the Obama administration. Those fears were founded. On July 26, 2017, the Trump administration proposed a ban on transgender people entering the military. As an article from the *Daily Beast* explains, "The policy reverses a 2016 decision by former President Obama that transgender individuals could serve their country openly, having found that they have minimal financial impact on the military" (McNamara 2019). Hope continued to wane when, in December 2019, the House of Representatives was unable to overturn the military ban (Burns 2019). Only days later, *HuffPost* announced that "President Donald Trump's Interior Department removed 'sexual orientation' from a statement in the agency's ethics guide regarding workplace discrimination" (D'Angelo 2019).

The diminishing rights of the LGBTQIA+ community extended beyond those at a national level. Individual states boldly began rescinding basic human liberties. In February 2019, Tennessee reintroduced the Tennessee Natural Marriage Defense Act, which restricts marriage to a union between a biological man and a biological woman. And on January 24, 2020, "Tennessee Gov. Bill Lee signed a controversial measure that would let religious adoption agencies deny service to same-sex couples" (Ebert 2020). Tennessee is now the eleventh state to have such a policy (Alabama, Kansas, Michigan, Mississippi, North Dakota, Oklahoma, South Carolina, South Dakota, Texas, and Virginia being the others). And while there are victories (like the Supreme Court denying an appeal to ban transgender people from using the bathroom congruent with their gender identity), numerous states are still working to curtail the rights of the LGBTQIA+ community. At this very moment, there is concerted effort to ban transgender people from athletics. As of October 2021, ten states "have enacted laws to bar transgender girls from participating in girls' sports at public schools" (Chen 2021). This blatant hostility toward the LGBTQIA+ community seems to increase on a daily basis. While many valiantly fight against this injustice, the "trend" shows no signs of abating.

Not contained to the political realm, this increasing oppression can be found in the arts. For instance, perhaps emboldened by the Trump administration, LGBTQIA+ portrayals in the arts have been subject to censorship. In May 2019, Alabama Public Television refused to air an episode of the long-running children's television show *Arthur* because it featured a wedding between two male animated characters. As reported by the BBC, "Programming director Mike McKenzie said broadcasting it would break parents' trust in the network" ("*Arthur*: Alabama Public Television Bans Gay Wedding Episode" 2019). Many viewed Alabama's decision as the beginning of a visible retaliation against the growing acceptance of the LGBTQIA+ community. In fact, in response to this ban on the *Arthur* episode, the *Week*'s Neil J. Young explained how this seemed emblematic of a new wave of hatred:

> The resistance to gay rights remains strongest among conservative Christians, and the churches they attend continue to oppose gay rights, some with growing stridency. Despite the seemingly favorable outlook for LGBTQ Americans in recent years, there's a sizable chunk of the country that has declared they won't capitulate to the cultural progress. Instead, they are working to set it back. (2019)

Unless there is radical change at all levels of business and politics, there is little doubt that more instances like the *Arthur* one loom on the horizon.

In an effort to extend compassion amid such cruelty, a multitude of artists have issued public apologies for previously using the LGBTQIA+ community as a source of comedic material. In January 2019, the executive producers of *Family Guy* stated that "gay jokes" would be phased out of the show. They specified, "Some of the things we felt comfortable saying and joking about back then, we now understand is not acceptable" (Swift 2019). However, since the show is a so-called "equal-opportunity offender," this reversal (in itself) seemed discriminatory. Here, leaving out the LGBTQIA+ community proved problematic for many queer viewers. In "Should *Family Guy* 'Phase Out' Gay Jokes?," *BBC News* offered the voices of LGBTQIA+ viewers as evidence that exclusion is not an acceptable choice. One viewer even (cleverly) noted, "I never felt like the gay jokes were at Stewie's expense, but rather an evolution of the character. . . . It seemed like the more queer he became, the less evil he was" (Rackham 2019). In under a year, the jokes were back, accompanied by a very "meta," very *Family Guy*–style acknowledgment. In season 19, episode 8, "Disney's *The Reboot*," Peter says of the embargo on gay jokes, "That quote was taken out of context and widely misunderstood." The results were similar when in May 2019 film actor Seth Rogen apologized for "gay jokes" like the ones found in *The 40-Year-Old Virgin*. In an interview with *GQ*, the actor reflected on his past work and the future. He simply noted, "We do not want people to feel bad when they're watching our movies" (McCloskey 2019). However, when *Queerty* addressed Rogen's announcement, the comment section lit up with consternation. Here, the feedback was vastly in favor of Rogen's old jokes with the sentiment that they were not told with "malice" (Reddish 2019). The complicated lesson learned by artists is that exclusion may be "safe" (and maybe even motivated by genuine compassion) but it is rarely the answer. Successfully navigating this complex environment has proven difficult for all artists who are allies of the LGBTQIA+ community. Certainly, this same fear is affecting the current cinematic depiction (and even inclusion) of the LGBTQIA+ community.

While many believe that current cinema can offer a more unfiltered and honest portrayal of the LGBTQIA+ community, that seems to be somewhat untrue. Recently, the awards-sweeping *Bohemian Rhapsody* came under serious scrutiny from the LGBTQIA+ community for "straightwashing" Freddie Mercury. Many reviewers and scholars pointed out that Mercury's bisexuality is suggested, but the rest is left for viewers to assume. While director Bryan Singer deflected the criticism by saying that he was not interested in making a cliché film about drugs and sex, actor Rami Maleck was more open in his reply:

> I totally understand. . . . He had a beautiful relationship with Jim Hutton, and we had a finite period in which we wanted to tell this story. . . . Believe me: There were conversations left and right about how to incorporate more of that story into this film. It was something I pushed for, to be quite honest, as much as possible and repeatedly brought to the attention of producers and directors and everyone who would listen. (Ryan 2018)

What remains most revealing is the sheer number of awards and accolades that this film earned. This seems to validate the concealing or coding of Mercury's sexual identity. And this is a dangerous precedent to set. In fact, "straightwashing" is shockingly common, even in current films. This especially applies to comic book heroes who are canonically queer: *Suicide Squad's* Harley Quinn, *Thor: Ragnarok's* Valkyrie, *Wonder Woman's* title character, *X-Men's* Mystique, and many more. When even comic book characters are "straightwashed" to protect the alleged sensibilities of viewers (and the bank accounts of Hollywood executives), the American film industry needs to be examined.

With the fundamental rights of the LGBTQIA+ community under constant threat and ripples of this oppression being seen in the arts, now is the time to closely examine the depiction of the LGBTQIA+ community in American cinema. This volume explores work from throughout American film history. Ethical and compassionate portrayals of the LGBTQIA+ community will be held in high regard. Conversely, cinematic missteps will be addressed. Contributors will explore where/how these works failed the community. Finally, deliberately cruel and destructive depictions of the LGBTQIA+ community will be dissected with care. Their detrimental nature/influence will be meticulously unpacked. Overall, the goal of the volume is to educate readers: to help guide them to see injustice more clearly and to inspire art that is both inclusive and thoughtful.

While this is a stand-alone volume, *The Encyclopedia of LGBTQIA+ Portrayals in American Film* serves as something of a companion to *The Encyclopedia of Sexism in American Films* (2019) as well as *The Encyclopedia of Racism in American Films* (2018). All address inequity as depicted by and located in American film. Likewise, as revealed in these volumes, there are countless examples of intersectionality that bring insensitivities and injustices even further into focus.

In this book, the explication of many of these films relies on the most common and problematic LGBTQIA+ tropes found in American film. While eight specific tropes affect the majority of the films selected for this volume, countless others exist and are also mentioned throughout this work.

The first trope this volume explores is LGBTQIA+ characters who are shown as one-dimensional. While allowing for an important degree of visibility, these characters lack depth. One such example of this character is the "gay best friend," whose role is to provide emotional support to the protagonist (most often, a heterosexual woman). Little is known about the personal life of the "gay best friend." This character is merely used to drive the narrative forward (and, frequently, to foster the happy resolution of the heterosexual plotline). In "The Queer 1990s: The Challenge and Failure of Radical Change," Michael Bronski calls the trope "a conservative rhetorical move that places gay male characters in major roles while, at the same time, sidelining them within a heterosexual narrative context" (2015, 341). In the motion picture industry, the inclusion of a "gay best friend" has the potential to draw the attention of both female viewers as well as gay viewers. In many ways, it is perceived as an ideal, financial "double dip." Films like Amy Heckerling's *Clueless* (1995), Michael Gottlieb's *Mannequin* (1987), and Michael Patrick King's *Sex and the City* (2008) provide prime examples of this figure.

The second category examines films that view LGBTQIA+ characters as disposable. This trope is so common that it has gained the popular expression "Bury Your Gays." This becomes particularly problematic when the sole LGBTQIA+ character is "killed off" in a film, and even more so if that person is killed as a result of her/his/their sexual/gender identity. While this trend has gained a great deal of criticism from LGBTQIA+ magazines like *Out* and *Diva*, even so-called mainstream magazines like *Vanity Fair* have addressed the issue. Given the pervasiveness of this trope and its destructive effect on the LGBTQIA+ community, *Diva* (a leading magazine for lesbian and bisexual women) released a brief article titled "10 Lesbian Films Where No One Dies" (2017). This was *Diva*'s way of creating a "safe" viewing list for members of the LGBTQIA+ community who have grown disheartened with this pervasive, deeply destructive trope. Examples of films that treat LGBTQIA+ characters as disposable include Tom Tykwer, Lana Wachowski, and Lilly Wachowski's *Cloud Atlas* (2012), William Friedkin's *Cruising* (1980), George A. Romero's *Land of the Dead* (2005), and James McTeigue's *V for Vendetta* (2006).

The third category pertains to LGBTQIA+ characters who are shown as an imminent threat to society. These characters are portrayed as sociopaths, psychopaths, sexual deviants, or otherwise harmful. In *Murder Most Queer: The Homicidal Homosexual in the American Theater*, Jordan Schildcrout notes: "The homicidal homosexual represents the sexual aggressor, duplicitous traitor, diseased corruptor, and evil destroyer of all that is good. In most narratives, these moral monsters exist in order to be eradicated, thus affirming the strength of traditional gender roles, heterosexuality, the family, and conservative values" (2014, 2). Here, the author makes the insidious nature of these roles abundantly clear. Moreover, in *Transgender on Screen*, J. Phillips says of films like Jonathan Demme's *Silence of the Lambs* (1991) and Geoffrey Wright's *Cherry Falls* (2000) that "transgender is negatively coded, associated directly with castration, madness, murder, and monstrosity" (2006, 85). As a whole, this trope is particularly problematic since it positions the public against the LGBTQIA+ community. Examples of films that depict members of the LGBTQIA+ community as a threat to society include Paul Verhoeven's *Basic Instinct* (1992), William Friedkin's *Cruising* (1980), Jonathan Demme's *Silence of the Lambs* (1991), Robert Hiltzik's *Sleepaway Camp* (1983), and Anthony Minghella's *The Talented Mr. Ripley* (1999).

The fourth category for analysis is the fetishization of LGBTQIA+ characters. Generally speaking, expressions of erotic desire between female characters are often employed for the sexual gratification of another male character or the male viewer. In an article for *Mic*, Anna Swartz explains, "Cinema history is littered with sensational depictions of lesbian sexuality. Sometimes lesbian sex, even just the implication of it, is tossed into a film apropos of nothing, and often just for the benefit of the male main character" (2018). In these instances, the main male character may be watching the women with their permission or may be engaging in an act of voyeurism. This act of voyeurism often extends to the male viewer watching the film. In these works, there is an overall sentiment that sex acts between women exist for the sexual pleasure of others. With this stated, it also warrants noting that this trend has increasingly been extended to women fetishizing gay male sexual encounters (though, currently, the vehicles for this fetishization are fan fiction and pornography). Undoubtedly, this is considered equally as problematic. As Victoria Brownworth writes, "fetishizing the sexuality of others is still a blatant form of sexism, homophobia, racism. When you fetishize another's sexuality, you make them less than. You make them Other" (2010). Examples of roles that are intended for the sexual gratification of another (including the viewer) are Darren Aronofsky's *Black Swan* (2010), Roger Kumble's *Cruel Intentions* (1999), Ivan Reitman's *No Strings Attached* (2011), and John McNaughton's *Wild Things* (1998).

The fifth category considers ambiguously gay characters. These roles suggest identification with the LGBTQIA+ community but fail to make it explicit. Disney films are notorious for including ambiguously gay characters. Examples of ambiguously gay characters in Disney films can be found in *Aladdin* (1992), *Beauty and the Beast* (1991), *The Emperor's New Groove* (2000), *Frozen* (2013), *The Incredibles* (2004), *Lilo & Stitch* (2002), and many more. In fact, entire academic works like Sean P. Griffin's *Tinker Belles and Evil Queens: The Walt Disney Company from the Inside Out* dig deeply into Disney's films as well as its history and practices, closely examining the company's complex relationship with the LGBTQIA+ community. Even outside of so-called children's films, this trope is still very much present. In "Movies and Wayward Images," Sharon Willis addresses ambiguously gay works. She particularly focuses on Jon Avnet's commercially and critically successful *Fried Green Tomatoes* (1991). Here, she mentions how the film "foregrounded 'friendships' that it couldn't fully account for narratively" (2008, 48). Ultimately, the author explains how this film was used to "challenge the frames of 'ambiguously gay' representations" in cinema (2008, 48). These films use "coded" moments and insinuation, but fall short of genuine inclusivity. Examples of roles that suggest identification with the LGBTQIA+ community but fail to state it outright include works such as Jonathan Levine's *All the Boys Love Mandy Lane* (2013), Kenny Ortega's *High School Musical* (2006), and Jack Sholder's *A Nightmare on Elm Street Part 2: Freddy's Revenge* (1985).

The sixth category is LGBTQIA+ characters who are employed for comedic relief. These are roles that appear to use LGBTQIA+ characters as a tool to create humor. These characters are created to be laughed at, not with. In Rob Epstein and Jeffrey Friedman's 1995 documentary *The Celluloid Closet*, the narrator states, "From the very beginning, movies could rely on homosexuality as a surefire source of humor." Moreover, in an article for the *Advocate*, Tracy E. Gilchrist and Daniel Reynolds note that "the representation that exists [in mainstream film] is, unfortunately, reduced to small parts that amount to sight gags or punch lines for outdated humor. . . . We can be hilarious—but not at the expense of our dignity" (n.d.). These films tend to use gay men with effeminate speech/mannerisms or female-coded attire for laughs. The reverse may apply to lesbian characters who dress in masculine-coded attire or have a lower vocal range. These characters can often be misgendered, with the "gender reveal" being the source of alleged humor. Examples of roles that appear to use members of the LGBTQIA+ community for humor include Dan Mazer's *Dirty Grandpa* (2016), Steven Brill's *Little Nicky* (2000), the *Pitch Perfect* franchise (2012, 2015, 2017), Jeff Kanew's *Revenge of the Nerds* (1984), Frank Coraci's *The Wedding Singer* (1998), and Ben Stiller's *Zoolander 2* (2016).

The seventh category for exploration involves LGBTQIA+ characters who are "straightwashed." These are roles that depict LGBTQIA+ characters/people from literature/history as heterosexual. Just as characters have been "whitewashed" in film, they have also been "straightwashed." Scholar Dragos Manea explains "straightwashing" as "the practice of erasing LGBTQ characters, characteristics, and/or events" (2016, 167). The aforementioned sanitized depiction of Freddie Mercury in *Bohemian Rhapsody* seemed to bring the term "straightwashing" into the general public, creating a keen awareness of this trend as well as the reasons why it must be opposed. This deliberate form of erasure can be found in works such as Ryan Coogler's *Black Panther* (2018), Matt Reeves's *Let Me In* (2010), Mel Gibson's *The Man Without a Face* (1993), Terrence Malick's *The Thin Red Line* (1998), Taika Waititi's *Thor: Ragnarok* (2017), and the *X-Men* franchise.

The eighth category addresses the trope of portraying LGBTQIA+ characters as cross-dressing/drag queens. These are roles that suggest all members of the LGBTQIA+ cross-dress. In "Gay Films Are a Drag," *Newsweek*'s David Ansen writes, "Hollywood has embraced cross-dressing as the safest way to pitch gayness to a mass audience. Drag queens are the cinema's favorite naughty pets, harmless if not quite housebroken" (1996). In regularly showing members of the LGBTQIA+ community as cross-dressing or as drag queens, the community is further Othered. This also seems to disregard the fact that the majority of those who cross-dress are heterosexual (Kendall 2016, 286). Examples of roles that suggest all members of the LGBTQIA+ community cross-dress include Mike Nichols's *The Birdcage* (1996), Joel Schumacher's *Flawless* (1999), and Zack Snyder's *Dawn of the Dead* (2004).

While many films involving the LGBTQIA+ community may be perceived as problematic (including some works that were once held in very high esteem), there are many that enlighten and inspire. Those are included here as well. They remain the goal for scriptwriters, directors, cinematographers, performers, and all involved in the filmmaking process. These films constitute hope. Perhaps, one day, there can be a revised version of this volume where these films represent the majority of the entries. That would be progress.

BIBLIOGRAPHY

"10 Lesbian Films Where No One Dies." *Diva*, August 31, 2017. Accessed January 15, 2020. https://divamag.co.uk/2017/08/31/10-lesbian-films-where-no-one-dies/.

Ansen, David. "Gay Films Are a Drag." *Newsweek*, March 17, 1996. Accessed January 2, 2020. https://www.newsweek.com/gay-films-are-drag-176014.

"*Arthur*: Alabama Public Television Bans Gay Wedding Episode." *BBC News*, May 21, 2019. Accessed December 2, 2019. https://www.bbc.com/news/world-us-canada -48350023.

Bronski, Michael. "The Queer 1990s: The Challenge and Failure of Radical Change." In *American Film History: Selected Readings, 1960 to the Present*, edited by Roy Grundmann, Cynthia Lucia, and Art Simon, 330–46. Hoboken, NJ: Wiley-Blackwell, 2015.

Brownworth, Victoria. "The Fetishizing of Queer Sexuality: A Response." *Lambda Literary*, August 19, 2010. Accessed December 17, 2019. https://www.lambdaliterary.org /feat/oped/08/19/the-fetishizing-of-queer-sexuality-a-response/comment-page-2/.

Burns, Katelyn. "Why Democrats Just Gave away Their Best Chance at Ending the Trans Military Ban." *Vox*, December 12, 2019. Accessed November 29, 2019. https://www .vox.com/2019/12/12/21013091/trump-trans-troops-ban-ndaa-house-democrats.

The Celluloid Closet. DVD. Directed by Rob Epstein and Jeffrey Friedman. Los Angeles: Sony, 1995.

Chen, David W. "Transgender Athletes Face Bans from Girls' Sports in 10 U.S. States." *New York Times*, October 28, 2021. Accessed November 17, 2021. https://www.nytimes .com/article/transgender-athlete-ban.html.

D'Angelo, Chris. "Interior Department Cut 'Sexual Orientation' from Anti-Discrimination Guideline." *HuffPost*, December 27, 2019. Accessed November 13, 2019. https:// www.huffpost.com/entry/sexual-orientation-interior-department-ethics-guidelines_n _5dff99e3e4b0b2520d0ca480.

Ebert, Joel. "Tennessee Gov. Bill Lee Signs Bill Allowing Adoption Agencies to Deny Gay Couples." *USA Today*, January 24, 2020. Accessed January 25, 2020. https://www.usa today.com/story/news/nation/2020/01/24/tennessee-gay-adoption-gov-bill-lee-signs -anti-lgbt-measure/4570788002/.

Gilchrist, Tracy E., and Daniel Reynolds. "17 LGBT Tropes Hollywood Needs to Retire." *Advocate*, n.d. Accessed December 3, 2019. https://www.advocate.com/arts -entertainment/2017/8/29/17-lgbt-tropes-hollywood-needs-retire#media-gallery -media-1.

Itkowitz, Colby. "LGBT Rights Page Disappears from White House Web Site." *Washington Post*, January 20, 2017. Accessed November 23, 2019. https://www.washingtonpost .com/local/2017/live-updates/politics/live-coverage-of-trumps-inauguration/lgbt -rights-page-disappears-from-white-house-web-site/.

Kendall, Diana. *Sociology in Our Times: The Essentials*. Boston: Cengage, 2016.

Manea, Dragos. "Leonardo's Paradoxical Queerness: *Da Vinci's Demons* and the Politics of Straightwashing." In *Queer TV in the 21st Century: Essays on Broadcasting from Taboo to Acceptance*, edited by Kylo-Patrick R. Hart, 159–77. Jefferson, NC: McFarland, 2016.

McCloskey, Caroline. "Seth Rogen and the Science of Rogenomics." *GQ*, May 21, 2019. Accessed January 2, 2020. https://www.gq.com/story/seth-rogen-cover-profile-june -july-2019.

McNamara, Audrey. "Trump's Transgender Military Ban Takes Effect Today." *Daily Beast*, April 12, 2019. Accessed November 29, 2019. https://www.thedailybeast.com /trumps-transgender-military-ban-takes-effect-today.

Phillips, J. *Transgender on Screen*. London: Palgrave Macmillan, 2006.

Rackham, Annabel. "Should *Family Guy* 'Phase Out' Gay Jokes?" *BBC News*, January 15, 2019. Accessed January 2, 2020. https://www.bbc.com/news/entertainment-arts -46878017.

Reddish, David. "Seth Rogen Is Really Sorry for His Homophobic Humor." *Queerty*, May 28, 2019. Accessed January 3, 2020. https://www.queerty.com/seth-rogan-really-sorry -homophobic-humor-20190528.

Ryan, Patrick. "Rami Malek 'Totally Understands' Criticism That Queen Film Straight-washes Freddie Mercury." *USA Today*, October 30, 2018. Accessed November 28, 2019. https://www.usatoday.com/story/life/movies/2018/10/30/rami-malek-gets-criticism -queen-film-straightwashes-freddie-mercury/1807059002/.

Schildcrout, Jordan. *Murder Most Queer: The Homicidal Homosexual in the American Theater*. Ann Arbor: University of Michigan Press, 2014.

Swartz, Anna. "Lesbian Sex Scenes Can Be Problematic in *Disobedience*, Rachel Weisz Tried to Avoid That." *Mic*, May 3, 2018. Accessed December 11, 2019. https://www .mic.com/articles/189148/lesbian-sex-scenes-can-be-problematic-in-disobedience -rachel-weisz-tried-to-avoid-that.

Swift, Andy. "*Family Guy* Takes on Trump: EPs Break down Peter Griffin's Presidential Brawl." *TVLine*, January 13, 2019. Accessed December 15, 2019. https://tvline.com /2019/01/13/family-guy-season-17-donald-trump-fight-explained-interview/.

Willis, Sharon. "Movies and Wayward Images." In *American Cinema of the 1990s: Themes and Variations*, edited by Chris Holmlund, 45–69. New Brunswick, NJ: Rutgers University Press, 2008.

Young, Neil, J. "Censoring Gay Marriage on TV Could Be an Ominous Sign of Things to Come." *Week*, May 25, 2019. Accessed December 7, 2019. https://theweek.com /articles/843202/censoring-gay-marriage-tv-could-ominous-sign-things-come.

• A •

ADAM (2019)

DIRECTOR: Rhys Ernst
SCREENPLAY: Ariel Schrag, based on the novel of the same name by Ariel Schrag
CAST: Nicholas Alexander (Adam), Bobbi Salvör Menuez (Gillian), Leo Sheng (Ethan), Chloë Levine (June), Margaret Qualley (Casey)
SPECS: 95 minutes; color
AVAILABILITY: DVD (Wolfe Releasing)

Adam is a socially awkward teenage boy from California with one remaining year of high school and no coherent plans for his future. He decides to spend the summer before his senior year in New York, living with his older sister, Casey. In New York, he stumbles into a queer new world: while he had expected to spend the summer surrounded by gay people (Casey is a lesbian in her twenties living in Brooklyn), he had not expected to be surrounded by so many transgender people. Casey's on-again-off-again boyfriend is a transgender man who is also named Casey—referred to as "(Boy) Casey"—and later in the film, (Girl) Casey pursues a transsexual woman named Hazel. Casey's roommate Ethan is a transgender man, although Adam assumes Ethan to be a cis man until toward the end of the film. Soon after arriving in New York, Adam finds himself talking to a young lesbian woman named Gillian at a party full of queer people. Adam realizes that Gillian has assumed that he is a transgender man and does not say otherwise. They begin to pursue each other in an awkward romance in which Adam consciously pretends to be a transgender man. They spend the summer exploring the gay world of early-2000s Brooklyn together, until the film concludes with Adam disclosing to Gillian that he is a cisgender man and Gillian admitting that she is bisexual.

Equally important to a synopsis of the film itself is a synopsis of the abundant discourse surrounding this film both before and after its release. There is functionally no academic scholarship regarding *Adam*, but commentary on the film proliferated colloquially in both online and in-person queer spaces. *Adam* is an adaptation of a novel of the same name written by Ariel Schrag, released in 2014. Schrag, who also wrote the screenplay for the film adaptation, is a prolific writer and cartoonist who first conceived of *Adam* while writing for *The L Word* in the early 2000s. In an interview shortly after the novel's release, Schrag details becoming obsessed, while working on *The L Word*, with the thought of a cisgender man who pretended to be a transgender man so as to date lesbians: "It did occur to me," she says, "that all these lesbians I knew were fawning over trans men who looked like teenage boys, and I thought a teenage boy could clean up if he got in there" (Gurba 2017). The suggestion that a lesbian woman would date a transgender man upset audiences to the point that there were calls for the film not to be released, to which Rhys Ernst, *Adam*'s director, responded: "The idea of boycotting or condemning projects before they're released is not progressive or beneficial. . . . There are other ways of engaging" (Keating 2019). From before it was released, the film understood itself as violating standards of political correctness. Rather than insist that the film did *not* violate such boundaries, it defended its right to cross these boundaries.

The backlash toward *Adam* is perhaps deserved, but it would be a mistake to allow the film's numerous and cascading ideological missteps to distract viewers completely from the complex and pressing questions about queer identity and community formation at work in the film. From the start of the film, characters make uncomfortable political missteps. On one of Adam's first evenings in New York, Casey invites him to an "*L Word* Party." The party scene opens with a shot of a room of young adults crowded around a small television that is recognizably playing an episode of *The L Word*. Someone asks jokingly, "Who wants to bet Tina's gonna fuck a guy this episode?," and almost everyone raises their hand. The film cuts to a shot of Casey, who is curled up romantically in the arms of an ambiguously transmasculine person, (Boy) Casey. "Yeah, I mean seriously," she says. "No one wants to watch Tina trolling for dick." She laughs nervously and looks up at (Boy) Casey, who also laughs. Someone shouts, "Traitor!," and another voice calls out, "I always knew she'd turn straight." There is more banter, after which Casey turns to Adam, who is sitting next to her, and says:

> Casey: Casey works at American Apparel, so he gets, like, crazy discounts.
>
> (Boy) Casey: Like, 40 percent.
>
> Adam: Cool. Wait, wait, you're a guy?
>
> (Boy) Casey: Yeah.
>
> Adam [to Casey]: I thought you were gay.
>
> Casey: Adam, shut up! [00:06:43–00:07:20]

The entire scene is interspersed with shots of the television, which is playing a scene from *The L Word* featuring the famously haphazardly depicted transgender character Max. Most significant in this scene is Casey's apparent humiliation at the suggestion that her interest in (Boy) Casey somehow contradicts her being gay. The scene plays not as though she is frustrated at Adam for misunderstanding the nature of her queerness but rather as though she is trying to hide from (Boy) Casey that she is gay. The tension between the apparently rigid identities of Casey's gayness and (Boy) Casey's "boy-ness" animates the scene.

After the party, the film cuts to Adam, Casey, and Casey's roommate June walking through the rainy streets of Brooklyn. They chat animatedly before Adam changes the subject by asking:

> Adam: So, Casey's like that guy on the show, right? Like, he used to be a girl, now he's a guy?
>
> Casey: Yeah, he's trans.
>
> Adam: Yeah, but he's not like, he's not like a real guy, with like a, with like a penis.

Casey: Trans guys are real guys, Adam. It has nothing to do with having a penis, okay?

Adam: Okay. But if you're gay, then like—

Casey: I'm *queer*, what*ever*. [00:08:12–00:08:38]

This exchange introduces "realness" to the film's imagination of transness. Casey is positioned here as the arbiter of queer identity, and insists that "trans guys" are the same as "real guys," revealing the film as invested in the question of whether transness is "real" or "pretend." This exchange also introduces a distinction between "queer" and "gay": "gayness" is defined as rigid with respect to the objects of its desire, while "queerness" incorporates desire more broadly. The relative realness of the multiple identities at play in this scene is in flux: either (Boy) Casey's "realness" necessitates the broadening of Casey's gay identity, or Casey's rigid gay identity throws (Boy) Casey's "realness" into crisis. This contrived tension between gayness and transness comes to structure the remainder of the film.

Soon after this exchange, Adam finds himself in a situation reminiscent of Casey and (Boy) Casey's tenuous romance. Adam follows Casey to a party at which he awkwardly begins chatting with a young lesbian named Gillian. She asks if Adam is here with (Boy) Casey and (Boy) Casey's friends, to which Adam says, "Yeah, they're my, they're my, they're my bros." "Cool," Gillian replies [00:24:20–00:24:29]. Gillian reads this interaction as communicative of Adam being a transgender man. Being (Boy) Casey's "bro" casts Adam as transgender in this space. The film instructs the viewer in its subtle language of transgender communication.

Adam and Gillian begin an awkward relationship. Following a visit to a quirky, fog-filled, dramatically lit art club, their first date finds them lunching at a café. Gillian asks, "So, what's your major?," at which point Adam begins to describe a life that is clearly fiction. At the party where he and Gillian first met, he told Gillian that he attended Berkeley, and so she inquires now as to whether he knows any of her friends who are Berkeley students. He claims to not know the first two people about whom she asks, but enthusiastically claims to know the third. Gillian excitedly asks what her friend is like these days, and Adam freezes as he realizes that he has talked himself into a corner. After a lengthy silence, Gillian stands to leave, at which point Adam confesses that he is not, in fact, a Berkeley student. Gillian sits back down. She reflects, and then assures him that this is okay. Adam continues to apologize:

Adam: At the gay marriage party thing, I made stuff up, because I thought you wouldn't like me. I don't— Here's the thing, though. I have to tell you something.

Gillian: Hey. My friend, Aiden, lied to his girlfriend. He's trans too. We went to Smith together, and he was so fucked up over gender stuff that he had to drop out his second year, and, well, he was really ashamed about it. And he just thought it was kind of funny because he was always open about trans stuff, and she was so supportive, but the, the big coming out was about school. What I'm trying to say, is, I think you, being yourself . . . it's really brave. [00:36:15–00:40:02]

Adam attempts to confess that he is cis, but Gillian cuts him off. Adam's claim to be a student at Berkeley and his claim to be transgender emerge in the same moment (at the party where he meets Gillian), and while these two "deceptions" emerge simultaneously as almost a single deception, this scene disentangles and presents them as separate deceptions. Adam *attempts* to confess to both deceptions in one move, but Gillian acknowledges only the Berkeley confession, pushing Adam deeper into his transgender charade. The juxtaposition of these deceptions prompts the viewer to compare them: what, if it exists at all, the film asks, is the difference between these lies? Gillian believes that Adam is about to confess that he *is trans*, and she assures him that his failure to explicitly disclose his transgender status is *not* equivalent to his Berkeley lie. But Adam is in fact attempting to confess that he *is not trans*. The irony at work in this scene (and across the film more broadly) plays like a joke on Gillian, which suggests that the film in fact regards Adam's two deceptions as equivalent.

As the film progresses, Adam's transgender deception is further presented as a lie that he consciously crafts. He is shown researching notable top surgeons so as to lie about having had top surgery. He watches instructional videos about binding. He is introduced to Gillian's friends and speaks as if familiar with the ins and outs of transsexual manhood (which is depicted, of course, monolithically).

While the film does a respectable job of kicking up dust with respect to nuances of trans identity, its politics crystalize in its resolution. Adam and Gillian attend a nature retreat for trans people (and friends of trans people) called "Camp Trans," where they finally speak explicitly about their individual self-conceptualizations. They go for a hike one evening and find themselves sitting in silence, until Adam finally speaks:

Adam: Gillian? . . . I love you.

[They kiss]

Adam: I'm not trans.

Gillian: I know. [01:19:05–01:19:45]

To borrow from Eve Sedgwick, Adam has built for himself a glass closet; Gillian already "knows" that he is cisgender. The next day, the two of them are once again on a hike, and Gillian elaborates that even though she knew that Adam was cisgender, she needed to pretend that he was trans for her own sake:

Gillian: I wanted you to keep pretending so I could pretend, too. Like, I needed you to be a trans guy for me to be able to like you.

Adam: Okay for you to like a guy?

Gillian: Yeah, which is pretty fucked up and transphobic if you think about it. [Screaming to sky] I'm bisexual! [Laughing] That wasn't as bad as I thought it would be.

Adam: [Screaming to the sky] I'm a straight cis male! [01:20:25–01:21:35]

In this scene, they accept each other and themselves as their "true" selves instead of their "pretend" selves. Adam was pretending to be trans, in contrast to "actual" trans people, who are imagined as somehow fundamentally or essentially transgender. In contradiction to Casey's suggestion at the beginning of the film that there is room in "queerness" for ambiguity and confusion, identity is ultimately constructed in the film as rigid and unyielding. Further, this exchange is presented as a moral resolution for both characters: they have been lying to themselves and to each other, and the correct thing to do (per the film) is to be clear about exactly who and what they are.

Adam asks: What happens when cisness is put in the closet? What happens to a cis person in a social world in which transness is the norm and cisness is rare? The film ironically positions a cisgender man as queer, in that Adam literally pretends to be queer, but also in that by way of being cisgender, Adam is a "queer" person in a transgender world. But in attempting to tell an ironic inverse narrative of a gay coming out story, *Adam* only reveals its own imagination of gay and queer identities as rigid and unyielding.

What is most compelling about this film is the ambiguities that it opens between "real" transness and "performances" of transness. Adam's ability to "pass" as a trans man casts critical doubt on the relative "realness" of both transness and cisness: perhaps transness is less about being "real" than the viewer assumes. Contrary to Casey's assertion that being a trans guy "has nothing to do with having a penis," the film critically suggests that Adam's relationship to transness has everything to do with having (or not having) a penis. Casey's liberal body-blindness is epistemologically insufficient for making sense of the complex gender operations of a transgender world. But although the film *attempts* to formulate a more complex epistemology of transgender genders, its framework of gender eventually collapses in on itself: its conceptualization of transness is ultimately organized around a series of rigid binaries. Adam is a cisgender and heterosexual man; Gillian is a cisgender and lesbian woman; Casey is a cisgender and lesbian woman; Ethan is a transgender and heterosexual man; and so on. The lines between various identities are momentarily blurred through intentional deception, but the film concludes with the suggestion that the apparent truth of all identities inevitably comes out.

The film is premised on the breaking down of sex/gender/sexuality binaries—the crossing of these strict binaries is presented as a taboo that *Adam* alone is brave enough to depict—but to make the crossing of these boundaries central to the film necessitates the reification of the very boundaries that the film claims to blur. If *Adam* truly offered a vision of a queer world that was not organized around strict sex/gender/sexuality binaries, the crossing of these boundaries in the film would not be presented as taboo. *Adam* works to reproduce the strict identity politics of the late 2010s even as it pretends to be a film set in a theoretically less rigid moment. *Adam*'s being set in 2006 is rhetorical sleight of hand. The film is set in 2006 not to construct an argument about queer history; rather, the temporal setting obscures the careless arguments that the film makes with respect to our current moment. If *Adam* makes a historical argument in any capacity, its argument is the rehabilitation of early 2000s Brooklyn as a historical scene exactly alike to our contemporary moment. *Adam* is a foundation myth that extends the rigid identity politics of its own historical moment (2019) into an imagined queer past. The film is uninterested in the actual historical ambiguities that are sometimes at work in the relationship between lesbianism and transmasculinity. *Adam* only invokes these ambiguities toward the end of reproducing rigid boundaries between transmasculinity and lesbianism, failing humiliatingly in the execution of an intellectually compelling premise.

See also *Cherry Pop*.

Bibliography

Gurba, Myriam. "The Rumpus Interview with Ariel Schrag." *Rumpus*, September 22, 2017. Accessed December 13, 2021. https://therumpus.net/2014/09/11/the-rumpus-interview-with-ariel -schrag/.

Keating, Shannon. "People Are Calling for This Queer Indie Film to Be Canceled before It Hits Theaters." *BuzzFeed News*, August 4, 2019. Accessed December 13, 2021. https://www .buzzfeednews.com/article/shannonkeating/rhys-ernst-adam-controversy-transgender-queer.

Sedgwick, Eve Kosofsky. *Epistemology of the Closet*. Berkeley: University of California Press, 1990.

—April Taylor Clark

ALGIE, THE MINER (1912)

DIRECTOR: Alice Guy-Blaché (with Harry Schenck and Edward Warren)
SCREENWRITER: Alice Guy (uncredited)
CAST: Mary Foy (Society Dowager), Billy Quirk (Algie)
SPECS: 10 minutes; black and white
AVAILABILITY: Blu-ray (Kino, "Pioneers: First Women Filmmakers")

This one-reel silent comedy begins as Algie, an unusually effeminate easterner, meets his fiancée's domineering father. Appalled by Algie's womanly manners and ambiguous sexuality, the father forbids him to marry his daughter—unless Algie can demonstrate his manliness within a year's time. Clad in dainty costume, Algie sets off for the Wild West to prove his mettle and immediately encounters two ruffians. Without hesitating, Algie kisses one ruffian after he provides Algie with directions. In his new western environs, however, Algie starts to become self-conscious of his effeminacy, especially when denizens of a saloon mock his tiny, insufficiently phallic pistol. Nevertheless, he finds employment as a miner and befriends Big Jim, who schools Algie in the ways of long guns, manly garb, and stout horsemanship. Soon enough, petite Algie becomes a valiant miner, discovering valuable ore and rescuing Big Jim from alcoholism and bandits. After a year has passed, a gun-toting Algie returns East to claim his bride—much to the shock of her uptight father, who, in contrast to the renovated Algie, now seems the effeminate one.

Dandyism and cross-dressing were commonplace tropes in silent slapstick, and at some point, nearly every silent clown donned feminine dress for the sake of misgendered farce. Indeed, comedies of gender confusion were especially suited to silent cinema, in which appearances alone defined diegetic reality and in which characters perceived (or mistook) superficial looks as operating truths. In *Algie, the Miner*, however, trailblazing female producer-director Alice Guy (later known as the married Alice Guy-Blaché) goes beyond the usual surface play of gender confusion, offering an ambisexual hero rather than a cross-dressed farceur. Usually, silent comedy presented clownish effeminacy as part of some masquerade, as in Chaplin's *A Woman* (1915) and *The Floorwalker* (1916); here, effeminacy reflects the hero's authentic character and personality. When Algie kisses a roving bandit as a way of thanking him for providing directions, viewers can only conclude that Algie is something other than devoutly heterosexual. Yet Algie is not gay per se: he rather embodies the anarchic spirit of clowning, which embraces ambisexuality but is not strictly constructed through it. Bret Wood's essentializing assertion that "Algie's character is defined as gay through certain visual indicators of behavior and dress" not only fails to appreciate the perversities of silent clowning but makes little sense within the framework of the story (Wood n.d.). Algie's goal, after all, is to marry a *woman*, a desire that is apparently sincere and not some sort of situational ruse. One might suggest that Algie (if gay) seeks a marriage of convenience, but were that the case, he could simply find another woman rather than spend an arduous year braving the wilderness and coal mines. Besides, marriages of convenience are only suited to men who want to "pass," a goal to which Algie does not initially aspire. To explain Algie's proposed marriage as a scheme of "passing" would also impose an existentialist rationale on a slapstick farce obviously lacking in any psychological depth.

While it might be tempting to claim a 1912 movie character as a watershed in gay representation, Algie's ambiguous sexuality is more in the tradition of the polymorphously perverse clown, who delights in violating boundaries, encompasses multiple sexual identities, and dallies with anyone who might cross his path. In his *Three Essays on the Theory of Sexuality*, Freud theorized that young, presocialized children experience pleasure in perverse and multiform ways, without regard to the social norms with which they are later indoctrinated. Freud's use of the word "perverse" does not imply moral judgment. He merely observed that small children—before the age of socialization—extract pleasure from nearly any scenario, including those that adults regard as deviant or taboo. For the presocialized child, ordinary bodily functions are sources of "clownish" pleasure rather than stigmatized shame. Pregenital children do not divide pleasures into sexual and nonsexual categories, nor do they understand the analogous distinction between privacy and publicity. Toddlers have yet to understand, too, the socially erected boundaries between heterosexual and "homosexual" identities. The silent-film clown—generally an overgrown, undersocialized child—recovers and reembodies these "lost" traits of childhood. His life consists of pranks, games, and idleness. He often finds himself in drag, flaunts ambisexual mannerisms, and, like Chaplin's Tramp, alternates between whimsical effeminacy and anarchic violence. Furthermore, the dichotomy of privacy and publicity mean little to the silent-film clown, who behaves in private as though there were spectators and in public as though there were none.

The plots of silent-film comedies often place the childish clown at a crossroads, forcing him—and silent clowns are almost always male—to become self-conscious of his infantilism and acclimate to "adult" social norms. Thus, Buster Keaton, Charlie Chaplin, and Harold Lloyd are always trying to land a job or get married, no matter how poorly steady employment or respectable monogamy would suit them. For Billy Quirk's Algie, conformity also means growing into heteronormative duties and developing the "correct" object choices that come with socialization and ego development. If viewers expect clowns to surrender their perversities in order to "win the girl" and please authoritarian fathers-in-law, the marriage plot in *Algie* still begs the question of *why* Algie wants to wed in the first place. His dress and mannerisms appear defiantly queer, and when he kisses the ruffian, his impulsive pursuit of bad object choices goes further than that of most clowns. Many silent comedies resort to mechanical plot devices to coerce deviant clowns into improbable (and thus comic) social conformities, particularly marriage. In *Seven Chances* (1925), for instance, Buster Keaton must wed within seven days, lest he forfeit his grandfather's fortune. But no external motivating force explains Algie's *fundamental* desire to marry this particular woman. Viewers might assume that, taking the clown's presocial transgressions to an extreme, Algie makes no distinction between gay and straight affections—like a child before the age of reason, he sees all human relationships as an extension and function of his own sexless ego.

Despite Algie's initial queerness, the film reiterates a variety of sexual and regional stereotypes. When "westernized" Algie returns home as a rugged frontiersman, he is as out of place among the effete bourgeoisie as his old, queerer self had been among western outlaws. The ensuing comedy is wholly conventional, that of a wild man outraging the monied classes. Perhaps the film means to comment on the impossibility of socializing the clown, who applies his manic hyperbole even to the process of his alleged "maturation." A less conservative—and indeed more comic—plotline might have seen Algie refuse to adopt masculine norms but claim his bride nonetheless, incongruously joining unmanly appearances with heterosexual desire. As it turns out, Algie learns to become ashamed of his ambisexuality—a trait Freud characterized as infantile but which spectators enjoy as a font of comic liberation. As with many "primitive" one-reel comedies of the early 1910s, the film ends suddenly, without closure or denouement. Viewers can only wonder what sort of husband Algie would actually make.

Theoretical concerns aside, Guy's comedy is a fascinating curio from cinema's inchoate years, when the intertwined rules of (conventional) narrative and gender had yet to be fully fixed. Recent years have witnessed a remarkable resurgence of interest in the works of Guy (1873–1968), often considered early cinema's foremost female auteur. French by birth, she served as the chief of production for France's Gaumont film company from 1896 to 1906 before moving to America (with her husband Herbert Blaché) to expand Gaumont's overseas production wing in 1910. Settling in New York and then in New Jersey, she and her husband formed the Solax Company, which would become America's largest film production force before the rise of the Hollywood studios. According to her own recollections, Guy directed, produced, or wrote more than one thousand films between 1896 and 1920, about 150 of which are extant. Of particular interest to queer and feminist historians is Guy's one-reel farce *The Consequences of Feminism* (1906), made in her native France. Caricaturing the perceived "goals" of feminism, this rumbustious comedy imagines a future of inverted gender roles, in which aggressive, hard-drinking women manhandle girlish, domesticated men.

See also *Cherry Pop*; *To Wong Foo, Thanks for Everything! Julie Newmar*.

Bibliography
Wood, Bret. *Algie the Miner*. TCM.com, n.d. Accessed March 5, 2021. http://www.tcm.com/this
-month/article/159633%7C0/Algie-the-Miner.html.

—Andrew Grossman

AMERICAN BEAUTY (1999)

DIRECTOR: Sam Mendes
SCREENPLAY: Alan Ball
CAST: Kevin Spacey (Lester Burnham), Annette Bening (Carolyn Burnham), Thora
    Birch (Jane Burnham), Chris Cooper (Colonel Frank Fitts), Allison Janney (Bar-
    bara Fitts), Wes Bentley (Ricky Fitts), Mena Suvari (Angela Hayes)
SPECS: 121 minutes; color
AVAILABILITY: DVD (DreamWorks)

Speaking postmortem, middle-aged suburban father Lester Burnham offers insight into the last months of his life before he is murdered. Plagued by a midlife
crisis and enduring ceaseless bickering with his bourgeois wife and his adolescent daughter, he suffers from a dreary life that makes his existence seem insig-
nificantly mundane. During his daughter's cheerleading performance, he immediately falls in love with her friend Angela. Fueled by his purpose of impressing
her, he starts working out and rediscovers the beauty of life. His determination
for change leads him to quit his unfulfilling job at an advertiser's office, thereby
extorting his boss for a twelve-month wage in order to purchase a 1970 Pontiac
Firebird. Meanwhile, his wife starts an affair with a success-driven realtor, which
does not bother Lester since he is certain that his marriage is beyond remedy.
The "first day of the rest of [his] life" finds a tragic end [01:20:05]: Lester's neighbor, Colonel Frank Fitts, a seemingly homophobic veteran who handles issues
with his son Ricky by executing physical as well as psychological violence on
him, observes Lester and Ricky smoking marijuana in Lester's garage, assuming
both being involved in a liaison. After beating up his son, the colonel pays Lester
a visit and kisses him, disclosing his probably lifelong repressed identity as a
gay man. However, the latter rejects him and is rather interested in exchanging
moments of endearment with Angela. The colonel cannot bear the repudiation,
heads back to Lester's house, and shoots him dead while Lester unknowingly
takes one last look at a family photo as he reminisces about the love he feels for
the "ordinary" life he once despised.

The multiple Academy Award–winning and critically praised film presents
LGBTQIA+ themes in order to point toward the unrealistic account of the com-
mercialized "American way of life" along with its social and cultural inconsistencies. Homophobia as one of the film's leitmotifs is predominantly conveyed
via the interactions between the actual queer character, Colonel Frank Fitts, his
son Ricky Fitts, and the film's protagonist, Lester Burnham. Colonel Fitts served
in the United States Army and "represents a conservative notion of masculinity,
which is based on an aggressive assertion of patriarchal dominance" (Nungesser
2010, 54). Until the remaining twenty minutes of the film, he, according to
scholar Erica Arthur, "project[s] an image of homophobic disgust" (2004, 134). He

does not shy away from derogatory remarks about the LGBTQIA+ community. However, toward the film's all-revealing final scene, his true self is unveiled. The veteran's journey of forcefully denying his "non-normative desire by adopting a hyper-masculine and homophobic stance" does not only issue criticism toward societal pressure but additionally carries the plot and ultimately leads to Lester's death (Nungesser 2010, 54).

The colonel's homophobic attitude can first be noted in an encounter with his gay male neighbors, Jim and Jim, who welcome him to the neighborhood. When both men express that they are partners, the colonel immediately interrupts them by asking what they are selling, believing them to be in a business partnership. Even after the couple clarifies their intent of just being friendly neighbors, he remains incredulous. His slight nodding is captured by the camera from a minimal low-angle shot, implying his disdain and his alleged emotional strength. The gay couple, according to Nungesser, "constantly confront[s] Frank Fitts with his fears and prejudices concerning homosexuality" (2010, 55).

The colonel's judgmental attitude toward the LGBTQIA+ community finds its course minutes after this encounter, during the father-son ride to school: "How come these faggots always have to rub it in your face? How can they be so shameless?" [00:24:32–00:24:39]. Ricky, a pot-dealing teenager who does not resemble his father in any way, explains that the men are not ashamed of their relationship. His father does not accept the response and warns him with a resentful countenance, wherefore Ricky abruptly responds in a militaristic manner: "Forgive me, sir, for speaking so bluntly, but those fags make me want to puke my fucking guts out" [00:24:59–00:25:04]. The smile on the colonel's face implies his contentment with his son's homophobic statement.

Wes Bentley as Ricky Fitts and Chris Cooper as Colonel Fitts in *American Beauty*. Courtesy of DreamWorks/Photofest.

Ricky certainly does not approve of his father's controlling and convention-driven mindset. In contrast, he sells and smokes marijuana, but deceives his father with fake urine samples he is forced to produce in order to prove his sobriety. He waits tables as a cover to justify his expensive possessions and money: "But my dad interferes less with my life when I pretend to be an upstanding young citizen with a respectable job" [00:33:21]. Creating this illusion by seemingly obeying the colonel's strict rules, Ricky fulfills his father's desire of fitting into society by following an authentic occupation and not stepping out of line. Even though he represents far different principles than the colonel, Ricky still tries to justify his father's ethically reprehensible mindset. When speaking to Jane about his father's aggressive and forceful nature, he says, "He's not a bad man" [01:16:40]. Additionally, when Ricky and Jane examine the colonel's gun cabinet, he proudly presents his father's "official state china of the Third Reich" and defends his questionable interest [00:58:50]. As Erica Arthur suggests, "Fitts's military background, violent homophobia, and possession of Third Reich dinnerware subtly align him with the right-wing militia movement" (2004, 133). The colonel's gun collection already indicates his patriotic stance in American society, but by proudly collecting memorabilia of World War II, which resulted in the extermination of millions of Jews, Mendes points toward the atrocity of Americans praising a historical sequence based on pure slaughter and guilt. After all, Ricky attempts to protect his father by pulling up a weak argument: "There's a whole subculture of people who collect this Nazi shit. But my dad just has his one thing" [00:58:58]. By trying to convince Jane of the innocuousness of his father's belongings, he does nothing but trivialize the colonel's antisemitic perversion along with his general politically and legally questionable attitude. Resulting from this scene, Ricky can be identified as a character fulfilling the function of the majority of real-life American society that does not, in any way, condone this mindset, but still is afraid of taking action or speaking against it. Therefore, Ricky represents a product of adaptation that is able to distinguish between ethical rights and wrongs but conveniently looks away when encountering racist, homophobic, or gun-violence-supporting attitudes. As Ricky puts it into words perfectly: "Never underestimate the power of denial" [00:47:57].

Throughout the narrative, the colonel manifests his impression of Lester being gay (or, at least, sexually fluid). The first time he encounters Lester, who jogs with his gay neighbors, the colonel expresses to his son: "Oh, what is this? Fucking gay pride parade?" [00:45:04]. Due to Ricky's regular visits to the Burnham household to provide the rebellious Lester with marijuana, which the colonel is not aware of, he quickly develops a misleading sense of both men having a liaison. Ricky's suspicious behavior is erroneously interpreted by his father as an indication of his son's secret sexual identity.

In the course of the film's plot, the colonel physically attacks Ricky after noticing he had accessed his personal cabinet and confronts him: "This is for your own good, boy. . . . You can't just go around doing whatever you feel like. . . . There are rules in life. You need structure. You need discipline!" [01:08:27–01:09:30]. In retrospect, the colonel's discipline-implying statement can refer to the life he forces himself to live. At this point, his façade starts crumbling. In this respect, Colonel Fitts's telling name hints at his repressed identity. During the majority of the colonel's screen time, the viewer is left with the impression of his desperate attempts at forced discipline and order toward his family, especially Ricky. He tries to prove his eligibility for being a well-respected, hypermasculine veteran who *fits* into a judgmental, primarily homophobic society. Hence, the colonel can be regarded as a "product" of his age, namely, a conservative Christian society that views the LGBTQIA+ community negatively.

The colonel's interactions with characters he assumes to be queer, namely, Lester and Ricky, point toward his own repressed sexuality. An early draft of the film's screenplay provides the colonel's backstory. Until reaching the vulnerable state of kissing Lester, the film hardly exposes any overt sign about the colonel's inner feelings. The draft, however, reveals a same-sex sexual experience during his time in the military. After he attacks Ricky for accessing his cabinet, the root cause for the colonel's anger becomes clear. A deleted scene presents him opening a box of old photographs:

> CLOSE on the grainy BLACK & WHITE PHOTOGRAPH IN his callused hands: it's of TWO YOUNG SERVICEMEN standing in front of a Jeep, both shirtless and wearing fatigues. Their muscular arms are draped lazily around each other's shoulders as they grin for the camera. One of these men is the Colonel himself, . . . almost thirty years younger. CLOSE on the Colonel's face as he studies the photo. His breathing has finally relaxed; his face has gone vacant. (Ball n.d., 70)

This scene would have given away the colonel's three-decade-long resentment of his own sexuality too soon. Pragmatically speaking, Mendes and Ball's decision to cut the revealing scene fosters the film's success, as it creates excitement during the revelation in the final minutes of run time. More importantly, the early disclosure of the colonel's sexual identity might have created a negative image of the LGBTQIA+ community since each scene following this moment in which he asserts homophobic remarks might have easily run the risk of indirectly rendering his sexual identity as the underlying cause for his hate-fueled actions (as opposed to his self-loathing).

Another scene that did not make the film's final cut would have catapulted the story to a different dimension. A deleted scene frames the film and presents Jane and Ricky being accused of Lester's murder. During the trial, the colonel hands the police a videotape, namely, the final film's first scene, in which Ricky jokingly asks Jane whether to kill Lester. The tape falsely proves his son guilty, and Ricky and Jane are convicted of murder. This changes the course of the plot from being tragically peaceful to an unjust crime narrative. Therefore, Mendes and Ball's major edit concludes the plot on a positive note and keeps the colonel from being portrayed a true villain (an all-too-common trope applied to the LGBTQIA+ community) who protects himself by any means necessary, framing own his son.

Toward the film's final third, Lester and Ricky's meeting at the Burnhams' garage is continually observed by the colonel. Here he is offered an unpleasant surprise for his unaccepting eyes. From his obstructed sight, the platonic situation of Ricky kneeling before the relaxedly sitting Lester to roll him a joint quickly turns into a horror scenario for the colonel. In his work *The History of Sex in American Film*, scholar Jody Pennington explains: "In one window, Lester reclines with a somewhat blissful expression on his face while in the other,

Ricky's head and shoulders seem to move downward toward Lester's crotch, a standard filmic device used in sexploitation, soft core, and Hollywood films to imply oral sex" (2007, 107). After Ricky comes home, his father confronts him with his personal nightmare, raising a gay son: "What does he make you do? . . . I will not sit back and watch my only son become a cocksucker. . . . I swear to God, I will throw you out of this house and never look at you again. . . . I'd rather you were dead than be a fucking faggot!" [01:29:58–01:30:29]. Ricky is finally fed up with his father's controlling behavior, which he provokes by falsely confirming his sexual identity as gay and even prostituting himself. Fitts cannot bear the disappointment, sends Ricky away, and strikes a self-defending pose by forming his hands into fists and starts crying, implying his inability to escape this uncomfortable situation he has been trying to avoid [01:31:22]. The medium close-up capturing his despair leaves the impression of a truth that has now been unveiled due to Ricky's fake confession, which paves the way for the colonel's expressing the truth about his own sexual identity in the next scene.

Moments later, Colonel Fitts pays Lester a visit and wants to be sure about the romantic signs he is certain of receiving from him: "Your wife is with another man and you don't care?" [01:36:03–01:36:08]. Lester speaks of his marriage being a "commercial for how normal we are when we're anything but" [01:36:12–01:36:21]. The colonel misinterprets Lester's suggestion to "get [him] out of these [wet] clothes" [01:36:34]. He cannot express his feelings and hugs Lester intensely, finally kissing him [01:36:42–01:37:09]. The camera presents a close-up of his face, which underlines the intimacy of this moment, revealing the colonel's shame and insecurity. Lester backs off gently and clarifies him receiving wrong signals, causing the colonel to leave Lester's garage ashamed. The final climax implies the improbability of the colonel's attraction to Lester being used as the motive for Lester's murder. The repression the colonel aggressively tries to uphold throughout his life indicates how an unsatisfying, reality-denying life can cause a person to psychologically deteriorate. The astutely inserted cuts leading to Lester's murder highlight the possibility of any of the film's relevant characters, whether it be Carolyn, Ricky, or Jane, having a motive for killing Lester. Each of those flawed characters are challenged during their search for their true identity. They reflect traits people in Western society share due to collective pressure, and even the murdering colonel falls under this category of pitiable people living an illusion by portraying their perceived opposite to enjoy social acceptance. In killing Lester, the colonel not only sends out an inner cry for help but, concurrently, tries to eliminate his true sexual desire and repressed feelings, because Lester was the only one who knows, although unwillingly.

Furthermore, Lester's final state of mind should not to be disregarded in order to understand the atmosphere during the last minutes of run time. Clearly, the film's ending leaves viewers in a mostly somber mood, notably due to Lester's sympathetic persona that evolves during the development of the plot. This remarkable transformation results in Lester's appreciation of "every single moment of [his] stupid little life" [01:50:59]. His death simulates a righteous call since he has reached a state of self-actualization he had been searching for. This circumstance explains the slight smile on his face after being murdered. Accordingly, Lester's death does not entirely convey sorrow; it is rather his happiness and satisfaction standing in the foreground. Lester's voice-over expressing gratitude intensifies this effect, which is why *American Beauty* ends on optimistic terms.

The happily tragic ending attenuates the colonel's desperate yet heinous deed and rather transmits the inner tragedy he experiences on a deeper note. Certainly, it might be argued that due to a queer character committing murder, the film connotes queerness on negative terms. However, this is not the case with *American Beauty*, as the film concentrates on the colonel's suppressing his real sexual identity in any way possible. Additionally, it is essential to consider that other LGBTQIA+ characters, namely, the neighbors Jim and Jim, are not portrayed as sinners or criminals. In fact, they coexist peacefully with the other protagonists. As scholar Kathleen Rowe Karlyn expresses accurately, "Fitts's pathology does not arise from his sexual orientation but his repression of it" (2004, 84). It is more the colonel's societal-driven mindset characterized by self-hatred that leads to murder rather than his sexuality. Therefore, Sam Mendes and Alan Ball fulfill a more than solid aim of illustrating the dangers repressive American society can cause. One of these hazards marks the problem with expressing sexual orientation, which people even in today's society, such as Colonel Frank Fitts, can be marginalized for. The colonel's case presents a severe issue with sexual identity that—to this day—various members of the LGBTQIA+ community endure. Nevertheless, *American Beauty* cautiously projects this problem onto the big screen without harming the LGBTQIA+ community's reputation. Ball, who identifies as gay, has also provided the screenplays for the successful series *Six Feet Under* and *True Blood*, where he "explores social, societal and political issues to create an immediate bond with the spectators," as Paquet-Deyris states (2012, 188).

Resulting from these findings, one can hardly label this film a negative account of the LGBTQIA+ community without being inexplicably judgmental and disregardful of the film's urge to criticize the American way of life. In order to assuage any remaining doubtful voices, as the film's promotional tagline implores: "Look closer."

See also *Fight Club*.

Bibliography

Arthur, Erica. "Where Lester Burnham Falls Down: Exposing the Facade of Victimhood in *American Beauty*." *Men and Masculinities* 7, no. 2 (2004): 127–43.

Ball, Alan. *American Beauty Early Draft. Screenplays and Scripts*, n.d. Accessed March 30, 2021. http://screenplaysandscripts.com/script_files/A/American_Beauty_early_draft.pdf.

Karlyn, Kathleen Rowe. "'Too Close for Comfort': 'American Beauty' and the Incest Motif." *Cinema Journal* 44, no. 1 (2004): 69–93.

Nungesser, Verena-Susanna. "Ways of Reclaiming Masculinity: Reactions to the 'Crisis of the White Man' in Paul Thomas Anderson's *Magnolia*, Sam Mendes' *American Beauty* and David Fincher's *Fight Club*." In *Gendered (Re)Visions: Constructions of Gender in Audiovisual Media*, edited by Marion Gymnich et al., 45–58. Göttingen: V&R Unipress, 2010.

Paquet-Deyris, Anne-Marie. "Alan Ball's California and Louisiana Series, *Six Feet Under & True Blood: A Troubled State of the Nation*." TV/Series, May 15, 2012. Accessed March 30, 2021. https://journals.openedition.org/tvseries/1195.

Pennington, Jody. *The History of Sex in American Film*. Westport, CT: Praeger, 2007.

—Tuğba Karaca

· B ·

BASIC INSTINCT (1992)

DIRECTOR: Paul Verhoeven
SCREENPLAY: Joe Eszterhas
CAST: Michael Douglas (Detective Nick "Shooter" Curran), Sharon Stone (Catherine Tramell), George Dzundza (Detective Gus Moran), Jeanne Tripplehorn (Dr. Beth Garner), Leilani Sarelle Figalan (Roxanne "Roxy" Hardy), Johnny Boz (Bill Cable)
SPECS: 127 minutes; color
AVAILABILITY: DVD (StudioCanal)

Basic Instinct is a neo-noir erotic thriller with Sharon Stone as bisexual novelist Catherine Tramell in the role of the Hitchcockian ice queen and Michael Douglas as Nick "Shooter" Curran in the role of the seedy and troubled San Francisco police detective. While Tramell is surrounded by accidental or unexplained death, Curran has his own checkered past, having been investigated by Internal Affairs for his role in the shooting of two tourists while undercover. The film opens with the lurid and brutal death of a one-time rock star, Johnny Boz, killed mid-coitus with an ice pick. Tramell is questioned as a suspect due to her relationship with Boz, which she refers to as sexual rather than emotional, based on passion and pleasure over and above intimacy during a graphic interrogation scene. Tramell's alibi for the murder is that her previous best-selling novel, *Love Hurts*, tells the story of a rock star killed in the manner of Boz himself, the argument being that she would not be "stupid" enough to write a book about a murder before committing that selfsame murder. Stupid she is not. Tramell has a dual degree in psychology and English, and viewers are reminded at key stages throughout the narrative that she is both "evil" and "brilliant." But what she is not, is arrested. Other characters in the film start turning up dead, including Tramell's live-in girlfriend Roxy Hardy as well as Curran's boss. Two hours of sex, violence, noirish plot twists, turns, and half-truths end with Curran shooting an unarmed Dr. Beth Garner as he believes her rather than Tramell to be the serial killer, before cozying up to Tramell, whom viewers find harboring an ice pick under their shared bed . . . in short, Tramell did it.

While Verhoeven and Eszterhas were the star names behind the screen, it was Michael Douglas who provided the Hollywood currency and credibility in front of the camera. That said, the film is routinely understood as a Sharon Stone star vehicle, as the tale of ultra sex and violence catapulted the performer to international stardom and, by extension, cemented her star status as a manipulating, duplicitous neo-noir femme fatale. While femme fatales are routinely punished or imprisoned at filmic closures for their social and sexual transgressions, Trammel is neither contained nor tamed at the end of the film, allowing her the rare chance of reprising the role in the sequel, *Basic Instinct 2* (2006).

Feminist critics and journalists such as Camille Paglia and Naomi Wolf present Sharon Stone's portrayal of Catherine Tramell as a sexually, socially, and economically empowered representation of bisexual womanhood during the postfeminist era. Indeed, Paglia has gone as far as to refer to *Basic Instinct* as her "favourite" film, providing audio commentary on the DVD release of the title in question (Haflidason 2014). And yet *Basic Instinct* could be variously reviled as a misogynist fantasy or celebrated as a feminist tour de force, condemned for blatant homophobia or celebrated as the ultimate cult lesbian movie. And Stone's portrayal of Tramell could be variously reviled, celebrated, or condemned accordingly. For some, Tramell is seen as a powerful feminist presence within popular culture, while for others, the character represents an antifeminist backlash and homophobia.

Basic Instinct does not shy away from depictions of same-sex attraction, which is rare for the period and remains so at the time of writing, and yet the film was held up as both misogynist and homophobic, with campaigning groups such as GLAAD releasing statements to the press protesting the negative portrayals of lesbians and bisexuals (Harris and Corwin 1992). Even before a single roll of film had been shot, the *Basic Instinct* film script became a boiling point for its negative portrayals of gay and lesbian characters in the media. Protests came from activist groups such as GLAAD, Queer Nation, LABIA, and NOW, and although the demonstrators were not successful in altering the film, they received so much coverage that review media found itself responding to activist charges in their writing (Cohan 1998). While NOW branded *Basic Instinct* one of "the most blatantly misogynistic films in recent memory" (Grant and McGregor 1992), GLAAD charged the film with presenting "negative portrayals that no self-respecting gay person would put up with" (Grant and McGregor 1992). After all, the lesbian and bisexual characters in the film are homicidal psychopaths. Hardy attempts to kill Curran, and after her death, graphic photos reveal that she slashed her two younger brothers to death with her father's razor, and Tramell herself is implicated in the murder of her parents and former lovers while Dr. Garner is eventually assumed to be the killer of a college professor, Lieutenant Nilsen, and Detective Moran. *Basic Instinct* was charged with depicting "exactly the kinds of stereotypes the gay community was trying to avoid in mainstream entertainment," and as such demonstrators tried to keep audiences away from the film by revealing the identity of the killer (Morrison 2016). However, such reception had little effect on the commercial success of the production because, either despite or due to the public protests, the film grossed $352 million worldwide, ranking it among the top five highest-grossing titles of 1992.

LGBTQIA+ activists critiqued the film for its perpetuation of gay and lesbian stereotypes at a time when homophobic violence was on the rise in the wider society. Although the central female protagonists in the film are presented as bisexual, it is of concern here that, first, the word "bisexual" is never used in the production; second, Garner refers to her bisexuality as both a phase and a source of embarrassment; and third, the film plays to stereotypes of both the "lipstick" and the "butch" lesbian without displaying genuine intimacy between bisexual characters. A particular low point of a title littered with problematic depictions of bisexuality comes when Curran asks Hardy about her sexual escapades, stating, "Let me ask you something Rocky, man to man. . . ." Moreover, although Tramell and Hardy live together, their passionate relationship is "all too conscious of creating an arousing spectacle" for Curran and the heterosexual male spectator (Nelson 2012). The openly bisexual Tramell is presented as a masochistic male fantasy whose bisexuality is inextricably tied to the threat of violence and death. Bisexuality, in this sense, could be understood as "one more feature of the male perception of the dangerous modern woman" (Deleyto 1997, 24–25). While the figure of the femme fatale, showcased in 1940s film noir and rearticulated in the 1970s and beyond, suggests an equation between female sexuality, death, and danger, *Basic Instinct* appears to foreground the unconscious weight of a culture that has inextricably linked the LGBTQIA+ community with criminality (Nelson 2012).

Basic Instinct would struggle to defend itself against charges of misogyny and homophobia, and there is clear evidence to suggest that the film's depiction of Tramell and her supporting cast of homicidal bisexuals was and continues to be a turnoff for LGBTQIA+ audiences, but so too there are members of the community who see power and empowerment in the neo-noir erotic thriller and the character of Tramell (Roberson 2018). With this more positive reading in mind, Adam Morrison begins what he terms a "gay movie trivia challenge" and asks readers to consider if they have ever seen a film where "a gay character" was either the wealthiest, smartest, or most successful person in the room. The answer, of course, being that Tramell is that rare LGBTQIA+ character who is all of the above. Writing over twenty years after the film's original release, on the back of the sequel, he reads the bisexual Tramell as omnipotent, concluding that the contemporary LGBTQIA+ community needs "more films like *Basic Instinct*" (Morrison 2016).

Not to detract from the problematic representations of bisexuality that are evident in the film in question, it is worth noting that *Basic Instinct* is an equal opportunity offender in that women, men, bisexuals, lesbians, heterosexuals, police officers, psychologists, academic professors, and novelists are all presented as devious or deviant at key stages throughout the film. In the director's own words, "nastiness is spread evenly among the film's characters" (Verhoeven, cited in Fox 1992). That said, Eszterhas and Verhoeven do seem to save their most vitriolic representations for the women of the film in general, and the insatiable and duplicitous bisexual women in particular.

See also *Cruel Intentions*.

Bibliography

Cohan, Steve. "Censorship and Narrative Indeterminacy in *Basic Instinct*: You Won't Learn Anything from Me I Don't Want You to Know." In *Contemporary Hollywood Cinema*, edited by Steve Neale and Murray Smith, 263–79. London: Routledge, 1998.

Deleyto, Celestino. "The Margins of Pleasure: Female Monstrosity and Male Paranoia." *Film Criticism* 11, no. 3 (1997): 20–42.

Fox, David. "To Protest *Basic Instinct*, Gay Groups Plan Oscars Disruption." *Seattle Times*, March 17, 1992. Accessed March 10, 2021. https://archive.seattletimes.com/archive/?date=19920317&slug=1481460.

Grant, Steve, and Alex McGregor. "Sex Crimes: Divide and Conquer." *Time Out* (London), April 22, 1992.

Haflidason, Almar. "*Basic Instinct* SE DVD." BBC Films—Review, September 24, 2014. Accessed May 20, 2021. http://www.bbc.co.uk/films/2002/05/17/basic_instinct_se_1992_dvd _review.shtml.

Harris, Scott, and Miles Corwin. "Opposition to Film *Basic Instinct* Rises: Entertainment: A Coalition of Women's and Gay Rights Activists Fears the Movie's Depiction of Bisexuals and Lesbians Will Result in Increased Violence against Women." *Los Angeles Times*, March 21, 1992. Accessed May 20, 2021. https://www.latimes.com/archives/la-xpm-1992-03-21-me -3817-story.html.

Morrison, Adam. "Essential LGBTQ Films: Adam Morrison on *Basic Instinct*." *Black List*, April 28, 2016. Accessed March 10, 2021. https://blog.blcklst.com/essential-lgbtq-films-adam -morrison-on-basic-instinct-bc3fb41510c8.

Nelson, Carrie. "Visi(bi)lity: Biphobia Bingo! A Look at *Basic Instinct*." *Bitch Media*, March 13, 2012. Accessed March 10, 2021. https://www.bitchmedia.org/post/visibility-biphobia-bingo-a -look-at-basic-instinct-feminist-film.

Roberson, Jennie. "The Unicorn Scale: *Basic Instinct*." bi.org, November 27, 2018. Accessed March 10, 2021. https://bi.org/en/articles/the-unicorn-scale-basic-instinct.

—Rebecca Feasey

BATMAN V SUPERMAN: DAWN OF JUSTICE (2016)

DIRECTOR: Zack Snyder
SCREENPLAY: Chris Terrio and David S. Goyer
CAST: Ben Affleck (Batman), Henry Cavill (Superman/Clark Kent), Amy Adams (Lois Lane), Jesse Eisenberg (Lex Luthor), Diane Lane (Martha Kent), Laurence Fishburne (Perry White), and Jeremy Irons (Alfred)
SPECS: 151 minutes (theatrical release)/183 minutes (ultimate edition); color
AVAILABILITY: DVD/Blu-ray (Warner Bros.)

Following the events of Zack Snyder's reboot of the Superman myth with 2013's *Man of Steel*, this film centers on Gotham City protector Bruce Wayne— Batman—dealing with the fallout from Zod and Superman's epic battle over Earth in *Man of Steel*. Personal loss and destruction trigger his feelings of loss over his parents, and he worries he cannot protect the world against someone with superhuman abilities. Meanwhile, protagonist Clark Kent—Superman— grapples with the idea that helping people has unexpected consequences for both him and his alter ego. Both of these heroes, in their insecurities, fall victim to Lex Luthor's scheme to pit them against each other and, as a result, become entangled in a misunderstanding that could have worldwide consequences.

In 2016, the PR for this film pitted these two heroes against each other with menacing glances and threatening poses—looking, supposedly, like one was ready to harm the other. However, even at this early stage, much of the feedback to these images focused on the tension between the two that actually looked a bit like sexual chemistry, as depicted in articles such as "Internet Has a Gay Old Time with New Images from *Batman v Superman*." Collecting various responses from online articles and tweets, Avery argues that these PR images are "supposed to be all gritty and serious" but instead "are giving us a campy gay vibe" (Avery 2016). Most of the feedback focused on the images where the two are shown together. Instead of prompting the threat of violence, the overall appearance of these men make it look like they are about to kiss: "If they weren't mortal enemies, it would make for a lovely climactic scene in a romantic comedy" (Avery 2016).

Since the film itself does not have a lead character who is LGBTQIA+, it cannot pass the Vito Russo Test. Categorizing a film as a "pass" means it meets three criteria, much like the Bechdel Test for strong female characters: "First, the film must include an identifiably LGBTQ+ character. Second, that character cannot be defined solely by their sexual orientation or gender identity. Third, the LGBTQ+ character must contribute significantly to the plot of the film" (them and GLAAD 2019).

Both Clark Kent and Bruce Wayne are clearly portrayed as heterosexual in both action and language. Clark has an emotional love scene with Lois Lane, wherein he clearly buys flowers for her and is worried about her safety, stating, "The woman I love could have been blown up or shot. Think of what could have happened" [00:25:29]. Similarly, Bruce's eyes wander to every pretty girl. When making small talk at a bar with someone who is Russian, Bruce casually quotes a popular saying, then chuckles and states, "Three nights with a Bolshoi ballerina, and that line was all she taught me" [00:38:46].

Ben Affleck as Batman and Henry Cavill as Superman in *Batman v Superman: Dawn of Justice*. Courtesy of Warner Bros./Photofest.

However, there is a third main character in the film, the antagonist Lex Luthor. In contrast to other portraits of Luthor over time, this version is young and presents the character as "effeminate and nebbish," a character who does not have any revealed love interest, male or female (Bartlebyscriven 2018). He does not flirt with any women—or men—on screen. However, in the third act, he creates a monster, literally, to kill Superman. This scene can be read as a reenactment, in a way, of Lois and Clark's romantic tub scene: it involves him gently caressing Zod's body in water, mixing it with his own bodily fluid to create something monstrous. "Doomsday is a manifestation of the worst sorts of heteronormative fears of homosexual copulation, basically, tinged with paranoia about what's 'unnatural'" (Bartlebyscriven 2018).

In interviews, Snyder denies that his movies are homophobic, stating, "Some people have said to me, 'Your movie is homoerotic,' and some have said, 'Your movie's homophobic.' In my mind, the movie is neither. But I don't have a problem with people interpreting it the way they'd like to" (Jensen 2007). However, one of the most quoted lines in the film could definitely be interpreted as homophobic: "The next time they shine your light in the sky, don't go to it" [01:19:37].

There are some positives in the film, as GLAAD points out in their assessment of each of 2016's new theatrical releases: "Anderson Cooper and Andrew Sullivan each appear in very brief scenes to deliver some super-hero related news. Though their cameo appearances do technically meet GLAAD's criteria for an onscreen LGBTQ impression, we continually hope that future superhero films will include substantial queer characters" (GLAAD 2017).

In the end, the film tackles the haves and have-nots—making social commentary on toxic masculinity and politics—effectively, but the film could address gay stereotypes and be more inclusive.

See also *Venom*.

Bibliography

"2016 Ratings." *GLAAD*, 2017. Accessed October 21, 2021. https://www.glaad.org/sri/2017/warner-brothers.

Avery, Dan. "Internet Has a Gay Old Time with New Images from *Batman v Superman*." *NewNowNext*, March 4, 2016. Accessed October 23, 2021. http://www.newnownext.com/internet-has-a-gay-old-time-with-new-images-from-batman-v-superman/03/2016/.

Bartlebyscriven. "Zack Snyder, Part IV: *Batman v Superman* v Toxic Masculinity." *Bart Cave*, September 3, 2018. Accessed October 23, 2021. https://bartcave.wordpress.com/2018/09/03/zack-snyder-part-iv-batman-v-superman-v-toxic-masculinity/.

Jensen, Michael. "300's Director Admits Using Homosexuality to Scare 20-Year-Old Men." *NewNowNext*, March 11, 2007. Accessed October 23, 2021. http://www.newnownext.com/300s-director-admits-using-homosexuality-to-scare-20-year-old-men/03/2007/.

them and GLAAD. "What Is the Vito Russo Test? A Smart Way to Gauge LGBTQ Hollywood Inclusion." *them*, April 10, 2019. Accessed October 23, 2021. https://www.them.us/story/vito-russo-test-glaad.

—Sandra Eckard

BATTLE OF THE SEXES (2017)

DIRECTORS: Jonathan Dayton and Valerie Faris
SCREENPLAY: Simon Beaufoy, inspired by real-life events
CAST: Emma Stone (Billie Jean King), Steve Carell (Bobby Riggs), Andrea Riseborough (Marilyn Barnett), Bill Pullman (Jack Kramer), Alan Cumming (Cuthbert "Ted" Tinling), Austin Stowell (Larry King)
SPECS: 122 minutes; color
AVAILABILITY: DVD (Twentieth Century Fox)

On September 20, 1973, tennis pros Billie Jean King and Bobby Riggs faced off in a televised match, watched by ninety million people worldwide. King won the match in three sets, and her win made great strides toward respect for women's tennis. This is the story of *Battle of the Sexes*, a 2017 film from directors Jonathan Dayton and Valerie Faris and screenwriter Simon Beaufoy. The film begins three years prior to the famed match, when nine female tennis players form what eventually becomes the WTA Tour. As the tour starts gaining attention and the Women's Tennis Association forms in 1973, Bobby Riggs proposes a match against the top female player, boasting he could beat her with ease. While he first pressures King to face him, she refuses, and Riggs ends up playing against Margaret Court in May 1973. Riggs beats Court, prompting King finally to accept his proposal. Riggs starts the match strong, but King eventually beats him in three straight sets. Though the film is billed as an adaptation of this great sporting event, its soul lies with Emma Stone's portrayal of Billie Jean King, both fighting for a spot in a male-dominated world and exploring and discovering her sexuality.

Early in the film, there is a sensual scene that takes place in a hair salon. As stylist Marilyn Barnett lovingly and intimately cuts King's hair, Billie Jean's breath hitches. The camera never wavers from Stone's poignant performance, realizing her feelings for Marilyn as Billie Jean. But she is married to a man, and she has never been with a woman before. This dawning realization is the through line of the movie, as is Billie Jean's relationship with Marilyn. The film's visual and audio style drastically change during this scene, suddenly becoming almost dreamlike as everything else in the salon, in the world at large, falls away, and the only thing left is Marilyn's fingers running through Billie Jean's hair. There is an acute sense of intimacy about the scene and no mistaking this scene for "gal pals"—it is intentional. As director Jonathan Dayton told *Vulture*: "We love tennis, don't get me wrong. But it was the love story that drove us to make this" (Buchanan 2017).

The film is the love story both between Billie Jean and Marilyn but also between Billie Jean and herself. Stone plays King with tremendous humanity without making her a one-dimensional figure, reduced only to her sexuality or feminism. It is, by far, one of Stone's most notable roles, especially coming off her Oscar-winning role in *La La Land*. She is simultaneously poised, strong, self-assured, and vulnerable. In portraying Billie Jean's fight for women's rights in professional sports, Stone is never more confident. As Billie Jean challenges Jack Kramer, a leader of professional tennis tours and misogynist, she blazes with glory. She knows she is risking her career, and the careers of the women who join her, but she does not back down. Her sexuality is trickier to navigate, particularly given the true nature of the film. The relationship depicted between Billie Jean and Marilyn is akin to that of first love, including both the thrill and fear of it, which is even heavier for Billie Jean as a public figure and trailblazer. Throughout all of this, including Billie Jean and Marilyn sleeping together for the first time, learning about each other, and falling in love, Billie Jean remains married to her husband, Larry King (stoically played by Austin Stowell). Larry is an ever-supportive husband of Billie Jean, leading the film to explore Billie Jean's conflict as not about her sexuality but about her relationship with Larry irrevocably changing. Her journey of discovery and self-acceptance is not a spectacle in the film, though it may be softened to make it more palatable for straight audiences.

That is one of the biggest critiques of the film—its mitigation of Billie Jean's coming-out story and her relationship with her sexuality. As Jill Gutowitz writes for *Vice*:

> Instead of a realistic take on one woman's struggle to square her private desires with life in the public eye—a struggle complicated by the 70s-era misogyny Billie Jean and her peers fought so fiercely against—we instead get a soft, unrealistic lesbian storyline that treats Billie Jean and Marilyn's romance with a forced gravitas that didn't match the tone of the movie. (2017)

The movie ends right after King defeats Bobby in the televised match. Conveniently, this also means the film ends long before the ugly dissolution of King and Barnett's relationship. The film gets to celebrate the revelatory relationship, albeit not without its obstacles, without the weight of depicting the actual outing of King and the aftermath. During the 1970s, King and Barnett's relationship ended, but Barnett continued to live in the Kings' Malibu, California, house rent free, until 1979 when the Kings asked her to move out (Ware 2011, 184). Not wanting to leave and armed with "letters from the tennis star at the height of their relationship as well as credit card receipts and paid bills that she had kept, Barnett threatened to go public" (Ware 2011, 184). The Kings stayed resolute; however, two years later, in May 1981, Barnett sued for both the title of the Malibu house as well as half of King's income from 1973 to 1979 (Ware 2011, 184). Over three decades later, King described these events as "horrible" but recalled to *NBC News* her choice to come out and claim her identity: "I said: 'I'm going to do it. I don't care. This is important to me to tell the truth.' The one thing my mother always said, 'To thine own self be true'" (Jackson 2017). Despite her mother's quoting of Shakespeare bolstering her at the time, her parents "remained deeply shaken by the revelations about her affair with Marilyn Barnett for years afterwards," though her husband stuck by her side (Ware 2011, 185). In the 2017 *NBC News* interview, King noted she was pleased the coming out process was becoming more acceptable in recent years but said no one should ever be outed, as the most important thing is for LGBTQIA+ people to "feel safe" and "have allies with you" (Jackson 2017). In speaking of the movie in the same interview, King hoped it would be relevant, particularly for younger generations.

How relevant can it be, however, if it more immediately turned King's story romantic and celebratory rather than acknowledge the truth of her struggles? It is a question constantly asked of art. That is, what responsibilities are creators beholden to when it comes to representing marginalized communities? It is not as easy to criticize *Battle of the Sexes* as, say, a movie with egregious stereotypes and offensive depictions of LGBTQIA+ characters. *Battle of the Sexes* celebrates King's sexuality, in a time when she had already become a lesbian icon, and offers audiences something triumphant and joyful, a revolutionary act in and of itself as too many stories focus exclusively on LGBTQIA+ trauma. In the film, Billie Jean King is also not the only positive LGBTQIA+ character. Beyond Marilyn, who, again, is given a much fairer shake than in real life, there is also Ted Tingling. Alan Cumming plays the role of the real-life gay tennis player who was also a spy before later transitioning into a fashion career. The way Ted is written comes close to being a negative stereotype, but the way Cumming endearingly embodies him saves the performance and makes the character far more earnest and heartwarming. In interviews, Cumming played into this by describing Tingling as a "fairy godfather" to King (Cohn 2017). At the end of the film, Billie Jean and Ted share a tearful embrace, as Ted emphatically tells her the world will change and they will be able to love who they want. Is it a bit of a cheesy line? Sure. Did the real Tingling actually say that? Unknown. However, that is not the point.

When Benjamin Lee, an editor for *The Guardian*, attended NewFest, New York's LGBTQ film festival, in 2018, he noticed all the films he watched had something in common, "a crushingly sad ending" (2018). Whether torn apart by death, homophobia, or the dissolution of a relationship, the common thread was that LGBTQIA+ characters were being torn apart by something. For years, it has

Emma Stone as Billie Jean King and Alan Cumming as Cuthbert "Ted" Tinling in *Battle of the Sexes*. Courtesy of Fox Searchlight Pictures/Photofest.

become a given that gay characters end up drowning in misery, as predictable a trope as a virginal brunette outsmarting a masked killer, or a beautiful straight couple who were sworn enemies ending up in a passionate kiss after an airport reunion. It is known by some as the "Bury Your Gays" trope. However, Benjamin Lee acknowledges the "great value and importance in sharing tough, grim, real stories and reminding many of the fatal consequences that can still meet being honest about one's sexuality," but he argues "it's also equally as important for us to see stories of resilience, hope, survival and romance" (2018). He ends his piece:

> There are still huge portions of gay history that need to be given space on-screen, undoubtedly, but they should be allowed to exist alongside more escapist fare as well. Homophobia persists for so many LGBT people in the real world with a terrifying rise in hate crime post-Trump but we don't always require a 120-minute reminder of it at the multiplex. I want to see gay characters thriving, falling in love, having fun, saving the day, overcoming challenges, staying together and being given the space to live happily ever after. Being queer isn't always easy but up on the big screen, it shouldn't always be this hard. (2018)

There is no right or wrong answer to this overall question, particularly in relation to this movie, which is not as easily condemned as a movie that fetishizes LGBTQIA+ trauma, but it highlights the complicated nature of representing for an entire community that does not exist as a monolith in society. The LGBTQIA+ community is vast and diverse and, therefore, LGBTQIA+ cinema should be as well.

See also *Behind the Candelabra*; *Can You Ever Forgive Me?*; *Kinsey*.

Bibliography

Buchanan, Kyle. "The Secret behind *Battle of the Sexes*' Most Sensual Scene." *Vulture*, September 22, 2017. Accessed May 27, 2021. https://www.vulture.com/2017/09/battle-of-the-sexes-haircut-hairdresser-scene-emma-stone.html.

Cohn, Paulette. "Alan Cumming on Why *Battle of the Sexes* Is Definitely Relevant." *Parade*, September 19, 2017. Accessed May 27, 2021. https://parade.com/603159/paulettecohn/alan-cumming-on-why-battle-of-the-sexes-is-definitely-relevant-in-2017/.

Gutowitz, Jill. "How 'Battle of the Sexes' Flubbed Its Lesbian Storyline." *Vice*, October 11, 2017. May 27, 2021. https://www.vice.com/en/article/a3kmbj/how-battle-of-the-sexes-flubbed-its-lesbian-storyline.

Jackson, Sierra C. "'It Was Horrible': Billie Jean King Recalls Being Outed in 1981." *NBC News*, September 25, 2017. Accessed May 27, 2021. https://www.nbcnews.com/feature/nbc-out/it-was-horrible-billie-jean-king-recalls-being-publicly-outed-n804451.

Lee, Benjamin. "LGBT Cinema Still Needs More Happy Endings." *Guardian*, October 31, 2018. Accessed May 27, 2021. https://www.theguardian.com/film/commentisfree/2018/oct/31/lgbt-cinema-still-needs-more-happy-endings.

Ware, Susan. *Game, Set, Match: Billie Jean King and the Revolution in Women's Sports*. Chapel Hill: University of North Carolina Press, 2011.

—Anya Crittenton

BEEFCAKE (1998)

DIRECTOR: Thom Fitzgerald
SCREENWRITER: Thom Fitzgerald
CAST: Carroll Godsman (Delia Mizer), Daniel MacIvor (Bob Mizer), J. Griffin
  Mazeika (Red), Jonathan Torrens (David)
SPECS: 94 minutes; color
AVAILABILITY: DVD (Strand Releasing)

A bittersweet homage to the golden age of male physique photography, director
Fitzgerald's biopic limns the life and times of Bob Mizer (1922–1992), arguably
America's most significant pioneer in the field of male erotica. Mixing documentary and drama, the film intercuts fictional reenactments of episodes from
Mizer's life, grainy footage from his short films, and present-day interviews with
former physique models, including Joe Dallesandro and Jack LaLanne. The film
begins with fictionalized scenes from Mizer's childhood, as he discovers his dual
obsessions with photography and the male form. In 1945, Mizer founds his now-
famous Athletic Model Guild (AMG), working as a skilled amateur photographer
from his Los Angeles home. Director Fitzgerald initially pictures Mizer living
a cheeky, idyllic lifestyle, surrounded by youthful models and assisted by his
indulgent mother, who fashions the models' censorship-mandated posing straps.
Much of the film portrays Mizer as a heroic, virtuous artist devoted to neoclassical beauty; in dramatized sequences, Mizer repeatedly blanches at the notion
that he is producing pornography. The film's tone darkens as Mizer encounters
increasing scrutiny from the authorities, who, beginning in 1945, prosecuted him
for skirting obscenity statutes and possibly exploiting models under the age of
eighteen. The film's final act hints at a viciousness beneath Mizer's rose-colored
sheen. After an underage, suicidal model struggling with his sexuality reports
Mizer to the vice squad, the narrative turns to Mizer's seedier colleagues, who
are more interested in exploiting young men than in preserving Hellenistic aesthetics. In an interview segment toward the film's end, ex-model Dallesandro
suggests that Mizer was not merely a disciplined voyeur but also procured his
models for sex ("It turns out he was a scuzz-bag after all!" Dallesandro exclaims).
Other interviewees contest Mizer's knowledge of and participation in sexual
exploitation, just as some of his straight, more naïve "fitness" models remained
unaware that they were disrobing for gay audiences.

A highly publicized queer film when first released, *Beefcake* offers a more
sentimental, late 1990s rejoinder to the militant New Queer Cinema of the earlier nineties. Whereas films such as Tom Kalin's *Swoon* (1992) and Gregg Araki's
The Living End (1992) were marked by AIDS-era angst and outrage, Fitzgerald
keeps *Beefcake*'s tone sanguine and playful. Many sequences in the film capture the joyful innocence that informed Mizer's 8-mm film loops, which often
parodied kitschy Hollywood tropes. Models would pose as cowboys and Indians,
James Dean–esque street punks, or scantily clad extras in ersatz biblical epics,
with wrestling substituting for sexual contact. Even the last third of *Beefcake*,
dealing with Mizer's legal prosecutions and persecutions, comes across as more
wistful than angry. A despairing history of political oppression nevertheless
underwrites the entire narrative, as Mizer operated AMG at a time when same-

sex conduct was an imprisonable offense and Hollywood could not even portray a heterosexual married couple sharing a bed. Mizer's photos and film loops— available by mail order through his in-house publication, *Physique Pictorial*— not only fostered semipublic venues for gay male desire but reproofed a Mc-Carthyite America that conflated nationalism with erotophobia. In the 1940s, as a voice-over in Fitzgerald's film explains, "penalties for nude art were more severe than those for bank robbery, manslaughter, or assault." "In San Francisco and New York," the narrator continues, "judges stated that . . . any form of nudity represented a public menace that must be dealt with severely." This sort of moral panic might seem the antiquated, neurotic symptom of prefeminist and prequeer times. Yet even in the twenty-first century there remain—in all fifty American states—laws that criminalize the public appearance of human skin and organs, even if nudity is no longer an *artistic* taboo. This lingering moral panic arguably has ideological motives, defining obscenity in narrowly sexual rather than broadly sociological or socio-ethical terms. Current state and local statutes repeatedly insist that public nudity will "cause alarm" to onlookers, as if the sight of an unobstructed gluteus should be more alarming (or obscene) than homelessness, rampant pollution, racial inequities, or other perfectly legal societal ills.

The pages of Mizer's *Physique Pictorial* directly addressed America's long-standing cultural panics over nudity. Alongside Mizer's photographs were polemical articles that bemoaned American prudishness and extolled lost Platonic ideals of natural beauty. A talented amateur, Mizer sought to produce commercial (homo)erotica for mass audiences in an era when the male nudes by highbrow photographers, such as George Platt Lynes, were yet unpublished or known only in private circles. Mizer was hardly alone in his quest to move homoeroticism into the mainstream. Contemporaries such as Bruce Bellas (known as "Bruce of Los Angeles") and Alonzo Hanagan ("Lon of New York") were likewise disseminating male seminudes through the mail-order marketplace, and alongside *Physique Pictorial* arose a myriad of digest-sized physique magazines—*Grecian Guild, Adonis, Fizeek, Male Figure*—that recycled the same models. Catering to underground audiences, Mizer did not need to replicate the techniques of the Mattachine Society, a pre-Stonewall gay rights organization that attempted (with little success) to advance a sterile, assimilatory image of gay men that would be palatable to middle-class America. Mizer's world was an erotic utopia, concerned only with aesthetics. Mizer was, in fact, the first American publisher to print the artwork of Tom of Finland. Not only offering a measure of queer visibility, physique magazines also fostered and facilitated invisible gay communities. According to physique magazine historian David K. Johnson, *Grecian Guild*, first published in 1955, sold its readers a trademark pin to wear "proudly," allowing "like-minded men" to identify one another discreetly (2010, 872). Through these identifications, members could develop "regional chapters, national conventions, [and] membership directories" for those dedicated to "the perceived ideals of ancient Greece" (2010, 872).

In the public spaces of their magazines, physique publishers openly argued for artistic freedom on First Amendment grounds. Mizer and his colleagues were well aware of the treacherous legal waters they were entering. *Physique*

Pictorial often featured editorials that railed against the escalating censorships endemic to postwar America. Mizer's appeals to freedom of expression sought to counter censors' quasi-nationalistic appeals to repressive decency. *Physique Pictorial* regularly printed subscribers' letters—many probably written by Mizer himself—that advise readers to be wary of postal inspectors tasked with rooting out indecent materials. In a 1955 issue of *Physique Pictorial*, Mizer offered a short polemic, titled "Crucifixion of the Arts," that praised the American Civil Liberties Union and traced governmental control of media to the Comstock Act of 1873, which banned the mailing of "obscene, lewd, or lascivious" writings or pictures (Mizer 1955, 2–3). Originally intended to prevent the spread of information about birth control, the Comstock Act was first used to suppress Ezra Heywood's *Cupid's Yokes*, an 1878 broadsheet that advocated women's bodily autonomy and what Heywood (an anarchist) called "sexual self-government." Comstock's vague wording allowed authorities considerable leeway in their crusade to drum up moral panic in later years. Once employed to suppress D. H. Lawrence's *Lady Chatterley's Lover* and James Joyce's *Ulysses*, Comstock was exploited by postal inspectors in the 1940s and 1950s to confiscate anything slightly titillating. The 1957 obscenity case surrounding Allen Ginsburg's *Howl* turned out to be a boon for physique photographers. In his landmark ruling, Judge Clayton Horn exempted controversial works from censorship if they possessed "redeeming social value," a legal construct allowing physique photographers to argue that their images promoted nonsexual ideals of health and well-being.

Purveyors of physique magazines nevertheless endured regular harassment by law enforcement, as the last third of Fitzgerald's film demonstrates. Mizer's work was directly attacked in *Perversion for Profit* (1965), a thirty-minute piece of antipornography propaganda that links photos of undraped young men to rampant communism, ungodly values, and the dissolution of the social fabric. Throughout the 1960s, liberal Supreme Court decisions increasingly struck down obscenity laws, and toward the end of the decade, nudity would enter the mainstream with the introduction of the MPAA (in 1967) and the international distribution of erotically frank art films, such as Vilgot Sjöman's once-scandalous *I Am Curious: Yellow* (1967). Adapting to liberalizing times, Mizer finally dispensed with the posing straps and ventured a (softcore) feature-length film, *Teacher's Pests* (1969), with full frontal nudity and only the semblance of a storyline. While *Beefcake* presents Mizer as a nearly asexual man appalled by explicit imagery, he did venture a few hard-core loops in the early 1970s. By that time, however, hard-core porn had already transcended the quaint form of the ten-minute loop, and underground auteurs like Tom de Simone and Wakefield Poole had begun to incorporate hard-core into 16-mm narrative features. Recent years have nevertheless witnessed a great resurgence of interest in Mizer's neoclassical sensibilities, and today the nonprofit Bob Mizer Foundation (www.bobmizer.org) not only preserves Mizer's photographic and cinematic legacy but celebrates him as a trailblazing activist.

See also *Cruising*; *The Genesis Children*; *Pink Narcissus*.

Bibliography

Bob Mizer Foundation. https://www.bobmizer.org. Accessed July 15, 2021.

Johnson, David K. "Physique Pioneers: The Politics of 1960s Gay Consumer Culture." *Journal of Social History* 43, no. 4 (2010): 867–92.

Mizer, Bob. *Physique Pictorial* 5, no. 2 (Summer 1955).

Padva, Gilad. "Nostalgic Physique: Displaying Foucauldian Muscles and Celebrating the Male Body in *Beefcake*." In *Queer Nostalgia in Cinema and Pop Culture*, edited by Gilad Padva, 35–57. London: Palgrave Macmillan, 2014.

—Andrew Grossman

BEHIND THE CANDELABRA (2013)

DIRECTOR: Steven Soderbergh, based on the memoir *Behind the Candelabra: My Life with Liberace* by Scott Thorson

SCREENPLAY: Richard LaGravenese

CAST: Michael Douglas (Liberace), Matt Damon (Scott Thorson), Scott Bakula (Bob Black), Debbie Reynolds (Frances Liberace), Dan Aykroyd (Seymour Heller), Rob Lowe (Dr. Jack Startz)

SPECS: 118 minutes; color

AVAILABILITY: DVD (HBO Films)

Behind the Candelabra is based on Scott Thorson's memoir, *Behind the Candelabra: My Life with Liberace* (1988). The book details the last ten years of Liberace's life and the six-year relationship he had with Thorson. The movie closely adheres to the book in recounting how Thorson, who was eighteen (and sometimes reported as seventeen) when he met Liberace, was propositioned by the world-renowned pianist forty years his senior to work as "a companion, a bodyguard, someone I can talk to" [00:22:20]. This offer also included the expectation of an ongoing sexual relationship, and Thorson, who spent most of his youth in foster homes, quickly agreed. The two form an all-encompassing, tumultuous attachment. The film traces the progression from their initial arrangement to a shared life together and the eventual dissolution of their relationship. *Behind the Candelabra* reveals the good, the bad, and the ugly, including the opulence of Liberace's life, the joys of domesticity, the endless effort to manage Liberace's claim of heterosexuality, the plastic surgery to make Scott look more like Liberace, Scott's eventual drug addiction, Liberace's leaving of Scott for an eighteen-year-old dancer, and the lawsuit that became the nation's first "palimony" case. It is reported that Hollywood studios refused to finance the biopic because it was "too gay," at which point Soderbergh turned to HBO (Child 2013). Though ineligible for an Academy Award due to being an at-home release, *Behind the Candelabra* won two Golden Globe Awards and eleven Primetime Emmy Awards, including Outstanding Miniseries or Movie and Outstanding Lead Actor in a Miniseries or Movie for Douglas.

The unmistakable beat of Donna Summer's "I Feel Love" introduces viewers to the last ten years in the life of Liberace, the pianist as flamboyant as he was eccentric. The song situates audiences in the days of disco before the introductory "HBO" is fully across the screen, and, for those in the know, the soundtrack locates Liberace and Thorson in a post-Stonewall, pre-HIV moment. The first scene is the interior of a gay bar, where Bob Black (played by a heavily mustachioed Scott Bakula) picks up Thorson (a feather-haired, cowboy-shirt-clad Matt Damon). Skipping the sexual encounter entirely, the scene cuts to Thorson's home life with his foster parents, Joe and Rose. During the dialogue that follows, "gay" identity becomes routed through geography.

After relaying that Scott has a message from "a man named Bob Black," Joe asks, "Is that one of them San Francisco fellas?" Scott says, "No, he's from here, West Hollywood" [00:03:30]. Only Joe, Rose, and Scott don't live in West Hollywood—known as an urban, flashy, gay mecca—they live on a ranch outside of LA. "For those in the know" thus proves important for both viewer and character alike. This exchange with Joe and Rose provides a fine example of the ways Soderbergh navigates multiple positions of viewership and insider/outsider knowledge of gay life. While Joe and Rose are both aware and accepting of Scott's "friends," no one asks about or directly acknowledges the matter of his sexual identity or gay *life*. (It should also be noted that Scott identifies as bisexual, though no one takes him seriously on this point for the duration of the film and thus treats his subject position as exclusively gay.)

The treatment of gay men (including bisexual men claimed as gay) in *Behind the Candelabra* deals mostly in established, easily available details that tend toward the universal. When Scott announces that he is going to work for Liberace, for instance, he assures Rose that Liberace "doesn't like me just for *that*" [00:24:37]. In this scene, the gaze is a collective one, as Rose, Joe, Scott, and audiences all understand "*that*" to mean sex in any orientation. However, the presentation of intimate knowledge about gay life and culture in particular is sometimes lost in translation. For instance, the sole question under "frequently asked questions" on IMDb's entry for this film reads, "What substance is being inhaled by Liberace during his love scene with Scott at the 39-minute mark?" (IMDb n.d.). The answer is "poppers," of course—but you would have to know in order to *know*; "poppers" are alkyl nitrites that relax smooth muscles throughout the body, particularly popular with gay men and the kind of vigorous sexual bottoming at the thirty-nine-minute mark.

In these ways, the film certainly foregrounds sexuality, objectification, and intimacy between men, but it does not seek to address the larger sociopolitical or cultural climate of the era. Stripped of the particularities of sexual orientation, theirs is a story seen time and again between wealthy, powerful men and their carefully groomed, decades-younger partners.

This trajectory is one that Carlucci, Liberace's tight-white-pant-clad houseboy, spells out for Scott early on:

> Here's what going to happen. You think you're so hot and sexy with your hard ass and that bisexual bullshit. You know how many there have been? Bobby, Hans, Chase, oh and some country boy stripper who was so dumb he wore his g-string backwards. He got rid of all of them, but I'm still here. And one day Lee (Liberace) is going to call Seymour and he is going to tell him to get rid of you. [00:33:50]

In terms of representation of a couple in the 1970s, *Behind the Candelabra* certainly trends more toward Ace and Ginger in *Casino* (1995) than Armand and Albert in *The Birdcage* (1996).

The love story portrayed between Liberace and Thorson—including the furs, the jewelry, the cars, the plastic surgery, the diet pills, the drug addiction, the cheating, the bitter separation—therefore provides a kind of litmus test. Is it only salacious because they are two men? Is it objectionable because it is Scott's face, rather than breast implants on a woman, that Liberace wants to alter? And is it only obscene because Liberace wants Scott's face altered to look like his own? Kobena Mercer suggests "an approach to ambivalence not as something that occurs 'inside' the text (as if cultural texts were hermetically sealed or self-sufficient), but as something that is experienced across the relations between authors, texts, and readers, relations that are always contingent, context-bound, and historically specific" (Mercer 2002, 188).

From this film, one would not, for instance, gain an understanding of what the gay liberation movement (1970–1980) offered, either politically or personally, for Liberace, for Scott, or for their relationship. This again pivots viewership to

Michael Douglas as Liberace and Matt Damon as Scott Thorson in *Behind the Candelabra*. Courtesy of HBO/Photofest.

a more universal, less politicized position. Whether or not it "works"—if one can truly see *beyond* the candelabra—is arguable. During a series of interviews with Matt Damon celebrating the film's release, one interviewer remarks, "The squabbles that these two men had were very much like the squabbles you hear going on in any house." Damon responds, "Right, exactly" (Vargas 2013). Though the house in question was draped in crystals, came with a houseboy, and is packed with pianos and portraits of Liberace's mother, the comment underscores ideas about a more essentialized difference. While it ought not have been remarkable in 2013 that a same-sex couple would have the same arguments "going on in any house," the reporter's simple on-camera realization speaks to the ongoing, uneven process of unlearning bias.

Perhaps more importantly, the absence of politicized content is an accurate reflection and deference to Liberace himself. His talent, fame, and star persona garnered decades of public interest throughout the world, and he very carefully produced, guarded, and defended the idea that he was heterosexual. This strategic, forward-facing denial of his sexuality is underscored throughout the film. The first time he sees Liberace, Scott says aloud, "Funny that they would enjoy something this gay," and Bob replies, "Oh they have no idea he's gay" [00:09:10]. Liberace tells Scott, "People only see what they want to see" [00:26:17]. Or, in the case of Liberace, what *he* wanted them to see: "Mr. Showmanship." To this effect, Liberace may be considered both the producer of content and, once established, as the representations and *idea* of "Liberace."

Ultimately, however, Liberace's glass closet was shattered in 1987 by the Riverside County coroner. Though Liberace's death was initially attributed to heart failure by his publicist and his physician alike, the coroner announced that Liberace died as a direct result of AIDS (Nelson 1987). While his agent and family denied the reports, HIV and AIDS nonetheless interrupted the exceptionalism and excess which had for so long produced a *not* "homosexual" subject position. In the film, an ailing Liberace echoes so many gay men of his generation when he says to Thorson, "I don't want to be remembered as an old queen who died of AIDS." Reflecting on Liberace's long and successful career, one critic offered: "Mr. Showmanship has another more potent, drawing power to his show: the warm and wonderful way he works his audience. Surprisingly enough, behind all the glitz, glitter, the corny false modesty, and the shy smile, Liberace exudes a love that is returned to him a thousand-fold" (Pyron 2000, 292). The danger is not in the stereotype, Richard Dyer advises, which is simply "an aspect of human thought and representation," but in "who controls and defines them, what interests they serve" (Dyer 2000, 246). A devout Catholic and a deeply closeted gay man, Liberace built his life rhinestone by rhinestone, and his rendition of "Ave Maria" sold over 300,000 copies.

See also *Battle of the Sexes; Can You Ever Forgive Me?; Kill Your Darlings; Kinsey.*

Bibliography

Child, Ben. "Steven Soderbergh: Hollywood Rejected Liberace Film for Being 'Too Gay.'" *Guardian*, January 7, 2013. Accessed June 3, 2021. https://www.theguardian.com/film/2013/jan/07/steven-soderbergh-liberace-film.

Dyer, Richard. "The Role of Stereotypes." In *Media Studies: A Reader*, 2nd ed., edited by Paul Marris and Sue Thornham, 245–51. New York: New York University Press, 2000.

IMDb. "*Behind the Candelabra* (2013) FAQ." n.d. Accessed June 2, 2021. https://www.imdb .com/title/tt1291580/faq?ref_=tt_faq_1#fq0039129.

Mercer, Kobena. "Skin Head Sex Thing: Racial Difference and the Homoerotic Imaginary." In *The Masculinity Studies Reader*, edited by Rachel Adams and David Savran, 188–200. Malden, MA: Blackwell, 2002.

Nelson, Harry. "Liberace Died of Pneumonia Caused by AIDS, Riverside Coroner Reports." *Los Angeles Times*, February 10, 1987. Accessed June 3, 2021. https://www.latimes.com/archives /la-xpm-1987-02-10-me-2349-story.html#:~:text=Liberace%20Died%20of%20Pneumonia%20 Caused%20by%20AIDS%2C%20Riverside%20Coroner%20Reports,-By%20HARRY%20 NELSON&text=Liberace%20died%20as%20a%20direct,certificate%20signed%20by%20 his%20physician.

Pyron, Darden Asbury. *Liberace: An American Boy*. Chicago: University of Chicago Press, 2000.

Vargas, Elizabeth. "'Behind the Candelabra' Interview: Matt Damon Says 'Candelabra' a 'Dream Role.'" ABC, May 21, 2013. Accessed June 3, 2021. https://abcnews.go.com/GMA/video/ candelabra-interview-matt-damon-candelabra-dream-role-19224337.

—Sasha T. Goldberg

BIG DADDY (1999)

DIRECTOR: Dennis Dugan
SCREENPLAY: Sid Ganis and Jack Giarraputo
CAST: Adam Sandler (Sonny Koufax), Joey Lauren Adams (Layla Maloney), Dylan and Cole Sprouse (Julian McGrath), Leslie Mann (Corinne Maloney), John Stewart (Kevin Gerrity)
SPECS: 93 minutes; color
AVAILABILITY: DVD (Sony Pictures Home Entertainment)

Big Daddy is a typical Adam Sandler comedy from the 1990s. That is, it is a romantic comedy geared toward adolescent men that features the mental and emotional maturation of a lovable loser, replete with gross-out, misogynistic, and homophobic humor.

In the film, Sandler plays Sonny Koufax, a former law student living through a self-inflicted arrested development after receiving a $200,000 settlement from a minor accident. At the beginning of the film, Sonny has a falling out with his girlfriend, Vanessa, over his lack of ambition and goals. Meanwhile, Sonny's roommate and law school classmate, Kevin, is given a going-away party for his visit to China. Sonny is the epitome of a slacker—working once a week at a tollbooth, sleeping well into the afternoon, and maintaining unkempt hygiene habits while living on stocks he invested in with his settlement money. Sonny's life turns upside down when Julian, Kevin's biological son, appears at his apartment. Sonny attempts to contact Social Services but gets a message explaining the office is closed for Columbus Day. Initially, Sonny is shown to be ill prepared to assume the role of a father (or functional adult). Across several scenes, he instructs Julian to urinate on the side of a restaurant, takes Julian to the park to trip Rollerbladers, and allows him to eat unhealthy foods (thirty ketchup packets). Along the way, Sonny meets Layla, his love interest, and gradually becomes a more competent guardian and responsible human being. *Big Daddy* concludes with a trial to determine the custody of Julian. It ends with Julian entering the custody of Kevin and with Sonny bonding with his estranged father and the presumption that Sonny will conscientiously resume his life. Just over a year later, Sonny is revealed to be a lawyer and married to Layla with a young child while maintaining a close relationship with Julian.

As a heterosexual romantic comedy, the film seemingly offers little by way of LGBTQIA+ commentary. However, two of Sonny's friends from law school, Tommy and Phillip, are involved in an openly gay relationship. In 1999, the portrayal of such unions was relatively rare in popular culture, especially in the wake of *Baehr v. Miike* (the 1999 Hawaiian Supreme Court case that determined state laws prohibiting same-sex unions violated the state's constitution) and the signing of the Defense of Marriage Act in 1996 (later deemed unconstitutional by *Obergefell v. Hodges* in 2015).

On the surface, Tommy and Phillip's portrayal is relatively positive. *Medium* critic Kevin Tash (2020), who reappraised the film when it started trending on Netflix in October 2020, points out that the couple is genuinely affectionate. Moreover, Sonny sticks up for the two when a mutual friend, Mike, negatively responds to their kissing. Sonny even entrusts the men to babysit Julian with Nazo (Sonny's racially stereotyped food deliverer) as he goes on a date with Layla, although it must be pointed out that the couple still allow Julian to engage in irresponsible behavior. A final positive note can be witnessed in that the couple are both professionals: each is a lawyer. However, when one digs beneath of surface of these superficial observations and explores the context of their portrayal, *Big Daddy* is revealed to have problematic baggage.

Critic Edward Guthmann of the *San Francisco Chronicle* rightly points out that Tommy and Phillip and their relationship serves mostly to generate homophobic jokes (1999). This fact is also discussed by Kevin Tash and will be given more attention below. While both critics rightfully problematize the portrayal of Tommy and Phillip, neither mentions the equally problematic character of Mike. Mike's sole purpose in the film is to register disgust for the purpose of cheap laughs at the expense of the gay couple. Nearly every scene with Tommy and Phillip ends with a perturbed response from Mike.

Mike can be said to represent public sentiment at the time. On one hand, he is friends with the couple. One the other hand, he dislikes and is disgusted by the fact that Tommy and Phillip are gay. He reluctantly accepts his friends but cares to know nothing of their personal lives and even resents mundane displays of affection in public. Mike would rather Tommy and Phillip keep their relationship behind closed doors and out of his sight or to revert back to their presumably heterosexual ways. Public opinion polls at the time showed many Americans were divided over gay rights. American's were beginning to "tolerate" the LGBTQIA+ community but were still hesitant to extend rights, such as protection against job discrimination and the right to marry. In other words, Americans desired LGBTQIA+ people to keep their affairs private and without any form of public endorsement. Mike's stance also reflects the "Don't Ask, Don't Tell" policy enacted by the US military between 1994 and 2011 wherein gays and lesbians enlisted in military service would not be asked about their sexual orientation and would not be allowed to discuss it.

As for Tommy and Phillip, Tash suggests scenes play the couple off as fix-ated on other men, as preoccupied with sex, or as just buffoonish (2020). All three observations are present in the babysitting scene. During Sonny and Layla's date, Layla asks about Julian. Sonny suggests that he is in good hands. The movie cuts to Sonny's apartment. Tommy is watching a movie with a shirtless Brad Pitt while Phillip and Nazo are playing cards with Julian and with Mike close by. Gazing in Phillip's direction, Tommy says, "Look at Brad's body, not an ounce of fat on it." In a somewhat indignant tone, Phillip asks, "What?" Tommy corrects himself, "Don't worry, I like yours better." Shortly thereafter, Arthur Brooks from the Social Services office shows up and witnesses Julian drinking ketchup straight from the bottle, suggesting Tommy, Phillip, and Nazo are just as incompetent at parenting as Sonny. As soon as Arthur leaves, Phillip tells Tommy, "My butt is definitely better than his." Tommy responds, "Without question," and both embrace. Significantly, in both sequences—leering over Brad Pitt and hugging—the film makes sure to register Mike's eye-rolling contempt for Tommy and Phillip.

Such mockery is sometimes counterbalanced in the film, but only for the purpose of laughs. A scene from Kevin's going-away party is illustrative. When Tommy and Phillip are first introduced, the audience does not immediately know their sexual orientation until the two kiss. As soon as this happens, the camera pans to Mike and Sonny, who are both sitting slightly away from the couple. Mike turns to Sonny to tell him, "I gotta admit. I'm still a little weirded out when they kiss." Sonny sticks up for Tommy and Phillip, stating, "Why? They're gay, that's what gay guys do." Mike's response suggests that he feels let down by their identity as gay men, that they have betrayed their once ap-propriately masculine relationship. Somehow, with their true sexual orientation known, they are not the same, "Yeah I know, but they were like our brothers to us back in school." Sonny's glib response represents another cheap laugh line for the film: "They're still like our brothers, our very, very gay brothers."

Another party scene is also instructive in that it demonstrates Tash's point that Tommy and Phillip are fixated on other men. In front of the party's attend-ees, Kevin announces his trip to China and his proposal to his girlfriend. He then jokingly states that his company chose the guy who shaved his buttocks for a five-dollar bet to represent them internationally. Immediately after mentioning the bet, Tommy shouts, "Prove it!" He then turns to those surrounding him, smiles, and insists that he was just joking.

In total, Tommy and Phillip appear for only a few minutes in the film. Per-haps because of this, they are more caricatures than characters. In spite of *Big Daddy*'s seemingly positive inclusion of a gay couple, the audience is meant to laugh at their difference.

See also *Blockers; Neighbors 2: Sorority Rising; Wet Hot American Summer.*

Bibliography

Adamczyk, Amy, and Yen-Chiao Liao. "Examining Public Opinion about LGBTQ-Related Is-sues." *Annual Review of Sociology* 45 (2019): 401–23.

Guthmann, Edward. "Bad 'Daddy'/Adam Sandler Comedy an Unholy Mix of Crudity and Corn." *San Francisco Chronicle*, June 25, 1999. Accessed February 1, 2021. https://www.sfgate.com /movies/article/Bad-Daddy-Adam-Sandler-comedy-an-unholy-mix-2922091.php/.

Morris, Charles E., and John M. Sloop. "'What Lips These Lips Have Kissed': Refiguring the Politics of Queer Public Kissing." *Communication and Critical/Cultural Studies* 3, no. 1 (2006): 1–26.

Tash, Kevin. "*Big Daddy* Is Trending on Netflix. But Has It Aged Well?" *Medium*, October 7, 2020. February 1, 2021. https://medium.com/cinemania/big-daddy-is-trending-on-netflix-but -has-it-aged-well-1f4897062699/.

—Todd K. Platts

BLOCKERS (2018)

DIRECTOR: Kay Cannon
SCREENPLAY: Brian Kehoe, Jim Kehoe
CAST: Leslie Mann (Lisa), John Cena (Mitchell), Ike Barinholtz (Hunter), Kathryn Newton (Julie), Geraldine Viswanathan (Kayla), Gideon Adlon (Sam), Ramona Young (Angelica)
SPECS: 102 minutes (theatrical release); color
AVAILABILITY: DVD (Universal Pictures Home Entertainment)

Blockers follows the story of three parents—Lisa, Mitchell, and Hunter—as they chase their kids throughout prom night in an attempt to stop them from enacting their sex pact, a plan the parents accidentally discover. The children, however, are hell-bent on losing their virginity on their prom night, and are even more determined not to let their parents interfere with their lives. As one group chases after the other, it is a battle between overbearing parents and independent millennials in a sex comedy where characters try to balance themselves on the tightrope between care and control.

The film opens with a flashback to the first day of preschool when the three kids and their parents met each other for the first time. The following montage—birthday parties, Halloween get-togethers, soccer games, and concerts—takes the viewers through the years until they finally meet eighteen-year-old Julie on the day of her prom. As she and Lisa sit and chat over breakfast, there is also a lingering sense of sadness. The mother-daughter duo, who are shown to be doing everything together, seem to be struggling to talk about Julie's college plans, with Lisa scurrying off as soon as Julie asks her if she is going to be okay when she leaves. The scene then shifts to Kayla's home, where her mother, Marcie, is giving an earful to Mitchell for interfering with their daughter's life. "Kayla is becoming a woman. This isn't the time to tighten your grip; it's the time to loosen it," she tells Papa Mannes when he wants to confront his daughter for buying lacey underwear [00:05:21–00:05:26]. These two scenes at Julie's and Kayla's homes set the background for the chaos that these overbearing parents cause in the hours to come.

The LGBTQIA+ theme of the film is introduced in the next scene, where Julie, Kayla, and Sam are sitting in the cafeteria discussing their prom night. While Julie and Kayla plan a sex pact where they both lose their virginity on the same night, the hesitation on Sam's face is apparent as she struggles to be a part of the conversation. The reason behind her hesitancy becomes evident when Angelica, a quirky Asian American student, walks into the cafeteria and dreamy music starts playing in the background. Sam starts to fumble with her words as soon as she catches a glimpse of Angelica, and her urgency to change the topic of conversation from heterosexual sex leaves no doubt in the minds of the viewers that Sam is gay. That she is also a geeky-looking kid, who doesn't seem to be a social outcast, feels like a fresh change from the stereotypical portrayal of queer teenagers in Hollywood. In an interview with *Vanity Fair*'s Joanna Robinson, director Kay Canon revealed that it was her decision to make Sam gay: "It was my idea to make Sam gay and that was one of the biggest changes. . . . I wanted to show three completely different relatable stories of who represents high school girls" (Robinson 2018). Later in the interview, the director also explains how "Sam's story was always leading with this idea of being worried that she wouldn't connect with her friends because they were losing their virginity to guys and she wasn't ready to lose her virginity, let alone confront her sexuality, and so she's full of fear" (Robinson 2018). At the same time, Canon also admits that casting the Chinese American Ramona Young as Sam's love interest was aimed to represent an even broader level of intersectional queerness in her film (Robinson 2018).

The next time viewers meet Sam is when she is in her room Photoshopping herself into pictures with the fictional character Xena. A famous 1990s series that ran for six seasons on NBC, *Xena: Warrior Princess* was born in a time when the LGBTQA+ movement was just starting to become part of the national conversation. The character Xena went on to attain a cult status, with fans across the world hailing her as a lesbian icon. Even Lucy Lawless, the actress who played Xena in the original series, admitted in her 2016 interview with *Entertainment Weekly*'s Natalie Abrams, "That friendship between Xena and Gabrielle transmitted some message of self-worth, deservedness, and honour to people who felt very marginalized, so it had a lot of resonance in the gay community" (Abrams 2016). This metareference of the fictional character is enough to erase all doubts regarding Sam's sexuality from the viewer's mind.

Shortly after this moment, the friends are shown getting ready for their big night, while all the parents come together to see them off. Sam's father, Hunter, who now lives separately after having cheated on his wife, lends them a limo for the night. It is also in this scene that a queer person's dilemma against peer pressure is fully explored—Sam is torn between telling her friends the truth about her sexuality, leaving her out of their heterosexual sex pact, or pretending to be straight for the night and losing her virginity to her date, Chad. While she gives in and chooses the latter, the parents get a hint of their plans and embark on their own hunt to stop the teens. But each parent has his or her own motive for doing so—for Julie and Mitchell, it is to preserve their twisted virginal visions of their "little girls"; for Hunter, it is to stop Sam from running away from who she really is. The camera, which until now had spent only half the amount of time on Hunter as it did on the other parents, for the first time stops to zoom in on Hunter's face as he tells Julie and Mitchell that Sam is a lesbian. When Julie asks him if Sam came out to him, he answers in the negative, telling her that he knows because "I am her dad" [00:31:11]. The camera angles from which Hunter is captured change drastically after this revelation; the long shots suddenly turn into close-ups, as if guiding the viewer's change in perspective on a man who was until now only perceived as, in Julie and Mitchell's terms, "a babysitter fucker" [00:18:30].

Before the three parents can even reach the prom venue, there are major developments in the friends' plans. Kayla and Lisa decide to leave for the after-party at a friend's lake house. Meanwhile, Sam approaches Angelica, who, as Sam learns, has recently broken up with her girlfriend, Lauren, because she was "a little confused" regarding her sexuality. When Sam asks Angelica how one learns to be sure of what they really are, Angelica replies, "It's probably different for everyone. . . . I guess you never know until you try" [00:34:15–00:34:30]. Decked out in a Galadriel cape, Angelica also looks every bit the powerful and wise Tolkienian character in this scene as she utters these words of wisdom. A 2010 survey by the *Guardian* revealed how it is common for lesbians to first have relationships with men, to an extent that many lesbians discover same-sex feelings only after they are married or in their thirties (Cochrane 2010). Thus, taking Angelica's advice to heart, Sam not only attempts to kiss Chad but also agrees to follow her friends to the lake house in order to go ahead with the sex pact. What is interesting in this scene is that Sam's disgust after kissing Chad is only shown momentarily before the manifestation of the same disgust is shown through Hunter's face, who walks into the room at the exact same moment and witnesses the kiss. But before he can reach to her across the room, Sam leaves with her group.

Losing their daughters' location, the three parents embark on their hunt anew, but this time it is Hunter's urgency that drives them. He even takes out his anger at seeing his daughter kissing a young man on Julie and Mitchell in a scene, screaming how they "raised a couple of bigots who have shamed my daughter into losing her virginity to the wrong sex" [00:39:33]. To which Julie retorts, "My daughter is not a bigot. We go to all the marches" [00:39:40]. It has often been a common misconception among heterosexuals that attending marches and slapping rainbow branding onto a product concludes their jobs as allies. GLAAD's 2013 ally PSA series "Coming Out for Equality" engages with similar conversations and explains how straight allyship needs to focus more on amplifying queer life experiences (Ratner 2013). In another scene in the film, Hunter accuses Mitchell of being homophobic, to which he replies, "I am not homophobic. My brother's gay and he's my best friend" [01:09:21]. In a *HuffPost* article titled "Can Someone Not Be Homophobic If They Have Gay Relatives and Friends?," Mark Baer (2017) explores this question and remarks how "my mother had a gay son and close friends who were gay and she was undeniably homophobic. I know because I lived it." In fact, this "gay best friend" stereotype, having made its way from the big screen into real life, has only resulted in producing tokenistic support from straight allies and has, in turn, been counterproductive to the LGBTQIA+ movement. And while the director's decision to add these two small scenes seems to stem from a desire to include an introspecting gaze—one that attempts to reflect over the shallowness of such superficial LGBTQIA+ support—the failure to build on this and explore the nuances of homophobia further defeats the purpose. The script's and the camera's inability to hold facile allies responsible for their crass remarks on the queer community reinscribes the very same stereotypes that these scenes seek to transform.

However, the climax of the film is cathartic in the way it treats the narrative of queer self-actualization. Sam, who is shown to be in bed with a naked Chad, realizes that she cannot go ahead with the sex pact the moment she touches Chad's genitalia. With both disgust and confusion evident on her face, she says no to Chad's offer of going ahead with the act. The camera focuses solely on Sam throughout the scene and carefully zooms in on her face during the moments when she finally comes to term with her queerness. The next few minutes are dedicated to her coming out to Hunter, who, in his quest, had come barging into the room Sam was in. Committed to helping her through the journey, Hunter lets her come out to him without revealing that he knew about it all along. What follows are hugs, tears, and an endearing father-daughter conversation where Hunter caresses away Sam's worry that she will lose her friends if she comes out to them as gay. "This is the stuff you tell people you care about," he tells her, urging Sam to share her news with Julie and Kayla [01:25:39]. The complexity of parenthood and "girlhood" are also explored thoroughly in this scene as Hunter tries to make sure that he gives his daughter enough courage to help her be who she is but also struggles to let go of her so that she can freely explore her sexuality and make her own decisions. Eventually, Sam tells her friends, and the second coming out scene is as powerful as the first one, with Julie and Kayla embracing Sam and putting an end to all her worries about them not accepting her. The prom party ends with Sam finally confessing to Angelica—their kissing scene with Hailee Steinfeld's voice singing the lines, "Gonna love myself; I don't need anybody else," almost feels like a cathartic denouement of Sam's journey to queerness [01:30:58].

Giving Sam equal screen time to that of her straight counterparts is not something that sex comedies often do, especially given the (historically) aggressively heterosexual nature of the genre. In her interview with *Vanity Fair*, Kay Canon herself accepts that she knows that "young women are starving to see themselves in films like this, where they're just normal kids going through 'normal' things" (Robinson 2018). She adds, "I put the second normal in quotes because the idea of a young woman struggling with her sexuality might be foreign to some parents. I hope that when kids watch it and parents watch it, it bridges this communication gap between a kid who might be going through something like this and their parents" (Robinson 2018). Indeed, in many ways, despite its shortcomings, *Blockers* lives up to its director's aspirations.

See also *Love, Simon; The Perks of Being a Wallflower; To All the Boys I've Loved Before.*

Bibliography

Abrams, Natalie. "Xena: Warrior Princess: An Oral Herstory." *Entertainment Weekly*, June 17, 2016. Accessed January 5, 2021. https://ew.com/article/2016/06/17/xena-warrior-princess-oral -history/.

Baer, Mark. "Can Someone Not Be Homophobic If They Have Gay Relatives and Friends?" *HuffPost*, December 28, 2017. Accessed January 8. 2021. https://www.huffpost.com/entry /can-someone-not-be-homophobic-if-they-have-gay-relatives_b_5a459384e4b06cd2bd03df10.

Cochrane, Kira. "Why It's Never Too Late to Be a Lesbian." *Guardian*, July 22, 2010. Accessed January 8, 2021. https://www.theguardian.com/lifeandstyle/2010/jul/22/late-blooming-lesbians -women-sexuality.

Ratner, Brett. "'Coming Out for Equality' PSA Campaign." *GLAAD*, April 18, 2013. Accessed January 6, 2021. https://www.glaad.org/ally.

Robinson, Joanna. "The Story behind *Blockers*' Unexpected Gay Romance." *Vanity Fair*, April 6, 2018. Accessed January 4, 2021. https://www.vanityfair.com/hollywood/2018/04/blockers-gay -romance-kiss-kay-cannon-gideon-adlon-ramona-young.

—Dyuti Gupta

BOOGIE NIGHTS (1997)

DIRECTOR: Paul Thomas Anderson

SCREENPLAY: Paul Thomas Anderson, based on the short film *The Dirk Diggler Story* by Paul Thomas Anderson, which was inspired by the documentary *Exhausted: John C. Holmes, the Real Story* by Julia St. Vincent

CAST: Mark Wahlberg (Eddie Adams/Dirk Diggler), Julianne Moore (Maggie/Amber Waves), Burt Reynolds (Jack Horner), Don Cheadle (Buck Swope), John C. Reilly (Reed Rothchild), William H. Macy (Little Bill), Philip Seymour Hoffman (Scotty J.), Heather Graham (Brandy/Roller Girl), Luis Guzmán (Maurice TT Rodriguez)

SPECS: 155 minutes; color

AVAILABILITY: DVD (Warner Bros.)

In the San Fernando Valley of California in 1977, a teenage busboy named Eddie Adams is discovered by adult film director and producer Jack Horner. His life is transformed when his special gift is unearthed on film. Eddie becomes the porn sensation Dirk Diggler. Not having a family to call his own, Dirk is welcomed into a supportive circle, including fellow exotic film actors Amber Waves, Roller Girl, and Reed Rothchild. When a venomous cocktail of drugs and egomania lead him down a dark path, Dirk's career, fame, and newfound sense of family is threatened.

Boogie Nights is a period drama written and directed by Paul Thomas Anderson, based on the life of John Holmes, a very successful adult film actor known for being well endowed. In an interview, Anderson explains how Dirk Diggler's film career in *Boogie Nights* was very much like that of Holmes. Anderson states: "With the '80s and the drugs, everything's taken a toll on him. That happened in John Holmes' life and it was reflected in the character he played (Johnny Wadd). We did the same thing with Dirk, and in the movie I blame the drugs and ego-building" (Ariano 2021).

The film is an expansion of a mockumentary short called *The Dirk Diggler Story* (1988), written and directed by Anderson as a student of film. In the short film, Dirk has a bodybuilder gay lover named Reed Rothchild. However, in *Boogie Nights*, Reed Rothchild is Dirk Diggler's partner in crime but not his lover.

Set in the late 1970s in Los Angeles's San Fernando Valley, the film seamlessly portrays the golden age of porn in filmmaking with a fifteen-million-dollar budget, respectively low, adding to the authenticity. The set looks realistic and wildly entertaining. Jack's swinging pad is complete with dark-paneled back-drops, sunken living spaces, gilded lamps, bumps of plentiful cocaine, wet bars, avocado kitchenettes, and shag carpets. The decor, hair, and makeup trends synonymous with the seventies (feathered hair, tight-fitting synthetic fiber clothing, platform shoes, no bras, Coppertone tans, and garish eye shadow) are cradled by a perfectly curated soundtrack of disco and beyond that spans the five-plus-year period (late 1970s to mid-1980s). High-budget professional sets and custom period clothing would not have suited this film.

According to Fernando Andrés, author of "The Unexpected Queerness of Paul Thomas Anderson," when the film crew was in search of a place to shoot *Boogie Nights*, most houses in Los Angeles had been updated between 1978 and 1996. Andrés continues: "They finally found a house in West Covina that the owners hadn't had enough money to update. According to cinematographer Mark Elswit, 'They had a kidney-shaped pool, a flagstone fireplace, all the original electric appliances, all the original light fixtures and almost the original draperies" (2017).

A three-minute-long take that introduces the main characters follows Jack Horner, adult filmmaker, accompanied by a stunning ethereal beauty and adult film star Amber Waves, into the Hott Traxx nightclub run by the zealous Maurice, who craves nothing more than to be an actor in one of Jack's films. The scene follows them to their corner booth in the club, panning the crowd of nightclub-goers, partying and dancing to the likes of the Emotions' "Best of My Love." It is pure disco perfection, with an air of optimism that foreshadows Jack's discovery and young Eddie's twist of fate.

Jack seems indifferent to the regular cast of characters who greet him. When young Roller Girl, renowned for her talents in Jack's films, skates to the table for a brief exchange, she is superficially acknowledged by Jack and met with words of concern from Amber Waves, who notices her fussing with her denim shorts; there seems to be discomfort in her pelvic region. Roller Girl explains that she has to pee and skates off across the dance floor. Jack pans the crowd and the camera follows, catching Roller Girl in a brief dance with some of her film cohorts, including Reed Rothchild and fellow actor Buck Swope. When she breezes back toward the bathroom and disappears, in her peripheral, the camera focuses on an unaffected-looking handsome young man collecting dirty dishes [00:04:05]. Jack is awestruck by the young man, captured in an extreme close-up. It is here where Eddie is first recognized by Jack as a potential moneymaker for his films; Jack stares knowingly at him, perhaps even longingly, a sentiment that bubbles up among adult characters of both sexes throughout the film. After being interrupted by a nonchalant exchange with Little Bill, a film crew member, about the logistics of the next shoot, Jack leaves the conversation and seeks out young Eddie in the kitchen of Hott Traxx.

He engages Eddie in small talk to unearth where he comes from [00:05:20]. Eddie thinks he is soliciting him for "5 or 10," referring to dollars for paid voyeuristic acts of masturbation. And when Jack asks him if that has happened already that evening, Eddie explains that it has "a couple of times" and continues to wash the dishes. Jack is intrigued by this, as this repetition and resilience is an asset for an adult film actor. He then introduces himself as "Jack Horner, filmmaker." Eddie, seventeen, recognizes him from something he had read and from films such as *Amanda's Ride* and *Inside Amber*. Jack refers to Eddie as "a 17-year-old piece of gold" and asks him to join them for a drink. Eddie declines, saying that he couldn't let down Maurice, his boss. The scene ends with Jack subtly professing, "I got a feeling that beneath those jeans there is something wonderful just waiting to get out" [00:07:30].

The next few scenes show the sad reality that each of three characters go home to. Amber Waves kisses Jack good night then sits on the side of her bed in his home where she resides, smoking, intoxicated, and begging her estranged husband on the phone to talk to her son, Andrew. Jack hits the wet bar in contemplation, and Little Bill goes home to his apartment only to discover his wife unabashedly having sex with another man she refers to as "stud," a trend that leads to their eventual demise. Eddie goes home to his Torrance, California, teenage bedroom with posters of seventies sex symbols, Bruce Lee, and shiny muscle cars pasted on his wall. He stands in his underwear before a mirror. There is an obvious protrusion in his briefs. Here, he practices his kung-fu moves to bestow confidence in his gifts that have been shattered by his abusive home life.

The next night in Hott Traxx, Jack whispers something into Roller Girl's ear, leading her to seek out Eddie to seduce him in a hidden closet at the club. It is an obvious manipulation by Jack to find out what is in Eddie's trousers and if his intuition about him is right. Later that evening, curious about Roller Girl's discovery, Jack, Amber, and Roller Girl ride up alongside of Eddie, who is walking home from work. They invite him out to dine, which later turns into an *audition* on Jack's couch.

Roller Girl, aimlessly searching for cocaine in the kitchen, is beckoned into the living room to have sex with Eddie in front of Jack. Casually, as if they are simply enjoying conversation, Roller Girl and Eddie proceed to indulge in each other while Melanie's 1970s classic tune "Brand New Key" plays on the stereo. Jack stares pensively, smoking and visually appraising their chemistry.

After a tragic scene where Eddie's mother verbally and physically attacks him upon his return home in the morning, Eddie leaves home distraught and runs to Jack, Amber, and Roller Girl, who take him in. They initiate him into their world and create their own tribe. Dirk befriends Reed Rothchild, fellow porn star. They become fast friends and confidantes, very similar in their childlike naïveté. Adams gives himself the screen name "Dirk Diggler"; his fast rise to success allows him to buy a new house, wardrobe, and a competition orange Corvette. Dirk and Reed collectively pitch a series of action-themed adult films to Jack, successfully launching a gold mine of films, funded by the Colonel, a friend of Jack's and industry mogul who, early on in the film, quietly asks Dirk to expose himself at a party. Jack eventually washed his hands of the Colonel, who is thrown in jail for possession of child pornography and pedophilia.

Scotty is another of Anderson's tragic characters. He is quirky, sexually repressed, and completely in love with Dirk. He works on set as the boom operator. He keeps the mic close enough to the actors to record with good sound quality, but not so close that it invades the shot. During a very steamy scene featuring a waist-up Amber Waves and Dirk Diggler having sex, Scotty is visually tortured, choking back his longing while holding the boom. Dirk's super friendly disposition leads Scotty to think that, just maybe, Dirk loves him too. He becomes a permanent fixture in Dirk's world, hanging on his every word and move.

Later, at a climactic New Year's Eve party at Jack's place that marks the year 1980, Dirk snorts copious amounts of cocaine for the first time with Amber Waves, portending his eventual crash and burn. In a cocaine-induced euphoria, he runs into Scotty, who leads him out into the driveway to see his new car. While they huddle and lean into the car to check out the interior, Scotty puts his arm around Dirk; when they stand up, he leans in and kisses Dirk passionately [01:19:34]. Shocked, Dirk pushes him away, asking him what he is doing. Scotty replies, "You look at me sometimes. I wanted to know if you like me." In a panic, Dirk tries to escape the conversation in an attempt not to hurt Scotty. Scotty disregards this and desperately asks Dirk, "Can I kiss you on the mouth? Please?" [01:19:46]. Dirk starts to show anger and repulsion and Scotty feels ashamed, resorting to apologies, blaming his drunkenness for his behavior. When Dirk storms off to ring in the new year, he leaves Scotty alone where he unravels in a very long, heartbreaking shot [01:20:50]. Scotty repeatedly cries, "I'm a fucking idiot." His face is twisted in anger and shame, his heart completely broken.

Then, just before the stroke of midnight, Little Bill discovers his wife having sex, yet again with another man at the party. Defeated, he retrieves a pistol from his car. As everyone celebrates the ringing in of 1980, he shoots his wife and the man, then turns the gun on himself.

In the new year and beyond, Dirk and Reed use mass quantities of cocaine on a regular basis, leading to Dirk's inability to maintain an erection. He becomes angry, detached, and jealous of a new leading man and is eventually fired by Jack during a heated argument. Dirk takes off with Reed, accompanied by the ever-faithful Scotty, to embark on a music career. Meanwhile, Jack rejects business overtures from Floyd Gondolli, a theater magnate in San Diego and San Francisco who insists on cutting costs by shooting on videotape. Jack becomes disillusioned with projects that seem lifeless, violent, and disrespectful to the women whom he considers family. He saw it as the end of an era of tasteful and artistic adult filmmaking. Having wasted their money on drugs, Dirk and Reed cannot pay a recording studio for demo tapes; their music dreams are shattered. Desperate for money, Dirk lands back where he started when he is solicited by a young man paying to watch him masturbate. The man assures him that he is "not gay." It is a setup, and he is brutally assaulted by a trio of guys who pull up in another pickup truck. "You shouldn't do this sort of thing, faggot," they cry before robbing him in a "darkly funny show of their hypocrisy" (Andrés 2017).

In the interim, Amber Waves finds herself in a custody battle with her ex-husband. The court determines that she is an unfit mother due to her involvement in the porn industry, criminal record, and cocaine addiction, while Buck Swope marries a fellow porn star, Jessie St. Vincent, who becomes pregnant. Because of his past, he is disqualified from a bank loan and cannot open his own stereo-equipment store, which is his dream. That night, he finds himself in the middle of a holdup at a donut shop in which the clerk, the robber, and an armed customer are killed. Buck escapes with the money the robber demanded. This heralds yet another twist of fate.

Dirk, Reed, and their friend Todd Parker attempt to scam local drug dealer Rahad Jackson by selling him a half kilo of baking soda as coke. Dirk and Reed decide to leave before Rahad's bodyguard inspects it, but Todd attempts to steal additional drugs and money from Rahad. In the ensuing gunfight, Todd shoots Rahad's bodyguard and Todd is killed by Rahad. Dirk and Reed barely escape. Dirk finds himself in Jack's kitchen, begging for forgiveness and help. He is welcomed by Jack, Amber, and Roller Girl's open arms.

There is a renewed sense of hope when Buck and Jessie give birth to their son. Reed takes a gig performing magic acts at a strip club, Roller Girl finally gets her GED, and the film closes with a close up on an exposed and healed Dirk in front of a mirror preparing to film, yet again, with Amber Waves.

Boogie Nights is the first film that film critic Fernando Andrés ever saw with a gay male character who is allowed greater range than a campy bit role, openly acting on his love for another man. Andrés states:

> I will always have a place in my heart for the way P.T.A.'s films captured the confusion and angst of my adolescence and coming out. When I say this to fellow film buffs who are queer, they usually aren't too happy: "but he's straight; what could he know about what we go through?" Or "but he's never had a gay protagonist." And yet I firmly stand by my belief that no greater filmmaker has more accurately translated the pathos and themes of the gay experience than P.T.A., even if he has a wife and four kids. (Andrés 2017)

There is a popular quote from drag icon RuPaul that encompasses what Anderson manages to capture in this film; a universal truth: "Gay people get to choose their own families." In Anderson's exploration of the porn industry during this era, he showed how those considered social misfits because of their contrasting interests came together and embraced comfort, creating their own family despite their differences.

See also *Score*.

Bibliography

Andrés, Fernando. "The Unexpected Queerness of Paul Thomas Anderson." *Film School Rejects*, January 6, 2017. Accessed December 3, 2021. https://filmschoolrejects.com/the-unexpected-queerness-of-paul-thomas-anderson-7cd04c78fd0b/.

Ariano, Ryan. "The Untold Truth of *Boogie Nights*." *Looper*, July 7. 2021. Accessed December 2, 2021. https://www.looper.com/454677/the-untold-truth-of-boogie-nights/.

—Amanda S. Grieme

THE BOONDOCK SAINTS (1999)

DIRECTOR: Troy Duffy
SCREENPLAY: Troy Duffy
CAST: Willem Dafoe (Paul Smecker), Sean Patrick Flanery (Connor MacManus), Norman Reedus (Murphy MacManus), David Della Rocco (David Della Rocco)
SPECS: 108 minutes; color
AVAILABILITY: DVD (Twentieth Century Fox)

Is vigilantism justified if one feels he has received a command from God? Within the first ten minutes of Troy Duffy's 1999 vigilante action film *The Boondock Saints*, viewers are aware that they are witnessing a Tarantino-esque film that will not take itself too seriously. The film follows two Irish Catholic twin brothers, Connor and Murphy, who become vigilantes to clean up organized crime in the city of Boston. Following a bar fight with members of a Russian crime syndicate, the brothers are later attacked by a member of the syndicate named Ivan Checkov. After narrowly defeating Checkov and being hailed as "saints" in the newspaper, the brothers receive what they believe to be a command from God to "Destroy all that which is evil. So that which is good may flourish" [00:27:05]. After recruiting another man named Rocco, the brothers wage a holy war against crime in Boston, ultimately emerging victorious with the assistance of an FBI agent named Paul Smecker. The film's excessive violence and mature language (over two-hundred instances of "fuck") are expected from a genre such as this. However, the level of depth given to some of the main characters is genuinely surprising for a genre that is often predicated on surface-level concepts. This is especially true for Agent Smecker.

Smecker is a complicated character. He is a brilliant FBI agent, piecing together crime scenes with ease while listening to Italian opera [00:13:12]. Furthermore, Smecker is knowledgeable about many different religious traditions, as he quickly updates the rest of the detectives on the reasons why the brothers are leaving coins on the eyes of their victims. Smecker is also one of the only characters in the film with any real depth. Dan Mecca would seem to concur. In an article titled "The Thing about *The Boondock Saints*, and Those Kind of Films in General," Mecca writes that "In *Saints*, the most interesting character interaction was Willem Dafoe's Paul Smecker with ANYBODY ELSE" (2009). Approximately half an hour into the film, viewers also learn that Smecker is gay, a fact that is made even more puzzling by Smecker's frequent use of derogatory homophobic slurs. For example, while Smecker is in bed with a male lover, he receives a phone call detailing a crime scene that he must investigate. During the phone call, the man he is sharing the bed with places his head on Smecker's abdomen. Smecker responds by slapping the man once on the head. The man is startled but once again places his head down on Smecker's abdomen. Smecker slaps him once again and hangs up the phone. After the man tells Smecker that he wants to cuddle, Smecker replies, "Cuddle? What a fag" [00:36:27]. Furthermore, a few moments later, a detective describes a victim as "the fag man" [00:37:19]. Smecker appears offended but the detective calls the victim "the fat man" after Smecker implores the detective to repeat himself [00:37:27]. It is left ambiguous if the detective really used the slur or if Smecker was imagining it. This would seem to suggest that Smecker is grappling with his own sexuality, and the slurs that he frequently hurls at others throughout the film could reflect his own inner turmoil. Later, while having some drinks at a bar frequented by gay men, Smecker is informed by the bartender that he has had enough to drink. Smecker replies, "Just pour the drink you fairy fuck" [01:23:47].

Following a confession at the same church Connor and Murphy attend, Smecker admits that he believes the brothers are right for purging the city of crime and he desires to join them in their mission [01:29:59]. It is following this confession that Smecker appears to find inner peace. He saves the brothers at the end of the film by infiltrating the base of the Italian mafia dressed as a woman and takes out as many of the guards as he can [01:35:01]. At the end of the film, while mafia don Joe Yakavetta is on trial, Smecker uses his clearances to open the side door of the courthouse for the brothers. This allows the brothers to execute Yakavetta with an audience watching as they proclaim to the city that they will be around if anyone chooses evil [01:42:44].

The plot leaves the viewer with a difficult question. Was Smecker portrayed in a positive light? There is no denying that Smecker was one of the most important characters in the film and that if it was not for Smecker's intelligence and ingenuity, the brothers would have failed in their mission of taking down Yakavetta. In an article published in *Sexuality & Culture*, Maria T. Soto-Sanfiel argues that "audiences manifest changes in their beliefs after being exposed to a narrative even when knowing that it is fictional. Fictions, indeed, can be as powerful as factual narratives in changing attitudes" (2018, 910). The fact that Smecker was clearly the most intelligent and capable character in the film underscores the message that Duffy is trying to convey. While Connor and Murphy were the main protagonists, they were portrayed as rather dim-witted in certain respects, such as the scene where the two brothers get into a fist fight in a vent just above the room where their targets are having a meeting [00:41:58]. This fight causes the brothers to fall through the vent. Smecker is not a character who would find himself in such a predicament. Smecker, despite his often cruel choice of words, is also a character who is not meant to be mere comic relief (even if that is the intention in a few scenes). Smecker is intelligent and blunt, portraying the sort of attitude one might expect from a stereotypically masculine, heterosexual character in this type of film. He is just as important to the plot as the two main protagonists themselves. For this reason, it seems fair to say that Smecker is the type of character who was meant to change attitudes, as Soto-Sanfiel has suggested.

Although Smecker's sexuality is an important part of his character, another important aspect is his ability to piece together elaborate crime scenes. This talent is shown using flashback. In some truly remarkable shots that show the brothers in the act of eradicating the evil in Boston, Smecker can be seen alongside them, narrating the events as they happen to his FBI partners and doing so using only his uncanny ability to create a narrative based on the available evidence at a crime scene.

The Boondock Saints is a film that has developed a cult following. This is not surprising given the film's close resemblance to some of the early work of Quentin Tarantino. The violence is unrestrained, and the language is graphic. These qualities often seem to take the place of character development in the film. Despite this fact, Paul Smecker's character is portrayed with such depth by Willem Dafoe that he becomes more than just a detective in a vigilante movie. Agent Smecker is, undoubtedly, the most interesting character in the film. His ingenuity as it pertains to investigative analysis makes him profoundly admirable. Smecker is also an interesting character because he is a multidimensional character who identifies as gay in a genre that historically has either ignored or

marginalized those in the LGBTQIA+ community. For this reason, *The Boon-dock Saints* is a film worth watching, if only to witness Dafoe's performance.
See also *Fight Club*.

Bibliography

Mecca, Dan. "The Thing about *The Boondock Saints*, and Those Kind of Films in General." *Film Stage*, September 21, 2009. Accessed November 27, 2021. https://thefilmstage.com/the-thing-about-the-boondock-saints-and-those-kind-of-films-in-general/.

Soto-Sanfiel, Maria T. "Positive Representation of Gay Characters in Movies for Reducing Homophobia." *Sexuality & Culture* 22 (2018): 909–30.

—Greggory S. Hanson

BOY CULTURE (2006)

Director: Q. Allan Brocka
Screenplay: Q. Allan Brocka and Philip Pierce, based on *Boy Culture: A Novel* by Matthew Rettenmund
Cast: Patrick Bauchau (Gregory), Derek Magyar (X), Darryl Stephens (Andrew), Jonathon Trent (Joey)
Specs: 90 minutes; color
Availability: DVD (TLA Releasing) and streaming (TLA, Dekkoo)

Boy Culture is narrated by and centered on the adventures of "X," a twentysomething high-end male escort. He lives in a chic loft in Seattle with two roommates, Andrew and Joey. Though he could afford to live alone, X explains that he took in roommates to avoid the IRS becoming suspicious about the real source of his income. The living arrangement sets up an archetypal romantic-comedy love triangle: X's attraction to Andrew is an open secret; Joey's infatuation with X is overt but unrequited, despite repeated attempts to seduce him. Andrew is less experienced with gay relationships; though he knew he was attracted to men, he had until recently been engaged to a woman. Andrew is interested in X but disapproves of his career, so he instead begins to bring home other men and, later, engages in a three-way with Joey. The film does not rest on archetypes, however; X's true feelings crystallize as a protective big brother toward Joey, and X's and Andrew's mutual attraction begins to blossom into full-fledged romance, with the requisite twists and turns of any burgeoning relationship.

The introduction of a new client to X's roster further complicates the dynamics of the group. Gregory, a wealthy older gentleman who, in recent years, has become a shut-in, begins paying handsomely for visits in which, initially, he does not solicit X's usual services. Rather, their "dates" look more like psychotherapy sessions, with X stretched out on Gregory's couch sharing details of his relationship troubles and Gregory perched on a nearby armchair listening, asking questions, and offering observations. The conditions of their relationship, as Gregory sets out at their first meeting, is that they must not become intimate until both men develop a mutual desire to do so. Gregory proceeds to seduce X—not with erotic overtures, but with stories of his youth and his past romances, particularly with a young man named Renaldo. Despite his cynical views about romance, X is swept in by Gregory's stories, and the fleeting possibility of true love despite all odds that they represent. The film's portrayal of septuagenarian Gregory as a sexual being, and the building of sexual tension between him and the much younger X culminating in a sex scene between the two, is remarkable in that the age difference between the men is considered unremarkable, neither handled with "kid gloves" nor fetishized as intergenerational romance often is in gay culture. Later, Gregory's stories are proven to be (at least partially) fabricated; X feels betrayed, and the experience retrenches X's cynicism, until Gregory redeems himself by explaining the truth of the situation to Andrew and encouraging him to follow his heart and be with X.

X is both the main character of the film and the narrator, providing additional exposition and insight throughout the film. Narrator X addresses the audience directly, even though on-screen X never breaks the fourth wall. His narration is often made in the form of a confession—"Forgive me, father . . ."—framing his various misdeeds as each of the seven deadly sins. X incorporates other religious references and iconography into his world as well, from the Virgin Mary statuette in his bedroom closet to the fact that he maintains a roster of twelve clients and refers to them as his disciples; only the death of one client allowed for the addition of another (i.e., Gregory). X further likens himself to a god or Christ figure when he describes the feeling of "omnipotence" he achieves during orgasm.

X's guardedness about his own feelings and experiences throughout the film is in stark contrast to his propensity for voyeurism. He recoils with jealousy when he sees Andrew kiss another man but doesn't break his gaze until Andrew catches him staring and moves out of sight. On another occasion, Andrew is unknowingly spied on in the shower by X, who begins to pleasure himself until interrupted by Joey. X revels in voyeurism at the film's eponymous gay bar, Boy Kultur, watching from his barstool perch and judging his fellow gay men participating in their public "mating rituals." This type of self-referential and, at times, self-deprecating critique of gay culture is widely seen today but was less common when the movie's source text was originally published. *Boy Culture* is based on the 1995 novel of the same name by Matthew Rettenmund. At its release, the book was celebrated as an example of a new and more sharply observant class of gay fiction, Rettenmund's background as a journalist lending itself to the incisive and candid portrayal of gay culture of this era (Lasky 2007, 14). This keen observation is echoed most clearly in X's detached and cynical critiques of "the scene," but X himself is not above or immune to the problematic qualities he decries in others. One biting example is heard in the opening exposition, when X notes his attraction to Andrew despite "not normally [being] into black guys" (a trope familiar from gay dating profiles/personals and amplified by the rise of hookup apps) followed shortly by Andrew calling out the racism of men who use "I'm not normally into black guys, but . . ." as a come-on line to try to pick him up, not knowing he is also calling out X [00:27:31].

In a flashback, one of few scenes in which X drops his guard and reveals more personal details about himself, he relates that his interest in his present career was rooted in his childhood:

I loved prostitute movies. Liz Taylor in *Butterfield 8*, Julia Roberts in *Pretty Woman*, Marlene Dietrich in every movie she made. As a kid, I thought prostitutes were the most beautiful creatures alive. You know, wisecracking, extravagant, you always learned from them. I felt destined to join the ranks of all the Hollywood actresses who had ever played a prostitute. I asked my mother if I could be a prostitute when I grew up. She simply said, "No." [00:27:57]

Despite regularly having sex with multiple clients, X considers himself nearly a virgin because he has had only limited experiences with men he felt a romantic connection with. His stance is clear: sex work with clients does not "count." Andrew, in contrast, cannot reconcile X's distinction between sex for pay and sex for love or pleasure. Eventually, however, Andrew seems to accept the situation—or at least accepts the fact that he will not be able to change X, so if he wants a future with him, he must trust X's ability to compartmentalize his sex work. In the final exchange in the film, viewers witness Andrew's new openness to X's stance, and they also see X becoming more vulnerable and open with Andrew, as evidenced by the fact that he has finally revealed his real name. Andrew calls him by the name "Alex," then asks if X is available—"X" now representing the escort persona separate from the man Andrew is in a relationship with. Andrew gives X his payment—a penny—and the film closes on a giant jar of coins on the men's bedside table.

In 2017, Rettenmund launched a successful crowdfunding campaign to reunite the *Boy Culture* production team (Rettenmund as cowriter, director and cowriter Q. Allan Brocka, and producers Philip Pierce and Stephen Israel) and lead actors Derek Magyar (X) and Darryl Stephens (Andrew) for a six-episode web series revisiting the *Boy Culture* characters ten years later. The web series is scheduled to launch in 2021.

See also *Jeffrey*.

Bibliography

Hornby, Nick. "Twentysomething." *New York Times Book Review*, October 15, 1995. Accessed July 16, 2021. https://www.nytimes.com/1995/10/15/books/twentysomething.html.

Lasky, David Jay. "In Bed with Derek." *Advocate*, March 12, 2007. Accessed July 17, 2021. https://www.advocate.com/politics/commentary/2007/03/12/bed-derek.

—Curt Lund

BOYS BEWARE (1961)

Producer: Sid Davis
Director: Sid Davis
Cast: None credited
Specs: 10 minutes; black and white
Availability: DVD (Reel Classic Films)

Intended for classroom exhibition, this ten-minute piece of antigay propaganda warns boys to steer clear of itinerant middle-aged pedophiles, who (according to the film) lurk throughout American suburbia. Equating (male) same-sex desire with predatory behavior, the film is divided into two segments that illustrate the respective perils of "passive" and "aggressive" "homosexuality." Each segment consists of silent, pseudodocumentary footage narrated by a stern police officer who offers homophobic admonitions to the tune of sprightly, upbeat music. In the first segment, schoolboy Jimmy is approached by Ralph, a middle-aged, balding predator who strikes up a friendship with the boy and gives him a ride home from school. The narrator informs viewers that Ralph, attempting to gain Jimmy's confidence, tells the boy "off-color jokes" and shows him "pornographic pictures," which arouse Jimmy's pubescent curiosity. The film cuts to Ralph and Jimmy ascending the outdoor staircase of a seedy motel. After a slow, ominous camera fade that signifies off-screen sexual abuse, Jimmy informs municipal authorities of the motel incident, and Ralph is summarily arrested. In the second sequence, the narrator informs viewers that Jimmy was among the lucky ones, for it turns out that "not all homosexuals are passive" and "some resort to violence." The film's second sequence introduces young basketball player Mike, who, accepting a ride with a middle-aged stranger, "realizes only too late that he is riding in the shadow of death," for "sometime later that evening, Mike . . . traded his life for a newspaper headline!"

Among the most notorious cinematic manifestations of the mental hygiene movement, producer Sid Davis's "educational" short, produced in cooperation with Los Angeles police and school boards, reflects the antiquated view that (male) same-sex desire is a nihilistic—and annihilating—pathology. Now a camp classic, *Boys Beware* should be understood as an artifact of hygiene-movement pseudoscience, which disseminated conformist values through the public health institutions that emerged in the early twentieth century. As Gerald Grob says, the hygiene movement marked a break from the psychology of the late nineteenth century, when the treatment of mental illness was limited to asylums. Frustrated by their lack of success with incarcerated, often untreatable individuals, some early psychologists began to focus on society at large, hoping to stem social ills before they metastasized into incurable pathologies. The hygiene movement's didactic qualities and propagandistic aims reflect the worldview of mental hygiene pioneer Thomas W. Salmon, who, in 1917, declared that "schools and prisons," rather than "institutions for the so-called insane," should be the primary venues for hygiene efforts (Grob, 1983, 154, 160). Bringing together "'scientific' modes of thought" and the "power of private institutions and public authority," the new hygiene crusade added a medical gloss to the era's puritanical mores (144). Most insidiously, the hygiene movement intersected with the anti-immigration and sterilization campaigns of the 1920s, which feared that an excess of "undesirables" would dilute the moral and intellectual fortitude of a "healthy" Anglo nation.

Yet the hygiene movement did not emerge from totally nefarious motives, nor can it be dismissed as pure folly. Today, much (if not all) of the hygiene movement seems both risible and unconscionable, but it was a moderately progressive force in its own time. It is important to remember that *any* discussion of sex education in America had been more or less unthinkable before the rise of the hygiene movement and its flagship organization, the National Committee for Mental Hygiene, founded in 1909. As Natalia Mehlman Petrzela observes, the hygiene movement faced an immediate backlash from religious conservatives who believed pioneering sex educators were nothing more than "perverts" interfering in familial or godly affairs (2015, 102). As early as 1913, conservatives mounted a "crusade to purge 'sex hygiene and personal purity education' from the Chicago public schools," one of the first steps in an ongoing campaign to remove even disease-prevention advice from public education (102).

Central to the hygiene movement were propagandistic, often ill-informed shorts, intended for exhibition in schools and steeped in the prejudices of their era. Hygiene shorts typically stressed conformity and obedience to authority through seemingly harmless topics: proper grooming, dating etiquette, pleasing one's parents, avoiding truancy, and so forth. In the late 1940s, hygiene movies began to focus more intently on issues of sexual morality, such as promiscuity, unplanned pregnancy, abortion, and syphilis. This heightened focus was a largely reactionary phenomenon. As Eric Schaefer notes, a midcentury rise in public school attendance mixed the genders to an unprecedented degree, stoking fears of ill-supervised adolescent sexuality (1999, 166). The period also witnessed a new consumer culture dedicated to middle-class pleasure and self-gratification; advertisements for makeup, perfume, and fashion sexualized young women in ways unknown to prior generations (166). The 1948 and 1951 Kinsey Reports on American sexual behavior further revealed that heterosexual promiscuity and gay and lesbian sex were more prevalent than previously assumed.

While Kinsey-stoked fears implicitly inform *Boys Beware*, the film is largely a symptom of the Cold War's cult of nationalistic masculinity. Any perceived queerness or gender nonconformity threatened to weaken the image of a virile America prepared to repel imminent Soviet onslaughts. Echoes of McCarthyite paranoia clearly run through *Boys Beware*, which repackages the era's "red scare" rhetoric. With only minor adjustments, the film's voice-over could apply to the era's Communist witch hunts: "One never knows when the homosexual is about . . . he may appear normal . . . and it may be too late when you discover he is mentally ill . . . so keep with your group." The narrator never considers the possibility that "one's group" could well contain gay people, nor does he mention the statistical fact that most sex abuse victims are assaulted not by wandering eccentrics but by elders they have long known and trusted.

Among sex hygiene films, *Boys Beware* was perhaps unique in its singular focus on "homosexuality." The standard villain of sex hygiene films was premarital heterosexual intercourse. In once-notorious hygiene films—such as *Mom and Dad* (1945) and *Because of Eve* (1948)—unplanned pregnancies inevitably lead to alcoholism, drug addiction, syphilis, petty theft, and the destruction of the social fabric. What *Boys Beware* shares with other hygiene films is a pervasive rhetoric of disease and contagion, here taken to parodic extremes. As schoolboy Jimmy is seduced by predatory, fortysomething Ralph, the narrator intones, "What Jimmy didn't know is that Ralph was sick—a sickness that was not visible like smallpox, but no less dangerous and contagious. . . . You see, Ralph was a *homosexual*, a person who demands an intimate relationship with members of their own sex." The film equates (male) same-sex attraction with depraved predation: gay men do not desire sexual gratification but "demand" it. Its camp value aside, *Boys Beware* could well be screened today in schools for an ironic reason—to inform students, straight and queer alike, of the state-sponsored misinformation and homophobia propagated by earlier generations.

For budgetary reasons, producer Davis shot his shorts without synchronous sound, but the film's diegetic silence also becomes thematically significant, as the gay men in *Boys Beware*—as well as the boys themselves—are literally robbed of their voices. The only person allowed to speak is the narrator, a heterosexist policeman who poses as a subject-matter specialist. As is typical with the era's social propaganda, the narrator acts as an invisible yet trustworthy personification of government authority, decreeing a litany of patriarchal norms. What will surprise contemporary viewers is the fate of young Jimmy in the film's first sequence. After informing authorities of his abuse in a motel room, Jimmy is "released on probation, in the custody of his parents," as the narrator says. That an underage victim would be punished with probation reflects the morality of the hygiene movement circa 1961: while the adult predator is irredeemably sick, the youth must undergo legal restraints to insulate him from further "contamination."

In 1961, producer Davis also distributed *Girls Beware*, a companion film that warns adolescent girls only of the threat of heterosexual predation. Like *Boys Beware*, *Girls Beware* features sternly didactic narration over silent footage, here accompanied by jazzy lounge music. The film concerns high schooler Judy, who advertises her babysitting services in a supermarket and is soon contacted by a predator in disguise. After Judy disappears and her fretful mother informs the police, the narrator reveals that "Judy's body had been found on a lonely desert road" after a "mentally sick person" had used her "innocent ad as an introduction to an act of violence!" The narrator concludes that adolescent dating should be restricted to malt shops, movie theaters, and other public venues in which the id is necessarily curtailed. Another Davis production, *Age 13* (1955), is more unusual. Relatively ambitious at twenty-five minutes, the film concerns Andrew, a thirteen-year-old driven to temporary madness by his mother's unexpected death. Spiraling into despair, Andrew attempts to commune with the departed through his transistor radio (!) and, trying to recall his mother's tactile presence, begins applying her old lipstick, perfume, and makeup. Though Andrew's confused flirtation with cross-dressing does not brand him as queer, it does instigate a slippery slope of deviance that continues with social isolation and culminates in gun-wielding violence. Eventually, Andrew is rehabilitated with the help of authoritarian school counselors and psychologists, at which point the soundtrack swells triumphantly with Tchaikovsky.

Though Davis's films are more or less police lectures, devoid of prurience, their antiqueer or sex-negative approach has a kinship with the road-show exploitation films of the 1930s and 1940s, which presented titillating subjects under the guise of moral hygiene education. Within the (tiny) subgenre of antigay hygiene films, *Boys Beware* had a rare precedent in Richard C. Kahn's *The Children of Loneliness* (1935), a now-lost film designed for the "adults only" road-show market. (Using tropes of the hygiene movement as a legitimation strategy, some early sexploitation filmmakers were able to skirt censorship guidelines by claiming their movies had educational value for adult audiences.) The film's poster, still extant, features a short-haired woman placing her hand on another woman's shoulders. A salacious caption reads, "Capable of love but . . . incapable of marriage . . . Life's a grim jest! Love's a hideous tragedy!" Purportedly, the film began as a young woman, Elinor, rebuffs the advances of her office colleague Bobby, a predatory lesbian. Whereas *Girls Beware* imagines a world of only patriarchal predation, this film also positions rapacious lesbians as a threat to naïve young women. Consulting a male therapist for advice, Elinor learns that Bobby offers a "barren substitute for the rich emotional life of a normal love" (O'Dell 2015). The story continues as Elinor unwittingly dates Paul, a closeted gay artist unable to perform (hetero)sexually. As if to reveal his orientation, Paul takes Elinor to a gay bar, where Elinor asks, "What sort of people are these?" Paul responds, "These are the children of loneliness, nature's tragic mistakes" (O'Dell 2015). The plot confirms its fatalistic thesis when a spurned Bobby clumsily attempts to throw acid in Elinor's face but only winds up scalding herself. Meanwhile, an art critic perceives effeminacy in Paul's paintings and concludes they must be the work of a woman hiding behind a male pseudonym. Fearful that he's been outed, Paul (for some reason) runs distraught into the street and is instantly flattened by passing traffic. The film's title presumably invokes Radclyffe Hall's groundbreaking lesbian novel *The Well of Loneliness* (1928), but the attempted connection is spurious. Dealing with lesbian lovers living a bohemian lifestyle in 1920s Paris, Hall's novel was a then-daring plea for tolerance, notably free of acid-throwing harpies and morally punitive traffic accidents.

It is worth noting that Sid Davis would repackage *Boys Beware* as *Boys Aware*, which overlays the same voice-over narration onto newly shot color footage. The more tepidly titled *Boys Aware* was released in 1973—the same year psychiatry's Diagnostic and Statistical Manual removed "homosexuality" from its list of pathologies.

See also *Far from Heaven*; *Hail, Caesar!*; *The Genesis Children*; *Kinsey*.

Bibliography

Grob, Gerald N. *Mental Illness and American Society, 1875–1940*. Princeton, NJ: Princeton University Press, 1983.

O'Dell, Cary. "Gay Cinema/Lost Cinema: 'Children of Loneliness' (1935)." Library of Congress, November 17, 2015. Accessed April 9, 2021. https://blogs.loc.gov/now-see-hear/2015/11/a-movie-missing-in-action-children-of-loneliness-1935/.

Petrzela, Natalia Mehlman. *Classroom Wars: Language, Sex, and the Making of Modern Political Culture*. New York: Oxford University Press, 2015.

Schaefer, Eric. *Bold! Daring! Shocking! True! A History of Exploitation Films, 1919–1959*. Durham, NC: Duke University Press, 1999.

—Andrew Grossman

BOYS DON'T CRY (1999)

DIRECTOR: Kimberly Peirce
SCREENPLAY: Kimberly Peirce and Andy Bienen, inspired by real-life events
CAST: Hilary Swank (Brandon Teena), Chloë Sevigny (Lana Tisdel), Peter Sarsgaard (John Lotter), Brendan Sexton III (Tom Nissen), Alicia Goranson (Candace), Alison Folland (Kate), Jeannetta Arnette (Lana's Mom)
SPECS: 118 minutes; color
AVAILABILITY: DVD/Blu-ray (Twentieth Century Fox)

A young trans man, Brandon Teena, explores his gender identity and falls in love in Nebraska in 1993. After getting into a drunken bar fight one night, Brandon wakes up in the small industrial town of Falls City and is taken in by a group of friends who spend most of their days drinking, getting high, and working dead-end jobs. Brandon meets Lana singing karaoke at the local bar. He instantly falls for her, and, eventually, Lana begins to feel the same. Lana's home life is difficult. She lives with her mom, who spends most of her days drinking and nights passed out in front of the television. The house is a meeting place for Lana's sister Candace, John, and his best friend Tom. John is the nominal father of the house and has served time in prison, during which Lana wrote him letters. He clearly longs to be with Lana and becomes jealous and volatile when Brandon moves in. Brandon also has troubles back home; he is summoned to court for a range of offences including larceny and grand theft auto. Eventually, his past catches up to him, his biological identity is revealed, and he is put in jail. Lana comes to bail him out, and Brandon tries to explain his gender identity to her, but Lana says she does not care and only wants to free him. But the damage has been done. The local newspaper prints Brandon's birth name, which John sees. He takes it to Lana's mom, and the group confronts Brandon. John and Tom forcibly expose Brandon's genitalia to Lana and then rape him later that night. They warn Brandon to keep quiet, but Lana convinces him to file a police report, which he does. Lana and Brandon plan to leave town, but before they can, John and Tom arrive at Candace's house, where Brandon is staying, and shoot him and Candace in front of Lana and Candace's baby. The final sequence shows Lana driving out of Falls City accompanied by Brandon's letter to her, heard in a voice-over.

Over two decades since its release, *Boys Don't Cry* remains a complex, provocative, and difficult film text that has the power to spark intense debate. Whether one believes the film to be a substantial entry in the canon of New Queer Cinema and an improvement in trans representation or a flawed depiction of Brandon Teena's story that consolidates his life and tragic death within a conventional lesbian romance and problematically erases a third victim, a disabled African American man named Phillip DeVine, from the film entirely, one thing is for certain: *Boys Don't Cry* is a rich text to analyze for the ways it complicates binary formulations of gender and fixed ideas of sexuality.

Boys Don't Cry follows Judith Butler's (1990) assertion that gender is culturally constructed. Rather than being fixed to and inseparable from biological sex, gender is instead performed based on cultural cues that are already in circulation. Spectators of these gender performances then use these cues to evaluate the performer's success at "being" masculine or feminine. Gender attributes can range from physical appearance, tone of voice, or social behaviors that have been built up over time to be accepted as normative. The film first introduces viewers to Brandon looking at himself in a mirror and, in so doing, establishes the significance of appearance and the framing of gender. Brandon combs his short hair, wraps his breasts, and stuffs a pair of socks between his legs. He wears a checked shirt, jeans, and (initially) a "ridiculous" Stetson hat in an imitation of that most masculine American figure, the cowboy. After the bar fight, which happens because of Brandon protecting a vulnerable young woman from the advances of another man, he is overjoyed at the fact that he has a black eye. For him this is an accessory of a "real" man. Later in Falls City, he has a go at bumper skiing, which involves attempting to remain standing in the back of a pickup truck driven at speed. After being thrown out of the vehicle several times, Lana asks him why he did it. "I thought that's what guys do here," Brandon replies. As Michele Aaron highlights, *Boys Don't Cry* is "a tale of passing" (2001, 92). In order to survive and be accepted in Falls City, Brandon must successfully pass as a man, which involves performing a certain type of masculinity. He is not performing as someone else but performing to be seen as himself. When that performance fails, due to Brandon's biology as identified by the state's legal system and news media, he is killed for it. Here, this essay focuses on analyzing two key scenes that occur toward the end of *Boys Don't Cry*—the "out of body" sequence as well as Brandon and Lana's third sex scene leading up to the shooting—by consolidating some of the critical responses these scenes prompted.

By this point in the film, Brandon and Lana have begun a sexual relationship, and there are indications that Lana knows there is something different about him. Their first sex scene is shown in flashback as Lana recounts the night to her friends. A series of shots suggests that she glimpses Brandon's cleavage. A trip to the town hall reveals Brandon's biological sex along with an array of outstanding criminal offences, which lands him in jail. Lana rushes to see him but is confused to find him in a women's cell. Brandon equivocates by saying that he is intersexed, to which Lana replies, "I don't care if you're half monkey and half ape, I'm getting you out of here." If Lana is put off by Brandon's declaration, she does not show it as they have sex for the second time soon after. When the pair arrive home, they are confronted by John and Tom (with Lana's mom, sister Candace, and friend Kate also present), who have seen Brandon's birth name printed in the local paper and have found leaflets about gender reassignment surgery in Lana's bedroom. Filmed using a handheld camera, Brandon is repeatedly pursued and cornered by John and Tom, who oscillate between faux jocularity and hostile menace. Representative of a heteronormative order built on a strict gender binary, John interrogates Brandon by asking, "It's simple. Are you a girl or are you not?" He also taunts Lana by saying that she should just admit it if she is a lesbian. This functions as a further link to Brandon, who was earlier posed the same question by his gay cousin. Lana attempts to defuse the situation by suggesting to John that she will get Brandon to reveal his sex to her in private. John reluctantly agrees, and Brandon and Lana retreat to her bedroom. Once they are alone, Brandon begins to unbuckle his pants, but Lana stops him saying that there is no need for him to show her: "I know you're a guy." Lana chooses to reaffirm Brandon's masculinity rather than subject him to the ordering power of heteronormativity that sees gender and sex as fixed and sexuality as a result of the biology of the sex object.

This is not enough for John and Tom. They force Brandon into the bathroom, pin him against the wall, and strip him to reveal his genitalia. It is at this moment, when Brandon appears at his most vulnerable with his male image threatened, that the film makes "the ultimate statement on the separation of gender from anatomy" (Aaron 2001, 94). The frenetic camerawork and editing halts appear to freeze on the tableau of Brandon being held upright by John and Tom. Lana sobs at his feet while Lana's mom, Candace, and Kate look on. A white glow floods the scene. Brandon gazes out toward those present (which includes the viewers) and locks eyes with another Brandon, this one fully clothed in his masculine attire. In this splitting of identity, the stripped Brandon is "sex" and the clothed Brandon is "gender." For Michele Aaron, the scene predicts Brandon's eventual martyrdom at the hands of John and Tom as well as making those present in the frame and those watching the film complicit in the attack (2001, 94). The film encourages viewer empathy. He is a charming, kind, generous, and free spirit. By now, if the film is working, viewers should care about the character and be deeply invested in what happens to him. Yet, in this scene, the viewer is helpless to intervene as the representatives of patriarchal, straight, and cisgender order attempt to violently expose Brandon's gender treachery. It is significant, then, that the film chooses to insert another Brandon at this moment of crisis. Jack Halberstam finds in this scene a clear example of what he calls the "transgender gaze," that is, "a look divided within itself, a point of view that comes from (at least) two places at the once" (2001, 296). In this view, the naked Brandon might be doomed as a result of the intolerance of the dominant social order, but the clothed Brandon represents an alternative future, one of survival, acceptance, and possibility. For Julianne Pidduck, however, Brandon's exposure represents a "point of no return" in *Boys Don't Cry* (2001, 101). For the historical Brandon Teena, his identity has been compromised, and he will be punished for his transgression. This comes in the next scene, where Brandon, cruelly questioned at the police station, reveals in flashback that he was raped by John and Tom later that night.

As the film moves toward its tragic conclusion, several writers comment that Brandon's masculinity is not only threatened by violent forces within the world of the film but also by the film's plot itself. For such critics, this occurs during Lana and Brandon's third sex scene as the latter hides out in a shed in Candace's backyard after filing a police report about the rape. The scene represents a shift from Brandon being seen and understood as a man toward a portrayal of him as a woman. Lana checks on Brandon, who lies on a sofa. Looking at him, Lana comments, "God, you're so pretty," whereas before he had been "handsome," and for the first time asks about what Brandon was like before: "Were you like me? A girl girl?" They start to have sex, at which point Lana says that she is unsure of how to do "this," in other words have lesbian sex. The scene dissolves, and they are seen lying next to each other on the sofa. According to Lisa Henderson, this scene confirms what the rape suggested—that Brandon is a woman—adding that "it is disturbing to watch Brandon be humanistically recovered by the script into a love that not-so-humanistically refuses the masculine gender he has struggled to become and for which, indeed, he is finally killed" (2001, 300–301) Contrasting the depiction of this sex scene to the previous two, Halberstam acknowledges that the "Hollywood-style" dissolve confers a greater legitimacy to this lesbian relationship, suggesting that "the couple are now making love as opposed to having sex" (297). Whereas the two earlier scenes showed frank, relatively graphic and prolonged sex, this sequence co-opts the visual tools mainstream Hollywood filmmaking uses to show (by not showing) acceptable sexuality. One could argue that by *not* showing this scene of lesbian sex, the previous two sex scenes are in fact given more legitimacy since the spectators can see them happening. Whichever way one reads the sequence, Lana's impression of Brandon has changed.

In the next scene, as they start to pack and prepare to leave town, Lana stops and says to Brandon, "Did you do something to your hair?" Brandon, once more, checks his appearance in the mirror and says, "I'll try to put it back." But Brandon cannot go back to the way it was before, and Lana cannot revert to her previous impression of Brandon as a man. This is made explicit when, in her final words to Brandon before John murders him, she calls him "Teena." It is a final misgendering that goes unanswered as John shoots him dead. What does Brandon feel at this moment? Does he now also view himself as a woman? How would he have replied to Lana in his final moments? It is precisely this ambiguity that keeps viewers coming back to *Boys Don't Cry*. Just like the highways that pepper the film, created using time-lapse photography that gives the film a science-fiction quality, *Boys Don't Cry* is a transgressive text. Just when viewers think they have it figured out, a character's gesture, frame composition, or musical cue appears to complicate understanding and prompts viewers to reevaluate what they think about it—a bit like how the film wants them to approach gender and sexuality.

See also *Transamerica*.

Bibliography

Aaron, Michele. "The 'Boys Don't Cry' Debate: Pass/Fail." *Screen* 42, no. 1 (2001): 92–96.

Butler, Judith. *Gender Trouble: Feminism and the Subversion of Identity.* London: Routledge, 1990.

Halberstam, Jack. "The 'Boys Don't Cry' Debate: The Transgender Gaze in *Boys Don't Cry*." *Screen* 42, no. 3 (2001): 294–98.

———. "Hiding the Tears in My Eyes." *Bully Bloggers*, December 7, 2016. Accessed June 7, 2021. https://bullybloggers.wordpress.com/2016/12/07/hiding-the-tears-in-my-eyes-boys-dont-cry-a-legacy-by-jack-halberstam/.

Henderson, Lisa. "The 'Boys Don't Cry' Debate: The Class Character of *Boys Don't Cry*." *Screen* 42, no. 3 (2001): 299–303.

Minkowitz, Donna. 2018. "How I Broke, and Botched, the Brandon Teena Story." *Village Voice*, June 20, 2018. Accessed July 15, 2021. https://www.villagevoice.com/2018/06/20/how-i-broke-and-botched-the-brandon-teena-story/.

Pidduck, Julianne. "The 'Boys Don't Cry' Debate: Risk and Queer Spectatorship." *Screen* 42, no. 1 (2001): 97–102.

—Adam Vaughan

BROKEBACK MOUNTAIN (2005)

DIRECTOR: Ang Lee

SCREENPLAY: Larry McMurtry and Diana Ossana, based on the short story of the same name by Annie Prouix

CAST: Heath Ledger (Ennis Del Mar), Jake Gyllenhaal (Jack Twist), Anne Hathaway (Lureen Newsome), Michelle Williams (Alma Beers Del Mar), Linda Cardellini (Cassie Cartwright), Randy Quaid (Joe Aguirre)

SPECS: 134 minutes; color

AVAILABILITY: DVD (Focus Features and River Road Entertainment)

Annie Proulx's short story "Brokeback Mountain" was originally published in the *New Yorker* in 1997 before being included in her short story collection *Close Range: Wyoming Stories* in 1999. Ang Lee's blockbuster film adaptation of the story was released in 2005.

In Wyoming in the early 1960s, Ennis del Mar and Jack Twist are recruited as shepherds. One evening, on an isolated mountainside, they drink excessively and have sex. The next morning, they agree that this was a one-time incident and deny their feelings for each other, though it is clear an attraction remains. At the end of summer, they move back to town and part ways. Ennis marries and has two daughters, while Jack moves to Texas, marries, and has a son. Ennis's and Jack's paths cross four years later, though Jack's attempts to build a life together with Ennis are rejected. They continue to meet occasionally for fishing trips, but Jack's desire for them to live together remains unfulfilled. Their last encounter ends in a conflict about the postponement of their next meeting. Later, Jack is killed by unknown assailants in a brutal homophobic attack. His widow tells Ennis that his death was caused by a road accident. The last scene shows Ennis in front of his wardrobe: the shirts he and Jack wore are hanging together, beside a postcard of the mountain.

Brokeback Mountain received many awards, including three Academy Awards in 2006 (Best Director, Best Adapted Screenplay, and Best Original Score), four Golden Globe Awards, and four British Academy of Film and Television Awards. It was selected by the Independent Film & Television Alliance as one of the most important films of the last thirty years.

The film's critical reception focused on a range of concepts, including masculinity (Rose and Urschel 2007; Barounis 2009); the environmental and natural surroundings of the story (Li 2007; Eric Patterson 2008); and religion (Geyh 2011; Henry 2007). Several reviewers praised Lee's film for opening the possibility of mainstream cinematic representations of sexual diversity. Che-ming Yang suggests that while "Ang Lee seems to have replicated the modes of heterosexual behaviors onto the gay couple," the love story central to the film appeals to a "universal" audience, "be they homosexuals or heterosexuals" (2010, 42).

However, the film's success was accompanied by debate about the explicit and implicit sexuality of the protagonists. Within this debate, most assume that Jack and Ennis are gay, while some argue that the sexuality of the characters is misinterpreted and that the characters remain bisexual and not gay (Brod 2007; Barker and Langdridge 2008). Others argue that the protagonists "are not gay enough and that the gay element of the narrative has been played down in the interests of mainstream marketability" (Keller and Goodwyn-Jones 2008, 22). Still others consider both arguments and characterize *Brokeback Mountain* as

> [a] story of traditional men who love in spite of their own masculinist assumptions and heterosexist paradigms, who love without becoming gay. While *Brokeback Mountain* does much for the visibility of same-sex desire, demonstrating that the love between two men can be moving and even tragic, it is not a movie about gay men. (Keller and Goodwyn-Jones 2008, 33)

Heath Ledger as Ennis Del Mar and Jake Gyllenhaal as Jack Twist in *Brokeback Mountain.* **Courtesy of Focus Features/Photofest.**

Brenda Cooper and Edward C. Pease analyzed 113 film reviews, finding that the film is praised as both a "universal love story" and a "gay cowboy movie" (2008). Cooper and Pease suggest that this dichotomy

> illustrates how efforts in the mainstream press to privilege queerness struggle to exist within heteronormative space. Comparing the film's queer protagonists to culturally familiar heterosexual symbols such as Romeo and Juliet, or Western icons John Wayne and Clint Eastwood, ironically elevates queer visibility while simultaneously relegating queers and queer experiences to the margins. Rather than celebrating *Brokeback Mountain* for its challenges to heteroideology, press reviews ultimately worked to appropriate Annie Proulx's voice, diluting her story's intended condemnation of brutal and destructive homophobia. (2008)

Ang Lee's *Brokeback Mountain* is a film that has invoked controversy and research on representations of sexuality in cinema. Important, however, is the degree to which debate around the film brought this discussion into the open.

See also *Kill Your Darlings; My Own Private Idaho.*

Bibliography

Barker, Meg, and Darren Langdridge. "Bisexuality: Working with a Silenced Sexuality." *Feminism & Psychology* 18, no. 3 (2008): 389–94.

Barounis, Cynthia. "Crippling Heterosexuality, Queering Able-Bodiedness: *Murderball, Brokeback Mountain* and the Contested Masculine Body." *Journal of Visual Culture* 8, no. 1 (2009): 54–75.

Brod, Harry. "They're Bi Shepherds, Not Gay Cowboys: The Misframing of *Brokeback Mountain*." *Journal of Men's Studies* 14, no 1 (2007): 252–53.

Cooper, Brenda, and Edward C. Pease. "Framing *Brokeback Mountain*: How the Popular Press Corralled the Gay Cowboy Movie." *Critical Studies in Media Communication* 25, no. 3 (2008): 249–73.

Geyh, Kathrin. *Das Helle braucht das Dunkle. Der biblische Sündenfall in Brokeback Mountain.* Konstanz: UVK, 2011.

Henry, Alley. "Arcadia and the Passionate Shepherds of *Brokeback Mountain*." In *Reading Brokeback Mountain: Essays on the Story and the Film*, edited by Jim Stacy, 5–18. Jefferson, NC: McFarland, 2007.

Keller, James, and Anne Goodwyn-Jones. "*Brokeback Mountain*: Masculinity and Manhood." *Studies in Popular Culture* 30, no. 2 (2008): 21–36.

Li, Xinghua. "From Nature's Love to Natural Love: *Brokeback Mountain*, Universal Identification, and Gay Politics." In *Reading Brokeback Mountain: Essays on the Story and the Film*, edited by Jim Stacy, 106–17. Jefferson, NC: McFarland, 2007.

Patterson, Eric. *On Brokeback Mountain: Meditations about Masculinity, Fear, and Love in the Story and the Film.* Lanham, MD: Lexington, 2008.

Rose, Jane, and Joanne Urschel. "Understanding the Complexity of Love in *Brokeback Mountain*: An Analysis of the Film and Short Story." *Journal of Men's Studies* 14, no. 2 (2007): 247–51.

Yang, Che-ming. "The Paradox of Transgressing Sexual Identities: Mapping the Micropolitics of Sexuality/Subjectivity in Ang Lee's Films." *Asian Culture and History* 2, no. 1 (2010): 41–47.

—Paul Venzo and Sabine Planka

BUT I'M A CHEERLEADER (1999)

DIRECTOR: Jamie Babbit
SCREENPLAY: Brian Peterson
CAST: Natasha Lyonne (Megan), Clea DuVall (Graham), Cathy Moriarty (Mary), Michelle Williams (Kimberly), Bud Cort (Peter), Mink Stole (Nancy), RuPaul Charles (Mike), Melanie Lynskey (Hilary)
SPECS: 85 minutes; color
AVAILABILITY: DVD (Artisan/Lionsgate)

Seventeen-year-old Megan Bloomfield is a popular high school cheerleader who dates a football player named Jared, although she does not enjoy kissing him. Instead, Megan enjoys watching the other female cheerleaders strut around and perform moves in their tight, revealing uniforms. When her parents begin to suspect her lesbianism, they send her to True Directions, a gay conversion therapy camp, to be cured of her "affliction." While there, she meets hard-nosed founder of True Directions Mary Brown, a conversion therapist named Mike (played by drag performer RuPaul), and other young people attempting to cure themselves of their "homosexuality." As the campers engage in True Directions' five-step therapy system, Megan slowly develops an attraction for Graham, another young woman at the camp, and the two begin a sexual relationship. When their relationship is discovered by the camp therapists, Megan, now at ease with her sexuality, is unrepentant, while Graham repents for her actions and remains to graduate the program. At the end of the film, Megan crashes the camp's graduation ceremony, where she convinces Graham to run away with her, and the two young women ride off into the proverbial sunset.

The director of the film, Jamie Babbit, conceived the plot based on an article about a young man who experienced a real-life conversion therapy camp. In an interview about the film, Babbit stated that she wanted Megan to be a cheerleader because cheerleaders are "the pinnacle of the American dream, and the American dream of femininity," figures least likely to be represented as lesbians on film (Grady 2005). As a cheerleader, Megan could have a "femme" quality, which would differ from existing "butch" representations in films such as *Go Fish*. Babbit also wanted to use the film to reflect on "gender roles, gender expectations, and the absurdity of them" (Dixon 2004, 161). The five-step program at True Directions seemingly parodies this absurdity of gender roles in society, particularly "Step 2: Rediscovering Your Gender Identity."

For the young women, this step involves practicing various stereotypical household chores, applying makeup, sitting in a "ladylike" fashion, changing diapers, and marriage rehearsal, whereas the young men practice very "masculine" tasks such as wood chopping, working on cars, playing ball, and adjusting their genitals. On an even more absurd level, the young men's coach, "ex-gay" Mike, is played by real-life openly gay drag performer RuPaul, who wears incredibly short shorts and a "Straight is Great" T-shirt. In her analysis of this film, Nikki Sullivan writes that Step 2 emphasizes "that far from being 'natural,' gender is learnt, often, with much difficulty and somewhat 'unsuccessfully'" (Sullivan

Clea DuVall as Graham Eaton and Natasha Lyonne as Megan Bloomfield in *But I'm a Cheerleader*. Courtesy of Lions Gate Films/Photofest.

2003, 54). In other words, Babbit and screenwriter Brian Wayne Peterson are using absurdity to represent the learned behaviors of gender and how these behaviors are very much a societal construct. In this way, the film works to "disorder,
denaturalize, [and] queer" the heteronormative (Sullivan 2003, 52–53). Part of
this absurdity is represented in Babbit's use of a distinct gender-specific color
scheme. The young women's rooms and clothes are represented in bright pink,
while the young men's rooms and clothes are designed in distinct bright blue,
which Chris Holmlund refers to as being "gender-tuned" or culturally specific to
either male or female (2005, 183).

Step 4: Demystifying the Opposite Sex and Step 5: Simulated Sexual Lifestyle
also call out the absurdity of gender roles, particularly Step 5, where in a final
assignment the campers must dress in skin-tight flesh-toned bodysuits decorated
with fig leaves, evoking images of the biblical Adam and Eve in the Garden of
Eden. Mary then guides the male and female campers into various simulated
sexual positions of male dominance and female submission, instructing them on
the "appropriate" manner in which to have sex and rejecting foreplay because
it's "for sissies." These scenes also represent Mary's desire to deny and cure her
own son Rock's "homosexuality," revealing the lengths one will go to reject
"alternative lifestyles." Holmlund comments that the film makes the straight
characters (Mary, Mike, the campers' parents) appear "more ridiculous and less
likeable than the queers" and that the queerness of the film is more "multifaceted" and complex (2005, 183–84). Indeed, Megan struggles with her sexuality
at first, finding it hard in Step 1: Admitting You're a Homosexual to articulate
this sexuality to Mary and her fellow campers. Megan does not believe that her
sexuality is "unnatural" and thinks her feelings toward other young women are
normal: "Everyone looks at other girls, all the time." Mary ultimately forces her
into admitting that she is "homosexual," and Megan is ashamed. However, she
is reminded later in the film by two older gay ex-campers "that there's no one
way to be a lesbian" and ultimately embraces her sexual identity, even after her
parents tell her she will be disowned if she refuses to complete the program.
There is undoubtedly a distinction being made here between the absurdity and
hypocrisy of heteronormativity and the much more reasonable understanding of
same-sex desire as normal, complex, and multidimensional.

But I'm a Cheerleader was released in the years following the New Queer
Cinema movement of the early 1990s, one in which queer films in film festival
circuits, or queer films that did not "share a single aesthetic vocabulary, strategy,
or concern," broke with previous films that "accompanied identity politics . . . irreverent, energetic, alternately minimalist, and excessive" (Rich 2013, 18). In all
of these more recent new queer films were "traces of appropriation, pastiche, and
irony, as well as a reworking of history with social constructionism very much
in mind" (18). Effectively, these films of the New Queer Cinema movement
were more transgressive and radical in their representations of queer identity,
working to alienate repressive heterosexual power structures or to reconfigure
traditional heterosexual concepts of marriage and family life. For Michele Aaron,
mainstream spectatorship has frequently been a place of queer "disavowal," but
she maintains the argument that New Queer Cinema has been an "intervention"
into this process of disavowal (2004, 187). Rather than the queer transgression

being contained or below the surface, New Queer Cinema "has been worked to divulge the knowingness or complicity at the heart of the spectatorship" (187). While queer representations have constantly been present in mainstream cinema in contained or sanitized ways, New Queer Cinema worked as an intervening measure to expose the complicity of the knowing mainstream spectator. Arguably, while *But I'm a Cheerleader* would not be considered a strict example of New Queer Cinema, the film echoes the sentiments of its earlier New Queer counterparts in its irreverent, excessive, and rather absurdist representation of heterosexuality and LGBTQIA+ identity in the late 1990s.

See also *Go Fish*; *Yes, God, Yes.*

Bibliography

Aaron, Michele. "The New Queer Spectator." In *New Queer Cinema: A Critical Reader*, edited by Michele Aaron, 187–200. Edinburgh: Edinburgh University Press, 2004.

Dixon, Wheeler Winston. "Jamie Babbit." In *Film Voices: Interviews from Post Script*, edited by Gerald Duchovnay, 153–65. New York: SUNY Press, 2004.

Grady, Pam. "Rah Rah Rah: Director Jamie Babbit and Company Root for *But I'm a Cheerleader*." *Reel.com*, March 6, 2005. Accessed March 20, 2021. https://web.archive.org/web/20050306182317/http://www.reel.com/reel.asp?node=features%2Finterviews%2Fcheerleader.

Holmlund, Chris. "Generation Q's ABCs: Queer Kids and 1990s Independent Films." In *Contemporary American Independent Film: From the Margins to the Mainstream*, edited by Chris Holmlund and Justin Wyatt, 177–91. New York: Routledge, 2005.

Rich, B. Ruby. *New Queer Cinema: The Director's Cut*. Durham NC: Duke University Press, 2013.

Sullivan, Nikki. *A Critical Introduction to Queer Theory*. Edinburgh: Edinburgh University Press, 2003.

—John Lynskey

• C •

CAN YOU EVER FORGIVE ME? (2018)

DIRECTOR: Marielle Heller
SCREENPLAY: Nicole Holofcener and Jeff Whitty, based on the memoir *Can You Ever Forgive Me?* by Lee Israel
CAST: Melissa McCarthy (Lee Israel), Richard E. Grant (Jack Hock), Dolly Wells (Anna), Jane Curtin (Marjorie), Ben Falcone (Alan Schmidt), Tim Cummings (Craig), Anna Deaveare Smith (Elaine)
SPECS: 107 minutes; color
AVAILABILITY: DVD (Twentieth Century Fox)

Based on Lee Israel's memoir of the same name, *Can You Ever Forgive Me?* depicts the trials and tribulations of Israel as a struggling writer in 1990s New York City. At the start of the film, her successful career as a biographer is waning. Though she hopes to write another biography, this time on Fanny Brice, her editor swiftly rebukes the idea and suggests Lee's declining career is her own doing. In order to make money, Lee begins selling personal valuables, such as original letters from famous authors. After being offered a low price for a "bland" letter, Lee realizes she can forge embellishments and even entire letters to make more money. She persuades her friend, Jack Hock, to join in her criminal enterprise, with the promise of financial gain appealing to both characters as a gay man and woman drowning in an oppressive and unforgiving city. Eventually, the FBI catches wind of the crimes and begins an investigation. Jack's subsequent arrest and cooperation lead to Lee's trial and her admission of guilt.

Due to the nature of the film being based on a true story, the sexual identity of both Lee and Jack are nonnegotiable. However, an adaptation is still just that: an adaptation. Any screenwriter or filmmaker could have depicted the characters' sexualities as they saw fit, regardless of real life, depending on what complemented the narrative they were trying to tell. With Nicole Holofcener and Jeff Whitty's script, as well as Marielle Heller's deft direction, Lee's and Jack's identities are complex, layered, and, most importantly, whole. Their sexual identities are both important to their characters and arcs, while not their only defining traits, thereby avoiding the two greatest sins of representing queer characters: sexuality being the only defining trait of a character or having a queer character in name alone. The movie centers the characters' queerness—audiences see Lee meet with an ex-partner, Jack takes a lover, and there are explicit references to the backdrop of the AIDS epidemic—without ever tokenizing or exploiting it. As Director Marielle Heller explained on *IndieWire*'s *Filmmaker Toolkit* podcast: "Their sexuality is not what defines these characters. The fact that she's a lesbian and he's a gay man are not what define who they are there. There's so much else that is important to them at this moment in their lives, but it is the truth of their circumstances" (Dry 2018). Such an explanation perfectly encapsulates the uniqueness of this film as a narrative that encourages both the individual parts and whole sums of its characters while also telling a larger and true story.

Examining Lee and Jack separately allows for the many layers of the film to come to light. While Lee's arc is largely confined to the film and her own, sometimes small-minded personal world, Jack exists within a broader scope. Think of it like this: Lee is the character of the writer, Jack is the character of the historian. Both are valid and both speak to different ways of incorporating queer characters and narratives in storytelling, especially true stories.

Lee is a mercurial character—often crude and tactless, she is selfish and jaded by a world and industry that has pushed her aside. While Lee may speak to larger problems of accessibility within the publishing industry and, even broader, a capitalist society, her story still primarily exists in a narrow vision. Lee cares— first and foremost—about herself, her well-being, her credit and acknowledgment as an author, her own self-preservation. There is nothing inherently wrong with this until it becomes clear such a character is a standard not everyone can meet. In the oft-discriminatory United States, this standard is steeper, riddled with obstacles, longer, and lonelier for some. Race, sexuality, gender, socioeconomic status, religion, neurotypical status, and more determine a person's standard and how whole that person can be in the eyes of society. *Can You Ever Forgive Me?* walks this line exceedingly well. Lee is an unlikable character, both to the audience and to the people who exist within her world, yet she is also not unforgivable. In storytelling, it is an outdated trope, and product of a judgmental society, that the Other is the villain—or, at least, not the hero. When this is the only way marginalized people are portrayed, it becomes dangerous, with their lives seen as lesser, their rights negotiable, their worth ancillary and offered, rather than inherent. If portrayed realities exclusively trade in negative stereotypes, "symbolic annihilation" occurs. This is a concept offered by Gerbner and Gross: "Representation in the fictional world signifies social existence; absence means symbolic annihilation" (1976, 182). In subsequent years, the theory of "symbolic annihilation" has expanded to include not only a lack of representation but negative or stereotypical representation as well. What happens, then, when an accurate and whole representation of Lee, as well as her narrative, hinges on her own nastiness, while being mindful of not perpetuating negative cultivations of a gay character? Writers Nicole Holofcener and Jeff Whitty walk that tightrope both carefully and nimbly.

What Lee does to earn the attention of the FBI is wrong but does not discount her struggles as a gay woman, her fame and talent as a gay woman, her *worth* as a gay woman. In Holofcener and Whitty's script, they take great pains to make this distinction. Their script allows Lee to be human and not have to represent or bear the representation of an entire community—this type of characterization is typically reserved for white, straight, cisgender characters who can carry enough complexities to make mistakes, even ones as egregious as a federal crime, and not be written off entirely. Lee is not above consequences, but neither is she deserving of blanket condemnation. Audiences understand this not only through Lee's individual character arc but through her relationship with Jack, which sits at the center of the film as, more than anything else, a love story. Both characters are culpable for the actions they knowingly commit, as Jack willingly aids Lee with her forgery, but what overwhelms this in the film is their friendship as two gay people finding solace in one another as society turns its back on them. There comes to be a trust between them—until Lee's beloved cat dies under Jack's care while Lee is away stealing authentic letters from various institutions. Lee ultimately ends their friendship over this but continues their criminal partnership out of necessity for both of their incomes. One of the final scenes in the film—after Jack has participated with the FBI, resulting in Lee's court summons—is a reconciliation between the two. Both have plenty to apologize for, but Lee's contrition pierces the heart more, as she is the one who originally dragged Jack into her mess, and now he is dying of an AIDS-related illness.

"I have no one to tell, all my friends are dead," Jack says to Lee early in the film. In *Can You Ever Forgive Me?*, which takes place in 1991, New York City had yet to reach its peak of AIDS-related deaths (1994, by which time nearly 50,000 people had died). In 1983, however, New York City accounted for more than half of all AIDS-related deaths and new infections in the country; in 1982, Rupert Murdoch's paper the *Australian* referred to HIV/AIDS as the "gay plague"; and it was not until 1985 that President Ronald Reagan finally said the word "AIDS" (Todd 2020, 81). Though Jack had not seen the peak, he had still lived through more than a decade of terror, the deaths of loved ones, and a complete lack of care from his country's government. While subtle, Jack's existence as a gay man in 1990s New York City was intentional on Heller's part. The quote at the start of this paragraph was one of the first things Heller added into the script, she told *IndieWire*'s Jude Dry (2018). Heller continued: "He says it in this very off-handed

Richard E. Grant as Jack Hock and Melissa McCarthy as Lee Israel in *Can You Ever Forgive Me?* Courtesy of Fox Searchlight Pictures/Photofest.

dark humor. There's no feeling sorry for himself in that moment. It's just kind of, it's not even a thing, he just says it and moves on. But hopefully we as an audience go, 'Oh right, this is New York City, a gay man, 1991'" (Dry 2018).

Jack's line about the death of friends and his own HIV-positive status is not the only detail referencing the time period or political backdrop. The film's production designer, Steven Carter, placed an ACT UP poster in the window of Julius, the bar Lee and Jack frequent, and also a real-world location often referred to as New York's oldest surviving gay bar. ACT UP stood for "AIDS Coalition to Unleash Power" and was formed in 1987 as a "nonviolent direct action group" (Todd 2020, 85). ACT UP demanded action over the unnecessary deaths of thousands of LGBTQIA+ people—and it worked. Shortly after ACT UP's first demonstration, the US Food and Drug Administration (FDA) announced a time reduction for the approval of new drugs treating HIV and AIDS-related illnesses. Though the film does not center on the AIDS epidemic nor Jack's reality living with the disease, its decision to include and, more importantly, *how* to include it speaks volumes.

Historians and researchers now agree the US government acted largely in a reactive way to the AIDS epidemic, rather than a proactive way. Though the disease was first recognized officially in the United States in 1981, President Reagan did not take any action until 1987 when he formed the Watkins Commission, "partly because the actions of ACT UP and other activist groups made it impossible for him to ignore the crisis any longer" (Todd 2020, 90). Even with such a commission and the attention—finally—of the government, AIDS-related illnesses became the leading cause of death among men aged 25 to 44 in 1992, and the leading cause of death among all Americans in the same age group only three years later (Altman 1995). This epidemic and the government's fatal inaction affected the LGBTQIA+ community in devastating ways, beyond the tragedy of the disease itself. As Matthew Todd writes in his book *Pride: The Story of the LGBTQ Equality Movement*, "By 1985, the world was in blind panic and, as the disease was seen as one only affecting only gay men [sic], a homophobic hurricane consumed the lives of those affected" (2020, 81). Throughout the film, Jack struggles with the realities of being a gay man in the 1990s, even in a city that boasted a known LGBTQIA+ community, including homophobia, homelessness, and the ravaging of a merciless and unrelenting disease. The freedom, then, of Lee allowing Jack to stay in her home and watch her cat, becomes clear. He has a bed to sleep in, a roof over his head, a comfortable and safe place to bring a lover home, away from the eyes of anyone who would judge or harm. Through a clever use of "show don't tell," the movie is able to convey the importance of Lee and Jack's friendship in such a time, regardless of any criminal activity. "The AIDS crisis was the moment that the lesbian and gay community really united, especially in New York City," Heller explains. "For a lot of men, lesbians were people who ended up taking care of them as they died. Lee and Jack represent that in some small way" (Dry 2018).

Can You Ever Forgive Me? is a riveting film full of riveting performances about a riveting, near-unbelievable true story. Its true accomplishment, however, lies in its exploration of LGBTQIA+ loneliness and the pain, desperation, and solace of finding companionship when completely left behind and forgotten by a cruel and close-minded world.

See also *Battle of the Sexes; Behind the Candelabra; I Am Michael; Kill Your Darlings.*

Bibliography

Altman, Lawrence K. "AIDS Is Now the Leading Killer of Americans from 25 to 44." *New York Times*, January 31, 1995. Accessed May 28, 2021. https://www.nytimes.com/1995/01/31/science/aids-is-now-the-leading-killer-of-americans-from-25-to-44.html.

Dry, Jude. "'Can You Ever Forgive Me?' Leads the Way for the Future of Queer Film." *IndieWire*, November 16, 2018. Accessed May 28, 2021. https://www.indiewire.com/2018/11/can-you-ever-forgive-me-queer-film-lgbt-melissa-mccarthy-1202021281/.

Gerbner, George, and Larry Gross. "Living with Television: The Violence Profile." *Journal of Communication* 26 (1976): 172–99.

Todd, Matthew. *Pride: The Story of the LGBTQ Equality Movement.* Richmond, CA: Weldon Owen International, 2020.

—Anya Crittenton

CAROL (2015)

DIRECTOR: Todd Haynes

SCREENPLAY: Phyllis Nagy, based on the novel *The Price of Salt* by Patricia Highsmith

CAST: Cate Blanchett (Carol Aird), Rooney Mara (Therese Belivet), Sarah Paulson (Abby Gerhard), Kyle Chandler (Harge Aird), Jake Lacy (Richard), Kennedy K. Heim (Rindy Aird)

SPECS: 118 minutes; color

AVAILABILITY: DVD (Anchor Bay Entertainment, StudioCanal)

Therese Belivet is a young aspiring photographer who works as a salesclerk in a department store in Manhattan. It is Christmas season, and Carol Aird, a wealthy suburban woman who lives in New Jersey, is looking for a doll for her daughter Rindy at Therese's counter. When Carol leaves, Therese realizes Mrs. Aird has left her gloves and decides to mail them to her address. As a gesture of gratitude, Carol invites Therese to lunch, initiating their acquaintance. Carol is corseted in an unhappy marriage and is now divorcing her husband, Harge, who threatens to take Rindy's full custody, alleging a morality clause on the basis of Carol's previous relationship with her longtime friend Abby Gerhard. For her part, Therese's misgivings in her relationship with Richard emerge as soon as she meets Carol. The two women become intimate and embark on a road trip at Carol's suggestion until the custody hearing. On New Year's Eve, they kiss and have sex. The next day, they find out that a private detective, hired by Harge, has audiotaped their sexual encounter through the wall and has sent the recordings to Harge's lawyer. Carol flies back home to fight for Rindy's custody while Abby drives Therese back to New York. In an attempt not to become estranged from her daughter, Carol complies with Harge's demands at first, shutting Therese out and isolating herself. However, she ends up signing over full custody to Harge in order to live her life truthfully. In the meantime, Therese focuses on her professional career and gets a position at the *New York Times* as a photographer. One day, Carol sees her in the street, writes her a note, and they meet at the Ritz. Carol hopes Therese will accept to live with her, but she does not. She also opens up the possibility to join her later if she has a change of heart, but Therese remains silent. Carol confesses that she loves her, but an interruption by an old friend of Therese's prompts Carol's leaving. In the last scene, Therese appears at the restaurant Carol is at and approaches her table; Carol spots her and smiles.

Based on Patricia Highsmith's 1952 romantic—and only openly lesbian—novel *The Price of Salt*, Todd Haynes's *Carol* retains the very essence of the book and transforms the story into a superb adaptation thanks to Phyllis Nagy's outstanding screenplay. Whereas in the book Therese is a set designer and Carol, mostly absent from the narrative, acquires a mythical quality magnified by Therese's infatuation, in the film Therese's profession as a photographer is in tune with her passive observation of Carol and allows her to materialize her obsession in snapshots. Longing gazes and subtle gestures carry out a great amount of subtext and highlight the oppressive social climate for the LGBTQIA+ community in the years prior to the gay liberation movement (Sullivan 1990). In fact, the same year *The Price of Salt* was published, "homosexuality" was classified as a mental disorder by the American Psychiatric Association (Patterson 2015). The antigay atmosphere had a great impact on Highsmith, who published the work under the pseudonym "Claire Morgan" after her publisher, Harper & Bros., rejected it. She was not ashamed of her sexuality, but she did not want to

Rooney Mara as Therese Belivet and Cate Blanchett as Carol Aird in *Carol*. Courtesy of The Weinstein Company/Photofest.

be labeled as a lesbian writer and, for years, denied any association with the book (Highsmith 2004, 291).

Set in 1950s New York, the aesthetics are reminiscent of Haynes's previous works *Far from Heaven* (2002) and *Mildred Pierce* (2001), and the oneiric reflections that pervade the film are influenced by the New York school of photography, in particular Saul Leiter's abstract pictures. An air of Grace Kelly in *Rear Window* is sensed in the architecture of Carol, and the character of Therese is conspicuously akin to that of Audrey Hepburn in *Sabrina*. Dressed in pinafores and a beatnik beret, Therese reinforces her image as a much younger woman than Carol and, along with her haircut—very similar to Carol's daughter's— might make the couple fall into rather stereotypical Freudian subjects, framing lesbian desire as a mother-daughter relationship. However, the film does not present a psychoanalytical approach to causation, nor does it explore sexual identity. Instead, *Carol* provides comments on class, age, and gender roles in a prejudiced society, and presents a love story between two characters who happen to be gay. The film exploits some dated clichés, such as the innocent and inexperienced young woman who is seduced by the predatory and older lesbian in furs, or the fact that Therese did not play with dolls but with train sets as a kid. Sexual identity can often be the main plot point in narratives that involve gay people, but in *Carol* lesbianism is not thematized as an element the plot revolves around and is not read as a problem or a trauma. The misery of the characters' lives does not derive from their sexual identity, and their relationship unfolds in the most natural way. There is no shame in feeling attracted to another woman, no momentous coming-out scene, and they never feel afraid of their emotions. This is depicted in Therese's organic response when her friend Dannie asks her about Carol, and especially in the custody hearing scene when an exhausted Carol admits to the affair with Therese, surrenders her custody rights in favor of Harge, and decides to start living authentically.

Many elements of Highsmith's novel stemmed from personal experiences. The plotline regarding Carol's divorce, custody, and the recording in the hotel room with another woman derive from the experience of Virginia Kent Catherwood, one of Highsmith's lovers (Dawson 2015). The character of Carol was inspired by a "blondish woman in a fur coat" who bedazzled Highsmith, who was, at that time, a young clerk working at Macy's, and is captured in the scene at the store in which Carol and Therese meet for the first time (Highsmith 2004, 298). In the opening scene, the camera follows a man into the Ritz Tower restaurant, where he interrupts a conversation between the two female protagonists. His point of view is then submitted to that of Therese's, who regains agency over the latent male gaze, utterly pervasive in the film industry (Marcus 2015). In addition to this defining shift of viewpoint, one of the most noteworthy accomplishments of this adaptation is the addition of Carol's point of view, which is subdued in the book. The scene in the Ritz at the beginning of the film triggers a flashback in Therese's mind that constitutes the story itself. At the end, when viewers see the scene again—"Everything comes full circle," anticipates Carol in her farewell letter to Therese [01:27:40]—the point of view has changed and now it is Carol's. The shifting perspectives allow viewers to have insight into the evolution of the characters, which, by the end of the story, is notable, as though their roles were swapped, Therese is distant and has an aura of unreachability, whereas Carol presents herself as vulnerable and expectant.

As Phyllis Nagy explains in an interview for Lambda Literary, there are implicit conversations about same-sex desire, but there is no queer language, and, for example, the word "lesbian" is never spoken (Jaffe 2016). Yet this subject matter is spoken about freely and never rejected or silenced. The most explicit allusion is manifested in a dialogue between Therese and her boyfriend, Richard. She naively asks him whether he has ever been in love with a boy or heard of it, which Richard denies in a simple and rather homophobic way and later refers to "homosexuals" as "people like that" [00:51:28]. In Carol's case, references to "homosexuality" are also implicit but more normalized, as she had relationships with women in the past. The dialogue between Carol and Abby is an exercise in reading between the lines, but the underlying meaning is clear. The coded language, the surreptitious glances and smiles provide enough context to understand that when Abby tells Carol she has met a redhead, this person is a woman, and when Carol acknowledges she does not know what she is doing with Therese and never did—meaning, she does not question the consequences of her actions—the reference to the past is intended to address Abby. The situation changes drastically in the scenes with Harge, where there is no coded language but an attempt to avoid anything that could hint at his wife's sexual ambivalence.

Even though "homosexuality" was perceived as a mental disorder—represented in the film by the psychotherapy sessions Carol is forced to attend during the battle for custody in order to allege a recovery from her "sexual deviation"—the film also suggests that Carol and Therese can go on a trip on their own without raising suspicions (other than those of Carol's husband) or could set up a home together because of the historical overlooking of lesbian desire in society, on one hand, and the way both women comply with the social conventions of femininity, on the other. In this sense, Carol sets a precedent for Therese, who follows suit. In the scene at the record store, the two women who stare at Therese—presumably lesbians—present themselves in a radically different way to her or Carol. The encounter seems to make Therese uncomfortable, given her reaction. This highlights that codification goes beyond the use of certain words or expressions, it is also related to corporal language, clothes, and everything with the power to communicate and convey information about one's identity.

The portrayal of "homosexuality" as a valid option is stressed by the uncommon ending for a love story involving same-sex desire. The Price of Salt is considered the first lesbian book with a happy ending where the characters are not doomed to a tragic fate as a metaphorical punishment for their sexual orientation—something that became the norm in the literature of the first half of the twentieth century if authors wanted to dodge obscenity charges and thus censorship. In the film, this moment is transmitted by a slow-motioned Therese walking toward Carol and a change in the point of view as Carol looks directly at the camera, making viewers into participants in the quiet happy ending that, as Haynes asserts, entails a beginning (Cooke 2015). The intensification of the music and its subsequent break with the sudden cut to black leaves the viewer pondering what comes next. For the director, it is clear: "They have a shot" (Cooke 2015). This last scene, with Carol's arresting face, almost still, slightly tilted, smiling, and addressing the camera, gives viewers "both a tantalizing taste of the past and glimpse of a queer future" (White 2015, 17).

The tranquil pace of the film, the minimal movement, and the sense of suspended happiness render the film as one of Therese's pictures. According to Susan Sontag, a photograph contains "a tiny element of another world" (2008, 11) and has the power to turn the ephemeral into an everlasting moment, "a perpetual sunrise" as Carol tells Therese [01:28:45]. With a sensitive approach to the ordeal same-sex desire supposed at the time, Haynes captures a piece of history and immortalizes these women's love story as "the image-world that bids to outlast us all" (Sontag 2008, 11).

See also *Far from Heaven.*

Bibliography

Cooke, Rachel. "Interview. Todd Haynes: 'She Said, There's a Frock Film Coming Up, with Cate Attached . . . It Sounded Right Up My Alley.'" *Observer*, November 15, 2015. Accessed March 20, 2021. https://www.theguardian.com/film/2015/nov/15/todd-haynes-interview-carol-frock-film-cate-blanchett-rooney-mara.

Dawson, Jill. "Carol: The Women behind Patricia Highsmith's Lesbian Novel." *Guardian*, May 13, 2015. Accessed March 20, 2021. https://www.theguardian.com/books/2015/may/13/patricia-highsmith-film-adaptation-carol-only-openly-lesbian-novel-cannes-cate-blanchett.

Highsmith, Patricia. *The Price of Salt.* New York: W. W. Norton, 2004.

Jaffe, Sara. "Phyllis Nagy: On Writing the Script for 'Carol' and Creating a Different Kind of Love Story." Lambda Literary, February 21, 2016. Accessed March 15, 2021. https://www.lambdaliterary.org/2016/02/phyllis-nagy-on-writing-the-script-for-carol-and-creating-a-different-kind-of-love-story/.

Marcus, Bennett. "Todd Haynes on Subverting the Male Gaze in *Carol.*" *Cut*, November 18, 2015. Accessed March 16, 2021. https://www.thecut.com/2015/11/todd-haynes-carol-male-gaze.html.

Patterson, John. "*Carol*: The Best Patricia Highsmith Adaptation to Date?" *Guardian*, November 23, 2015. Accessed March 16, 2021. https://www.theguardian.com/film/2015/nov/23/carol-patricia-highsmith-todd-haynes.

Sontag, Susan. *On Photography.* London: Penguin, 2008.

Sullivan, Gerard. "Discrimination and Self-Concept of Homosexuals before the Gay Liberation Movement: A Biographical Analysis Examining Social Context and Identity." *Biography* 13, no. 3 (Summer 1990): 203–21.

White, Patricia. "Sketchy Lesbians: *Carol* as History and Fantasy." *Film Quarterly* 69, no. 2 (Winter 2015): 8–18.

—Layla Ferrández Melero

CHERRY POP (2017)

DIRECTOR: Assaad Yacoub
SCREENPLAY: Nick Landa
CAST: Lars Berge (The Cherry), Dequan Johnson (Blanqueesha), Matthew Sanderson (White Chocolate), Miguel Sagaz (Choriza), Caldwell Tidicue (Kitten Withawhip), Cole Hartley (Delusia), Patrick Holt (Lady Zaza), David McKee (Ariella)
SPECS: 79 minutes; color
AVAILABILITY: DVD (Wolfe Video)

Cherry Pop follows the story of a heterosexual singer who aspires to perform at a local drag club, Cherry Pop, to advance his career. The club's shows regularly feature a "Cherry," or a drag performer who has yet to make a live debut. For the entirety of the film, the protagonist's true name is hidden, and he is only referred to as "the Cherry." The nightclub's staff unquestionably assumes that the Cherry is gay as he prepares to perform in drag. However, his true identity is revealed when one of the club's regular drag queens answers a phone call from his girlfriend. Knowing his true sexuality, the queens confront him in an explosively verbal altercation that forces the Cherry to leave before his set. However, he returns to perform despite his alienation. At the cusp of performing his lip sync, the building's power is mistakenly turned off. The Cherry continues to perform his set of "Ave Maria" acapella. The angelic performance not only wins the acceptance of the queens who first rejected him but also earns him the favor and awe of the club's most prized queen, Zaza.

As a whole, the film frames the experience of the minority in society, but does so through a role reversal, as a seemingly traditional heternormative character is forced into the position of the societal "Other." Dr. Zuleyka Zevallos, applied sociologist, contextualizes the concept of Otherness as an inherently dichotomic power structure within society: "The concept of The Other highlights how many societies create a sense of belonging, identity, and social status by constructing social categories as binary opposites" (2018). The narrative is an ambitious and ironic satirization of society that paints queer individuals as the oppressors in this binary relationship, but it also questions the viability of discrimination against the Other in the scope of the LGBTQIA+ community. Despite this, the film does not negatively portray queer individuals. Moreover, it poses that superficial assertions of identity create a dichotomic conflict of the societal Other versus the conventional expectations of culture.

The film's opening presents the protagonist's role as an unorthodox minority. The initial sequence begins with a voice-over monologue set to a black backdrop; the Cherry describes his hunger for a self-fulling authenticity as he performs:

> This is my memory about a dream I once had—a dream to perform in my own way, and as long as I got to do that, nothing else really mattered at the time. . . . I had this dream; I wanted the experience of giving others an experience, but finding the stage to kick-start your dreams on is not an easy task, and that is how I ended up at Cherry Pop. [00:00:50–00:04:21]

The language of the monologue is semantically reminiscent of queer narratives; the narrator longs for a sense of freedom that seems out of reach. Additionally, the progression of finding an alternative stage is discretely coded to reflect the experience of freshman drag performers. The ideas communicated by the monologue introduce the protagonist's role as a nontraditional minority; although he is part of the macroculture, his purpose in life is socially unorthodox and theoretically places him in similar circumstances to the drag performers at Cherry Pop.

However, the Cherry's motivations are immediately challenged by the hostile environment of Cherry Pop as the sequence transitions to a medium shot of him walking to the entrance of the nightclub. As he is admitted into the club, the Cherry is advised by the doorman, "Don't make eye contact with them. . . .

Fucking queers." [00:02:22–00:02:29]. The authenticity and hopefulness of the opening monologue are undercut by the sobering discontent of the doorman's advice. Much like the doorman, there is an ironic hostility that each employee holds for their fellow workers and cast members. This irony is dependent on an assumption that queer spaces are geared toward empowering the communities they serve. However, the cast of drag performers is far from the basis of this assumption. Not only does the cast habitually refuse to accept new performers, but they routinely speak to one another with transphobic, racist, and classist slurs. Repeating the same oppressive language used by the macroculture, Cherry Pop is shown as a volatile by-product of society in which minorities refuse to question the social ideas that marginalize one another. Moreover, the trauma of marginalization motivates the cast of Cherry Pop to discriminate against each other as a futile way to reject their own status as societal Others. Simone de Beauvoir explains the power transaction of establishing marginalized sociological roles in the introduction of *The Second Sex*: "No subject will readily volunteer to become the object, the inessential; it is not the Other who, in defining himself as the Other, establishes the One. The Other is posed as such by the One in defining himself as the One" (1949, 7). Cherry Pop is an arena in which those who are already seen as societal Others fight for supremacy among other minorities within the dynamic described by Beauvoir.

Different from the abusive cast of drag performers, Ariella is the only queen of the night's cast to show humility and kindness to the Cherry. Additionally, her character is one of the most troubled as a whole. The film draws a connection between Ariella's own struggles with her family and having the capacity to show empathy to the protagonist. Much like the Cherry is assumed to be gay, Ariella is assumed to be heterosexual by her mother. Although her mother routinely attends her shows, she is firmly delusional in thinking that Ariella is playing a stage role at a local theater. Meanwhile, Ariella's boyfriend shows no interest in her struggle to convince her mother of her true sexuality. Like the protagonist, Ariella is caught between the expectation of a third party and her own truth. Although her position is presented as a comedic subplot, it is still presented as a mirrored reflection of the Cherry.

Although Ariella and the Cherry find a substantial kinship with each other initially, Ariella is quick to join the other queens in their violent treatment of the protagonist once he is outed as a heterosexual. Just before White Chocolate, a regular performer at Cherry Pop, bursts into the bathroom to confront the Cherry about his sexuality, Ariella is found assuring him that she would support him should he ever need emotional support. As the Cherry asks her about the drastic change in behavior once he is outed, she answers, "Let's not dwell in the past" [00:35:13]. This shift between the protagonist and a mirroring character highlights how minorities are deprived of intimacy and solidarity. The dramatic change in tone also emphasizes how the true character of the protagonist is never compromised by his sexuality, but the treatment he receives is dependent on meeting the assumptions of those around him. Although the film features queer characters as the aggravators, the conflict, as a whole, is a metaphor for the treatment of queer individuals in contemporary Western society. Just as LGBTQIA+

individuals are denied empathy or human value on the basis of not being seen as social equals, the protagonist receives the same treatment at Cherry Pop.

However, as the Cherry is harassed to the point of leaving the club before his set, the queens realize the importance of his participation in the show. The role of the Cherry is vital to the club's nightly performance as it is the essential finale. Without a performer to fulfill this role, they recognize that they have effectively ruined their own show. The queens' realization highlights the destructive nature of their ignorance; they have compromised their own show for the sake of their preconditioned prejudice. Even Ariella pushes herself to apologize to the protagonist as he returns to perform. The film recounts the sincerity and intimacy the two formerly shared to reflect the warmth of true comradery that transcends the barriers of prejudice. The need for the Cherry's participation in the night's show also comments on the role of the minority in society; despite the hostile and stigmatized treatment that the societal Other faces, society still garners value from the parties that it oppresses. The absence of the abused protagonist is the first moment in the film that the antagonists realize the error of their ways.

Nonetheless, the climax of the film featuring the protagonist's performance is the ultimate transcendence of the social barriers that create the narrative's main conflict. On the cusp of performing a lip-synced performance of "Ave Maria," the lights are accidentally turned off by a lost patron trying to find the bathroom. Although comedic in setup, this is a symbolic disabling of formal, structured society. Left without a track to perform to, the Cherry continues to perform a capella. Stripped of the enhancements of modern society that would otherwise force him to perform without his true voice, he delivers an organic and hauntingly beautiful performance of the classic song. Leaving patrons in tears and the rest of the cast in awe-struck astonishment, the performance elevates the completion of the authenticity that he craves at the beginning of the film. Not only is the performance organic, but the protagonist establishes that connection with his viewers that he also describes in his opening monologue. The film asserts that art, acting as an expression of the pure human desire for acceptance and agency, will overcome the dichotomy of society and the societal Other.

Although the film ironically follows the narrative of a heterosexual performer, the themes are based on the experiences that queer minorities face in society. Moreover, the film speaks to the capacity of art to break down the barriers that bar LGBTQIA+ individuals from finding the acceptance that all humans crave. Despite portraying queer archetypal characters as the oppressors, the film's conclusion shows that breaking down barriers of preconditioned conception is not only freeing but creates a strengthened bond within the community. The film serves as an optimistic critique of modern queer spaces to transcend the struggles of the sociological and binary mechanisms of Otherness and to, instead, empower and support the communities that they serve.

See also *To Wong Foo, Thanks for Everything! Julie Newmar*.

Bibliography

De Beauvoir, Simone. *The Second Sex*. Translated by Constance Borde and Sheila Chevallier. New York: Random House, 1949.

Zevallos, Zuleyka. "What Is Otherness?" *Other Sociologist*, June 17, 2018. Accessed May 30, 2021. https://www.othersociologist.com/otherness-resources/.

—Sean D. Catino

CLOUD ATLAS (2012)

DIRECTORS: Tom Tykwer, Lana Wachowski, and Lilly Wachowski
SCREENPLAY: Tom Tykwer, Lana Wachowski, and Lilly Wachowski, based on the novel of the same name by David Mitchell
CAST: Tom Hanks (Dr. Henry Goose / Hotel Manager / Isaac Sachs / Dermot Hoggins / Cavendish Look-a-Like Actor / Zachry), Halle Berry (Native Woman / Jocasta Ayrs / Luisa Rey / Indian Party Guest / Ovid / Meronym), Jim Broadbent (Captain Molyneux / Vyvyan Ayrs / Timothy Cavendish / Korean Musician / Prescient 2), Hugo Weaving (Haskell Moore / Tadeusz Kesselring / Bill Smoke / Nurse Noakes / Boardman Mephi / Old Georgie), Jim Sturgess (Adam Ewing / Poor Hotel Guest / Megan's Dad / Highlander / Hae-Joo Chang / Adam [Zachry's brother-in-law]), Bae Doona (Tilda / Megan's Mom / Mexican Woman / Sonmi-451 / Sonmi-351 / Sonmi Prostitute), Ben Whishaw (Cabin Boy / Robert Frobisher / Store Clerk / Georgette / Tribesman)
SPECS: 172 minutes; 134 minutes (Mainland China Cut Version); color
AVAILABILITY: DVD (Warner Home Video)

Six narratives intersect across millennia. Pacific Islands, 1849: a young lawyer named Adam Ewing befriends an escaped slave, and they combine to overcome the murderous plans of a greedy doctor. Cambridge, 1936: Robert Frobisher, an aspiring young musician, hides in a rundown hotel after shooting renowned composer Vyvyan Ayrs, who blackmails the younger man to give up his credit to the "Cloud Atlas Sextet" piece or have his identity as a gay man revealed and his reputation ruined. San Francisco, 1973: investigative journalist Luisa Rey works to reveal a conspiracy to cover up the design flaws in a nuclear power plant. London, 2012: down-on-his-luck book publisher Timothy Cavendish has a windfall when the author of his latest title kills a literary critic. However, when the author's lowlife henchmen come to collect their boss's earnings, Cavendish cannot pay up. He goes on the run and ends up in a retirement home that treats its residents as prisoners. He hatches a plot to escape. Neo Seoul, 2144: a worker clone called Sonmi-451 becomes the living symbol for a rebel network to overthrow the oppressive ruling classes. Before the rebels are killed and she is captured, she manages to broadcast a political manifesto. An unnamed location, a century later: the global sea level has swallowed most civilizations. Zachry is a tribesman carrying guilt and grief for the killing of his brother-in-law and nephew by a rival tribe. The community is visited by Meronym, a member of the technologically advanced Prescients, who needs a guide to take her up the mountains. She warns that all remaining humanity will become extinct unless she reaches a communication satellite and contacts the off-world colonies. Zachry reluctantly agrees, battling his personal demons in the shape of the sinister "Old Georgie." A coda reveals an older Zachry telling his story to a group of children on one of the colonies where he now lives with Meronym.

There are two explicitly LGBTQIA+ characters in the Wachowskis and Tom Tykwer's adaptation of David Mitchell's novel. They are gay lovers Robert Frobisher and Rufus Sixsmith, who hide their relationship in 1930s Cambridge. Frobisher, as played by openly gay actor Ben Whishaw, is an eloquent and charming opportunist. Sixsmith, meanwhile, is a quiet and dignified character, a student at Cambridge, and seemingly caught in the whirlwind that is Robert's hectic life. The young composer's narrative arc begins and ends on the run in a hotel. He is first seen in bed with Sixsmith as the hotel manager angrily bangs on the door not wanting "their sort" lodged in his establishment, a sentiment echoed by Chinese film censors, who cut nearly forty minutes from the film, including some gay content, on its release in January 2013. Frobisher jumps out of bed, hastily grabs his belongings (including Sixsmith's elegant waistcoat), and darts out of a nearby window toward his next adventure. It just so happens that this will be his last; he shoots himself as Rufus arrives too late to rescue him. The film encourages the viewer to sympathize with Robert's plight. It reveals his thoughts in a voice-over as he writes letters to his beloved Sixsmith, and he composes the orchestral piece that gives the film its title. Vyvyan Ayrs, the composer Robert assists, is a caricature of embittered old age and long-held privilege. As he orders his assistant around, belittles him, and eventually blackmails him for being gay, the viewer is expected to align with Robert. Ayrs's reaction to Robert's sexual identity is indicative of well-worn stereotypes. He uses the term "buggery" and, when confronted by an armed Frobisher, mockingly says, "You won't pull that trigger. Your kind never does." In other words, gay men are cowards and weak willed, an accusation Robert arguably disproves when he (possibly by accident) shoots Ayrs and later commits suicide. Rufus Sixsmith suffers a similar fate. However, his death by gunshot is staged as a suicide when, in fact, he is murdered for his knowledge about a political coverup in the 1970s that threatens to kill thousands of innocent people.

On the one hand (and similar to the treatment of lesbian and gay characters in *V for Vendetta*, which the Wachowskis scripted), by prematurely dying, Robert and Rufus suffer the fate of many LGBTQIA+ characters in so-called popular cinema. In Robert's case, his existence is incompatible with the current society, and he is forced to end his life rather than suffer the persecution he will no doubt endure. Shortly before his suicide, in a letter to Sixsmith, Robert imagines a "better world" waiting for them both. In Rufus's case, a gay character is sacrificed to allow a (presumably) straight character, Luisa Rey, to complete the work he has started. On the other hand, one could argue that these characters do not truly die in the sense that their progenitors and descendants appear in each of the different timelines. This is the central conceit of Mitchell's novel and Tykwer and the Wachowskis' film; we are all connected. (The directing team would later reunite to explore similar themes in the Netflix series *Sense8*). Clone Sonmi-451, whose fight to be recognized as equal to the "pure-blood" humans and not socially deviant chimes with the LGBTQIA+ rights movement, encapsulates the film's central tenet when she says, "Our lives are not our own. From womb to tomb we are bound to others, past and present, and by each crime and every kindness, we birth our future." Therefore, the numerous other characters played by Ben

Whishaw and James D'Arcy throughout the film are to be understood as the traces of Robert Frobisher and Rufus Sixsmith.

These two characters are transgressive in terms of their sexuality. Yet nearly all the characters in *Cloud Atlas* are transgressive in one way or another because the directors decide to cast the same actors in opposition to assigned identity markers, such as ethnicity, gender, social standing, and age. In this way, South Korean actor Bae Doona can portray a nineteenth-century white middle-class American woman, a Mexican laundress in the 1970s, as well as a human clone in twenty-second-century Neo Seoul. Halle Berry, who is biracial, plays a Jewish woman, an Indian woman, and an East Asian man. Finally, Whishaw, in addition to young white gay male Frobisher, is depicted as elderly, white, and female in a later sequence. Indeed, it is Whishaw-as-Frobisher who writes "all boundaries are conventions waiting to be transcended. One may transcend any convention if one can first conceive of doing so." It is heard in a voice-over and plays over a montage of sequences showing sociocultural transgressions as a white man and Black slave form a friendship and a human man has sex with a female clone. It is also the case that Tykwer and the Wachowskis (the Wachowskis both identify as trans women) are crossing certain representational boundaries. While one might question how effective or politically correct their choices are, there is no doubting that it results in a particularly "queer" viewing experience.

See also *V for Vendetta*.

Bibliography

Benshoff, Harry M., and Sean Griffin. "Introduction: What Is Queer Film History?" In *Queer Images: A History of Gay and Lesbian Film in America*, edited by Harry M. Benshoff and Sean Griffin, 1–18. Lanham, MD: Rowman & Littlefield, 2006.

Keegan, Cáel M. *Lana and Lilly Wachowski*. Urbana: University of Illinois Press, 2018.

Pearson, Wendy G., Veronica Hollinger, and Joan Gordon, eds. *Queer Universes: Sexualities in Science Fiction*. Liverpool: Liverpool University Press, 2008.

Trinder, Stephen. "Encounters with the Other: Transcultural Possibilities in the Wachowskis' and Tykwer's *Cloud Atlas*." *Open Cultural Studies* 3, no. 1 (2019): 232–44.

—Adam Vaughan

CLUE (1985)

DIRECTOR: Jonathan Lynn
SCREENPLAY: Jonathan Lynn, based on the board game of the same name
CAST: Eileen Brennan (Mrs. Peacock), Tim Curry (Wadsworth), Madeline Kahn (Mrs. White), Christopher Lloyd (Professor Plum), Michael McKean (Mr. Green), Martin Mull (Colonel Mustard), Lesley Ann Warren (Miss Scarlet)
SPECS: 96 minutes; color
AVAILABILITY: DVD (Paramount)

Based on the classic board game of the same name, *Clue* is a campy-murder-mystery-turned-cult-classic comedy set in 1954 New England. Opening on a dark and stormy night, the film centers on the butler, Wadsworth, preparing Hill House, the requisite creepy mansion, for a dinner party. One by one, guests arrive—three men and three women—and each are instructed to use aliases (all of which are derived from the board game: Colonel Mustard, Mrs. White, Professor Plum, Mrs. Peacock, Miss Scarlet, and Mr. Green) rather than their real names, although none knows the reason why. The last guest, Mr. Boddy, arrives, and Wadsworth reveals each of the guests is being blackmailed by his employer, Mr. Boddy, for various suspicions and crimes. Wadsworth indicates he has the evidence Mr. Boddy has been using, all of which he is prepared to hand over to the police, who will arrive within the hour if the guests are prepared to face the allegations to be free from blackmail. Mr. Boddy offers each guest a gift (a candlestick, a rope, a knife, a revolver, a wrench, and a lead pipe) and an alternative: kill Wadsworth instead and their secrets will remain safe, but the blackmail will continue. When the lights flicker off, it is Mr. Boddy and not Wadsworth who appears to be dead on the floor. The capers commence as the guests and Wadsworth attempt to figure out who the killer is, splitting up, searching the mansion, and using the secret passages they discover to move from room to room. Instead of finding resolution, the bodies stack up as the maid, the cook, a singing telegram, a passing motorist, and an off-duty police officer all end up dead in the mansion. In the theaters, viewers randomly received one of three possible endings to the film; the DVD of the film offers all three endings and also indicates one of them is the *real* conclusion: Wadsworth is the actual blackmailer, Mr. Boddy was *his* butler, and each of those murdered had been an accomplice or informant killed by the guest in the house who knew who they were. Only Mr. Green is innocent—an undercover FBI agent sent to monitor the situation. All guilty parties are arrested at the conclusion of the film, with the exception of Wadsworth, who is fatally shot by Mr. Green. While the film generally received lukewarm reviews, as one reviewer rightfully noted, "1985's *Clue* adaptation still has a rabid fan base," due in large part to its stellar cast and campy nature; as of February 2020, it was being reported that Ryan Reynolds and his production company were considering a reboot of the film (Hilburn 2020).

Much of the film relies on stereotypes for its humor, creating over-the-top characters who embody particular ideas for a laugh. The female characters fall into two main categories: highly sexualized or overly matronly. Thus, Mrs. White is the Black Widow character, a woman who has had five husbands, many of whom mysteriously end up dead. Miss Scarlet runs a brothel and gets propositioned repeatedly by Professor Plum. Yvette, the maid, spends her time in the film in a sexualized French maid's outfit, frequently attracting attention from the majority of the male characters. Thus, as Wadsworth introduces Colonel Mustard to Yvette, he states, "Yvette, would you attend to the Colonel and give him anything he requires? Within reason that is," suggesting Yvette's appearance and position also speak to her sexual availability [00:05:31–00:05:36]. Conversely, Mrs. Peacock and the cook are placed in less revealing clothing, indicating their matronly, desexualized positions, as the jokes, both verbal and physical, tend to focus on their body sizes, movements, and speech instead of their sexuality.

Similarly, the men fit predictable types as well, with Colonel Mustard and Professor Plum, as well as Mr. Boddy, repeatedly staring at, commenting on, or touching women's bodies, often without consent or interest on behalf of their female counterparts. Almost all of the characters fit traditional, heteronormative tropes. Set in the 1950s and filmed in the 1980s, it is perhaps not surprising that the film embraces and reifies heteronormative sexuality.

Mr. Green is the one exception in the film, at least for the majority of the action. Whereas Colonel Mustard is a less-than-sharp military man's man known to frequent Miss Scarlet's brothel and Professor Plum is a sexually aggressive intellectual (who lost his license to practice psychology after sleeping with a female patient), Mr. Green is tall, thin, and bespeckled: a bit nerdy and unassuming. When he first arrives at the mansion, Wadsworth reprimands the home's barking German shepherds, yelling at them to sit, but it is Mr. Green who quickly finds a bench and shrinks his body onto it, demonstrating a clear subservience to a more dominant male in the scene.

As Wadsworth begins revealing each guest's secret to the assembled guests, allegedly attempting to encourage them to free themselves from the shame of blackmail, Mr. Green nervously stands, stating, "I have something to say. I'm not going to wait for Wadsworth here to unmask me. I work for the State Department and I'm a homosexual. I feel no personal shame or guilt about this, but I must keep it a secret or a I will lose my job on security grounds. Thank you" [00:23:23–00:23:49]. Given that the film is set in 1954, this reference to the purging of LGBTQIA+ men (and women) from government service is an important historical reference. As Craig M. Loftin noted:

> Gay men and lesbians became entangled within a growing postwar anti-communist hysteria when the U.S. Senate held hearings in 1950 on homosexuals "and other sex perverts" working for the government. These hearings spurred the purge of thousands of gay men and lesbians working in government agencies, and they exacerbated police surveillance of homosexual communities nationwide during the 1950s and into the 1960s. The penalties of homosexual visibility were often severe during these years. (2007, 577)

The destructiveness of what became known as the "Lavender Scare," where anything outside of traditional heterosexuality was seen as perversion, had far-reaching impacts on the LGBTQIA+ community as "thousands of suspected homosexuals were investigated, interrogated, and dismissed by government officials and private employers" (Friedman 2005, 1105).

While it is important to give *Clue* credit for highlighting the Lavender Scare, a historical moment often overshadowed by the Red Scare, the film's overall treatment of the character of Mr. Green is problematic. Two important moments immediately follow Mr. Green's brief speech. As he sits back down following his confession, Professor Plum abruptly leaves the shared couch, while Mrs. Peacock, the eldest woman at the party, grimaces in disgust. Their reactions represent an ongoing distrust and distaste for Mr. Green throughout the film. Similarly, following the confessions, Wadsworth notes his own wife was supposedly a victim of the blackmail as well; in her case, she was known to have friends who were Communists, playing into another fear prevalent in 1950s America. Wadsworth states through his false tears, "He hated my wife for the same reason that he hated all of you. He believed that you were all thoroughly un-American" [00:31:56–00:32:04]. While this moment would theoretically unite those in the room under the umbrella of their "crimes," the film uses this moment to highlight Mr. Green as the table he is resting against collapses, sending glassware crashing to the ground and pulling focus directly to him. This shift of attention to Mr. Green immediately following Wadsworth's comments about "un-American" behavior tells viewers to see Mr. Green as the recipient of the "un-American" label, perpetuating the myth common in the 1950s—and beyond—that his sexual identity is somehow a crime against the country.

This Othering is repeated throughout the film. Mr. Green's "feminine" attributes, such as his immediate deferral to Wadsworth in the beginning of the film, his lack of attraction to the sexually available women, and other characters' distaste for him become the running jokes that surround his remaining time in *Clue*.

Viewers repeatedly see Mr. Green as a klutz, as decidedly unmanly. When the dinner gong is struck, he accidentally throws his glass of champagne on Mrs. Peacock. At dinner, when the doorbell rings, he mistakenly spills soup on Miss Scarlet, prompting him to admit, "I'm sorry. I'm afraid I'm a little bit accident prone" [00:13:20–00:13:25]. This physical humor focuses on his nervousness and his lack of male bravado. As Alan Sinfield notes, "Lesbians and gay men have found two tendencies in Freudian theory particularly hard to deal with. One is the implication that gay men are in some fundamental way feminine and lesbians correspondingly masculine" (2002, 122). By portraying Mr. Green as more nervous and flighty, his masculinity is called into question.

This emasculation or demasculinization occurs in less obvious ways throughout the film. As the guests sit around the dinner table before the reasons for their visit are revealed, Mr. Green lets on that he knows who Mrs. Peacock really is. With a sly look on his face, he intones, "I know who you are. . . . I work in Washington, too" [00:12:47–00:12:53]. He reads as underhanded, almost sneaky in this scene, traits more often associated with women than men, given his indirectness and his pleasure in his secret. Similarly, when Mrs. Peacock screams when she fears she may have been poisoned, it is Mr. Green who slaps her across the face. He is the only male character willing to violate the sanctity of the older woman's space, a fact that seems to be attributed to his refusal to obey traditional gender roles. In one of the false endings of the film, one that portrays Mrs. Peacock as the sole murderer, Wadsworth, upon seeing her arrested, states, "You see, like the Mounties, we always get our man," to which Mr. Green asks, incredulously, "Mrs. Peacock was a man?" [01:27:53–01:28:01]. He is immediately slapped by both Wadsworth and Colonel Mustard. By placing him in the position of the recipient of a violence he perpetrated earlier, he is being directly associated with his victim: a woman. He is also, once again, shown as the least dominant male character in the room. In another possible ending, when Wadsworth reenacts the evening to show how each murder was accomplished, he once again uses Mr. Green's body, this time by repeatedly throwing Mr. Green to the floor and assaulting him as part of the reenactment. Mr. Green attempts to stand up for himself, screaming, "Will you stop that?," to which Wadsworth replies, simply, "No" [01:14:33–01:14:35]. Mr. Green is not taken seriously as a man or as a person, denigrated and used because of his perceived lack of masculinity.

Similarly, when the group searches the house midfilm, the cook, a large and sexually nondescript woman, falls out of the walk-in freezer. She is already dead, and her body falls toward Mr. Green. He attempts to stop her from hitting the floor, but she is significantly larger than he is; indeed, this body mismatching is supposed to be the main humor of the scene: the large (unfeminine) woman being caught by the lithe (unmasculine) man. Mr. Green calls out for help repeatedly, but none come to his aid, instead allowing the bodies to fall to the floor, with Mr. Green trapped under the cook's dead weight. Again, the humor seems to be focusing on the incongruity of their bodies, as well as Mr. Green, the only non-heterosexual man in the group, trapped under a female body.

Similar physical humor is used when those remaining in the house split up to search for clues. After drawing lots to determine partners, Mr. Green is paired with Yvette, the buxom, French-maid-outfit-wearing blonde who is ogled by every other man in the home. Mr. Green's visible distaste at being partnered with Yvette is palpable. Neither one of them wants to go first in climbing the stairs to the attic, so they end up traversing a narrow staircase together with Yvette's body thrust up against Mr. Green's in a way that highlights his lack of interest in her sexualized body, once again demonstrating his "Otherness" in the film.

Perhaps the most damning element of the film, however, is the "real" ending. In this version, Wadsworth is revealed as the blackmailer, and each of the guests, with the exception of Mr. Green, has killed someone in the house, most likely the informant who provided information on them to the blackmailer. Mr. Green is the exception: when the dust settles, he is the only person who was not responsible for a death. When he is asked directly if he is a police officer, he responds, "No, I'm a plant"—to which Miss Scarlet retorts, "A plant? I thought men like you were usually called a fruit"—before revealing himself as an FBI agent [01:32:32–01:32:46]. The use of language here, particularly "fruit," is problematic, but even more complicated is the character shift that happens in Mr. Green in this moment. His voice drops; he becomes self-assured. All of his awkwardness is suddenly gone. Indeed, it is Mr. Green who fatally shoots Wadsworth, triggering fellow agents and police officers to stream into the mansion. As the guests turn on each other with blame, the newly entered chief demands to know who is guilty. Mr. Green announces, "They all did it. But if you want to know who killed Mr. Boddy, I did. In the hall. With the revolver. Okay chief, take them away. I'm going to go home and sleep with my wife" [01:32:58–01:33:12]. This is the closing moment of the film, the final scene in the "real" ending. Mr. Green's restored confidence comes not from his position but rather his sexuality. He is revealed to be "straight," immediately conforming to heteronormative traditions of masculinity and leaving viewers with an assurance of his virility.

Clue, despite its cult-classic status and clear fan base, relies on problematic gender and sexuality stereotypes for much of its humor. As GLAAD President Sarah Kate Ellis has noted, "Leaving LGBT people out of the picture—or including them only as a punchline—keeps old prejudices alive and creates an unsafe environment, not only here in America, but around the world" (Donnelly 2016). Basing the entirety of Mr. Green's character on his sexuality and on harmful stereotypes makes the humor of this film fall flat in many places. Certainly, the film also calls on other overdone stereotypes surrounding gender, sex work, virility, body size, and more; upon close examination, however, the film becomes harder and harder to find funny. It is possible that viewers are meant to read

Mr. Green's portrayal of a gay man as a parody, as an identity that would not be looked at too closely or questioned by his fellow houseguests, a ruse meant to protect his actual identity. As the only LGBTQIA+ character in a film set in the 1950s and filmed in the 1980s, however, this reading does not improve the film's contemporary reception; it will be interesting to see if a remake adheres to or complicates this outdated portrayal.

See also *Basic Instinct*; *Midnight in the Garden of Good and Evil*.

Bibliography

Donnelly, Matt. "Hollywood Movies Still Stereotype LGBT Characters, Depict 'Gay Panic' Scenes." *Wrap*, May 2, 2016. Accessed March 26, 2021. https://www.thewrap.com/gay-panic-stereotype-lgbt-glaad-study-2015-movies-get-hard/.
Friedman, Andrea. "The Smearing of Joe McCarthy: The Lavender Scare, Gossip, and Cold War Politics." *American Quarterly* 57, no. 4 (2005): 1105–29.
Hilburn, Trey, III. "Ryan Reynolds Onboard for 'Clue' Adaptation; Eyes Director James Bobin." *iHorror*, February 11, 2020. Accessed March 23, 2021. https://www.ihorror.com/ryan-reynolds-onboard-for-clue-adaptation-eyes-director-james-bobin/.
Loftin, Craig M. "Unacceptable Mannerisms: Gender Anxieties, Homosexual Activism, and Swish in the United States, 1945–1965." *Journal of Social History* 40, no. 3 (2007): 577–96.
Sinfield, Alan. "Lesbian and Gay Taxonomies." *Critical Inquiry* 29, no. 1 (2002): 120–38.

—Meredith M. Malburne-Wade

CLUELESS (1995)

DIRECTOR: Amy Heckerling
SCREENPLAY: Amy Heckerling, inspired by the novel *Emma* by Jane Austen
CAST: Alicia Silverstone (Cher), Stacey Dash (Dionne), Brittany Murphy (Tai), Paul Rudd (Josh), Donald Faison (Murray), Justin Walker (Christian)
SPECS: 97 minutes; color
AVAILABILITY: DVD (Paramount)

This comedic update of Jane Austen's *Emma* moves the story to a Beverly Hills high school where the popular Cher enjoys a privileged life centered on shopping and fashion. Feeling judged as selfish and superficial by her stepbrother, Josh, Cher begins to meddle in the lives of others via matchmaking and makeovers. Her interference in the love life of her adopted protégé Tai is disastrous, and her infatuation with a new student is based on a misunderstanding of his sexuality. Once Cher realizes she is in love with Josh, she realizes how "clueless" she is about life and determines to become a better person.

Most of the characters in *Clueless* work as analogues of the characters in Jane Austen's *Emma*. Cher's classmate Christian Stovitz takes the place of Frank Churchill, whose charm and attentiveness is misconstrued by a heroine eager to convince herself that she is in love. In each case, this theoretical object is inaccessible to her romantic interest. In Frank's case, it is because he is secretly engaged, and in Christian's, because he is gay. Given the social environments in which they operate, both of these male characters can be seen as complicit, to some extent, in the misunderstandings. Christian is a likeable character, and his dilemma engages the audience's sympathy when the specter of hypothetical romance intrudes on his friendship with Cher. But for both him and the flirta-tious Frank Churchill, there's a high likelihood that their intentions would be interpreted as romantic ones.

A monologue from Cher about the slovenly style and bad manners of boys her age segues to the scene in which "the elusive Christian," who attends school in California part of the year, appears in her classroom. The first thing Christian says to her is "nice stems," referring to her legs, which suggests a level of attrac-tion. He furthers their interactions by asking generally about the local "clam-bakes" (i.e., "social scene") in his retro-infused style, and they immediately find an event to attend together (Sachs 2015). Christian's phrasing, presenting himself as the new kid in search of guidance from someone in the know, is ambiguous about his intentions. When he arrives to pick her up though, the event has been framed as a date, for which he comes to the door, meets her father, and acts as her escort. Once the truth is revealed, this can be reinterpreted as his operating in the hope that she will take their evening together seriously. With his theatrical persona based on retro style, there may be an assumption that a sense of ironic fun is running through their interactions. Cher's own game playing, making herself appear more sought after by sending herself flowers and chocolates from fictional admirers, may give him the idea that she has a boyfriend or is otherwise not interested in him as anything but a potential friend.

For their second, one-on-one date, Cher unilaterally decides to lose her virginity, setting the stage with a revealing outfit and a failed attempt at cook-ing, playing up a traditional, heteronormative feminine role. Christian, though, provides more overt cues to nudge her toward an understanding of the situation, based on the gay iconography of the films he brings to watch, *Some Like It Hot* and *Spartacus*, and tries to keep her focused on that. "Christian had a thing for Tony Curtis," she innocently narrates, remaining oblivious to the homoerotic themes. Here, she attempts to initiate physical contact by putting her foot on his, and he immediately reacts, almost jumping out of her reach. She excuses the action by saying her feet are cold, and he covers them for her. When she offers him some wine, and he notes its connection to feeling "sexy," she meaningfully replies, "That's okay." Realizing her misunderstanding, he immediately cuts the night short, and there's a legitimate sadness to their farewell at the door, when he says, "You're great. We're friends, right?"

Christian has tried to lead Cher to fathom his secret without directly ex-plaining his sexuality, reflecting a time in which there were still mixed attitudes toward the LGBTQIA+ community. Therefore, the "intrigue" and "mystery" surrounding his character were not necessarily of his own making. Nonetheless, when this fails, he is quick to withdraw from the romantic misunderstanding, even if it means withdrawing from her company.

Before the revelation about his sexuality, Christian is coded as gay in mul-tiple ways, reading William Burroughs in class and judging Tai's female rival as "Hagsville." During the first date, although he is fairly flirtatious with both Cher and Tai, he also talks very animatedly to the bartender, which is noticeable in retrospect. A reaction shot of Josh shows him noticing that Christian talks to another young man on the dance floor, seeming to dance with him, which tips off the viewers. Finally, when Christian calls Cher about the second date, he is in an art gallery, in front of a painting of three men with their arms around each other.

The significance of gay coding appears in full force during the scene when Cher learns the truth. In the car with her best friend Dionne and Dionne's boyfriend, Murray, she discusses the failed date, which has made her feel unattractive, and that her feminine persona failed to be well crafted enough. She says, "He does dress better than me," when Murray realizes who they are talking about, leading to a full string of stereotypical gay symbolism:

> Murray: Are you bitches blind or something? Your man Christian is a cake boy!
>
> Cher, Dionne: A what?
>
> Murray: He's a disco-dancing, Oscar Wilde–reading, Streisand ticket–holding friend of Dorothy, know what I'm saying?
>
> Cher: Uh-uh, no way. Not even.
>
> Murray: Yes, even. He's gay.
>
> Dionne: He does like to shop, Cher. And the boy can dress.

His sense of style, one of his main initial attractions, is ultimately what makes Cher understand his unavailability, and after coming to terms with her mistake, the two develop a closer friendship. She calls him "one of my favorite shopping partners," and when she later lists the positive attributes of her friends, viewers see them together in an art gallery, while she says, "He always wants everything to be beautiful and interesting." While the emphasis on Christian as fashionable and focused on aesthetics might contain some problematically stereotypical coding, he is never depicted as effeminate or as physically weaker than the heterosexual male characters. In fact, he is the one who viewers see perform a heroic physical action, rescuing Tai from the young men at the mall who almost drop her from a railing.

Like with Austin's *Emma*, heteronormative marriage rituals are still foregrounded in the film's conclusion, despite the early puncturing of the perceived sanctity of marriage by Cher's dismissal that her father was "barely even married" to an ex-wife, "and that was five years ago." Cher and Tai have been paired up with their ideal matches, joining Dionne and her boyfriend at their teachers' wedding—a relationship that Cher masterminded. At the wedding, Elton and Amber, the minor antagonists, are shown sitting together, apparently still a couple. Christian is in attendance, seen in the audience and later standing by the groom during the bouquet toss, but he is barely visible and is excluded from the traditional happy ending received by the other major characters. He remains uncoupled.

This reticence is likely a result of the time in which the film was made, as mainstream comedy was expected to reach a wide audience. Visibility of gay characters was beginning to be more common in the mass media, but many still existed in neutered environments, where they were accepted by other characters but not allowed to have sex lives, or even much in the way of romance. For example, only a year before, in May 1994, a controversy erupted over the popular nighttime soap opera *Melrose Place* when the show's gay character almost had a brief on-screen kiss. While "the scene included a kiss when it was filmed," as aired, "viewers only saw the two men shake hands and share a meaningful look" (Elber, "Fox Executive Defends Removal," 1994). Fox Broadcasting Co. executives stated that "the bottom line is, we're in a business . . . we would have lost up to $1 million by airing that kiss," since they believed "advertisers would have pulled out in droves" (Elber, "Fox Executive Defends Removal," 1994). This response was described by another news source as "predictable," what any network could expect (Pergament 1994). A spokesman for the Media Research Center ("conservative watchdog group") told the Associated Press, "I don't want a program that teaches homosexuality is wrong. I don't want a program that teaches it's right. If you want to entertain, entertain. If you want a documentary on this, put it on PBS" (Elber, "Show's Gay Kiss Too Racy," 1994). This viewpoint reinforces the idea that depictions of heterosexual characters are normative, and apolitical, while the inclusion of LGBTQIA+ characters is outside the norm and presenting a political agenda.

Clueless existed in this context, a forerunner of more inclusive representation. In another manifestation of the "predictable," actor Justin Walker understood that "Christian's sexuality would change many things, for characters moving forward but in particular, for me. The fact is, when that is your first known role, people label you. In my case, I became the gay guy from *Clueless*" (Vincent 2015). Still, Walker does not express any bitterness about being identified in this way, but the film's popularity did not lead to the kind of career success for him it did for many of his costars. For her part, when asked what "responses to the film at the time . . . were particularly meaningful" to her, Alicia Silverstone replied, "I was really well-received by the gay community after *Clueless* came out. . . . That has always been my favorite aspect of the film. Particularly what it means to gay boys" (Bell 2020).

While the character of Christian was, in the end, relegated somewhat to the role of "gay friend," the story line adds a bit of depth within the froth. Their relationship is certainly treated with more gravity than many aspects of the film; even the potentially traumatic scene where Cher is robbed at gunpoint is played for laughs. For a comedy of its time, Cher's confusion and Christian's conflict over it were handled with a degree of sensitivity, and gave important, if imperfect, visibility to a gay character.

See also *Blockers*.

Bibliography

Bell, Keaton. "Alicia Silverstone on the Legacy of *Clueless*, 25 Years Later." *Vogue*, July 19, 2020. Accessed March 29, 2021. https://www.vogue.com/article/alicia-silverstone-clueless -25th-anniversary-interview.

Elber, Lynn. "Fox Executive Defends Removal of *Melrose Place* Gay Kiss." *AP News*, July 15, 1994. Accessed March 29, 2021. https://apnews.com/article/64c83d73dde08db10cdc514e309a 93ea.

———. "Show's Gay Kiss Too Racy Even in Daring TV Year?" *AP News*, May 5, 1994. Accessed June 8, 2021. https://apnews.com/article/cedd5b851d4f643c29081039a2d40ffd.

Pergament, Alan. "*Melrose Place* Season Finale Backs Off on Gay Kiss Scene." *Buffalo News*, May 18, 1994. March 29, 2021. https://buffalonews.com/news/melrose-place-season-finale -backs-off-on-gay-kiss-scene/article_686ae60e-43c5-586b-a040-b969073d7fb6.html.

Sachs, Amy. "How to Use 10 Words from 'Clueless' in Convo Today." *Bustle*, July 10, 2015. Accessed June 7, 2021. https://www.bustle.com/articles/95952-10-words-made-famous-by -clueless-that-we-can-totally-still-use-in-our-lives-today.

Vincent, Alice. "Whatever, Forever: An Oral History of *Clueless*." *Telegraph*, July 13, 2015. March 29, 2021. https://www.telegraph.co.uk/film/clueless/making-of-cast-interviews-anniversary/.

—Karen Kohoutek

THE CRAFT: LEGACY (2017)

DIRECTOR: Zoe Lister-Jones

SCREENPLAY: Zoe Lister-Jones, based on characters created by Peter Filardi
CAST: Cailee Spaeny (Lily), Zoey Luna (Lourdes), Gideon Adlon (Frankie), Lovie Simone (Tabby), David Duchovny (Adam), Michelle Monaghan (Helen), Nicholas Galitzine (Timmy)
SPECS: 97 minutes; color
AVAILABILITY: DVD (Sony Pictures Home Entertainment)

In 1996, Columbia Pictures released *The Craft*, a supernatural horror film about four Los Angeles teens at a parochial high school who form a coven. As they start practicing magic, they face unforeseen negative consequences. Nearly twenty-five years later, in 2020, Columbia Pictures released a sequel to the film titled *The Craft: Legacy*. The movie follows protagonist Lily Schechner, who moves to a new town with her mother to live with her mother's new husband. At school, Frankie, Tabby, and Lourdes take notice of Lily, and when they discover she has magical abilities, they welcome Lily into their coven. The four high school witches start practicing magic, with their first targets being misogynistic boys at school who harass female classmates. As in the original film, unforeseen consequences develop, and the four witches must combine their powers to save the day. The movie, as directed and written by Zoe Lister-Jones, is a calling card for Millennials and Gen Z, presenting itself as unabashedly "woke," progressive, and diverse. Nonetheless, the film's representation of the LGBTQIA+ community is genuinely refreshing.

Every year, GLAAD puts out its *Studio Responsibility Index*, a thorough report of LGBTQIA+ representation in major studio films. The report looks at films theatrically released by eight major studios—Lionsgate, Paramount Pictures, Sony Pictures, STX Films, United Artists Releasing, Universal Pictures, Walt Disney Studios, and Warner Bros.—as well as four smaller imprints, including Focus Features, Roadside Attractions, Searchlight Pictures, and Sony Pictures Classics. An intersectional document, the *Studio Responsibility Index* analyzes not only the number of LGBTQIA+ characters in films released by these companies but how much time they have on screen, sexual orientation, gender identity, race, LGBTQIA+ characters with disabilities, and genres. For repeat years, GLAAD found a troubling lack of bisexual+ characters, transgender characters, and LGBTQIA+ characters of color, all of whom *The Craft: Legacy* depicts with authenticity. Despite bisexual+ people making up the majority of the LGBTQIA+ community, the report found in 2019 that bisexual+ characters decreased by one percentage point from 2018, and only three of the eight major studio films had bisexual+ characters (2020, 12). Further, none of the bisexual+ characters from 2019 were male-identifying (2020, 12). In terms of transgender characters, "film continues to lag behind other media as a third straight year passes with zero transgender characters in major releases" (2020, 15). A majority of 2019's LGBTQIA+ characters were also white and male-identifying (2020, 12). These statistics have been the trend in Hollywood according to the *Studio Responsibility Indexes*, which first began in 2013.

First in *The Craft: Legacy* is Lourdes, a transgender member of the coven, who is also played by transgender actor Zoey Luna. Furthermore, Luna is also a woman of color. The film quickly establishes Lourdes's gender identity in an affirming and nonexploitative way. As the witches discuss their periods and tampons at school, Lourdes jokes about not being able to relate. Her friends quickly apologize and the scene moves on, simple as that. "They did it in such a beautiful way that I had been waiting for, I guess, studios and movies to address it," Luna told *IndieWire*'s Jude Dry (2020). It is important that Lourdes is both explicitly made transgender and also played by a transgender actor. In the *2020 Studio Responsibility Index*, GLAAD acknowledges four transgender or nonbinary actors appeared in major studio films, and while the organization noted they were "pleased to see trans actors being cast in roles that are not explicitly written as transgender," the lack of acknowledgment or making the characters they played explicitly transgender did lend itself to a lack of representation and ability to be included in the report (2020, 15). In the film, Lourdes's gender identity is a fact, something that can be acknowledged, but it is not the only part of her identity, nor is it a spectacle; it is as simple as the color of her hair. She is also depicted as good and powerful, without any of damaging stereotypes often attached to LGBTQIA+ characters, particularly that of transgender people as "duplicitous" or "dangerous." Further, Hollywood has been mired by numerous controversies surrounding cisgender actors playing transgender characters and the lack of opportunities for transgender actors. Luna noted in the same *IndieWire* interview that Lister-Jones "was willing and able to listen to anything I had to say" (Dry 2020). Because of Lister-Jones's prior work with GLAAD, Luna found she did not have to share as much because Lister-Jones had already taken on the responsibility of educating herself.

Another crucial character in the film is Timmy, a classmate of Lily, Frankie, Tabby, and Lourdes. He starts off in the film as one of their first targets—a young man at their school who harasses and humiliates young women. When the coven performs their first major spell on someone outside of their foursome, they perform a spell to "awaken Timmy to his highest self, aka a 'woke spell'" (Menta 2020). There is certainly a conversation to be had about the coven performing spells on people without their consent, but likely the film wants the audience to see the spell less as brainwashing or changing Timmy, but rather as giving him a chance to be his true self. In fact, he becomes a close friend of the four leads and an outspoken ally. In one scene, he hilariously uses the phrase "womxn with an 'x,'" which again, may be a little obvious or heavy-handed, but it is also equal parts endearing. His most important scene comes later in the film when he plays "Two Truths and a Lie" with the leads. When it is his turn, he states, "My mom gave me this [necklace], I'm a virgin, and, um, Isaiah and I hooked up." At first, Lily, Frankie, Tabby, and Lourdes think the last statement is the obvious lie, but as Timmy begins tearing up and crying, they realize, in fact, it is one of the truths. In an emotional and vulnerable admission, he opens up to his new friends about his sexual orientation. "It's felt good when it's been with girls as well, so. It's just hard for dudes," he confesses. "I feel like there's no room to be . . . everyone assumes you're just gay, and that's fine, there's nothing wrong with that at all, I just . . . I like both." This scene is revolutionary not only because it depicts a bisexual male-identifying character, which, as the *Studio Responsibility Index* revealed, is sorely lacking in film representation, but also because of how bisexuality is treated in media.

One of the most harmful stereotypes and impressions of LGBTQIA+ people are about those who identify as bisexual. Because bisexuality is the attraction to two or more genders, a grossly inaccurate view of them is that they are overly sexualized, unfaithful, promiscuous, or indecisive. Media frequently falls into this trap when depicting LGBTQIA+ characters. In the Netflix film *Alex Strangelove*, for example, the titular main character explores his sexuality, first identifying himself as bisexual and then ultimately deciding he is gay by the end. While this is undoubtedly a realistic experience for some, when it is too often the depiction of LGBTQIA+ characters in media, it sends the harmful message that being bisexual is not as valid or is simply a stop on the way to being gay. Likewise, some shows, from Hulu's *Love, Victor* to HBO's *Sex and the City*, also suffer from intense biphobia. In Netflix's wildly popular *Orange Is the New Black*, the show never acknowledges its lead character's bisexuality until the seventh season. There is context and history to explain why bisexual+ people experience a prejudice and erasure very differently. As Abby Webb writes for *Study Breaks*, research in the 1980s labeled bisexuality as "secondary homosexuality," and, "dominated by bias toward monosexuality, researchers presumed that heterosexuality and homosexuality were the only legitimate orientations; therefore, anyone claiming to be bisexual was either a closeted gay clinging to heterosexual norms, or just experimenting beyond their actual preference" (2019).

Throughout the entirety of *The Craft: Legacy*, Timmy remains both a good person and bisexual, never suddenly deciding he is gay or that his bisexuality was just a "phase." Moreover, he was not ever shown through a biphobic lens. Anna Menta explains why this subversion of people's expectations and assumptions about teen boys is so powerful:

> Suddenly, in retrospect, so many things about Timmy's behavior make sense: Compensating for his insecurities by acting aggressively heterosexual. Taking out his fear, anger, and loneliness on Lily. Striving to fit himself into the box that society expects him to slot into. None of that makes his behavior right—or even forgivable—but it does make it make *sense*. (2020)

Unfortunately, the movie then, however unintentionally, falls into the "Bury Your Gays" trope. In the last third of the film, Timmy dies. The students at school are told he killed himself, but it later becomes clear that he was murdered by the movie's antagonists. Though the film does this from purely a narrative and plot standpoint, it is disappointing regardless to include the death of an LGBTQIA+ character, especially one who has a newfound sense of freedom and happiness by coming out to a support network. As Menta acknowledges, however, his coming out scene is an "undeniable grand slam out of the park," and if that scene "helps even just one confused bi teen, that's a net win" (2020). It does not make up for the movie killing him off, but it showcases that representation is not always as neat or black-and-white as one may wish it could be.

The original *The Craft* movie has a large LGBTQIA+ following. *North Texas Daily*'s Davion Smith explains:

> The film analyzes a lot of the gay experiences of othering and alienation and uses the contextual history of the occult to provide an enriching experience. The girls find each other through longing glances, realizations that they are like one another and are different from everyone else. In a society that does not accept you and actively seeks to harm you for your differences, it makes sense to hide who you are. The whole encounter mimics the search for the romantic attention and affection queer teenagers often engage in. (2020)

The Craft franchise has clearly always had its LGBTQIA+ fans. Nonetheless, it is very different for a film to be queer-coded and adopted by LGBTQIA+ fans, and for a film to be explicitly queer. This is why *The Craft: Legacy* is so groundbreaking and exciting in terms of its LGBTQIA+ representation—it does not shy away from representation or using clear, affirming language. It is also intersectional in its LGBTQIA+ representation, which is especially crucial for transgender women of color, who face a high rate of violence in the United States. In 2019, the American Medical Association (AMA) labeled the increase in violence against transgender people as an "epidemic," and the media doubles down on the experienced pain by misgendering transgender victims (Torres et al. 2019). Lourdes gets not only to survive as a transgender woman of color in the film but to win and experience happiness and success.

Of her decision to depict LGBTQIA+ characters in a positive and progressive manner, Lister-Jones said:

> For me as a filmmaker I've taken the responsibility very seriously when it comes to representation. So this film was an incredible opportunity to portray the world as it actually exists. And especially when looking at young people and the ways in which young people can be other-ed. I really wanted to include queer and trans characters in that conversation. Whether or not I would category this film as feminist, in any discussion of feminism or looking at feminist issues, trans and queer voices must be included. So that was really important to me. (Chichizola 2020)

The Craft: Legacy exists as a successful example of LGBTQIA+ representation, especially in regards to fictional storytelling, but also, and just as importantly, in real life.

See also *Mean Girls*; *The Perks of Being a Wallflower*.

Bibliography

Chichizola, Corey. "*The Craft: Legacy* Director Reveals Why There Are So Many LGBT Stories." *CinemaBlend*, November 4, 2020. Accessed May 27, 2020. https://www.cinemablend.com /news/2558237/the-craft-legacy-director-reveals-why-there-are-so-many-lgbt-stories.

Dry, Jude. "'The Craft: Legacy' Star Zoey Luna Is Just One of the Witches." *IndieWire*, November 3, 2020. Accessed May 27, 2020. https://www.indiewire.com/2020/11/the-craft-legacy -zoey-luna-trans-lgbtq-1234596772/.

GLAAD. *2020 Studio Responsibility Index.* https://www.glaad.org/sites/default/files/GLAAD%20 2020%20Studio%20Responsibility%20Index.pdf.

Menta, Anna. "'The Craft: Legacy' Has a Bi Coming Out Scene I Wish I'd Seen as a Teen." *Decider*, October 29, 2020. Accessed May 27, 2021. https://decider.com/2020/10/29/the-craft -legacy-timmy-coming-out-scene-bi/.

Smith, Davion. "'The Craft': How Queer-Coding Empowered a Generation." *North Texas Daily*, November 27, 2020. Accessed May 27, 2021. https://www.ntdaily.com/the-craft-how-queer -coding-empowered-a-generation/.

Torres, Ignacio, et al. "For Trans Women of Color Facing 'Epidemic' of Violence, Each Day Is a Fight for Survival: 'I'm An Endangered Species . . . but I Cannot Stop Living.'" *ABC News*, November 20, 2019. Accessed May 27, 2021. https://abcnews.go.com/US/trans-women-color -facing-epidemic-violence-day-fight/story?id=66015811.

Webb, Abby. "Why Bisexuals Can't Catch a Break from Erasure." *Study Breaks*, August 23, 2019. Accessed May 27, 2021. https://studybreaks.com/thoughts/biphobia-and-erasure/.

—Anya Crittenton

CRUEL INTENTIONS (1999)

DIRECTOR: Roger Kumble
SCREENPLAY: Roger Kumble, inspired by the novel *Les Liaisons Dangereuses* by Pierre Choderlos de Laclos
CAST: Sarah Michelle Gellar (Kathryn), Ryan Phillippe (Sebastian), Reese Witherspoon (Annette), Selma Blair (Cecile), Joshua Jackson (Blaine)
SPECS: 97 minutes; color
AVAILABILITY: DVD (Sony Pictures Home Entertainment)

Stepsiblings Sebastian Valmont and Kathryn Merteuil live a carefree and careless existence in their lavish New York City home, where they treat the rest of their Manchester Prep classmates as pawns in an erotically charged and sadistic game. Sebastian keeps a journal of his sexual conquests, briefly reveling in the emotional wreckage left in his wake before he moves on to his next challenge. Kathryn is a social climber, willing to employ both her sexual prowess and her manipulative cunning to keep control of every situation. She is responsible for many incredibly campy and iconic moments throughout the film, storing a private stash of cocaine in a cross necklace that she wears at all times, for example. When two new students, Cecile and Annette, appear over the summer, the stepsiblings waste no time in working toward the ruination of both. Sebastian agrees to help Kathryn corrupt childlike Cecile while Kathryn promises to sleep with her stepbrother (which he has long desired) if he is able to successfully woo Annette, whose vow to stay celibate until marriage has been published in *Seventeen* magazine—a vow that Sebastian views as a personal affront and an irresistible challenge.

The film is a loose retelling of Pierre Choderlos de Laclos's eighteenth-century epistolary novel *Les Liaisons Dangereuses*. Borrowing both character names and plot points from this source material, *Cruel Intentions* substitutes the French nobility with wealthy young Millennials, an updated aristocracy. Through this reframing, the film was hailed as an innovative adaptation in its shift to a more contemporary retelling with "changes from the original book reflect[ing] demographics as well as trendiness" (Levy 1999). Among these changes was the inclusion of new gay characters, a still fairly novel choice for a mainstream production at the end of the twentieth century. Joshua Jackson, who played the film's only openly gay character, later emphasized this idea, commenting on the significance of being able to portray Blaine in such a way that the character "still felt like a real person" (Li 2019). Despite this claim around authenticity, however, his portrayal has not held up. In the years since its release, *Cruel Intentions* has been deemed "melodramatic, openly rude, mean, sometimes grotesquely sexy, and anti-LGBTQ" (Gruttadaro 2019). Even at the time of its release, Roger Ebert wondered at the treatment of the film's gay characters: "Surely kids as sophisticated as those in this story would be less homophobic?" (1999).

Indeed, both Kathryn and Sebastian use homophobic slurs. For instance, at the film's start, Sebastian informs his stepsister that Annette and her boyfriend, Trevor, plan to wait until marriage to have sex. To this, Kathryn interrupts to say, "Trevor's a fag" [00:13:33]. At the close of this conversation, Sebastian sets off for his room, where he plans to write about his latest sexual conquest. Kathryn yells after him: "Oh gee, your journal. Could you be more queer?" [00:14:16]. And while Kathryn uses these terms as a means of emasculating and demeaning her stepbrother, Sebastian uses the same terms for similar purposes. Frustrated in his first advances toward Annette, he complains to Blaine that "some fag—no offense" warned Annette of his "lascivious tactics" [00:20:23]. And although the term is overtly offensive, especially in the demeaning way that Sebastian calls upon it, Blaine is used to soften and excuse its use as he shows that no offense has been taken.

If viewers are to see Kathryn and Sebastian's manipulation and misconduct around sex as part of their "cruel intentions," Blaine employs his sexuality to a similar end. A conventionally attractive, bleach-blond prep, Blaine is first introduced to the viewer as he weighs out Sebastian's marijuana. Viewers are to understand that Blaine is not only another wealthy classmate of Sebastian's; he is also his drug dealer. In response to the complaint voiced by Sebastian above, Blaine tells him that Annette's informant was likely Greg, whom Blaine goes on to suggest is gay as well, but not openly so. Letting on that he and Greg are sexually involved, Blaine arranges for Sebastian to catch him in bed with Greg later that night: "Don't think this one's not going to cost you," says Blaine, to which Sebastian sets down a wad of cash and walks away [00:22:04]. While Sebastian's sexuality is linked to power and hedonism, Blaine's is thus linked to monetary gain, Blaine being more than happy to blackmail his lover for the right price.

In this way—portraying Blaine as a blackmailer and a drug dealer—the film adds to the economic configurations of gay identity in the media at the turn of the century. In *Learning Queer Identity in the Digital Age*, Kay Siebler observes the impact of capitalism at this time; gay men were increasingly being shown in

film and television, but often through a lens constrained by wealth and material-
ism. "The Great White Queer," as Siebler referred to this depiction, "embodies
affluence and 'whiteness,' teaching young gay men that being gay means assimi-
lation through consumption" (2016). Blaine's character continues to reproduce
this idea, narrowly defining what it means to be gay.

As planned, Sebastian walks in on Blaine and Greg, pulling the covers off
the pair, who recoil from their assailant, both clad solely in their underwear.
Greg immediately begins to bargain with Sebastian, appealing to his discretion.
Instead, Sebastian snaps a few photos of the men while a smug Blaine leans back
and watches the interaction with amusement. The message is clear; being gay is,
itself, a *liaison dangereuse*. According to *Cruel Intentions*, it leads to blackmail
and extortion [00:31:37–00:32:58]. And while Blaine is here shown to be on the
more lucrative end of this ordeal, Greg hardly comes off as a victim. Despite
being outed, he elsewhere brags to his teammates about a young woman whom
he assaulted on a date, suggesting to the audience that he is not a character who
deserves much sympathy, making his blackmail feel almost justified [00:22:20–
00:22:36]. In the context of his extortion, Sebastian drives home the limited
representation available to Greg. "What about your family?" he asks. "I mean,
can you imagine the humiliation your father's going to feel when he finds out
his pride and joy is a fudge-packer?" [00:31:55–00:32:02]. These derogatory terms
have no effect on Blaine; instead, bemused, he admits that it probably never was
Greg who warned Annette after all. And so, as Caetlin Benson-Allott observes,
"anal sex triumphs as the ultimate cruel intention" (Benson-Allott 2005). It is a
side plot, but one that nevertheless manages to make light of the multilayered
competition between Kathryn and Sebastian through the nonchalant humor of
inexplicably cruel Blaine.

Between the setup and execution of Blaine and Sebastian's blackmail plan,
Kathryn brings about her own moment of potential same-sex desire in what is
easily the film's most discussed scene. Here, Kathryn brings Cecile to a park,
where the two picnic together and discuss how Cecile ought to navigate the
social scene of Manchester Prep. As Kathryn pries for information about an
ex-boyfriend, who she knows has shown interest in Cecile, the unaware Cecile
confesses that she has never even kissed a boy. To this, Kathryn suggests Cecile
practice with one of her girlfriends, promptly turning Cecile toward her, offering
her a few quick tips, and then moving in for such a "practice" kiss. The first kiss
lasts only a moment, but when Cecile replies that it was no big deal, Kathryn
moves on to inform her that they are going to try it again, "only this time, I'm
going to stick my tongue in your mouth" [00:24:02]. This next kiss is nothing
like the first. Not only does it last far longer—a full twenty seconds [00:24:20–
00:24:40]—it's accompanied by a slow zoom in of the camera that directly frames
the lip-locked women; the background music gently swells with the prolonged
shot, which ends as an infamous thread of spit stretches out between the two
when they finally pull apart.

This kiss was controversial though celebrated. Embraced by the young voting
constituents of the MTV Movie Awards, who crowned it the "Best Kiss" in 2000,
critics spent more time debating the kiss than they did the film's haphazard inclusion of rape, coercion, and dubious consent (Benson-Allott 2005). A gesture

toward an increasing acceptance surrounding same-sex desire, the kiss seems only that—a gesture. Following the kiss, Cecile's eyes remain closed. She is still enraptured in the moment, leaning in for more. Kathryn pulls back with a mild look of annoyance, and Cecile seems to snap out of it, turning off her desire for Kathryn—and other women—altogether, never to return to it again. Accordingly, the kiss is to be read more as a demonstration of Cecile's innocent, sex-starved state than it is an indication of potential lesbianism. Indeed, Cecile's childishly unrefined but assertive sexuality is a running joke throughout *Cruel Intentions*. In a later scene, for instance, she unwittingly directs her music tutor's gaze beneath her skirt in an attempt to impress him with a headstand. But while her kiss with Kathryn might therefore register as her broader desire boiling over (not indicative of any actual same-sex desire), it nevertheless caught viewers' attention more noticeably than did the blackmail scene between Blaine and Greg. As Shannon Keating observed, this scene "spurred the sexual awakenings of an untold number of straight men and lesbians" (Keating 2019). Expanding on such a claim, however, Tricia Jenkins observes that "it is important to ask whether or not these teen movies are helping to welcome a new era in lesbian visibility, or if these movies merely capitalize on male heterosexual fantasies, further epitomizing the male gaze" (Jenkins 2005). Jenkins ultimately views the kiss between Kathryn and Cecile fitting within this latter trend, noting that the pretense for the kiss was Cecile's desire to kiss her music tutor, a man.

The result is a heterosexualized same-sex kiss, and what it indicates, according to Jenkins, is mainstream producers' discomfort with "authentic lesbianism" (Jenkins 2005). This heterosexualizing of same-sex desire is revealed twice over in the next film that would go on to win the MTV Movie Award for "Best Kiss" between two members of the same sex. In 2002, Jason Biggs and Sean William Scott won the award for their kiss in *American Pie 2*. Yet this kiss has none of the eroticism that exists in the *Cruel Intentions* kiss. In the later film, Biggs's and Scott's characters delight over two women they believe to be lesbians; after enjoying a kiss between the two women, the men are coerced into a kiss of their own. Yet this kiss is anything but sexual. Instead, their characters show physical duress, immediately turning away from one another when the kiss ends in order to gag. The message is clear: homosexuality disgusts, but when two women kiss for a man's enjoyment, that's something else entirely. *Cruel Intentions* may be less explicit, but the idea is similar; whereas the film is willing to show a passionate kiss between two ostensibly straight women, no affection or romance is displayed between the two explicitly gay male characters.

In moving from an analysis of explicitly gay characters to a kiss between two women that both suggests and rejects a lesbian reading, it is also important to consider the impression apparently left on so many gay male viewers of the film. According to a number of accounts, it was not the out gay character Blaine or the prolonged kiss between two women that impacted them most; instead, it was a brief scene in which the aggressively heterosexual Sebastian shows off his naked figure from behind. As Annette approaches him at the swimming pool early on in the film, the viewer's gaze aligns with Annette's own as she stumbles upon the naked Sebastian. Turning to face Annette, Sebastian (now visible from the waist up) implies that she has caught him as he was putting on his bathing suit. Reflecting on the scene, Ryan Phillippe claimed a number of fans had told him over the years, "That's the moment I knew I was gay" (Li 2019). This sentiment is reaffirmed in an article published in the *Advocate* that credits the nude pool scene as being responsible for many gay men's "sexual awakening" (Reynolds 2020). And while this might seem a strange aspect to attach such weight to, there is nevertheless evidence that for queer men at the time of the film's release, this scene was a meaningful one. As David Levithan has observed in relation to literature that calls forth a particular response from an interpretive community—although his observations could certainly extend to a film like *Cruel Intentions*—"there is what it is meant to mean, and then there is what it means to any given reader because of what that reader brings to it, and the time (and age) at which that reader encounters it" (Levithan 2003).

Although *Cruel Intentions* might have been unique in its inclusion of gay characters and potentially queer content at the end of the 1990s, it offered a fairly standard, typically negative treatment of this material. As a review published in the *Guardian* for the twentieth anniversary of the film in 2020 observed, "The film's satirical forays into the realms of gay sexuality . . . jar a bit" (Bradshaw 2020). The film remains an enjoyable time capsule, cementing a grungy decadence at the turn of the Millennium, sweeping through plush Manhattan mansions with Placebo's "Every You Every Me," but hindsight is 20/20, and in looking back, it is easy to wonder what audiences found redeemable in the film.

See also *Clueless; Mean Girls*.

Bibliography

Benson-Allott, Caetlin. "The 'Mechanical Truth' behind Cruel Intentions: Desire, AIDS, and the MTV Movie Awards' 'Best Kiss.'" *Quarterly Review of Film and Video* 22, no. 4 (2005): 341–58.

Bradshaw, Peter. "*Cruel Intentions* Review—Young Love Still Looks Laboured 21 Years On." *Guardian*, July 17, 2020. Accessed December 12, 2020. https://www.theguardian.com/film/2020/jul/17/cruel-intentions-review-ryan-phillippe-sarah-michelle-gellar-reese-witherspoon.

Ebert, Roger. "Cruel Intentions." RogerEbert.com, March 5, 1999. Accessed December 16, 2020. https://www.rogerebert.com/reviews/cruel-intentions-1999.

Gruttadaro, Andrew. "How *Cruel Intentions* Killed the '90s Teen Movie—and Became an Instant Classic." *Ringer*, March 27, 2019. Accessed December 15, 2020. https://www.theringer.com/movies/2019/3/27/18281534/cruel-intentions-1999-90s-teen-movies.

Jenkins, Tricia. "'Potential Lesbians at Two O'Clock': The Heterosexualization of Lesbianism in the Recent Teen Film." *Journal of Popular Culture* 38, no. 3 (Feb. 2005): 491–504.

Keating, Shannon. "It's Been 20 Years Since *Cruel Intentions* and There's Never Been Another Movie Quite Like It." *BuzzFeed New*, March 5, 2019. Accessed December 18, 2020. https://www.buzzfeednews.com/article/shannonkeating/cruel-intentions-20th-anniversary-1999-sarah-michelle.

Levithan, David. "Afterword." In *A Separate Peace*, edited by John Knowles, 205–8. New York: Simon & Schuster, 2003.

Levy, Emanuel. "Cruel Intention." *Variety* 374, no. 2 (March 1, 1999): 77.

Li, Shirley. "*Cruel Intentions* Cast Spills All the Details on Making the Seductive Teen Drama." *Entertainment Weekly*, March 21, 2019. Accessed December 16, 2020. https://ew.com/movies/2019/03/21/cruel-intentions-oral-history/.

Reynolds, Daniel. "Ryan Phillippe's Parents 'Shunned' Him Over Gay Role, *Cruel Intentions*." *Advocate*, November 18, 2020. Accessed December 16, 2020. https://www.advocate.com/tele vision/2020/11/18/ryan-phillippes-parents-shunned-him-over-gay-role-cruel-intentions.
Siebler, Kay. *Learning Queer Identity in the Digital Age*. London: Palgrave Macmillan, 2016.

—Jon Heggestad

CRUISING (1980)

DIRECTOR: William Friedkin
SCREENPLAY: William Friedkin, inspired by the novel *Cruising* by Gerald Walker
CAST: Al Pacino (Steve Burns), Paul Sorvino (Captain Edelson), Don Scardino (Ted Bailey), Richard Cox (Stuart Richards), Karen Allen (Nancy Gates)
SPECS: 102 minutes; color
AVAILABILITY: DVD (Arrow Video)

Cruising is a basic police procedural starring Al Pacino as Steve Burns, a police officer tasked with going undercover to investigate a series of brutal killings in Manhattan's gay community. When given the assignment, Burns is informed by Captain Edelson that he is not investigating conventional gay life but the leather and sadomasochistic scene. While on assignment, Burns befriends Ted Bailey, a neighbor in an apartment complex with seemingly exclusively gay tenets. Bailey serves as his guide to the city's gay enclaves. As Burns gathers clues, he frequents numerous leather bars, in which patrons are dancing, kissing, taking part in a variety of light sadomasochistic activity, and generally enjoying themselves. Burns's immersion into his assignment is shown to have a negative impact on his own personal relationship with girlfriend Nancy. Burns's first major suspect is Skip Lee, a waiter who is viewed with suspicion and derision by bar regulars. Burns witnesses Lee beaten and coerced into a confession before police discover his fingerprints do not match those found at a murder scene. Burns gets upset with Lee's treatment and expresses a wish to leave the assignment. Edelson convinces him to stay and to follow a new lead—Stuart Richards, a student at Columbia University and former student of victim Professor Paul Vincent. Burns begins surveilling Richards, eventually finding letters Richards addressed to his deceased father asking for acceptance. Believing he has found the killer, Burns hoodwinks Richards into a sexual tryst in Morningside Park wherein Burns stabs Richards before Richards is able to draw his knife. With Richards in custody, Bailey's murdered body is discovered. The police, however, write it off as a lover's quarrel, as throughout the film Bailey had been arguing with his boyfriend, Gregory. With the case seemingly solved, Burns moves back in with Nancy. While Burns shaves his face, Nancy adorns the leather attire Burns wore undercover. The film ends with a shot of the sun viewed from the harbor.

When assessing *Cruising*'s relevance to LGBTQIA+ issues, its text is less important (which is not to say it is unproblematic) than the circumstances of production and the controversy that surrounded it. *Cruising* is based on a 1970 novel of the same name by Gerald Walker and the experiences of detectives Randy Jurgensen and Sonny Gross. Walker's book, reportedly based on real cases, involves an undercover detective, John Lynch, entering New York's gay, sadomasochistic scene, posing as a potential victim to capture the killer. Perhaps unintention-ally, the book homophobically paints gay men as different from "normal" city inhabitants and suggests Lynch has awakened his homoerotic feelings, which are closely associated with his new murderous impulses. That is, his sexual identity is equated with pathology. Jurgensen and Gross patrolled the New York streets, including its gay enclaves, between 1962 and 1979. Friedkin's screenplay loosely borrowed from their case files as well; he also used the men as tour guides of gay subculture. The title of the film and novel derives from a slang term for the practice of frequenting an area in the search for casual and anonymous sexual encounters.

Cruising evoked intense debate over its cultural politics and what it repre-sented. It drew protest from gay activists and allies during production and after its release. LGBTQIA+ media and LGBTQIA+ supporters in the media wrote scathing articles on the production. Chief among these writers was Arthur Bell, a gay writer for the *Village Voice*. Bell acquired an early version of the script and told readers that it was dangerous and to sabotage the production. Bell's reader-ship and his ability to rile them proved strong enough to inspire energetic pro-tests to disrupt filming. Protestors pointed mirrors onto the set from rooftops to interfere with lighting, others blew whistles and blasted air horns to drown out the film's sound recording, some even threw bottles at Pacino and Friedkin after a day of shooting. Every time the crew shot outdoors, they were met with boos, chants, and other distractions that were effective enough to cause extensive redubbing of dialogue. Bell also feuded with numerous prominent columnists over *Cruising*, most notably with Pete Hamill and Rex Reed, both of the *New York Daily News*. Hamill, who was sympathetic to gay rights, argued attempts to censor *Cruising* were fascistic. For his part, Reed proclaimed that Bell's hyper-bole was more homophobic than the content of Friedkin's film.

Fears within the LGBTQIA+ community over the content of *Crusing* were not misplaced. Attitudes toward LGBTQIA+ people were decidedly negative across the 1970s and into the 1980s. The American Psychological Association only removed "homosexuality" from its list of mental illnesses in December 1973. As per the General Social Survey, which began tracking opinions and civil liberties questions regarding the gay community in 1973, attitudes toward LGBTQIA+ people were decidedly low. The vast majority of Americans felt same-sex relations were wrong, that those who identified as gay should not be hired as elementary school teachers, and that same-sex marriages were not le-gitimate. Repeated negative portrayals risked marginalizing the community even further in the public eye.

While many in the LGBTQIA+ community condemned the film, others worked as extras, causing a minor civil war in the gay community. Protestors ar-gued the gay actors were self-oppressive traitors, while the gay actors countered that the protestors were discriminating against the community of which they were a part. Some in the LGBTQIA+ community felt the infighting was giving the film too much attention and could result in the sale of more tickets. Those critical of the film countered that Friedkin was a prominent director and the film would receive publicity regardless of protests.

Despite the controversy and events that surrounded its production, *Cruising* was released in February 1980 and received mostly negative reviews from critics, LGBTQIA+ and straight alike. In a lengthy critique of the film, *Los Angeles Times*'s Charles Champlin noted, "It is like taking a Hamburg brothel as the site for an examination of heterosexuality" (1980). Vincent Canby of the *New York Times* called it "a homosexual horror film" that presents "a distorted view of homosexual life" that makes no attempt to "comprehend" the culture it dramatizes (1980). At screenings, gay groups across the United States picketed theaters, particularly in larger cities like New York and San Francisco. For these protesters, the film represented the latest in a problematic Hollywood tradition of equating homosexuality with homicidal tendencies. At a time when LGBTQIA+ communities were advocating for rights, the film, in their view, portrayed a deviant and distorted image of gay men. The film showed a sadomasochistic community that was characterized by depravity, danger, and seediness. The film made no earnest attempt to understand the people involved in the sadomasochistic leather subculture; everything in the film is spectacle for viewers. Unsurprisingly then, *Cruising* flopped, pulling in just under seven million dollars against its eleven-million-dollar budget in the year of its release and disappeared from theaters relatively quickly. *Cruising* was even nominated for three Golden Raspberry Awards: Worst Film, Worst Director, and Worst Screenplay.

For his part, Friedkin maintained that *Cruising* was neither a condemnation nor a celebration of gay life. Rather, the director used the gay leather scene as a backdrop for a murder mystery, failing to see the potential danger of depicting a misunderstood and denigrated community in such a light. Friedkin and distributor United Artists, however, made a few concessions. The film contains a disclaimer stating, "This film is not intended as an indictment of the homosexual world. It is set in one small segment of that world, which is not meant to be representative of the whole," the inclusion of which was criticized as an admission guilt. It is significant to note that the disclaimer has been deleted in recent DVD and Blu-ray releases of the film. Likewise, Edelson's qualifier of describing the leather scene as atypical of gay life was also added. Today, the film is viewed more ambiguously. Some notable academics such as R. Barton Palmer, Eugenio Ercolani, and Marcus Stiglegger have even encouraged revisionist readings.

See also *Basic Instinct; Summer of Sam.*

Bibliography

Canby, Vincent. "Screen: Pacino Stars in Friedkin's *Cruising*." *New York Times*, February 15, 1980. Accessed February 1. 2021. https://www.nytimes.com/1980/02/15/archives/screen-pacino-stars-in-friedkins-cruisinganother-country.html/.

Champlin, Charles. "*Cruising*—Looking Past the Images." *Los Angeles Times*, February 10, 1980. M1, M47–M50.

Ercolani, Eugenio, and Marcus Stiglegger. *Cruising*. Liverpool: Anthem, 2020.

Guthmann, Edward. "The *Cruising* Controversy: William Friedkin vs. the Gay Community." *Cinéaste* 10, no. 3 (1980): 2–8.

Kates, Steven. "Gay Men on Film: A Typology of the Scopophilic Consumption Pleasures of Cultural Text." *Consumption, Markets and Culture* 4, no. 3 (2000): 281–313.

Miller, D. A. "*Cruising*." *Film Quarterly* 61, no. 2 (2007): 70–73.

Palmer, R. Barton. "Redeeming *Cruising*: Tendentiously Offensive, Coherently Incoherent, Strangely Pleasurable." In *B Is for Bad Cinema: Aesthetics, Politics, and Cultural Value*, edited by Claire Perkins and Constantine Verevis, 85–104. Albany: State University of New York Press, 2014.

Schoell, William. *Stay Out of the Shower: 25 Years of Shocker Films Beginning with "Psycho."* New York: Dembner Books, 1985.

Wilson, Alexander. "Friedkin's *Cruising*, Ghetto Politics, and Gay Sexuality." *Social Text* 4 (1981): 98–109.

Wood, Robin. *Hollywood from Vietnam to Reagan . . . and Beyond.* New York: Columbia University Press, 2003.

—Todd K. Platts

• D •

DAWN OF THE DEAD (2004)

DIRECTOR: Zack Snyder
SCREENPLAY: James Gunn, inspired by the film of the same name by George Romero
CAST: Sarah Polley (Ana), Ving Rhames (Kenneth), Jake Weber (Michael), Ty Burrell (Steve), Michael Kelly (CJ), R. D. Reid (Glen)
SPECS: 101 minutes (theatrical release), 110 minutes (unrated director's cut); color
AVAILABILITY: DVD (Universal Pictures Home Entertainment)

A remake of George A. Romero's 1978 film of the same name, Zack Snyder's *Dawn of the Dead* opens at the genesis of the zombie apocalypse. A nurse, Ana, flees her infected husband and encounters a small group of survivors. They attempt to take refuge in the Crossroads Mall. Here, the crew is soon detained by mall security, who mistake those seeking shelter for unsavory opportunists. With the help of a compassionate security officer, the group is able to subdue their captors. Later, the modest community expands when they grant safe harbor to more survivors. As resources dwindle and danger becomes imminent, the group evacuates the mall in hopes of reaching a zombie-free island. Nonetheless, their well-constructed escape plan disintegrates when the survivors' vehicles are attacked by a horde of the undead. Bloodshed abounds. The few who live through this trial set sail (to what, ultimately, appears to be calamity).

Dawn of the Dead's opening credits feature a montage of modern images: a CDC update, a White House briefing, and a variety of news reports. However, Johnny Cash's "The Man Comes Around" croons an ancient prophesy. Using imagery from the Book of Revelation, the song describes the Last Judgment. Here, early in the film, there is an insinuation that a religious scourge is underway. This is later supported as the de facto head of mall security, CJ, intently watches a televangelist sermonize. From a remote location, the preacher explains that the sins of humanity have created this hell on earth. He cites premarital sex, abortion, and "man-on-man relations" as the reasons for the apocalypse [00:36:15]. And while this seems target all alleged "sinners," the speaker adds "same-sex marriage" to his list, appearing to doubly accuse the LGBTQIA+ community [00:36:19]. While preposterous, the scene does not permit this moment to be read as anything other than genuinely terrifying. Here, skillful cinematography stresses this man's authority. The camera slowly and continuously zooms in on the television screen where he appears. The televangelist becomes increasingly more pixilated (i.e., more monstrous) as he menacingly fills the screen. There is a keen sense that the fourth wall is being broken. He looks at the viewer and quietly offers: "How do you think your god will judge you? Well, friends, now we know" [00:36:21–00:36:28]. The viewer, like CJ, is left feeling overpowered and rebuked. Moreover, it warrants noting that the actor who portrays the televangelist is one of two survivors of the Monroeville Mall massacre in George Romero's *Dawn of the Dead*. This actor and his iconic voice are instantly recognizable by cinephiles. His character in the 1978 original is the epitome of resilience in a zombie apocalypse. Simply put, he is a hero. Here, a thrilling cameo, becomes something slightly more. Though the actor is (presumably) not portraying the same character in this remake, his words carry tremendous weight.

Shortly after this moment, the security officers are shown waking up and preparing for a new day of survival. Terry, the more empathetic of the three, laments not being able to get his favorite coffee, a "soy mocha latte with foam" [00:37:52]. His colleague Bart responds with an expression of revulsion and the word "faggot" [00:37:53]. While Terry does not react to this homophobic slur, CJ does. The store in which the security guards have taken shelter is tiered according to product. Standing on the highest tier, CJ literally and metaphorically looks down on Bart and flatly says, "What are you doing?" [00:38:01]. While it is likely that CJ is concerned about dissention in his small group, his words can also be viewed as an admonition. And, undoubtedly, this moment of decency primes the viewer to accept CJ's "fifth-act conversion." Nonetheless, what ultimately warrants notice is that both Bart and the televangelist are authority figures. Though both are depicted as grotesque, the voices of both are influential. And both are not allies of the LGBTQIA+ community.

The only character who identifies as gay is introduced forty-four minutes into the film. Glen enters the mall with a group of survivors, two of whom are infected with the zombie virus. Holding the hand of a critically ill woman be-

Ty Burrell as Steve, Ving Rhames as Kenneth, Kim Poirier as Monica, Boyd Banks as Tucker, Jake Weber as Michael, R. D. Reid as Glen, Kevin Zegers as Terry, and Michael Kelly as CJ in *Dawn of the Dead*. Courtesy of Universal/Photofest.

ing transported in a wheelbarrow, Glen is initially portrayed as compassionate. However, when asked by Ana for information about the woman, he cannot help. Though he seems composed, he says, "Uh, yeah, sure. Just gimme a moment to collect myself, okay?" [00:44:25]. However, there is no "moment" to waste. Immediately, Glen's character is established as ineffectual. This remains consistent throughout the film: he contributes nearly nothing to the group of survivors. When asked for help with the sick or even in formulating a simple prayer for the dead, Glen always declines to act. Now, there are other members who also offer little to the group, but each provides social commentary and furthers the narrative. For instance, Steve, a wealthy cynic, spends the film sipping coffee and directing others. It is the promise of fleeing on his yacht that allows him the privilege of leisure. Steve's character demonstrates that even though society is crumbling, status still has meaning. And all of this viewer resentment culminates in his gratifying death at the hands of Ana (after Steve has been zombified). The same applies to Nicole, a young woman who appears to be in her late teens or early twenties. She has no practical skills; however, Nicole's innocence and compassion are most welcome in a film predicated on death and doom. Moreover, it is Nicole who forces the evacuation from the mall by trying to save a stray dog, leading to the zombies infiltrating the sanctuary. By contrast, Glen, a middle-aged man, is shown as having the ability to be an asset (off screen, he sheltered a small cluster of survivors in a church until they were rescued by a tractor-trailer driver), but he remains inert. He does virtually nothing to help the survivors or to further the story. As a result, the viewer is left with a relatively negative impression of the film's only LGBTQIA+ character.

Equally as troubling is the climax of the film. A montage depicts the survivors attempting to enjoy their time in the mall. Richard Cheese's cover of Disturbed's "Down with the Sickness" plays in the background as the characters pair off: Kenneth and Andy play chess, Nicole and Terry stargaze, Ana and Michael watch a film, Monica and Steve have sex, and Bart and CJ gamble for cigarettes. With the exception of Tucker, who is shown gleefully riding a bicycle throughout the halls of the mall, Glen is the only character without a counterpart. His segment opens with a close-up of a woman's black slingback. The person trying on the shoe is wearing a sheer, calf-high stocking (slightly rolled down). A white kitten-heel sandal is shown on the other foot, implying that these belong to the shopper. A cut then reveals that it is Glen trying on these feminine-coded shoes. By initially concealing the identity of the "customer," the director elicits shock and amusement, both of which are problematic. Gender identity/gender expression should not be employed as artistic tools to provoke negative audience reaction. Moreover, showing Glen (who identifies as a gay man) as "cross-dressing" is equally as troubling given that the *Diagnostic and Statistical Manual of Mental Disorders: DSM-5* asserts that the majority of "cross-dressers" identify as heterosexual (American Psychiatric Association 2013, 703). Showing a gay man "cross-dressing" is a vicious stereotype with little basis in reality. Finally, it is worrisome that Glen has sequestered himself in this store to try on so-called women's shoes alone. While others are sharing companionship in what appears to be their final days of life, Glen is shown as self-isolating to experiment with women's accessories. Not only is he denied an ally, but he is shown as having skewed priorities. The scene that follows this montage seems to be a reflection on this moment of "sickness" (as the song seems to suggest).

Approximately two minutes after the montage's conclusion, Glen is seen speaking with the imprisoned security guards. A lattice-style grate keeps the men confined. As the scene opens, the viewer is positioned with the detainees, seeing Glen on the other side of the grate. He begins with, "I guess the first time I knew I was gay, I was thirteen. This guy . . . Todd. He was building a deck in our backyard" [01:00:06–01:00:20]. The grate, the placement of the camera, and Glen's quiet admission all seem to suggest a form of confession. This positions Glen as a sinner, the type referred to by the televangelist. It is equally as telling that this follows the montage where Glen was shown experimenting with feminine-coded attire. It insinuates that he *needs* to confess. Compounding the disquieting nature of this moment, the jailed security guards are seated and changing their clothes as Glenn stands over them, watching. There is a minute hum of viewer discomfort as Glen discloses his sexuality while viewing the caged men perform this intimate task. In fact, one confined guard, CJ, says, "Please, just stop" [01:00:23]. Glen disregards this earnest request and continues to relate his sexual awaking. In frustration, CJ responds, "Oh my god. I'm in hell" [01:00:33]. He then covers his ears and grimaces. In *Gospel of the Living Dead: George Romero's Visions of Hell on Earth*, Kim Paffenroth optimistically views this moment as "[using] humor to satirize homophobia" (2006, 106). However, it is important to understand that these men are not consenting to this conversation or to be observed while performing their daily personal-care routine. Here, Glen's sexuality becomes a sort of unintended torture. And a sweet memory gains a lascivious undertone. Certainly, there is little humor to be found here.

As the film speeds to its conclusion, there are moments where it seems Glen is given a measure of redemption. For instance, when the survivors transform the mall vans into *Mad Max*–style vehicles, Glen is seen handing Ana a socket wrench. Though a minor gesture, he is doing more than most. And, as the crew flees the horde, Glen pushes Terry into the van when he resists being separated from his girlfriend. This may have saved Terry's life, and it certainly saved time. Nonetheless, these hopeful moments are obliterated when Glen accidentally kills Monica. As the modified mall van takes a sharp corner, Glen nearly bisects Monica with a running chain saw. The death is brutal and graphic. His error is horrific since he needs only to release the trigger to stop the chain saw. In fact, it would be a natural reaction to do so. David Roche addresses this moment in *Making and Remaking Horror in the 1970s and 2000s: Why Don't They Do It Like They Used To?* Here, the scholar notes that "by inadvertently killing [Monica], the homosexual character is both ridiculed and made complicit with the heterosexual imperative that characterizes the slasher genre [the explicit death of the sexually active female character]" (2014, 99). Undoubtedly, there is ample support for Roche's assessment of Glen being *used* to fulfill the demand for Monica's death. At this point in the film, (perceived) salvation is moments away. Monica, Ana, and Nicole are the sole remaining women. Throughout the film, Ana and Nicole are depicted as "wholesome," engaging in entirely chaste activities with their newfound love interests. Using Glen to remove this "transgressor" (Monica has sex with a virtual stranger, she allows the sex act to be recorded, she smokes cigarettes, she drinks alcohol, etc.) is unsurprising, but insidious. It underscores Glen as an incompetent stereotype.

While Glen is accountable for Monica's gruesome death, his own death is unexplained and anticlimactic. When Glen's van overturns, Ana leaves her own vehicle to offer assistance. As she peers in the van, Ana is visually assaulted by pure carnage. The camera showcases Monica's body (underscoring Glen's appalling folly) and then moves to Glen. While no injuries can be seen, his shirt and face are blood drenched. Just minutes from the conclusion, he becomes a silent casualty. No one discusses the incident any further as all attempt to move on to safety. As a "transgressor" himself, perhaps Glen's death was inevitable.

In 2007, Zach Snyder said of *300*'s Xerxes, "What's more scary to a 20-year-old boy than a giant god-king who wants to have his way with you?" (Daly 2007). Accusations of homophobia spilled onto headlines. It would seem that the director's remake of *Dawn of the Dead* may have provided an early indication of this insensitivity. As a result of its suspect portrayal of the LGBTQIA+ community and its tendency to fall victim to stereotyping, this film cannot be considered a positive contribution in the fight toward equality.

See also *Fright Night; Let Me In; May*.

Bibliography

American Psychiatric Association. *Diagnostic and Statistical Manual of Mental Disorders: DSM-5*. Arlington, VA: American Psychiatric Association, 2013.

Daly, Steve. "Double-Edged Sword: How *300* Was Positioned to Be a Box Office Hit." *Entertainment Weekly*, March 11, 2007. Accessed March 3, 2020. https://ew.com/article/2007/03/11/how-300-was-positioned-be-box-office-hit/.

Paffenroth, Kim. *Gospel of the Living Dead: George Romero's Visions of Hell on Earth*. Waco, TX: Baylor University Press, 2006.

Roche, David. *Making and Remaking Horror in the 1970s and 2000s: Why Don't They Do It Like They Used To?* Jackson: University Press of Mississippi, 2014.

—Erica Joan Dymond

D.E.B.S. (2004)

DIRECTOR: Angela Robinson

SCREENPLAY: Angela Robinson, based on the short film of the same name by Angela Robinson

CAST: Sara Foster (Amy), Jordana Brewster (Lucy), Meagan Good (Max), Devon Aoki (Dominique), Jill Ritchie (Janet), Geoff Stults (Bobby), Jimmi Simpson (Scud), Holland Taylor (Ms Petrie), Michael Clarke Duncan (Mr. P/Mr. Phipps)

SPECS: 92 minutes (theatrical release); color

AVAILABILITY: DVD (Sony Pictures Home Entertainment)

Initially a short film by Angela Robinson, *D.E.B.S.* was adapted into a feature by the same director after it landed the backing of Screen Gems production house and Sony Pictures Entertainment. The story revolves around four female spies—Amy, Max, Janet, and Dominique—in a paramilitary agency who are on a mission to catch the mafia queen Lucy Diamond. But things take a turn when Amy starts to fall for Lucy and has to balance her growing feelings for the supervillain and her loyalty to her job as a spy. Added to this, her ex-boyfriend Bobby, with whom she recently broke up, is trying to win her back. Between love, secrecy, and lots of gunfights, the action-comedy follows Amy and Lucy, the two star-crossed lovers, as they struggle to seek a happy ending for themselves.

The film's opening montage presents a panning shot of a classroom where students are taking the SAT exam as a voice-over explains how hidden within the paper is another secret test through which a paramilitary academy recruits secret service spies. This secret test measures "the student's innate ability to lie, cheat, fight, and kill" [00:00:36]. The viewers are introduced to the four protago-nists as they get their recruitment letters, while a voice-over explains in a comi-cally serious tone: "Some call them seductresses, some call them spies, fools call them innocent, they call themselves D.E.B.S." [00:00:48].

In the next scene, the D.E.B.S. are summoned to action in a *Mission Impos-sible* style by Mr. P, who informs them that the mafia boss Lucy Diamond is back in the country and is the most dangerous of all enemies they have faced—no federal agent has ever lived to tell the story after facing her. The scene then shifts to Lucy Diamond's underground den, where the mafia boss herself is introduced as the film's first LGBTQIA+ character. Lucy's chief henchman and best friend Scud is shown to be setting Lucy up with an ex-KGB assassin and forcing her to go out on a date. Meanwhile, not knowing what this meeting is about, the D.E.B.S., Homeland Security, FBI, and CIA stake out Lucy's date from the rafters of a ridiculously high-ceilinged restaurant. It is of note that the movement of the camera straight up from Lucy's table to the D.E.B.S. hideaway quotes from the famous stage scene in Orson Welles's *Citizen Kane*, where the camera moves upward past the catwalks, ropes, and pulleys in an exactly similar manner. Erstwhile director Angela Robinson admitted in an interview with *IndieWire* that she was "really influenced by Bob Fosse, Spielberg, John Hughes, and more recently, Sam Raimi, Peter Jackson, and Robert Rodriguez, plus a lot of T.V. . . . I kind of 'riff' on a lot of genre influences in my work, [and] in 'D.E.B.S.' I'm constantly quoting other movies. It's kind of a 'mish-mash' of influences" (Her-nandez and Brooks 2005).

Unsurprisingly, the date is a complete disaster that ends up in a shooting spree. Lucy almost escapes the venue but is intercepted by Amy, the very D.E.B. who mentioned in a pervious scene that she is writing a thesis on Lucy Diamond. Amy is surprised to learn that Lucy is a lesbian, and even more astounded that she feels charmed by the mafia boss's personality. This is also the first time that the film hints at a lesbian plotline as the chemistry between the two women on screen is obvious. But the scene abruptly ends with Lucy running away the mo-ment Amy's attention wavers. The fellow D.E.B.S. find Amy standing among a heap of diamonds, which are Lucy's calling card. Assuming that Amy actually fought with Lucy Diamond and chased her away, the team members praise her for her bravery. Lucy, however, is smitten by Amy's innocent charm and decides to meet her again. In one of the many poorly done green-screen moments in the film, Lucy is shown to be breaking into the D.E.B.S. mansion by first trac-ing Amy's bedroom through her phone-like gadget, which has a peculiar facial-recognition ability, and then ninja flipping through some absurd laser fields built around the house. Once inside, she manages to con Amy into going with her to a nightclub, and even drags Janet along when she accidentally catches the two on their way out. The scene at the nightclub, which can easily pass as Lucy and Amy's first date, is one of the pivotal moments of the film. Amy tells Lucy about her hypothesis that "as a woman operating in a male dominated field, you felt a need to overcompensate by being exponentially more ruthless and diabolical than your established male counterparts" [00:29:20]. She even goes as far as to psychoanalyze Lucy: "I think that the psychological forces combined to create a kind of emotional void in which you're incapable of loving or being loved" [00:29:46]. But the tide of conversation eventually changes, and soon it is Amy who is telling Lucy how she broke up with her boyfriend a few hours ago because she did not love him. In the next moment, Lucy leans in for a kiss, and for the first time since they sat on the table, the camera shows both her and Amy in a single frame. It is as if all the previous over-the-shoulder shots were merely building up each's perspective of the other, and it is finally as Amy starts to realize that she is attracted to Lucy that they are included in one frame. Janet stops them before they can kiss—her cry of "Oh my god, she almost kissed you!" comes off as multilayered since her shock stems not just from the fact that her fellow D.E.B. was breaking federal statutes by kissing an enemy but also from the realization that Amy is queer, as her next utterance "and you almost let her" clearly indicates. Janet's homophobia is clear in the next few scenes, where she keeps pointing out to Amy that "it's a girl" that she was going to kiss and even goes to the extent of calling Amy "a gay slut" [00:33:57–00:36:10].

Unaware of her situation with Lucy, the head of the D.E.B.S. agency, Mrs. Petrie, promotes Amy to the position of squad captain, a move that is not taken well by ex-captain Max, who feels that Amy is undeserving of the post. Unknowingly, though, Mrs. Petrie comes dangerously close to the truth in this scene when she tells Amy that "you identify with Lucy Diamond because I think she sees your pathos. You've got some dangerous union symbiosis going on" [00:38:53]. But since she means it in a different context, one where Amy is the hero who fought Lucy and defended herself, Mrs. Petrie's words are not taken seriously by anyone apart from the viewer, who can understand the hidden connotations behind them. Throughout the scene, the camera zooms in on Amy's face as she sits in discomfort while her seniors are showering her with praises. It is almost absurd that nobody in a paramilitary agency that trains spies is able to see through Amy's ridiculously obvious act, although this underlines the film's intention of satirizing the spy-thriller genre. After all, even to this day the illustration on the back of the DVD version of the film describes itself as a "smart and sexy spy spoof about love at first gun sight."

In her first assignment as a captain, Amy is given the task to stop a bank heist and catch Lucy Diamond in action. Unfortunately, Amy has no experience in giving orders and operating independently, and as a result, she ends up leading her team into a booby trap set by the mafia boss. Lucy also makes sure that while the rest of the D.E.B.S. are trapped, Amy is with her. It is in this scene that the pair eventually kiss, although there is utter chaos erupting around them. It is interesting that this time it is Amy who stops Lucy from walking away and initiates the kiss, even though moments before she tells Lucy that "I really like you. But I don't 'like' like you" [00:46:35]. That Amy's acceptance of her identity as a queer person is not followed by a dramatic coming-out story is refreshing to see, not because coming out stories are passé, but for once, it would have neither fit the parameters of the story nor the tone of the film. That Amy's realization of her own sexuality does not manifest into a violent reaction is then a testament to the variety of ways queer people come to terms with their identities. Jill Ritchie remarked in a promotion interview for the film, "I think ultimately for Lucy and Amy, especially for Amy because she has to face disappointing a lot of people and coming forth with who she really is, what she really wants and eventually she gets there . . . So take that into life, don't worry about what others think and eventually they will come around if they're true to themselves" (B 2005). In the next montage, the viewer sees the love story blooming on-screen while the entire D.E.B.S. agency, along with Amy's ex-boyfriend Bobby, work day and night to find Amy, who they believe has been kidnapped by Lucy Diamond. Lucy and Amy, conversely, are in their honeymoon phase, where they are shown to be driving around in cars, going on dates, and watching the sunset together. Amy even confesses her feelings to Lucy in one of the most heartfelt conversations in the film: "I'm here because I feel more like me when I'm with you than I do when I'm with me" [00:53:27]. Although the duo is caught in flagrante delicto by the D.E.B.S. team, who are tipped off about Amy's location, there is an internal shift in Amy's character after this point in the film. She takes all the scolding and punishments without speaking a word in response, but Amy's subordinate demeanor feels less a consequence of her shame of having an affair with an enemy and more a result of her confusion of whether Lucy is the right person for her. This is further underlined by the fact that Lucy tries to right her past wrongs by returning all the wealth she acquired through underhanded means in order to prove to Amy that she is willing to change for her.

The next time the viewers meet Lucy is when she has cut all ties with the mafia world and is now trying to gate-crash the D.E.B.S. year-end dance, where Amy is being awarded "D.E.B. of the Year." She reaches the auditorium just in time to hear Amy read her speech of how disgusting her experience was with Lucy. But all it takes is for their eyes to meet before Amy publicly announces that everything she had said until then was a lie, and that "the days I spent with Lucy Diamond were the happiest days of my life. And the only brave thing I've done this whole time is what I'm doing now. So if you'll excuse me, I have a date with the devil" [01:18:18]. That bravery is equated with love also comes off as a ringing battle cry from a queer person, who is all set to break through the heterosexual standards of society and find her own happy ending. The next scene shows Amy and Lucy running toward each other in slow motion, and the setting is in a storage room that looks exactly like the place where they both met for the first time. The two share a long-awaited kiss but soon get caught by Amy's squad members. However, the four D.E.B.S. make up with each other; likewise, Max, Janet, and Dominique are shown to be reconciling with the fact that one of their teammates is in love with an enemy. The acceptance of such a relationship follows soon after, and as Meghan Good remarked in a promotional interview, Amy's friends realize "that the most important thing was for [their] friend to be happy, whatever that was for her. Stop focusing on what [they] thought was best for her and let her do her thing" (B 2005). And with their help, Amy and Lucy get out safely, evading the rest of the spies.

The film ends with a scene that mimics countless heterosexual love plots in Hollywood: of the couple driving into the night, heads on each other's shoulders. Only this time, it seems to defamiliarize the same by showing a lesbian couple in such a frame, both in an attempt to support as well as normalize LGBTQIA+ relationships. In the above-quoted interview, director Angela Robinson herself stressed the film's LGBTQIA+ theme: "This film is really about following your heart and being who you really are. I think that is a really positive message" (Hernandez and Brooks 2005). Seeing how *D.E.B.S.* has remained alive in pop-culture imagination as one of the first spy-action films to be created by a queer director, it is safe to say that the message somewhat hit home.

See also *Blockers*; *Bound*.

Bibliography

B, Brian. "Get into *D.E.B.S.* with a New Contest, an Interview with the Girls, and Loads of New Content!" *MovieWeb*, March 25, 2005. Accessed December 9, 2021. https://movieweb.com/get-into-debs-with-a-new-contest-an-interview-with-the-girls-and-loads-of-new-content/.

Hernandez, Eugene, and Brian Brooks. "5 Questions for 'D.E.B.S.' Director Angela Robinson." *IndieWire*, June 13, 2005. Accessed March 15, 2021. https://www.indiewire.com/2005/06/5-questions-for-d-e-b-s-director-angela-robinson-78194/.

—Dyuti Gupta

DESERT HEARTS (1985)

DIRECTOR: Donna Deitch
SCREENPLAY: Natalie Cooper, based on the novel *Desert of the Heart* by Jane Rule
CAST: Helen Shaver (Vivian Bell), Patricia Charbonneau (Cay Rivvers), Audra Lindley (Frances Parker)
SPECS: 91 minutes; color
AVAILABILITY: DVD (Criterion Collection)

Uptight Columbia University English Professor Vivian Bell arrives at a Reno, Nevada, divorce ranch in the 1950s, where she will spend six weeks to establish residency. At a time when most states only allowed women to divorce in cases of adultery or abandonment, business is booming in Reno, but Vivian finds little in common with fellow residents or ranch owner Frances Parker. Instead, she throws repression to the wind in her unexpected attraction to Parker's stepdaughter Cay Rivvers, a younger, carefree artist who works at the nearby casino. A dance of desire follows, culminating in a sensual love scene and an uplifting hope for the future.

For a generation, *Desert Hearts* remains a touch point as the first lesbian romance film to be distributed by a major studio (Samuel Goldwyn Co.) in mainstream theaters. The Sundance Film Festival winner features a Western landscape with its promise of new lives and loves, a 1950s nostalgic country and rockabilly soundtrack, and the first tender, lesbian sex scene of its kind. One might imagine treading both eagerly and apprehensively into the theater, since positive movies about women in love did not yet exist on cable television (the vampires of *The Hunger* aside) and indie VHS tapes in the local video store would not appear until the 1990s. Perhaps audiences breathed a sigh of relief that Vivian and Cay did not commit suicide or join a bisexual tryst, watching in virtual disbelief at being allowed to witness a nonvoyeuristic sex scene between two women on the big screen.

Directed and produced by Donna Deitch when female directors were even more rare than they are today, the romance is adapted from the 1964 novel by Jane Rule, *Desert of the Heart*—itself a milestone in published fiction for lesbian readers. After raising the movie's budget herself with help from people like Gloria Steinem and Lily Tomlin, Deitch ran into another wall when casting. Most actors would not think of taking a lesbian or gay role in the 1980s, and Helen Shaver and Patricia Charbonneau both later revealed that their agents warned that these parts would ruin their careers. But the combination and contrasts of Shaver and Charbonneau produce lightning with sexual tension—one blonde, one brunette; one older, one younger; one a professor in a proper buttoned-up suit, one a maverick in cowboy boots, denim shorts, and low-cut shirt.

In his 1986 review, prominent film critic Roger Ebert remarks that the movie's "undeniable power" comes from the chemistry between the two actors, especially in their "sex scene of surprising power." It does not read as another exploitative portrayal but something sweet, sensuous, explorative, steering clear of the male gaze. The women here are not presented as objects of desire for heterosexual male viewers, since Deitch eschews the standard erotic angles, framing, and soundscape that are so familiar to audiences. It is a lesbian gaze, the mutual gaze between two women who connect and desire one another as Vivian nervously experiences a sexual awakening (Hollinger 2012). In the 1980s, this is revolutionary. Ebert's television partner Gene Siskel writes that *Desert Hearts* "may have accomplished on film what hasn't been achieved in society—the desensationalizing of lesbianism" (1986).

Although not by any means monolithic, audience members like controversial feminist commentator Camille Paglia, who saw the film eleven times, often overwhelmingly agreed with these mainstream reviewers, while lesbian critics still had a good deal to challenge. The movie and the relationship it depicts are not without faults, and the standard plot has been seen hundreds of times before, except here girl meets girl, girl pursues girl, girl loses girl, girls get together. Deitch intentionally avoided making this an issue film and designed the story to parallel the heterosexual world. For some reviewers, that makes *Desert Hearts* not queer *enough*, duplicating heteronormative relationships rather than modeling something unique (Hollinger 2012).

The easterner arrives on the train, dropped into the West in all its expansive glory. Hair tight in a bun, dark glasses shield her eyes. The desert and the possibilities for letting go await as the local wild child roars down the highway in a Ford Fairlane convertible. The eastern intellectual has sophisticated tastes and cannot relate to the gum-popping prospective divorcées at the ranch. The local works a cash till at the casino but wants something more out of life. A glimpse of the westerner as a ceramic artist shows the easterner that this one is not like the others. Again, moviegoers are familiar with this plot involving couples overcoming barriers of class, education, culture, and age. Carpe diem. Here it is not just the West, but Reno, where the theme of gambling and taking risks is reinforced. And this time, the driver who causes life to career out of control is a woman.

Although the warnings from Frances to stay clear of Cay are evident—Cay was expelled from college for "unnatural acts"—the dangers of lesbian life in the conservative 1950s are not explored in depth. Instead, audiences must intuitively understand that Vivian struggles not only with internal homophobia but a potential loss of profession and the life she has known. However, as a jackpot winner in the casino says, "If you don't play, you can't win." Director Deitch plays this role herself and literally reveals what the film is all about. To fall in love and change your life, you have to take a chance. As the train back to New York begins rolling down the tracks, Vivian reaches for Cay, and the two at least ride to the next stop in uncertainty, but with a future. Although our media landscape today is not as bereft of positive images as the 1950s or the 1980s, that chance for a future together, for a happy ending, is still defiant, subversive, and meaningful.

See also *Carol*; *Far from Heaven*.

Bibliography

Ebert, Roger. "*Desert Hearts*." RogerEbert.com, June 6, 1986. Accessed March 20, 2020. https://www.rogerebert.com/reviews/desert-hearts-1986.

Hollinger, Karen. *Feminist Film Studies*. London: Routledge, 2012.

Rich, B. Ruby. "*Desert Hearts*: The Thrill of It All." Criterion Collection, November 14, 2017. Accessed March 20, 2020. https://www.criterion.com/current/posts/5118-desert-hearts-the -thrill-of-it-all.

Siskel, Gene. "Flick of the Week." *Chicago Tribune*, August 8, 1986. Accessed March 20, 2020. https://www.chicagotribune.com/news/ct-xpm-1986-08-08-8602270452-story.html.

—Angela Beauchamp

DODGEBALL: A TRUE UNDERDOG STORY (2004)

DIRECTOR: Rawson Marshall Thurber
SCREENPLAY: Rawson Marshall Thurber
CAST: Vince Vaughn (Peter LaFleur), Christine Taylor (Kate Veatch), Ben Stiller (White Goodman), Rip Torn (Patches O'Houlihan), Justin Long (Justin Redman), Stephen Root (Gordon Pibb), Alan Tudyk ("Pirate" Steve Cowan)
SPECS: 93 minutes; color
AVAILABILITY: DVD (Twentieth Century Fox)

A modern retelling of the age-old David and Goliath tale, *Dodgeball: A True Underdog Story* follows Peter LaFleur, the everyman owner of Average Joe's Gym, a gym for regular folk looking more for community than for an extreme level of fitness. Peter is in over his head financially, as he is told by attractive and competent lawyer, Kate Veatch, and has thirty days to come up with fifty thousand dollars or his gym will be bought out by White Goodman, the vain and villainous owner of the competing (and next door) Globo Gym. Several of Peter's similarly downtrodden clients (and close friends) band together to devise a way to save the gym they love, and after several failed (and terrible) ideas, Gordon (an obscure-sports aficionado) suggests they enter a Las Vegas dodgeball tournament whose grand prize happens to be the exact amount of money needed to save

Average Joe's. The Average Joe's crew stumble their way into the semifinals of the competition aided by aged dodgeball legend Patches O'Houlihan and the strong athletic skills of new team member Kate Veatch. The team learns to embrace their weaknesses as strengths and is able to defeat Globo Gym, retain Average Joe's, and earn a small fortune along the way.

Opening on a television advertisement for the soon-to-be antagonist Globo Gym, *Dodgeball: A True Underdog Story* quickly cements itself within the realm of the male gaze. The camera pans over disembodied, physically fit, attractive, mostly female customers while an announcer questions whether the viewer is overweight or "out of luck with the opposite sex" [00:00:31]. The message sent by Globo Gym and its ironically named owner, White Goodman, is of heterosexual desire and inclusion.

This film quickly switches perspective to that of Peter LeFleur, the owner of Average Joe's. His business represents the much less intimidating, down-to-earth counterpart to Globo Gym. And Peter himself is depicted as more oafish and amiable than the high-energy White. Peter wakes up after a night of sleeping on the couch and quickly brushes his teeth while listening to his voice messages, one of which informs him that he has three rented videos overdue: *"Drunken Hussies 3, Backdoor Patrol 5,* and *Mona Lisa Smile"* [00:02:52–00:02:56]. The joke is not only the juxtaposition of the two pornographic films with a mainstream feature film but between the pornography and a stereotypically "feminine" film like *Mona Lisa Smile.* Here Peter's minor deviation from the rigid demands of heterosexual masculinity is the source of laughs.

Average Joe's is populated by traditionally "unimpressive" masculine specimens, all of whom the film exploits (in its attempt at humor) by highlighting their physical or sexual weaknesses. For instance, Justin is a slender and somewhat artless high schooler seeking help in winning the heart of a young woman. Similarly, Owen is a tall but not physically athletic man who struggles with attracting women. And Gordon is an older, overweight man married to a mail-order bride who seemingly "emasculates" him. However, as much as non-normative heterosexual masculinity is employed to amuse viewers, queerness fairs even worse.

The dodgeball team's trainer, Patches O'Houlihan, spends his entire screen time humiliating the players into being better at the sport. While he calls the team "ladies" on more than one occasion and "a bunch of females" on another, he goes so far as to refer to Justin as "queer bait." Moreover, when it is revealed that Kate, who has become an ally of Peter's and Average Joe's, can play dodgeball, Patches repeatedly refers to her as "lesbo," "dyke," and "Billie Jean King." It is a running joke that because Kate is adept at sports, she must be a lesbian. This is repeatedly denied by Peter, who is romantically interested in her.

However, rumors of Kate's sexual identity do not turn out to be altogether unfounded when, after winning the championship, a woman, Joyce, comes onto the court and kisses Kate passionately. Dwight, who was insisting that Kate is a lesbian, is about to have an "I told you so moment" when Kate turns around and declares, "Hey! I'm not a lesbian. . . . No, I'm bisexual" [01:26:41–01:26:49]. She then pulls Peter by his shirt and kisses him as passionately as she kisses the aforementioned Joyce. This is a blatant example of the male gaze that is rampant in this film; from the camera lingering on two women kissing while the men stare in awe to upskirt shots of twirling cheerleaders. Kate's bisexuality is only there to satisfy a heterosexual male fantasy.

Interestingly, Kate's sexual identity is alluded to (whether intentionally or not) earlier in the film in a way that viewers less knowledgeable about queer women might not be aware of. After fending off White Goodman's advances with the help of Peter, Kate invites Peter into her home, which he discovers is adorned with unicorns from top to bottom. He looks at her while she self-consciously describes herself as a unicorn lover. In the LGBTQIA+ community, a "unicorn" is a bisexual woman who dates couples (consisting of a man and a woman) and usually has threesomes. There is much debate about this term in the community and whether couples looking for a "unicorn" are actually just objectifying queer women. For Kate's unicorn obsession to be such a core part of her personality seems unlikely to be an accident but a coy way of her foreshadowing her queerness, even though it only exists to serve Peter in the long run.

For all of the film's flaws, there are moments of progress here: nontraditional masculinity emerges victorious against hyper-, toxic masculinity without having to conform to heterosexual ideals. Nonetheless, because of the (1) homophobic and biphobic language that is not demonized but used for comedic purposes and (2) the use of the male gaze (especially as it applies to Kate's same-sex relationship), the film cannot be considered a positive representation of the LGBTQIA+ community.

See also *Big Daddy*; *Neighbors 2: Sorority Rising*; *Wet Hot American Summer.*

—Genevieve Ruzicka

DREAM BOY (2008)

DIRECTOR: James Bolton
SCREENPLAY: James Bolton, based on the novel of the same name by Jim Grimsley
CAST: Stephan Bender (Nathan), Maximillian Roeg (Roy), Randy Wayne (Burke), Owen Beckman (Randy), Thomas Jay Ryan (Nathan's father), Diana Scarwid (Nathan's mother), Rooney Mara (Roy's girlfriend), Rickie Lee Jones (Roy's mother)
SPECS: 90 minutes; color
AVAILABILITY: DVD (Peccadillo Pictures)

Based on Jim Grimsley's 1995 novel of the same title, *Dream Boy* is set in the late 1970s. It dramatizes the story of two young men from the US rural South who fall in love. While the film follows the development of the relationship between the two main characters, Roy and Nathan, it also focuses on Nathan's family: in particular, Nathan's sexually abusive father. Roy appears to provide Nathan with a sense of safety and protection. As their relationship progresses, viewers observe both Roy coming to terms with his sexuality and Nathan becoming more confident. At the point where both young men appear to be ready to enjoy their relationship, one of their friends rapes and murders Nathan.

The story is situated in rural America, where church appears to be the center of social life. The opening scene of the film introduces not only the context of the story, but also its core aspects. Viewers see a family returning home from worship. Once they arrive, the son, Nathan, stares at a cute neighbor. At home, Nathan is shown as sad. For instance, when he was in the car with his parents, returning from church, there is little to no discussion among them. Both his mother and his father appear to be preoccupied with something of minor importance. It is understood that he is alone. However, in the following scene, viewers see Nathan looking out of his window. He sees the cute neighbor again and stares at him attentively, examining every movement. Feelings of loneliness inside the house are juxtaposed to finding interest in what he sees looking out the window, suggesting family problems and Nathan's need to escape his home.

The next day, Nathan gets on the school bus. The driver is the neighbor Nathan was looking at the previous day, Roy. Viewers see them exchanging looks through the rearview mirror of the bus. Despite the fact that they both appear to be reserved, there is a sort of interest between them. However, this changes in the next scene. Roy is also a student, and viewers see him in the cafeteria having lunch. However, at school, Nathan and Roy do not exchange any looks, and the same is true during the ride back home. Here one can infer that they are careful about what the other students might say if they understand that these young men are romantically interested in each other, which further highlights the traditional mindset of the society they live in. When Nathan returns home, viewers see him again looking out the window, carefully examining his neighbor tend to his animals. The scene ends with Nathan having dinner with his mother. The father is absent from the scene. Yet his absence is not discussed between Nathan and his mother, possibly because it is not a rare occurrence, which further contributes to establishing the existence of family problems.

The next set of scenes focuses more on the relationship between Nathan and Roy. Viewers first see Roy attending Sunday school. There is a young woman there with whom Roy exchanges a few smiles. One might find this confusing, but considering how traditional this society appears to be, it is not surprising that, despite the fact that Roy might be romantically interested in other young men, he is also involved in a relationship with a young woman either because he is bisexual or as a result of social pressure and expectations. This scene is contrasted with the next one, in which Roy and Nathan are on the bus returning from school. Viewers see them exchanging looks again. This time they appear to be less reserved, and after the last student gets off the bus, Roy invites Nathan to sit closer to him. They do not talk, but viewers see them being content with the fact that they are closer to each other. When they arrive home, Roy invites Nathan to his house to help him with an English assignment. The section then ends in a similar manner with the one it started. Roy attends Sunday school again. When it is over, he exits with the same young woman viewers saw him with at the opening scene of this section. They are holding hands, and they get inside a car. They start kissing and touching each other. Apart from the fact that viewers get to learn more about Roy, this scene being placed immediately after the first exchange between the two young men makes viewers wonder whether Roy is looking for some sort of sexual gratification because of his interest in this young woman or whether he does so because of his interest in Nathan.

The next scene finds Roy visiting Nathan's house. They do their homework together, and they also discuss the place they live in. It appears that Nathan is there for the summer, while Roy lives there permanently. Roy expresses his dislike of the place. Nathan tells Roy that he is used to changing homes every so often because of his father's job. Even though this could be possible, it does not appear to be true. So far in the film, viewers have either seen the father being preoccupied with something of little interest at home, or he is absent at times when one would not be expected to be at work. The discussion does not develop any further. Nathan's mother appears by the door, calling for bedtime. The mother seems to be concerned and not at ease with Roy's presence. Does she suspect that her son is attracted to other young men and does not know whether to let him pursue his interests? Another look at this suggests that the mother is concerned because she does not want Nathan's father to return home and find Roy there. This would suggest that both the mother and the father know about Nathan but the father is not accepting. In any case, what is important in terms of family dynamics is that the mother is, in a sense, closer to Nathan and that both she and Nathan are intimidated by Nathan's father.

The following day, viewers see Nathan in the school cafeteria. Roy and two of his friends sit with Nathan. They arrange a deer hunt over the weekend, and they invite Nathan along. Despite the friendly gesture of the invitation, though, they do not appear to be really friendly with him. The way they look at him suggests that this relationship might be problematic. Back at Nathan's house, viewers see a similar scene to the one that introduced them to Nathan's family life. The mother is preoccupied with some house chores, and Nathan's father is sleeping on the couch in the middle of the day. Viewers still do not know much about Nathan's father, but it has certainly been established by now that when he is around, silence and order prevail. Later, Roy visits Nathan to study. Nathan is unable to concentrate, though. While they do their homework, viewers see Nathan touching Roy's hand. Roy takes it away momentarily, but after a second he holds Nathan's hand. They touch each other's bodies, and they leave the house to go for a walk. When they reach the local graveyard, they start touching and kissing. They undress, and they spend the next moments looking at each other's eyes, touching and hugging each other's bodies. One cannot but wonder: Is a graveyard the only place they can truly be themselves? Does this suggest that only in death can they really be free?

When Nathan returns home, his father approaches him in the kitchen and invites him to watch a Western with him. Nathan declines. At this stage in the film, it is unclear why Nathan declines. Given how little time they spend together as a family doing meaningful and bonding things together, one would expect Nathan to take this opportunity. By declining this offer, viewers are made to consider what the reasons might be for Nathan not to want to spend time with his father. The next scene finds Nathan and his family attending church. At night, Roy and his girlfriend also attend church. When it is over, Roy declines an offer from his girlfriend for some company. He is distant and uninterested. This might not be surprising for the viewers. Roy has developed an interest in Nathan. Therefore, turning his girlfriend's offer down possibly justifies the view that he was with her out of necessity. What is of significance, though, are the parallels between Nathan declining his father's request for company and Roy declining his girlfriend's request for some company. Could it be that the type of company Nathan's father and Roy's girlfriend are looking for is the same? For the first time in the film, audiences start worrying about Nathan's relationship with his father.

The relationship between the two young men continues to develop. After school, when everyone has gotten off the bus, Nathan and Roy find an opportunity to undress and touch each other. Later in the day, Nathan visits Roy and his mother. They discuss and have a good time, the three of them. Later, Roy asks Nathan out. Nathan cannot respond without asking his mother first, and he asks Roy to go to Nathan's home and ask his mom. When he does, Nathan's mother explains that she is concerned because his father will not like this, and that he has been worrying about their relationship, but she eventually agrees. Nathan, Roy, and his two friends go swimming. Nathan does not know how to swim, but one of the boys tries to throw him into the water, confirming the awkward looks they exchanged in the school cafeteria when they first met. Roy intervenes, and the friend leaves Nathan alone. On the way back, Roy pulls over. The two kiss, undress, and rub against each other, imitating a sexual act. Nathan appears to have some experience. This makes Roy jealous, and he tries to hit Nathan. They get dressed and drive back home. Nathan tries to speak to Roy, but he does not respond.

At home, Nathan looks out of the window, trying to see Roy. His mother's voice interrupts him. She calls him to join her and his father downstairs. Nathan seems not to want to do so. He gets in bed and pretends to be sleeping. His father opens the door of Nathan's bedroom. He asks him questions about his day, and Nathan replies but does not elaborate. The father asks Nathan to open his eyes, but Nathan refuses to do so. Viewers see the father getting upset with Nathan, but his mother intervenes and asks him to go downstairs. The father says that it was wrong for Nathan to skip church and go out with his friends instead, and he goes downstairs. When the father leaves Nathan's room, Nathan gets out of bed and sets a trap so that anyone who enters his room will trip and fall. Instead of sleeping in his bed, he stuffs it with pillows so that it looks like he is under the covers and sleeps on the floor instead. At night, the father opens the door and while approaching what he thinks to be a sleeping Nathan is caught by the trap. Nathan wakes up, runs downstairs, leaves the house, and spends the night at the graveyard. All suspicions that were previously hinted at are now confirmed. Nathan's father has been sexually abusing his son. This explains Nathan's declining his father's requests for company, Nathan's mother being scared of what his father would think if Nathan went out with his classmates, but also the overall hostile environment in Nathan's house.

Nathan's parents are looking for him, but he remains in hiding at the graveyard. It is unclear for how long Nathan sleeps outdoors. One morning, viewers see Nathan sleeping in the school bus. When he wakes up, he goes quickly to his house to take a shower, change clothes, and have breakfast. His mother sees him and prays for him. He continues spending time in the woods. Roy is looking for him as well. One evening he finds him at the graveyard, and he invites him to stay at his barn. Roy asks Nathan what has happened, but Nathan does not reveal the truth. He tells Roy that his parents had a fight. Roy makes a bed for Nathan in the barn and reassures him that he would be safe there. In the morning, he wakes him up with a kiss. Nathan goes to his house for breakfast. While Nathan is eating, his father wakes up and attempts to start a fight, but he fails to do so because Nathan's mother intervenes.

After almost fighting with his father, Nathan escapes to Roy's barn. There, Roy tells Nathan that he is going camping with his two other friends over the weekend, and he asks Nathan to go with him. Nathan agrees, and viewers then see the four friends out in the woods, around the fire, sharing a drink. They start a discussion about stories of people who have died in the woods, and they ask Roy to tell a story. While Roy narrates a scary story, one of his friends realizes that Nathan is looking at Roy in a manner that suggests romantic interest, not just friendship. This is the same friend who attempted to throw Nathan into the water when they had gone swimming. Later in the night, Nathan and Roy leave their tents to collect some wood for the fire. They hear a few odd sounds, and they get back in their tent area. While they are going into their tent, the camera focuses on the face of the other friend, who is staring at Roy and Nathan. It becomes apparent that he understands that something is going on between Nathan and Roy. What is not clear yet is why this concerns him. At this moment in the film, one can argue that he is jealous, homophobic, or both.

Inside the tent, while Nathan and Roy undress and kiss, Roy tells Nathan that Nathan's father came to see him and, among other things, warned Roy that Nathan makes things up. Perhaps the father sensed that the two young men were close and thought that Nathan might want to share what he has been going through with his father. It is possible that this is something that has happened before, and a possible explanation for why the family keeps moving houses. The father wanted to ensure that Roy does not believe what Nathan might tell him about his father. For the first time in the movie, Nathan and Roy engage in oral sex, with Roy being on the receiving end, asking Nathan if he minds that he does not reciprocate. Nathan seems not to care about this. Arguably, he might be deriving pleasure only by the fact that someone cares for and protects him. The next morning, the four friends go exploring. While walking, the suspicious friend takes off his top and gives Nathan aggressive looks. They reach a plantation house and, at night, they decide to break in to see if it is haunted. Inside the house, Nathan listens to someone talking to him. It is his father's voice, asking him whether he remembers what they did when he was little. It is now explicit that the father raped Nathan when he was young.

Roy finds Nathan. They get intimate again, and they engage in oral sex. This time, Nathan is on the receiving end. During the act, the two friends see them. Roy asks them to leave and then runs after them. Nathan gets dressed and tries to find the others. While he is walking, someone hits him in the head. In the next scene, viewers see the suspicious friend beating and eventually raping Nathan, who is in a near-unconscious state. When he finishes, he takes a piece of furniture and hits Nathan in the head. Nathan is on the floor, unconscious, with blood coming from his head. Roy finds him dead. The next scene shows the father, having been summoned to identify the body. The final scene finds all the characters attending Nathan's funeral. Nathan is also present as a ghost. The next shot shows Nathan's house where viewers see Nathan's ghost waking up, walking around the woods. He stays at the graveyard. From there, he sees his mother leaving his father. The next morning, Nathan's ghost visits Roy at his barn. Roy is crying, but he eventually sees Nathan's ghost. The two hug each other. The final shot finds Roy driving the bus. Looking through the rear mirror, sometimes he sees Nathan and sometimes not.

See also *Boys Don't Cry; Shelter; Summer of Sam.*

—Angelos Bollas

· E ·

EVERY DAY (2018)

DIRECTOR: Michael Sucsy
SCREENPLAY: Jesse Andrews, based on the novel *Every Day* by David Levithan
CAST: Angourie Rice (Rhiannon), Lucas Jade Zumann (Nathan), Nicole Law (Kelsea), Jeni Ross (Amy), Colin Ford (Xavier), Justice Smith (Justin), Debby Ryan (Jolene), Maria Bello (Lindsey)
SPECS: 97 minutes; color
AVAILABILITY: DVD (Warner Bros.)

In *Every Day*, A is a consciousness, a spirit, who wakes up in a different body each morning. "Always someone my age. Never too far from the last. Never the same person twice. I have absolutely no control over any of it," A explains to Rhiannon, a sixteen-year-old young woman with whom A has fallen in love [00:26:13–00:26:28]. The main concern of the film thus becomes how A and Rhiannon navigate the romance between the two of them. When first introduced to Rhiannon, for example, A is inhabiting the body of Justin, Rhiannon's then boyfriend, but by the time the conversation noted above occurs, A has moved on to the body of Megan, a petite brunette who looks nothing like Rhiannon's usual type. While Rhiannon learns how to fall in love with someone who appears in a new form every day, A is met with an obstacle course of different embodied experiences: navigating one host's depression, avoiding a flight scheduled for another host that would take A to Hawaii, and waking one day in the body of Rhiannon, herself.

Every Day is one of many books by young adult author David Levithan that has been adapted for the screen. Both book and film have been celebrated for breaking down binaries of gender and sexuality, depicting instead a wide range of identities. Indeed, Levithan is the recipient of three Lambda Literary Awards for his work exploring LGBTQIA+ themes, and *Every Day* certainly adheres to these themes as well. The novel advocates for inclusivity of sexualities and gender expressions as A inhabits hosts who identify as gay, lesbian, transgender, cisgender, and straight. Through A's inner monologue, readers hear A's reflections on these subjects. For example, while inhabiting the body of Hugo, who is celebrating his one-year anniversary with boyfriend, Austin, at a Gay Pride parade, A reflects, "In my experience, desire is desire, love is love. I have never fallen in love with a gender. I have fallen for individuals. I know this is hard for people to do, but I don't understand why it's so hard, when it's so obvious" (Levithan 2012). Similarly, when inhabiting the body of Vic, a transgender man, A excites in the relatability of Vic's experience:

> There were days I felt like a girl and days I felt like a boy, and those days wouldn't always correspond with the body I was in. I still believed everyone when they said I had to be one or the other. Nobody was telling me a different story, and I

was too young to think for myself. I had yet to learn that when it came to gender, I was both and neither. (Levithan 2012)

As Levithan later observed, "A is really agender more than transgender, there's certainly a kinship [between A and Vic]" (Nunn 2018).

While both book and film recount many of the same events, the way in which the events are presented to the audience is, necessarily altered to account for the affordances of the different medium. The novel clearly establishes A as the main character, whereas in the film, Rhiannon gets considerably more screen time. In a review of the film, Matia Burnett even refers to Rhiannon, and not A, as the central figure in the story (Burnett 2018). This shift might largely be due to the fact that the book is narrated in first person, in A's own voice, with the reader's being privy to A's own inner monologue; the film, however, has no narration, and as a result, Rhiannon's experiences learning about and interacting with A ground the narrative instead. Nevertheless, "the notion of A being defined entirely by an interior life, not the way the world sees A," what Levithan cites as the appeal that enticed him to first write *Every Day*, is lost in the film (Nunn 2018). In retelling the story through film, director Michael Sucsy relies heavily on the visual cues of the medium—like A's gestures and habits—to allow both Rhiannon and the viewer to keep tabs on which body the spirit is inhabiting at any given moment.

Still, despite this narratorial shift, the film drives home a message of inclusivity, advocating for—as Patricia Kennon notes—"an admirable range of sexualities and gender expressions" (2015). But it does so without interior monologue. These musings become dialogic instead, as Rhiannon asks A, "So, do you consider yourself a boy or a girl?" After a brief pause, A simply replies, "Yes" [00:57:41–00:57:48]. The character of Vic still makes an appearance, played by Ian Alexander, an actor who is, himself, transgender. Yet the film does away with the focus that the book pays to Vic, his relationship to girlfriend Dawn, and his movement through different spaces and groups of family and friends. Instead, Vic's body serves as a way for Rhiannon to draw attention to the changeability of A's appearance. Upon first expressing how much of a challenge it would be to pursue a romantic relationship with someone who changes bodies every day, Rhiannon emphasizes her point by gesturing to Vic. In response, A observes, "Not everyone's body aligns with their mind, but I'm not asking you to give Vic a chance, Rhiannon; I'm asking you to give me a chance" [00:39:12–00:39:21]. Notably, this dialogue identifies a larger pattern within the film. The gender and sexual identities that are explored more fully in the pages of the novel are neglected by the film. Not only is Vic's backstory cut out, but A's other gay and lesbian identities are glossed over as well. While the book shows A in the bodies of those who identify as LGBTQIA+, the film—perhaps in its focal shift to Rhiannon—loses these dynamics.

In focusing more on Rhiannon, however, other aspects appear more prominent. Although A's shifting gender presents an initial problem in both versions of *Every Day*, the film allows viewers to see Rhiannon's movement toward acceptance more fully. A nice addition in the film is a conversation in which Rhiannon describes her "type" to A as "tall, slim, nice shoulders" [00:21:45–00:21:50]. And even though she, herself, seems unsure of this description, it at least articulates a clearer basis for why she is drawn more to some of the bodies A inhabits than others. In response to Rhiannon's description, however, A predicts, "I just know that you can be attracted to way more people than you think" [00:22:38–00:22:41]. And, as A predicted, Rhiannon finds herself kissing a wide range of her peers: tall, short, Black, white, athletic, and less athletic. Yet only once does Rhiannon kiss another girl, and this kiss is more hesitant and reserved than those that have come before, with A asking for permission where none was required previously [01:11:52–01:12:03]. Kate Erbland regards this directorial choice as one that undermines the central theme of the film, that "love knows no boundaries" (2018). And Kennon has pointed out the same issue within the novel, viewing Rhiannon's resistance to certain bodies as a mode of "maintaining hegemonic gender codes, conceptualizing A as both male and heterosexual" (2015). Still, Rhiannon certainly tries to move past this more rigid way of thinking, and the scene just described helps to demonstrate this aspect of her narrative. Worth noting here is that the film and its resulting critiques are more about open-mindedness than they are about sexuality-as-biology or sexuality-as-choice. The film is not suggesting that everyone could be pansexual if they just tried hard enough; rather, it seems to imply that if viewers—like A—break away from preconceived notions of gender and sexuality, they will find many of these constructs (perhaps even those about biology and choice) are just that: constructs.

This being the case, A ultimately concludes that the two need to go their own ways, that there is no future for their queer relationship. In deciding to move on, A leaves Rhiannon with a parting gift: a date with Alexander, whom A is currently inhabiting. This plot point is bittersweet, simultaneously thoughtful and "creepy" (as Erbland [2018] points out), even raising concerns about consent, which the novel does a much better job of fleshing out. In addressing why a separation is necessary, A pitches Alexander to a distraught Rhiannon, first drawing attention to Alexander's appearance: "Alexander's perfect for you. He's your type. . . . He's tall, slim, nice shoulders." But Rhiannon protests, quickly volleying back, "You're my type" [01:23:15–01:23:51]. And, indeed, the film ends as Alexander—who is now back to being inhabited by the real Alexander—walks down the school hallway with Rhiannon. In this way, the film, despite including a wide range of gender expressions and sexual identities, seems to echo the well-known chorus sung to so many LGBTQIA+ individuals: for them, there can be no future, at least not one that looks like those waiting for their heterosexual peers.

The book also builds a substantial subplot around Western religion's long-standing positioning against gender and sexual minorities, and this discourse is largely absent from the film. Within the novel, A inhabits an evangelical Christian named Nathan who is left with a vague sense of A's possession of his body. Fitting this experience within the framework he knows, he gains media traction in his attempt to explain what happened to him. After Nathan claims it was the devil that possessed him, another character informs A that "now the religious crazies want to make him a poster child" (Levithan 2012). In his accusations against A, Nathan operates as a loose metaphor for those religious institutions that have historically persecuted those who identify as gay. This theme is further expanded by A's frequent return to the subject; at the Gay

Pride parade mentioned above, A catches sight of a protestor whose sign reads, "HOMOSEXUALITY IS THE DEVIL'S WORK" (Levithan 2012). To this, A makes an astute observation: "People use the devil as an alias for the things they fear. The cause and effect is backward. The devil doesn't make anyone do anything. People just do things and blame the devil after" (Levithan 2012). Although, in this, A seems to be forgetting that in inhabiting Nathan, Nathan's body was, in fact, made to do certain things that he had no control over, and that this experience of having his body overridden is what led Nathan to regard A as the devil. This detail aside, Nathan's religious persecution of A does map nicely onto many an LGBTQIA+ individual.

The film, however, only pays a brief homage to this entire subplot. A social media post about Nathan makes Rhiannon aware that the Nathan she danced with one night at a party was not who she thought he was. When she goes to interview Nathan later, posing as a journalist, she confirms that he has no knowledge of the time they spent together, and this aids her in later processing A's claims of body hopping. So, once again, the movie glosses over what was an emphatically queer theme from the book, subjecting it to a more central narrative focused on Rhiannon.

In conclusion, the film still displays a wide range of LGBTQIA+ identities, petitioning for a celebration of these identities and for diversity more broadly. However, it does this to a lesser extent than the novel on which it is based. While some of the perspective that A offers from within the embodied experience of these diverse hosts is lost along with a number of the book's subplots, which offer nuance to the romance narrative, other insights are gained. Through the visual medium of film, for example, the audience better witnesses the different embodiment of A's hosts, as fifteen separate actors were cast to play A over the course of the movie (Burnett 2018). This point is harder to grasp, A's body swapping seeming less drastic, when narrated by the consciousness in the book. In discussing the film, Levithan was quick to note that these many embodiments of A was something that he hoped viewers of all genders, orientations, and backgrounds would be able to identify with. "One of the most amazing things about the book's life, so far, is [that] a lot of people who would not otherwise gravitate toward a queer story come around to it," Levithan noted (Burnett 2018). Turning to the film, he added, "I hope non-queer viewers will start to question the notion of gender and how we're defined by our bodies after seeing the movie, too" (Burnett 2018). Certainly, viewers will be drawn to the film's expansive and talented cast. Likewise, the concept of the film is unique enough to entertain audiences even if fans of the book find it a bit simplistic in its representation of the novel's themes. In reflecting on films from 2018, the critic Peter Bradshaw awarded the film a unique accolade "for the quirky film overlooked by the complacent MSM gatekeeper-establishment which might be a future cult classic" (2018). For those looking for a view of gender and sexuality beyond their overly characterized binary relationship, *Every Day* certainly stands out as a prominent offering.

See also *Love, Simon; The Perks of Being a Wallflower; To All the Boys I've Loved Before.*

Bibliography

Bradshaw, Peter. "And the 2018 Braddies go to . . . Peter Bradshaw's Films of the Year." *Guardian*, December 10, 2018. Accessed December 21, 2020. https://www.theguardian.com /film/2018/dec/10/braddies-peter-bradshaw-films-of-the-year.

Burnett, Matia. "In Theaters: *Every Day*." *Publishers Weekly Online*, February 27, 2018. Accessed November 20, 2020. https://www.publishersweekly.com/pw/by-topic/childrens/childrens -industry-news/article/76174-in-theaters-every-day.html.

Donner, Mathieu. "'I Have to Figure Out Who I Am': Embodied Self, Time, and the Ethics of Adolescence in David Levithan's *Every Day*." *Journal of the Fantastic in the Arts* 28, no. 3 (2018): 402–24.

Erbland, Kate. "*Every Day* Review: YA Adaptation Packs Timely Message about Acceptance, but Buries It under Creepy Plot Twists." *IndieWire*, February 22, 2018. Accessed December 23, 2020. https://www.indiewire.com/2018/02/every-day-review-ya-adaptation-david-levithan -novel-1201931011/.

Kennon, Patricia. "'If the Inside Was the Outside': Gender, Heteronormativity and the Body in David Levithan's *Every Day*." *Foundation* 44, no. 122 (2015): 58–67.

Levithan, David. *Every Day*. New York: Alfred A. Knopf, 2012.

Nunn, Jerry. "David Levithan Brings 'A' Game in New Movie." *Windy City Times* 33, no. 23 (February 2018): 24.

—Jon Heggestad

• F •

THE FALLS TRILOGY (2012, 2013, 2016)
The Falls (2012)

DIRECTOR: Jon Garcia
SCREENPLAY: Jon Garcia
CAST: Nick Ferrucci (RJ), Benjamin Farmer (Chris), Brian J. Saville Allard (Rodney), Quinn Allen (Elder Harris), Harold Phillips (Thomas)
SPECS: 91 minutes; color
AVAILABILITY: DVD (Lake Productions, Breaking Glass Pictures)

The Falls: Testament of Love (2013)

DIRECTOR: Jon Garcia
SCREENPLAY: Jon Garcia
CAST: Nick Ferrucci (RJ), Benjamin Farmer (Chris), Hannah Barefoot (Emily), Bruce Jennings (Noah), Harold Philips (Thomas)
SPECS: 133 minutes; color
AVAILABILITY: DVD (Lake Productions, Breaking Glass Pictures)

The Falls: Covenant of Grace (2016)

DIRECTOR: Jon Garcia
SCREENPLAY: Rodney Moore
CAST: Nick Ferrucci (RJ), Benjamin Farmer (Chris), Curtis Edward Jackson (Ryan), Bruce Jennings (Noah), Harold Philips (Thomas)
SPECS: 119 minutes; color
AVAILABILITY: DVD (Lake Productions, Breaking Glass Pictures)

The eponymous first film of the *Falls* trilogy tells the story of two young Mormon missionaries: RJ Smith and Chris Merrill. RJ and Chris are roommates and mission companions, sharing a small apartment while stationed in Oregon. They are not particularly successful at converting others to the Church of Jesus Christ of Latter-day Saints (LDS), but during their time together, they befriend a Vietnam veteran, Rodney. In Rodney's company they experiment with smoking marijuana, watch movies, and begin to neglect their duties as missionaries. One evening at a diner, RJ confronts Chris about their situation. Their conversation is witnessed by a group of agitators who taunt them with homophobic slurs. They get into a fight, and RJ punches one of their attackers. After the fight, the two young men appear to demonstrate affection toward each other: Chris tenderly holds ice on RJ's injured hand, and later, RJ watches Chris while he is sleeping. Soon after, their growing attraction for each other culminates in sexual intercourse near a deserted railway line.

In the unfolding story line, their continued lack of success in their mission work eventually comes to the attention of their missionary zone leader when he walks in on the two young men in bed together. The incident is reported to the LDS authorities, forcing RJ to return to his family. However, through the influence of his father, Chris is allowed to complete his mission. The film concludes with Chris following the advice of Rodney to write to RJ and propose a road trip together.

The Falls: Testament of Love picks up the story after RJ and Chris have parted ways as lovers. RJ now lives in Seattle. He is estranged from the church, has a new boyfriend named Paul, and is an emerging writer and magazine editor. Chris has instead embraced his faith, married a woman named Emily, and is now a father to daughter Kaylee. The two former missionaries reunite briefly at Rodney's funeral, but their relationship is strained. RJ is extremely unsettled, breaking up with Paul and flying to Salt Lake City to confront Chris. Chris is angry that RJ's presence threatens his life as a straight Mormon family man. Eventually, however, they meet at RJ's hotel and have sex. Chris calls a family meeting and reveals that he is in love with RJ. His family is outraged at what has happened, directing all blame toward RJ.

In the unfolding story line, during his parents' twenty-fifth wedding anniversary, Chris sings a religious song but is interrupted by RJ, who storms into the gathering and kisses Chris passionately. Having rejected the LDS church in its entirety, RJ returns to Seattle alone. Although he receives a letter from Chris forgiving him for disrupting the anniversary celebrations, the status of their relationship remains unresolved.

At the opening of *The Falls: Covenant of Grace*, Chris is living alone in Salt Lake City—divorced but still connected to the church. Chris visits RJ, who lives in Portland, yet there is tension between them because of their differing relationships to the church. During a run together, they begin to fight, and RJ suffers a panic attack over their continued arguing about religion.

Back in Salt Lake City, Chris's mother dies suddenly. RJ quickly decides he must go to support Chris by traveling to Salt Lake City, accompanied by his father, Tom, who has grown increasingly supportive of his son. Their attendance at the Merrill family home at a time of mourning causes tension. RJ returns to Portland and the support of his queer friendship group. Though still unsure of his relationship with Chris, he rejects the advances of a young gay man who has a crush on him. Chris's father, Noah—once utterly opposed to his son's sexual identity and his relationship with RJ—begins to recognize the love that exists between them. Noah (Elder Merrill), a senior member of the LDS church, unsuccessfully lobbies its highest leadership group to change church teaching on same-sex relationships. Eventually, RJ and Chris reunite: Chris proposes marriages and RJ accepts.

According to *Variety*, the first film in the trilogy was made over twenty-five days on a budget of just seven thousand dollars. *The Falls* achieved cult status among indie viewers, a popularity that was leveraged to attract fan funding to make the subsequent films. Despite the relative lack of financing, viewer responses were overwhelmingly positive: the final installment, *The Falls: Covenant of Grace*, has a *Rotten Tomatoes* positive rating of 95 percent (2016).

At just an hour and a half of screen time, *The Falls* is somewhat short for a feature-length movie, and its somewhat clunky dialogue, rough plotting, and patchy acting go hand in hand with its lack of big financing. The production values of the subsequent films improved, but the almost unscripted and impromptu quality of the dialogue of the original is maintained across the trilogy. The simple aesthetic of these films is devoid of artificial cinematic effects, and the soundtracks are subtle; for example, silences are often left unfilled by nondiegetic music. Unconstrained by big-budget financing, the focus is very much on the growing intimacy of two young men, without recourse to sophisticated production values or high-profile actors who could bring established star personas to their roles. Together with the somewhat erratic nature of the plot, these features are arguably part of the realist charm of this trilogy.

Male nudity and gay sex scenes are included rather than omitted from these films. While the sex is not explicit or pornographic, it is quite clear that the main protagonists engage in foreplay, oral, and anal sex. Brett Farmer, the actor who plays lead character Chris Merrill, appears in full-frontal nudity in a shower scene, and the kisses between Farmer and fellow actor Nick Ferrucci are passionate and full of longing. Both actors identify as straight, and yet there is an obvious chemistry between them. Farmer observes that "kissing Nick was just as nerve-wracking as kissing any female co-star. It puts you in a very vulnerable place, but there was and is a lot of trust between Nick and myself. He's a very lovable man and a tremendous actor" (Cromer 2018).

Director and writer Jon Garcia highlights the physical, emotional, and spiritual intimacy of the two male protagonists. This is not simply the story of two gay Mormons who meet each other and are compelled to come out by their love—or lust—for each other. Rather, the films explore the difficulties the protagonists have in their attempts to reconcile faith, family, and sexuality. The consequences of this struggle are made apparent and include the splintering of family relationships, divorce, financial strain, shared parenting, and betrayal.

The Falls trilogy follows C. Jay Cox's 2003 movie *Latter Days* in its critical engagement with homophobic attitudes and beliefs in the Church of Jesus Christ of Latter Day Saints. Garcia does not, however, make fun of Mormonism. Unlike the musical-comedy stage show *The Book of Mormon* (first staged in 2011), the films in *The Falls* trilogy do not make lewd jokes or rely on clichés about "magic underpants." In fact, the aesthetics and traditions of Mormonism—the uniforms of the missionaries, the androcentric culture of the LDS leadership, the white veil of the temple, and the sacred undergarments worn by RJ and Chris—are woven into the most visually sumptuous elements of the cinematography, as well as the narrative focus on the central relationship between the two young men.

The resolution of *The Falls* trilogy points toward a heteronormative, monogamous relationship between RJ and Chris as the desired/desirable outcome. The final voice-over tells audiences that RJ and Chris are married and live together in Salt Lake City, the spiritual center of Mormonism. In an interview with *Beliefnet* in 2004, C. Jay Cox suggested that being gay and being Mormon are incompatible, an idea he explored in his own film about gay Mormon missionaries. Jon Garcia's approach is more nuanced. Indeed, embedded in the classic romantic narrative closure to the trilogy is the idea that religion—in this case,

Mormonism—can be folded into a gay love story. This is, arguably, the hallmark of the queer politics of these films: they do not suggest that abandoning religion or family is the only or automatic route open to the pursuit of same-sex love.

See also *I Am Michael*; *Yes, God, Yes*.

Bibliography

Cox, C. Jay. "A Topic Deeply Buried." *Beliefnet*, 2004. Accessed February 2, 2021. https://www .beliefnet.com/faiths/christianity/latter-day-saints/2004/02/a-topic-deeply-buried.aspx.

Cromer, Ruby. "Benjamin Farmer: Advocate." *A&U*, May 4, 2018. Accessed February 2, 2021. https://www.aumag.org/2018/05/04/benjamin-farmer-advocate/?fbclid=IwAR1GVsbAX2 _hQ_Oj2U9fI-8blZ0-PMLgjgi0q7VZ01pJ3lQEpDh0luEWRHQ.

Harvey, Dennis. "Film Review—*The Falls: Testament of Love*." *Variety*, October 29, 2013. Accessed February 2, 2021. https://www.variety.com/2013/film/reviews/the-falls-testament-of -love-review-1200776127/.

"The Falls: Covenant of Grace." Rotten Tomatoes, 2016. Accessed February 2, 2021. https:// www.rottentomatoes.com/m/the_falls_covenant_of_grace.

—Paul Venzo

FAR FROM HEAVEN (2002)

DIRECTOR: Todd Haynes
SCREENPLAY: Todd Haynes
CAST: Julianne Moore (Cathy Whitaker), Dennis Quaid (Frank Whitaker), Dennis Haysbert (Raymond Deagan)
SPECS: 107 minutes; color
AVAILABILITY: DVD (Universal Pictures Home Entertainment)

Cathy and Frank Whitaker are the ideal suburban postwar power couple; Frank is a top salesman for a Westinghouse-like company called Magnatech, while Cathy is a doting housewife and mother of two cookie-cutter children, a boy and girl. They live in an attractive home in Hartford, Connecticut, with all of the modern amenities, making them the envy of their neighbors. They wear pastel-colored clothing, they drive practical cars, they go to ballet recitals, they have a "Negro" maid and gardener while also being "friends" to the NAACP; in essence, they have what most white all-American couples want—everything—that is, until they lose it all when Frank's dark secret bubbles to the surface and opens a Pandora's box of same-sex longings and miscegenation. Written and directed by Todd Haynes and starring Julianne Moore, Dennis Quaid, and Dennis Haysbert, *Far from Heaven* (2002) is an homage to director Douglas Sirk and the 1950s melodrama films that were censored by the Hollywood production code.

According to "The Motion Picture Production Code" (Board of Directors of Motion Picture Producers and Distributors of America Inc. 1931), "No picture will lower the moral standards of those who see it. Hence the sympathy of the audience should never be thrown to the side of crime, wrongdoing, evil or sin" (595). Further: "The sanctity of marriage and the home shall be upheld," and motion pictures "shall not infer that low forms of sex relationship are the accepted or common thing" (595). Some of those low forms include "sexual perversion" and "miscegenation," which run parallel with "White slavery" and "seduction

or rape." Because of these restrictions, directors, including Sirk, although compli-
ant, continuously needed to find ways to work around the code even if it meant
using subversive tactics like placing hats on beds, lighting another person's
cigarette, or having couples kiss, break, then kiss again. As discussed in his
article about Sirk's relationship to German filmmakers, Eric Rentschler writes,
"Films like *All that Heaven Allows* and *Written on the Wind* [were a] popular
form [that] could be recast to appeal to audience expectations while simultaneously undermining them" (2005, 156). The "popular form" Rentschler speaks of
is melodrama, a marketable form of filmmaking heavily produced after World
War II and primarily promoted to mothers and war-weary wives. As Kenneth
MacKinnon states:

> [The] movies never seem to corroborate fully the family's self-image or to avoid
> exposure of the gaps between what is and what is willed to be. The families end
> with a new fiction, more securely insulated against the inroads of unwelcome
> actuality, or else transform themselves into a muted form of bourgeois nuclear
> family which has somehow been transformed by love. (2004, 36)

In other words, women could go to these movies, watch exaggerated familial conflict, which is far worse than what they have at home and is magically "resolved"
by the end credits, leaving the women properly satiated. What these women failed
to realize, or maybe realized but did not want to address, was although these
melodramas kept the family whole, how could it be after what has happened to it?

Far from Heaven is what film directors like Sirk wanted to create but could
not. The film opens with the happy nuclear family but ends with a family that
has gone nuclear. Ultimately, Cathy becomes a divorced mother of two, alone
and waving goodbye to a Black man she has fallen in love with while her ex-
husband is hunkered down in a seedy hotel room with his male lover. This breakdown is because Cathy, in an attempt to get her husband to stop working and
start eating, goes to his office to find him passionately kissing another man he
picked up in a gay bar. This leads to Frank trying to live the life of a straight man;
he even goes to a conversion therapist to get "fixed" of his "perversion." The
characters never seem to gain their footing, however. Frank tries to make love to
his wife while in a drunken stupor, they try to converse about their issues, they
even try to go on vacation to get some much-needed relaxation; however, it is
all for naught. During this vacation, Frank meets the man he falls in love with.
In a way, *Far from Heaven*, like any good pastiche, pays homage to a time when
Hollywood cinema was grand but shows viewers what the reality of situations
like this may be: we cannot hide from our true selves, because it will destroy
not only us as individuals but the families we so desperately want to hold on to.

See also *Gilda; Hail, Caesar!; The Uninvited.*

Bibliography

Board of Directors of Motion Picture Producers and Distributors of America Inc. "The Motion
   Picture Production Code." March 31, 1930. Accessed June 26, 2021. https://www.asu.edu
   /courses/fms200s/total-readings/MotionPictureProductionCode.pdf.
MacKinnon, Kenneth. "The Family in Hollywood Melodrama: Actual or Ideal?" *Journal of Gender Studies* 13, no. 1 (March 2004): 29–36.

Rentschler, Eric. "Douglas Sirk Revisited: The Limits and Possibilities of Artistic Agency." *New German Critique* 95 (Spring/Summer 2005): 149–61.

—Douglas C. MacLeod Jr.

FATHER OF THE BRIDE SERIES (1991, 1995, 2020)
Father of the Bride (1991)

DIRECTOR: Charles Shyer
SCREENPLAY: Charles Shyer and Nancy Meyers, inspired by the film of the same name by Vincente Minnelli
CAST: Steve Martin (George Banks), Diane Keaton (Nina Banks), Martin Short (Franck Eggelhoffer), Kimberly Williams (Annie Banks-MacKenzie), Kieran Culkin (Matty Banks), George Newbern (Bryan MacKenzie), BD Wong (Howard Weinstein)
SPECS: 105 minutes; color
AVAILABILITY: DVD (Buena Vista Entertainment)

Father of the Bride Part II (1995)

DIRECTOR: Charles Shyer
SCREENPLAY: Nancy Meyers and Charles Shyer, inspired by the film *Father's Little Dividend* by Vincente Minnelli
CAST: Steve Martin (George Banks), Diane Keaton (Nina Banks), Martin Short (Franck Eggelhoffer), Kimberly Williams (Annie Banks-MacKenzie), Kieran Culkin (Matty Banks), George Newbern (Bryan MacKenzie), BD Wong (Howard Weinstein)
SPECS: 106 minutes; color
AVAILABILITY: DVD (Walt Disney Studios Home Entertainment)

Father of the Bride Part 3(ish) (2020)

DIRECTOR: Nancy Meyers
SCREENPLAY: Nancy Meyers
CAST: Steve Martin (George Banks), Diane Keaton (Nina Banks), Martin Short (Franck Eggelhoffer), Kimberly Williams (Annie Banks-MacKenzie), Kieran Culkin (Matty Banks), George Newbern (Bryan MacKenzie)
SPECS: 25 minutes; color
AVAILABILITY: YouTube

The *Father of the Bride* films are light comedies that focus on the Banks family. Patriarch George Banks, proprietor of an athletic shoe company, is married to Nina. The Banks have two children, Annie and Matty. Annie marries Bryan in the first film. The sequel sees Annie and Nina both pregnant. In the third installment, a short filmed during the COVID-19 pandemic, the characters reunite some fifteen years after the sequel for the marriage of Matty. A major supporting character in the films is Franck Eggelhoffer, a much-in-demand wedding planner whose grand vision and expensive tastes drive George's wedding costs astronomically high. In the short-film sequel, Franck returns, this time as a family friend and an interior decorator.

Father of the Bride is the work of frequent collaborators Charles Shyer and Nancy Meyers, who were married when making their films together. The inspiration for the first film was Vincent Minnelli's 1950 film of the same name (the sequel was inspired, in part, by the 1950 film's sequel, *Father's Little Dividend*). The thrust of the comedy lies in the escalating costs and stresses that George experiences as he pays for his daughter's wedding; additionally, comedy resides in his midlife crisis. The films were produced by Touchstone Pictures, a film company that operated under Walt Disney Studios Motion Pictures. Both studio films were released during the Christmas season and were marketed toward wide family audiences. The tone of the films—and the aesthetics—are bright, sunny, and aggressively mainstream. The characters are moneyed, white, heterosexual, and cisgendered. The only disruption to the homogeny is the appearance of Franck, an extravagantly flamboyant man, who appears as a counterpoint to the seemingly middle-of-the-road "normal" George. Reportedly inspired by Hollywood wedding planner Kevin Lee, Franck is a loud and cacophonous riot of gay male stereotypes as well as European clichés. Though not explicitly queer, his appearance and his characterization perform many of the expectations of queerness, particularly in men: his labor is gendered and Othered, and his function is a comically exaggerated variation on the fairy godmother. His relationships to the other characters and their approach to him also reveal clues to his vague queerness: namely, he is inscrutable to the more traditionally masculine George, but he immediately hits it off with Nina and Annie. But because the *Father of the Bride* films are carefully coordinated and planned to appeal to a wide audience, there is little to actually offend in Franck's character: his conception, as delivered by comedian Martin Short, manages to avoid charges of homophobia because his character is rendered so broadly; the result is a character so cartoonish and artificial he becomes nearly asexual.

Franck's character is introduced in *Father of the Bride* forty minutes into the film. The Banks family meets Franck at his place of business, a celebration of wedding excess. The showroom of his shop is stuffed with baroque, ornate furnishings and decors. There are small tables crowding the space, elaborately carved chairs, an impressively constructed wedding cake, and it seems as if any available space is crammed with extravagant flower arrangements. The space is dominated by traditionally feminine concerns, and therefore a power imbalance is struck: though George is the primary breadwinner in the situation (he is paying for the wedding), it is Nina, Annie, and Franck who dominate in this space. The environment is not only traditionally feminine but also an alter to consumerism—but more specifically, *gendered* consumerism. George in his tasteful-if-bland gray suit is visually out of place, and Nina and Annie—in their lovely creams and pastel pinks—fit right in. Though Franck's workplace is sumptuous and beautiful, meant to impress his clients, it is nonetheless an important center for commerce, consumerism, and queer- and female-centered labor—not to mention an industry that is predicated on wealthy and busy women. As academic Kristin Blakely writes, "Wedding planners are a form of outsourced labor; the unpaid work of mothers and daughters are transported from the home to the public marketplace" (2008).

Diane Keaton as Nina Banks, Steve Martin as George Stanley Banks, Martin Short as Franck Eggelhoffer, and Kimberly Williams as Annie Banks in *Father of the Bride*. Courtesy of Buena Vista Pictures/Photofest.

Before viewers are introduced to Franck, they see his assistant Howard Weinstein (played by openly gay actor BD Wong). Like Franck, Howard is a character with visual cues that indicate queerness: his role as Franck's assistant speaks to the gendered notion of labor, particularly gendered connotations of the assistant, a role largely seen as feminine—according to one study, all jobs seen as "gay" were also seen as stereotypical female jobs (Hancock, Clark, and Arnold 2020). Like George, Howard is dressed in a suit, but he is far more fashionable and trendier in his clothing—though the fashion is slightly stylized to make a visual gag; and unlike George, who is nonplussed with the environment, Howard is at home. There are also the vaguely feminine cues of his pseudo-European affectations.

When viewers finally meet Franck, he breezes into the room, announcing his arrival with his comically indecipherable European accent that renders "Mister and Missus Banks" to "*Master* and *Moooses Bahnks*." Like Howard Weinstein, Franck's visual presentation is meant to convey a cartoonishly safe rendition of the campy fop. Franck's hair is teased and sculpted into a pompadour, and he is chicly attired in a sharp black suit, a bright red tie (emblazoned with a heart), and a fancy waistcoat. When he greets Nina and Annie, he is a caricature of officiousness, slathering the women's hands with kisses, before launching into an incomprehensible monologue, punctuated by his limp-wristed gesticulations.

Due to George's voice-overs, viewers are privy to his personal thoughts, and he is baffled by Franck's suggesting that the wedding planner will have to work in "subtitles." Though there is little to indicate that George is homophobic or contemptuous of Franck's fey carriage, there is a giant maw that is carved between the two men because of the masculine/feminine binary that the two characters are playing out; George, the stolid, straight family man who is paying for his daughter's wedding versus the partnerless, sexless Franck who is an assemblage of fruity gags. Director Charles Shyer frames the interactions very deliberately to highlight the feminine atmosphere that Franck curated: The wall is covered in a thick, floral tapestry. Though it is the middle of the afternoon, Franck's desk is lit with a Liberace-like candelabra. Expensive china dots the space. As Franck boasts he designed his workspace, viewers see that it is ornate and extreme, though over-the-top and gaudy. When addressing the Banks family, he is flanked by a bouquet of tropical flowers and a gigantic crystal and bronze candelabra. A huge bouquet of roses peek from behind Franck as he stands in front of a riot of lush and deep reds and golds.

Though Franck was by most accounts the breakout character of *Father of the Bride*, his presence in the film is remarkably brief—roughly fifteen minutes. This is due to the power of Short's performance as well as the nearly vaudevillian comedy of the character who looms so large in the film. Like many minorities in mainstream, white-centered narratives, Franck's sole role in the film is to serve and to provide a service, to support the genial, straight white people, and not to have a personal life of his own; his character is defined by his stereotypically gay job as well as what he can do to help the Bankses. The film seems almost a precursor for *Queer Eye for the Straight Guy*, in which fashionably queer men are dispatched to make the lives of straight folks more stylish. Research has shown that "gay male consultants in [wedding planning] are in the most demand . . . gay men are able to command a higher service fee because of preconceived, stereotypical notions that brides have about working with them" (Blakely 2008). Some studies have supported the theory that sexual minority status could be seen as a benefit and impart certain privilege to queer people, and some research has shown that some would be "more likely to hire a gay or lesbian applicant" for certain roles (Hancock, Clark, and Arnold 2020). The space that Franck created for himself professionally tracks with what studies show when examining trends in queer labor, particularly queer professionals who are "more likely to work in occupations with higher task independence" (Vieira 2016); Franck operates in a space—self-curated and self-managed—in which he is solely in charge and where his professional interactions lie solely in delegating and supervising.

Father of the Bride Part II's plot charts the predictable progression of the characters: after getting married, Annie discovers she is expecting. Due to the film's convoluted machinations, viewers also discover that Nina is pregnant, so George is facing impending grandfatherhood and fatherhood simultaneously. As with the first film, viewers are reunited with Franck and Howard about forty minutes into the film, when Nina and George run into their former wedding planner at the doctor's office after learning that she is pregnant. As George stresses and fusses, his voice-over frets about having a baby at their age and declares ominously that nothing could top his news, but he is wrong, as the elevator doors open to reveal Franck in mid-wrist-flapping soliloquy with Howard. Upon spying their old friends, Franck greets the perpetually reticent George with a jolly kiss. He then launches into a confession of the various minor cosmetic procedures he has had at the office, again, leaning into stereotypes of gay male vanity, which intersect with clichés of feminine vanity.

The return of Franck in the sequel translates to more over-the-top consumerism and spending. Not only does Franck create a massive baby shower for Nina and Annie, but he also evolves from just a party planner to an interior decorator, insinuating himself into the family's life by conducting a major renovation to the family home, which includes a horrifyingly expensive nursery for Nina's infant. As with the first film, Franck's role again is one of servitude—though paid servitude. He seems to have suspended his personal life to serve as a helper for the family. Again, though none of the characters of the *Father of the Bride* could be considered well rounded or complex, Franck's character is especially one-note and truncated. Whether hauling fabric samples to the Banks home or leading the pregnant women in a farcical aerobics class, Franck again performs the role of the fairy godmother, his sole purpose to provide assistance to the straight Banks family. Because of Franck's murky sexuality and sexual identity, masculinity is not much of a topic when looking at his characterization—another reason why he does not seem to feel the need to assert any traditional masculinity nor exhibit any anxieties about his alleged lack of traditional masculinity.

In *Father of the Bride Part 3(ish)*, viewers see Matty marrying his fiancée, a frontline worker. The characters meet to celebrate Matty's nuptials via Zoom, as millions of other families have during pandemic lockdowns. Franck's return with a few new characters (including a cameo by Robert DeNiro as Matty's future father-in-law) again serves as marginal character, though, as in the second film, he is folded into the Banks family as an honorary member (a flamboyant gay uncle). Though some may see Franck as a base stereotype of gay male clichés, the films cannot be taken seriously as an objectionable or homophobic representation of male queerness because the sentimental and friendly tone of the films take the sting out of any potential offense and the overwhelming friendliness and good-natured tone of the films ensure that any kidding or joking done in the films is all in good fun.

See also *Big Daddy*; *Just Go with It*.

Bibliography

Blakely, Kristin. "Busy Brides and the Business of Family Life: The Wedding-Planning Industry and the Commodity Frontier." *Journal of Family Issues* 29, no. 5 (2008): 639–62.

Doyle, Alison. "Top 10 Jobs in the LGBTQ Community." The Balance Careers, February 13, 2020. Accessed March 20, 2021. https://www.thebalancecareers.com/top-lgbtq-jobs-2059651.

Hancock, Amanda, Heather Clarke, and Kara Arnold. "Sexual Orientation Occupational Stereotypes." *Journal of Vocational Behavior*, April 13, 2020. Accessed March 25, 2021. https://www.researchgate.net/publication/340801225_Sexual_orientation_occupational_stereotypes.

Vieira, Helena. "There May Be Some Truth to the 'Gay Jobs' Stereotypes." London School of Economics blog, January 18, 2016. Accessed March 20, 2021. https://blogs.lse.ac.uk/business review/2016/01/18/there-may-be-some-truth-to-the-gay-jobs-stereotype/.

—Peter Piatkowski

FIGHT CLUB (1999)

DIRECTOR: David Fincher
SCREENPLAY: Jim Uhls, based on the novel *Fight Club* by Chuck Palahniuk
CAST: Edward Norton (Narrator), Brad Pitt (Tyler Durden), Helena Bonham
  Carter (Marla Singer)
SPECS: 139 minutes; color
AVAILABILITY: DVD (Walt Disney Studios)

Fight Club's unnamed narrator is an IKEA-living/loving insomniac debilitated by
and discontented with his life. Clearly suffering from sleeplessness, the narrator
seeks help from a physician but is refused medication. The narrator is scolded,
"You want to see pain? Swing by First Methodist Tuesday nights. See the guys
with testicular cancer. That's pain." While the doctor is being facetious, the narrator visits Remaining Men Together at First Methodist and experiences instant
catharsis. As a result, he assumes a number of identities in order to join various
other support groups, finding relief and, by extension, sleep after each meeting.
However, this respite is short-lived. The narrator encounters the destitute Marla
Singer at Remaining Men Together. She is soon discovered to be a support group
"tourist" (i.e., a fraud) whose very presence leads to tension and a repeated bout
of insomnia for the central protagonist. Meanwhile, in another "chance encounter" on a plane, the narrator meets the mysterious Tyler Durden. Durden quickly
takes the narrator down a self-destructive path that begins with his carefully
curated apartment being blown up and ends with half of his face being blown off.
Between these two explosive events, the men establish an underground fighting
club as a way to enable them to cope with their dissatisfaction with society, as
it spans consumer culture, gender roles, and work-place aspirations. As the club
grows, the two men spiral out of control. Durden begins a sexual relationship
with Singer, the narrator blackmails his boss, and they both begin a shady business of selling (human-based) soap to high-end boutiques. The film reaches its
climax when the narrator uncovers Durden's hidden agenda for Fight Club, Project Mayhem, an attempt to erase consumer debt by way of chaos and destruction.
However, one plot twist remains. In a dingy hotel room, the narrator is revealed
to suffer from dissociative identity disorder, and Durden is exposed as his "alter
ego." The film slams to a conclusion as the narrator attempts to expel Durden
and stop Project Mayhem's destruction.

   Fight Club is a film about hegemonic masculinity, and irrespective of whether
the title is read as critical commentary on male power and aggression as part of a
discourse on masculinity in crisis or as an endorsement of male brutality, there
is no denying that the film presents a myriad of punished and punishing male
bodies in close physical contact. Men of all shapes and sizes are seen delivering
and experiencing pain as a cathartic release and relief against the backdrop of a
consumer-driven society. Although there is scope to talk about muscular bodies
as a site of erotic display for spectators in the way that Western, war, action, and
adventure movies are routinely examined as a site for spectacular bodies, the difference here is that these are not heroic bodies destined to take on the form of an
on-screen surrogate; rather, these are seemingly interchangeable bodies who are
deemed disposable in the narrative (Neale 1994; Fradley 2004).

Brad Pitt as Tyler Durden and Edward Norton as the narrator in *Fight Club*. Courtesy of Twentieth Century Fox/Photofest.

That said, there does remain scope to read *Fight Club* as a queer narrative, based in part on the "homoerotic overtones of gay author Palahniuk's novel" (Eloise 2019). This reading is not because of any openly LGBTQIA+ characters in the film, but rather because of the film's dramatic and climactic opening and closing sequence whereby the narrator is tied up with Durden's gun in his mouth, a sequence that leans a little heavily on phallic power and mastery. Phallic dominance is taken further with the split-second penis frames that are spliced into the family-friendly films within the text and *Fight Club* itself. Moreover, when the underground Fight Club emerges and flourishes, viewers are told that the first rule of Fight Club is that no one talks about Fight Club, a phrase that leaves audiences with the uncomfortable reality that such secrecy would have been and continues to be used in all-male bars and clubs that enable gay men to meet in a homphobic society. In short, the fight club in *Fight Club* could be read as "an analogy for homosexual sex" (Holmes 2021).

However, even if one overlooks the phallic symbolism and potentially closeting rule of the club, the relationship between the narrator and his alter ego has routinely been read as queer. Feeling trapped at work and home, a chance meeting followed by fighting and moving in with Tyler Durden gives the narrator a new outlook on life. Relocating from a carefully curated apartment to a large, dilapidated house finds the narrator balancing his old life while succumbing to the charisma and opportunities that stem from his friendship with Durden. Jude Dry refers to the narrator as "ardently pining" for his doppelganger (2017), while fan theories talk about the narrator being sexually attracted to Durden, stating that it is only when he merges with his alter ego that he can find and feel affection and attraction for Marla Singer (r/FanTheories 2016). After all, although the narrator had contact details for both Singer and Durden, it was Durden whom he chose to call when he needed a place to stay, and it is therefore Durden rather than Singer with whom he sets up a house in the manner of a 1950s sitcom. The narrator even goes so far as to describe life with Durden as reminiscent of "Ozzie and Harriet." This is an unabashed reference to the married couple of the long-running American sitcom of that name. Clearly, the narrator enjoys their time together, excluding work and support groups for their domesticated days and aggressive nights and becoming jealous and possessive when Durden gives his attention to other characters, male or female, in the narrative.

Although the film could be accused of homophobia, for interweaving "homosexuality" with toxic masculinity and for conflating homoeroticism with sadomasochism, it is equally possible to read the film as a liberating site of male camaraderie and a debunking of heteronormativity. In this later reading, the narrator kills Durden not as a "rejection of homosexuality, but as a rejection of toxic masculinity . . . as a healthy embrace of the narrator's feminine side, in contrast to his earlier misogynistic rejection of it" (Holmes 2021). Therefore, even though Karen Ashcroft and Lisa Flores suggest that *Fight Club* flirts with the homosocial before concluding with compulsory heterosexuality (2000, 21), the film could be read as queer because of its ability to disrupt "predetermined gender identities" (Peele 2001, 868). That said, even though Marianne Eloise offers up a number of homoerotic "teasings" (2019), Robert Alan Brookey and Robert Westerfelhaus have argued that such elements cannot be read as queer when watched in tandem with the extratextual materials provided on the DVD. Although the narrative might be read as homoerotic or homosexual, the running commentaries provided by the film's "director, actors, and writers use denial, dismissal, and distraction to undermine the validity of a homosexual interpretation" (Brookey and Westerfelhaus 2002, 30). In short, rather than leave the film open to interpretation, the DVD constrains queer readings via a "digital closet" and "homosexual erasure" (21–43).

Fight Club is a fascinating film in terms of its commentary on gender, sexuality, and society, but it remains for individuals to decide how they read the central protagonist(s) here, based on how much time and attention they give to review media, supporting commentaries, or subsequent theories from within the fields of queer, feminist, or media theory.

See also *American Beauty*.

Bibliography

Ashcraft, Karen, and Lisa Flores. "Slaves with White Collars: Persistent Performances of Masculinity in Crisis." *Text and Performance Quarterly* 23, no. 1 (2000): 1–29.

Brookey, Robert Alan, and Robert Westerfelhaus. "Hiding Homoeroticism in Plain View: The *Fight Club* DVD as Digital Closet." *Critical Studies in Media Communication* 19, no. 1 (2002): 21–43.

Dry, Jude. "The Best Queer Films You Didn't Know Were Queer, from *Fight Club* to *Who Framed Roger Rabbit*." *Indiewire*, July 7, 2017. Accessed March 29, 2021. https://www.indie

wire.com/2017/07/best-lgbt-films-you-didnt-know-were-queer-fight-club-gay-lesbian-movies -showgirls-1201851309/2/.

Eloise, Marianne. "Why We Shouldn't Take David Fincher's Masterpiece So Seriously." *Games-Rader+*, October 15, 2019. Accessed March 29, 2021. https://www.gamesradar.com/uk/fight -club- anniversary-david-fincher-toxic-masculinity/.

Fradley, Martin. "Maximus Melodramaticus: Masculinity, Masochism and White Male Paranoia in Contemporary Hollywood Cinema." In *Action and Adventure Cinema*, edited by Yvonne Tasker, 235–51. Oxford: Routledge, 2004.

Holmes, Ivor. "Interpreting *Fight Club*: Masculinity and Homoeroticism." *Muse*, March 3, 2021. Accessed March 29, 2021. https://nouse.co.uk/2021/03/03/interpreting-fight-club-masculinity -and-homoeroticism.

Lindgren, Simon. "A Copy, of a Copy, of a Copy? Exploring Masculinity under Transformation in *Fight Club*." *Scope: An Online Journal of Film and Television Studies* 19 (2011): 1–27.

Neale, Steve. "Masculinity as Spectacle: Reflections on Men and Mainstream Cinema." In *Screening the Male: Exploring Masculinities in Hollywood Cinema*, edited by Steve Cohan and Ina Rae Hark, 9–22. London: Routledge, 1994.

Peele, Thomas. "*Fight Club's* Queer Representations." *JAC* 21, no. 4 (2001): 862–69.

r/FanTheories. "*Fight Club*—My Theory Is That the Protagonist Is Gay. **Spoilers Included**." Reddit, May 30, 2016. Accessed March 29, 2021. https://www.reddit.com/r/FanTheories /comments/4xwf1v/fight_club_my_theory_is_that_the_protagonist_is/.

—Rebecca Feasey

FRIGHT NIGHT (1985)

DIRECTOR: Tom Holland
SCREENPLAY: Tom Holland
CAST: William Ragsdale (Charley Brewster), Amanda Bearse (Amy Peterson), Chris Sarandon (Jerry Dandridge), Jonathan Stark (Billy Cole), Stephen Geoffreys (Edward Thompson), Roddy McDowall (Peter Vincent)
SPECS: 106 minutes; color
AVAILABILITY: DVD (Sony Pictures Home Entertainment)

Fright Night (1985) is a vampire film catering to the then-burgeoning teenage horror market of the mid-1980s. It focuses on Charley Brewster and his girlfriend Amy as Charley discovers his new next-door neighbor, Jerry Dandridge, is a vampire and is responsible for a series of murders in town. Of course, no one believes Charley, not even Amy and his friend Ed, initially. With nowhere to turn, Charley draws on his love of horror films and attempts to enlist the help of Peter Vincent, a washed-up actor who once played a vampire hunter in movies and now hosts a program called *Fright Night Theater* that often features vampire movies, to confront Jerry Dandridge. Vincent refuses, assuming Charley is a kooky fan. However, after Vincent is given an eviction notice, Amy and Ed offer him five hundred dollars to humor Charley's conviction that Dandridge is a vampire. At first, Dandridge seems immune to holy water (Vincent only gave him tap water) and a crucifix (one must believe for it to work), but Vincent notices that Dandridge is not visible in a pocket mirror, causing him to leave with the group in a panicked state, dropping the mirror on the way out. Dandridge becomes aware that the group knows of his vampiric nature by discovering a shard of Vincent's mirror. Dandridge follows Charley, Amy, and Ed as they try to walk home. When Ed ventures on his own, Dandridge turns him into a vampire. Dandridge then turns his sights on Charley and Amy, who have taken cover in a nightclub. Now a full-blown vampire, Ed attempts to attack Vincent in Vincent's apartment. Ed is thwarted when Vincent burns him with a crucifix. At the nightclub, Charley tries to call the police while Amy is hypnotically lured to and kidnapped by Dandridge. At his house, Dandridge dresses Amy in an evocative evening gown as the two caress one another. The scene ends with Amy moaning in ecstasy as she is bitten and turned into a vampire. Charley and Vincent regroup and confront Dandridge in his house but are interrupted by Dandridge's assistant, Billy. Billy is not a vampire but rather an undead supernatural being. With Billy seemingly getting the better of the two, Vincent retreats to Charley's house, where he is surprised by Ed. Vincent manages to stab Ed through the heart with stake, seemingly killing him. Vincent rejoins Charley, and the two are able to vanquish Billy, who turns to goo, sand, and bones when killed. With morning approaching, Dandridge tries to hide in the basement but is killed when Charley and Vincent break the black-painted windows, letting the sun shine through. With Dandridge slain, Amy returns to normal. *Fright Night* ends with Vincent back as the host of *Fright Night Theater*, which is taking a hiatus from the showing of vampire films, and Charley and Amy where they started the film—in Charley's room. Charley looks into Dandridge's house and notices a set of glowing red eyes, ignoring them before turning his attention back to Amy. Before the credits roll, Ed's laugh can be heard from Dandridge's home, spouting the line, "Oh, you're so cool Brewster!"

Though *Fright Night* foregrounds a heterosexual romance between Charley and Amy, the film is rife with homoerotic subtext. At the beginning of the film, Charley and Amy are making out. Amy tells him to stop, much to Charley's chagrin. While Charley expresses heterosexual frustration over his girlfriend's unwillingness to go "all the way," Charley also becomes obsessed with his new neighbor, Jerry Dandridge. He begins spying on Dandridge from his room with binoculars, seemingly putting a halt to his interest in and relationship with Amy. Indeed, at one point Amy breaks up with Charley for not giving her the attention she wants. It is only when Dandridge and Ed are out of the picture that Charley places his focus back on Amy. Even then, his attention is still attracted to the house next door.

Moreover, the characters of Jerry Dandridge, Ed Thompson, and Billy Cole have been read as gay (or metrosexual). Dandridge is impeccably dressed, suave, debonair, and preoccupied with his appearance, traits stereotypically associated with gay men or metrosexuals. Dandridge's relationship with Billy Cole also warrants further mention. Dandridge presumably has the ability to vampirize anyone of his choosing. It is thus telling that his chosen assistant is another well-dressed and immaculately manicured man. Likewise, Billy seems absolutely devoted to his master. Numerous scholars have pointed to a scene wherein Billy tends to an injured Dandridge, fixated mostly on the vampire's midsection, an implied act of fellatio. Ed offers another case of strongly implied same-sex desire. Throughout the film, he is not shown to have a girlfriend or as sexually desiring women. In the scene where Ed is turned into a vampire, Dandridge tells him, "I know what it's like to be different," and tells Ed, "They won't pick on you anymore. Or beat you up. I'll see to that," both possible insinuations of Ed's "homosexuality." Though *Fright Night*'s homoeroticism is strongly implied, editor Kent Beyda told John Kenneth Muir that the undertones were "very conscious" and that Director Tom Holland wanted to experiment with the sexual nature of vampirism (Muir 2012, 445).

See also *Dawn of the Dead; Let Me In.*

Bibliography

Benshoff, Harry M. *Monsters in the Closet: Homosexuality and the Horror Film.* Manchester: Manchester University Press, 1997.

Leeder, Murray. "Forget Peter Vincent: Nostalgia, Self-Reflexivity, and the Genre Past in *Fright Night.*" *Journal of Popular Film and Television* 36, no. 4 (2009): 190–99.

Muir, John Kenneth. *Horror Films of the 1980s.* Jefferson, NC: McFarland, 2012.

Ní Fhlainn, Sorcha. *Postmodern Vampires: Film, Fiction, and Popular Culture.* New York: Palgrave Macmillan, 2019.

—Todd K. Platts

• G •

THE GENESIS CHILDREN (1971)

DIRECTOR: Anthony Aikman
PRODUCER: Billy Byars
SCREENPLAY: Anthony Aikman and Billy Byars; Barbara Smith ("narration written by")
CAST: Vincent Child (Priest), Greg Hill (Greg), Peter Glawson (Peter)
SPECS: 84 minutes; color
AVAILABILITY: VHS/DVD (Award Films International)

A psychedelic allegory awash in religious symbolism and youthful male nudity, *The Genesis Children* begins as a quasi-Luciferian figure summons American children to perform a religious rite on a desolated Roman beach. Appearing alternately as a priest, pedagogue, and military policeman, he gives the boys only vague instructions; left to their own devices, the boys cast off their clothes and their civility, some discovering enlightenment and others only confusion. As they engage in male bonding, presumably in preparation for their ritual performance, they realize only too late that their act has already begun—that they, in effect, are their own audience. In the process, they descend into an innocent noble savagery, immolating an abandoned bus (symbolic of ugly modernity) and discovering the joys of playacting (they pretend to stab one other, at which point the film cuts not to spurting blood but to a cow's life-giving milk). As the adult world gradually disappears, the film escalates its religious imagery, proposing that the boys' *Robinson Crusoe*-esque adventure might usher in a second Genesis orchestrated by the omnipresent, pantheistic Lucifer figure.

The only feature film of British naturalist and travel writer Anthony Aikman (1942–2011), *The Genesis Children* is a fairly pretentious mix of new-age mysticism and Christian allegory, as the plot synopsis suggests. The film attracted considerable controversy—and is mainly remembered for—the abundant nudity of its young male cast, aged about ten to seventeen. Given present hysterias about pedophilia and even the slightest hints of underage nudity, it is difficult to imagine such a film being distributed today. At once naïve and voyeuristic, *The Genesis Children* is more or less the cinematic residue of the physique magazines of the 1950s and 1960s, which packaged nudity (for gay audiences) under the façade of fitness modeling.

The Genesis Children grew out of producer and cowriter Billy Byars's Lyric International, a company that in the 1960s had produced physique magazines and 8-mm and 16-mm shorts of adolescent (nonsexual) nudes, available to an underground clientele by mail order. In 1971, Lyric attempted to break into the (semi)mainstream with *The Genesis Children*, shot in 35 mm. In the same year, the company also launched *Zipper*, a *Playboy*-esque periodical for gay men that featured nude photo spreads alongside "legitimate" interviews with the likes of

Rod Stewart, David Cassidy, and Rock Hudson. Lyric International came to an ignominious end through the legal troubles incurred by Byars's relationship with Guy Strait (*not* a pseudonym), who engaged several of Lyric's underage models in illicit sexual relations. The publisher of pre-Stonewall gay newssheets such as the *League for Civic Education News* and the *Citizen News*, Strait was a notable (if also sketchy) figure in San Francisco's early gay rights movement. Strait's dalliances with the "Lyric boys," as they were called, exiled him from mainstream gay rights circles, and his subsequent 1973 trial for sexual abuse, spotlighted by the Attorney General's Commission on Pornography (aka the Meese Commission), catalyzed a mid-1970s panic over child pornography. Byars was immediately tainted by his business relationship with Strait, and Lyric International collapsed, sabotaging a planned follow-up to *The Genesis Children* called *Peter and the Desert Riders*, of which only production stills seem extant.

While many viewers undoubtedly will see *The Genesis Children* as exploitative, and some might deem it quasi-pornographic, discrepancies over the film's ratings certificate shed new light. While the film received an X rating in the United States, it was rated only G in Canada, proof in itself that prurience lies in the eye of the beholder (or is construed arbitrarily by unelected government bureaucrats). Even then, the ratings board of the Motion Picture Association of America did not grant the film its X in a knee-jerk fashion. A notoriously puritanical institution, the MPAA gave an X more reluctantly to *The Genesis Children* than to mainstream films such as *Midnight Cowboy* (1969) and *A Clockwork Orange* (1971), films originally rated X and later reclassified as R. According to a 1972 article in *After Dark* magazine, MPAA chief (and psychiatrist) Aaron Stern confessed, "*The Genesis Children* is really a very benign film . . . only the cumulative amount of nudity and the closeup shots of the pelvic area . . . brought about the X decision" (Swisher 1972, 18). On its face, Stern's reasoning makes little sense: if the film is in fact "very benign," why should it be stigmatized? Historically, the MPAA's one-size-fits-all guidelines have rarely parsed or contextualized nudity. "Closeup shots of the pelvic area" are seen as intrinsically indecent, even if their presentation would seem "benign" to the vast majority of the population not aroused by young boys. The X rating automatically categorizes the film as lewd, not by surveying a community's actual perceptions of the film but by assuming *some* audiences will see the film as inescapably pornographic. Ironically, the film was forbidden to boys who have presumably seen themselves naked before a mirror and whose gaze likely lacks predatory intent.

Once the film was freighted with the X rating, the filmmakers had little choice but to play both sides of the fence. On the one hand, they expressed indignant surprise that their Edenic allegory had been branded as pornography; Aikman's own website describes the film as akin to *Lord of the Flies*, never mentioning the contentious nudity. On the other hand, the film's advertising campaign capitalized on the stigmatic X, though in all fairness the filmmakers had little choice, for few theaters would screen X-rated films. A sensational ad in the *Los Angeles Free Press* featured the following caption over a silhouetted image of a torch-wielding boy: "If beauty offends you, do not, *do not*, see this film—for here are naked young boys on an Italian beach, searching for *the real meaning of life*! Rated X . . . Now playing!" ("The Genesis Children" 1972, 10). Needless to say, the ad neglected to expound the connections between nude beachfront boys and the "real" meaning of life, though it did guarantee patrons "free parking."

Reviewing *The Genesis Children* in the *Los Angeles Times* when it debuted at Hollywood's Encore Theater, critic Kevin Thomas tried to give Aikman and Byars the benefit of the doubt. "There's enough earnestness to *The Genesis Children* . . . to allow for the possibility that its makers had something more in mind than an adolescent male nudie," he suggests (1972, B-5). Thomas was unpersuaded by the religious allegory in which Aikman clothes the proceedings, however. He concludes that the film becomes a nudie "by default, so murky . . . is [the filmmaker's] philosophizing" (B-5). Many viewers will likely concur with Thomas's conclusion. The film's young, nonprofessional performers, many of whom appeared in Lyric's photo publications, were clearly chosen for their boyish looks and not their abilities to spin philosophical subject matter. The actors mostly fumble through their few line readings, and the lead boy's voice-over narration struggles to create meaning from disconnected musings about dreams, watchtowers, lost seashores, and various poetic clichés. Director Aikman does create a few memorably lyrical sequences, crosscutting attractive images of Roman streets with sunsets and the boys' nude frolics, often filmed in slow motion and accompanied by monastic chanting or a lush orchestral score.

The potential sexualization of underage performers extends, of course, into other media, as evidenced by the legal troubles that have plagued photographers such as Jock Sturges and David Hamilton, whose collections of artistic adolescent nudes have been pulled from bookstore shelves. At the same time, the 1992 Supreme Court decision *United States v. Knox*, which dealt with mail-order videos of underage girls "in underwear, leotards, or other thin but opaque clothing," claimed that intentional child pornography can exist in the absence of nudity, as long as the child is engaged in "actual or simulated lascivious exhibition." Despite its full nudity, *The Genesis Children* was not regarded by the court as "lascivious" (a subjective term, derived from the Latin *lascivia*, "lust"). Most notably and paradoxically, *The Genesis Children* was *not* banned but rather reframed, by dint of its X rating, as legal pornography (unlike *Midnight Cowboy* and *A Clockwork Orange*, *The Genesis Children* retains its X to this day). If protectors of public morality suspected—even correctly—that the film appealed to pedophilic interests, one would expect that they would have banned it outright. Instead, the film was categorized as pornography and shown only in art houses to a designated audience. As a result, the rating effectively created an adult gaze, ensuring that the only people who can see the film are precisely those most likely to have prurient interests.

See also *Beefcake*; *Boys Beware*; *Pink Narcissus*.

Bibliography
"The Genesis Children." *Los Angeles Free Press*, August 18–28, 1972, 10.
Swisher, Viola Hegyi. "Generating *The Genesis Children*." *After Dark*, September 1972, 18.
Thomas, Kevin. "*The Genesis Children* a Gambol on the Beach." *Los Angeles Times*, August 1, 1972.

—Andrew Grossman

GEOGRAPHY CLUB (2013)

DIRECTOR: Gary Entin

SCREENPLAY: Edmund Entin, based on the novel of the same name by Brent Hartinger

CAST: Cameron Deane Stewart (Russell Middlebrook), Justin Deeley (Kevin Land), Meaghan Martin (Trish), Andrew Lewis Calwell (Gunnar), Ally Maki (Min), Teo Olivares (Brian Bund), Allie Gonino (Kimberley)

SPECS: 84 minutes; color

AVAILABILITY: DVD (Shoreline Entertainment)

Geography Club is based on the young adult novel of the same name by Brent Hartinger (2003). The film is set in middle-class suburbia, surrounding the fictitious Goodkind High School, and centers on the teenage character Russell Middlebrook. Russell meets the handsome football player Kevin Land in a gay internet chat room, and a romance begins. Russell confides to his friend Min that he might be gay, and she, in turn, comes out to him as bisexual. Together, with a number of other "outsider" students, they form an undercover gay–straight alliance group at school, under the pseudonym "Geography Club," believing that a name of such mundanity will help to keep their identities a secret. Meanwhile, Kevin discovers that Russell has a talent for playing football. This is Russell's opportunity to become an insider with the school jocks. Added to this, another character named Brian Bund—a member of the Geography Club—is tormented by popular football players who accuse him of being gay (he is not).

An important subplot in the movie involves Russell's childhood friend Gunnar, who has no idea that Russell might be gay. Gunnar pressures Russell into double date with classmates Trish and Kimberley that ends in Russell's dismay as the entire school learns that he is gay. The narrative denouement occurs when Min and Russell have a falling out over Russell's unwillingness to stand up to the popular bullies on Brian's behalf. Kevin and Russell then have a falling out over Kevin's unwillingness to admit he is gay, and the Geography Club momentarily dissolves. To make things right, Russell finally defends Brian, apologizes to Min for being an unsupportive friend and ally, and comes out to the rest of the school. Gunnar and Russell eventually resolve their differences. At the film's conclusion, Russell and Kevin are no longer together.

Brent Hartinger's novel *Geography Club* was part of the vanguard of LGBTQIA+ writing for young adults that emerged in the late 1990s and early 2000s, including the work of writers such as David Levithan, whose novel *Boy Meets Boy* was also published in 2003 (Cart and Jenkins 2018). An important difference between the novel and its cinematic adaptation is the focus on interteen relationships: whereas in the book the narrative is primarily concerned with the romance between Russell and Kevin, the film focuses more on the relationships between Russell and his peers—particularly his friendships with Min and Gunnar. Viewers never find out if Russell and Kevin have sex, and the narrative of the film gives equal or greater airtime to Gunnar's lack of prowess in dating young women than to Russell's exploration of his hitherto latent same-sex desire. In this manner, the film version plays up the idea of "compulsory heterosexuality"

(Rich 1981), the degree to which being straight allows teenagers to gain social capital and compete in the homophobic environment of high school.

The overarching metaphor of spatial geography is used to describe the school and small-town American suburbia in terms of insiders and outsiders. This film suggests that spaces such as the locker room, athletic field, classrooms, and school cafeteria remain off-limits to anyone who is gay. Ultimately, the eponymous Geography Club is rendered as a venue for different forms of "Otherness," rather than as a beachhead into the decolonization of heteronormative spaces.

The references to an online gay chat room—a queer space that allows Russell and Kevin to meet and communicate—is indicative of the importance of Internet communities to young queer people that flourished in the early 2000s. While *Geography Club* does not deliver a critical analysis of the pros and cons of Internet interaction for gay teens, this is a theme that becomes a staple in more recent YA literature, including David Levithan's novel *Two Boys Kissing* (2013) and in Becky Albertelli's *Simon vs. the Homosapiens Agenda* (2015)—a popular gay YA novel that was made into the feature film *Love, Simon* in 2018.

See also *Every Day; Love, Simon; Mean Girls; The Perks of Being a Wallflower.*

Bibliography

Cart, Michael, and Christine A. Jenkins. *Representing the Rainbow in Young Adult Literature: LGBT+ Content aince 1969.* Lanham, MD: Rowman & Littlefield, 2018.
Rich, Adrienne. *Compulsory Heterosexuality and Lesbian Existence.* Chicago: University of Chicago Press, 1981.

—Paul Venzo

GHOSTBUSTERS (2016)

DIRECTOR: Paul Feig
SCREENPLAY: Paul Feig and Katie Dippold
CAST: Melissa McCarthy (Dr. Abigail L. "Abby" Yates), Kristen Wiig (Dr. Erin Gilbert), Kate McKinnon (Dr. Jillian Holtzmann), Leslie Jones (Patty Tolan), Chris Hemsworth (Kevin Beckman), Neil Casey (Rowan North)
SPECS: 117 minutes (theatrical release), 134 minutes (extended edition); color
AVAILABILITY: DVD (Sony Pictures Home Entertainment)

Physicists Dr. Erin Gilbert and Dr. Abby Yates are so convinced of the existence of ghosts that they quite literally wrote a book on the topic. However, while Yates, teaming up with the eccentric Dr. Jillian Holtzmann, remains dedicated to proving the existence of paranormal phenomena, Gilbert disowns the research and by extension, their friendship. Although working toward tenure at Columbia University, Gilbert agrees to one last ghost bust in a deal that would see Yates remove the offending book from sale; however, the ensuing reputational damage results in her being fired from her professorial role. The three women become four, joined by subway worker Patty Tolan, teaming up as the catchily named "Conductors of the Metaphysical Examination." The full force of New York's paranormal problem is unleashed when hotel employee and occultist Rowan North looks to bring about the end of the world. The newly dubbed Ghostbusters hire a beautiful but vacant secretary, invent proton containment lasers, face off with the local mayor, nod at the original franchise, and ride the Ecto-1 all before saving the city from the fourth cataclysm.

Ghostbusters (2016) was the first of a number of recent female reboots within a genre routinely committed to male action. And although there is much to applaud in the film from in-jokes and knowing franchise winks to quippy dialogue and a multitude of femininities on screen, the film was not well received by the original *Ghostbusters* (1984) fan base, due in part to the gendered recasting. Cowritten by Katie Dippold and Paul Feig and starring some of the most popular comedic actors of their generation, the reboot was assumed to be a commercially successful summer blockbuster, and yet the trailer reached over a million negative votes when it was first streamed online. These votes, it turned out, were part of a wider trolling campaign that was steeped in misogyny but thinly veiled under the guise of franchise fidelity (Rich 2016). Sam Adams of *IndieWire* sums it up when he states that "reviving the franchise with women in the leading roles"' was the "the ultimate desecration" for fanboys (2016). And although there is evidence that the film was not universally popular with female audiences, even a cursory look at IMDb polling makes it clear that female audiences rated the movie twice as highly as their male counterparts. In short, "it takes some seriously tortured logic to argue that gender has nothing to do with the anti-*Ghostbusters* backlash" (Adams 2016).

Outside of the misogynistic backlash and looking at the film itself, something the naysayers were routinely accused of failing to do before casting their vote, it is frustrating to see the central female protagonists so routinely undervalued and dismissed at key stages throughout the narrative. And although this enables the plot to unfold, there was room for balance here. A Ghostbuster being ousted from a prestigious university for her wayward mission makes sense for the plot and story; repeated public humiliation, infantilization, and dehumanization within the screen narrative does not. These moments give the impression that the studio is having to carefully weigh up an all-female franchise against that of a depiction of female empowerment.

In an era that seemed confused as to how to depict engaging, complex, empowering, multifaceted female characters on the big screen, *Ghostbusters* (2016) manages to give audiences a multiplicity of femininities that push back against a heterosexual imperative that dominates much mainstream movie fare and the notion of woman as object. There are a couple of jokes at the expense of the characters' punctuality and sartorial choices, but these are easily forgiven and forgotten in a movie that otherwise looks to encourage and embrace the diversity of the female experience. Indeed, diverse femininities are simply a fact of the movie, beyond hierarchy or commentary within the narrative. Rather, it is the depiction and commentary surrounding the "terrible" yet "pretty" and muscled Kevin that is uncomfortable to laugh at or with here. But back to the central protagonists, are they diverse in terms of class, race, and broader manners and characteristics? Yes. Diverse in terms of a depiction of nonbinary sexualities? Of a fashion!

Casting Kate McKinnon, an openly lesbian comedian and writer known for *The Big Gay Sketch Show* (2006–2010) and *Saturday Night Live* (1975–) as the steampunk-esque Holtzmann meant that early buzz around the film left audiences asking if the franchise had written not just female Ghostbusters but a gay central character. Whether they did or not depends on who you ask and how you watch the film. While much popular commentary predicted McKinnon playing a lesbian lead, *Autostraddle*'s Kayla Kumari Upadhyaya announced that all the women in the film are lesbians or bisexual. Upadhyaya provided a very thorough breakdown of her argument as it spans relationships, rebounds, flings, and love stories between the four women of the reboot (2016). In her film review, the author concludes, "Say it loud, say it proud: *Ghostbusters* is gay" (Upadhyaya 2016). Even still, one might argue that there is little more than lesbian hints and subtext within the film.

McKinnon's zany, irrepressible, and endearing engineer Holtzmann is an infectious ball of energy, wit, and curiosity. To those looking for a gay female/fantasy superhero, she is front and center. For those reading the film more literally, her queer identity is nowhere to be seen. One can choose to put the knowing winks and come-hither one-liners down to a lack of traditional feminine etiquette or to one of the greatest lesbian performances in genre filmmaking. In terms of the latter reading, Feig admitted he thought the character was gay and directed McKinnon to allow for this reading, but studio constraints to keep the film family-oriented prevented any explicit references within the title (Kies 2017). In short, Holtzmann is marked as queer, she can be read as queer, she is played by an openly lesbian comedian, but her sexuality is never mentioned or monitored in the narrative.

Kate McKinnon as Jillian Holtzmann in *Ghostbusters*. Courtesy of Columbia Pictures/ Photofest.

Although it is disappointing to realize that, even in 2016, mainstream studios are nervous about including an openly lesbian character, in part due to international audiences, it is worth highlighting the ways McKinnon frames her performance. In a broad range of news, reviews, interviews, and other ancillary materials, McKinnon "makes no attempt to hide her sexuality"; she is clearly "passionate about delivering gay characters, as opposed to playing straight ones" (Dunstall 2017, 224), telling audiences that "I don't want to be some straight girl in the movies, I want to be doing what I want and using who I am authentically" (cited in Dunstall 2017, 224). If both writer and performer situate the character as queer, then this is no longer just reading between the lines and looking for subtext. Indeed, McKinnon's depiction of the fearless, charismatic, all-singing, all-dancing, cartoonish Holtzmann, even without being labeled as queer within the narrative, offers a fascinating iteration of womanhood that challenges existing stereotypes and social boundaries of femininity. Holtzmann is self-assured, professionally driven, exuberant, and bold. She is comfortable with and confident in her own gender-blending suits and smoking jackets, cherished and adored by old friends and new.

The loyalties, camaraderie, and female friendship evident on screen is notable and valuable, and irrespective of whether the different combinations are read as hookups, exes, future partnerships, or friendships, it is important to see love and loyalty shared between the big-screen protagonists. Indeed, at the time of writing, there is a petition for Feig and Dippold to create a sequel to *Ghostbusters* (2016), in part because it legitimizes STEM fields for girls and young women, transcends romance narratives, demonstrates the value of female friendship, and encourages acceptance as it relates to "genders, backgrounds, heritages and sexualities" (Marshall 2016). I signed the petition.

See also *Can You Ever Forgive Me?*; *Dawn of the Dead*; *Let Me In*.

Bibliography

Adams, Sam. "Why The *Ghostbusters* Backlash Is a Sexist Control Issue." *IndieWire*, July 14, 2016. Accessed March 23, 2021. https://www.indiewire.com/2016/07/ghostbusters-reboot-backlash-1201705555/.

Dunstall, Hannah. "Kate McKinnon: From Holtzmann to Hilary." *Comedy Studies* 8, no. 2 (2017): 223–25.

Kies, Bridget. "Ghostbusters." *Queer Studies in Media and Popular Culture* 2, no. 2 (2017): 265.

Marshall, Hannah. "Petition: *Ghostbusters* Answer the Second Call—2nd Female *Ghostbusters* Film." Change.org, 2016. Accessed March 23, 2021. https://www.change.org/p/ghostbusters-fans-ghostbusters-answer-the-second-call-2nd-female-ghostbusters-film-b7421c4f-b18a-4a93-bc2d-da66ca99ea9b.

Rich, B. Ruby. "What Is at Stake: Gender, Race, Media, or How to Brexit Hollywood." *Film Quarterly* 70, no. 1 (Fall 2016): 5–10.

Upadhyaya, Kayla Kumari. "Look, All the Women in *Ghostbusters* Are Gay—Deal with It." *Autostraddle*, July 21, 2016. Accessed March 23, 2021. https://www.autostraddle.com/look-all-of-the-women-in-ghostbusters-are-gay-deal-with-it-345763/.

—Rebecca Feasey

GILDA (1946)

DIRECTOR: Charles Vidor
SCREENPLAY: Marion Parsonnet, Jo Eisinger, and Ben Hecht (uncredited); E. A. Ellington (original story)
CAST: Joseph Calleia (Detective Maurice Obregon), Glenn Ford (Johnny Farrell), Rita Hayworth (Gilda), George Macready (Ballin Mundson)
SPECS: 110 minutes; black and white
AVAILABILITY: DVD (Columbia Pictures)

On the seedier side of Buenos Aires, dandyish, middle-aged gangster Ballin Mundson takes under his wing young, down-on-his-luck gambler Johnny Farrell. More than employer and employee, the pair become unusually fast, intimate friends and share a bond fraught with unsubtle sexual symbolism and homoerotic overtones. Johnny is therefore shocked to discover that Ballin has suddenly married Gilda, a voluptuous singer with whom Johnny had a mysterious and presumably stormy prior relationship. Soon there develops an implicit bisexual love triangle awash in sadomasochism, as the evil Ballin becomes sexually excited by both the tension between Gilda and Johnny and the possibility that Gilda might cuckold him with his "intimate" friend. When Ballin later commits a murder, he flees the country, leaving alone Johnny and Gilda, who ruminate on their possible future together and plot to free themselves from Ballin's domineering grip.

A film that sometimes awkwardly straddles film noir and overheated melodrama, Gilda exemplifies the ways Hollywood screenwriters of the classical era tried to circumvent the homophobia of the Hays Code through the use of subtext, symbolism, and double entendres. The implied same-sex relationship between young hustler Johnny and decadent mobster Ballin was sufficiently submerged to escape not only the Hays censors but (amusingly) director Vidor himself, who in later interviews claimed that he was unaware of the screenwriters' intended subtext (much as Jimmy Stewart was oblivious to the gay subtext of Hitchcock's Rope [1948]). Vidor may have been alone in his ignorance: Macready and Ford create a palpable, dangerous intimacy between Ballin and Johnny, perhaps the only queer characters in classical noir who are not relegated to the margins. Generally, identifying queerly coded characters in noir is a relativistic proposition. Noir heroes are so absurdly manly and femme fatales so womanly that any hint of unmanliness (in male roles) or "butchness" (in female ones) can code subsidiary characters as "relatively" queer (e.g., Peter Lorre in The Maltese Falcon [1941] or Van Heflin's inebriated intellectual in Johnny Eager [1941]). Nevertheless, contemporary viewers might find the men's relationship in Gilda remarkably suggestive for its time and far less "coded" than one might expect. Today's audiences may only wonder how average moviegoers in 1946 interpreted Ballin's blatantly phallic, dagger-sprouting cane, a weapon he and Johnny describe as their "third friend." The pair continually declare that "gambling and women don't mix"—while the two of them seem to mix perfectly. In the context of the men's thinly closeted relationship, the panoptical headquarters of Ballin's gambling den is particularly revealing. While Ballin and Johnny can surveil gamblers from above, their windowed office is also equipped with automatic shutters when privacy is needed, signaling the shifting moments of visibility and invisibility that define their bond.

In one of the film's most iconic moments, Johnny first discovers Gilda, Ballin's new fiancée, dressing in the older man's bedroom, effortlessly flinging her long hair above bare shoulders. Suddenly realizing Ballin's bisexual tendencies, Johnny exclaims, "I never expected to see a woman here!" In a flat tone of voice, Ballin responds, "My wife does not come under the category of woman." Even acknowledging that the film frames its relationships in the doubled shadows of noir and closeted queerness, Ballin's bizarre retort is still difficult to unpack. Perhaps Ballin means that Gilda, like so many women of noir, is damaged goods—she and Johnny, it turns out, share their own tortured romantic history, which the film never fully explicates. Well aware of the film's gay subtext, *Village Voice* critic Molly Haskell zeroed in on Ballin's odd line and sarcastically called Gilda "a female impersonator" who sits "between 'the older man' and 'the stud'" in what amounts to a "sexual masquerade" (1974). To call Gilda a "female impersonator" seems as absurd as Ballin's comment itself, given that Hayworth was Hollywood's ideal bombshell. Yet Gilda's (and Hayworth's) idealization might protest too much. Only an "unreal" vision of female beauty, perfectly manufactured by Hollywood, could distract viewers from the men's relationship and the men from one another. Gilda's beauty is as unreal as the two men's love is impossible.

Once Ballin announces his intentions to marry Gilda, Johnny makes no effort to hide his jealousy and resentment. In a pivotal scene, Gilda proposes a toast as the three dine together. "Just a few weeks ago we drank to the three of us," Johnny replies, implying that he and Ballin had enjoyed a toast with their "third friend," Ballin's piercing (if also hidden) phallic sword. Gilda, puzzled by the enigmatic remark, asks of the third friend, "Was it a him or a her?" Given the film's subtext, Gilda's remark about the mysterious friend's gender carries an obvious double meaning, suggesting that Ballin rather capriciously switches the gender of his object choice. The film does not demonize Ballin for his bisexuality, however, as Johnny is bisexual too; rather, Ballin's villainy and criminal doings mark him as deviant. Indeed, early on, Ballin does business with ex-Nazis, who so often appear in postwar noir as tokens of enduring, festering evil.

Accusations of sexism have often dogged noir, and *Gilda* is no exception. The queer attraction between Johnny and Ballin, facilitated by their male-dominated criminal milieu, is clearly muddied—perhaps even stirred—by misogynist overtones. Though Gilda shares with the femme fatale an unbounded sexuality, she is more pawn than seductress, bouncing between the two men and winding up with Johnny simply because the film never offers her a third choice. In the justly famous scene in which she sings "Put the Blame on Mame" while slowly stripping off a glove before a rapt audience, Gilda marshals her sexual power and drives both Johnny and Ballin to jealousy. But her potential power is sabotaged by the song's misogyny: the lyrics identify the seductress "Mame" as the root of all evil, a mythic woman whose kiss burned down Chicago and whose "ice-cold 'no'" to an eager suitor plunged all of Manhattan into a deep freeze. Importantly, the "Mame" sequence transpires on the stage of Ballin's nightclub, where Gilda is effectively his prisoner and subject to his misogynous domination. After Ballin kills a man and flees the country, she runs off with Johnny, leaving behind her femme fatale persona and becoming a vulnerable, suffering, and *redeemable* woman.

Many critics have subjected the "Mame" sequence to feminist analysis, particularly in light of its hypocritical, Old Testament moralism. Gilda's song at once extols the erotic power of feminine beauty and "blames" that beauty for the downfalls of men—even bisexual men, as this film would have it. Through her song, Gilda becomes a prisoner of her own excessive beauty, much as Hayworth was the mythic confection of Hollywood publicity men. If Gilda's unreal beauty wedges apart Johnny and Ballin, Gilda is herself wedged into designer Jean Louis's black strapless dress, a specially cantilevered marvel that resiliently clings to Hayworth's torso and bosom as she performs her mock striptease. Given the impossibility of *actually* stripping in a 1946 Hollywood movie, the allure of Gilda's ostentatious outfit substitutes for her unseeable skin. For critic Zoe Kurland, Gilda is practically swallowed up by her couture, the interior workings of which were so intricate that "even if that zipper did come down, it would simply reveal more dress, a never-ending vortex of clasps and corsets leading to nowhere" (2020). Kurland wonders if stripping is "the only way" Gilda can "achieve autonomy," as she tries to cast off her Hollywood costume and the straight male fantasy it represents (2020). Yet Gilda's performance—what Haskell calls "the most erotically abortive striptease in cinema"—is more sham than tease (1974). Triply bounded by her male-designed costume, Hayworth's bombshell image, and the puritanical Hays Code, Gilda is allowed to discard only a single, vestigial glove that extends to her elbow. Unable to strip off her shackles, she must turn to Johnny, finding painful refuge in their former relationship.

Understandably, some critics have tried to salvage from Gilda's stage performance and overall predicament some measure of sexual power. While admitting that Gilda is impossibly caught in a tug-of-war between the two men, Julie Grossman emphasizes the intensity of Gilda's erotic personality. "Johnny Farrell can't abide Gilda's verbal, psychological, and sexual power over him," Grossman suggests (2009, 28). "He reacts so violently and cruelly to her (comparing women to insects, for example) that the movie enacts in the story the annihilating process of 'putting the blame on Mame'" (28). Though Gilda provokes and manipulates Johnny, her power is a largely sadomasochistic one, potent enough to drive Johnny to despair but not potent enough to free herself from Ballin.

In its second half, *Gilda* parts company with film noir, but not through the bisexual themes that seem to undercut noir's binary of stalwart machismo and feminine iniquity. Rather, after Ballin goes on the lam, Gilda and Johnny find themselves in a series of melodramatic scenes that reveal Gilda as a multilayered, sympathetic character, quite unlike the single-minded, irredeemable femme fatale. As Gilda's moments of fleeting power give way to feminine self-sacrifice, the film segues into the masochistic ethos of the "woman's film," a Hollywood trend contemporaneous with noir. In a sense, the film's scenario inverts the premise of the previous year's *Mildred Pierce* (directed by Michael Curtiz), which begins as an angst-ridden melodrama but eventually makes Joan Crawford's tortured heroine into a noirish figure complicit in murder. Starting from noir and mutating into melodrama, *Gilda* suddenly returns to the world of noir in a hastily staged climax, as fugitive Ballin and his symbolic blade return to confront Johnny and Gilda, now committed lovers. In the violent confrontation that follows, Ballin is offed with his own phallic spear, heterosexuality emerges triumphant, and Gilda is afforded a happy ending unavailable to noir's usual array of temptresses.

If the abrupt conclusion seems unsatisfactory, the film's nearly improvised script is largely to blame. As Otto Friedrich explains, "The original screenplay was the work of one Marion Parsonnet, but [producer] Virginia Van Upp, who had . . . written [Hayworth's previous film] *Cover Girl*, kept rewriting *Gilda* . . . only a page or two at a time, often on the night before a scene was scheduled for shooting" (1986, 113–14). Director Vidor confessed, "We never knew what was coming next, and we even started the picture without a leading man" (Friedrich 1986, 114). Furthermore, scenes near the end of the film, in which Gilda rouses Johnny to jealousy by painting herself as promiscuous, had to be rationalized to appease Hays Code guidelines. "The censors had to be placated," Friedrich continues, "so Miss Van Upp produced a finale in which it turned out that Gilda had always been faithful and virtuous and had just pretended otherwise to arouse her tormentor" (114).

As a result of its sexual mirages and semi-improvisatory screenplay (which an uncredited Ben Hecht further retooled), *Gilda* has produced some frankly inexplicable commentary over the years. Writing in *Film Noir: An Encyclopedic Reference to the American Style*, Elizabeth Ward asserts that "the friendship between Ballin Mundson and Johnny Farrell is remarkable for its lack of self-consciousness in the face of its overt pathological aspects" and claims that the men's "sexuality is completely suppressed, whether toward one another or toward women" (1982, 112). Apart from failing to define "pathological aspects"—it is not clear whether Ward refers to criminality, homosexuality, or the cruelty underpinning the men's relationship—Ward clearly overstates matters. Of course, Hays-era filmmakers had to *largely* suppress the men's sexual relationship, but if it were *completely* suppressed, it logically would not be apparent without the most painful stretches of the imagination. Today, even mainstream critics acknowledge the flagrancy of Johnny and Ballin's erotic relationship. Turner Classic Movies' noir historian Eddie Muller, for instance, has not only reiterated the queer reading of *Gilda* but has argued that it is the *only* reading that makes sense of the film's opaque romantic triangle (2018).

The film's noir credentials are bolstered by finely etched black-and-white cinematography courtesy of the legendary Rudolph Maté, a Polish émigré whose credits range from Carl Dreyer's *The Passion of Joan of Arc* (1928) to Alexander Korda's *That Hamilton Woman* (1941). The film's uneasy slide from foggy noir into tidy melodrama perhaps reflects the prosaic sensibilities of Vidor, a middlebrow director mainly remembered for "prestige" biopics such as *A Song to Remember* (about Frederic Chopin) and *A Song without End* (about Franz Liszt), as well as the ill-fated 1957 production of *A Farewell to Arms*. Despite Maté's technical contributions, Vidor never exploits the dingy, sleazy mood that animates the best of noir, nor does he invest Buenos Aires with the searing hothouse atmosphere that Robert Montgomery brings to the American Southwest in *Ride the Pink Horse* (1947). Though *Gilda* is a crucial, often fascinating example of classical Hollywood's negotiations of (and around) the closet, one could only imagine how a noir auteur like John Huston or Robert Siodmak might have reshaped the film's enigmatic allure.

See also *Rope*.

Bibliography

Dyer, Richard. "Homosexuality and Film Noir." *Jump Cut* 16 (1977): 18–21.

Friedrich, Otto. *A City of Nets: A Portrait of Hollywood in the 1940s*. New York: Harper Perennial, 1986.

Grossman, Julie. *Rethinking the Femme Fatale in Film Noir*. New York: Palgrave Macmillan, 2009.

Haskell, Molly. "Heroines Cool and Languorous." *Village Voice*, January 17, 1974. Accessed August 20, 2021. https://news.google.com/newspapers?id=wKIeAAAAIBAJ&sjid=B4wDAAAAIBAJ&pg=6249,1071873.

Kurland, Zoe. "Put the Blame on Mame: Fragmentation and Commodification in *Gilda*." *Bright Lights Film Journal*, June 29, 2020. Accessed August 20, 2021. https://brightlightsfilm.com/put-the-blame-on-mame-fragmentation-and-commodification-in-gilda/#.YR9X84hKgaY.

Muller, Eddie. "Noir Alley." Television Broadcast of *Gilda* on Turner Classic Movies, October 9, 2018.

Ward, Elizabeth. "Gilda." In *Film Noir: An Encyclopedic Reference to the American Style*, edited by Alain Silver and Elizabeth Ward, 112. Woodstock, NY: Overlook Press, 1982.

—Andrew Grossman

GO FISH (1994)

DIRECTOR: Rose Troche
SCREENPLAY: Guinevere Turner and Rose Troche
CAST: Guinevere Turner (Camille "Max" West), V. S. Brodie (Ely), T. Wendy McMillan (Kia), Migdalia Melendez (Evy), Anastasia Sharp (Daria)
SPECS: 83 minutes; black and white
AVAILABILITY: DVD (MGM)

Go Fish is the feature debut of Rose Troche, the director of *The L Word* series (2004). It was cowritten by her then partner Guinevere Turner, featuring in the role of Max, one of the four central lesbian characters of the film. Inspired by the Chicago lesbian community of the early 1990s, it chronicles a few weeks in the lives of some of its members—an African American college professor, Kia; her Latino girlfriend and nurse, Evy; Camille aka "Max," a student and budding writer; the unashamedly promiscuous Daria and her roommate Ely. Max and Ely start to fall in love, with vehement support from their friends, yet first they must overcome a series of obstacles, one of them being the existence of Ely's long-distance partner. After the long-distance breakup, Max and Ely consummate their relationship, and the film closes on a "happy ending" note.

The triteness of the plot indicates how important style, narrative strategies, and character construction are in *Go Fish*. The film was groundbreaking in several aspects. As one of the early representatives of what critic B. Ruby Rich dubbed the New Queer Cinema, *Go Fish* premiered at the Sundance Festival in 1994 and became a major crossover hit almost overnight, convincing MGM to buy its distribution rights and making both Troche and Turner into stars. As B. Ruby Rich notes in her account of the film's early fame:

> Turner had a whole page in *Interview* with her hair arranged in front of her face like a beaded curtain, touting her as a writer to watch; Rose got a pitch in *Rolling Stone* as the hot director for 1994, all pierced and intense-looking; and the two together got the number 2 slot in the *New Yorker* Talk of the Town section, which would be a major status symbol. It was unprecedented respect for a lesbian movie. And keep in mind, all that time *Go Fish* hadn't even opened yet. (2013, 60)

The film presents several forms of lesbian identity, yet none of it is shown as problematic. In this way, it was received as a most welcome breach from the mainstream tradition of showcasing lesbians as comic or tragic characters, discovering for its audience, as Lisa Henderson puts it, "a historically invisible character type: the happy lesbian in love," whose "source of conflict is romance itself and not (hallelujah) lesbianism" (1999, 57).

Troche and Turner's choice of characters is clever and varied and deserves a closer look. The women in *Go Fish* are all young and urban. They, however, differ in their conditions and background. The first of the four major characters viewers encounter is Kia, an African American lesbian. The audience steps right into her class on the history of the lesbian movement, in which her students are asked to recount the names of historical and present lesbians, confirmed or assumed. After several humorous attempts, one of the students asks about the purpose of such an exercise when most of the women from history are only hypothetically lesbian. At this point, Kia, the oldest of the crowd, establishes herself as the spokesperson for the whole community (and the film), stating that "throughout lesbian history there has been a serious lack of evidence . . . lesbian lives and lesbian relations barely exist on paper. And it is with that in mind and understanding the meaning and power of history that we begin to want to change history."

Kia is also the matchmaker operating behind the central romantic relationship of *Go Fish*—it is she who picks Ely for Max in a café and who arranges a collective visit to the cinema from which she excuses herself in a last-moment fashion, letting Ely and Max go by themselves. This visit results in their first kiss, interrupted by a call from Ely's partner. It is also Kia whose suggestion for the designation of female genitalia, "the honey pot," wins the discussion in one of the scenes. Making the voice of reason Black is a pioneering step on the part of the filmmakers, as most earlier lesbian theory was white centered, marginalizing the perspective of women of color. It needs to be said, however, that Kia's Blackness is nowhere shown as an issue, or her viewpoint as formed by her race. She dates Evy, a Latino nurse, with whom she is passionately in love yet who lives with her mother. In one scene, Evy comes home to find her ex-boyfriend with her infuriated mother, who was just informed about her daughter's sexual identity. A quarrel ensues, and Evy is kicked out of the house. In desperation, she returns to Kia's apartment, where she is somewhat clumsily comforted by Max, who offers her to replace her biological family with a lesbian one, comprising Kia and Max.

This scene is one of the very few in the film where discordance pertaining to lesbian identity is presented, and it is quite instructive to realize that the core of the problem is not racial or ethnic but strictly sexual. Even though Troche herself is of Puerto Rican origin, the specificity of non-white lesbian experience is omitted from the film, probably for the sake of the chosen genre, romantic comedy.

Leaving race/ethnicity aside does not prevent the makers from complicating the romance by the discussion of lesbian identity itself, if solely from the angle of sexuality. The central character in this respect is Daria, who also contributes to the communal effort of bringing Max and Ely together (she throws a party where the two finally commit themselves to each other) yet serves another important role in a more general and political way. New Queer Cinema, as the label suggests, is grounded in queer theory, proposing one's identity as nothing fixed, given by birth, but very much a social project, prone to fluidity, formation, and change. The character of Daria is highly instructive in this sense. Toward the middle of the film, viewers watch Kia and Evy joking, kissing, and caressing each other in bed. Cut, and the audience is presented with a series of close-ups of two naked bodies having sex. At first, viewers tend to see these as Kia and Evy; soon, however, it is revealed that it is Daria, in bed with a man. This conflation of gender identities may puzzle viewers, yet it prepares them for the following scene in which Daria is attacked on a dark street by an anonymous crowd of lesbians and interrogated about the activity just shown. Most of the female examiners are appalled and disgusted, questioning Daria's proclaimed lesbian sexual identity, framing her intercourse with a man as a threat to the lesbian community as a whole. One of the women snaps, "How are we supposed to establish some kind of identity if lesbians are going around having sex with men?" At first, Daria tries to diffuse the situation: "We're not talking life commitment here, we're talking sex, just sex." Soon she begins to dismantle the idea of a fixed and uniform lesbian identity and conduct, asking, "What is the amount of time that has to pass before I regain my lesbian status?"

The mise-en-scène of this sequence supports the oppressive tribunal feeling— in an anonymous, dark, back-alley space, the faces are framed mostly in close-ups, lit from below as if performing in a B horror movie. The accusations are serious, yet the viewer tends to side with Daria, a feeling supported by their memory of their own mystification just a scene ago. It is a surprisingly sophisticated moment in a film finely attuned to the establishing of proper lesbian style in terms of clothing and haircuts. (Max, at first, dismisses Ely because she dresses like her mom. Ely's makeover begins with the cutting of her long hair not to look so "hippieish." Max herself wears cropped shorts, a white T-shirt, and Dr. Martens almost as a uniform.)

The crossover success of *Go Fish* tends to be explained by the choice of genre. Troche and Turner use the basic tropes of traditional Hollywood romantic comedy, which, on one hand, secures them a bigger audience (the 1990s were a decade when romantic comedy came to the spotlight of popularity again), and, on the other, allows the queering of the typically heteronormative couple to look natural. As Henderson notes, "In *Go Fish*, the generic conventions, transformations, and refusals typical of romantic comedy secure lesbian identity as unproblematic, while also challenging the heteronormative presumption of Hollywood romance" (1999, 45). At the same time, as noted earlier, the choice of genre may explain the lack of a deeper commitment of the film on the level of race, ethnicity, and class, to which only lip service is paid.

The romcom format is complicated in more ways in *Go Fish* than just by switching genders. The flow of the narrative is interrupted on so many occasions that there is barely a coherent linear structure. This is very much the heritage of independent cinema as such, differing on purpose from the classical temporal structures of storytelling, perfected by Hollywood, yet it owes much to avant-garde cinema as well. Throughout the whole film, the story of the two women falling in love is complemented by various abstract shots—of a wooden spinning top moving across a checkerboard, of crackling light bulbs, of milk mixing with coffee in a tall glass, of newspapers falling from above, of close-ups of hands performing various gestures. Apart from highlighting self-reflexiveness of the medium and drawing the spectator out of the romantic narrative, these visual digressions pay homage to the tradition of feminist filmmaking that focused on the display of the domestic and unspectacular (Henderson 1999, 53). The feeling of intimacy, sensuality, and commitment is reinforced by the film's fondness for close-ups, mostly capturing parts of caressing bodies or faces of the characters.

Self-reflexivity, or the fact that the film knows about its own existence as film, is at the core of the second group of narrative ruptures, which could be called "enter the lesbian chorus." On three occasions, Kia, Evy, Daria, and Daria's actual girlfriend meet to comment on the progress of the Max–Ely romance, literally putting their heads together (these scenes are framed in close-up, from a high angle above the characters), directing the narrative development, writing the script. This has a pleasurably disorienting effect on the spectator at times because the characters are obviously stepping out of their prescribed roles of fictional beings, becoming proxies for the filmmakers themselves. In the very first entry of the chorus, Daria lasciviously comments on her own interest in Max, despite their goal of matching Max with Ely, while Evy puts her back on track semijokingly: "Get over it, Daria. It's called *Go Fish*, not *All You Can Eat*." Their second séance, closed by their common decision to "get on with it," is followed by a prolonged sequence of the cutting of Ely's long hair, edited in a nonchronological order accentuating its liminal and transgressive function in the romantic line of the narrative—as if by magic, the short-cropped hair lures Max from her den into the local bookstore, where she meets the transformed Ely (viewers see her new haircut only in this scene).

The third major breach in the romcom narrative tradition is situated around Max, in her visualization of her fears in claiming her lesbian identity. From the beginning of the film, viewers know Max attempts creative writing. A scene picturing her seated on a sofa with a notepad and pen, in fact, directly follows the title sequence set in Kia's class, interweaving images, introducing the audience to the major characters in their domestic settings, some of the images from the avant-garde sequences, and her voice-over narrating a story of missed meetings and relationships culminating with claiming her identity with, "It's Max, my name is Max." From this opening, Max establishes herself as the nexus of the story (this is, of course, sealed by the fact that she is played by Turner, the author of the script). It is she who makes the first moves in her relationship with Ely, supported by her community. Hers, as viewers can infer from the beginning, are the poetic interventions. Toward the second half of the film, the audience sees Max writing again, and her account expands into the most condensed and complex audiovisual digression of *Go Fish*. In a voice-over, Max delineates her anxieties vis-à-vis social pressures and expectations and spurs an alternative story of her being heterosexual:

> What if I black out and I wake up alone, midday, in a house and I've been napping, and I find out I'm married to a man. An honest man, who's devoted to me, and I'm late to pick up the kids. . . . I imagine the joy of kissing my husband in the supermarket and the wistful smile of the old woman who sighs quietly "Young love." . . . I can sink into the comfort of being mother, wife, sister-in-law, grandmother, not strapped with the awkward title of aunt. I could live a life of gender-specific pronouns and answer truthfully about boyfriends and mean only good friends when I say, and leave out that desperate qualifier, really good friend. . . . I am not waiting for a man. I just hate this eerie feeling that a man is waiting for me.

The visuals present Max in a white wedding dress with a lace veil, standing awkward and rigid, facing the camera, as her co-lesbians come to kiss her on the cheek. Later, two other brides appear, in the same dress, positioned next to each other as if undergoing the marriage ritual together. Only a second later, viewers learn that it is a superimposition. When Max, in a voice-over, describes her cool and detached attitude to the idea of heteronormative sex, the three brides remove their veils and start undressing. After a moment, the image is reversed, and the veils are back in their places. Max's talk about the contrast in her feelings about lesbian sex is visualized rather directly—one of the crew comes to her and they start kissing passionately, but then, she puts the veil down again and leaves Max standing alone with "that eerie feeling." The wedding dress is an evident metaphor for heteronormativity—all the lesbians from this sequence wear black civil clothes. The blessings of married life recounted only semi-ironically are, however, betrayed by the position of the bride—alone, removed from the community, and with stiff posture. A wedding changes into a sort of funeral in Max's imagination.

Just as in the "lesbian chorus" scene, the film here foregrounds the importance of community in lesbian identity, the protection and support that finally leads to a happy ending in the romantic line as well. The focus on the communal, permeating the very production of the film as well (in the beginning, the crew were only women, working mostly for free [Rich 2013, 58–60]), immerses *Go Fish* in a relaxed and joyful halo, radiating even after more than twenty-five years and leading Adrian Martin to dub the film "a frankly utopian fantasy" (1995). The genius of the film, however, lies not only in providing one of the first lesbian romcoms but in mixing the light with the ominous, as the bigoted community reaction in Daria's sequence manifests, and at least nodding to the range of lesbian experience, racial, ethnic, class, and other.

See also *The Kids Are All Right*; *Kissing Jessica Stein*; *The Uninvited*.

Bibliography

Henderson, Lisa. "Simple Pleasures: Lesbian Community and *Go Fish.*" *Signs* 25, no. 1 (1999): 37–54.

Martin, Adrian. "Go Fish." Film Critic: Adrian Martin, January 1995. Accessed April 30, 2021. http://www.filmcritic.com.au/reviews/g/go_fish.html.

Rich, B. Ruby. *New Queer Cinema: The Director's Cut.* Durham, NC: Duke University Press, 2013.

—Veronika Klusakova

THE GRAND BUDAPEST HOTEL (2014)

DIRECTOR: Wes Anderson
SCREENPLAY: Wes Anderson
CAST: Ralph Fiennes (M. Gustave), Tony Revolori (Zero Moustafa), F. Murray Abraham (Zero, adult), Saoirse Ronan (Agatha), Tilda Swinton (Madame D), Adrien Brody (Dmitri), Jude Law (Author, young)
SPECS: 100 minutes; color
AVAILABILITY: DVD (Fox Searchlight)

The Grand Budapest Hotel is a story of last days: the last best days of the titular European hotel, the last days of a vanishing civilization before the triumph of brute barbarism, and the last days of the film's protagonist, Monsieur Gustave H. The film's story is triply framed, an elaborate architecture even by the standards of Wes Anderson, a director for whom framing is a frequently employed device. The outermost frame of the film features a young woman paying homage to an unnamed author in the Old Lutz Cemetery. The film then shifts back in time to 1985 as this unnamed author (based on the novelist Stefan Zweig) speaks to the camera about his craft until he is abruptly interrupted by a young child bearing a toy gun. These two framing devices open onto yet another scene set in 1968, which finds the author as a younger man convalescing in the baths at a desiccating European hotel called the Grand Budapest ("a picturesque, elaborate, and once widely celebrated establishment" that is now "an enchanting old ruin"). There he befriends the proprietor of the hotel, a mannered, sorrowful, and deeply lonely man named Zero Moustafa. Zero unfolds the story of his life and how he acquired the hotel to the author, and this story (which is set in a fictional Eastern European land called Zubrowka in 1932) makes up the bulk of the narration. Indeed, neither Zero nor the author stands as the true protagonist of the film; this role belongs to M. Gustave, Zero's first boss and the fastidious concierge of the Grand Budapest Hotel. M. Gustave is a man who prides himself on his own personal refinement and on his ability, as a concierge at a high-end hotel, to anticipate and meet every need of his wealthy, mostly female, mostly elderly clientele (these needs sometimes express themselves sexually, as will be discussed later). The flamboyant and earnest M. Gustave regards his role as concierge not as a job but as a vocation, and he passes his ideals and the ideals of the Grand Budapest Hotel on to his protégé, Zero, a young orphaned refugee who applies for the position of lobby boy at the hotel. When Madame D, a frequent guest of the hotel and a lover of M. Gustave, dies under suspicious circumstances and bequeaths a priceless work of art to Gustave, Gustave finds himself accused of wrongdoing by her greedy and pernicious family. The main narrative arc of the film describes M. Gustave's valiant efforts to save first himself and second the Grand Budapest Hotel from the encroaching forces of fascism, personified by the character Dmitri, Madame D's violent son who is also a member of the ZZ Party (a fictionalized, Anderson-ized version of the Nazi Party). Along the way, Zero falls in love with Agatha, a beautiful young baker who, in turn, helps Gustave escape from a brief period of imprisonment. Zero's deep affection extends to Gustave, who represents to Zero a code of behavior, a father/brother figure, and a dying way of life that he longs to preserve through his own dedication to the hotel they both loved and served. Although Zero eventually loses both his cherished wife and his beloved mentor, he maintains the fading Grand Budapest Hotel as a monument to Gustave, Agatha, and the life Zero lived when he loved them.

Love, devotion, and a somewhat esoteric and intellectualized sense of passion emerge as themes in many of Wes Anderson's films, including this one. Yet for all of desire's prominence, critics of Anderson's work frequently note that actual love stories between characters in his films are often immature, impossible, and nearly or completely sexless. Andrew Karpan, in "Wes Anderson's

Ralph Fiennes as M. Gustave and Tony Revolori as Zero in *The Grand Budapest Hotel*. Courtesy of Fox Searchlight Pictures/Photofest.

Manly Men," argues that most of Anderson's early films feature a love triangle between a young or childish man, an older defeated man, and a woman who is unavailable to them both (the love triangles in *Rushmore, The Life Aquatic,* and *The Royal Tenenbaums* all bear this observation out nicely) (2017). Love stories are rarely consummated; indeed, sex and physical intimacy of any kind are virtually absent, giving way instead to love of an ideal (*Rushmore*), a thing (the hotel in *The Grand Budapest Hotel*), or a pursuit (*The Life Aquatic, The Darjeeling Limited*). Critics also note that, excepting two offhand mentions of temporary gay entanglements, all of the romantic relationships, limited though they may be, are, as Ryan Reft writes in his article "The Sexuality of 'Whimsy,'" "firmly entrenched in heterosexuality" (2012).

Until, it would seem, *The Grand Budapest Hotel*, although scholars and critics frequently find themselves at a loss to describe exactly *how* this film is more inclusive in terms of its representation of LGBTQIA+ characters. Many agree that M. Gustave is a new type of character for Anderson yet struggle to delineate what, exactly, Gustave represents; critics variously describe him as bisexual, polysexual, "a gay gigolo," a fop, and a character "who may be gay" or whom people "[assume] to be gay, but he's not." Judy Berman (whose article identifies most of the examples cited above) writes that although Gustave "has no sex life with other men . . . he is the closest Wes Anderson has come to a queer character," but she finally concludes that "Gustave's sexuality remains a mystery" (2014). Joshua Encinias echoes Berman's take nearly word for word; he claims that "M. Gustave is the closest Anderson has come to a queer character in his universe" and situates Gustave among other characters in Anderson's body of work who have subtle, brief "moments of gay desiring and identifying" (2018). (Encinias also writes of Anderson's own aesthetic and personal "dandy[ism] in style, if not in deed," a categorization that could be extended to the character of Gustave as well [2018].) Andrew Karpan sees *Budapest* as an example of a "more curious expression of desire" than Anderson's previous films, which cover the "more conventional terrains of the heterosexual relationship and its discontents," but ultimately concludes that the world represented in *Grand Budapest* is "not quite gay. Not yet" (2017).

The critics' confusion regarding Gustave's sexuality is mirrored in the movie itself as various characters struggle to define Gustave. Gustave's sexuality attracts curious attention in all five of the "chapters" of the main film; indeed, Berman argues that Gustave's sexuality is nothing less than "the driving force of the story" (2014). Yet, despite its centrality to the film, Gustave's sexuality ultimately defies categorization, as most starkly illustrated by the confrontation between Gustave and Dmitri in part 2 of the film. The scene takes place at the reading of Madame D's will, and Dmitri, her violent, fascist son, furiously confronts Gustave upon learning that Madame D bequeathed a priceless work of art to him:

Dmitri: That fucking faggot! He's a concierge. What are you doing here?

M. Gustave (*stiffening*): I've come to pay my respects to a great woman whom I loved.

Dmitri (*turning to the room*): This man is an intruder in my home! You're not getting [the painting] *Boy with Apple*, you goddamn little fruit!

M. Gustave (*genuinely offended*): How's that supposed to make me feel?

Dmitri: Call the police. We're pressing charges. This criminal has plagued my family for nearly twenty years. He's a ruthless adventurer and a con artist who preys on mentally feeble, sick old ladies—and he probably fucks them, too!

The three sisters look horrified. One of the little old ladies gasps. Shocked faces look to M. Gustave. He shrugs and says tentatively:

M. Gustave: I go to bed with all my friends.

Dmitri coldcocks M. Gustave an uppercut to the jaw and drops him with one punch.

Dmitri: If I learn you ever once laid a finger on my mother's body, living or dead, I swear to God, I'll cut your throat! (*screaming*) You hear me?

M. Gustave (*clever though dizzy*): I thought I was supposed to be a fucking faggot.

Dmitri (*hesitates*): You are, but you're bisexual!

M. Gustave (*pause*): Let's change the subject.

Gustave's sexuality both eludes and infuriates Dmitri, as evidenced by both his verbal ineptitude and physical violence in this scene. Gustave is somehow both a sexually voracious lothario who takes advantage of women and simultaneously a "little fruit" or, later, a "candy ass" whose very self-assured and visible flamboyance offends Dmitri. Either way, to Dmitri, Gustave is sexually transgressive, be it in his desire to sleep with old women or in his homosexuality/bisexuality, and for his sexual transgressions, he must be punished or destroyed. This is crucial to remember: to stray outside of, or to elide entirely, accepted roles governing sex and sexuality is, in the encroaching world of fascist domination, punishable by death. Gustave darkly hints at such immediately after this scene with Dmitri when he says to Zero, "Something about those lunatic foot-soldiers on the express—I think this could be a tricky war and a long dry spell in the hotel trade. For all we know, they could board us up tomorrow. *Zero looks alarmed*." In her monograph *The Cinema of Wes Anderson: Bringing Nostalgia to Life*, Whitney Crothers Dilley notes:

> During the prohibitive environment of Eastern Europe during World War II, the elements of society most often attacked along with the Jews (represented by Zweig) were non-white immigrants (represented by Moustafa) and homosexuals (represented by Gustave). These were the vulnerable groups most often condemned to death in the concentration camps. (2017)

Both Zero, as a refugee, and Gustave, as a "sexual deviant," face the very real threat of imprisonment and death under a regime such as the one that men like Dmitri are bent on erecting and enforcing.

That Gustave knows this is made clear in the third part of the film, which takes place at "Checkpoint 19: The Internment Camp." In this section of the film, Gustave wears not the meticulous uniform of the concierge but instead faces the camera and the audience wearing a grim prisoner's uniform and an alarming black eye. The script elaborates: "His face is purple and misshapen, covered almost entirely with bruises and abrasions, with one eye swollen completely shut." When Zero asks, horrified, what has happened, Gustave replies:

> What happened, my dear Zero, is I beat the living shit out of a sniveling little runt called Pinky Bandinski who had the gall to question my virility—because if there's one thing we've learned from penny dreadfuls, it's that, when you find yourself in a place like this, you must never be a candy ass. You've got to prove yourself from Day One. You've got to win their respect. Of course, I've got about a foot and a half of reach on Pinky, so once I'd pried him loose out from under my armpit, it was short order before I whipped him into scrambled eggs (*drinks a sip of water*). You should take a long look at his ugly mug this morning (*spits blood back into the cup*). He's actually become a dear friend. You'll meet him, I hope. So.

Gustave is aware that the world perceives him as gay; he is also aware that to be gay or gay appearing in prison and in the world at large is to risk bodily injury, if not death. This scene in the prison acts a microcosm of the world that threatens Gustave and his beloved hotel: because of the fascist insistence on sexual and racial purity, Gustave *must* assert a heterosexual—or at least virile—façade in order to avoid violence from the world as a whole. Yet after he does enact this version of exaggerated masculinity through his own display of protective violence, Gustave reverts immediately to his cultivated manners and his inherent civility ("He's actually become a dear friend. You'll meet him, I hope."). Gustave *must* complicate the world's understanding of him if he wishes to live even in the margins of this world and its shifting ethos. Gustave's ability to confound men like Dmitri and Pinky is indeed, ultimately, a means of survival, and his defiance can be defined as an essentially *queer* one.

"Queer," I would argue, is the term not only most useful to describe Gustave but also to describe the entire aesthetic and thematic stance of the film itself. The following brief exchange between Gustave and his newly befriended band of convict brothers reveals the aptness of "queer" as the term essential to Gustave's sexuality and to comprehending his purpose as a character:

> Pinky: Me and the boys talked it over. We think you're a real straight fella.
>
> M. Gustave: Well, I've never been accused of that before, but I appreciate the sentiment.
>
> Pinky: You're one of us now.
>
> M. Gustave (*somewhat moved*): What a lovely thing to say. Thank you, dear Pinky. Thank you, Günther. Thank you, Wolf. I couldn't ask for a finer tribute. *M. Gustave bows slightly. He hesitates.*

Whatever Gustave's sexuality is, he is, most importantly, *not straight*; he is, in fact, a queer character par excellence because of his ability to transgress boundaries and transcend definitions. Queerness sets itself both in opposition to and as a liberating sexual and an intellectual alternative to straightness; indeed, as

Kerry Mallan notes in her article on queer tropes in children's literature, *"queer* is a term that resists identity categorizations based on sexual orientation. . . . As a theoretical strategy, *queer* reveals the social and historical constructions of identity formation and dualistic concepts that govern normative notions of gender and sexuality" (2021). A queer stance (or in this case, a queer character) is one that eschews the limits of *either/or* and replaces it with the possibilities of *both/and*. The reason Gustave is impossible to define (by characters and critics alike) is that it is his very nature to defy definition; in short, to be queer, and to introduce queerness as a concept into the world of Wes Anderson films. Gustave is an example of what Mallan identifies as "a 'binary outlaw'" in that he "refus[es] to abide binary distinctions between . . . [gay] and straight" (2021). If Anderson's other films are variously described as "sexless" or as possessing a "pubescent vision," *Grand Budapest* differs because it is, from its protagonist to its ethos, queer.

Queerness extends beyond the question of Gustave's sexuality, even if that is what introduces it to the film, in two notable ways: the way the film dramatizes a queer family structure, and the way it employs a style that can be understood as a type of queer resistance. As many scholars point out, family structures that operate along lines of chosen kinship rather than biological lines can be understood as queer. These supportive networks honor bonds that develop outside of the heteronormative family structure and become, to use Kath Weston's famous phrase, "the families we choose" (1997). Gustave and Zero build this type of queer kinship over the course of the film: both separated from their families of birth, they repeatedly refer to themselves as brothers and recognize themselves as sharing a bond that is nothing less than familial. Indeed, once we recognize the queer family structure within this film, the prevalence of queer kinship structures in Anderson's other films becomes apparent. Films such as *Rushmore* and *The Life Aquatic* in particular feature the formations of families of choice that extend or replace families of biological origin.

Finally, Anderson's distinctive framing devices can themselves be understood as a type of queer resistance. Tom Hertweck, in his essay "The Great Frame-Up: Wes Anderson and Twee Narrative Contrivance," argues that Anderson's elaborate framing devices around his main narratives clear space for stories about softness, manners, and beauty and attempt to protect this sensibility from the harsh reality of the unforgiving world around it (2018). In this way, Anderson's narrative frames become a type of "buffer zone delimiting fantasy—but a fantasy that is always just about to rupture" (2018). Hertweck argues that this framing allows Anderson to "[tell] a personal story about civility in a hard world," in effect, to hold up a counternarrative that emphasizes care, service, and kinship in the sneering face of fascism (2018). What Hertweck calls *twee* (which he defines as an aesthetic insistence on the "quaint, pretty, or sentimental" but also as "a desire for 'the freedom (and often the daring) to be soft in an increasingly hard world'") we might also understand as a form of queer resistance to the hypermasculinity represented by characters such as Dmitri (2018). If Anderson's elaborate framing devices ultimately cannot keep the relentless forces of history at bay in *The Grand Budapest Hotel*, M. Gustave, as Anderson's first and most well-developed queer character, briefly and brightly illuminates a different way of being in the world, and a different type of character in Anderson's cinematic universe.

See also *The Life Aquatic with Steve Zissou*.

Bibliography

Berman, Judy. "Where Do Queer Characters Like *Grand Budapest Hotel*'s Gustave Fit into Wes Anderson's Sexless Universe?" *Flavorwire*, March 26, 2014. Accessed November 21, 2021. https://www.flavorwire.com/447727/where-do-queer-characters-like-grand-budapest-hotels -gustave-fit-into-wes-andersons-sexless-universe.

Dilley, Whitney Crothers. *The Cinema of Wes Anderson: Bringing Nostalgia to Life*. New York: Wallflower Press, 2017.

Encinias, Joshua. "Could *Isle of Dogs* Be Wes Anderson's Queerest Film Yet?" *Into*, March 23, 2018. Accessed November 21, 2021. https://www.intomore.com/culture/could-isle-of-dogs-be -wes-andersons-queerest-film-yet/.

Hertweck, Tom. "The Great Frame-Up: Wes Anderson and Twee Narrative Contrivance." *Texas Studies in Literature and Language* 60, no. 2 (2018): 129–50.

Karpan, Andrew. "Wes Anderson's Manly Men." *Film School Rejects*, April 20, 2017. Accessed November 21, 2021. https://filmschoolrejects.com/wes-anderson-men-d32f77bb6842/.

Mallan, Kerry. "Queer." In *Keywords for Children's Literature*, 2nd ed., edited by Lissa Paul and Philip Nel, 161–63. New York: NYU Press, 2021.

Reft, Ryan. "The Sexuality of 'Whimsy': Gender and Sex in the Films of Wes Anderson." *Tropics of Meta*, September 24, 2012. Accessed November 24, 2021. https://tropicsofmeta .com/2012/09/24/the-sexuality-of-whimsy-gender-and-sex-in-the-films-of-wes-anderson/.

Weston, Kath. *Families We Choose: Lesbians, Gays, Kinship*. New York: Columbia University Press, 1997.

—Cara McClintock-Walsh

· H ·

HAIL, CAESAR! (2016)

DIRECTOR: Ethan Coen and Joel Coen
SCREENPLAY: Ethan Coen and Joel Coen
CAST: Josh Brolin (Eddie Mannix), George Clooney (Baird Whitlock), Alden Eh-renreich (Hobie Doyle), Ralph Fiennes (Laurence Laurentz), Scarlett Johansson (DeeAnna Moran), Tilda Swinton (Thora Thacker/Thessaly Thacker), Chan-ning Tatum (Burt Gurney)
SPECS: 106 minutes; color
AVAILABILITY: DVD (Universal Pictures Home Entertainment)

Set in 1951, *Hail, Caesar!* is about the studio films of the 1930s, 1940s, and 1950s. At the center of the story is Eddie Mannix, a studio executive and so-called Hollywood fixer. Baird Whitlock, one of the studio's most famous stars, is kidnapped and held for ransom while filming *Hail, Caesar! A Tale of the Christ*. A "study group" of Communists working in Hollywood, who call themselves "The Future," is responsible for the kidnapping. Meanwhile cowboy-turned-actor Hobie Doyle struggles to fit into movies that are not Westerns as the studio sees their decline. Mannix also tries to contain the sexuality of actress DeeAnna Moran, while Burt Gurney is a gay actor tap-dancing his way into audiences' hearts. Mannix tries to manage all the studio personalities, including prevent-ing reporters Thora and Thessaly Thacker from covering a "scandal" involving Whitlock, all while trying to get Whitlock back.

The studio, and by extension studio executive Eddie Mannix, has a preoc-cupation with the sexuality of many of their actors (Mannix was an actual Hol-lywood fixer, while the rest of the characters are composites of or allusions to actors from the time). *Hail, Caesar!* uses the figure of Mannix to illustrate the ways sexuality is both contained and policed in the name of compulsory hetero-sexuality. Writer Anne Helen Peterson describes it as the "legislation of female and queer sexuality" (2016). One of the first scenes is of Mannix coming to "res-cue" one of his rising young starlets from taking photos for "French postcards" (erotic postcards of the era). The actress DeeAnna Moran is pregnant, not sure of the father, and is pressured by the studio to get married to maintain her image. She tells Mannix that she has had rotten luck with men, that they all turn out to be "pretty boys, saps, and swishes." This in part is an allusion to the sexualities of her fellow actors, who Mannix is also managing. Unlike her costars, Moran's "sexual deviance [is] within societal 'bounds'" (Peterson 2016). Mannix seeks to have Moran adopt her own baby, and in the process, she marries the surety agent who is assisting with the adoption, much to Mannix's relief.

Laurence Laurentz is directing a period piece in which Hobie Doyle, cowboy-cum-actor, is being asked to star in as a crossover from his usual cowboy films. (Laurentz himself is an ode to Director Noël Coward.) Doyle is awkward and clumsy in the role—and it becomes clear that maybe he is not really an actor—maybe he has just been playing himself this whole time. Doyle is being forced into a new role in films and simultaneously out on a date as a publicity stunt. Western films are seen as anachronistic; thus, Doyle is seen as in need of an update. While his sexuality is never explicitly discussed, the desire to pair him with one of the studio's female leads, Carlotta Valdez, suggests there is a question of his sexuality, or at least the public reception of it. While he enjoys the company of Valdez and seems to attract female suitors, without assuming compulsory heterosexuality, he reads as asexual. In the clip of his latest Western, it is unclear if Doyle is serenading the young woman or perhaps the moon itself is the object of his affection.

Burt Gurney plays a singing and dancing sailor is a throwback to Gene Kelly and musical sailor films like *On the Town* (1948) and *Anchors Aweigh* (1945). Gurney is first shown on a set for a bar named "The Swinging Dinghy" (a phallic allusion and double entendre) alongside fellow sailors also perhaps pointing to the "swinging or vacillating nature of the sailors' sexuality" (Karpinski 2019, 32). There are a few women in the bar, but they quickly leave the sailors to their own devices.

The sailors sing a song titled "No Dames" in which they seemingly lament the eight months they will be out to sea without women. The lyrics highlight the lack of "dames" and the fact that they will all be in very close quarters:

> When we're out there on the sea
> We'll be happy as can be
> Or so the Captain claims!
> But we have to disagree.
> Cause the only guarantee
> Is I'll see a lot of you
> And you'll see a lot of me!

What becomes evident in the song is despite the lack of female companionship (or maybe because of it) the men are all excited to be in each other's company. The bartender tries to close the bar and is scandalized by the sexualities of the sailors. He shouts at them, "This ain't that kind of place!" and tries to kick them out. Instead, the place erupts into celebration, with the sailors dancing in each other's arms. Gurney, when trying to exit the bar, finds himself caught between two sailors as he spins to face more sailors at the entrance to the bar. Instead of being taken aback by the homoerotic happenings at said bar, the sailors cheer and gladly join in on the fun.

With the sailor films of the 1940s as a reference point for this musical number, Burt Gurney is, in many ways, the actualized queer sailor that Gene Kelly could never be: "The men dance with each other in ways that are alluded to in the Gene Kelly films but here the viewer, gay or straight, knows for a fact that there is desire between the dancing sailors" (Karpinski 2019, 32). The cadence and syllables of the character's name is even a throwback to Kelly. While Kelly marched and protested against HUAC (House Un-American Activities Committee) blacklisting of Hollywood actors, Gurney is actually a Communist and the head of the group the Future. In his final scene, the Future rows him out in a small boat to meet a Soviet submarine, which he boards to go fight for the cause in Russia. His entire affect betrays him (perhaps he was one of the "swishes" referenced by costar Moran)—he even boards the submarine by gracefully leaping from the rowboat to its side.

Writer Lee Weston Sabo explains, "The post-war setting is used not as a screen against which to project anachronistic gay jokes from a modern perspective, but as a spotlight for highlighting the homoeroticism already evident in films of the period" (2016, 6). The film is able to illuminate the characters' sexualities instead of just alluding to them:

> In many ways, *Hail, Caesar!* is the fantasy realized—what us queers have been wanting all along from Gene Kelly: those gay sailors are finally able to fulfill their desire for each other without shame. They are able to play up the overt queerness and camp for today's audiences in a way that wasn't previously possible. *Hail, Caesar!* makes the subtext of *Anchors Aweigh* and *On the Town* explicit. (Karpinski 2019, 33)

Sabo also draws a parallel between Channing Tatum's starring role in the *Magic Mike* films to Kelly's sailor musicals:

> On one hand, it points out the openly secret Hollywood traditions of concealing homoeroticism within films about supposedly straight characters. . . . On the other hand, it also expresses a kind of sadness at what we've lost: compared to the exhausting, in-your-face sensuality of *Magic Mike*, the double entendres and cheeky naïveté of *No Dames* feels a lot dirtier, a lot edgier, a lot more subversive. (2016, 7)

The twin sister reporters Thora and Thessaly Thacker keep alluding to *On Wings as Eagles* starring Baird Whitlock and that they have a salacious item they want to publish. It is later revealed that this film was directed by none other than Laurence Laurentz. Whitlock is accused of "engaging in sodomy" with Laurentz for the lead role in *On Wings as Eagles*. This film is credited as his big break, which he allegedly achieved only through his relationship as Laurentz's "young protégé." In conversation with Thora, Mannix mentions that Burt Gurney is Laurentz's "current protégé" (in other words, his lover). The audience never sees Gurney and Laurentz interact (or Whitlock and Laurentz, for that matter)—this information is all relayed through secondhand gossip.

Hail, Caesar! passes GLAAD's own Vito Russo Test, which is modeled on the Bechdel Test and named after the author of the famous queer film text *The Celluloid Closet*. Passing the Vito Russo Test does not ensure that a film is queer friendly, just as the Bechdel Test does not mean a film is feminist, only that it meets these qualifications. In their *2017 GLAAD Studio Responsibility Index*, GLAAD writes about *Hail, Caesar!*:

> The trope of predatory gay characters bribing or pressuring a straight man into sex is both offensive and incredibly overdone through the years. Concurrently, closeted actor Burt Gurney—the star of the musical number "No Dames" who is referred to as "Laurentz' new protégé"—is revealed as the head of the Communist cell before he boards a Soviet submarine. (2017)

George Clooney as Baird Whitlock in *Hail, Caesar!* **Courtesy of Universal Pictures/ Photofest.**

This review assumes that Baird Whitlock is straight while the film itself tells a much more nuanced story. Whitlock constantly brings up his womanizing although viewers never see him with a woman. When he wakes up in the hands of the Future, he even says, "I'm thinkin', 'What the hell?' I've woken up in some strange houses before, but never without a broad next to me." Given the time period and his overcompensation, he appears to be covering for his own sexuality in one way or another. In the discussion of Whitlock and director Laurentz, it is never said nor implied that Whitlock "engaged in sodomy" against his will. In the film, Whitlock is meant to read as closeted—gay or even bisexual. Peterson refers to it as Baird's "sexual flexibility" (2016).

GLAAD also asserts that Burt Gurney is closeted although, unlike other stars, there is no mention of his relationships with women or a denial of his sexuality. If anything, through the queer sailor dance number and his relationship with Laurentz as his new "protégé," he is the most "out" character, perhaps akin to actors in the 1940s and 1950s whose sexuality was the best kept secret in Hollywood. GLAAD also reveals their anti-Communist bias as they list Burt Gurney's Communist ties among the other issues they see with the film. Aaron Lecklider's "*Hail, Caesar!* Shows Hollywood's Hidden History of Queer Communists" looks at this connection: "The Cold War indeed saw a stepped-up persecution of homosexuals in federal employment and society at large, which occurred alongside the politicization of gay women and men through an emerging movement of radicalized 'homophiles'" (2016). Lecklider continues:

> Burt's blond hair and pursed lips suggest Soviet-era propaganda as he gazes powerfully into the future. At the same time, his strong masculinity channels familiar gay male depictions popularized in physique magazines from the 1950s. He embodies the hope and promise of the Soviet utopia alongside the highly sexualized prettiness of the matinee-idol queer. (2016)

In "Camping Out in Hollywood: The Coen Brothers' *Hail, Caesar!*," Sabo argues that while *Hail, Caesar!* might be the Coen Brothers' film most explicitly to deal in camp, in fact all of the Coen Brothers' films engage with camp in one way or another (2016). Sabo writes, "There's nothing overtly homosexual about the Coens' imitation of an Ester Williams seaside musical, but, considered alongside the rest of the film's kitsch iconography—sailors, cowboys, Roman bacchanalia— it screams of not just camp, but gay camp" (2016, 4). He continues, "The homoerotic underpinnings of male bonding is one of their hallmarks: think of how many times in their films two or more men share hugs, sleeping quarters, intimate meals or ritualistic exchanges of phallic symbols" (2016, 5). Thus, Gurney leaving for Russia aboard the phallic symbol of the submarine seems all the more apt.

One of the many films inside the film is the titular *Hail, Caesar! A Tale of the Christ* (which takes its subtitle from the equally homoerotic film *Ben Hur*), starring Baird Whitlock as a Roman soldier. Not only does the film include a Roman bacchanalia but it also includes the homoerotic element of Whitlock's character's transformation upon meeting Christ (even if Whitlock himself cannot remember his line that ends in "faith").

In "How the Coens Tricked You into Thinking 'Hail, Caesar!' Is about Nothing," Anne Helen Peterson writes that utopia is aesthetically proffered only to be narratively unraveled:

> Johansson's sexual drive manifests in a literal inability to fit into her performing costume; the Western hero's anachronism makes it impossible for him to fit into society; Tatum's queerness overfills the masculine space of the Navy ship; Clooney is alienated from the Christian awakening at the *Hail, Caesar!* film-within-a-film, increasingly compelled by a competing, secular, class-based explanation for why the world is the way it is. (2016)

Peterson adds, "And as for Tatum, he's too much for Mannix to even attempt to address," but it is important to consider that Mannix does not even try (2016). Mannix and Gurney are never seen interacting. Mannix reveals that he knows that Gurney is Thora Thacker's source for the gossip on Whitlock's relationship with Laurentz because Gurney was uniquely positioned as Laurentz's current lover to attain such information. Mannix also reveals that because of Gurney's role as the head of the Future, publishing such information would be detrimental to Thacker's career because it would associate her with a known Communist, which would have been a career-ending move at the time.

In conclusion, *Hail, Caesar!* both shows the ways that sexuality is contained and controlled in Hollywood and the film industry but also illuminates the ways queerness has been present all along.

See also *Gilda; The Uninvited*.

Bibliography

GLAAD. *2017 GLAAD Studio Responsibility Index*. May 16, 2017. Accessed June 6, 2021. https://www.glaad.org/sri/2017/universal-pictures.

Karpinski, Kel R. "Performing Desire in Times Square: Sailors, Hustlers and Masculinity." CUNY Academic Works, 2019. Accessed June 6, 2021. https://academicworks.cuny.edu/gc_etds/3002.

Lecklider, Aaron. "*Hail, Caesar!* Shows Hollywood's Hidden History of Queer Communists." *Slate*, February 15, 2016. Accessed June 6, 2021. https://slate.com/human-interest/2016/02/hail-caesar-shows-hollywoods-queer-communist-hidden-history.html.

Peterson, Anne Helen. "How the Coens Tricked You into Thinking 'Hail, Caesar!' Is about Nothing." *BuzzFeed News*, February 11, 2016. Accessed June 6., 2021. https://www.buzzfeednews.com/article/annehelenpetersen/how-the-coens-tricked-you.

Sabo, Lee Weston. "Camping Out in Hollywood: The Coen Brothers' *Hail, Caesar!*" *Bright Lights Film Journal*, March 6, 2016. Accessed June 6, 2021. https://brightlightsfilm.com/camping-out-in-hollywood-the-coen-brothers-hail-caesar/.

—Kel R. Karpinski

HOME FOR THE HOLIDAYS (1995)

DIRECTOR: Jodie Foster
SCREENPLAY: W. D. Richter
CAST: Holly Hunter (Claudia Larson), Robert Downey Jr. (Tommy Larson), Anne Bancroft (Adele Larson), and Charles Durning (Henry Larson)
SPECS: 103 minutes; color
AVAILABILTY: DVD (MGM)

At first glance, Director Jodie Foster's 1995 *Home for the Holidays*, starring Holly Hunter, Robert Downey Jr., Anne Bancroft, and Charles Durning, is a holiday film where a cold-stricken young woman, who gets fired from her job as an art restorer and then accidently makes out with her former boss, flies back to her parents' house to have Thanksgiving with most of the family, the one holdout being her little brother, Tommy (who shows himself about twenty minutes into the film). The movie is seemingly popcorn fodder; most critics at the time thought of it as a common lighthearted farce where eccentric characters get together in a fishbowl and aggressively bump into one another and the glass, until finally the bowl bursts and the pressure is released. One reviewer, Emmanuel Levy of *Variety*, concludes: "Pandering to its audience, 'Home for the Holidays' is not so much an uncanny as a canned picture, reaffirming viewers' dreaded anxiety of spending yet another predictably chaotic Thanksgiving in the clutches of their families—while also suggesting why next year they'll do the same thing again" (1995).

What is interesting, however, is *Home for the Holidays* is not as typical in other ways, in that it deviates from farcical norms when it comes to how it characterizes the one gay character in the film, Tommy, played by Downey. Earlier in his review, Levy mentions this by lauding Downey's performance as "multi-nuanced" and "notably unstereotypical" (1995), which is important to place to the forefront, because prior to the 1990s, in most films, LGBTQIA+ characters were represented as "as an object of ridicule and laughter" or were "dangerous, violent, predatory, or suicidal" (Media Smarts n.d.). In the 1990s, however, queer characters became more recognized and normalized, even though the country was still quite homophobic and discriminatory; generally, gay characters were not the protagonists but were supporting characters helping the main characters through their conflicts, like in the case of *Home for the Holidays*. Claudia, played by Hunter, adores Tommy, who is a whirlwind of energy, love, and happiness. He is out and he is proud, and, more importantly, it is known by the family that he is gay (and is not the central focus of Tommy's identity). Viewers are led to assume that the family has known about Tommy's sexual identity for some time; the straight members of the family, in fact, are more eccentric and zanier than the one commonly represented as eccentric and zany in most Hollywood films prior to the 1990s, which is an important but necessary shift from the norm. Much of that may have to do with Jodie Foster, who, much to the surprise of many, came out publicly during an acceptance speech in 2013 when receiving the Cecil B. DeMille Lifetime Achievement Award at the Golden Globes but had apparently and quietly been out in Hollywood since "the Stone Age" (Abramovitch 2013).

Much of that, however, may also have been because of the slow shift in an understanding of the gay community during the Clinton era, a time that was still problematic with the passing of "California's Proposition 8 banning same-sex marriage and the 1996 Defense of Marriage Act, which prohibits federal recognition of same-sex marriages by the states" (Franke-Ruta 2013) and coming off of the heels of Reagan, Bush Sr., and the AIDS epidemic, then considered "the Gay Disease." With films like *The Birdcage, Interview with the Vampire, Philadelphia, The Crying Game*, and *The Wedding Banquet*, the queer community, through the mass media industry, was being regularly seen and experienced by the general public, to the point of being ordinary.

In *Home for the Holidays*, even with the biting intolerance expressed by Joanne during the Thanksgiving dinner sequence, and even with the lack of complete understanding from his parents, Tommy and his surprise marriage to Jack (which is also exposed during the dinner sequence) are looked at as being part of the family dynamic. It is just another argument to be had in what is a series of arguments from a family like most other families in the country, functional in its dysfunction. Tommy is not strange because he is gay; he is strange and gay, which allows the viewer to be more at ease and ultimately love him, very much like his entire family does, even if they do not understand him or his identity.

See also *Father of the Bride* Series.

Bibliography

Abramovitch, Seth. "Jodie Foster's Stirring Golden Globes Speech: 'I Already Did My Coming Out a Thousand Years Ago' (Video)." *Hollywood Reporter*, January 13, 2013. Accessed June 26, 2021. https://www.hollywoodreporter.com/news/general-news/jodie-fosters-stirring-golden-globes-411953/.

Franke-Ruta, Garance. "How America Got Past the Anti-Gay Politics of the '90s." *Atlantic*, April 8, 2013. Accessed June 26, 2021. https://www.theatlantic.com/politics/archive/2013/04/how-america-got-past-the-anti-gay-politics-of-the-90s/266976/.

Levy, Emmanuel. "Home for the Holidays." *Variety*, October 29, 1995. Accessed June 26, 2021. https://variety.com/1995/film/reviews/home-for-the-holidays-1200443218/.

Media Smarts. "Queer Representation in Film and Television." Mediasmarts.ca. Accessed June 26, 2021. https://mediasmarts.ca/digital-media-literacy/media-issues/diversity-media/queer-representation/queer-representation-film-television.

—Douglas C. MacLeod Jr.

THE HOURS (2002)

DIRECTOR: Stephen Daldry
SCREENPLAY: David Hare, based on the novel of the same name by Michael Cunningham
CAST: Nicole Kidman (Virginia Woolf), Meryl Streep (Clarissa Vaughan), Julianne Moore (Laura Brown), Ed Harris (Richard Brown), Stephen Dillane (Leonard Woolf), Miranda Richardson (Vanessa Bell), Toni Collette (Kitty), John C. Reilly (Dan Brown), Claire Danes (Julia Vaughan)
SPECS: 114 minutes; color
AVAILABILITY: DVD (Paramount)

The Hours consists of three parallel narratives—interconnected by Virginia Woolf's 1925 novel *Mrs Dalloway*—about a day in the life of three women living in different places and different times: writer Virginia Woolf in Richmond, 1923; suburban housewife Laura Brown in Los Angeles, 1951; and editor Clarissa Vaughan in New York City, 2001. Early in the morning, Virginia Woolf wakes up and starts working on the first draft of her next novel after the usual visit of her doctor; Laura Brown's day begins in bed reading *Mrs Dalloway* while her husband makes breakfast for their son; and Clarissa buys flowers first thing in the morning and plans a party for her friend Richard, a gay poet who is dying of AIDS and just received a prestigious literary prize.

Virginia is deep in thought about her novel. Her sister Vanessa and her children visit her one day and Virginia remarks how she is longing for London life. After the kids find a dead bird, Virginia ponders death and decides not to kill her heroine but someone else in the book. Before leaving, Virginia violently kisses Vanessa on the lips. Afterward, she goes to the station to take a train to London, but Leonard finds her and an argument about her mental health follows: on doctors' orders, they moved to Richmond, but Virginia misses London—she confesses, "My life has been stolen from me. I'm living in a town I have no wish to live in. I'm living a life I have no wish to live" [01:18:07].

Laura's day revolves around making a cake for her husband's birthday. After kissing her neighbor Kitty, she dwells on the claustrophobic roles as mother and wife that constrain her and thinks about killing herself. Having finished the cake, Laura drops her son at the babysitter's house and drives to a hotel with the intention to commit suicide, but she changes her mind. Instead, she decides to abandon her family.

Clarissa is absorbed in preparing the party. Richard thinks he failed as a writer, does not want to attend the party, and feels he is staying alive to satisfy Clarissa, whom he calls Mrs Dalloway. Later in the day, Louis—Richard's former lover—shows up at Clarissa's apartment and she reminisces about their youth and the summer she and Richard were romantically involved, the happiest moment in her life, as she tells her daughter Julia. When she goes to help Richard get ready for the party, he jumps out of the window in front of her. At night, Laura Brown, Richard's mother, arrives at Clarissa's apartment and tells her that, even though nobody will forgive her, she does not regret having abandoned her family: "It was death. I chose life" [01:41:55].

Based on Michael Cunningham's Pulitzer Prize–winning 1998 novel *The Hours*, named after Woolf's working title (Mullan 2011)—a postmodern reading of Virginia Woolf's *Mrs Dalloway*, or "retelling" as the author posits (Cunningham 2011)—Daldry's adaptation presents "a woman's whole life in a single day" from different space-time settings, in which characters of different sexual identities converge to offer a glimpse into their lives [00:16:26]. The three elements more thoroughly explored in both the novel and the film adaption and which the protagonists must face are time—its passing, duration, and rupture—sexuality—by means of kisses—and suicide.

The opening and closing scenes break with the one-day timing of the story in order to show Virginia Woolf writing her suicide notes and walking into the River Ouse in Sussex in 1941. The rest of the film is timed according to the hours of a day: morning, afternoon, and evening/night. The shared experiences of the three protagonists (and Woolf's Mrs. Dalloway), that is, their pondering over social conventions, gender roles, and sexual identity, convene in the present time of the story. Cunningham makes use of Woolf's "tunnelling process" to connect his characters to the present moment, something Daldry carefully transposes to the big screen. The result is the portrayal of the writing, the reading, and different reenactments of a novel written in the 1920s but very much alive in the 2000s.

The film shows the evolution of the social implications of same-sex desire, but it does not delve into it. The characters' queer sense of self is represented by kisses: in the case of Virginia Woolf and Laura Brown, secret romantic encounters with other women, and in Clarissa Vaughan's case, her singular heterosexual experience. Kate Haffey (2010) posits that the kisses stand for "the power of the moment" (151) and are "consistently placed in opposition to the work of continuance" (152), which is symbolized in the limiting gender roles imposed on women. In 1923, Woolf, sexually ambivalent herself, creates the character of Mrs. Dalloway, for whom a kiss with her friend Sally Seton in youth meant "the most exquisite moment of her whole life." However, this is never mentioned in the film. Instead, Virginia kisses her sister in a desperate act, which irritates Vanessa. Far from the tender and reciprocated kiss in Cunningham's book—which leads Woolf to include the kiss between Clarissa and Sally Seton in her novel—the scene in the film seems to aim at revealing Virginia Woolf's same-sex desire in a rather forced way. In 1951, Laura, feeling entrapped in her life as a housewife, kisses Kitty after explaining that she needs to go to the hospital to have a growth in her uterus checked. Kitty decides to ignore the incident, downplaying Laura's impulse, and leaves. Whereas in the book, the kiss awakens a latent desire toward Kitty, in the film the kiss seems to have a merely comforting function. The kiss is the turning point in Laura's day and increases her distress, which eventually pushes her to the hotel room where she plans to commit suicide. In 2001, Clarissa, the only openly lesbian of the three protagonists, kisses Richard and Sally. In the present, Clarissa and Richard exchange two greeting kisses, passionless but sentimental, to which Clarissa reacts awkwardly, as, for her, it supposes a deviation from her relationship with a woman and thus represents a transgression (Haffey 2010, 152). As she tells Louis, she is stuck in the past, in the summer she and Richard were together, and the kiss she remembers so fondly acquires a special significance because it transcends gender and fixed sexual orientations by reverting the original idea from *Mrs Dalloway* [00:54:36]. According to Haffey, the past kisses in the three time lines "exist outside an imaginable, scripted future" (152). This is why Clarissa and Sally's kiss at the end of the film is seen in a new light, as the scene provides a sort of happy ending and a prospect of futurity.

The different queer identities in the film are attached to certain stereotypes, such as depression, suicidal thoughts, and AIDS. The multiplicity of points of view and the disruption of the chronology with space-time leaps that take viewers from the beginning of the twentieth century to the beginning of the twenty-first century provide a site of reflection as to how sexually fluid identities have been dealt with at different times in the last hundred years. The dialogue between Woolf's and Cunningham's novels is mirrored in that of *The Hours* (the novel) and Daldry's adaptation. The film offers three different resolutions for the characters' sexual ambiguity. In Woolf's novel, Clarissa cherishes the kiss with Sally, but her sexuality is resolved as she accepts heteronormativity, complying with the norm and acquiescing in the roles of wife, mother, and hostess. For her part, Woolf, although unconventionally, married as well, providing herself with a sort of social shield, like many other lesbians at the time. Laura Brown, feeling as constrained as Mrs. Dalloway, falls into a depression, attempts suicide, and ends up running away from domesticity, a fate that resembles the one met by female characters in lesbian pulp fiction of the 1940s and 1950s. By abandoning her husband and two children, Laura becomes "the monster," as Clarissa's daughter states [01:31:04]. Clarissa Vaughan, however, is the paradigm of the postmodern sexually fluid character and the reversal of Clarissa Dalloway: she accepts a lesbian identity, but the most exquisite moment in her life was shared with a man. In the end, once Richard is gone and Clarissa's nurturing is finished, as though she felt the same relief Louis did when he ended his relationship with Richard—"The day I left him . . . I felt free for the first time in years," he concedes [00:55:24]—she is able to resume her life and her relationship with Sally.

See also *Far from Heaven; A Single Man*.

Bibliography

Cunningham, Michael. "Virginia Woolf, My Mother and Me." *Guardian*, June 3, 2011. Accessed March 10, 2021. https://www.theguardian.com/books/2011/jun/04/virginia-woolf-the-hours -michael-cunningham.

Haffey, Kate. "Exquisite Moments and the Temporality of the Kiss in 'Mrs. Dalloway' and 'The Hours.'" *Narrative* 18, no. 2 (May 2010): 137–62.

Mullan, John. "The Hours by Michael Cunningham." *Guardian*, June 24, 2011. Accessed March 10, 2021. https://www.theguardian.com/books/2011/jun/24/the-hours-michael-cunningham -bookclub.

—Layla Ferrández Melero

• I •

I AM MICHAEL (2015)

DIRECTOR: Justin Kelly
SCREENPLAY: Justin Kelly and Stacey Miller, inspired by the *New York Times Magazine* article "My Ex-Gay Friend" by Benoit Denizet-Lewis
CAST: James Franco (Michael), Zachary Quinto (Bennett), Charlie Carver (Tyler), Avan Jogia (Nico), Emma Roberts (Rebekah)
SPECS: 101 minutes; color
AVAILABILITY: DVD (Brainstorm Media)

I Am Michael follows a decade in the life of Michael Glatze, a gay-activist-turned-fundamentalist-Christian. An accomplished writer for queer publications like *XY* and *Young Gay American* through most of his twenties, Glatze later renounced "homosexuality," leaving his long-term boyfriend in order to pursue a career in the church and marrying a woman he met at Bible school. Justin Kelly's film, produced by Gus Van Sant, is based on Glatze's real-life story with much of the source material borrowed from Benoit Denizet-Lewis's 2011 *New York Times Magazine* article titled "My Ex-Gay Friend." While the film has been characterized as "ambiguous" in its portrayal of Glatze and the antigay rhetoric he adopted—an aspect that has frustrated many of the film's critics—*I Am Michael* explores what is so frequently framed as a dichotomy between sexuality and religion from a new and nuanced perspective.

The film opens with a halting conversation between Michael and a young man who is "having some trouble" with his sexuality. Their conversation—a confession, really—is a common trope found in Western works addressing gay identity and the church. When the youth, visibly distressed, says, "I just don't understand why God made me like this," referring to his romantic and sexual desire toward other men, Michael is quick to correct this idea with his own doctrine. He begins, "He didn't. You should never define yourself by your choices or your desires. 'Gay' doesn't exist. It's a false identity. . . . You always have a choice. You want to go to heaven, right? . . . If you're a moral person, then you'll choose heterosexuality in order to be with God" [00:01:05–00:02:12]. And with that, the stage is set; Michael's beliefs, beliefs that he is hoping to see reproduced in this youth, are among those that have historically been cited to justify discrimination and even violence against the LGBTQIA+ community (Karslake 2007).

But Michael's dogmas are more complicated than they first appear. As the next scene illustrates, he hasn't always held these antigay beliefs. In fact, the film transitions to ten years earlier and shows Michael living with his then boyfriend Bennett in San Francisco, working as the editor of a prominent gay magazine, and enjoying the company of queer friends and colleagues [00:02:18]. The rest of the film moves chronologically, following Michael and the events in his life that would lead him to the opening scene's conversation with the other young man.

A number of compelling juxtapositions in the film suggest why Michael might have moved from one outspoken position to the extreme opposite. Early on, for example, Michael stands amid a crowd at a quiet vigil being held for Matthew Shepard, who, the victim of a well-reported hate crime, was murdered for being gay in 1998 [00:05:00]. A contemplative Michael is spurred on in his activist work following this event. Working alongside the rest of his team, he attempts to navigate *XY* magazine's response to the hate crime. And his later work continues to combat discrimination by making stories of LGBTQIA+ youth known. At a speaking engagement later on, he is even seated next to Judy Shepard, Matthew Shepard's mother, who, along with her husband, founded the Matthew Shepard Foundation in memory of their son.

While Matthew Shepard's death prompted his mother to become a prominent LGBTQIA+ rights advocate, the death of Michael's own mother is a source of anxiety for him that draws him away from LGBTQIA+ activism and toward a rigid understanding of a Christian afterlife. Through flashbacks and a trip to the spot where his mother's ashes are scattered, viewers see the strength of their familial relationship [00:09:39–00:11:55]. The memory of his mother functions as a major motivation for Michael's later actions, funneling many of his experiences into his apparent reflections surrounding death. Michael sets off to make "a documentary about queer youth in America, because discrimination against LGBTQIA+ youth must be eliminated" [00:18:38–00:18:47]; for example, Christianity's positioning against LGBTQIA+ youth is a recurring theme in many of the interviews that Michael conducts [00:18:57–00:20:36]. Nevertheless, Michael is most captivated by an interview with a gay Christian student at Liberty University (whose real-life campus website celebrates being ranked the "Most Conservative College in America"). While interviewing this Liberty student, Michael falls silent and becomes introspective as the student excuses himself in order to attend to a fellow classmate whose mom has just passed away. Michael watches, entranced by the comforting words and prayers offered to the grieving woman [00:20:37–00:22:01]. A number of close-ups on Michael's face and a POV shot of his later perusal of a website titled "Why I Am a Gay Christian!" continue to shed light on the character's inner struggle regarding his sexuality [00:22:16]. At the premiere of his documentary, Michael mulls over the student's words once more: "I didn't come out to friends and family until last year. I'm a Christian . . . which a lot of people think is impossible, but I think that's just as ridiculous as the antigay right" [00:22:35–00:22:49]. Following this introspective trajectory, Michael begins attending church and pulling away from Bennett.

This introspective turn is further connected not only to his mother's death but to his father's as well, and a growing fear around mortality in general. Crawling into bed one night alongside Bennett, whose growing anxieties about his boyfriend match Michael's own, the latter asks, "Do you think when we die, we just disappear like we never existed?" [00:28:10–00:28:19]. Bennett assures him that he and Michael will always be together, but a subsequent montage indicates that Bennett has misunderstood Michael's concerns. Images from the tree where Michael scattered his mother's ashes and the Liberty student's prayer for his classmate are interspersed into an already disorienting club dance scene, illustrating the actual struggle that Michael is going through as he attempts to deal with his fears around death, doubts regarding his sexuality, and general attraction to religion [00:28:56–00:29:10]. Following this montage, Michael experiences his first panic attack, his anxiety now making itself manifest physically. But Michael sees the onset of these attacks as a sign from God. Refusing to believe that they are, in fact, panic attacks, he fears his chest pains are a misdiagnosed heart condition. When tests reveal that there is no underlying condition, he thanks God for saving him and turns his efforts toward a new magazine called *YGA* (*Young Gay Americans*), dedicating an early issue to Christianity and "homosexuality," hoping to bring the two together. His interest, however, quickly loses its symbiotic direction. As Michael listens to a sermon recording by a pastor who frames rejecting "homosexuality" as a form of love, the camera spins around him with swelling music, making his resulting paradigm shift visible, corporeal [00:44:20–00:45:10].

While the question of death and mortality is here displayed as an explanation for Michael's redirection, his trajectory is also put forth—oddly enough—as an extension of his "queer theory." "Gay and straight are just social constructs," Michael tells his editorial team at *XY*. "God, you and your queer theory. Class is in session with Professor Michael Glatze," a coworker quips back. But Michael doubles down, responding, "We need to put out the message that being attracted to the same sex doesn't define who you are" [00:06:32–00:06:48]. At first, he presents this postgay understanding of identity as a means of positioning being gay within a wider array of identity markers. At a later speaking engagement, Michael expands on this idea: "What a lot of people aren't aware of is that the terms 'heterosexual' and 'homosexual' were only introduced about a hundred years ago," offering a history of sexuality well known to those who have read Foucault on the subject [00:08:45–00:08:53]. But while here Michael, like Foucault, is attempting to move away from the limitations of discursive constructions of sexuality in order to add nuance and complexity to the narratives of LGBTQIA+ youth, he employs this same framework to later renounce "homosexuality" as a "false identity" (as noted in the confessional scene from the start of the film).

Although this narrative depicts Michael's trajectory as a natural progression of his intellectual thought—as he breaks away from limiting labels and rejects not only the binary of gay and straight but many forms of sexuality altogether—the film seems to be giving this idea more credit than it deserves. After all, the real Michael Glatze repeated trite arguments that framed same-sex desire as a "deficit of masculinity," adhering to conservative rhetoric far more than to queer theory (Denizet-Lewis 2011). Furthermore, while the film might portray Michael deconstructing homosexuality, he simultaneously reinforces the construction of heterosexuality. Writing on his personal blog, he reasons, "I was a heterosexual person with a homosexual problem, and I took care of that problem" [01:02:07–01:02:13]. This is not a continuation but a break from his earlier understanding of sexuality and its constructs.

Looking to the conservative rhetoric Michael employs in the film, viewers see another interesting juxtaposition as the ex-gay man condemns what he perceives as Christian persecution against him and his newfound beliefs in much the same way that he had previously fought LGBTQIA+ discrimination. For example, when he is asked to leave a Buddhist meditation retreat after making other participants uncomfortable as a result of his growing intolerance, he expresses his sense of injustice. "So, because I'm Christian, and I express my opinions, I have to leave? That's so messed up" [01:03:09–01:03:18]. But his sense of being a martyr positions him in opposition to other in-members of his new faith as well. Butting heads with a teacher at the Bible college he later attends, Michael complains to a number of his classmates—"We're here to serve God, not to identify as the exact kind of Christians they want us to be"—before quickly apologizing for the outburst [01:25:38–01:25:48]. A fellow student named Rebekah, however, encourages him: "You know what's best because that's God speaking through you" [01:25:51–01:25:54]. Her comment seems to add to Michael's already dangerous sense of religious grandeur. Already, Michael has read a number of signs—his panic attacks, for instance—as indicators that God is speaking directly to him. Michael decides to leave the school, and Rebekah leaves with him. They declare their love for one another, and Michael professes to have successfully "uprooted" his same sex desires as a result [01:32:22].

His grandiose delusions are both explained and validated by Michael's desire for social clout within the film. Accustomed to the publicity and accolades of being an LGBTQIA+ advocate, his switch to the ex-gay movement was just as visible, just as blogged about. As demonstrated by his own online writing, his excitement at Rebekah's encouragement, and his drive to become a pastor of his own congregation, Michael appears as a person who desires both attention and followers. In response to the antigay rhetoric Michael employs in *I Am Michael*, pointing specifically to his reference to being gay as a choice, film reviewer William Blizek questions "why anyone would take that claim seriously, especially when it's coming from someone who is always seeking public attention" (Blizek 2015).

Indeed, many critics wondered why the film dedicated so much time to creating a three-dimensional depiction of someone they saw as a two-dimensional hypocrite (Catsoulis 2017). Director Justin Kelly similarly notes that confused critics were quick to ask him, "Why give this guy [Michael] a voice?" (Setoodeh 2015). But Kelly saw a larger, unexplored narrative in Glatze's life, although he added, "It's not like I'm going to rally and say I'm on his side" (Setoodeh 2015). Still, this is half the reason why so many critics were confused, claiming that neither Kelly nor the film seems to take a side at all. Blizek wonders who the film is intended for—too risqué for a conservative audience, too indifferent about religious intolerance for a queer audience. Framed as both impartial and ambiguous, the film seemed to frustrate a number of viewers who wished to see the film fall into one camp or another. Ambiguity seems to be the predominant response to the film; following an early screening, even the real-life Michael Glatze expressed his approval to interviewer Jake Reynolds in the vaguest of terms, hoping that the film would open a dialogue about "a variety of these things," later hinting at the reason for his ambiguity: "We want to be very careful about it because we don't want to be starting another fight" (Reynolds 2015). Despite conducting a cordial interview, Reynolds, an out gay vlogger, followed the clip with his own push to demystify what was going on in the film. Addressing his viewers, he concludes that *I Am Michael* "doesn't really have a point of view one way or the other. I mean half of it was really, really gay . . . and half of it, I think the Christian fundamentalists would love" (Reynolds 2015). Dissatisfied with this ambiguity, he looks for a response to the film by reasserting a more binary-oriented lens: "So who's going to like it more: the gay activists or Christian fundamentalists?" In restructuring this binary, Reynolds seems to be undoing the narrative that the film successfully conveys—the idea that there needs to be more room for open dialogue and for more compassion in general. For, as the ending of the piece indicates, Kelly deals with the film's main subject compassionately but not indifferently.

I Am Michael ends with the just-married Michael and Rebekah greeting their new church congregation [01:35:30–01:36:10]. As patrons filter in, a close-up of Michael shows a look of discomfort as it settles across his face. A subsequent close-up of Rebekah, who is watching her new husband, reveals a similar expression, her eyes and the corners of her lips falling downward as she observes Michael's slight shift in features. The film abruptly transitions to the end credits after a final close-up on Michael's face shows he is beginning to breathe heavily, suggesting the beginning of another panic attack. The message is clear: although the film has granted Michael a great deal of sympathy and nuance of character throughout his homophobic trajectory, he has not yet attained the sense of peace that he believed "renouncing homosexuality" would provide. If his panic attacks are an indication of his need to change from the person he was, he is still on the wrong path. By ending on a sour note, Kelly cues the audience's understanding that Michael is not yet (and perhaps never has been) in the right. He is someone who is in over his head, uncertain. The film may be called *I Am Michael*, but it does not—and possibly cannot—definitively tell viewers who Michael truly is, as he does not yet seem to know himself.

See also *Yes, God, Yes.*

Bibliography

Blizek, William. "I Am Michael." *Journal of Religion and Film* 19, no. 1 (2015). https://digital commons.unomaha.edu/jrf/vol19/iss1/22.

Catsoulis, Jeannette. "Review: *I Am Michael* Portrays a Gay Activist Seeking to Be Straight." *New York Times*, January 27, 2017. Accessed January 2, 2021. https://www.nytimes.com/2017/01/26 /movies/i-am-michael-review-james-franco-zachary-quinto.html.

Denizet-Lewis, Benoit. "My Ex-Gay Friend." *New York Times Magazine*, June 16, 2011. Accessed January 1, 2021. https://www.nytimes.com/2011/06/19/magazine/my-ex-gay-friend.html.

Karslake, Daniel. *For the Bible Tells Me So.* First Run Features, 2007.

Reynolds, Jake. "Exclusive Interview with Michael Glatze of *I Am Michael* (starring James Franco)." YouTube, January 30, 2015. Accessed January 4, 2021. https://www.youtube.com /watch?v=DERC4kpd5Ag&feature=emb_logo.

Setoodeh, Ramin. "Story of Ex-Gay Man Stirs Sundance." *Variety* 326, no. 16 (2015): 16.

—Jon Heggestad

IT (2017) AND *IT CHAPTER TWO* (2019)
It (2017)

DIRECTOR: Andy Muschietti

SCREENPLAY: Chase Palmer, Cary Fukunaga, and Gary Dauberman, based on the novel *It* by Stephen King

CAST: Jaeden Lieberher (Bill Denbrough), Bill Skarsgård (Pennywise the Dancing Clown), Jeremy Ray Taylor (Ben Hanscom), Sophia Lillis (Beverly Marsh), Finn Wolfhard (Richie Tozier), Wyatt Oleff (Stanley Uris), Chosen Jacobs (Mike Hanlon), Eddie Kaspbrak (Jack Dylan Grazer)
SPECS: 135 minutes; color
AVAILABILITY: DVD (Warner Bros.)

It Chapter Two (2019)

DIRECTOR: Andy Muschietti
SCREENPLAY: Gary Dauberman, based on the novel *It* by Stephen King
CAST: Jaeden Lieberher/James McAvoy (Bill Denbrough), Bill Skarsgård (Pennywise the Dancing Clown), Jeremy Ray Taylor/Jay Ryan (Ben Hanscom), Sophia Lillis/Jessica Chastain (Beverly Marsh), Finn Wolfhard/Bill Hader (Richie Tozier), Wyatt Oleff/Andy Bean (Stanley Uris), Chosen Jacobs/Isaiah Mustafa (Mike Hanlon), Eddie Kaspbrak/James Ransone (Jack Dylan Grazer)
SPECS: 170 minutes; color
AVAILABILITY: DVD (Warner Bros.)

Together, *It* (2017) and *It Chapter Two* (2019) tell the story of seven close-knit friends, affectionately known as the Losers Club, as they battle Pennywise the Dancing Clown, an evil, supernatural being who feeds on the fear of children every twenty-seven years. The first film focuses on the club's formation and culminates in the temporary defeat of Pennywise. Initially, the club includes Bill Denbrough, Richie Tozier, Stanley Uris, and Eddie Kaspbrak. Bill is the de facto leader and struggles with stuttering. Richie is the group's wisecracking, bespectacled jokester. Stanley is a pensive Jewish boy preparing for his bar mitzvah. And Eddie is a sickly (and possibly hypochondriac) boy with a smothering mother. As the summer begins, Bill tries in vain to find his missing younger brother Georgie (Pennywise's first victim in the film), as the Losers Club also deals with bully Henry Bowers and his ruffians. Along the way, three more friends are added to the club, Ben Hanscom, Beverly Marsh, and Mike Hanlon. Ben is teased for his obesity and brought into the group after escaping an attack from the Bowers gang. Beverly is ostracized for her perceived promiscuity while suffering through an abusive relationship with her father and is recruited when she runs into Losers at the pharmacy while buying tampons. Mike, seemingly the lone African American youth in Derry, joins the Losers Club after being saved by them during an attack from the Bowers gang. Separately, each member of the Losers Club receives disturbing visions conjured by Pennywise that prey on their worst fears. Together, they travel to his lair and seemingly defeat him. Only wounding the demonic clown, the Losers bicker among themselves before momentarily splitting up. When they reunite, it seems like they have vanquished Pennywise for good. To be sure, Bill makes each of the Losers swear an oath to come back and defeat Pennywise should he return to Derry twenty-seven years later.

It Chapter Two sees the reunion of the Losers as adults. They only have vague memories of the events that bonded them together. Stricken by fear, one Loser, Stanley, decides to commit suicide instead of staring down Pennywise once more. Mike feels that if the Losers perform the Ritual of Chüd associated with the Shokopiwah tribe, they can defeat Pennywise. The ritual requires the retrieval of a token from their childhood for an offering. The ritual also requires that they retrieve the token alone as they had temporarily disbanded the summer they encountered Pennywise. While alone, each member flashes back to past encounters with Pennywise while also experiencing new ones as adults. Before long, all the Losers except Mike and Bill express misgivings and desires to leave Derry. After fending off an adult Henry Bowers, who just escaped a mental institution with the help of Pennywise, the Losers coalesce and resolve to perform the ritual. During the ritual, Pennywise transforms into a spider-like creature and mortally wounds Eddie. The remaining Losers taunt Pennywise to make him feel small, an act that regresses the clown to an infant, whereupon Mike rips out the creature's heart for the remaining Losers to crush. With Pennywise fully vanquished, the Losers must escape his lair. Richie, however, is crestfallen over Eddie's death and initially refuses to leave his side. Upon escaping, they head to the quarry, where Bill, Mike, Ben, and Beverly speak fondly of Eddie. Richie can only sob before he is embraced by the group. The film ends with the reading of a letter Stanley wrote before committing suicide. Each of the Losers is highlighted as both a teenager and an adult reading portions of the letter as the Losers go their separate ways once more.

In assessing the duology's significance to LGBTQIA+ issues, it is best to parse out specific aspects of the film, including the town of Derry and its homophobia as well as the homoerotic relationships within the Losers Club, especially Richie's sexual orientation and his relationship with Eddie. Though the duology portrays Richie as a person struggling to come to terms with his sexuality and as a heroic character, the films fall short of achieving any milestones for LGBTQIA+ representation in cinema.

In the films, Derry is an evil place, hiding the prejudices and hatreds of the past as they continue to manifest in the present, including but not limited to homophobia. The beginning of *It Chapter Two* offers the strongest illustrative example. After playing a game at the Derry carnival, Adrian Mellon and his partner Don Hagerty are accosted by a group of local teenagers led by Webby, who tells the men they "wouldn't want to give people the impression we allow a bunch of fucking fairies like you in this town" before savagely beating them. Adrian is thrown over the bridge, where he is eaten by Pennywise. Don chases after Adrian and witnesses Pennywise but is spared. During the attack, no one in town notices the hate crime despite it barely happening on the outskirts of the carnival. It is also not mentioned again the rest of the film. The couple is singled out solely because their sexuality is overt and open. Much as Derry has ignored its missing children, it too has ignored its homophobia, thereby condoning it. It bears noting that the incident as portrayed in the novel (and, therefore, the movie) was inspired by the real-life murder of Charlie Howard, a young gay man beaten and drowned in Bangor, Maine, on July 7, 1984. It also bears noting that Charlie and the character of Adrian both had asthma.

Homophobia is also seen as one of Bowers's tactics to bully the Losers. On the last day of school, the Losers and Bowers engage in a heated exchange. After imitating Bill's stutter, Bowers tells him, "This summer's gonna be a hurt train for you and your faggot friends." Likewise, as discussed below, Bowers uses homophobic slang to insult Richie in a scene where Richie's sexuality is strongly insinuated.

The relationship between the Losers can be said to be rife with homoerotic undertones. For instance, Stanley describes dumping his school supplies into the garbage as the "best feeling ever." Richie interjects, "Yeah. Try tickling your pickle for the first time." And when the boys decide to play at the quarry, they all strip down to their white underwear. Even with the arrival of Beverly, Richie, Stanley, and Eddie are preoccupied, splashing each other while Bill and Ben set their eyes on the lone girl/young woman. Even when dry, the boys remain in their underwear.

Along these lines, one of the more famous aspects of *It Chapter Two* was the decision to make Richie gay, something that is strongly implied at various points in the film. When Richie retrieves his artifact for the Ritual of Chüd, he walks into an abandoned theater, which triggers a flashback to his adolescence. In the flashback, Richie is playing *Street Fighter* against a boy named Connor, who is later revealed to be the cousin of Henry Bowers. While playing Connor, Richie glances over to him in a manner that might connote attraction, especially considering how the scene plays out. When Richie wins, he slaps Connor five and compliments him on the good game, but there is an awkward pause. As before, the subtlety of the interaction can be missed were it not for what happens next.

Isaiah Mustafa as Mike Hanlon, Bill Hader as Richie Tozier, James McAvoy as Bill Denbrough, Jessica Chastain as Beverly Marsh, and Jay Ryan as Ben Hanscom in *It Chapter Two*. Courtesy of Warner Bros./Photofest.

Richie offers Connor a token to play him again. Sensing tension over Richie's gesture, Connor asks why he is being weird. At this point, Bowers becomes part of the scene. Connor looks at Bowers and says, "You assholes didn't tell me your town is full of little fairies." For his part, Bowers exclaims, "What? You're trying to bone my little cousin?," before yelling to Richie, "Get the fuck out of here, faggot!" Overcome with embarrassment, Richie retreats from the theater and to the park, where he is terrorized by a statue of Paul Bunyan, who asks him, "Want a kiss, Richie?" After coming out of the flashback, Pennywise appears atop the statue, mocking Richie by asking if he wants to play a game. He suggests Truth or Dare, noting that Richie would not want anyone to pick truth because of what he is "hiding." Pennywise continues, "I know your secret. Your dirty, little secret. Oh, I know your secret. Your dirty, little secret. Should I tell them, Richie?" When delivering the last sentence of the quote, Pennywise looks straight at the camera, seemingly breaking the fourth wall. It is clear that the audience is supposed to assume that Richie is gay, something that evinces itself with Eddie.

Much has been written about the homoerotic relationship between Richie and Eddie in the novel. Throughout the book, Richie calls Eddie "cute," and when Eddie is felled by Pennywise, Richie kisses him on the cheek. The nature of their relationship is subtle in the first film (at best) but more apparent in the second film, even more prominent than the novel. In the first film, Richie glances at Eddie during several telling interactions. With Eddie revealed to be gay in the second film, the scenes take on a new tenor. When the Losers first encounter Beverly, they discuss her presumed promiscuity when she leaves. Richie says the list of boys she has slept with is longer than his penis, looking at Eddie while doing so. Likewise, when Pennywise appears in Bill's slide projector, Richie clutches onto Eddie. Finally, when the Losers take their blood oath at the end of the film, Richie and Eddie are the only two to hug before leaving. The homoerotic nature of these interactions as teenagers gains new significance when *It Chapter Two* reveals that a teenage Richie carved "R+E" on a bridge in Derry. Producer Barbara Muschietti told *IGN*'s Jim Vejvoda, "The way I interpreted it was that there was love there. I don't know if romantic, I don't know. But it feels totally natural that it would be unrequited love" (2019).

Though implicit in the first film, Richie's sexuality is explicit in *It Chapter Two*. Writer Gary Dauberman, for instance, discusses the conscious decision to strongly insinuate Richie's feelings for Eddie:

> There is a subtext in the novel and Andy [Muschietti, director] and Barbara [Muschietti, producer] and I talked about it, but it didn't feel like a choice, it just felt like a natural part of his character. But I love that love story. I think that is a special part of the movie and a special part of the character. Because it felt like it was part of his character. I think we pulled it out more, and it is more prominent in the movie. It is a part of the many things that define him. The carving of the initials, I give credit to Andy on that. It was a great way to button that up. (Parker 2019)

Indeed, in *It Chapter Two*, Richie takes Eddie's death hardest. Initially, he is in denial, trying to convince the Losers that Eddie can still be saved. After escaping Pennywise's lair, Richie sobs in the quarry before the Losers embrace him. Just before leaving Derry, he recarves "R+E" into the bridge. This is done while

Stanley is narrating his letter to the group. Stanley's letter seemingly encourages Richie to embrace his sexual identity: "I live my whole life afraid. Afraid of what would come next. Afraid of what I might leave behind. Don't. Be who you want to be. Be proud." It is, however, uncertain at the end of the film if Richie will let his true feelings be known. As mentioned below, the film suggests this is something he wishes to keep secret.

The films are also not breakthroughs for progressive LGBTQIA+ portrayals in cinema. Richie's show of affection to his dead friend provides a counterbalance to the brutal death of Adrian Mellon, but it is weak. The ending for Richie is, at best, ambiguous, while the heterosexual couple to emerge from the Losers Club (Ben and Beverly) seems a happy one. Richie's feelings for Eddie only emerge at the end of the second film, giving the narrative no opportunity to explore his sexuality in depth. It also bears noting that Pennywise has the uncanny ability to read his victim's worst fears. That adult Richie's biggest fear is his outing as a gay man casts doubt on whether he will come out even though Stanley's encouragement to "be proud" seemed directed at him.

See also *Dawn of the Dead; Fright Night; Let Me In.*

Bibliography

Burbatt, Jaime. "Stephen King and the Ambiguously Gay Trope." *Vocal*, September 7, 2017. Accessed April 2, 2021. https://vocal.media/geeks/stephen-king-and-the-ambiguously-gay -trope-1/.

Grace, Dominick. "Doing *It*: Sex and the Monster." In *The Many Lives of It: Essays on the Stephen King Horror Franchise*, edited by Ron Riekki, 44–55. Jefferson, NC: McFarland, 2020.

Itzkoff, Dave. "Bill Hader Discusses Richie Tozier's Secret in *It Chapter Two*." *New York Times*, September 6, 2019. Accessed April 2, 2021. https://www.nytimes.com/2019/09/06/movies/bill -hader-it-chapter-two.html/.

Keaney, Quinn. "Let's Discuss Richie's 'Secret' in *It Chapter Two* for a Sec." *Pop Sugar*, September 12, 2019. Accessed April 2, 2021. https://www.popsugar.com/entertainment/Is-Richie -Gay-in-It-Chapter-Two-46584437/.

Mercer, Erin. "The Difference between World and Want: Adulthood and the Horrors of History in Stephen King's *It*." *Journal of Popular Culture* 52, no. 2 (2019): 315–29.

Opie, David. "The Scariest Thing about *It Chapter 2* Is the Film's Limited Portrayal of Queerness." *Digital Spy*, September 13, 2019. Accessed April 2, 2021. https://www.digitalspy.com /movies/a29020986/it-chapter-2-richie-gay-sexuality-lgbtq/.

Parker, Ryan. "*It: Chapter Two* Writer Explains Decision to Include Richie Tozier's 'Secret.'" *Hollywood Reporter*, September 12, 2019. Accessed April 2, 2021. https://www.hollywood reporter.com/heat-vision/why-it-chapter-2-bill-hader-explored-richie-toziers-secret-1237100/.

Peitzman, Louis. "*It Chapter Two* Reckons with Stephen King's Troubling Legacy of LGBTQ+ Representation." *Them*, September 5, 2019. Accessed April 2, 2021. https://www.them.us/story /it-chapter-two/.

Pulliam, June. "'Best Not to Look Back': Monstrosity, Medium and Genre in Tommy Lee Wallace's *It* (1990)." In *The Many Lives of It: Essays on the Stephen King Horror Franchise*, edited by Ron Riekki, 84–94. Jefferson, NC: McFarland, 2020.

Vejvoda, Jim. "*It Chapter Two*: How Richie's Secret Comes from Stephen King's Book." *IGN*, September 6, 2021. Accessed May 21, 2021. https://www.ign.com/articles/2019/09/07/was -richie-gay-in-it-chapter-2.

—Todd K. Platts

• J •

JEFFREY (1995)

DIRECTOR: Christopher Ashley
SCREENPLAY: Paul Rudnick, based on the play of the same name by Paul Rudnick
CAST: Steven Weber (Jeffrey), Michael T. Weiss (Steve Howard), Patrick Stewart (Sterling), Bryan Batt (Darius)
SPECS: 92 minutes; color
AVAILABILITY: DVD (Shout! Factory)

Jeffrey is a handsome gay man living in New York City in the mid-1990s. Coming of age during the AIDS crisis means that Jeffrey looks at dating and sex with an extreme wariness. His best friends are Sterling, a rich and imperious interior decorator, and his much-younger partner, Darius, an actor appearing in Andrew Lloyd Weber's *Cats*. Though Jeffrey likes dating and enjoys sex, he is so worried about AIDS that he vows complete celibacy to guarantee safety. But despite his commitment to his plan, he meets Steve, a ruggedly handsome man who reveals he is HIV-positive. As Jeffrey's reserve starts to crumble, he must confront his crippling fear of AIDS and embrace living. And as an example, he has the idyllic relationship of Sterling and Darius to look to—the latter is also HIV-positive, and the two repeatedly assure Jeffrey that HIV-positive does not necessarily translate to a death sentence.

Jeffrey's screenplay is adapted by Paul Rudnick from his stage play. A hit as an off-Broadway play, *Jeffrey* is an important entry in queer cinema as it addresses the AIDS crisis with humor and empathy. The film—an independent feature from Orion Classics—was part of an emergence of queer pop culture of the mid-1990s, a period that was relatively fruitful for queen cinema. The same year that saw *Jeffrey*, Hollywood films like *Boys on the Side*, *Home for the Holidays*, and *To Wong Foo, Thanks for Everything! Julie Newmar* as well as seminal documentaries like *The Celluloid Closet* and *Wigstock* were released; during this time, pop artists like k.d. lang, Melissa Etheridge, and RuPaul were enjoying success. As comedian/talk-show host Arsenio Hall remarked to RuPaul on his eponymous chat show, "There seems to be . . . this *freedom* that's going on [in the 1990s], people coming out, being themselves," which RuPaul attributed to the Clintons' being elected to the White House after three terms of Republican presidencies ("RuPaul Interview on Arsenio 1993" 2018). This moment in queer cinema can be best summarized by Lily Tomlin's narration during a montage of 1990s-era queer cinema in *The Celluloid Closet*: "The long silence is finally ending. New voices have emerged, open and unapologetic. They tell stories that have never been told. About people who have always been there" (Epstein and Friedman 1996).

When looking at *Jeffrey*, it is important to note that it is a romantic comedy about AIDS. So much of queer cinema, and AIDS cinema in particular, is about trauma, and the idea of an AIDS comedy seems to be antithetical to the subject matter. Rudnick himself noted that during the play's initial run, audiences would laugh and then suddenly stop when a character announced his HIV status: "There were certain moments, especially when one character announced that he was HIV positive, when the audience stopped laughing. It was just total silence, and you could tell they thought, 'Oh, this is not a comedy anymore. . . . That's impossible.' And then a few seconds later, they were roaring again" (Rudnick 2021). What viewers are seeing in *Jeffrey* is a work that chooses to address the AIDS crisis—similarly to artists such as Larry Kramer and Tony Kushner—but instead of telling a sad story, Rudnick chose to use comedy as his form of activism. He packages his story in the way Nora Ephron or Woody Allen would by telling it as a romantic comedy. The history of AIDS and gay culture does find its way into the film—viewers see images of Gay Pride, Christopher Street, artist George Segal's *Gay Liberation Monument*—but the concerns of the main character are packaged as a gay version of *When Harry Met Sally* or *Sleepless in Seattle*.

The allusion to Ephron and Allen is important when analyzing *Jeffrey* because aside from being a story about AIDS and queer life, it is about AIDS and queer life in New York City. New York City is particularly important when looking at American queer history. It is the site of the Stonewall Rebellion, which took place in the summer of 1969 and sparked the contemporary gay rights movement (as well as being the inspiration for Gay Pride), and New York City was one of the first—and hardest hit—cities during the AIDS crisis. In 1997, the *New York Times* reported that over sixty thousand people had died in New York City, with over one hundred thousand people living with HIV and thirty thousand with full-blown AIDS. Aside from San Francisco, New York City had become the city most affected by the AIDS crisis (Altman 1997).

But New York is also seen as an important cultural hub for queer America. Like San Francisco, Los Angeles, Chicago, and other major cities in the United States, New York City was a destination for many queer people who sought to leave stifling small towns or rural environments for the seemingly more progressive big cities, in which the anonymity and diversity of larger populations meant that they could be more open with their sexual and gender identities. So the New York–ness of *Jeffrey* is almost as important to the film as the queerness and the AIDS narrative. Rudnick himself described the film, in part, as a "valentine to Manhattan," and he wanted to "use Manhattan as a kind of Gershwin romance capital," a clear reference to the use of Gershwin's "Rhapsody in Blue" in Woody Allen's 1979 classic *Manhattan* (1995).

Jeffrey's opener is vaguely reminiscent of Allen's use of Gershwin's classic piece in *Manhattan*. Over Stephen Endelman's jaunty, jazzy score, sweeping shots of Manhattan are presented (inadvertently poignant because the Twin Towers stand majestically in the skyline), with the sun setting, casting majestic silhouettes of the gorgeous skyscrapers of the city, before the montage goes into night, and the crazed neon-sluiced Broadway and Times Square flash across the screen. And as the title is splashed across the screen, viewers are introduced to the title character with the frank and declarative statement, "I love sex. It's just one of the truly great ideas. I mean, just the fact that our bodies have this built-in capacity for joy, it makes me love God." While viewers hear this monologue, director Christopher Ashley, rather bluntly, times Jeffrey's speech with the exploding of fireworks.

The film's first proper scene shows two men in bed having sex, moaning with ecstasy, their coitus interrupted by a broken condom. Much was made of this scene as the opener for the original play, and it is telling that Rudnick places it further down, only after viewers get a cinematic tour of Manhattan. The scene is at once funny and troubling: Jeffrey is calm, but his partner is panicked, repeating with heightened frenzy and alarm, "It broke?"

What follows is a mordantly funny montage in which sex and AIDS collide in a grim kaleidoscope. Images of condom wrappers ordering "Safe Sex" and a *Time* cover announcing gloomily "AIDS: New Research, New Danger" juxtapose with AIDS-skittish potential partners suggesting cuddling, one partner who requires an extensive background history and a series of AIDS tests results, and even a man wearing a face mask who is covered in cling film. Images of presidents, ACT UP protestors, HIV-positive activists Magic Johnson and Pedro Zamora climax with a terrified Jeffrey waking up, screaming, "No!" as if AIDS was a nightmare.

For queer people—particularly gay or bisexual men—who came of age in the 1980s, AIDS was a constant thrum, becoming part of the landscape and soundtrack of growing up and discovering their sexuality. The dominant message of queerness during this time was one of fear and gloom. Viewers meet Jeffrey again, in Washington Square Park, and he speaks directly to the camera, breaking the fourth wall. He recounts a sad moment when he was with a man in bed, but his sex partner was crying. "I'm sorry," the man said through tears, "this used to be so much fun." The emotional heft of this line lies in the complex, layered grief that AIDS left among gay men: not just the immediate grief for friends and lovers, but also the grief of losing a way of life. The gay men who lived through the first decade of the AIDS crisis experienced their sexuality go through a seesaw: they were condemned for their sexuality, later they defiantly celebrated their sexuality, and now they were facing a forbidding fatality from their sexuality. Though it is difficult not to apply metaphor to their illness, it felt like a judgment of some kind.

But again, because this is a comedy, viewers are immediately given a break. When the audience returns to Jeffrey, he announces his celibacy as a response to the AIDS crisis. As soon as he makes this announcement, he is interrupted by a very handsome, muscular, *shirtless*, friendly man who asks him for directions. It is clear that though Jeffrey is determined, his pledge will not be easy.

One of the conventions of romantic comedy is the "meet cute," when the romantic leads meet in a funny, amusing way. Looking to channel his pent-up sexual energies elsewhere, Jeffrey decides to become a "gym bunny" (another classic—if clichéd—trope of gay male culture). As the groovy club beats of the soundtrack score the montage of muscular and sweaty bodies, Jeffery is optimistic that he will be able to forgo sex for exercise. Until he meets Steve, the impossibly handsome Adonis who offers to be his spotter.

Christopher Ashley is doing a lot in this scene with Rudnick's script. He indulges in some slapstick humor when it comes time for Jeffrey to go through a set of bench presses, moaning orgasmically as Steve encourages him with some lusty cheers of support (Ashley also stages the scene cheekily by having Steve's groin just inches away from Jeffrey's panting face). As with most romcoms, there is instant chemistry, and the two men kiss—viewers get another break from the fourth wall, but this time, they plunged into a parallel universe, one in which an audience of teens is watching this in a cinema. The man-on-man kiss prompts homophobic disgust from the two male adolescents, while their female dates coo in esteem. It is as if the film wants to predict—and lampoon—the bigoted reaction man-on-man affection inspires. When the original play was performed, Rudnick and company had concerns about the response to the work—he was particularly worried about the elderly matinee crowd who may look at these themes with disapproval. Though his fears were unfounded, the visceral reaction of the male teens is a pointed way to ease some of the possible homophobic responses from real audiences. (It is important to remember that this film was released in 1995.)

Though sexuality is a dominant theme in the film, the other important relationship highlighted is Jeffrey's friendship with Sterling and Darius. Again, Rudnick's script explores the convention of queer cinema of "found" or "created" families; gay men leave their biological families behind and create adopted families of friends. Sterling is the epitome of the witty, self-possessed dandy, a younger take on Quentin Crisp, who is impossibly stylish (just approaching vulgarity) and is unable to get through a sentence without throwing out a quip or a well-placed bit of shade. When Jeffrey recounts being impossibly helped by Mother Teresa, Sterling asks of her looks, sniffing bitchily, "Oh, *please*. She's had work done," when informed that she looked "great."

The union of Sterling and Darius is presented as an ideal "marriage." The topic of gay marriage was not yet a prevailing issue in the national discourse, but it would only be roughly a year before Bill Clinton signed the Defense of Marriage Act (DOMA), essentially guaranteeing that states would be able to deny recognition of gay marriages from other states as well as codifying a federal denial of gay marriages for federal purposes. The monogamous relationship that Sterling and Darius enjoy is presented to Jeffrey as a safe, holistic, and fulfilling answer to his fear of AIDS as well as his angst about what has happened to recreational sex in the virus's looming specter. Sterling is an interior decorator with money, and Darius is a young Broadway hoofer who appears in his first scene in the film wearing a *Cats* costume. In their well-appointed Manhattan apartment, Sterling and Darius make for a striking scene: among the expensive furniture, Sterling is dressed in a foppish set of silk pajamas, and Darius is casually sitting on a couch in his cat costume. Despite the seeming absurdity of their visual trappings, Sterling muses, "Sometimes I think we should be on a brochure for Middle America, then everyone can say, 'Oh, look, a wholesome gay couple.'" (Darius is wearing a studded collar while Sterling says this with a straight face.) Rudnick's penchant for quippy humor has Jeffrey coin the decorator and dancer not a wholesome couple but "Martha Stewart and Ann Miller" (two very imposing figures in camp gay male culture).

But there is something a little more interesting going on with Jeffrey's dismissal of his friends as "wholesome" in that he bristles at the idea that gay people are expected to be role models who ape straight culture. The discussion then delves into something quite substantive as issues of identity and representation come up. Rudnick has talked about including "clichéd" images of queer

Bryan Batt as Darius, Patrick Stewart as Sterling, Steven Weber as Jeffery, and Michael Weiss as Steve Howard in *Jeffery*. Courtesy of Orion Classics/Photofest.

male sexuality in the past because he worried about leaving out gay characters who are campy, effeminate, or flamboyant. The scene is an astute repudiation of respectability politics.

Though the film is about a man who vows never have to sex because of his fear of AIDS, viewers also see the treatment of HIV-positive people. Much of the discourse around AIDS and HIV in the late 1980s and early 1990s centered on the disease and the tragedy. Little attention was given to the lives of HIV-positive people outside of their status. What *Jeffrey* looks to correct is the notion that someone with HIV or AIDS is defined by the illness or the virus. As Rudnick pointed out, the film works to

> show that people who are HIV positive or have full-blown AIDS also have the rest of their lives, that it is not necessarily an immediate death sentence and that sometimes, even out of compassion, we can reduce people to just their disease, even if it's not AIDS. They suddenly become nothing more than a red ribbon. In this movie, we have many characters with AIDS who have full sex lives. (1995)

When Jeffrey finds out that Steve has HIV, viewers get to the root of his worries, which inspired his celibacy kick. Not only is Jeffrey worried about getting HIV, but he also worries about the implications of having a lover with AIDS. Jeffrey is facing a knotty dilemma in which he is "torn between feelings of overwhelming romantic love and, 'What are you letting yourself in for?' in terms of someone being sick, in terms of someone who you may then need to be taking quite a bit of care of, and just the idea of falling in love with someone who may very well not live forever" (Rudnick 1993a).

Unlike Rudnick, Jeffrey struggles not to reduce Steve to his HIV status. In a particularly distressing moment, Jeffrey's fears are realized when Darius passes out due to the side effects of his medication. At the theater, Darius suddenly feels light-headed and faints, tumbling down a winding staircase. As a crowd assembles, Sterling manages to be calm and Darius attempts to rally; a woman in the crowd is familiar with the medication Darius is on and offers helpful advice (a telling nod to AIDS's omnipresence in New York City). At this moment, Jeffrey witnesses a future he fears, which only seems to confirm his plans for celibacy.

Though Rudnick's script and Ashley's direction work to leaven the serious themes of AIDS, they do not ignore reality. So much of Rudnick's work on this film is defined by his experiences losing loved ones to AIDS. He described writing the film with "helpless motivation" as he was surrounded by so much sickness and dying (Rudnick 2021). The audience does not see Darius's death; instead, they witness Sterling's slow processing of it, stoically thumbing through a copy of *Outdoor Photography* in a hospital waiting room. The scene starts off with some foreboding: it is set in a hospital, never an auspicious place for a film about AIDS, no matter how funny it is. Sterling's demeanor, his leonine carriage, is replaced by a subdued appearance. When he finally reveals that Darius is dead, it is an offhand comment after tersely answering Jeffrey's concerned questions. With his efforts at consolation spurned by a grief-stricken Sterling, Jeffrey retreats only to be confronted by Darius, now an angel, wearing his *Cats* costume, though now with white fur and complete with studded collar. Darius admonishes his friend for attempting to live a life devoid of happiness because of fear and urges Jeffrey to "Hate AIDS, Jeffrey, not life." When asked how, Darius suggests that Jeffrey view AIDS as "the guest that won't leave."

When writing about *Jeffrey*, Richard Corliss mused, "In the age of AIDS, there is something heroic about the task [Rudnick] has set himself: to put the gay back in gay." *Jeffrey* is a romantic comedy—an oft-uproarious one—about a very serious topic. Because he was inspired by those around who have died, Rudnick took care because he "never wanted to trivialize the issue at all. But, on the other hand, I thought the challenge of it, to see you could find the humor also right next to the nightmare of it seemed that, if you could pull it off, it would be exhilarating" (1993b). In the years since *Jeffrey* was released, advancements in the treatment of AIDS have changed the way people look at AIDS and HIV. Narratives that once recognized the tragedy of the illness were beginning to draw out other stories that acknowledged the complexities of AIDS and HIV, accompanying the tragedy with optimism, joy, and even mundanity. *Jeffrey* is a stirring film because it seeks to complicate the prevailing discourse of AIDS cinema by adding humor and filtering the story through a mainstream, pop romcom lens.

See also *Philadelphia*; *To Wong Foo, Thanks for Everything! Julie Newmar*.

Bibliography

Altman, Lawrence K. "Deaths from AIDS Decline Sharply in New York City." *New York Times*, January 25, 1997. Accessed March 18, 2021. https://www.nytimes.com/1997/01/25/nyregion /deaths-from-aids-decline-sharply-in-new-york-city.html#:~:text=More%20than%20 60%2C000%20people%20have,per%20day%20in%20November%201995.

Corliss, Richard. "Laughing on the Inside Too: Paul Rudnick." *Time*, May 3, 1993. Accessed March 20, 2021. http://content.time.com/time/subscriber/article/0,33009,978390-4,00.html.

Epstein, Rob, and Jeffrey Friedman. *The Celluloid Closet*. Sony Pictures Classics, 1996. Amazon, https://www.amazon.co.uk/Celluloid-Closet-Lily-Tomlin/dp/B00H381SZS/ref=sr_1_1?crid=N FFVSLVSTACO&dchild=1&keywords=the+celluloid+closet&qid=1617394867&sprefix=lesli e+jo%2Cdigital-music%2C188&sr=8-1.

Rudnick, Paul. Interview by Doug Write. "Inviting Outrage: Doug Write in Conversation with Paul Rudnick." New Theatre Workshop, January 19, 2021. Accessed February 20, 2021. https://www.youtube.com/watch?v=EwJ9aW1YsG0.

———. Interview by Charlie Rose. *Charlie Rose*, August 9, 1995. Accessed March 25, 2021. https://charlierose.com/videos/2691.

———. Interview by Terry Gross. *Fresh Air*, December 10, 1993a. Accessed March 20, 2021. https://freshairarchive.org/guests/paul-rudnick.

———. Interview by Charlie Rose. *Charlie Rose*, February 25, 1993b. Accessed March 25, 2021. https://charlierose.com/videos/2691.

"RuPaul Interview on Arsenio 1993." YouTube, August 16, 2018. https://www.youtube.com /watch?v=WbINxJJY7u4.

—Peter Piatkowski

JENNIFER'S BODY (2009)

DIRECTOR: Karyn Kusama
SCREENPLAY: Diablo Cody
CAST: Megan Fox (Jennifer), Amanda Seyfried (Needy), Johnny Simmons (Chip), Adam Brody (Nikolai), Chris Pratt (Officer Roman Duda), J. K Simmons (Mr. Wroblewski)
SPECS: 102 minutes; color
AVAILABILITY: DVD (Twentieth Century Fox)

Two high school friends, Needy and Jennifer, have seemingly nothing in common. Jennifer is a popular cheerleader, and Needy is an insecure and studious "nerdy" type. One night, Jennifer brings Needy to a local dive bar to attend a concert by indie rock band Low Shoulder. The bar catches fire, and the two girls escape, only for Jennifer to leave with the band, despite Needy's protests. Later, Jennifer comes to Needy's house, covered in blood and vomiting a thick trail of black fluid. Jennifer appears at school the next day, seemingly fine, but soon begins killing and eating her male classmates. She reveals to Needy that on the night she left the bar with Low Shoulder, they took her to the woods and murdered her as a virgin sacrifice to Satan to gain fame and fortune. Because Jennifer was not a virgin, she has become permanently possessed and must feed on men to exist. After doing some research, Needy discovers that Jennifer must be a succubus, a female demon that seduces men in order to feed on them. After Jennifer seduces Needy's boyfriend and kills him, Needy breaks into Jennifer's bedroom and stabs her through the heart, killing her and destroying the demon. In an asylum, Needy has manifested some of Jennifer's supernatural abilities and breaks out of her cell, later tracking down the Low Shoulder band members and murdering them.

The screenplay for the film was written by Diablo Cody, who is known for writing films such as *Juno* (2007), *Young Adult* (2011), *Paradise* (2013), and *Tully* (2018) and for creating the television program *United States of Tara* (2009–2011). Before her career as a screenwriter, Cody worked as an exotic dancer and peepshow performer, which she detailed in her memoir *Candy Girl: A Year in the Life of an Unlikely Stripper* (2005). Cody's involvement in *Jennifer's Body* is particularly important because of her former engagement with what society often considers a socially transgressive form of spectacle but what others may view as a form of female empowerment (Schweitzer 2000, 65).

Similarly, the director of the film, Karyn Kusama, is also known for representations of female empowerment in her work. Kusama has directed films such as *Girlfight* (2000), *Æon Flux* (2005), and *The Invitation* (2015). With the exception of *The Invitation*, Kusama's films are known for their strong feminist themes and flawed female protagonists. In an interview, she called herself a "feminist unapologetically" and, in regard to *Jennifer's Body*, noted that an "emotionally honest story about toxic friendships between women is not going to be easily understood by the sort of mainstream—I want to say—male horror fans" (Puchko 2018). While Kusama does not highlight or acknowledge LGBTQIA+ representation in this film, her comments on the mainstream, particularly of the male audience's lack of acceptance, speak to a representation of female empowerment present within the central protagonists. For example, scholars such as Aidatul Chusna and Shofi Mahmudah suggest the transgressive image of the two female characters exemplifies Barbara Creed's definition of the monstrous-feminine, where "woman as monster can transgress the border which separates the living subject from that which threatens its extinction" (Creed 1993, 14). This image of female monstrosity signals a transgression in *Jennifer's Body* that facilitates female empowerment, but also one that enables a queer connection between the two women.

The queer connection between Jennifer and Needy develops through Needy's relationship with the transgressive monster, in this case, Jennifer. Through their deep connection and a very evident same-sex attraction, Needy ultimately becomes transgressive by association as a result of Jennifer's monstrosity and influence. This queer relationship between the two women, the one that leads to Needy's eventual transgression, is demonstrated in several scenes throughout the film. The first scene occurs near the start of the film, when Needy is watching Jennifer cheer at a school pep rally. They make eye contact and wave at each other. In a voice-over, Needy says, "Sandbox love never dies," implying that their bond is steadfast and perhaps deeper than friendship. The reverse shot of Jennifer is seen through Needy's gaze in slow motion, as she admires Jennifer's beauty. One of their classmates, Chastity, who is seated behind Needy, leans down to her and says, "You're totally lesbi-gay." Although Needy defends this by saying, "What? She's my best friend," the LGBTQIA+ representation here is quite evident.

This image of Jennifer, as seen through Needy's gaze, works as a reversal of the "active/male and passive/female" gaze identified by Laura Mulvey (1975, 11). Needy, as a woman, possesses the active male position or the "active power of the erotic look" (12), while Jennifer is in the passive female position, her appearance

Megan Fox as Jennifer and Amanda Seyfried as Needy in *Jennifer's Body.* **Courtesy of Twentieth Century Fox/Photofest.**

"coded for strong visual and erotic impact" (11). Needy's gaze represents a queer subversion of the male gaze, with Needy taking on the more dominant role of "looking" and Jennifer the object of this gaze. Yet the representation of Jennifer as erotic spectacle and sexual object is also subverted through her monstrosity. In monstrous form, Jennifer becomes bestial, "ranging from the reptilian to the ruminant" (Wills and Roberts 2017, 16). Her body becomes abject, leaking and expelling bodily wastes and developing into an object of repulsion, or the filth and defilement the clean body rejects (Kristeva 1982, 3). Here the scopophilic gaze that constructs the woman as erotic object is subverted by Jennifer's abject monstrosity, and as a result of this monstrosity, Needy becomes transgressive in order to reject it.

There are several examples throughout the film of Jennifer's influence on Needy that later motivate her transgression. In one scene, Jennifer has been possessed and turned into a full-fledged monster. Needy and her boyfriend, Chip, are having sex, while Jennifer has lured their classmate Colin to a vacant house to seduce and kill him. As Needy is having sex, she envisions blood dripping from the ceiling and Jennifer in the corner of the room. She begins to make high-pitched whimpers at the sight of it, which her boyfriend mistakes for moans of pleasure. Through some supernatural connection, Needy can see and hear Jennifer murdering Colin. She leaves in a panic and almost immediately drives into Jennifer on the road, covered in blood in her demonic state. Needy envisioning Jennifer kill while having sex is not only very telling of their queer connection but also represents a transgressive embodiment of bodily excess through pleasure, fear, and pain.

Representations of excess (bodily or otherwise) are often considered transgressive in the mainstream. Linda Williams notes what she refers to as the "pertinent features of bodily excess" in pornography, horror, and melodrama (1991, 4). The first is "the spectacle of a body caught in the grip of intense sensation or emotion" (4), which builds on Carol Clover's discussion of films that privilege sensational body genres (Clover 1987, 187). For Williams, the bodily spectacle of intense sensation or emotion is most often seen through the portrayal of orgasm in pornography, in horror's portrayal of violence and terror, and the portrayal of weeping in melodrama. While *Jennifer's Body* is hardly pornography or melodrama, these portrayals of the bodily spectacle are all present within this scene. Needy experiences the intense sensation or emotion of sex with Chip yet envisions Jennifer in the process, and the horror and violence of witnessing Jennifer brutally murder Colin ultimately leads to intense weeping and overwrought emotion. Yet because Jennifer is the source of this bodily excess for Needy, and given the already preconceived attraction between them, there is a queer embodiment of bodily excess that is present here. Aside from the fact that Needy envisions Jennifer at the height of all this bodily emotion, Jennifer is the solitary source of the bodily sensations (pleasure, sadness, anger) that leads Needy to become transgressive.

There are multiple examples in this film of queer representation between these two characters, and the one that inspires Needy's transgression is most strongly identified or acknowledged. On the same evening that Needy envisions Jennifer killing Colin, she returns home after encountering Jennifer on the road and finds Jennifer in her bed. The two kiss passionately for several moments before Needy revives herself and pulls away, but the kiss remains unspoken between them. Another scene takes place on the night of prom, when Jennifer has lured Needy's boyfriend, Chip, to an abandoned pool and attempts to kill him. Needy comes to his rescue and taunts Jennifer, calling her "insecure" and no longer "socially relevant," which intensely angers Jennifer. Needy tells her, "I thought you only murdered boys," to which Jennifer replies, "I go both ways." This informal term (sometimes phrased "swing both ways") works as a double entendre, implying versatility in terms of sexual orientation or attraction (bisexuality) and Jennifer's choice of victims.

In a later scene, Jennifer is at home lying in bed recovering from her confrontation with Needy and Chip. Needy breaks through her bedroom window and attacks her, trying to stab her with a utility knife in the heart to expel the demon. As they struggle, Jennifer says, "Do you buy all your murder weapons at Home Depot? God, you're butch." By calling Needy "butch," Jennifer is using a term for a lesbian subculture that ascribes masculine identity and its various characteristics to lesbian women. Gayle Rubin defines "butch" as "the lesbian vernacular term for women who are more comfortable with masculine gender codes, styles, or identities than with feminine ones" (1992, 467). Jack Halberstam discusses the pejorative nature or stereotypes often constituted by "butch" yet writes that "the butch" often exceeds these stereotypes through their societal representation and disrupt "the dominant systems of representation that depend on negative queer images" (1998, 180). Jennifer is undoubtedly using the term in a pejorative way, attempting to subjectify Needy's queer identity and make her a victim. However,

Needy is ultimately able to transcend and liberate herself from these stereotypes and dominant systems of representation yet still remain transgressive.

Jennifer's body represents the same transgressive monstrosity often observed in the monstrous-feminine: she is "from virgin to whore, defined in terms of her sexuality" (Creed 1993, 3). In contrast, Needy's body liberates itself from social categories and conventions of the feminine, represented as "an emancipatory hybrid that resists genre conventions and cultural expectations" (Wills and Roberts 2017, 19). She is simultaneously represented as the outwardly bookish, nerdy type, wearing glasses and using the library to solve the problem of Jennifer's possession, as well as a sexually active and self-secure progressive representation of womanhood. The more intimate scenes of Needy and her boyfriend "possess a joyous eroticism that answers and supplements Jennifer's exaggerated pastiche of vampy sexuality" (Wills and Roberts 2017, 19). She also represents a contradictory image of the "Final Girl," a long way from the sexually reluctant, androgynous image identified by Clover who is ultimately saved by a male figure (1987, 204). She is neither virginal nor androgynous, instead fighting Jennifer on her own after Jennifer kills Chip. When Chip tries to fight Jennifer, she fights alongside him. In this sense, she has liberated herself from the confines of male/female hierarchy and the traditional horror image of the woman in distress.

Although Needy does manage to liberate herself from social stereotypes of the feminine and more traditional female horror film images, she nevertheless becomes transgressive through her friendship with the monster. When Jennifer bites Needy during their final confrontation, she seemingly passes on some of her supernatural powers. Needy escapes the asylum where she is being housed and murders the members of Low Shoulder in a similar manner to Jennifer as succubus. Although the women's attraction to each other is not explicit, the moments that have been illustrated above show an unmistakeable queer representation. Through this relationship with Jennifer as monster, Needy herself becomes a type of monstrous-feminine.

See also *Dawn of the Dead; Fright Night; Let Me In.*

Bibliography

Chusna, Aidatul, and Shofi Mahmudah. "Female Monsters: Figuring Female Transgression in *Jennifer's Body* (2009) and *The Witch* (2013)." *Humaniora* 30, no. 1 (2018): 10–16.

Clover, Carol. "Her Body, Himself: Gender in the Slasher Film." *Representations* 20, no. 1 (1987): 187–228.

Creed, Barbara. *The Monstrous-Feminine: Film, Feminism, Psychoanalysis.* London: Routledge, 1993.

Halberstam, Jack. *Female Masculinity.* Durham, NC: Duke University Press, 1998.

Kristeva, Julia. *Powers of Horror: An Essay on Abjection.* New York: Columbia University Press, 1982.

Mulvey, Laura. "Visual Pleasure and Narrative Cinema." *Screen* 16, no. 3 (1975): 6–18.

Puchko, Kristy. "Karyn Kusama on Destroyer, Sexism in Filmmaking, and the Redemption of Jennifer's Body." *Syfywire*, October 11, 2018. Accessed May 28, 2021. https://www.syfy.com/syfy wire/karyn-kusama-on-destroyer-sexism-in-filmmaking-and-the-redemption-of-jennifers-body.

Rubin, Gayle. "Of Catamites and Kings: Reflections on Butch, Gender, and Boundaries." In *The Persistent Desire: A Femme-Butch Reader*, edited by Joan Nestle, 466–83. Boston: Alyson Publications, 1992.

Schweitzer, Dahlia. "Striptease: The Art of Spectacle and Transgression." *Journal of Popular Culture* 34, no. 1 (2000): 65–75.

Williams, Linda. "Film Bodies: Gender, Genre, and Excess." *Film Quarterly* 44, no. 4 (1991): 2–13.

Wills, Deborah, and Toni Roberts. "Desiring Monsters: Femininity, Radical Incontinence, and Monstrous Appetite in *Ginger Snaps*, *Jennifer's Body*, and *Deadgirl*." *Reconstruction: Studies in Contemporary Culture* 17, no. 2 (2017). Accessed May 28, 2021. http://reconstruction.digital odu.com/issues/contents_172/172_wills_roberts/.

—John Lynskey

JUST GO WITH IT (2011)

DIRECTOR: Dennis Dugan

SCREENPLAY: Allan Loeb and Timothy Dowling, inspired by the film *Cactus Flower* by Gene Saks

CAST: Adam Sandler (Danny), Jennifer Aniston (Katherine), Nicole Kidman (Devlin Adams), Nick Swardson (Eddie), Brooklyn Decker (Palmer), Dave Matthews (Ian Maxtone Jones), Bailee Madison (Maggie), Kevin Nealon (Adon)

SPECS: 116 minutes; color

AVAILABILITY: DVD (Columbia Pictures)

Just Go with It begins with Danny, age twenty-two, suffering a painful breakup from his unfaithful fiancée. Cutting through the following decades, viewers watch as Danny then uses his wedding ring as a gimmick to pick up young women at bars and trick them into sex. The plot thickens at a glamorous party at which Danny begins pursuing a young, attractive, and kindhearted math teacher named Palmer. Spending the night with her on the beach, Danny begins to feel a serious connection with Palmer. As they leave the beach the next morning, however, Palmer finds the wedding ring in Danny's shorts, after which she refuses to date Danny, thinking he is still married. Instead of being honest, Danny tells Palmer that he is in the process of divorcing his unfaithful wife, "Devlin." Danny then persuades Katherine to pretend to be his soon-to-be ex-wife. The web of lies becomes entangled further as Katherine takes a call from her kids in front of Palmer, thus causing her to believe Maggie and Michael are Danny's children. The kids then blackmail their pretend father into taking them on a trip to Hawaii. Despite Danny's plans to propose to Palmer on the vacation, Katherine and Danny fall in love on the trip and later marry.

Released in 2011, this romantic comedy was inspired by the plot of the 1969 film *Cactus Flower*, starring Walter Matthau, Ingrid Bergman, and Goldie Hawn. In the original film, which is based on the French play *Fleur de Cactus*, a middle-aged dentist avoids telling awkward truths to his twenty-one-year-old girlfriend by having his loyal office assistant pretend to be his wife. *Cactus Flower* was a box-office success: it was the seventh highest-grossing film of the year, and Goldie Hawn won an Academy Award and a Golden Globe for her work. Much like the original, *Just Go with It* follows the main characters as they become tangled in a web of lies. *Cactus Flower*'s plot is adapted into the 2010s with Adam Sandler (who coproduced the film) portraying Daniel "Danny" Maccabee, a forty-five-year-old plastic surgeon living in Beverly Hills, California. Much like the original, Danny pursues a younger woman only to realize he is in love with his longtime assistant, Katherine Murphy, as she pretends to be his wife. Unlike the original, *Just Go with It* was poorly received by critics and "won" two Golden Raspberry Awards for Worst Actor and Worst Director.

Throughout *Just Go with It*, viewers watch as five characters—Danny, Katherine, her children Maggie and Michael, and Danny's cousin Eddie (who finagles his way into the trip as well)—practice what they frame to be improvisation in order to maintain Danny's relationship with Palmer. LGBTQIA+ representations and queer-coded characters are scattered throughout the film as the main characters fumble their way through a series of comedic lies only to eventually become more vulnerable and honest with one another by the conclusion. *Just Go with It* uses LGBTQIA+ characters as plot devices and sites of humor within the narrative's progression.

The first queer-coded character given dialogue is Ernesto, a flamboyant, Black hair stylist who helps Katherine make her transformation into "Devlin." As a plot device, Ernesto makes catty remarks about Katherine's hair but ultimately helps amplify her beauty.

Fifty-two minutes into *Just Go with It*, the film first depicts its most central LGBTQIA+ character, Ian Maxtone Jones (Dave Matthews). Ian is the sham husband of Katherine's rival from her collegiate sorority, the real "Devlin Adams." Katherine and Danny have a chance encounter with Devlin and Ian at the resort. Devlin and Ian's relationship thus throws a wrench into the improvisation. Nonetheless, the time Katherine and Danny spend with Ian and Devlin causes them to begin confessing their feelings for each other.

The character of Ian Maxtone Jones is wealthy, vain, and a liar at his core. Viewers are introduced to him beginning with the farce that he invented the iPod; later, Devlin reveals that Ian got his money from suing the LA Dodgers after getting hit by a foul ball. In this same instance, as Devlin comes clean to Katherine, she reveals her marriage is failing and that Ian is gay. Ian is then depicted flirting with and touching the muscles of several handsome, young sailors by the bar. Ian's true sexual identity is hinted at before Devlin reveals the truth to Katherine. Most notably, Ian attempts (but ultimately fails) to win a competition with Devlin against Katherine and Danny by carrying a coconut between his buttocks. Ultimately, Ian helps fuel the film's heterosexual romance plot but fails to be a nuanced representation of the LGBTQIA+ community.

Just Go with It is certainly no model for progressive sexuality nor a positive contribution toward LGBTQIA+ acceptance (and it never claims to be such). Released in 2011, the film follows its era's heteronormative formulations of romantic comedy, intimacy, and social norms. Although the film is generally lighthearted, it should be noted the film's humor is built on body shaming, ageism, racial and ethnic stereotypes, toxic masculinity, and misogyny.

See also *Big Daddy*; *Dodgeball: A True Underdog Story*; *Neighbors 2: Sorority Rising*.

—Michael Diambri

· K ·

THE KIDS ARE ALL RIGHT (2010)

DIRECTOR: Lisa Cholodenko
SCREENPLAY: Lisa Cholodenko and Stuart Blumberg
CAST: Annette Bening (Nicole/Nic), Julianne Moore (Jules), Mark Ruffalo (Paul),
  Mia Wasikowska (Joni), Josh Hutcherson (Laser)
SPECS: 107 minutes (theatrical release); color
AVAILABILITY: DVD (Focus Features)

The Kids Are All Right tells the story of a queer family, comprising a lesbian couple, Nic and Jules, and their children, Joni and Laser. All hell breaks loose when the kids decide to look for their biological father, Paul. With Joni's impending shift to another city for college, Laser hanging out with questionable company, and Jules's frustration at not being successful in her career, the family already seems to have enough on its plate before Paul comes barging in as the newest addition to the household. Insecurities start to run high as Paul is seen as a competitor who is trying to win the kids over. To make things even more complicated, Jules cheats on Nic with Paul. Between hurt and betrayal, love and forgiveness, Lisa Cholodenko places the concerns of a lesbian couple and LGBTQIA+ parenting in the twenty-first century.

The film loses no time in introducing its LGBTQIA+ characters, and three minutes in, the viewer gets a glimpse of the married couple and their children. The film takes an even bolder step in the next few minutes as it shows a few intimate scenes between Nic and Jules. The angles from which the scenes are shot are similar to how mainstream Hollywood films usually portray heterosexual sex scenes, focusing strictly on the face of one of the partners as the other performs oral sex. What is striking is the "ordinariness" of the entire scene, one of the first attempts that the film makes to unhinge the characters from their sexual identities and focus on them as any other married couple. There is also an interesting caveat to the sex scene as Nic and Jules make love while watching gay porn on their television. In 2015, sexuality researcher Lucy Neville published an article titled "Male Gays in the Female Gaze: Women Who Watch M/M Pornography" that astonished many, arguing that women are responsible for one-third of viewership of gay male porn on the online pornography site Pornhub. Neville surveyed a total of 275 women of various sexual orientations, including bisexual, lesbian, heterosexual, and pansexual women. The reports of her study stated that "a total of 82 percent of participants preferred gay male pornography to other genres" (Neville 2015). Continuing the same conversation in her 2018 book *Girls Who Like Boys Who Like Boys*, Neville suggested that one of the biggest reasons behind such a statistic is how women have always been portrayed in mainstream pornography. The degradation, objectification, and dehumanization of women in straight porn is a turnoff for many women, and it was the conclusion of the study that most women have a strong desire to consume porn that is ethical in some way (Neville 2018). Neville also explained how versatility is another motivation for the rising viewership of gay male porn: "What women liked most about male-male porn is versatility, and with heterosexual porn you are going to get penetrated eventually, and that's dull. A lot of ways it can play out with men is more exciting, more experimentation, more open to negotiation" (2018). In this film, Jules takes this conversation even further when she explains how "human sexuality is complicated and sometimes desire can be counterintuitive. For example, women's sexual responsiveness is internalized, sometimes it's exciting for us to see responsiveness externalized, like with a penis" [00:23:30–00:23:50].

Meanwhile, the kids embark on their own mission to find their biological father and, after a lot of snooping and prying, they manage to get hold of a name and a phone number. They soon schedule a meet with Paul, a well-built, motorcycle-owning organic farmer who uses his garden-grown vegetables to run a restaurant. Paul, as they soon notice, is the complete opposite of everything that they have been familiar with—not only is he a cisgender heterosexual man, but he also lives in a way that has always been looked down on by Nic and Jules. He rides motorcycles at a dangerous speed, does not have a stable job or a career, and squanders away his time with a new woman every day. Conversely, the parents, in their quest to be more open-minded and liberal, are not able to say no when Joni and Laser ask them if they can invite Paul to their home. "We have to be smart about this. If we act like grubby bitches, we are just going to make it worse. Let's just kill him with kindness and put it to bed," says Nic to Jules when they are alone in their room [00:26:04–00:26:34].

Despite that decision, neither of them is able to warm up to him when he visits, especially not Nic, who is not only appalled at Paul's rugged way of life but is also battling with an inner crisis of being rendered irrelevant in her kids' life with the entry of this new member. Her anxiety had already been summed up in a previous bathroom scene where she tells Jules that even though she gets it that Paul is "their biological father . . . it still feels really shitty. Like we're not enough or something" [00:25:40]. The garden scene where Paul is introduced to Nic and Jules is one ridden with discomfort and awkwardness. Paul is slightly confused about what to expect out of a queer family, and the camera keeps losing its focus whenever he looks at the married couple from his viewpoint. But when Nic and Jules start to share the story of their first meeting, the camera zooms into the couple's faces from the point of view of their children, reiterating the normalcy of their stories from the perspective of the two kids raised outside homophobic hysteria.

The climax of the movie hinges on Jules's infidelity when she cheats on Nic with Paul. Working in the backyard of his house (her newest venture being landscape gardening), the two kiss by mistake. But soon sparks fly and, frustrated by a near-insipid sex life, Jules gives in to sleep with Paul. While the two try their best not to repeat their deed, they continually find themselves back in bed with each other. To be sure, to depict a lesbian having an affair with a straight man reeks of a shameless Hollywood trope, one that affirms the worst stereotypes about LGBTQA+ relationships. It would have been fine to use this plotline had the director wanted to focus on Jules's stifled sexual fluidity, but the larger point of her affair in the film is merely to throw light on her ailing relationship with Nic. The film peddles the heterosexual myth that all lesbians secretly long for men and uses it to push the story forward. In an interview with *Independent*, Dr. Lisa Blackman, a professor of media and cultural studies, said the film only satisfied the fantasies of a heterosexual viewer not the one belonging to the LGBTQIA+ community:

> One of the biggest discourses that comes from a hetero-normative place is that "all a lesbian needs is a good fuck" [by a man]. The adventure of the film lies in the heterosexual romance while the women's relationship is more about habit, monotony and routine. . . . I have heard people say, "Thank God it was not a film about earnest lesbians taking about lesbianism that I would not be interested in." (Blackman 2010)

That Lisa Cholodenko, a filmmaker who identifies as gay, crafts a story around a lesbian woman sleeping with a straight man and does not address the issue behind it is then a big blow to the seemingly queer-friendly conversations that the film initiates.

The second half of the film deals with Nic's shock at discovering Jules's betrayal and the latter's repentance for the same. The first time Nic learns of her partner's affair is when she and the children are having a dinner at Paul's place. The dinner scene is one of the most pivotal moments in the entire film, one which director Quentin Tarantino termed "one of the scariest scenes he'd ever seen on screen" (Donnelly 2020). Nic and Paul are finally shown to be getting along—they discover that they have the same taste in music, and in one extraordinary shot, they start singing a cappella to Joni Mitchell's "Blue." The picture of this happy household, with two stepsiblings, two lesbian mothers, and a donor father, mirrors the epitome of the queer family, where all the societal norms of marriage, partnership, and bloodline fall apart. But soon in the scene, Nic discovers strands of Jules's hair all across Paul's bedroom and bathroom. The realization of her partner's infidelity comes with a tracking shot, where the camera rotates and zooms into Nic's facial expressions. It is also a shot that, as many critics have insisted, landed Annette Bening a nomination for Best Actress at the Eighty-Third Academy Awards.

The confrontation scene between the couple is set in their bathroom, which is also one of the central settings in the film. From a lovemaking scene, to major decision-making moments, to Nic finding out about Jules's betrayal in Paul's bathroom, the repetition of the setting is a conscious decision to reaffirm the normality of such occurrences in a couple's day-to-day life, despite the sexual orientation of the people involved. Jules, in her apology to the entire family, surmises the reality of marriage quite precisely:

> Marriage is hard. It's two people slogging through this shit, year after year, getting older, changing. . . . Sometimes you're together for so long that you stop seeing the other person. You just see some weird projection of your own junk. And instead of talking to each other you go off the rail and you make stupid choices. [01:33:54–01:35:12]

The relatability of her words is perhaps what earned the film lasting cinematic admiration—for portraying an image of queer people that elevates their average-ness, instead of exploiting the community's struggles and experiences. Mark Ruffalo points out in an interview with *Variety*, "What made that movie so powerful is that it wasn't a polemic. It was people watching themselves—their own relationships, whether they were straight or gay, that's why it had such a cultural impact. Folks saw these people are really no different than them" (Donnelly 2020).

Nevertheless, the film does falter on the representation front since both Moore and Bening are straight actors playing queer characters. As a director, Cholodenko is of the opinion that "it's of the discretion of the director who's the most compelling for that job. While I want to promote gay people represent-ing gay people, trans people, all the rest, queer people—it's also a commercial prospect" (Donnelly 2020). On the other hand, Moore herself addressed such criticisms in one her promotion interviews for the film: "I've thought about that a lot. Here we were, in this movie about a queer family, and all of the principal actors were straight. I look back and go, 'Ouch. Wow.' I don't know that we would do that today, I don't know that we would be comfortable. We need to give real representation to people" (Donnelly 2020). Nevertheless, despite tum-bling at certain places, the film is refreshing in the way it does not show any of the characters in a bad light; there are no villains in this story. Each adult and, to a lesser degree, the kids are merely trying to make sense of the complicated situations they keep finding themselves in. They battle their dreams and desires while trying to make their family work. In short, everyone in the film is trying to be all right, kids and adults alike.

See also *Kissing Jessica Stein*; *The Wedding Banquet*.

Bibliography

Blackman, Lisa. "The Kids Are All Right? Not According to the Lesbian Lobby." *Independent*, November 23, 2010. Accessed February 27, 2021. https://www.independent.co.uk/arts-enter tainment/films/news/the-kids-are-all-right-not-according-to-the-lesbian-lobby-2141111.html.

Donnelly, Matt. "'The Kids Are All Right' Turns 10: The Untold History of the Queer Family Classic." *Variety*, July 30, 2020. Accessed March 3, 2021. https://variety.com/2020/film/news /the-kids-are-all-right-oral-history-10-years-annette-bening-julianne-moore-1234719810/.

Neville, Lucy. *Girls Who Like Boys Who Like Boys: Women and Gay Male Pornography and Erotica*. Cham, Switzerland: Palgrave Macmillan, 2018.

———. "Male Gays in the Female Gaze: Women Who Watch M/M Pornography." *Porn Studies* 2, no. 2–3 (September 2015): 192–207.

—Dyuti Gupta

KILL YOUR DARLINGS (2013)

DIRECTOR: John Krokidas
SCREENPLAY: John Krokidas, Austin Bunn, based on real-life events
CAST: Daniel Radcliffe (Allen Ginsberg), Dane DeHaan (Lucien Carr), Michael C. Hall (David Kammerer), Ben Foster (William S. Burroughs), Jack Huston (Jack Kerouac)

SPECS: 104 minutes; color
AVAILABILITY: DVD (Sony Picture Classics)

Based on a true story, *Kill Your Darlings* depicts the college years of the Beat poet Allen Ginsberg, a period marked by the development of his antiestablishment outlook, an embrace of sexual liberation, and the blossoming of relationships with a number of the other writers who would become the core of the Beat Generation, namely, Jack Kerouac and William S. Burroughs. The film shows that many of these introductions came by way of Lucien Carr, an older undergraduate at Columbia University who takes Allen under his wing. Despite being the main character of the movie, Allen nevertheless takes a back seat to Lucien, who drives the entire plot of the film. Captivated by Lucien in the first minutes of the film, Allen spends the rest of *Kill Your Darlings* spending time with, dwelling on, and writing for and about the other man. Lucien, viewers discover, is only passing his classes thanks to an older friend of his, David, who—also enthralled by Lucien's charm—writes the younger man's essays for him as part of a complicated romantic relationship. As Allen learns more about the manipulative nature of this relationship, he urges Lucien to leave David for good. Lucien does, but Allen suddenly finds himself in the role that David had previously occupied. Lucien begins to use Allen in the same way he used David, but the continued repetition of this relationship dynamic is foreclosed by Lucien's sudden murder of the older man.

Dane DeHaan as Lucien Carr and Daniel Radcliffe as Allen Ginsberg in *Kill Your Darlings*. Courtesy of Sony Pictures Classics/Photofest.

As far as gay and queer portrayals in the film go, the first half is more homosocial than "homosexual," as Allen navigates his newfound friendship with Lucien. Lucien, however, introduces Allen to the gay social scene of Greenwich Village. Here, they observe primarily as outsiders, watching—for example—as police officers escort two gay men from a bar. Around the same time that Allen learns of the romantic ties between Lucien and David, he begins to envision himself in a more intimate relationship with Lucien as well. The latter half of the movie develops this dynamic more explicitly, and the film's climactic sex scene was hailed as "about as graphic as we've seen . . . a mainstream movie go in the gay sex department" (Avery 2013). The film, which might therefore be seen as depicting a wide range of shifting and evolving relationships, illustrates well the differences that Eve Kosofksy Sedgwick observes between homosocial and "homosexual" dynamics between men, as well as their existence not as separate categories but on a continuum (as noted below).

Lucien and Allen initially bond over Brahms and Whitman [00:10:23–00:11:10], signaling a connection founded on intellect, art, and a shared outlook on the academy around them. In an earlier scene, Allen disagrees with a professor while the latter lectures on the necessary "rhyme, reason, conceit [and] balance" of good poetry. Allen interrupts, noting that Walt Whitman was a poet who "hated rhyme and meter." For Whitman, "The whole point was untucking your shirt" [00:08:21–00:08:28]. This notion is the seed from which his antiestablishment views will emerge—views that will be both fuel and foundation for his relationship with Lucien. Even at the close of this confrontation, the camera pans to Lucien, who is staring at Allen from the back of the classroom, engaged with what the other has to say.

Whitman, himself, is a useful touchstone for Allen's embrace of same-sex attraction. As John D'Emilio and Estelle B. Freedman observed regarding nineteenth-century writers, "Whitman served as the most important reference point for men who aspired to the ideals of 'manly affection' and comradeship" (D'Emilio and Freedman 1998). That Whitman and his writing bring Allen and Lucien together therefore cues the reader into anticipating the trajectory of their relationship.

As the two become closer, working together to create "A New Vision"—a writerly community that would lay the groundwork for the Beat Generation—Allen becomes confused by and jealous of Lucien's relationship with David. When he draws attention to their relationship, Lucien grows distressed, explaining, "He [David] is a goddamn fruit who won't let me go. . . . A queer" [00:31:11–00:31:33]. Although Allen seems taken aback by this choice of words, he proceeds to comfort Lucien. As Lucien rests his head in Allen's lap, the slurs he used seem to allow Allen a new grasp on the way he feels about the other man. Allen's desires are depicted through an imagined scenario in which he plays with Lucien's hair, his head still in his lap, before Lucien turns toward Allen, opening his mouth in order to take Allen's fingers into it. An abrupt cut back to their earlier positioning—Lucien resting his head peacefully on Allen's lap while the latter watches him, tense with apparent longing—reveals that the erotic encounter was only Allen's secret desire being played out in his mind [00:31:55–00:32:39].

Later, this desire becomes slightly more manifest through an oral sex scene in which a young woman working as a librarian unknowingly operates as a go-between for the two men. The act is part of a ploy to steal the librarian's keys for a later break-in. Allen distracts her, luring her into the stacks. As she proceeds to give Allen oral sex, Lucien makes a copy of the key, but also watches the act, the two men holding eye contact as the librarian brings Allen to climax [00:49:20–00:50:05]. In *Between Men*, Sedgwick observes that male-male relationships remain safely in a homosocial state through the intercedence of a woman who might triangulate the desire (1985). Following this framework, the moment shared by Lucien and Allen is here made somehow acceptable and safe through the librarian's presence. The librarian, like all of the women in the film, fairs poorly. She is merely a pawn in a game that Allen and David are playing. As A. O. Scott observed regarding the film, "If you are looking for critical perspective on the misogyny of postwar America's most famous literary radicals, you will not find it here" (Scott 2013). The scene's formation of triangulated desire, misogynistic in nature, seems to teeter at the very edge of homosociality and homosexuality, thanks to the two men's almost complete disregard for the librarian—their desire for one another fairly evident.

While neither of these acts are explicitly gay, it is clear by the midpoint of the film that Allen has slipped into the same role previously (or perhaps simultaneously) occupied by David. Already a conversation between Allen, David, and William has indicated that Lucien is only interested in manipulating those whom he can use for his own benefit. Commenting on this element of the film, John-Paul Pryor even suggests Lucien might be "a cold-blooded psychopath" (Pryor 2013). Despite seeing Allen as a threat to his relationship with Lucien, David warns his rival that as soon as he thinks he knows Lucien, "he'll find someone else; maybe he already has" [00:35:04–00:35:17]. Both David and Allen's hopes to be cast as Lucien's love interest certainly seem to go unfulfilled. Yet, despite the fact that the nature of Lucien and David's relationship is never explained in full, an emotion-packed scene in which Allen tells Lucien to break things off with David, who has interrupted an enjoyable evening out, certainly reads as an uncomfortable breakup. A distraught David immediately begins to plead with Lucien: "Look at me, Lu. . . . You said I was everything to you. You are everything to me. Everything to me" [00:56:10–00:56:55].

Yet, in the following scene, Allen finally makes his move. As he and Lucien, drunk and laughing, rest beneath a tree, they bask in the events of the night (namely, Lucien's departure from David). It is a sweet moment that they share, and Allen, taking advantage of it, leans in and kisses Lucien. Lucien pulls away for a moment, but the two come together again for a long and passionate kiss [00:58:25–00:59:37]. When their friend Jack stumbles up to them, they pull apart, and Lucien quickly draws Jack away, turning to tell Allen that he has "work to do"—composing an essay that David had previously written for Lucien but which he, in the scene prior, had made a show of rejecting. Allen curses as he realizes the arrangement that he has unintentionally re-created.

This event leads to two vastly different outcomes. First, turning to Lucien, viewers see that he is unable to turn off others' desires in the same way that he has—to some degree—mastered in himself. Hoping to reunite with Lucien, David returns to him, appeals to him, even threatens him. Fragments of the events that result from this confrontation are then displayed through a nonlinear mode of storytelling. It is unclear how much of this story is the "true" narrative of events and how much Allen has composed through his own investigative writing. At any rate, Lucien apparently stabs David and drags his body into the Hudson River. When Allen hears of the news, he finds Lucien in jail, being held for the crime, but the newly minted murderer explains to Allen that he'd killed David out of self-defense: "He wanted to hurt me, I had no choice" [01:13:45–01:13:51]. Hoping to enlist Allen to now write his deposition for him, Lucien goes on to explain that he hopes to frame the murder as an "honor slaying" [01:15:46].

An "honor slaying," as Allen later learns in preparing Lucien's deposition, refers to "a lethal attack committed when the accused is defending himself against a known homosexual. If the accused is heterosexual, he shall be pardoned. But if the accused is homosexual, the charge of murder in the first degree shall stand" [01:15:50–01:16:20]. And so, Allen begins to wrestle with understanding what David's relationship with Lucien meant and what his own relationship with Lucien means. According to Lucien's mother, Lucien is a victim of David's obsessive fascination: "He spun a web to ensnare my son," she tells Allen. Demonstrating that Lucien's manipulative charm is a hereditary trait, she adds, "Thank God Lu has you in his life. He talks about you all the time. . . . He calls you his guardian angel." To this, Allen replies, "That's what he called David" [01:17:36–01:17:55]. While Allen struggles to piece together these broken relationships, he discovers evidence that David deeply loved Lucien and that Lucien loved him back, that David even saved Lucien after the younger man had attempted suicide [01:20:18–01:22:20]. And so Allen writes the deposition to reflect this:

> He loved you. And the truth is, once you loved him back. But this secret ate away at you. So, in Chicago, you tried to kill yourself. He rescued you. He saved your life. You needed him as much as he needed you. Some things once you love them become yours forever. And if you try to let them go, they only circle back and return to you. They become part of who you are, or they destroy you. [01:24:50–01:27:29]

Lucien's story is one in which his homophobia becomes internalized. At a time when same-sex relations were outlawed, Lucien turns his desires into weapons. Running away from the truth of his desires, he brings about pain—hurting first himself and then those around him.

Allen, however, accepts his desires and grows through them. Although the entire plot is driven by Lucien, Allen emerges as the film's hero in the end, the character who learns the most and comes away with a clearer knowledge not only of himself but of his family, friends, lovers, and rivals. Realizing that his relationship with Lucien brings no satisfaction, he approaches a stranger at a bar. The stranger, a sailor, looks remarkably like Lucien from behind—tall, lean, blonde. In fact, Allen at first mistakes the man for Lucien, but seeing that the sailor is not Lucien, and observing instead the sailor's evident interest in him, Allen proceeds to engage him, ultimately going home with and having sex with the man. This is, presumably, Allen's first time being penetrated by another man. Radcliffe has been praised for his performance in this scene, and the scene itself has been lauded as a more realistic version of gay sex than what audiences typically see in the movies—if, indeed, the act is shown at all (Avery 2013; Pryor 2013). While the gay sex scene in *Brokeback Mountain* might give the viewer pause, raising a number of questions regarding the mechanics and even physics of gay sex, Allen's facial expressions, the positioning of his legs, the pleasure and pain in this moment of *jouissance* are all more believable. Commenting on these choices, Radcliffe, who plays Allen in the film, notes that in discussing the scene with director John Krokidas (an openly gay man), he was told that "gay sex, especially for the first time, is really fucking painful. And [Krokidas] said that he had never seen that portrayed accurately on film before" (Pryor 2013).

While his portrayal might be laudably more accurate, a new set of concerns nevertheless spring up concerning the scene's sequencing within the film. The scene occurs within a wide range of penetrative experiences. Allen's sexual encounter is spliced with scenes of William as he injects himself with heroin, Jack as he receives gut-wrenching news of his friend's death in World War II, and Lucien as he stabs and kills David [01:09:51–01:12:15]. While these climactic moments work well in theory, placing them side by side forces the viewer to equate sex between men with destructive behavior, loss, and death. This perhaps extends the gay-sex-as-painful display considerably too far. At the end of the sequence, Jack observes that his friend—in his last message from overseas—had been reciting Percy Shelley's "Adonais: An Elegy on the Death of John Keats." When his girlfriend asks Jack why the poem is significant, he replies, "It means he's dead" [01:12:12]. This conclusion clearly maps onto the scenes of Lucien and David, begging the question: Is the audience to view William's drug use and Allen's anal penetration as deaths as well?

Yet, while the fall of Lucien's knife is paired with a grimace on Allen's face as he pushes his head back upon the pillow [01:11:30–01:11:32], the effects of these various deaths are not the same. William is lost; Jack, forlorn; David, gone; Lucien, ensnared. Yet Allen reaches up to the soldier's face, bringing it to his own, passionately covering it in kisses, ecstatic. Perhaps Krokidas is more interested in the fruits of these penetrative experiences than in depicting them as similar to one another. In threading these acts together, he displays how wide ranging the results of these experiences ultimately are.

While repeating the same unfortunate trope present in so many cinematic works that focus on gay characters, almost entirely erasing women from the narrative and portraying same-sex relationships as manipulative imbalances of desire, *Kill Your Darlings* nevertheless tells a compelling story that is "at once a lurid true-crime chronicle and a coming-out story" (Scott 2013). Its focus on Allen Ginsberg's college years offers viewers a worthwhile origin story not only for someone who would go on to become one of the most outspoken gay rights advocates in twentieth-century America, but for the entire Beat Generation as well. If nothing else, watch it for the dream sequence in which Dane DeHaan sucks on Daniel Radcliffe's fingers [00:32:28–00:32:36].

See also *Battle of the Sexes; Behind the Candelabra; Brokeback Mountain; Can You Ever Forgive Me?*

Bibliography

Avery, Dan. "Daniel Radcliffe Delivers Graphic Gay Sex Scene in *Kill Your Darlings*." *Logo*, October 15, 2013. Accessed January 13, 2021. http://www.newnownext.com/daniel-radcliffe -bottoms-kill-your-darlings-gay-sex-scene/10/2013/.

D'Emilio, John, and Estelle B. Freedman. *Intimate Matters: A History of Sexuality in America*. Chicago: University of Chicago Press, 1998.

Kramer, Gary M. "*Kill Your Darlings* Has Enthralling Moments but Ultimately Fails." *San Francisco Bay Times*, 2013. Accessed January 13, 2021. http://sfbaytimes.com/kill-your-darlings -has-enthralling-moments-but-ultimately-fails/.

Pryor, John-Paul. "Daniel Radcliffe." *Flaunt*, October 24, 2013. Accessed January 14, 2021. https://flaunt.com/content/people/daniel-radcliffe.

Mondello, Bob. "Beat Manifesto: *Kill Your Darlings*, Figuratively and . . ." NPR, October 16, 2013. Accessed January 12, 2021. https://www.npr.org/2013/10/16/234832821/beat-manifesto -kill-your-darlings-figuratively-and.

Scott, A. O. "The Watchful Years, before the Howling Began." *New York Times*, October 15, 2013. Accessed 12, 2021. https://www.nytimes.com/2013/10/16/movies/kill-your-darlings -stars-daniel-radcliffe.html.

Sedgwick, Eve Kosofsky. *Between Men: English Literature and Male Homosocial Desire*. New York: Columbia University Press, 1985.

—Jon Heggestad

KING COBRA (2016)

DIRECTOR: Justin Kelly
SCREENPLAY: Justin Kelly, inspired by real-life events
CAST: Garrett Clayton (Sean Lockhart/Brent Corrigan), Keegan Allen (Harlow), James Franco (Joe), Christian Slater (Stephen), Molly Ringwald (Amy), Alicia Silverstone (Janette)
SPECS: 92 minutes; color
AVAILABILITY: DVD (Shout! Factory)

The opening sequence of *King Cobra* shows Sean Lockhart (better known by his stage name Brent Corrigan) as he walks into the grainy shot of what looks like a home video. It quickly becomes clear, however, that this is the casting couch of gay porn producer Stephen, the founder of Cobra Video. The opening credits roll on with clips of Sean and Stephen's banter interspersed with the former's journey to Stephen's home studio. With this banter, set to a sexy synthesizer score, writer and director Justin Kelly foreshadows many of the film's later events. Upon first meeting each other in person, for example, Stephen tells Sean that he looks great, and when Sean replies, "Thanks, you look good, too," Stephen dismisses the compliment. "No, no, I'm an old man." But Sean disagrees, "Old men can look good, too" [00:03:36–00:03:45]. And he is not wrong—Slater, being a veteran heartthrob, has aged into this role quite nicely. And although his character seems unsure of how to respond to the younger man's flirtations, quickly changing the subject, the exchange hints at the romance that will build between the older producer and his protégé.

The dangers of their ensuing romance, however, are previewed in these opening minutes of the film as well. Lying across Stephen's couch, Sean tells the camera that he is eighteen, and Stephen zooms in on Sean's amused smile before adding, "I had to double check that ID a couple of times, didn't I?" [00:02:34–00:02:43]. But as the audience later discovers, the ID was a fake, and this fact will work as a point of contention between Stephen and the underage actor. Sean's smile is both naive and knowing, as is the look he gives the camera just before the opening sequence ends. "Let's loosen things up a little bit, and take off some of those clothes," directs the pornographer. "Show the Cobra fans what they really want to see" [00:05:09–00:05:18]. And as Sean's hand slides into his pants, the camera tilts up to his face, which already shows signs of pleasure. Suddenly glancing up, Sean gives a knowing smirk. "Want to see it?" he asks. The shot cuts to a completely entranced Stephen on the other side of the camera, looking greedily at Sean before replying, "Yeah, show me that cock" [00:05:32–00:06:09]. Whereas pornography generally places the viewer in the role of a voyeur, the perspective here places the voyeur, himself, in the viewer's gaze—the shot being not of Sean's penis, but of Stephen's pleasure. In the midst of this shifting perspective, the film's tone is vaguely ominous, both light and dark, fun and dangerous.

These points of tension all work well for a film based on the real-life events leading up to the murder of gay porn producer Bryan Kocis (whom the film renames Stephen). In a *Rolling Stone* article that covered the murder, Kocis is described as "a reclusive middle-aged man with a paunch who liked to troll the Internet for boys" (Wilkinson 2007). Although the film reimagines him as leading-man material in the form of Slater, it otherwise re-creates this description, making Stephen at once passive and predatorial, even "lecherous" (Cheshire 2016). But director Justin Kelly does justice to the dark narrative, playing with the stereotypes recorded in the pages of *Rolling Stone* while adding depth to Sean, Kocis (Stephen), and even Kocis's murderers.

Much has been written on the capitalistic and hierarchical structure of the gay porn industry (Escoffier 2003; Bishop 2015) that makes a profit on the desires of those who have, historically, been marginalized and rejected—often violently—by a heterosexual majority. *King Cobra*, despite offering those in gay porn a greater degree of complexity and depth, similarly presents the larger industry as superficial at best, dangerous—even lethal—at worst. While one producer's murder at the hands of his competitors is the most obvious example of this depiction, all of the same-sex relationships on-screen are framed as manipulative, dubious, and dangerous. After Sean's first performance, for example, Stephen enters the younger man's bedroom wearing a revealing robe. "Are you going to sleep in here tonight?" Stephen asks. It barely registers as an invitation, and its awkwardness makes itself apparent on Sean's confused face. "Uh, yeah?" he responds. Stephen reassures Sean that that will work fine, telling the actor once more that he has something "very, very special," but the scene then cuts to Stephen, alone in his own bed, masturbating to the thought of the younger man [00:06:45–00:08:04]. Mimicking the implicitly masturbatory fantasy offered by pornography, the film depicts Stephen as he climaxes with audible groans before the scene cuts once more, now showing Stephen as he photographs a happy-looking family of husband, wife, and two children. Although it is possible to read this moment as one that shows a greater range to Stephen's character, it comes across instead as a kind of double act, suggesting that the subject is a preying producer at night and a meek family photographer by day.

Still, Stephen interacts with his sister and her family (the family he has been photographing) in a way that feels wholesome, even sweet, as he jokingly tries to circumvent his sister's attempts to set him up on a date with her female co-worker [00:09:37–00:10:01]. He is shy, hiding from those closest to him, despite his online reputation as "a big, bad . . . King Cobra" [00:10:55–00:11:11]. Even in his first attempts to seduce Sean, he is raw and vulnerable. Despite the power differentials between the two—Stephen being an older, wealthier man of independent means, Sean an underage dependent lacking the capital or resources to make it on his own—Stephen initially approaches Sean with a kind of nervous vulnerability. At one point, for example, Stephen tries to explain some of the technical aspects of filming to Sean; the latter, being uninterested in receiving these instructions, begins recording and interviewing an embarrassed Stephen instead, the result being a clear role reversal. Although Stephen insists that he is a "behind-the-camera guy," Sean persists, and Stephen opens up about his own first time sleeping with another man in college. He recalls that when his friends found out, they rejected him, and Stephen, taking the camera back and setting it once more on Sean, concludes, "So, a few years ago, I decided to just do what I love. Even if people despise it, think it's dirty, trashy, I don't give a fuck" [00:25:11–00:25:47]. Turning the camera off, he pulls Sean toward him, kissing him. Sean looks apprehensive, but Stephen continues. "Please just make me feel wanted," he says, and Sean seems to comply although the question of consent still lingers [00:26:32–00:26:56]. Thus, while the scene highlights Stephen's liberation, it does the opposite for Sean. In the ensuing sex scene, the younger man appears detached and visibly distressed, glancing at Stephen with frequent looks of contempt [00:27:18–00:27:24]. Already, Sean appears trapped.

But it does not become apparent how trapped Sean is until much later. Although he initially seems to put up with Stephen's advances because of the benefits that complicity affords, Sean later begins to bicker with the producer concerning his pay. Stephen tries to skirt the problem, but Sean pushes on, saying, "You just bought a fucking Maserati, Stephen. Do you think I'm an idiot?" [00:37:20–00:37:23]. Although Stephen offers a raise, he also grows hostile, reminding Sean that "according to the contract that you signed, I don't have to give you a raise until we make five more videos" [00:38:01–00:38:08]. "Read before you sign, darling," Stephen concludes before shifting gears and pulling yet another power move. "You know what? I'm only going to give it to you under one condition. . . . You have to tell me that I fucked you better than your little boy toy," referring to Mikey, Sean's costar-turned-love-interest [00:38:15–00:38:32].

In following the tradition of many existing narratives surrounding pornography, Stephen is here depicted as both an exploitative consumer and producer while Sean is a site of erotic fantasy, subjected to financial coercion. And in the next scene, these power moves continue as Sean cleans Stephen's toilets for him [00:39:13]. When Sean discovers that Stephen made nearly $240,000 for the video that he was paid $500 for, the actor finally puts an end to their romantic and professional relationship. Stephen, outraged, calls the youth "a whore" as he leaves Stephen's home for good [00:42:36].

But Sean is not depicted solely as a victim of Stephen's vacillating moods. He, too, is fully capable of playing power games. Frustrated by the sexual turn of his relationship with Stephen, he tells the older man's neighbors that Stephen makes gay porn, knowing that it will shock them; he is happy—in fact—to be outing the older man without his consent [00:28:24]. Later, Sean unconvincingly apologizes for arriving late to a film shoot, where he then ignores Stephen's direction, before calling him "too old" and flaunting his new sexual relationship with his scene partner, Mikey, in front of Stephen [00:28:35–00:31:36]. When Sean realizes that he is unhireable after leaving Stephen—his former producer having copyrighted the name "Brent Corrigan," ensuring that Sean would be unable to work with anyone else—the younger man retaliates by informing Stephen that he had been underage and using a fake ID when he first began working with Cobra. "If you don't give me my name back, I'll tell everyone you made kiddy porn," Sean threatens [00:49:18–00:49:44]. Stephen doesn't believe Sean will go through with it, but he does, and it immediately ruins both of their careers. Speaking with another producer, Sean is informed that he "kind of made the industry look a little bad with the whole underage thing" [00:50:50–00:50:54]. Sean seems surprised at this news, and it perfectly illustrates the tension between worldliness and naïveté that runs throughout the film.

For the most part, Sean's cunning seems centered in his body, his looks, and how to use these assets best to his advantage. Outside of that, the actor comes across as materialistic, vain, even foolish. When left alone at Stephen's house, for example, he flips through several channels discussing politics and current events (including coverage of Hurricane Katrina), only to land on an Animal Planet program about horses. Having dismissed what might be thought of as more pressing or substantial programming, Sean exhibits a look of passive contentment as he watches the animals nuzzle one another. The camera cuts away to show Sean, standing zombielike in his underwear, facing the TV [00:10:01–00:10:33]. While this childish simplicity makes it all the more disturbing as the audience realizes Sean was underage upon first coming under Stephen's wing, it also depicts the star as a simpleton, more style than substance.

Yet this narrative about Sean is not the only one being told about him in the film. When he meets up with Mikey once more near the end of the film, hoping to rekindle their relationship and to enlist the other actor in a new porn venture, Mikey responds negatively, questioning Sean as to why he is still invested in porn instead of "real filmmaking" [01:05:40]. Sean, dejected, plows forward with his plan anyway. In the end, he succeeds, directing his own porn video in the final scene of King Cobra [01:26:51–01:28:31]. Yet, despite the suggestion of independence, the overwhelming effect is still a sense of entrapment. He may be at top of the gay porn industry again, but the film suggests that the industry ultimately functions as nothing but a capitalistic spectacle run by greedy gay men who would forgo healthy, balanced relationships for monetary gain.

Although Stephen and Sean are both portrayed in tenuous roles of victim and perpetrator, fluctuating between stereotypes of the dangers of sex work and more rounded explorations of their individual characters, neither seems as extreme as two of the film's other characters: Joe and Harlow. A parallel narrative runs alongside Stephen and Sean's as Joe and Harlow, the producers of a competing gay porn site called Viper Boyz, navigate their own volatile relationship before meeting up with Sean in hopes of securing the young star for a future production. When they hear of the legal issues surrounding Sean's stage name, Joe and Harlow decide the only solution is to murder Stephen. And although the couple shows the sincerest affection and intimacy of anyone in the film, their violent turns are more extreme as well. Much of this is due to Joe's apparent jealousy of and for Harlow, which constantly flares up as a direct result of the escort service that the men also operate. At one moment, Joe lays out a list of rules, insisting that Harlow offer "no passionate kissing and no anal" to his clients [00:17:27–00:17:34]. The next, Harlow lustily pulls down Joe's swimming trunks before performing fellatio. Here, their banter about rules seems playful, but later, the volatility of Joe and Harlow's relationship becomes more striking. As Harlow hands a client's money over to Joe, the latter glares back. "You promised me you were going to be good," he says, and despite Harlow's protests that he had behaved himself with the client, that he was just doing business as Joe had instructed him, Joe shoves the money back into Harlow's face. "You think this means anything to me?" he spits. "You're more important to me than any fucking amount of money. Do you understand that?" [00:20:04–00:20:45]. When Harlow insists that it was Joe who wanted him to get into the escort business, Joe explains that he is only envious of Harlow for being preferred by their clients. Joe apologizes and the two embrace one another, insisting that they have only ever loved each other and engaging in what is certainly the most passionate kissing of the entire film [00:21:39–00:22:09]. This scene also serves as a unique counterpoint to Sean and Stephen's arrangement, which lacks real intimacy, turning instead on monetary concerns. Conversely, Joe and Harlow are quick to demonstrate the real passion of their relationship, casting money, morality, and all other concerns aside. The film, of course, shows that neither relationship is a particularly good model.

Although Joe's rages seem upsetting, Harlow flirtatiously entertains them. After denying Joe's accusations that he is sleeping with their new assistant, for example, Harlow smiles back at him, saying, "Baby, it is so hot that you'd rather kill me than let someone else have me" [00:34:55–00:35:00]. Their explosive romance even leads the two to pull a gun on one another as they argue about their financial problems (even this fight is not caused by money, but rather over the efficacy of shooting their debt collectors). Joe begins this confrontation, but it ends with Harlow commandeering the gun—thanks to his military training—and holding it to Joe's head. Both collapse to the floor as Harlow apologizes to Joe [00:45:02–00:45:16].

Nevertheless, a number of tender moments between these two men appear throughout the film, with Joe and Harlow's violent sincerity acting as a foil to Sean and Stephen's manipulative games. Joe and Harlow are clearly enamored with one another, and Harlow showers Joe with presents and attention while also repeatedly referring to him as "my little piggy bank" [00:16:27–00:16:45]. They work out together, consume their protein shakes together, lay out in the sun together, all the while exchanging frequent flirtations and getting physical as often as they can [00:16:45–00:17:56]. At one point, Harlow tells a client (a dumpy looking man with his arm in a sling who excitedly rubs his face on Harlow's feet) that Joe "helped [him] get honorary discharge for being a fag" [00:18:57–00:19:25], and when Harlow later becomes distressed while filming a sex scene with a co-star who reminds him of his own abusive stepfather, Joe helps him work through the resurfaced trauma [00:40:44–00:43:10].

Still, the film culminates with Harlow violently stabbing Stephen to death. Having partially reconciled over the phone, Stephen tells Sean that he has to get going; he has a new actor auditioning for him tonight [01:03:58–01:04:23]. Stephen then answers the door to reveal that his new talent is, in fact, Harlow. As the audition begins, in much the same way that Sean's did at the start of *King Cobra*, Harlow quickly takes over, telling Stephen where to sit and what the older man is and is not allowed to touch. While flipping the dynamic between actor and producer in a way that is, again, not dissimilar to Sean's earlier recording of Stephen, this moment holds none of the sweetness that the earlier instance did. Eerie music builds as Harlow moves from seductive to aggressive. Standing above Stephen, his voice loses its flirtatious edge as he asks the producer, "Is that what you like to do, huh? Touch all these little boys whenever you want?" [01:11:04–01:11:11]. Stephen begins to dismiss this idea, but Harlow quickly silences him by repeatedly plunging a knife into Stephen's neck and chest. Joe walks into the room and asks Harlow if he had to be so messy. Although shaken, Harlow is still able to respond: "I did it, for everyone who's ever taken advantage of me" [01:12:58–01:12:58]. The parallel discourse between Stephen and Sean from earlier in the film and Stephen and Harlow at this moment casts Sean in Harlow's role as Stephen's killer. Harlow's claim extends not only to include Sean but perhaps all underpaid workers whose bodies bring a profit to the porn industry. It seems important then, that Harlow is shown "directing" the scene before the violence occurs, suggesting the implicit violence of the industry while being manifested through an act of stabbing that might, itself, be rendered as phallic. Nevertheless, it is somewhat of a surprise that Stephen's murder is at Harlow's hands when Joe has previously shown himself to be the more violent of the two; upon Stephen's death, it is Joe after all who happily congratulates the shaken Harlow on a job well done [01:12:56–01:13:38]. More surprising still is the scene leading up to the couple's arrest. As the Viper Boyz get into their car for a drive sometime after the murder, Joe suddenly turns to Harlow, his face distressed. "What have we done?" he asks. Moments later, police lights begin to flash, and the two realize that their actions have caught up to them [01:24:13]. Although movie critic Godfrey Cheshire notes that the Viper Boyz recall "the days when gay people in movies were all portrayed as dangerous psychos," even Joe and Harlow hint at a level of engaging complexity (2016).

Expanding on this topic in his review, Cheshire observes that the "softcore prurience in the areas of both sex and violence," so central in *King Cobra*, has existed "at least since content restrictions on movies were relaxed in the late '60s," but while director Justin Kelly may draw on this earlier, limiting cinematic history of gay men in film, his direction nevertheless incorporates more nuance, nodding to past stereotypes while offering his characters a more rounded treatment (2016). No one comes out of the film unscathed, but nobody seems entirely irredeemable either—a true feat for a film based on the events of a real-life murder. As David Ehrlich observes, the film "pounds with empathy for those who want to live in a world that's only comfortable with them in its margins, those men who decide that it's better to own the sewers than to live on the streets" (Ehrlich 2016). In their quest to own anything at all, they fail, but even if *King Cobra* is a cautionary tale, it is one with a great deal more depth than what its toned and superficial façade might at first suggest.

See also *Boogie Nights; I Am Michael*.

Bibliography

Bishop, CJ. "'Cocked, Locked and Ready to Fuck?': A Synthesis and Review of the Gay Male Pornography Literature." *Psychology & Sexuality* 6, no. 1 (2015): 5–27.

Cheshire, Godfrey. "King Cobra." RogerEbert.com, October 28, 2016. Accessed December 30, 2020. https://www.rogerebert.com/reviews/king-cobra-2016.

Ehrlich, David. "*King Cobra* Is the *Boogie Nights* of Gay Porn (Tribeca Review)." *IndieWire*, April 17, 2016. Accessed December 31, 2020. https://www.indiewire.com/2016/04/king-cobra-is-the-boogie-nights-of-gay-porn-tribeca-review-289836/.

Escoffier, Jeffrey. "Gay-for-Pay: Straight Men and the Making of Gay Pornography." *Qualitative Sociology* 26, no. 4 (2003): 531–55.

Holden, Stephen. "Review: It's Pornographer vs. Pornographer in *King Cobra*." *New York Times*, October 20, 2016. Accessed December 28. 2020. https://www.nytimes.com/2016/10/21/movies/king-cobra-review-james-franco-christian-slater.html.

Lee, Ashley. "Tribeca: Christian Slater, James Franco Explain Why They Made Gay Porn Drama *King Cobra*." *Hollywood Reporter*, April 18, 2016. Accessed December 31, 2020. https://www.hollywoodreporter.com/news/general-news/king-cobra-884731/.

Smith, Nigel M. "*King Cobra* Review: James Franco at His Lurid Best in Gay Porn Shocker." *Guardian*, April 22, 2016. Accessed December 30, 2020. https://www.theguardian.com/film/2016/apr/22/gay-porn-star-king-cobra-review-james-franco-brent-corrigan.

Wilkinson, Peter. "Death of a Porn King." *Rolling Stone*, September 30, 2007. Accessed July 17, 2021. https://www.rollingstone.com/culture/culture-news/death-of-a-porn-king-71027/.

—Jon Heggestad

KINSEY (2004)

DIRECTOR: Bill Condon
SCREENPLAY: Bill Condon, inspired by real-life events
CAST: Liam Neeson (Alfred Kinsey), Laura Linney (Clara McMillen), Peter Sarsgaard (Clyde Martin), Chris O'Donnell (Wardell Pomeroy), Timothy Hutton (Paul Gebhard), John Lithgow (Alfred S. Kinsey)
SPECS: 118 minutes; color
AVAILABILITY: DVD (Fox Searchlight)

Kinsey presents the life of sex researcher Alfred Kinsey through a series of flashbacks as he trains one of his researchers. The film begins with Kinsey's childhood in the early twentieth century as the son of a fundamentalist pastor. After college, Kinsey becomes a zoology professor at Indiana University, where he meets Clara McMillen, a graduate student who soon becomes his wife. He becomes involved in researching sexuality upon recognizing the lack of sexual knowledge his students have and begins teaching sexual education in the 1940s. Eventually, this course leads to his broader sexual research and a sexual relationship with Clyde Martin, a student turned researcher. Kinsey finds both success and controversy with his report on male sexuality published in the 1950s, but the public sentiment turns against him with his later report on female sexuality, which is coupled with his declining health from overuse of barbiturates. The film ends with Kinsey and McMillen reaffirming their relationship and Kinsey continuing his research.

Considering the film's release in 2004, amid the LGBTQIA+ community's continuing fight for marriage equality and other rights during Bush-era Christian conservatism, the queerness of *Kinsey* operates in an uncertain fashion, wanting to validate the experiences of those who exist outside the boundaries of "conventional" sexuality while not wanting to alienate straight audiences. The character of Kinsey himself sits at the center of the film's internal conflict. While his queer feelings are often discussed throughout the film, they are rarely shown. The only noteworthy instance is the first time he has sex with Clyde Martin during a research trip to Chicago. This encounter takes place after they finish conducting interviews at a gay bar: the two men are seen getting ready for bed, with Martin's penis clearly on display, as much a focus of the camera as it is for Kinsey. The two men then discuss Kinsey's scale of sexuality, with Martin asking Kinsey where he feels he falls. After some moments of hesitation, Kinsey identifies himself as a "3," in the bisexual range. They quickly become intimate, kissing and embracing in a passionate manner. However, this is undercut by the next scene of Kinsey's wife crying as Kinsey tells her about his sexual encounter. As film reviewer Robert Corber notes, "In representing Kinsey as emotionally tone deaf, the film endorses the view that he did not adequately consider the psychological aspects of sex but reduced it to a set of physiological reactions" (2005, 469). While Kinsey describes other same-sex liaisons during his framing device interview, Martin is the only male partner with whom viewers see Kinsey become intimate. While the film aims to respect the range of sexual experiences Kinsey had in his lifetime and for which he advocated in his research and writings, this is diluted in the face of the heteronormative emphasis placed on Kinsey's relationship with his wife, particularly in the film's final scene of the two reaffirming their love.

Clyde Martin's presence in the film is noteworthy in how much he does and does not participate in the queer representation of the story. Martin is the character the story is most comfortable identifying as bisexual and initially represents the freedoms that Kinsey believes his research will bring to society. He is frequently seen in emotional intimacy with both men (Kinsey) and women (Clara McMillen as well as his wife, Alice); the film emphasizes the latter as he has an explicit sex scene with McMillen compared to the more sensual moment with Kinsey in the hotel room. However, his queerness throughout the film is often minimized compared to his evolving relationship with Kinsey and his research methodology. His challenge to Kinsey toward the end of the film, about Kinsey viewing sex more in terms of "fucking," or sexual behavior, rather than intimate relationships, showcases how "[director Bill] Condon validates the shift in contemporary gay and lesbian life toward an emphasis on family and couple formation" and the broader family values of the time (Corber 2005, 470). In essence, Clyde's purpose as a queer character is to help Kinsey better understand his own queerness before convincing him that it is not the path for him.

Kenneth Braun, the extensive research subject whom Kinsey and one of his assistants interview partway through the film, represents the most significant source of homophobia and general anxieties around queer identity. The scene featuring Braun is one of the most overtly stylistic and sexual in the film, beginning with his public masturbation in front of the two men interviewing him. The film's framing of Braun being positioned above Kinsey and the assistant illustrates how threatening he feels, not only to them but to the audience as a whole, in this moment of sexual prowess. His tales of widespread incest, pedophilia, and bestiality are presented in a montage, similar to the earlier montage of interview subjects throughout the country, but the Braun montage is more concerning. Whereas the national montage of various interviewees illustrates the spectrum of sexual experiences Kinsey was interested in exploring, the Braun montage presents the troubling aspects of sexuality that his research was uncovering. Braun's scientific description of his sexually related memories and catalogue of diverse sexual encounters seems to indicate he is trying to downplay his queer, predatory behavior through the guise of research, something that Kinsey's opponents accused him of (although this criticism is not present in the movie). The specific statement that sends Kinsey's assistant away from the interview in disgust, wherein Braun describes his observations of prepubescent boys achieving orgasms, is presented as the most horrifying not only for its pedophilia but for its pederastic implications. The last lines of the scene showcase one of the film's most telling moments. Braun asks Kinsey if he makes sure that all of his assistants are trained to be neutral in their behavior during interviews, wherein Kinsey responds that some statements can still be disturbing to hear even after being trained. Braun then questions whether Kinsey advocates for an "anything-goes" philosophy of sexuality, as Braun believes, but Kinsey makes it clear that he does not want anyone to be hurt during a sexual activity. The halfhearted ending of the scene shows, for all of the emphasis on trying to remove stereotypes and fears regarding queer sexual behaviors, the film still presents one of its most overtly queer characters as a sexual predator.

Two other scenes in the film are more positive in their representations of queer characters but still fall into tropes that are typical both of the time period in which the movie was made and of contemporary queer media. As mentioned earlier, Kinsey and Martin go to Chicago to interview gay men; as Kinsey describes it, these men are an untapped well of sexual information that differs from the heterosexual experiences he hears about from his students and peers. This statement also describes how the film sees queer characters outside of Kinsey and Martin: people to study and listen to in order to "understand" the "Other" sexualities that exist alongside straight people without being asked to consider them as individuals. The first couple Kinsey asks to interview brushes him aside in a very camp manner before another man comes up, interested in discussing his sexual experiences. The scene then moves to Kinsey and Martin talking with a third man, who relates a time he had a sexual experience with another man as a teenager before his father caught them and assaulted them. While this moment is meant to create sympathy within the viewer (as similar events would be seen as contemporary for the audience of 2004), this description of gay pain, combined with the camp couple from earlier, create a very stereotypical view of gay men in the film. The only clear lesbian character in the movie is the final research subject Kinsey is seen interviewing, an elderly woman played by Lynn Redgrave.

Her story details how she fell in love with a woman she met at her workplace, causing rifts in her family and private life, only to be healed when she entered into a relationship with her friend. This moment, one of the last scenes of the film and occurring at a moment when Kinsey has become a professional outcast, ends with the woman walking over to Kinsey, touching him on the shoulder, and saying, "You saved my life." However, this focus on how much Kinsey has helped this woman undercuts any potential focus on the queer awakening this woman has undergone; in addition to portraying stereotypes about lesbians and their relationships, "[this scene] reproduces an image of lesbianism that lesbians have long disputed, that they do not like sex as much as gay men, that . . . [lesbians] have a deeper . . . commitment to monogamy and domesticity, and that above all what they look for in relationships is emotional intimacy" (Corber 2005, 468). Ultimately, both of these scenes with incidental queer characters use these characters to further the plot of the (mostly) straight main character while limiting audience sympathy toward these queer characters.

However queer or progressive *Kinsey* wants to be (especially with an openly gay man helming it), the period, viewpoints of the filmmaker, and overall focus of the film prevent it from treating queerness as anything but an odd sidestep for its characters. If the film were made ten or fifteen years later, it might have embraced the fluid sexuality of its characters better and given the queer characters a better representation; instead, its early 2000s-based ideology means it is stuck figuring out how even to describe who these characters are. It is also hampered by the fact that Condon, who previously made a film about the gay director James Whale in *Gods and Monsters* (1998), appeared to be uncomfortable with some aspects of Kinsey's life and personality. In an interview for *NPR* promoting the film, Condon stated, "I think anyone who's unsympathetic to [Kinsey] will find plenty in [the film] to kind of confirm that view" (Corber 2005, 464). This distance can also explain the inconsistent tone the film takes with Kinsey's sexuality, initially seeming willing to present his full range of sexual feelings before ending with a heteronormative recommitment between him and Clara. Finally, the film paints Kinsey and the queerness of his research in a way that lightly illustrates the idealism it contained while restraining the explosive potential of its ideas. Kinsey believed that identifying people by the behaviors they performed sexually is more important than the identities they claimed to inhabit, an idea that is uncomfortable to both straight and queer populations. Ultimately, while *Kinsey* is noteworthy for focusing on queer people in the time it was made, it has become overshadowed by past and contemporary productions that have fully embraced Kinsey's ideas of sexual freedom, openness, and a desire to help others find their true selves.

See also *Battle of the Sexes*; *Behind the Candelabra*; *Can You Ever Forgive Me?*

Bibliography

Corber, Robert J. "Rethinking Sex: Alfred Kinsey Now." *American Quarterly* 57, no. 2 (June 2005): 463–74.

—Jacob DeBrock

KISSING JESSICA STEIN (2001)

DIRECTOR: Charles Herman-Wurmfeld
SCREENPLAY: Heather Juergensen and Jennifer Westfeldt, based on the off-Broadway play *Lipschtick* by Heather Juergensen and Jennifer Westfeldt
CAST: Heather Juergensen (Helen), Jennifer Westfeldt (Jessica), Tova Feldshuh (Judy Stein), Scott Cohen (Josh Meyers), Jackie Hoffman (Joan)
SPECS: 97 minutes; color
AVAILABILITY: DVD (Fox Searchlight)

Jessica Stein, age twenty-eight, strives for balance as a newspaper writer, painter, jogger, daughter, and friend, but she remains alone and perpetually disappointed in single male suitors in New York City. Pressured by her mother and grandmother to pair off before she grows "old," she eventually answers a "woman seeking woman" personal ad in the newspaper, drawn to the author's use of poet Rainer Maria Rilke. Helen, an assistant director of an art gallery, meets Jessica at a bar despite Jessica's repeated attempts to leave because, as she says, "This isn't me." She's drawn, however, to Helen's literary turn of phrases in a world of, to Jessica, near illiterate people. Helen opens Jessica up to new ideas: from blending lipsticks to finding more people attractive. Jessica and Helen begin quietly dating, and Jessica realizes that she will have to come out to her family and friends and date Helen publicly or else she will lose her. Jessica does just that, but Helen leaves her after several months together due to their lack of sex. They remain friends, Helen finding another woman and Jessica remaining single but more fulfilled after quitting her newspaper job to pursue her art.

Jessica's identity as a Jewish woman is firmly established in the first scene during a Yom Kippur service that Jessica's mother and grandmother are scanning for single, available men on the Day of Atonement. This scene of suffering combined with humor, a classic Jewish comedy trope, also introduces a theme of the film: that heterosexuality is normalized and expected among the Jewish middle class. These cultural expectations of Jessica weigh on her throughout the film, which depicts her as anxious and uncomfortable with sex with women. Whether she is comfortable having sex with men is never discussed.

In this film, which is based on a scene from a 1997 off-Broadway play by Jennifer Westfeldt and Heather Juergensen called *Lipschtick*, lesbianism is positioned as an alternative to heterosexuality once Jess is exhausted with dating men who are intellectually inferior: men who mispronounce "narcissistic," men who rub their nipples, men who order for her, and men who split the check with her based on how many lettuce leaves she ate in a salad.

Jessica's brand of neurotic, therapy-obsessed, insomniac, self-declared unhappy Jewish New Yorker was well established by 2001 by comedian Woody Allen and later by Jerry Seinfeld, and Jessica squarely fits within this role. On her second date with Helen, Jessica says, "Whenever I've thought about lesbianism in the past, I've always said, 'Ew. I can't go there. Can't get excited.' I mean, what would we do?" [00:30:45]. She brings leaflets about lesbian sex to Helen's home and discusses strap-on sex accessories that she says have a "gross-out factor." By the end of the night, it becomes clear that Jessica and Helen enjoy kissing one another, but Jessica physically jumps when any other touching or intimacy occurs.

They continue to see one another and make out, but Helen grows increasingly impatient with Jessica's time line for approaching sex. Helen complains that Jessica is a straight, neurotic tease, a "Jewish Sandra Dee."

Helen's sexuality is juxtaposed with Jessica's throughout the film, from the very first scene in which she is introduced. Helen is immediately portrayed as a sexually in-charge career woman, balancing multiple sexual relationships with men, one of them married. Her pleasure is privileged above the men's feelings and priorities. She is also a person with gay friends, and she discusses her interest in women with her colleague Sebastian and his partner, Martin. "It's the one thing I haven't experienced," she says [00:11:25]. Her pleasure, which drives her, is a stark contrast to Jessica's lack of desire, which hinders their intimacy from beginning to end. Together, the portrayals of Jessica and Helen's desire and their sexual identities communicate to viewers a range of queer sexual expression.

Yet not all of Helen's friends support her sexual fluidity. While Sebastian supports her, Martin feels that her dating women is a whim and likens her decision to enjoying a fad like henna tattoos. Once Helen has a steady girlfriend, Martin and Helen argue in the street about Helen's relationship, Martin saying that he cannot put black shoe polish on his face and join a gospel choir as a Black person [00:59:32]. Helen says you are born Black, and Martin responds that is his point—that Helen cannot choose or become a lesbian after having dated men. A spectrum of sexualities is never discussed, nor is bisexuality, underscoring third-wave feminist Jennifer Baumgardner's argument in her 2007 *Look Both Ways: Bisexual Politics*, in which she walks readers through a history of bisexuality, from Sigmund Freud to Masters and Johnson, tracing the ways bisexuality has long been "denied or diminished" in American culture and history (2008, 50).

Lesbianism treated as porn or a subject of heterosexual men's fascination is critiqued in the film. Two men approach Jessica and Helen at a restaurant to debate who is more beautiful. Helen then inquires why men are obsessed with lesbianism. They inadequately respond and stumble over themselves, calling it "double sexy." Nonetheless, while this unfolds, Helen strokes Jessica's thigh under the table. This nearly leads the two women to a more intimate experience at Helen's apartment—but they are immediately interrupted by a visit from one of Helen's male lovers.

It becomes clear at Jessica's mother's Shabbat dinner that a barrier to Jessica living as an out lesbian is her Jewish family and friends normalizing heterosexuality. While Helen attends this dinner under the guise of being Jessica's single friend, she is able to see more of Jessica's background. Viewers never have the privilege of seeing Helen's background. It is when a storm leaves them stranded overnight in Jessica's childhood bedroom that Helen and Jessica are able to finally have sex—in the center of Jessica's controlled and controlling past.

Once Jessica and Helen are officially a couple, Jessica still keeps Helen at length, not sharing that her brother, Daniel, is getting married. She does not tell her mother about Helen being her girlfriend; moreover, she does not invite Helen to accompany her to the wedding. Helen tells her, "This didn't just happen to you" [01:06:55]. Helen feels that when Jessica fails to acknowledge her role in her life, Jessica is ashamed of her. The notion of losing Helen because of keeping her a secret motivates Jessica to come out to her family and friends. The film devotes several scenes to Jessica coming out to colleagues; she asks her friend, Joan, "Do you find me disgusting?" and tearfully tells Josh that she is *with* Helen. There is also a moving scene in which Jess's mother sits with her on her porch during the evening. "Sometimes I think I'm going to be alone forever . . . you can jump in any time," Jessica tells her. Her mother tears up. "I think she's a very nice girl" [01:14:05]. Jessica cries and they embrace.

Always in the background in this film is Josh Meyers, Jessica's boss, brother's friend, and former boyfriend at Dartmouth. At the start of the film, when viewers see Jessica in her newsroom, Josh tells her she "practically went down on" the male artist she profiled, sexualizing her writing. The environment of sexual harassment and a hostile workplace created by Meyers is appalling throughout the film as he ogles her openly and rifles through Jessica's desk in her absence, violating her personal privacy. He corners her at work to ask who her "new guy" is, normalizing heterosexuality, and criticizes her at a work dinner party for not being open to love, telling her that she is her own problem, not the men she rejects (including him). Josh is always peering behind her like a stalker: at the office, at Shabbat dinner, and at her brother's wedding. While this is not intended as threatening throughout the film, it also is a throwback to the early aughts, still decades prior to the #MeToo movement.

As Josh watches from afar, viewers see Helen and Jessica move in together, spend holidays together, and hang out with Martin and Sebastian. Sex remains an issue of difference for Helen and Jessica throughout the film, Helen asking why Jessica never makes noise in bed. In the end, their mutual love of art does not change that Jessica avoids sex with Helen. Helen explains that they are best friends, but that she needs to be with someone who wants to rip her clothes off. This ultimately ends the relationships, and each finds new love: Helen, with another woman, and Jessica, perhaps with Josh, or so viewers are led to believe when they see the two bump into one another in a bookstore where Jessica is posting a flyer. Does she want to rip off Josh's clothes? Is she attracted to men? The film does not explore this.

In the film's final sequence, viewers are supposed to see that Jessica has grown and changed, quitting her copyediting job, attempting to meditate, wearing a new hairstyle, but she also winds up back where she began: in Josh Meyer's orbit. The original ending for the film, however, left audiences even angrier, with Jessica going to Josh's house to seek him out after dating Helen. In many ways though, even the characters' flaws are a flashback and microcosm of this time period: the Ally McBeal fashion aesthetic, the slow trickle of lesbian characters and actors coming out in Hollywood and in film scripts, and even the attentive male gaze always in the background.

See also *Go Fish; The Kids Are All Right.*

Bibliography

Baumgardner, Jennifer. *Look Both Ways: Bisexual Politics*. New York: Farrar, Straus & Giroux, 2008.

Benshoff, Harry M., and Sean Griffin. *Queer Images: A History of Gay and Lesbian Film in America*. Lanham, MD: Rowman & Littlefield, 2006.

Cadenas, Karensa. "The Secrets behind *Kissing Jessica Stein*, a Rare LGBTQ Romcom." *Entertainment Weekly*, February 8, 2019. Accessed March 8, 2021. https://ew.com/movies/2019/02/08/kissing-jessica-stein-secrets/.

Kissing Jessica Stein. LGBT Info Wiki. Accessed March 8, 2021. https://lgbt.wikia.org/wiki/Kissing_Jessica_Stein.

—Jamie Wagman

• L •

LADY BIRD (2017)

DIRECTOR: Greta Gerwig
SCREENPLAY: Greta Gerwig
CAST: Saorise Ronan (Lady Bird McPherson), Laurie Metcalf (Marion McPherson), Tracy Letts (Larry McPherson), Lucas Hedges (Danny), Timothée Chalamet (Kyle), Beanie Feldstein (Julie)
SPECS: 94 minutes; color
AVAILABILITY: Blu-ray/DVD (Lionsgate)

Christine "Lady Bird" McPherson is a precocious, pink-haired teenager in 2002 who dreams of fleeing her hometown of Sacramento, California, for somewhere with more culture. Before she can realize her ambitions, Lady Bird must navigate her family, friendships, and nascent love life as she completes her senior year at a Catholic high school. Despite wishing for a lead role in the fall musical, she is in the chorus line; despite beginning a relationship with her dream boy, Danny, he turns out to be more interested in his male costar. When she does lose her virginity to another crush, Kyle, it is quick and unexciting. Family tensions also abound as Lady Bird's father, Larry, loses his job, and her already overworked mother, Marion, struggles to understand her daughter's erratic choices, leading to frequent fights. Unwilling to attend UC Davis close to home, Lady Bird secretly applies to New York universities behind her mother's back. Although this spurs the biggest fight yet between the two, just one day in New York is enough for Lady Bird, now back to using the name Christine, to understand Marion's complicated relationship with their life in Sacramento.

Only one scene in *Lady Bird*, featuring Lady Bird and Danny, explicitly invokes gay identity. Nevertheless, Greta Gerwig's debut as a sole director is suffused with queer themes. Lady Bird's attempts to discover and define her own identity—which is not avowedly LBGTQ yet still related to gender and sexuality—speaks to similar occurrences during the establishment of LGBTQIA+ identity. Although she is coming of age rather than coming out, Lady Bird's clashes with her family, difficulty assimilating to her school's social hierarchy, and discovery of her sexuality take on a queer tone. Lady Bird's romantic relationships with Danny and Kyle and platonic friendships, especially with Julie, contribute to Lady Bird's understanding of sexuality and identity.

An early scene depicts Lady Bird and Marion arguing while driving, among other things about Lady Bird's self-selected name. Marion insists that "your name is Christine," while Lady Bird implores her mother to "call me Lady Bird, like you said you would" [00:03:10]. This crisis of naming sets up the tension between mother and daughter as a key theme of the film while also foregrounding Lady Bird's determination to set the terms of her identity. Although Lady Bird never compares her determination to choose her own name to LGBTQIA+

identity, her struggle mirrors the challenges often faced by LGBTQIA+ people, especially youth, attempting to become individuals in a family space. LGBTQIA+ historian John D'Emilio notes how by the early twentieth century, "the ideology surrounding the family described it as the means through which men and women formed satisfying, mutually enhancing relationships and created an environment that nurtured children" (1983, 103). Both then and in *Lady Bird*'s early 2000s, this dominant family ideology prioritizes the mother and father's heterosexual relationship as the nucleus of the family and makes them responsible for disciplining their children to society's rules. Lady Bird responds to these demands by jumping out of the moving car, a bold act of refusal that sets up Lady Bird's position toward her family and the ideology they represent; if her family wants her to be someone she is not, she will leave.

Lady Bird's independent disposition extends to her private Catholic high school. Lady Bird attends Immaculate Heart on a scholarship, although Marion also frequently remarks that the family's financial contribution is still significant. Neither Lady Bird nor her family appear to be practicing Catholics, and Lady Bird is often framed as a cultural outsider in the school's wealthy, conservative social ecosystem. She runs for class president with posters featuring, in her words, "a bird head on a lady body, or vice versa" [00:05:05]. This visual representation of her chosen name is aesthetically jarring—photographed bird heads adorned with plastic googly eyes topping the bodies of kneeling schoolgirls, or Lady Bird's smiling face atop a stork that also bears a human arm—mixing media and bodies to convey both an abstract and concrete image of how she understands her name. Queer and trans theorist Jack Halberstam describes bodily collage as "made up of not only different body parts but different perspectives . . . and different modes of representation," creating an artistic form that can mark the fraught situation of trans bodies in contemporary art (2005, 98). Lady Bird never invokes claims of transgender identity, but her artistic expression demonstrates a moment in which Lady Bird's navigation of identity in her life aligns with an LGBTQIA+ perspective.

The film showcases Lady Bird's daily life in an unassuming manner, prioritizing the content of her movements and conversations above cinematic showmanship. Her best friend, Julie, is a frequent interlocutor with whom Lady Bird discusses her frustrations. Julie is another teenager at Lady Bird's school, and she is Lady Bird's only classmate to apparently come from a similar socioeconomic background. While their classmates drive Range Rovers and chat on cell phones—which were pricey luxuries for a teenager in 2002—Lady Bird and Julie swipe magazines off the grocery store rack and walk through wealthy neighborhoods to imagine their lives if they lived in such large houses. Lady Bird and Julie also discuss sexuality in frank terms, in one scene casually discussing masturbation while eating Communion wafers. Lady Bird wonders if "maybe it's different when you actually have a penis in there, like's more intense," prompting Julie to quip that "mine is pretty intense, I think" [00:11:50]. Such a nakedly sexual conversation occurring in a religious space shifts the typical Catholic discourse about sex—described by philosopher Michel Foucault as "the confession of the flesh"—as a sacred act to something more casual and fluid (1978, 19). While Lady Bird and Julie are still discussing heterosexual intercourse, their conversation draws a contrast between Lady Bird's perspective and the dominant ideologies and institutions that surround her.

The film moves directly from their explicit conversation to auditions for the fall musical, another form of artistic expression Lady Bird aims to make her own. The auditions are where she first sees Danny, who is portrayed as an awkward yet charming teenage boy. Lady Bird is immediately smitten, writing Danny's name on the wall above her bed and plotting how to spend more time with him. Although she only makes the chorus in the fall musical—Stephen Sondheim's *Merrily We Roll Along*—while Danny and Julie are both cast in more significant roles, Lady Bird is undeterred in her advances, initiating conversation and buying Danny gifts related to the musical. When the two eventually kiss after a school dance, it is because of Lady Bird's efforts. This narrative of romantic perusal contradicts what feminist film critic Laura Mulvey identifies as the traditional male gaze, in which "the man controls the film fantasy and also emerges as the representative of power in a further sense" (1999, 63). Danny demonstrates no control over his relationship with Lady Bird or the broader film; instead, it is she who drives the film's narrative and is more closely aligned with the viewer.

The audience continues to view events through Lady Bird's perspective as her relationship with Danny progresses, usually at her pace rather than his. Lady Bird is the one who, while cuddling and looking at the stars, says, "You know, you can touch my boobs, right?" [00:23:50]. Danny declines, saying, "I respect you too much for that," prompting Lady Bird to joke that "if you had boobs, I wouldn't touch them either" [00:24:10]. Later, Lady Bird joins Danny for Thanksgiving at his grandmother's house, after which they meet up with Julie and another student from the musical to smoke marijuana and attend a coffee-shop concert. The camera follows Lady Bird's gaze as she looks at one of the band members in particular, later to be introduced as Kyle, another privileged teen at their school. The brief glance is not remarked on by any of the characters but foreshadows the later relationship between the two. The viewer understands Lady Bird to be the primary narrative force in *Lady Bird*, with the film tracing her search for identity rather than forcing an identity on her as so often occurs in Hollywood cinema.

Danny's queerness is entirely subtextual for the first third of the film, perhaps alluded to but with no overt signifier. It thus comes as a shock to both viewers and Lady Bird when, facing a long line at the women's restroom, she barges into the men's room to find Danny and his male costar kissing in a bathroom stall. The camera tracks behind Lady Bird but subtly shifts to center the two young men embracing in the frame before moving back to capture Lady Bird's shocked face as she storms away, all contained within the same shot [00:34:15]. The film quickly cuts to a long take of Lady Bird and Julie crying as they listen to the Dave Matthews Band song "Crash into Me," giving their heartbreak caused by the young men kissing more screen time than the kiss itself. Danny's queer perspective and narrative is not brought forward in *Lady Bird* and, while Gerwig often returns to similar themes throughout her films, it is unlikely she would develop a direct sequel/remake detailing Danny's experience. Although Danny's queerness is made explicit, it is not a narrative focus of the film. Thematically, though, Danny's hidden story aligns with the film's broader motifs of sexuality and identity.

A subsequent scene with Lady Bird and Danny more concretely weaves Danny's queerness into the film's thematic register. Since ending their relationship, Lady Bird has started initiating conversations with Kyle, whose name is inscribed next to where Danny's is now crossed out. Although Lady Bird appears to have moved on, Danny's arrival at the coffee shop where she now works unnerves her. She heads out the back door only to be met by Danny, who begins by making small talk about their families only for Lady Bird to emphatically cut in by saying, "You're gay" [00:44:20]. Danny responds, "Can you not tell anyone, please? I'm so sorry about everything. I'm so ashamed of all of it. It's just, it's going to be bad, and I just need a little bit of time to figure out how I'm going to tell my mom and my dad" [00:44:35]. Lady Bird promises to keep his secret, a delicate piano soundtrack playing over a profile shot of the two embracing, Danny weeps as she consoles him. Although the details of Danny's situation are only suggested, his language suggests an understanding of his identity that is far more precarious than Lady Bird's understanding of herself. That *she* is the one to name his gayness rather than him emphasizes this. Lady Bird again moves the narrative forward, producing Danny's identity in her words and comforting him when the reality of that identity overwhelms him. This moment of grace from Lady Bird offers a salve to the relatively rough prior treatment of his sexuality and marks growth of her character. As Lady Bird becomes more secure in her self-made identity, her capacity increases to help others understand theirs. Anthropologist and media scholar Mary L. Grey describes queer identity formation as "labor carried out among and through people, places, media texts, and a host of other circuitous routes" (2009, 21). *Lady Bird*'s routes to representing gay identity are indeed circuitous, but the braiding of Lady Bird and Danny's stories brings LGBTQIA+ representation into a narrative otherwise about heterosexual coming of age. Danny also endures struggles similar to Lady Bird's with her family and school. His own perspective is not the film's focus, but the queer valances of those struggles are more brightly illuminated by his presence.

Danny mostly fades from *Lady Bird* after this scene as Lady Bird's East Coast dreams and relationships with Kyle, Julie, and her mother drive the remainder of the narrative. Danny does briefly appear near the film's conclusion after high school graduation, and the two appear to be on good terms. Comparing their postbreakup friendship to Lady Bird's disastrous relationship with Kyle offers a final note for reflection. Although probably heterosexual—he does enigmatically describe his past sexual partners as "people" rather than "women"—Kyle emerges as an antagonist in the film's middle third. Initially lying to Lady Bird and describing himself as a virgin, the two have on-screen sex that can only be described as painfully awkward. Lady Bird is furious upon learning of Kyle's lie, primarily because of its impact on her understanding of their actions. "I just had a whole experience that was wrong," she says [01:00:40]. "Who the fuck is on top their first time?" [01:00:55].

Lady Bird reacts with visibly more anger to Kyle's deception than Danny's. The film's thematic presentation of sexual identity thus problematizes *deception* rather than queerness. In the final analysis, although Lady Bird has sex with Kyle

rather than Danny, it was her experiences with Danny that proved more enduring, pleasurable, and formative. Her decision at the film's conclusion to go by
Christine, her birth name, is more thematically aligned with Danny's eventual
realization of his truth than Kyle's unabashed lying. Christine is not rejecting the
sense of identity she gained while going as "Lady Bird" but is instead understanding how to fully express her identity as a gendered, sexual adult regardless of the
name that requires.

See also *But I'm a Cheerleader; Yes God Yes.*

Bibliography

D'Emilio, John. "Capitalism and Gay Identity." In *Powers of Desire: The Politics of Sexuality*,
    edited by Ann Snitow, Chistine Stansell, and Sharon Thompson, 100–13. New York: Monthly
    Review Press, 1983.
Foucault, Michel. *The History of Sexuality: Volume One.* Translated by Robert Hurley. New York:
    Random House, 1978.
Grey, Mary L. *Out in the Country: Youth, Media and Queer Visibility in Rural America.* New
    York: New York University Press, 2009.
Halberstam, Jack. *In a Queer Time and Place: Transgender Bodies, Subcultural Lives.* New York:
    New York University Press, 2005.
Mulvey, Laura. "Visual Pleasure and Narrative Cinema." In *Feminist Film Theory: A Reader*,
    edited by Sue Thornham, 58–69. New York: New York University Press, 1999.

—Sam Hunter

LET ME IN (2010)

DIRECTOR: Matt Reeves
SCREENPLAY: Matt Reeves, inspired by the novel *Låt den rätte komma in* by John
    Ajvide Lindqvist and the film *Låt den rätte komma* by Tomas Alfredson
CAST: Kodi Smit-McPhee (Owen), Chloë Grace Moretz (Abby), Richard Jenkins
    (The Father), Cara Buono (Owen's Mother)
SPECS: 116 minutes; color
AVAILABILITY: DVD (Anchor Bay Entertainment)

Life is hard for twelve-year-old Owen. His mother is a religious zealot who
spends her evenings drinking and crying. Meanwhile, his father remains a disembodied voice on the telephone, instructing Owen to disregard his mother's fanati-
cism and promising visits that never materialize. Home may be depressing, but
school is worse. There, Owen endures ever-escalating physical and psychological
abuse by a trio of bullies. Nonetheless, the arrival of a twelve-year-old girl promises friendship. This new neighbor, Abby, provides Owen with a needed reprieve
from his mother as well as the courage to confront his tormentors. Nonetheless,
while Abby may appear to be Owen's peer, she is soon revealed as a centuries-
old vampire. Abby's arrival in Los Alamos brings a plague of death and fear. And
with every brutal assault and dead body, law enforcement draws a little closer.
Presented with the option to remain in New Mexico or accompany Abby in her
escape, Owen trades his life of pain for one of servitude to this perpetual child.

Let Me In is not an original cinematic contribution. Prior to this American
version, it was both a best-selling Swedish novel and an awards-sweeping Swedish

film. In both works, LGBTQIA+ themes are prominent. Those same themes are omitted from the American interpretation: the piece being stunningly straight-washed. As a result, before an examination of *Let Me In* can be conducted, the film's source material must be addressed. This, in itself, is problematic. As noted by scholar Maria Holmgren Troy, "In commonsensical terms, it is not easy to determine whether the American film, for which Reeves wrote the screenplay, should be regarded as an adaptation of the novel or a remake of the Swedish film" (2015, 26). During an interview with NPR's Guy Raz, Matt Reeves himself seems to confirm that both works shape his film: "It's not a shot-for-shot remake, but there are places where in a certain way it's a scene-for-scene remake. There are definitely scenes that are in the novel and in the Swedish film that are in our film" (Raz 2010). Therefore, given that Reeves's film appears to draw inspiration from both, it is necessary to address the Swedish novel and Swedish film to establish a foundation for comparing and explicating the American version.

John Ajvide Lindqvist's novel *Låt den rätte komma in* (*Let the Right One In*) is a genre-busting juggernaut that combines crime, romance, fantasy, and horror. It also offers a complex examination of both sexual and gender identity. In Lindqvist's novel, Eli (changed to "Abby" for the American film) presents as biologically female. However, as it becomes clear that Oskar (changed to "Owen" for the American film) has romantic feelings for her, Eli hints at her former life:

"Oskar, do you like me?"
   "Yes. A lot."
   "If I turned out not to be a girl . . . would you still like me?"
   "What do you mean?"
   "Just that. Would you still like me even if I wasn't a girl?"
   "Yes . . . I guess so."
   "Are you sure?"
   "Yes, why do you ask?" (Lindqvist 2004, 125)

Readers quickly interpret the subtext of Eli's words to mean that she is not a child but an adult vampire confined to a child's body. However, as the novel incrementally reveals, the name "Eli" is a truncated variation of "Elias" (Lindqvist 2004, 289). Born biologically male, Eli was sexually assaulted by a vampire at the age of twelve. This vampire removed Eli's genitals and cursed the child with immortality. When Oskar meets Eli, he believes she is biologically female. And he falls in love with her before he fully understands that she is biologically male. While the novel may have fantastical elements, Oskar's internal struggle reflects reality. Though he identifies as heterosexual, Oskar's affection for Eli challenges this identity. Throughout the duration of the novel, this life-altering conflict is explored. For instance, readers find Oskar bravely seeking external guidance. While on a school trip, he privately asks a trusted teacher if two men can be in love. Though she initially misinterprets Oskar's question, Marie-Louise ultimately reaches a compassionate answer: "That's friendship. That's also a form of love. Or, if you mean . . . well, two guys can also love each other in that way" (Lindqvist 2004, 191). When Oskar asks how love between men can work, she gently elaborates, "You form a covenant with someone, a union. Regardless of whether you're a boy or a girl you form a covenant saying that . . . that it's you and that person. Something just between the two of you" (191). While his teacher is a supportive ally, Oskar is depicted as continuing to struggle with being in a queer relationship: "he could somehow accept that she was a *vampire*, but the idea that she was somehow a *boy* that could be . . . harder. He knew the word. Fag. Fucking Fag. Stuff that Jonny [the lead bully] said" (307). Though the text shows Oskar contending with these issues, it also shows him striving never to hurt Eli. He realizes that many of his negative thoughts are the product of wholly negative people. For instance, when Eli directly asks Oskar about her biological sex, she inquires, "Are you . . . disappointed?," to which Oskar replies, "Why would I be?" (348). While Oskar's answer hums with avoidance, it is because he realizes the problem may reside within himself. Throughout this novel, readers experience Oskar's confusion with his sexuality, his concern about society's perception of those who identify as LGBTQIA+, and, ultimately, his resolution to continue his relationship with Eli. This is slow and painstaking. It is very much grounded in reality. Moreover, Lindqvist's love for his fans (and for those in the LGBTQIA+ community) becomes clear in "Let the Old Dreams Die" (the short story follow-up to *Let the Right One In*). Here, the author has Oskar and Eli seal their union by exchanging blood (instead of wedding rings since the setting is the 1980s) so that they can spend eternity together. That the novel is a bestseller and the short story was enthusiastically anticipated by the public underscores a society eager to embrace LGBTQIA+ themes. This carries over to the Swedish film.

The original Swedish film adaptation retains the spirit of Lindqvist's novel. Tomas Alfredson even lifts many lines directly from the text. However, in the film, Oskar more readily accepts Eli's biological sex. Like in the novel, Eli suggests that she is not biologically female but only when Oskar sees her undressed does he realize that she is biologically male. Here, while Eli changes her clothes, Oskar quickly peeps through a door that has been left ajar. Viewers are presented with his point of view as he sees a scar where Eli's genitals once were. There are no musical or cinematic prompts to indicate how viewers should feel. They will take their cue from Oskar. And, as Eli dons a dress, Oskar seems to process this moment and move on entirely. "The gender reveal" is not positioned as traumatizing or horrific. It is simply a resolution to Eli's allusions. Moreover, early on, the film appears to prepare viewers for Oskar's relatively casual reaction. When Oskar stays at his father's home, a male adult drops in. The gentle background music and the knowing looks exchanged by the two men seem to strongly suggest a romantic connection. In *The Pleasures of Structure: Learning Screenwriting through Case Studies*, Julian Hoxter refers to this visitor as the "gay lover" of Oskar's father (2015, 187). He is not alone in making this connection. Renowned horror film scholar Ken Gelder suggests the same in *New Vampire Cinema*, going so far to suggest that this person may actually cohabitate with the father (2012, 38). With this noted, it also needs to be stated that the film's director seems to be astonished by (though amenable to) this interpretation: "At several screenings in the US, I've heard people say that the father's a homosexual! This for me came as a total surprise, but of course I found it interesting" (Blake 2008). It is uncertain if Alfredson is gaslighting viewers and critics or if the scene's romantic elements are merely accidental; however, what is certain is that following "the gender reveal," nothing changes. Oskar and Eli remain entirely romantically entwined. The final scene of the film is of them peacefully leaving to a new destination where they will continue their lives together. In this instance, white sunlight pours through the windows of the train. A wooden trunk containing Eli sits in front of Oskar. The two "exchange kisses" via Morse code [01:49:13]. Appearing genuinely content, Oskar allows his head to fall back on the seat. These final seconds solidify the romantic plot and provide viewers with a semblance of closure. Like the novel, the film ends in love. The same cannot be said of the American version.

As a result of his extraordinary cinematic and storytelling prowess, Alfredson was offered the opportunity to reshoot the film in English for an American audience. However, this request was placed as his own film was still receiving critical acclaim and countless awards. Understandably, Alfredson refused, saying, "I am too old to make the same film twice and I have other stories that I want to tell. I think that it is a little sad. I wish that American viewers would just see the foreign language version" (Waddell 2009). However, what remains most remarkable is that American action/horror director Matt Reeves immediately committed to the project. Given that he was most recognized for his work on the broadcast television series *Felicity* and the mainstream sci-fi thriller *Cloverfield*, Reeves seemed like an unlikely choice for this complex piece. Alfredson did little to conceal his contempt for Reeves as well as his disdain of the predatory nature of the American cinema machine. In an interview with *IndieWire*'s Kevin

Lina Leandersson as Eli in *Let the Right One In* (Låt den rätte komma). Courtesy of Magnolia Pictures/Photofest.

Jagernauth, he said: "I think that there's something dishonest about copying someone's work. I think it's much stronger if you do something personal of your own that's original" (2012). However, when he said this, Alfredson was unaware of how significantly Reeves had both replicated and altered his film. Uninspired and misguided, the American film became a crude shadow of its former self. And that Reeves wrote the screenplay as well as directed leaves little room to place blame elsewhere.

A Hammer film, *Let Me In* has all of the production company's infamous hallmarks: buckets of blood, mounds of gore, an abundance of grotesque sound effects . . . and surface-level commentary. This is apparent from the first moments of the film. While the original adaptation opens with the ambient sounds of winter and gauzy images of Oskar gazing into the night, the American film opens with screaming ambulance sirens and ghastly images of a badly burned man. The difference in audience and genre is instantly apparent. But the alterations go deeper. Gone are the potent observations about immigration. Eradicated is the message that teachers are often unwitting accomplices to bullying. And, most shocking, omitted is the entire LGBTQIA+ story line. In this instance, when Abby states that she is not a girl, she means that she is a vampire. She means that she literally turns into a snarling abomination with mottled skin and white-out eyes (which is unique to this American interpretation). This monstrousness is not confined to her physical being. As is progressively made clear, Abby callously indoctrinates her caretakers as children and uses them until they no longer serve a purpose. In essence, unlike Oskar, Owen is disposable. Here Abby is not the tortured and reluctant vampire of the Swedish novel and original film; she is an opportunistic, manipulative, unrepentant fiend. By replacing the LGBTQIA+ story line with a more traditional supernatural story line, Reeves brutally sanitizes the film so as to be instantly acceptable to American horror lovers: ones who might cheer on a woman chewing a hole in her own arm but cringe at two biologically male characters kissing.

For all that Reeves removes from the original works, what he does retain is often baffling. For example, Reeves preserves the iconic moment where Oskar peeps on Eli changing clothes. Like in the original film, the bedroom door remains ajar. However, in this case, Owen ambles over and watches Abby change. His gaze is cold and unchanging. Since there are no revelations, there is no point-of-view shot. This only seems to intensify the invasive nature of his behavior and the severity of his transgression. As Owen briefly lingers, viewers become keenly aware that he does not have Abby's explicit consent to observe her naked body. He is not a curious twelve-year-old trying to unravel clues. He is a voyeur, a violator. There is no reason for him to spy on Abby. It does not further the narrative (as it does with the revelation of Eli having been born biologically male). However, it does make a formerly sympathetic character like Oskar into a genuine miscreant like Owen, which contributes to the surface-level horror of the piece. What seems most surprising is that in the director's commentary for this scene, Matt Reeves states:

> This is, of course, a key moment. And, a lot of people reference it to the original
> film because it's a moment where you see . . . umm, you see . . . Eli's scar on her

genitalia. And, it's a very *known* sort of moment, too. It's one that kind of alludes to a very, very . . . umm . . . deep backstory from the novel. and, . . . umm . . . it's one that actually, we didn't include here. But, by holding on Kodi [Owen], that interpretation for people who have read the book, still applies. [01:29:31–01:29:57]

It seems that the director is implying that if viewers understand "Abby" as biologically male from the previous works, that could pertain here as well. However, this attempt at placating the knowing audience is unsuccessful since there are no allusions to the LGBTQIA+ community anywhere in Reeves's film. LGBTQIA+ themes are not to be used as "Easter eggs." They are not to be held as a secret for those "in the know." And to conceal such an allusion and make it a "footnote" on a little-used DVD audio track is to push the entire community back into the closet. This is a grievous error on Reeves's behalf.

As a result of their contribution to the LGBTQIA+ community, the original Swedish works are held in high esteem. When discussing Lindqvist's novel, perhaps Marie Levesque best describes its impact:

> By performing multiple gender and sexual identities, Eli(as)'s character in *Let the Right One In* is not only a potent illustration of several gender and sexual spectrum positions which can be performed in real LGBTQIA2+ circles, but it strives to open up closed social spaces and broken societal views concerning different genders and sexualities. Therefore, the figure of the vampire is more than a simple cultural figure; it is a social tool capable of providing a safe space to further comprehend and, hopefully, change gender and queer issues for the better. (2020, 101)

This may also be the reason why *Bloody Disgusting*'s Chris Eggertsen noted that the American film "unfortunately failed to find much of an audience during its theatrical run" (2011). Reeves's erasure of the LGBTQIA+ community virtually obliterates the message and meaning of the original works. And it needs to be stated that because of the profoundly diluted nature of this thoroughly American horror film, an LGBTQIA+ story line would have been both disastrous and insulting. Abby would have been one more queer character portrayed as a remorseless threat to society. Certainly, there are far too many of those films (e.g., Jonathan Demme's *Silence of the Lambs*, Brian De Palma's *Dressed to Kill*, and Robert Hiltzik's *Sleepaway Camp*). As a result, Americans would be sage do as Tomas Alfredson suggests: watch the original Swedish adaptation.

See also *Dawn of the Dead*.

Bibliography

Blake. "NIFFF 2008—*Let the Right One In* Interview." *Screen Anarchy*, July 25, 2008. Accessed July 4, 2020. https://screenanarchy.com/2008/07/nifff-2008-let-the-right-one-in-interview.html.

Eggertsen, Chris. "Interview: *Let Me In* Director Matt Reeves!" *Bloody Disguising*, February 1, 2011. Accessed June 22, 2020. https://bloody-disgusting.com/interviews/23271/interview-let-me-in-director-matt-reeves/.

Gelder, Ken. *New Vampire Cinema*. New York: Bloomsbury Academic, 2012.

Hoxter, Julian. *The Pleasures of Structure: Learning Screenwriting through Case Studies*. New York: Bloomsbury Academic, 2015.

Jagernauth, Kevin. "Tomas Alfredson Says There Is 'Something Dishonest' about Matt Reeves' *Let Me In* Remake." *IndieWire*, February 27, 2012. Accessed July 3, 2020. https://www.indiewire.com/2012/02/tomas-alfredson-says-there-is-something-dishonest-about-matt-reeves-let-me-in-remake-112633/.

Levesque, Marie. "Amid and Beyond Gender(s): The Vampire as a Locus of Gender Neutrality in John Ajvide Lindqvist's *Let the Right One In*." In *The Global Vampire: Essays on the Undead in Popular Culture around the World*, edited by Cait Coker, 90–103. Jefferson, NC: McFarland, 2020.

Lindqvist, John Ajvide. *Let the Right One In.* New York: St. Martin's Griffin, 2004.

Raz, Guy. "The Perils of Remaking a Beloved Swedish Vampire Film." NPR, October 10, 2010. Accessed May 3, 2020. https://www.npr.org/templates/story/story.php?storyId=130475811.

Reeves, Matt. Audio Commentary. *Let Me In*. Anchor Bay Entertainment, 2011.

Troy, Maria Holmgren. "Dealing with the Uncanny? Cultural Adaptation in Matt Reeves's Vampire Movie *Let Me In*." *American Studies in Scandinavia* 48, no. 1 (2015): 25–41.

Waddell, Calum. "Tomas Alfredson: New Wave Vampires." *Total Sci-Fi Online*, April 9, 2009. Accessed June 4, 2020. https://web.archive.org/web/20101201235025/http:/totalscifionline.com/interviews/3356-tomas-alfredson-new-wave-vampires.

—Erica Joan Dymond

THE LIFE AQUATIC WITH STEVE ZISSOU (2004)

Director: Wes Anderson
Screenplay: Wes Anderson and Noah Baumbach, inspired by the French ocean explorer Jacques Cousteau
Cast: Bill Murray (Steve Zissou), Owen Wilson (Ned Plimpton), Cate Blanchett (Jane Winslett-Richardson), Angelica Huston (Eleanor Zissou), Willem Dafoe (Klaus Daimler), Jeff Goldblum (Alistair Hennessey)
Specs: 119 minutes; color
Availability: DVD (Criterion Collection)

Steve Zissou is an award-winning oceanographer and documentarian who is now faced with a faltering career. At the Loquasto Film Festival, he premieres the first part of his latest adventure to a chilly reception. During the filming of this installment, Steve's best friend and collaborator, Esteban, was killed by a "jaguar shark" (a name coined by Steve). He tells the audience that for the film's second part, he will hunt down this shark and kill it for revenge. As he plans his reprisal, Steve is joined on the *Belafonte* (his ship) by Eleanor Zissou (his sometimes-estranged wife), Ned Plimpton (a stranger who may be his adult son), Jane Winslett-Richardson (a pregnant reporter assigned to write a cover story on Steve), the crew of the ship, and a group of unpaid interns. As the crew attempts to film part 2, Steve and Ned also explore the potential for a father-son relationship. Financing woes, aging equipment, backbiting rivalries, attacking pirates, and a kidnapping attempt beset the voyage. All of this leads to the film's most sobering moment: Ned's tragic death in a helicopter accident. Following the onslaught of calamity, the remaining crew piles into a submersible and films the jaguar shark as Steve comes to terms with the loss of his friend Esteban as well as potential son Ned. In the final scene, Steve returns to the theater from the opening sequence and waits outside as the second part of the film is screened to thunderous applause.

The crisis of modern masculinity resides at the fore of *The Life Aquatic with Steve Zissou* (Robé 2013, 101). Steve is something of an anachronism. His fame peaked at a moment when cisgender, heterosexual, risk-taking masculinity was at its zenith. Steve and some crew members still voice a longing for this older version of manhood. For example, old footage that Team Zissou watches of themselves trapped on an ice floe features Steve rescuing a wounded snow mongoose and her babies. Reminiscing on this moment, crew member Klaus tells Ned, "That's what it used to be like." In this statement, Klaus is alluding to the broader idea of men embarking on adventures, diving into glacial pools, rescuing a mother and children, and so on. To contemporary sensibilities, this footage seems stagey and outdated; nonetheless, Steve does not see this and struggles to understand his fading fame. Evidence of Steve's obliviousness resides in an interview with Jane. The reporter inquires about Steve's apparent decline in popularity: "So, what happened, in your opinion?" This bold question elicits hostility but no reflection. Only much later, when Steve approaches Eleanor for help after a pirate attack and kidnapping, does he wonder, "What happened to me? Did I lose my talent? Am I ever gonna be good again?" His first glimmer of understanding appears during a half-botched mission to rescue the pirates' hostages, when he begins to see the fraud underlying his self-presentation, but only after his carelessness causes Ned's death is he finally faced with a consequence that cannot be salvaged through traditional masculine bluster.

Steve's understanding—or lack of understanding—of the LGBTQIA+ community springs from this same archaic worldview and is exemplified in his casual use of homophobic invectives. For example, Steve repeatedly refers to Jane as a "bull dyke" when speaking about her to Ned. In these moments, the term "bull dyke" is intended as an insult, detached from an accurate description of Jane's sexual identity. The insult is a reaction to her rejection of him—her negative appraisal of his recent work and her rebuff of his sexual interest in her. Steve also uses homophobic slurs to describe his much more successful rival Alistair Hennessey, who was his former roommate and also Eleanor's first husband. During the opening scene at the film premiere, Steve asks Eleanor, "How could you lay that slick faggot?," to which she responds, "Well, I was in love with him at the time." This same language resurfaces when Steve visits Eleanor at Alistair's home, "You know, I'd be jealous about you staying at Allie's place . . . except I always thought he was kind of a closet queer." While these moments could be Steve again using homophobic slurs without connection to a character's actual identity, in a later exchange between Alistair and Steve, Alistair self-identifies as bisexual. Speaking about Eleanor, Alistair says, "We've never made great husbands, have we? Of course, I have a good excuse. I'm part gay," to which Steve replies, "Supposedly everyone is"—a more nuanced reaction than his earlier insults would lead viewers to expect.

Steve's embracing of an older model of masculinity hampers his ability to connect deeply with other men, bond with his son, and mourn the loss of his best friend Esteban (Robé 2013, 111). For example, Steve seems oblivious that Klaus is growing desperately jealous of his relationship with Ned until Klaus has an outburst when Steve assigns Ned to Team A and Klaus to Team B for the raid on the pirates. Steve responds, "Listen. You may be on 'B' Squad, but you're

Jeff Goldblum as Alistair Hennessey and Bill Murray as Steve Zissou in *The Life Aquatic with Steve Zissou*. Courtesy of Touchstone Pictures/Photofest.

the 'B' Squad leader. Don't you know me and Esteban always thought of you as our baby brother?" Klaus responds, "I've always thought of you two as my dads. Please don't let anyone make fun of me for saying so." The moment captures the contradictions of the *Belafonte*'s homosocial environment. The strict definition of masculinity that is so closely tied to Steve's success encourages him to define male friendships in terms of family to legitimize them. Simultaneously, Steve and Ned both struggle for an understanding of what a father-son relationship should be. Ned has never had a father. While he does not discuss this with Steve, his feelings about his fatherless childhood surface in a conversation with Jane when he states that she would be a "good single mother" but then points out that it puts her "at a tremendous disadvantage." And while Steve initially claims he first heard about Ned only five years previously, he later admits he has known he might have a son since Ned was born. Resistant to fatherhood, he says he had never contacted Ned, "Because I hate fathers and I never wanted to be one." Equally as revealing, just before the helicopter crash that kills Ned, Steve admits to saving the fan letter Ned sent seventeen years earlier. Here Steve displays a private tenderness that he has heretofore concealed, perhaps for fear of being viewed as less than his hypermasculine image would permit.

By the film's conclusion, Steve has come to understand himself as "a showboat and a little bit of a prick," and while he does not undergo a complete metamorphosis, he shows signs of moving past his hegemonic understanding of masculinity. He has made peace with Alistair and Jane, reunited with Eleanor, and abandoned his plan to kill the jaguar shark. As the jaguar shark is seen from the submersible, Steve openly cries, remembering Esteban. At the film festival, he publicly acknowledges the relationship with his son, Ned (a relationship still technically unproven), and while waiting for public reaction to the film, he gives Ned's childhood Zissou Society ring to Klaus's young nephew and says, "This is an adventure"—the adventure being entering the future with a changed world-view. As the credits roll, he is walking away from the screening with Klaus's nephew on his shoulders.

See also *The Grand Budapest Hotel.*

Bibliography

Robé, Chris. "'Because I Hate Fathers, and I Never Wanted to Be One': Wes Anderson, Entitled Masculinity, and the 'Crisis' of the Patriarch." In *Millennial Masculinity: Men in Contemporary American Cinema*, edited by Timothy Shary, 101–21. Detroit: Wayne State University Press, 2013.

—Katherine Walker

LITTLE MISS SUNSHINE (2006)

DIRECTOR: Jonathan Dayton and Valerie Faris
SCREENPLAY: Michael Arndt
CAST: Abigail Breslin (Olive), Greg Kinnear (Richard), Paul Dano (Dwayne), Alan Arkin (Grandpa Edwin), Toni Collette (Sheryl), Steve Carrell (Frank)
SPECS: 101 minutes; color
AVAILABILITY: DVD (Fox Searchlight)

A middle-class family from Albuquerque, New Mexico, embarks on a road trip to California so seven-year-old Olive Hoover can compete in the "Little Miss Sunshine" beauty pageant. Loading the entire family into the Volkswagen bus and driving eight hundred miles is neither a vacation nor a popular idea; however, several factors contribute to this decision. Olive's father, Richard, declares they cannot afford to fly; Olive's mother, Sheryl, is unable to drive the bus because it has a manual transmission; their other car is a two-seater, and Grandpa insists on going to watch Olive perform the dance he choreographed; and Sheryl's brother, Frank, was just released from the hospital after a suicide attempt and cannot be left alone. Also along for the ride is Olive's brother, Dwayne, a Nietzsche-following teenager who has taken a vow of silence until he can fulfill his dream of becoming a jet pilot. The combination of these six personalities makes for a dysfunctional road trip, and the failing yellow bus that the family has to push to get started adds comic relief. Along the way, Richard continually lectures his family with nuggets from the self-help program he has developed and is trying to market. Grandpa Edwin—Richard's foul-mouthed father—who was evicted from a retirement home for snorting heroin, gives Dwayne unsolicited sexual advice. And what is obvious throughout the film but not discussed until the climax is that Olive is not typical beauty pageant material. Her straight, waist-length hair, large glasses, and slightly round belly give her the appearance of an average kid, unlike her sexualized young competitors. But her family believes in her, which is what brings heart to this otherwise sadistic comedy.

The film opens with Olive standing in front of the TV watching the Miss America pageant. After the winner is crowned, Olive rewinds the video so she can study the beauty queen's reaction. While Olive brings her hands to her face to mimic surprise and overwhelming joy, viewers hear the voice of Olive's father saying, "There are two kinds of people in this world: winners and losers." The scene cuts to Richard giving a presentation on his nine-step self-help program, and then the lights go up to reveal four unenthused students scattered in a class-room. Meanwhile, Olive's mother is driving to pick up her brother, Frank, who is being released from the hospital after a suicide attempt.

Once Olive's parents arrive at home, they call the family to the dinner table. Grandpa spots the bucket of takeout chicken and protests, "Every night it's the fucking chicken," providing immediate insight into Grandpa's uncouth charac-ter. While the family is passing the food around the table, Olive notices a white bandage on each of Frank's wrists. She asks her uncle what happened, and he says he had an accident. When the inquisitive girl persists, Sheryl decides to tell her daughter the truth about Frank's suicide attempt, to Richard's dismay. Olive asks with concern why her uncle tried to kill himself. Richard responds, "Frank gave up on himself, which is something winners never do," spouting one of the tenets from his program. Frank explains that he was unhappy because he fell in love with someone who didn't love him back. When Frank refers to his love interest as "he," Olive responds with confusion, "A boy? You fell in love with a boy? That's silly." Juxtaposed with Olive's innocence is Grandpa's disdainful reply, "That's another word for it." While Frank proceeds to recount the events that contributed to his depression—getting fired from his job at the university and a rival professor being named the preeminent Proust scholar, a title Frank proudly claims repeatedly—Grandpa disruptively blows his nose. The fact that Sheryl decides to openly talk about suicide yet Olive is surprised to learn that men could fall in love with each other shows an incongruous priority of the important discussions between parent and child. In addition to Grandpa being blatantly homophobic and rude, Richard judging Frank's depression as weakness, and Sheryl neglecting to normalize her brother's identity as a gay man to her young daughter, Frank is infantilized with children's cartoon sheets on his cot and a McDonald's glass at dinner. Here, viewers note that the only LGBTQIA+ character in the film is continually marginalized.

During the road trip, the film perpetuates heteronormativity and continues to make a joke of Frank's sexuality. In the VW bus, Grandpa asks Dwayne if he's "getting any" and gives a vulgar lecture on the importance of having sex with a lot of women. Grandpa even tries to bring Frank into the conversation and employs a homophobic slur. When they stop for gas, Frank asks Grandpa if he wants anything from the convenience store. Grandpa requests some "nasty" porn, gives Frank money, and says to get himself a "fag rag." Inside the store, Frank happens to run into the graduate student with whom he was in love. Frank awkwardly greets the young man, asserts that he is doing just fine, and tries to obscure the "hetero" pornography visible on the counter behind him. Frank's anguish in this scene is apparent. Viewers do not know if Frank has had successful relationships or if he is comfortable with his own sexual orientation. They only see that Frank is a gay man with depression and a failed relationship. Without further development of Frank's character, the audience is left with the impression that LGBTQIA+ individuals are suffering. The Centers for Disease Control and Prevention (2016) actually confirms that gay men are eight times more likely to have tried to commit suicide than straight men; however, studies have found that depression among gay men is directly related to discrimination and stigma. If people treat Frank the way Edwin treats him, it is understandable that he would suffer from depression.

In another scene, the family stops for breakfast. Frank orders a fruit plate and chamomile tea, and Grandpa orders an entree called "The Lumberjack." The contrast in their food orders once again perpetuates stereotypes. "Fruit" is a known insult to demean those who identify as gay, while lumberjacks are depicted as being the epitome of masculinity. Olive orders waffles a la mode, and Richard tells his daughter that beauty queens do not eat ice cream because they do not want to get fat. In an effort to counter Richard's hurtful comment, support Olive's food choice, and reject the sexist ideal body image, Grandpa, Frank, and Dwayne dig into Olive's ice cream and encourage her to do the same. While the film does a good job of admonishing fat shaming, it neglects to bolster the image of the gay character.

Alan Arkin as Grandpa, Steve Carell as Frank, Paul Dano as Dwayne, Abigail Breslin as Olive, Toni Collette as Sheryl, and Greg Kinnear as Richard in *Little Miss Sunshine.* **Courtesy of Fox Searchlight Pictures/Photofest.**

The next day, Grandpa does not wake up, and when they take him to the hospital, he is pronounced dead. When the bereavement liaison tells Richard he can neither take the body across state lines nor leave the body in the hospital, he decides to steal his father's body. The family rallies to help drop the sheet-clad corpse out the hospital window and hide him in the trunk. Along the way, Richard gets pulled over and is obviously nervous about the contents of the trunk, which rouses suspicion in the police officer. The cop opens the trunk, and the stack of pornographic magazines falls to the ground. Not even noticing the dead body wrapped in a sheet, he picks up the magazines and in a moment of heterosexual male bonding, praises Richard for his taste in porn. The officer is surprised to see the gay magazine, which is designed to elicit a laugh, with the LGBTQIA+ community once again being the punch line.

At the pageant, the young contestants are all adorned with teased-up hair, too much makeup, and plastic smiles. In contrast, Olive looks like a normal kid, and until she compares herself to the other contestants, this does not seem to be an issue. After the bathing suit competition (for little girls!), Olive is seen examining herself in the mirror and sucking in her stomach, obviously impacted by the expected standard of beauty.

Meanwhile, outside near the beach, Dwayne is distraught and has given up his vow of silence after learning that he cannot become a jet pilot because he is color-blind. In an effort to counsel Dwayne, Frank talks about his subject of study, Marcel Proust. Frank describes Proust as a loser, echoing Richard's self-help program. It is no accident that Frank is a Proust scholar. In addition to being gay and experiencing unrequited love, another parallel that can be drawn between the two men is that Proust spent time in a sanitarium (Hustvedt et al. 2016). Drawing from Proust's writing, Frank tells Dwayne that "all those years he suffered, those were the best years of his life, because they made him who he was." The advice Frank has for his nephew is not to miss out on life. It is interesting that Frank, whose wrists are still bandaged, has this perspective. It is a noble effort on the filmmaker's part to give Frank this awareness, but the character is not developed enough for espousal of these values to be realistic. The lack of character development can also be seen as marginalization.

Back on the pageant stage, the other contestants' performances are over-the-top and hokey. Frank and Dwayne tell Sheryl that Olive should not perform because she will be laughed at. "We've got to let Olive be Olive," Sheryl replies in one of the most poignant moments of the film. Olive takes the stage and performs a surprising striptease to Rick James's "Superfreak," unaware of the sexual nature of the moves her Grandpa taught her. Some audience members walk out and others heckle her. Uncle Frank stands up to cheer her on, and the rest of the family follows suit. Olive continues her routine, which includes crawling on the stage and growling, and the pageant director tries to stop her performance. Richard runs on stage to protect and support his daughter and starts dancing with her. Soon the whole family joins in, dancing and celebrating Olive's uniqueness. Sheryl's comment about allowing Olive to be who she is and the family's celebration of the child's individuality are what redeems this family. This attitude of acceptance could be applied to the gay character, but not all audiences would make that leap.

In 2006, *Little Miss Sunshine* was a comedy that poked fun at the dysfunctional American family. Alan Arkin's timing and delivery is definitely comedic, and he even won the Oscar for Best Actor in a Supporting Role; however, using an LGBTQIA+ character for a joke is not funny to the progressive, "woke" audiences of today. *Little Miss Sunshine* certainly was not the first movie to marginalize gay characters. A *New York Times* article astutely observes that "film comedy is littered with ugly and painful stereotypes that emasculated, infantilized and diabolized gay men" (Piepenburg 2018). If America is to become the accepting nation it claims to be, its film industry needs to examine its negative portrayal of the LGBTQIA+ community.

See also *Carol; Fight Club; The Kids Are All Right; My Own Private Idaho.*

Bibliography

Centers for Disease Control and Prevention (CDC). "Gay and Bisexual Men's Health." February 29, 2016. Accessed November 13, 2020. https://www.cdc.gov/msmhealth/stigma-and-discrimination.htm.

Hustvedt, Siri, et al. "Six Writers on the Genius of Marcel Proust." *Literary Hub*, July 11, 2016. Accessed November 13, 2020. https://lithub.com/six-writers-on-the-genius-of-marcel-proust/.

Piepenburg, Erik. "Gaysploitation Upends the Stereotypes That Make Us Wince." *New York Times*, June 1, 2018. Accessed November 13, 2020. https://www.nytimes.com/2018/06/01/arts/gaysploitation-upends-the-stereotypes-that-make-us-wince.html.

—Caryn S. Fogel

LOOKING FOR MR. GOODBAR (1977)

DIRECTOR: Richard Brooks

SCREENPLAY: Richard Brooks, based on the novel of the same name by Judith Rossner

CAST: Diane Keaton (Theresa), Richard Gere (Tony), Tuesday Weld (Katherine), Tom Berenger (Gary), William Atherton (James), Alan Feinstein (Martin)

SPECS: 136 minutes; color

AVAILABILITY: DVD (La Entertainment)

Theresa grew up in a repressive Irish Catholic household, but once she gets to college and into the New York working world, the feminist and sexual revolutions of the 1970s influence her to break away from traditional morality. Wholesome teacher of deaf children by day, at night Theresa discovers her own sexual liberation in bars and increasingly risky encounters with men. Meanwhile, Gary struggles with internal homophobia and self-hatred after a gay-bashing incident. Their two worlds violently collide under the destructive pressures of heteronormativity and sexual repression, ending in one of the most shocking rape/murder sequences in Hollywood cinema.

At first glance, it might appear that *Looking for Mr. Goodbar* is just another 1970s gay psycho-killer story or a morality play about "bad girls" being punished for sexual transgressions. A "good girl" moves to the city and is seduced into a licentious life of sex and drugs, rejecting marriage and children, until one night goes too far. A man's impotence "reveals the underlying psychosis that accompanies homosexuality," and his mental illness results in a brutal crime against a woman who put herself into a dangerous position. However, a closer look at the film reveals a much more complex tale about personal choices, male rage, and women as independent actors, sexual beings, and objects of men's control. The liberation of women and gay men are equated in the struggle against oppressive societal norms. Yet at the same time, ideological inconsistencies may suggest reading the film's discourses as misogynist and antigay.

Loosely based on a real-life story and subsequent novel by Judith Rossner, the movie version stars Diane Keaton as Theresa, a saintly teacher of deaf children who becomes what one of her lovers calls a "bar-hopping slut" at night. Initially escaping a controlling Irish Catholic father at home, Theresa finds as a first lover her English professor, who is a serial manipulator of young women. Significantly, when she loses her virginity to him, the professor prematurely ejaculates, leaving her to wonder why he is "done" when, from her point of view, they have just begun. At the end of the semester when he dumps his student for the next conquest, she asks, "Is my sex too straight?" An affair with a conventional, older man seems "too straight" in the middle of the sexual revolution, and so Theresa begins to look for something else in the bars at night, with drugs and a string of one-night stands and sex-only relationships with men that are all unsatisfactory.

Tony is one of these, objectified and sexualized as an object of what appears to be more a gay male gaze than what viewers might expect of a straight woman's gaze. He wears an open denim shirt with short sleeves rolled up to reveal muscular arms, jumping up in a revealing jock strap to do pushups on the floor. Continuing the seventies gay aesthetic, he later appears in a black leather jacket and tight jeans. When Tony pauses their first sexual encounter, she wonders why he does not finish. Afterward, Theresa asks him to leave and not spend the night, a behavior usually ascribed to men after sex, rather than women, and when Tony wants to move in, she soundly rejects the idea.

A social worker she meets on the job is too good, too Catholic like her father, and she taunts him when he does not jump into bed with her, suggesting that he is gay instead: "Maybe you don't like women. Maybe you go for men." When they do begin to have sex, James puts on a condom, and Theresa laughs at him, blows it up like a balloon, and asks which one of them it is supposed to protect. He leaves, humiliated. As different as they are, both Tony and James want to control her and insist on a relationship she does not want. Tony wields a glow-in-the-dark switchblade and repeatedly breaks into her apartment, while James stalks her at night. Another date takes her to a gay bar for drinks, and she questions his proclivities. He says, "Me, queer? Jesus, I'm a married man!" She remains unconvinced, but before he can prove anything, Tony arrives, demanding, "Who the hell are you? . . . What are you, a faggot?"

On New Year's Eve, Theresa revels in the streets with gay men and drag queens, and when gay bashers appear, Gary successfully fights back and then runs away in lingerie, heels, and a blonde wig to meet a stereotypical sugar daddy: "Don't you ever ask me to wear this crap again! Never, you hear! I'm no God damn Nellie. . . . We're a couple of freaks. We're freaks!" The older man cries while Gary, now in his jeans with a muscled torso, tells him that he is leaving. Drinking from a bottle and enraged, the younger one, who appears to hate himself, yells, "I'm a pitcher, not a catcher, and don't you ever forget that!"

In a bar afterward, Theresa approaches Gary and engages him in conversation to avoid James, who is stalking her nearby, and then takes her new find back to the apartment. But in bed, something is amiss. He tries to arouse himself and says, "In my neighborhood, if you didn't fight, you were a fruit. In prison, if you didn't fight, you spread ass." Concerned, Theresa tells him, "Maybe it's me, whatever. It's not your fault. It happens." He angrily replies that all women have to do is lie there while men do all the work, which leads Theresa to laugh and try to get him out of the apartment. When he won't leave, she asks, "What are you trying to prove?" That sets Gary off: "Prove? Prove what? I don't have to prove nothing to you! You think I'm some kind of flaming faggot!" Then, accompanied by a strobe light, he "proves" his manhood, calling Theresa a "bitch," raping and simultaneously stabbing her to death with the knife viewers had seen James washing in the sink earlier. It is a disturbing sequence, implicating all of the men in Theresa's life as potential killers who really desire men but choose to dominate women when they are impotent with them—because that is what society and the heteronormative model tell them is the proper thing to do. Theresa's dead, frozen face in the strobe transitions into black.

In the series of black and white stills that begin the movie, gay men in clubs are pictured, even a gay couple kissing, all accompanied by disco music. They are integral to the world created in the film, right from the opening, perhaps presaging Theresa's experience that all men are really only aroused by other men. The sexual repression of this desire causes men to hate women after literal impotence blows the cover of heterosexual normalcy. Tony, James, and Gary all must wield phallic knives to substitute for sexual performance with women. For Gary, the oppression he faces from society is what makes him snap, not same-sex longing.

When it was first released, feminist critic Molly Haskell called *Looking for Mr. Goodbar* "harrowing, powerful, appalling" and suggested that it might be not only an important film but a great one (1977). In Theresa, viewers see a woman reaching and grasping sexual ecstasy, rejecting love for bliss in the here and now in a portrayal from her intimate point of view, something exceedingly rare on screen. The film is filled with dualities and mirrors, and it is as if Theresa leads the life of a gay man, enjoying the kind of anonymous sex associated with the gay community before AIDS. In more recent online forums, gay men who were young in the 1970s mention that they identified with Theresa, who lived a sort of fantasy gay life in the big city (LaBruce 2016). Back in 1977, *New Yorker* critic Pauline Kael observed that Theresa "cruises singles bars the way male homosexuals cruise gay bars and s-m hangouts."

Or was this a blatant backlash against both the women's movement and gay pride? On the surface, the film does what would now be labeled "blaming the victim," making Theresa the responsible party for what happened. She even renders men impotent during sex and laughs at them. The other individual to blame is the gay man who goes home with Theresa in order to prove to himself that he is capable of sex with a woman. Gary is the stereotypical homicidal gay man, so viewers may blame the murder on the "sexual pervert" spawned by the new social mores.

Looking for Mr. Goodbar's presentation of contradictions indicates that writer/director Richard Brooks purposely engaged viewers in an examination of the confusion of the times and challenged audiences to make sense of changing attitudes around gender and sexuality.

After a home video release on VHS, reported problems with music clearance for the now classic disco soundtrack mean that today the film is only available on late-night television, European DVD imports, or YouTube uploads.

See also *Cruising*.

Bibliography

Haskell, Molly. "Exposing a Nerve." *New York Magazine*, October 31, 1977, 116, 118–19.

Kael, Pauline. "*Goodbar*, or How Nice Girls Go Wrong." *New Yorker*, October 24, 1977. Accessed August 11, 2021. https://www.newyorker.com/magazine/1977/10/24/goodbar-or-how-nice-girls-go-wrong.

LaBruce, Bruce. "Bruce LaBruce's Academy of the Underrated: *Looking for Mr. Goodbar*." *Talkhouse*, July 19, 2016. Accessed August 4, 2021. https://www.talkhouse.com/12795.

—Angela Beauchamp

LOVE, SIMON (2018)

DIRECTOR: Greg Berlanti

SCREENPLAY: Elizabeth Berger and Isaac Aptaker, based on the novel *Simon vs. the Homo Sapiens Agenda* by Becky Albertalli

CAST: Nick Robinson (Simon), Katherine Langford (Leah), Alexandra Shipp (Abby), Keiynan Lonsdale (Blue/Bram), Jorge Lendeborg Jr. (Nick), Clark Moore (Ethan), Logan Miller (Martin), Jennifer Garner (Emily), Josh Duhamel (Jack), Tony Hale (Mr. Worth).

SPECS: 110 minutes; color

AVAILABILITY: DVD (Twentieth Century Fox)

Simon Spier, a student at Creekwood High School, has not come out as gay to his family or friends. When Martin (a classmate) reads Simon's private email to an anonymous person named "Blue" about being gay, he forces Simon to help him get closer to Simon's friend Abby, or else Martin will reveal Simon's secret. After Martin gets publicly embarrassed by his failure to gain Abby's affection, he leaks Simon's emails on CreekSecrets, an online chat room that is a platform for gossip. Simon comes to terms with his sexual identity being public knowledge and, because he has fallen in love with Blue, invites Blue to meet him on the Ferris wheel at the carnival. With admiring onlookers, Simon and Blue share a romantic kiss and begin dating.

Rated PG-13, *Love, Simon* is considered the first film by a major Hollywood studio to focus on gay teenage romance. Its success can be noted in the awards the movie won. *Love, Simon* earned the GLAAD Media Award for Outstanding Film—Wide Release. Likewise, it earned the Movie Comedy Award and the Movie Breakout Star Award at the Teen Choice Awards. And Simon and Bram's kiss atop the Ferris wheel won Best Kiss at the MTV Movie and TV Awards.

Love, Simon is adapted from Becky Albertalli's *Simon vs. the Homo Sapiens Agenda*. The "Simonverse" continues in print with *Leah on the Offbeat* (2018) and *Love, Creekwood: A Simonverse Novella* (2020). It has also been extended to television with Hulu's 2020 series *Love, Victor*. Considering the success of this franchise, some readers questioned how Albertalli writes so vividly about a gay character when she is in a heterosexual marriage. It was eventually revealed by Albertalli herself that she is bisexual (Albertalli 2020).

Challenging heteronormativity, *Love, Simon* advances valuable messages. For example, Simon's voice-over asks, "Why does straight have to be the default?" Here, an imagined, comic scene depicts a series of Simon's friends telling their parents they are heterosexual, with the families having various reactions. As a result, the film exposes and questions the expectation that gay people must come out because being straight has been made normative.

Additionally, the inappropriateness of "outing" someone is conveyed clearly in *Love, Simon*. Martin's exposure of Simon's sexual identity devastates Simon. His little sister comes into his room after finding out online. She tells him he could deny it, but Simon lashes out, "Why the hell would I deny it? I'm not ashamed of it." The next day, on Christmas, Simon comes out to his parents and says, "I'm still me." Simon has been wondering whether he was gay since he was thirteen. He intended to be "out" once he got to college. Nonetheless, in an important moment of atonement, Martin later apologizes for taking away Simon's decision about when to "come out."

Concerning *Love, Simon*, intersectionality is attempted but could have been explored in more depth. In Simon's suburban high school only one student, Ethan, is openly gay. Ethan is an African American, gender-fluid character specifically created for the film adaptation. A potential misstep in adding this character concerns the unexplored loneliness that Ethan could feel. This is not given nearly enough attention since he is shown verbally responding to harassment. For instance, a scene in the school cafeteria has two students publicly bullying and ridiculing Ethan and Simon by mimicking sexual activity. This leads to a conversation between Simon and Ethan that accentuates Simon's privilege. Communication scholar Jessica Rauchberg critiques how the film depicts Ethan "as a person of color whose purpose in the film is to perform emotional labor for Simon's emotional growth" (2019, 47). While the movie's tagline, "Everyone deserves a true love story," underscores the importance of LGBTQIA+ representation, Rauchberg perceives that "the film only presents white (gay) characters as able to make choices about romantic relationships" (20).

Even with occasion stumbles, *Love, Simon* challenges heteronormativity and offers a romantic, happy ending for an LGBTQIA+ teen audience.

See also *The Perks of Being a Wallflower*.

Bibliography

Albertalli, Becky. "I Know I'm Late." *Medium*, August 31, 2020. Accessed April 17, 2020. https://medium.com/@rebecca.albertalli/i-know-im-late-9b31de339c62.

Corbett, Sue. "Spring 2015 Flying Stars: Becky Albertalli." *Publisher's Weekly* 262, no. 26 (June 29, 2015): 17.

Rauchberg, Jessica. "Interrogating Homonationalism in *Love, Simon*." MA thesis, University of South Florida, 2019. https://scholarcommons.usf.edu/etd/7901.

—Amy Cummins

· M ·

THE MAN WITHOUT A FACE (1993)

DIRECTOR: Mel Gibson

SCREENPLAY: Malcolm MacRury, based on the young adult novel of the same name by Isabelle Holland

CAST: Mel Gibson (Justin McLeod), Nick Stahl (Charles E. "Chuck" Norstadt), Margaret Whitton (Catherine Palin), Fay Masterton (Gloria Norstadt), Gaby Hoffman (Megan Norstadt)

SPECS: 115 minutes; color

AVAILABILITY: DVD (Icon Home Entertainment)

The film *The Man Without a Face* takes its name from the character of Justin McLeod, a former teacher and now a recluse who lives in a cottage at one end of an island off Maine. One half of McLeod's face and body is horribly burned. Conjectures abound in the island community about the cause of the disfigurement. The phrase used by the local people to describe him—"the man without a face"—is a reference to his facial disfigurement. Twelve-year-old Chuck Norstadt arrives on the island with his family to spend the summer. He is desperate to get into St. Matthews, a prep school, to escape his mother and two stepsisters, Gloria and Meg, and to ready himself to join the Air Force like his late father, who he believes is a war hero. He approaches McLeod to tutor him. Initially reluctant to do so, McLeod eventually agrees. Their interaction is productive both academically and emotionally. Chuck develops an interest in his studies as well as self-confidence, and as the summer progresses, he seems increasingly likely to pass the entrance that would help him secure admission to St. Matthews. An unusual bond of friendship also develops between the man who had shut himself off from the world and the boy from a dysfunctional family. However, fearing disapproval of family, peers, and the community, Chuck keeps his friendship with McLeod a secret. After a series of incidents reveal certain truths about Chuck's father, he is shocked and runs for comfort to the only person he considers a friend, McLeod, and ends up spending the night at his house. This precipitates a series of occurrences that conjure up McLeod's past, the accident that caused his disfigurement, the boy who died in the accident, and McLeod's relationship with the deceased boy, who was also his student. It is revealed that McLeod became a recluse after he was wrongly accused of sexually abusing his student, lost his job, and was sentenced to three years in prison for involuntary manslaughter. As Chuck's mother and other people on the island come to know about McLeod's friendship with Chuck, their latent homophobic attitudes manifest, and there are insinuations of child sexual abuse with regard to Chuck. For a second time and without any substantiating proof, and in spite of Chuck's assertions to the contrary, McLeod is thought to have abused Chuck and is forbidden by the authorities to have any further contact with the boy. Chuck expectedly gets into St. Matthews. Having tried to maintain communication with McLeod, he learns that his letters were not delivered, sneaks out of school, and reaches McLeod's house, only to find that his friend moved to an unknown location. He finds a letter from McLeod thanking Chuck for his gift of trust and friendship in a world that had misjudged him, and for unexpectedly giving him a new lease on life. Not completely out of Chuck's life, at his graduation ceremony, McLeod attends from afar, and the film ends as Chuck trains his eye on McLeod and waves to him as he gradually walks away.

The film is a story of an ideal platonic friendship between an adult and an adolescent that the public misinterprets as entering taboo domains. The relationship between Chuck and McLeod is initially that of mentor and mentee, but over the summer they grow inexplicably close. The bond between them treads the finer, more intricate dimensions of friendship, guidance, and even love. But against a backdrop and atmosphere of general fear—the fear of being different— the relationship is problematized. Chuck, who is perceived to be *different* from his peers, is stigmatized by his own family, particularly by his mother and elder sister, for not being as bright as his siblings. McLeod is a much-discussed mysterious entity on the island. Most discussions center on what marked him *different* from others—his face. Homophobic comments and suggestions are recorded from the very beginning of the film. It is evident in the change in people's reactions during the party scene at the beginning of the movie as the narrative shifts from rumors about McLeod killing his wife [00:27:01] to those of McLeod killing his boyfriend [00:27:14]. Mrs. Norstadt's apprehensions about sending Chuck to St. Matthews are also based on such homophobic perceptions [00:06:02].

The relationship between McLeod and Chuck is built on an important element, trust, despite the fact that Chuck lies to McLeod about his father, about his mother, and about having gotten her permission to study with McLeod. McLeod's trust stems from his strong conviction that it was the student's (Chuck's) desire to learn that made him lie. That trust is an important element in the relationship between the two is made evident on more than one occasion. McLeod does not hesitate to share the presumably private details about the car accident that resulted in the death of his young student and ultimately changed his life forever. His trust in Chuck overrides any other consideration. McLeod tells Chuck about Patrick. Patrick was fixated on McLeod and decided to do something rash knowing that his feelings were not reciprocated by his teacher. While it was Patrick whose actions led him to his own death as well as to McLeod's face being burnt, McLeod is always portrayed as being in deep sorrow for losing him that day. For him, the tragedy that occurred that day was much more than the disfiguration of his face, bringing with it a restructuring of his life and the enormous sense of guilt that accompanied the loss of Patrick.

When Chuck divulges these details to his friends, leading to a fresh wave of gossip that eventually makes life more difficult for McLeod, McLeod is still sympathetic in assessing Chuck, attributing any unintentional transgressions to his age. The element of trust is further underscored in a scene where Chuck comes to know the truth about his father. Shaken and unable to cope, he finds solace and comfort with McLeod.

Affection is another sentiment that is crucial to the development of the film plot. Once trust is established between the two central characters, the intensity of and need for reciprocation is very strong. Even when Chuck inadvertently divulges the truth about McLeod, he pleads with his friends not to bad-mouth McLeod and is deeply perturbed that words have taken a different turn in passing from one person to another, resulting in his being projected in a much worse light. When wrong impressions are created due to McLeod letting Chuck stay the night at his place, McLeod goes to Chuck's house despite being aware that he might be treated badly, just to make sure that the boy is alright [01:28:10]. Toward the end of the movie, when Chuck finds out that the letters he wrote to McLeod remained undelivered, he does not think twice about escaping boarding school the same night to reach McLeod's place and ascertain the reason. He finds that McLeod has moved, but there is a painting and a letter for him from McLeod in the empty house. The final scene, which marks the essence of this relationship, highlights the extent to which the two care for each other. Legal strictures forbid McLeod from meeting Chuck but cannot prevent him from attending his graduation ceremony. As soon as he notices McLeod's presence at the edge of the crowd, Chuck leaves his group of friends and gazes longingly at his mentor. There is the glint of love and friendship and the hint of a tear in his eyes.

Why do the authorities and the local community behave in such a biased and narrow-minded way toward this relationship? Each of the responses seems to make evident how difficult it is for the community to conceive of a platonic relationship between the tutor and his protégé. It seems as if the vigilantism of the homophobic gaze has implanted itself in the mind of every adult member of the community, and they "see" only what they want to, scrutinizing every action in terms of what constitutes appropriate behavior in a heteronormative society. Even though neither Chuck nor McLeod expresses sexual desires individually or toward each other, fallacies from the Patrick incident come to bear on public opinion. The fact that they are friends who enjoy being in each other's company is something that transgresses community norms and comprehension as McLeod is neither peer, family, nor a respected institutional/community elder. Consequently, this intergenerational friendship is reduced to a child sexual abuse narrative. This is evident in the conversation between Chuck and his mother:

Chuck: See, he's my tutor. But he's also my friend. I can tell him anything.

Gloria: Last night, did he . . . or at any other time, did he . . . touch you?

Chuck: Yeah, sure.

Gloria: How did he touch you?

Chuck: Why are you asking me this? I told you he is my friend, didn't I? Just tell me.

Gloria: Chief Stark told me something about your friend. A boy was killed in a driving accident.

Chuck: Ya, ya, I know. He told me. So what?

Gloria: He went to prison for three years. The boy that was killed was a pupil of
his. He was in the car with McLeod and they were having—he was abusing the
boy, Charles! Do you understand what that means? [01:26:12]

Chuck is so disturbed by what he hears that he risks driving dangerously down
a busy street to meet his tutor. In response to Chuck's repeated queries, McLeod
asks him:

McLeod: Did I ever abuse you? Did I ever lay a hand of anything but friendship
on you? Think Norstadt. Reason. Could I? Can you imagine me ever doing so?
And what about the past? What do you see?

Chuck: Just tell me you didn't do it, I'll believe you. [01:36:50]

Michel Foucault, in his work on the discourse of sexuality, writes about a repressive Victorian understanding of sexuality where, in an industrial and postin-
dustrial world, sexuality was confined to peoples' bedrooms and no other form
of sexuality was to be talked about other than the procreational one. Sexuality
was thus repressed and relegated to the domain of the unspoken and unknown.
One can say that the basic aversion that comes into play in a homophobic society is an aversion to this unknown. This unknown might be something that is
common knowledge and yet repressed to a state of mystery and denial through
a chain of legal and social commands that control what one should know. And
what starts as a conscious Victorian repression becomes a question of "true
belief" in terms of societal values (Foucault 1978, 4–8). The film exemplifies
this very fear of the unknown. The status of the teacher in the film is expressed
entirely through speculation. The island community has no knowledge of who
the person is and deals wholly in rumors, conjectures, and fantasies, especially
ones that generate a sense of fear, anxiety, or horror about his identity. He is a
subject of silenced speech and need not be acknowledged when out in the open.
Nobody tries to ascertain what his true identity is on account of his supposedly
scandalous history. Over a period of time, his own identity has been a subject of
repressed morality. It is more comfortable for society to let him be a mystery that
creates fear than to let him be known and accepted.

Malcolm MacRury's script is based on a 1972 young adult novel of the same
name by Isabella Holland. An understanding of the novel and of the relation
between the novel and the film is important in understanding perceptions of
"homosexuality" and homophobia in the film. There are significant differences
between the film and the novel. In the novel, there are clear indications of a
sexual incident between Chuck and McLeod the night Chuck stays over at his
tutor's house:

Justin reached me and put his arms around me and held me while I cried out of
some ocean I didn't know was there. I couldn't stop. After a while he lifted me
up and carried me to the bed and lay down beside me, holding me.
    I could feel his heart pounding, and then I realized it was mine. I couldn't stop
shaking; in fact, I started to tremble violently. It was like everything—the water,
the sun, the hours, the play, the work, the whole summer—came together. The

golden cocoon had broken open and was spilling in a shower of gold. (Holland 1972, 111)

The dialogue between the two the next morning, in which McLeod tries to help Chuck make sense of what happened the previous night, leaves the question of Chuck's sexuality open-ended:

There's nothing about it to worry you. You reacted to a lot of strain—and shock— in a normal fashion. At your age, anything could trigger it.
    You mean it doesn't have anything to do with you?
    It has something to do with me, sure. But nothing of any lasting significance. It could have been anyone—boy or girl. It could have been when you were asleep. You must know that. (Holland 1972, 112)

In the novel, many would assume that Justin McLeod is probably gay. "I've known what I was for a long time," he says at one point in the novel (Holland 1972, 112). The novelist is suggestive when narrating the relationship between the two. In the film though, all ambiguity about both McLeod's and Chuck's sexuality is done away with. They are depicted as straight, and the relationship is narrated as an ideal platonic friendship. The nuanced and evocative explorations of the relationship between Chuck and McLeod in the novel, in which the relationship seems to negotiate desire by transforming it into something valuable and productive and which some critics interpret as child grooming, are totally muted. Instead of being the coming-of-age story that the novel was written as, the film is more about how an inspirational teacher and good human being is misunderstood, focusing more on how much of a positive impact the relationship has on the child, before homophobia and suspicions of child sexual abuse shift focus to McLeod and present him as a misunderstood and maligned tragic hero.

That the "sexual subtext in the novel" is removed and the theme of same-sex desire, dealt with at considerable length in this young adult novel by Holland, is altered has been seen in conjunction with the director and lead actor Mel Gibson's views about the LGBTQIA+ community (Advocate.com Editors 2010; *Telegraph* 2017). However, some reports contend that "the decision to alter the character's sexuality" was made well before Gibson became part of the project. It was a commercial decision made on account of the fact that McLeod's being gay "was prohibitive in selling the book" (Yant 1993).

The novel itself is not without its own deficiencies, as pointed out by Cart and Jenkins, who are of the opinion that the novel ends up reinforcing the then prevalent ideas about gay men instead of critiquing them (2006, 21–22). In its association of gay identity with disfigurement, loneliness and exile, rejection, and ultimately death, the novel articulates the character of McLeod through certain stereotypically negative markers that being gay was associated with in the time the story is set. The film script retains all these negative tropes except the ending (in the novel the protagonist dies in a far-off country, leaving his inheritance to the boy) but at the same time portrays both McLeod and Chuck as heterosexual, giving the relationship between the two and societal responses to it an entirely different dynamic. The unfounded allegations of an exploitative relationship that come up in the film once the relationship between adult and child becomes public bear testimony to how a homophobic culture stigmatizes this intergenerational friendship based on its own sociocultural norms about what is acceptable or unacceptable, consolidating beliefs and perceptions under the imaginary specter of pedophilia.

See also *The Perks of Being a Wallflower.*

Bibliography

Advocate.com Editors. "Mel's Early Day Antigay Meltdown." *Advocate*, July 11, 2010. Accessed March 10, 2021. https://www.advocate.com/arts-entertainment/entertainment-news/2010/07/11 /mels-meltdowns-included-antigay-speech.

Cart, Michael, and Christine Jenkins. *The Heart Has Its Reasons: Young Adult Literature with Gay/Lesbian/Queer Content, 1969–2004.* Lanham, MD: Scarecrow, 2006.

Foucault, Michel. *The History of Sexuality, Volume 1: An Introduction.* Translated by Robert Hurley. New York: Pantheon Books, 1978.

Holland, Isabelle. *The Man Without a Face.* New York: Bantam Books, 1972.

Telegraph. "'I Have Been Digging a Ditch for the Past 10 Years': Mel Gibson's Life in Pictures." November 24, 2017. Accessed March 16, 2021. https://www.telegraph.co.uk/films/0/mel -gibson-life-career-pictures/.

Yant, Monica. "A Look Inside Hollywood and the Movies: Risky Business: 'Man' Without a Homosexual Face." *Los Angeles Times*, September 5, 1993. Accessed March 10, 2021. https:// www.latimes.com/archives/la-xpm-1993-09-05-ca-31784-story.

—Banibrata Mahanta

MAY (2002)

DIRECTOR: Lucky McKee
SCREENPLAY: Lucky McKee
CAST: Angela Bettis (May), Jeremy Sisto (Adam), Anna Farris (Polly), James Duval (Blank), Nichole Hiltz (Ambrosia)
SPECS: 93 minutes; color
AVAILABILITY: DVD (Lionsgate)

May Canady is desperate for a connection with another person. As a child, a lazy eye alienated May from other children. May's only friend was Suzie, a doll enshrined in a glass case that was a birthday present from her seemingly well-meaning but overbearing mother. As an adult, May is still lacking a bond with anyone other than Suzie. May finally feels a connection when she meets Adam, a local mechanic, but her social awkwardness leads to Adam rejecting her. May's mental health deteriorates as her attempts at romance and friendships fail, resulting in a series of murders and May's attempt to literally "make" a friend out of the best parts of those who have scorned her.

The first half of *May* focuses on the title character's pursuit of Adam. During this period of the film, the only LGBTQIA+ character directly represented on screen is May's lesbian coworker Polly. After May is ultimately rejected by Adam, May and Polly become intimate, revealing May's bisexuality.

Up until committing her first murder, May is portrayed as a sympathetic figure. She is lonely, lacks confidence, and just wants to feel accepted and loved by someone. In that regard, May is an easy character to sympathize with and root for. At the same time, even before May commits her first murder, her behavior is obsessive and predatory. This is exemplified in her relationship with Adam.

When May sees Adam, she becomes fixated on him and, specifically, his hands. When getting contact lenses to correct her lazy eye, May remarks to her optometrist that she has a date coming up. The "date" May mentioned was her timing a walk across an intersection at the same moment Adam would be coming from the opposite direction in hopes that they would strike up a conversation. When Adam fails to notice her on the street, May follows him to a coffee shop. After Adam falls asleep at his table, May approaches him and begins touching his hand, going so far as to rub her face against his hand before retreating when Adam awakens.

Adam and May finally have a proper introduction and a conversation later at a laundromat. May then, once again, attempts to orchestrate she and Adam running into each other while crossing the street. This time, she is successful and the two have an impromptu lunch in a park before agreeing to a proper date. After their date, May leaves Adam a phone message and then stares at the phone waiting for his return call. When the call fails to arrive, May simply waits outside his front door. When Adam emerges, he informs her that he had not returned her call because he was busy but agrees to a second date with May. After having dinner, the two go to Adam's house, where he shows her a short horror film he made of a couple engaging in cannibalism with each other. Adam and May then begin to be intimate, but May awkwardly bites Adam's lip to the point of drawing blood. She tells him that she was just mimicking what happened in the movie he showed her. Adam is disturbed by this and leaves. Later, May goes to see Adam at his home but overhears him telling his roommate that he plans to avoid May from now on.

While the relationship between May and Adam progresses and deteriorates, viewers see glimpses of May at work as a veterinary assistant, including her interactions with Polly. Until her relationship with Adam comes to an end, May does not appear sexually interested in Polly. May does, however, comment to Polly that she believes her neck is beautiful (much in the same way May focuses on Adam's hands). Throughout their scenes together, Polly frequently attempts to flirt with May, including seductively sucking her thumb as May walks by and coaxing May to slow dance with her in the office.

The night May overhears Adam's plans to distance himself from her, she receives a message from Polly inviting her over to her home. With Polly, May is despondent over what has occurred with Adam, but Polly begins to kiss and undress her. May does not object to Polly's advances, but May does not actively participate either. It is not until May refers to herself as "weird" and Polly responds that she "loves weird" that May becomes an active participant in the sexual experience. When May returns to Polly's home on a subsequent day, she finds Polly with another woman. In a later scene, Polly introduces this new woman as Ambrosia. May, once again, feels rejected by someone she believed she had a connection with. At home, May accidently kills a cat that Polly asked her to adopt when, in a fit of anger, she throws an ashtray because the cat will not come to her.

While May lacks confidence and is sexually timid, Polly is exceedingly confident and driven by sex. For instance, while dancing together at work, Polly attempts to persuade May into adopting her cat by asking May, "Do you like pussy ... cats? Do you like pussy cats? Geez, you're a nasty little thing, aren't you?" [00:32:16–00:32:26]. When May and Polly become intimate, the experience holds meaning for May and makes her feel accepted. For Polly, however, this was just another sexual conquest. When May finds Polly with Ambrosia, Polly asserts that Ambrosia was "an opportunity that I just couldn't pass up" [00:52:47–00:52:49] before offering May the opportunity to join them and then asking May if they can talk later because she's "gotta hit this" [00:53:01–00:53:02]. Ambrosia is treated as a sex object. When the character is introduced, only her legs (which May comments on later) are portrayed on screen. Ambrosia only fully appears in two other scenes in the movie where she is either flirting with Polly or being rude to May.

May's attempts to connect with someone go beyond just adult relationships. After seeing a group of blind children playing in the park, she volunteers at their school. May feels drawn to one child, Petey, who, likely reminding May of herself, is playing alone. May's attempt to bond with Petey and the other children also does not end well. When May brings Suzie to the school to show the children, Suzie's glass case falls to the floor as the children wrestle over it. The case shatters, spraying glass across the floor, and the children badly cut themselves when they crawl through it looking for Suzie.

Suzie's glass case was used as a metaphor for May's mental health throughout the film. With each rejection May suffered, more cracks appeared in the glass case, reflecting May's moving closer to a breakdown. When Suzie's case finally shatters, May only needs one final push to be sent over the edge. That push comes in the form of another rejection. May meets Blank, a punk rocker, at a bus stop. May invites him home with her and comments on his torso. Blank then finds the corpse of the cat in May's freezer. When May asks if they are best friends now that Blank has discovered May's secret, Blank responds by calling her a freak and emphatically stating that they are not going to be friends. May then kills Blank by stabbing him in the head with a pair of scissors. Calmly smoking a cigarette while surveying the body of Blank on her floor, May remarks that she "needs more parts" [01:06:36–01:06:38] and, later, that "if you can't find a friend, make one" [01:11:07–01:11:10].

May buys a large cooler on wheels and steals surgical knives from her workplace. On Halloween, May dresses as Suzie and puts her plan into action. First, May kills Polly and Ambrosia. May harvests Polly's neck and Ambrosia's legs before packing them in her cooler and moving on. Next, she visits Adam, who is with his new girlfriend. May kills them both and adds Adam's hands and his girlfriend's earrings to her cooler before returning home. May stitches together the parts she's collected from her victims along with pieces of fabric to create a friend for herself who she names "Amy." Worried that her creation cannot see her, May cuts out her own lazy eye and lays it on the effigy. As she passes out, May appears to hallucinate Amy reaching over and stroking her face with what used to be Adam's hands.

May is revealed to be bisexual about halfway through the film but is portrayed as being less interested in sex and more interested in feeling connected with someone else, whether that person is a man or a woman. This is further demonstrated in her creation of Amy, which is composed of parts of the men and women who have rejected her. Due to her persistent loneliness since childhood and spiraling mental state, May is willing to commit multiple murders to finally have a friend to call her own.

Lucky McKee's *May* qualifies as a horror movie mostly thanks to its finale, but for the majority of the run time, *May* is a character study of a damaged woman. The film is effective in this regard but also incorporates some stereotypical depictions of LGBTQIA+ individuals. The three LGBTQIA+ characters in the film are portrayed as either severely mentally disturbed (May) or preoccupied with sex (Polly and Ambrosia). By the time the film ends, none have survived.

See also *Dawn of the Dead*; *Let Me In*.

—Corey Call

MEAN GIRLS (2004)

DIRECTOR: Mark Waters
SCREENPLAY: Tina Fey, inspired by the nonfiction book *Queen Bees and Wannabes* by Rosalind Wiseman
CAST: Lindsay Lohan (Cady Heron), Rachel McAdams (Regina George), Lacey Chabert (Gretchen Wieners), Amanda Seyfried (Karen Smith), Tina Fey (Ms. Norbury), Tim Meadows (Mr. Duvall), Lizzy Caplan (Janis Ian), Daniel Franzese (Damian)
SPECS: 97 minutes; color
AVAILABILITY: DVD (Paramount)

Sixteen-year-old Cady Heron has spent her life being homeschooled while living with her zoologist parents on a research assignment in Africa. When they return to America, Cady starts attending school for the first time at North Shore High, where she meets and befriends "art freaks" Janis and Damian. The two friends educate Cady on the various cliques at North Shore, including three popular young women referred to as "The Plastics." Among the members of the Plastics are the manipulative and beautiful "queen bee" Regina George, the insecure but wealthy Gretchen Weiners, and the sweet but dimwitted Karen Samuels. One day at lunch, the Plastics invite Cady to sit with them in the cafeteria, where Regina welcomes Cady into the group. Soon after, Cady, Janis, and Damian devise a plan for Cady to infiltrate the Plastics and ruin Regina's popular reputation . . . with disastrous results.

The film was written by and costars Tina Fey, former cast member and writer for *Saturday Night Live* and creator of *30 Rock*. Fey based the film on the nonfiction self-help book *Queen Bees and Wannabees* (2002) by Rosalind Wiseman, which focuses on high school–aged young women forming harmful cliques and how to combat clique mentality. One scholar writes that Fey's screenplay works to avoid any sentimentality, trivialization, or homogenization of the teenage experience, instead using "a blend of the familiarly absurd to critique the excesses of teenage behavior for its meanness and insensitivity" (Simmons 2011, 133). The Plastics are, no doubt, the epitome of this harmful and absurd high school clique dynamic, using what they refer to as a "Burn Book" to write insults, rumors, and secrets about their classmates and teachers. It is this clique-like behavior that isolates many of their nonpopular classmates, including Janis, who they simply label in the Burn Book as a "dyke" due to her outward, somewhat "alternative" appearance. Janis never explicitly discusses her sexuality with anyone but instead finds herself labeled as such because of her differences. This marginalization of high school "artsy" types or outcasts, or indeed any person who does not conform to a strict binary of masculinity or femininity, is central to the theme of *Mean Girls*. However, these binaries and differences between the marginalized and the vain popular "girls" are ultimately demystified by Fey in the screenplay.

For instance, Janis playfully refers to her friend Damian as "too gay to function" and makes it clear that this expression is only acceptable when *she* says it. After Cady hears this, she repeats it to the Plastics, who then write it in the Burn Book next to Damian's picture. At the start, this particular element of the film reflects a central theme of "girls" behaving badly, given that Janis and Damian are not the only marginalized characters to receive this abuse from the Plastics. In their Burn Book, Dawn Schweitzer, a softball player and "sporty girl," is referred to as a "fat virgin" with a "huge ass." Trang Pak, leader of the clique Janis and Damian refer to as the "Cool Asians," is a "grotsky little byotch" who made out with the football coach. Bethany Byrd, a member of the "Desperate Wannabes" clique, is referred to as a "slut" because she uses super jumbo tampons, and Tina Fey's character, math teacher Ms. Norbury, is a "sad old drug pusher." Yet the very fact that the already marginalized Janis and Damian introduce these different cliques to Cady, ones that they have undoubtedly constructed themselves, exemplifies the film's tendency to expose this "mean girls" cliché.

In this way, the marginalized are continuing this cycle of exclusion by situating others into their own constructed cultural and subcultural binaries. In a scene where Cady, Janis, and Damian are first getting acquainted, Janis informs Cady about the different cliques at North Shore: "Freshman, ROTC guys, Preps, JV Jocks, Asian Nerds, Cool Asians, Varsity Jocks, Unfriendly Black Hotties, Girls Who Eat Their Feelings, Girls Who Don't Eat Anything, Desperate Wannabees, Burnouts, Sexually Active Band Geeks." As Janis lists these cliques, viewers hear her voice-over as the camera moves across the cafeteria, showing each clique behaving in a stereotypical way that suits their identification. Janis tells Cady that where she sits in the cafeteria is crucial, that she and Damian are "The Coolest People You Will Ever Meet," and that the worst clique is "The Plastics": "Beware of the Plastics." One could argue that Janis's stereotypical identification of others works as a type of defense mechanism. About this sequence from the film, Simmons writes that "'differences' are compressed into a socially accurate microcosm of the volatile rivalries that characterize the student population" (2011, 135). As someone who has been bullied and marginalized because of her dissimilarities, Janis designates others into these stereotypical binaries as a way of overcoming her own marginalization.

Similarly, the character of Damian is represented as somewhat of a gay cliché but also simultaneously a rejection of stereotypical gay physicality. He performs a Christina Aguilera ballad at the school talent show, hangs out with Janis and Cady in the girl's bathroom, and is responsible for some of the film's campiest dialogue: "That's why her hair is so big. It's full of secrets." Yet, physically, Damian does not conform to the stereotypical representation of gay men having perfect bodies. He is larger, more overweight, but still exudes a tremendous confidence. In an early draft of the script, when Fey first introduces Damian, she writes: "Damian is possibly fat and definitely gay" (Fey 2003, 6). Even though his representation avoids a physical cliché, Damian still engages with Janis in her marginalization of others as a possible form of defense. He is, in many ways, representing the qualities of a "mean girl." While walking Cady through the halls on her first day at North Shore, Damian singles her out by loudly proclaiming, "New meat coming through." When a girl calls him out for being in the girl's bathroom, he calls her "Danny DeVito" because of her size and stature. He believes Regina George, the head of the Plastics, is "fabulous but evil," and when he sees Ms. Norbury at the mall with Janis and Cady, he asks Janis if he is "morally obligated to burn [her] outfit." In this manner, Damian is fulfilling a "sassy" gay stereotype of bitchy cattiness while simultaneously working to overcome his alienation as a marginalized individual.

Yet, in many ways, those who appear marginalized in *Mean Girls* are relegated not only because of their sexuality but also because of their gender. Among some of the academic scholarship written on the film is the subject of feminism and the film's representation of femininity. Deidre M. Kelly and Shauna Pomerantz write that, either intentionally or unintentionally, *Mean Girls* operates under a discourse that "overtly and covertly ignores or ridicules feminism," one that privileges "projects of individual but not collective empowerment" (2009, 2–3). Later in the film, when Regina learns of Cady's backstabbing, she takes the contents of the Burn Book, photocopies them, and distributes them around the school. This causes pandemonium and forces Ms. Norbury to stage an intervention in the gymnasium with all the young women at the school (plus Damian). In a speech to the room, Ms. Norbury tells them, "You all have got to stop calling each other sluts and whores. It just makes it okay for *guys* to call you sluts and whores. Who here has ever been called a slut?" Kelly and Pomerantz believe that this particular scene identifies a lack of implication and culpability on the part of men, "a lack of acknowledgment concerning broader issues—such as patriarchy, compulsory heterosexuality, and the complexity of female competition" (2009, 7). In this regard, bullying and marginalization among women is represented as not a wider social problem also involving men but rather a "mean girl" problem, and Kelly and Pomerantz believe the film ignores these complexities.

While *Mean Girls* has arguably not aged well since its release, the film has maintained consistent popularity and even developed a cult following with a strong, devoted fan base. Its representation of LGBTQIA+ characters, or those named as such, is somewhat problematic but also honest and forthright. In the present day, this clique mentality among young people and the "mean girl" problem are still very much prevalent, especially given issues with cyberbullying and online harassment toward LGBTQIA+ people. The Plastics' Burn Book, and the chaos it causes upon its distribution, acts as a sort of precursor to this online hate and the effects it has, exposing a consistent problem that has stood the test of time.

See also *The Perks of Being a Wallflower; To All the Boys I've Loved Before.*

Bibliography

Fey, Tina. "*Mean Girls*." StudioBinder, June 3, 2003. Accessed March 18, 2021. https://www
.studiobinder.com/blog/mean-girls-script-screenplay-pdf-download/.

Kelly, Deidre M., and Shauna Pomerantz. "Mean, Wild, and Alienated: Girls and the State of
Feminism in Popular Culture." *Girlhood Studies* 2, no. 1 (2009): 1–19.

Oppliger, Patrice A. *Bullies and Mean Girls in Popular Culture.* Jefferson, NC: McFarland, 2013.

Simmons, Gary. "Mirrors, Make-Up and Meanings in 'Mean Girls.'" *Screen Education* 60 (2011):
132–38.

—John Lynskey

MIDNIGHT IN THE GARDEN OF GOOD AND EVIL (1997)

DIRECTOR: Clint Eastwood

SCREENPLAY: John Lee Hancock, based on the nonfiction book *Midnight in the
Garden of Good and Evil: A Savannah Story* by John Berendt

CAST: John Cusack (John Kelso), Kevin Spacey (Jim Williams), Jack Thompson
(Sonny Seller), Irma P. Hall (Minerva), Jude Law (Billy Hanson), Lady Chablis
(Chablis Deveau), Alison Eastwood (Mandy Nicholls)

SPECS: 155 minutes; color

AVAILABILITY: DVD (Warner Bros.)

When up-and-coming writer John Kelso arrives in Savannah, he thinks he is
there for a few days to write a five-hundred-word piece on Jim Williams's annual
Christmas party at the historic Mercer House for *Town & Country*. He meets
the charismatic Jim as well as other Savannah locals (including the Lady Chablis,
played by herself), attends the party, and happens to be in town when Jim shoots
and kills one of his employees (and clandestine lover), Billy Hanson. John inserts
himself into the case, deciding to stay in Savannah to monitor the case and write
a book, the one he hopes will make his career. John gets close to Jim, believing
in his innocence, and interviews those who knew Jim and Billy. His support of
Jim is eventually shattered by Jim's private confession to him, soon after which
Jim dies mysteriously; John, however, finds love and friendship in the city that
has, at least for now, won him over.

Midnight in the Garden of Good and Evil is a complicated film. It is based
on John Berendt's own time in Savannah and his best-selling 1994 nonfiction
text of similar name. As Clara Juncker notes, "both book and film versions have
a distinctly postmodern flavor," combining "travel narrative, tourist brochure,
detective fiction, (auto)biography, and courtroom drama" (2005, 182). The film
takes many liberties with the text, something Clint Eastwood, the film's director, acknowledged, including an enhanced portrayal of John and Jim, multiple
characters rolled into composites (including Mandy and Minerva, pivotal in the
film but not widely discussed here), and the condensing of the four actual trials
of Jim Williams (whose name was not changed) into one; the changes were made
without Berendt, who, according to Eastwood, "was convinced it couldn't be
adapted" (Wilson 2013, 170).

It is also difficult to proceed without referencing the ongoing allegations
against Kevin Spacey. In 2017, actor Anthony Rapp alleged Spacey assaulted him

in 1986 when Rapp was underage (Francescani 2019). Spacey claimed no memory of the incident but "apologized for 'what would have been deeply inappropriate drunken behavior'" (Francescani 2019); he also came out as a gay man. Several other accusations from multiple parties, many of whom were underage at the time of alleged interactions, followed (Francescani 2019). In 2020, Rapp and an anonymous man filed an ongoing lawsuit against Spacey for sexual assault (Associated Press 2020). There are troubling overlaps between the alleged incidents and the film. Certainly, Billy Hanson is of age in the film, but Spacey's character is the older and richer man; the power differential is, in retrospect, even more disturbing. It should be acknowledged, however, that these allegations were not public knowledge at the time of the film.

The film itself, while deeply flawed, delves into topics ranging from identity and sexuality to acceptance and resistance. John is supposed to be the more progressive northerner who does not, as a cisgender and straight man, always pick up on the social or sexual cues around him, but who seems to be generally accepting once he catches on to the unspoken-but-generally-known facts of his surroundings. It is unclear, for example, when he figures out that Jim has relationships with men and women (although the implication is that his relationships with men are more important to him) why John becomes one of Jim's staunchest supporters while quietly rebuffing his potential romantic interest. After sending over a suit for John to wear to the party, Jim observes him, flirtatiously noting, "Good fit. 44 long. I have an eye for framing things" [00:19:24–00:19:32]. Jim will indeed have an eye for "framing" his discussion of the future shooting, painting himself as innocent, but he also clearly has an eye interested in "framing," or capturing, John. Viewers see this interest mount when Jim questions, "Would you care to see something a little more . . . unusual?" [00:24:21–00:24:26]. The extended eye contact is not something John shies away from, agreeing to tour the home with Jim. As they ascend the staircase, the camera pans to a statue of a young man that obscures the men, zooming in on the statue's genitalia, highlighting both Jim's implied interest in John and his later-disclosed interest in younger men.

The moment is heightened when Jim reveals one of his treasures to John: "This is the dagger that Prince Yusupov used to murder Rasputin. He sliced off his cock and balls with it. True story and deliciously evil, don't you think?" [00:25:06–00:25:22]. John also spies a loaded gun in the treasure box as Billy Hanson enters, drunk, demanding money and threatening both Jim and John. The murderous and emasculating dagger placed alongside the gun, immediately followed by the entry of Billy, foreshadows the eventual death of both Jim and Billy, tied together due to their tumultuous, and eventually fatal, relationship, driven by desire and power. John is nonetheless intrigued by Jim, and his confusion during the interaction with Billy shows he is trying to piece together the men's relationship. When the party ends and Jim asks him to stay and chat, alone, John declines, seemingly acknowledging and politely rebuffing Jim's overtures.

Yet John is one of the first (and only) to defend Jim. He has a vested interest in the case since he wants Jim's help to write a book, but he genuinely supports Jim repeatedly. When interviewing Jim in prison before his trial, John asks Jim to explain his relationship with Billy: "Billy and I had a bond. That's not something that they're ever going to understand. They'll just see the sex, and the age difference. But Billy was going to make something of himself. . . . He needed what I gave him, and I needed what he gave me. Now, do you wish to pass judgment on that?" [01:07:19–01:07:54]. While there are obvious power differentials at play between Jim and Billy, Jim's openness about needing his lover is poignant, one of the first seemingly real moments with the overly genteel and guarded Jim (although, given his desire to befriend the man who will write his story, it is also likely contrived). His question of "judgment" is sound, as much of the town begins to turn on him.

Learning of the betrayal of his friends, who refuse to testify on his behalf, Jim quietly responds, "They clamored for my friendship, hoping and praying for invitations to my parties. Where were their judgments then?" [01:54:04–01:54:13]. The newly found indignation regarding Jim is explained by one of Jim's friends: "Those who are happy that Billy is no longer burning rubber through the squares are the exact people who think that Jim picked a very unseemly way to exit the closet, if you will" [01:12-57–01:13:11]. Mandy, a composite of multiple characters in the text who becomes the love interest of John in the film, notes, "Well normally there wouldn't be a problem seeing as the general rule is rich people get off. Problem is, they're usually straight" [01:16:55–01:17:02]. She continues, "Jim's friends knew he was gay. Secretly, they congratulated themselves on being so cosmopolitan. But if they knew he was completely open with his sexuality, they would've shunned him. Maybe the jury will too" [01:17:07–01:17:21]. The film raises several important points here: Jim's sexuality, a well-known secret, is acceptable only when it remains undiscussed in polite conversation; Jim's class (and privilege) has limits when pushed up against the prejudice surrounding LGBTQIA+ individuals, and the liberal self-congratulatory friends of Jim realize they are not quite as progressive as they had originally thought. Although these are brief moments in the film, they stress the extent of the prejudice surrounding LGBTQIA+ individuals as well as the difference between perceived acceptance and *actual* acceptance, particularly among "progressives."

John sees himself as one of the most progressive in town—the northerner looking down on the less liberal South. Mandy questions John's objectivity, wondering if he is assuming Jim's innocence prematurely, something John rejects:

> John: Objectively speaking, it's starting to look like they're going to hang a guy for his sexuality.
>
> Mandy: Something that would never happen in New York, right?
>
> John: Well, you said it, not me. [01:17:36–01:17:47]

Of course, anti-LGBTQIA+ prejudice extends beyond the South. John's inability to see such a clear claim due to his own beliefs and his desire for it to be better in the North calls into question his own objectivity at the moment he most wants to defend it.

Part of the anger aimed at Jim, aside from his breaking of the unspoken rule of silence surrounding his sexuality, is his choice of lovers (and victims). One of John's interviewees states:

Well, honey, there's bound to be a certain resentment about Jim having killed that boy—that boy, in particular, I mean. Why? Well, Billy was a very accomplished hustler. By all accounts, very good at his trade, and very much appreciated by both men and women. The trouble is, he hadn't finished making the rounds, no. Billy Hanson was known to be a good time, but a good time not yet had by all. [01:13:21–01:14:00]

Another town member puts it more simply: "They're saying that Jim Williams killed the best piece of ass in Savannah" [01:14:00–01:14:04]. Some of the anger expressed toward Jim is not solely about his outing of his own sexuality but rather the potential outing of other members of polite society, those who wished to have sexual relationships with men and women without discussion or consequence. However, these moments also problematically associate a stereotypical rampant and assumed promiscuity as part of the gay or bisexual male lifestyle.

Viewers see more negative views toward queerness in the film during Jim's trial. Jim's lawyer, Sonny Seller, tries to prevent the prosecution from discussing Jim's sexuality, noting the lead attorney's "intention is to paint Jim Williams pink and then rely on some prejudice in the jury" [01:32:45–01:32:52]. Sonny's objection is overruled, and witness George Tucker discloses Jim and Billy's sexual relationship. When Sonny asks George if he himself is a "homosexual," [01:36:19–01:36:21], George becomes flustered, "Naw sir, I ain't no fairy, okay, look, uh, I've had some experiences, but I'm out of it now" [01:36:46–01:37:00]. When pressed, he tells the court, "It's wrong. Bible says so" [01:37:10–01:37:13]. It is clear, despite Sonny's objectionable language about painting Jim "pink," that the prosecution is hoping to use the jury's antigay prejudices to sway the outcome of the trial, as even George, despite his own sexual preferences, calls on the Bible and negative terminology to distance himself.

Jim's own telling of his relationship with Billy on the stand is important, but it is also contrived. By this point, John knows Jim lied about the shooting and carries more blame than he is letting on; John questions, and thus the viewer questions, everything Jim says. Jim admits, "Over time, it evolved into something less formal. We became intimate. Billy could be very charming. He had his girlfriends and I had mine. But to me, sex is a perfectly natural thing. Didn't bother me, didn't bother him. It was just an occasional natural occurrence between consenting adults" [02:10:04–02:10:27]. Viewers could see Jim's view on sex as evolved and fluid, or they could see it as a denial of his true sexuality (assuming his interest in women is social necessity, not desire). More important, however, are the disgusted reactions from some on the jury and the bailiff. They are not questioning his authenticity; they take him at his word, displaying discomfort surrounding anything outside "traditional" heterosexuality. Sonny seemingly uses this discomfort in his closing argument: "Now if you don't like, or if you don't cotton to, his lifestyle, just think about this: we deal with these people all the time—some good, some bad. They're a part of our community, and you can't judge a man for that. This is God's world. Let God be the judge of that. And let you good folks be the judge of this" [02:14:53–02:15:26]. As fraught as Sonny's language is ("these people"), when he sits back down, he leans over to touch Jim in a supportive manner, one that demonstrates their clear friendship. This is not a moment of triumph, but it is a moment of alliance that stands in contrast to the previous distrust and disgust aimed at Jim. Sonny is by no means a progressive character, but viewers see his personal relationships can trump his prejudices.

Outside the portrayal of Jim and Billy, the film includes several moments with Lady Chablis, an African American transgender club performer featured in the text who plays herself in the film. John tries to interview Miss Chablis, who repeatedly refuses him, noting she is in mourning and no one has brought her flowers; Jim follows her around town to her doctor's office, this time offering an apology and roses before driving her home. Despite mentioning "Chablis" is a show name and that she becomes "Lady Chablis" in her act, and despite her references to being hot because her "shots are kicking in" [00:45:16–00:45:25], John does not realize she is transgender until he asks what the "F" stands for in the "F Deveau" phonebook entry: "The F stands for Frank, hon, that's me," she replies with a smile [00:46:02–00:46:16]. John's shock is momentary, but Sonny reacts differently: "She's a he? . . . You're shitting me. . . . Proper folks don't discuss such things" [00:46:30–00:46:39]. Again, the film emphasizes the role silence so often plays in LGBTQIA+ lives, silence that can be harmful.

Chablis runs the risk of being a caricature in the film, one called on for humorous moments and admittedly amazing one-liners. In some ways, viewers certainly see that portrayal. But she also has some of the best, most poignant moments in the film. She explains to John what her "T" is, her "Truth," as she talks about "hiding her candy" from John and others [01:03:13–01:03:26]. But she also tells John not to tell her new boyfriend her "Truth." When John mentions he is bound to find out eventually, she remarks, "When I'm ready for him to find out he'll find out," just as, she notes, John found out when she was ready and not before [01:03:50–01:04:24]. The moment is couched in humor, but it is an important discussion of self-determination, one John (and potentially the viewer) needs to understand.

When Chablis, who knew Billy before his murder, agrees to testify (albeit after she ambushes John at the Alpha Phi Beta cotillion), she acknowledges she is doing it for John: "I've thought about it, and I realize how nice you've been to me. You know what? You've treated me like a prefect lady; you've even made me feel so very special. You know, people can be so mean sometimes. But not you" [01:46:42–01:47:01]. John, burdened by the weight of her confession, finally begins to worry about the scrutiny she will face, urging her to reconsider. Chablis, in a powerful statement for self-worth, argues, "John, I have nothing to hide and I'm not ashamed of anything I've ever done" [01:47:30–01:47:34]. John notes her testimony may be an indictment of Billy, and she questions him:

> Chablis: So let me get this right now, so what you're saying is because Billy hung out with the "drag queens," he deserved to die?
>
> John: It's fucked up, but yeah.
>
> Chablis: Yeah, that's fucked up. [01:47:39–01:47:49]

So much of the film is about lying, about hiding identity and desire, about keeping secrets. Chablis defies those moments and calls out the social constructs and judgments for what they are: "fucked up."

Chablis recognizes she will be challenged in the courtroom for who she is, but she sees the moment as one in which she can hold power: "You see, those folks think they're using the Doll, but the Doll's using them right back. I'm going to use that courtroom as my coming out party. See John, you know who I am? I am the Lady Chablis: hear me roar" [01:48:02–01:48:19]. In typical style, when asked to explain her "Truth" to the jury, Chablis does not falter in the face of an unforgiving room: "I could throw words and labels at all of you, but you seem like nice people, so I'm going to be open and honest. I have a man's toolbox but everything else about me is pure lady. I love to dress in women's clothes. I love to go shopping. I love to have my nails done. And I love men" [01:49:42–01:50:10]. During her closing line, she reaches out to touch Sonny's hand. He recoils as disgust and confusion appear on many faces throughout the courtroom. And yet Chablis, true to her word, is not deterred. One of the most powerful scenes occurs as the judge reacts to her standing up unbidden:

Judge: You sit down Mr. Deveau.

Chablis: Miss Deveau. I'm a single girl, your Honor.

Judge: Miss Deveau, whatever, have a seat. [01:52:40–01:52:48]

Chablis refuses to engage with the negativity that comes from the judge's denial of her identity, and she corrects his misgendering in a way that acknowledges his position of power but also refuses to cede her own. While Jim and Billy often come off as flat, power-hungry, violent, and dishonest, Chablis reads as kind, approachable, unchanged by the opinions of those around her. Her strength and humor often carry the film in ways it does not always deserve.

Midnight in the Garden of Good and Evil is not an easy film. The film conjures many images viewers have seen repeatedly associated with LGBTQIA+ characters, from the rich, cultured, sly Jim to the hypermasculine, violent, bisexual Billy. And yet, for all its faults, it sometimes quietly challenges expectations; if not for the whole film, then for important moments.

See also *Basic Instinct; Clue.*

Bibliography

Associated Press. "Kevin Spacey Sued for Alleged Sexual Assault of Two Teenagers in 1980s." *Guardian*, September 10, 2020. Accessed April 1, 2021. https://www.theguardian. com/cul ture/2020/sep/10/kevin-spacey-sued-for-alleged-sexual-assault-of-two-teenagers-in-1980s.

Francescani, Chris. "The Rise and Fall of Kevin Spacey: A Timeline of Sexual Assault Allegations." ABC News, June 3, 2019. Accessed April 1. 2021. https://abcnews.go.com /US/rise-fall -kevin-spacey-timeline-sexual-assault-allegations/story?id=63420983.

Juncker, Clara. "Simulacrum Savannah: *Midnight in the Garden of Good and Evil.*" *Literature Film Quarterly* 33, no. 3 (2005): 182–90.

Wilson, Michael Henry. "'Truth, Like Art, Is in the Eyes of the Beholder': *Midnight in the Garden of Good and Evil* and *The Bridges of Madison County.*" In *Clint Eastwood: Interviews, Revised and Updated,* edited by Robert E. Kapsis and Kathie Coblentz, 168–77. Jackson: University Press of Mississippi, 2013.

—Meredith M. Malburne-Wade

MONSTER (2003)

DIRECTOR: Patty Jenkins
SCREENPLAY: Patty Jenkins, inspired by real-life events
CAST: Charlize Theron (Aileen Wuornos), Christina Ricci (Selby Wall), Bruce Dern (Thomas)
SPECS: 110 minutes; color
AVAILABILITY: DVD (Sony Pictures Home Entertainment)

Determined to put an end to her miserable life, Aileen finds a bar and seeks to spend the last five dollars in her pocket. She meets Selby, who tries to befriend her. With no place to sleep overnight, Aileen accepts Selby's offer to stay at her aunt's house, where the latter lives. They begin a romantic relationship and live on the road. Leaving her home does not prove difficult for Selby since her evangelical aunt and uncle disapprove of her sexual orientation. To keep her ever-demanding girlfriend satisfied, Aileen continues her occupation as a prostitute. However, Aileen becomes the victim of a traumatizing crime; one of her johns abuses and rapes her in his car. In self-defense, Aileen shoots the man dead with his own gun. She robs him, disposes of his body, and steals his car. Selby does not seem to feel much empathy for Aileen's situation. Both live from motel to motel with Aileen procuring money for Selby, and soon after a second murder, Aileen ends up killing two innocent men for Selby. Her subsequent endeavor to live a crime-free life proves disastrous as she is not able to obtain legitimate employment. Ultimately, Selby causes a car accident with one of her victims' vehicles, which attracts the attention of the police. In one of the film's last scenes, after being arrested, Aileen is called by Selby, who is being supervised by the police. She lures Aileen into confessing her deeds. The closing credits inform viewers of Aileen's death sentence in 1992 and execution in 2002.

In her first full-length film, then unknown director Patty Jenkins ventures to tell the story of the infamous female American serial killer Aileen Wuornos. The biopic is loosely based on Aileen's life and depicts sections of her criminal path in the late 1980s, consisting of seven murders. The story's emotional climax focuses on Aileen's relationship with Selby Wall, a character who is fictionalized and bears no resemblance to Aileen's real-life partner, Tyria Moore.

Patty Jenkins's Monster displays the darkest stage of Aileen Wuornos's criminal path and attempts to garner sympathy for her by providing insight into her early childhood and her destructive relationship with Selby. The film's ending purposely leaves viewers with a dramatic and melancholic impression of Aileen's outcome. However, it must never be forgotten that she killed several men. As a result, the film's dramatic display of Aileen's "fate" should be regarded critically. In fact, it is essential to note the film's biases. In the DVD's bonus material, Jenkins elaborates on her motivation for making the film:

> Monster is the story of a person crossing from one side to the other, from good to evil. It's about this last attempt to get love, which ended up culminating in a string of murders. I felt extremely responsible to be very clear about the fact that she did some horrible things, and she knew that she did some horrible things. I am not telling the story of a glorified serial killer but rather to service the greater truth, which I saw. [00:01:14–00:01:39]

Searching for a "greater truth," however, does not negate the undeniable fact that Aileen committed murder. Even if this truth is deeply rooted in Aileen's lifelong search for love and security, it does not excuse her actions. In the DVD's bonus material, Charlize Theron also tries to clarify the film's intent: "It's a love story. This is not the diaries of a serial killer. This is really somebody's journey in finding light in the darkest room you can possibly imagine. Somehow she found this little sliver of light and ran with it" [00:05:02–00:05:18]. Evidently, the sentimental nature of the film is designed to lead viewers to pity Aileen and her life circumstances. It seems to attempt to justify her unethical and criminal deeds. This is troubling, but equally as disconcerting is Jenkins's decision to fictionalize Aileen's relationship with Selby and interweave it with her criminal path. The film becomes disquieting, making Aileen's relationship with Selby appear to be the catalyst for her homosocial spree.

Soon after the film begins, *Monster* introduces its supporting character, Selby, who tries to test her small-talk skills on a despondent Aileen drinking her beer. After initially rejecting Selby and clearly informing her she is not gay, Aileen gives her a chance and agrees to stay at Selby's place out of necessity. This commences a rocky relationship that finds its first emotional highlight on Selby's bed, where she touches Aileen's face delicately. This moment is backed by a soft piano melody. The repeatedly appearing soundtrack elevates the romantic moments between both women to a level of melancholy that belies the profoundly unhealthy and dangerous nature of this relationship. Therefore, it is salient to register how the musical elements manipulate viewers, drawing the focus away from the murders and onto the women's liaison.

Moreover, the presentation of Aileen and Selby's physical appearance and relationship demands attention. Both women (in real life) fit into perceived stereotypes of the LGBTQIA+ community. However, their on-screen counterparts warrant examination. While Charlize Theron's transformation is implemented authentically (her resemblance to Aileen is uncanny), the portrayal of Selby remains problematic. The character shows no connection to real-life Aileen's partner, Tyria Moore. In real life, Tyria Moore's personal style is shown in testimony, interviews, and photographs as masculine leaning: wearing functional clothing and having a short haircut. Her body type is larger, and her features are relatively unrefined. However, her film counterpart, Selby, is a slender, delicate, and feminine-looking young woman with soft facial features. While real-life-inspired Aileen portrays the misandrist yet "masculine" lesbian who cannot find her place in society, Selby's portrayal marks a product of the filmmaker's imagination. With Aileen's role as a provider in this nomadic relationship, it is worth questioning whether the film retreats to heteronormativity or rather tries to render Selby's persona more accessible/acceptable to mainstream viewers.

In addition to discrepancies in appearance, the differences between real-life Tyria and fictional Selby deserves further attention. Throughout the plot and especially while cohabitating, Selby demands financial security from Aileen: "You can take care of me, right? Cause I spent all that money" [00:36:55–00:37:03]. After Aileen expresses her disdain for prostituting herself, Selby shows no empathy toward her girlfriend: "I thought you said it wasn't that bad" [00:37:20]. In an online article, Anoushka Rego clarifies Aileen's real-life love interest Tyria's attitude on prostitution: "In the documentary, 'Aileen Wuornos: Mind of a Monster,' Tyria divulges, 'Once I found out that she was prostituting, I did everything I could to help her stop doing that. But Aileen was adamant and would not relent'" (2020). With this in mind, one is left to wonder why Jenkins constructed Selby to be this callous. This problematic portrayal of Selby impacts LGBTQIA+ people negatively, portraying members of the community as cruel and self-centered.

In this same vein, the fictional Selby is shown as an opportunist. To keep her lover satisfied, Aileen strives for a legal job and attends job interviews, which do not prove fruitful. Nonetheless, Selby does not shy away from directly pressuring Aileen to provide for her: "Lee, what are you gonna do? . . . I am kinda starving here" [00:42:22–00:42:34]. She adds: "Why did you quit hooking? . . . You said that we were gonna party, party, party. But there hasn't been a fucking party." It is here that Aileen divulges the self-defense murder to Selby: "I fucking killed my last john. . . . All I had to think about was having the rest of your fucking life to think I stood you up. . . . And I didn't want to die thinking that maybe . . . you could have loved me. So I killed him" [00:46:06–00:47:13]. Selby's demanding nature becomes the underlying cause for Aileen's criminal deeds. And Selby's indifference to Aileen's pain, again, shows the LGBTQIA+ community in a negative light—as practically pathological.

Another aspect that creates a negative perception of this fictional relationship is its slow transformation into one-sided love. Aileen reveals her genuine investment in her relationship with Selby while observing her in an amusement park:

> I loved her. And the thing no one ever realized about me or believed was that I could learn. I could train myself into anything. People always look down their noses at hookers. Never give you a chance cause they think I took the easy way out. But no one can imagine the willpower it took to do what we do. Walking the streets, night after night, taking the hits and still getting back up. But I did. And they'd all missed out. Cause they had no idea what I could discipline myself to do when I believed in something, and I believed in her. [01:05:40–01:06:25]

This powerful monologue is performed through a voice-over and is accompanied by supporting camerawork. As Aileen's voice reaches the audience, the camera captures, from Aileen's perspective, Selby, who does not reciprocate any of the affection Aileen expresses toward her. While Aileen's voice-over discloses the difficulties of prostitution and the abuse it entails, there is a shot of Selby and then a reverse shot of Aileen, which elevates her inner speech and seems to show the disparity in their relationship. Aileen suffers verbal and psychological abuse from Selby. Considering Aileen's traumatic childhood memories, she has barely had the chance to experience a secure and healthy relationship; therefore, she is eager to keep her connection to Selby alive. By offering intense insight into the seemingly tough Aileen's vulnerability along with her steadfast desire to keep Selby, the film also emphasizes her humanity rather than her monstrousness. The filmmaker, especially in this very scene, provides an image of Aileen far removed from the real-life misandrist.

Finally, after being arrested, Aileen receives a phone call from Selby, who reminds her of the car accident, which Aileen claims not to remember. Selby tries to lure her into confessing to save herself: "I just wanna live, Lee. . . . Why did you do this?" Aileen understands that she is being monitored by the police and yet she divulges her motivations to protect Selby: "Cause I love you. . . . I love you with all my heart, my soul, my mind. And I'd never let you down, alright? Cause it was me, it was only me. And I will tell them that, alright?" [01:35:32–01:36:10]. When they see each other in court, Selby barely looks at her, shows virtually no emotions, and testifies against her. Again, this fictionalized character is shown as self-serving.

As a whole, *Monster* focuses on a destructive and difficult same-sex relationship resulting in a string of murders. The fictional Selby radiates irresponsibility; she is capable of doing anything not to get caught for a horrible act, even if that means turning in the only person in her life who understands and supports her. This one-sided relationship was doomed from the beginning. Although Aileen had seemingly been aware of the improbability of her relationship's future due to her crimes, she attempted everything in her power to sustain a greedy Selby. Aileen is undoubtedly responsible for her deeds because she chose this criminal path, being conscious of its consequences. Unlike the real-life Aileen, the *Monster* protagonist does not kill men out of pure disgust. Although she expresses her misandry during the film's plot, the main catalyst of those heinous deeds is Selby's unrealistic desires. The film tries to find a way to display the fate of her relationship by presenting its emotional and legal intractability. Therefore, it is necessary to understand the film's intention. Although the producers/director/artists at least attempt to show Aileen's unethical deeds and her poor motivations, they are more eager to put the couple through an emotional journey to create empathy in the viewer. The addition of Selby creates a sentimental tone that tries to connect viewers to Aileen Wuornos's perspective and her dramatic life as an outcast. *Monster* "attempt[s] to reveal the private person behind the public [figure] of . . . Wuornos and interrogate[s] the ways in which [its] fame circulated and what it represented" (Bell-Metereau 2015, 86). As a result, and perhaps unintentionally, the film leaves a questionable impression of the LGBTQIA+ community.

See also *Battle of the Sexes*; *Behind the Candelabra*; *Can You Ever Forgive Me?*; *I Am Michael*.

Bibliography

Bell-Metereau, Rebecca, and Colleen Glenn. *Star Bodies and the Erotics of Suffering*. Detroit: Wayne State University Press, 2015.

Rego, Anoushka. "Who Was Aileen Wuornos' Girlfriend? Where Is She Now?" *Cinemaholic*, September 2, 2020. Accessed July 25, 2021. https://thecinemaholic.com/aileen-wuornos-girlfriend/.

—Tuğba Karaca

MOONLIGHT (2016)

DIRECTOR: Barry Jenkins
SCREENPLAY: Barry Jenkins, based on the unpublished semiautobiographical play *In Moonlight Black Boys Look Blue* by Tarell Alvin McCraney

CAST: Alex R. Hibbert (Little), Ashton Sanders (Chiron), Trevante Rhodes (Black), Mahershala Ali (Juan), Naomie Harris (Paula), Janelle Monáe (Teresa), Jaden Piner (Kevin age nine), Jharrel Jerome (Kevin age sixteen), André Holland (Kevin)
SPECS: 111 minutes; color
AVAILABILITY: DVD (Altitude Film Distribution)

A young African American man named Chiron comes of age in Miami, Florida. The film is divided into three parts, each dealing with a different period of Chiron's life and his struggles with identity, and each with a different title that describes aspects of the character's identity. The first part, "Little," focuses on Chiron's childhood and his relationship with Juan, a drug dealer who takes him under his wing on seeing the boy bullied and living in a neglectful home with his mother, Paula. Little suspects that he might be different to the other boys and goes to Juan and his girlfriend Teresa to ask if he is a "faggot." Part 2, "Chiron," focuses on Chiron (Little's birth name) in high school. He is still bullied by the other young men but remains friends with Kevin from his childhood. Despite Juan's death, Chiron continues to visit Teresa as an escape from his turbulent home life with his mother, whose behavior is becoming increasingly erratic due to her drug addiction. One night, Chiron spends the evening at the beach and is joined by Kevin. They smoke some marijuana and end up kissing. Kevin manually pleasures Chiron. Soon after, at school, tired of being harassed, Chiron goes into class, picks up a wooden chair, and attacks one of the bullies, knocking him out. Chiron is arrested and taken away by police as Kevin looks on. The concluding section, "Black," begins with Chiron about ten years older, now a drug dealer and living in Atlanta. He receives a phone call from Kevin, who is working as a cook in Miami. Kevin invites Chiron to meet up for a free meal. On his way back to his hometown, Chiron visits Paula, who is living in a drug rehabilitation center. She apologizes for how she treated him growing up, and they tearfully make amends. Chiron arrives at Kevin's restaurant, and the pair catch up over food, wine, and music. They go back to Kevin's apartment, where Chiron reveals that he has not been touched like Kevin touched him that night on the beach. They sit on the bed, Chiron's head resting on Kevin's shoulder, who cradles him, gently stroking his head. The final image of the film is of Little standing on the shore at night looking out to sea. He turns and looks to the camera.

"Who is you?" It is a repeated question in *Moonlight* and strikes at the heart of the film's central themes of identity and finding one's place in the world. It is spoken twice. The first time is by Paula to Juan when he brings Little home. He has spent the night at Juan and Teresa's house after hiding from a gang of kids who tease him. The second occurs when Kevin asks Black the question at the end of the film. Both times, the question is asked of a grown adult male who deals drugs. Based on appearance alone, Juan and Black encapsulate a certain type of masculinity. They appear physically strong, wear gold "grills" over their teeth, have do-rags on their heads, and drive expensive cars, all iconography associated with social status and gang cultures. Yet both characters also subvert the simplistic stereotypes popular culture consistently attributes to these images. Contrary to his imposing physical presence, Juan is a gentle, softly spoken, nurturing character who cares for Little when he is bullied at school. And Black's characterization problematizes normative understandings of masculinity through his sexuality.

Naming, and how it relates to Chiron's sense of identity, including coming to terms with his gay identity, is significant in the film. Each of the titles given to the three sections of the film correspond to aspects of the central character's identity and are often used interchangeably within these parts. The nickname "Little" corresponds to Chiron's diminutive stature. At the dinner table with Juan and Teresa, when he finally speaks, he declares, "My name is Chiron, but people call me Little," and the viewer is supposed to infer that it is a name he has not chosen himself but has been assigned to him by others, including his bullies. It also denies him a name insofar as an adjective, in this case "little," usually accompanies that which it describes. When they first meet, Juan calls Chiron "little man," thus giving Chiron more of an identity and establishing the mentoring role he will play in the boy's early life. Later, Juan tells Little/Chiron about his time growing up in Cuba. He was a handful in childhood, he says, and one night he came across an elderly woman who stopped him and said, "In moonlight, black boys look blue. That's what I'll call you: Blue." Juan uses this story to teach Little/Chiron that it is up to him to decide who he will be in life, not anybody else. The film is suggesting a cycle to Juan and Chiron's narratives, one that comes true through the youngster's transformation by the film's conclusion.

As the second of the three narrative parts, the section titled "Chiron" functions as a point of transition. Chiron is now a teenager and experiences growing pains, both physical and metaphorical. From being small, he is now tall and lanky, an outcast who is often seen alone hugging his backpack close to himself, coiled, as if always ready to run away from danger. It is noteworthy that in this section he is called all three names that he has or will have over the course of the film. In other words, his identity is even more indeterminate during this time. He is called "Little" by his bullies, a throwback to his small stature in childhood. Various people call him "Chiron," among them his mother and Teresa. His childhood friend, Kevin, is the only one to call him "Black." Once again, however, it is a name Chiron has not chosen. This is also the section where viewers first see Chiron acting on his same-sex desires. Part 1 hints at Chiron's gay identity, such as when Paula rails at Juan, asking him whether he has seen the way Chiron walks and if he knows why the other boys pick on him. Little/Chiron then asks Juan and Teresa, "What's a faggot?" To which Juan replies, carefully and considerately, "A faggot is a word used to make gay people feel bad." When Little/Chiron asks him whether he is a faggot, Juan quickly responds, "No. You could be gay, but don't let anyone call you that [faggot]." Here Juan is understanding and sympathetic, and even accepting of the possibility that Little/Chiron could be gay. This scene also connects naming to statements of sexual identity by referring to Juan's lesson of not letting others determine who you are; you might be gay, but never a faggot.

Later, teenage Chiron escapes his turbulent home and school life by traveling to the beach. It is portrayed as a space with happy memories for Chiron and time spent safe with Juan growing up. One night, sitting on the beach, Chiron is joined by Kevin, who says that he comes here to smoke marijuana. Chiron uses the opportunity to ask Kevin why he calls him "Black." Kevin says that it is his nickname for him, which Chiron explains is strange for one man to do for another man. They continue talking and smoking and share their troubles and sensitivities (Chiron becomes especially interested when Kevin hints that he could sometimes cry). They eventually kiss, and Kevin manually pleasures Chiron. This is important due to this being Chiron's first sexual experience in the film. Kevin also calls him "Chiron" before they kiss, thus linking his legal birth name with his gay identity. As a result, the film consolidates same-sex desire within a framework of acceptability.

It is surely not incidental that this scene contains a focus on hands, given that the name Chiron comes from the Greek word *kheir*, meaning "hand." Besides the association with the sexual activity Kevin performs, the camera lingers on a shot of Chiron digging his hand and fingers into the sand, a sign of his sexual pleasure. When Kevin drives Chiron home that night, they leave by shaking hands, the same hands that were shown as part of their encounter, which the film emphasizes through slow motion as their hands touch in the car. Incidentally, in Greek mythology, Chiron was a centaur, the son of Cronus and Philyra, and, unlike other centaurs, who were often aggressive and cruel, he was known to be extremely wise and knowledgeable. Just like the mythical creature that was part man and part horse, Chiron in *Moonlight* is a man with no singular identity.

In part 3, Chiron runs his own small drug-dealing business out of Atlanta. His underlings call him "Black," and it seems that Chiron has chosen this as his name and identity. Time has changed him. Gone is the small child and gangly teenager; he is now muscular and imposing. It is quite a transformation. This is a theme found throughout the film, mainly focused on water. In part 1, Juan performs a symbolic baptism on Chiron as he teaches him to swim and about his shared Black history. Chiron emerges changed and is seen dancing excitedly at school and more talkative. The sight and sound of waves occur throughout and symbolize change through their constant shaping of the shoreline. They are the first sounds heard and the last images seen as Little/Chiron stands on the beach and turns toward the camera. Taken together, these moments suggest the constant becoming of identity that is never fixed and always subject to fluid change.

Of course, the viewer realizes that "Black" is also the nickname Kevin gave to Chiron, so even as he presents a hard, threatening, and "straight acting" self, the name carries queer significance. When Kevin calls Chiron, his demeanor changes. It is the first time either has spoken since Kevin watched Chiron being arrested at school for attacking a student with a chair. From an authoritative presence barking orders at his dealers, he turns into the shy, awkward, stuttering Chiron from the earlier parts of the film. This is not to suggest that the latter is his authentic self, even if viewers might draw their own conclusions. Rather it emphasizes that the persona "Black" is just that, a performance meant to guard Chiron against the kind of harassment he has been on the receiving end of throughout his life. This is made clear when he visits Paula in a drug rehabilitation center on his trip back to Miami. As they are reconciled, Paula says, "Your heart ain't gotta be black like mine, baby. You hear me, Chiron?" This emotional scene is the catalyst for Chiron shedding his identity as Black when meeting up with Kevin. The setup to the sequence suggests a performance when Black/

Chiron checks his appearance in his car window before entering the restaurant. Once inside, on hearing about Chiron's drug dealing, Kevin says, "That's not you, Chiron." When the pair go to Kevin's apartment, Chiron's answer to Kevin's question "Who is you?" is answered by his confession that Kevin is the only man who has ever touched him the way he did on the beach all those years earlier. In other words, Chiron is the young man on that beach being embraced by another man. The film's penultimate image is of Chiron and Kevin on a bed in the same pose as on the beach: this time filmed from the front, Chiron resting his head on the shoulder of Kevin, who caresses him. It is a closing tableau of tenderness between the two men and an indication of Chiron's acceptance of his (gay) identity.

See also *Naz & Maalik*.

Bibliography

Alexander, Bryant Keith. *Performing Black Masculinity: Race, Culture, and Queer Identity*. Lanham, MD: Altamira Press, 2006.

Harris, Keith M. *Boys, Boyz, Bois: An Ethics of Black Masculinity in Film and Popular Media*. New York: Routledge, 2006.

Johnson, E. Patrick, and Mae G. Henderson. *Black Queer Studies: A Critical Anthology*. Durham, NC: Duke University Press, 2005.

O'Brien, Daniel. *Black Masculinity on Film: Native Sons and White Lies*. London: Palgrave Macmillan, 2017.

—Adam Vaughan

MOTHER'S DAY (2016)

DIRECTOR: Garry Marshall
SCREENPLAY: Garry Marshall, Tom Hines, Anya Kochoff, and Matthew Walker
CAST: Jennifer Aniston (Sandy), Kate Hudson (Jesse), Sarah Chalke (Gabi), Britt Robertson (Kristin), Jason Sudeikis (Bradley), Julia Roberts (Miranda), Timothy Olyphant (Henry), Margo Martindale (Flo), Aasif Mandvi (Russell)
SPECS: 118 minutes; color
AVAILABILITY: DVD (Universal Pictures Home Entertainment)

For a film that begins with Atlanta mothers running after their kids and taking care of them only as mothers can, and then showcasing a giant womb float for an upcoming Mother's Day parade, Garry Marshall's *Mother's Day* makes the viewer anticipate that his film is all about mothers. Which it is. And yet, while it hails mothers who are both human and flawed, the film also deploys the mother figure to articulate some of the deepest prejudices that create fault lines within the national fabric of the United States. The film begins with the giant womb float, which Jesse's lesbian sister Gabi creates along with her partner, Max, and about which Gabi mentions that "it's symbolic that we all come from the same place: gay, straight, transgender, black, white, [and] purple" [00:05:04–00:05:14]. Gabi has to compulsively lie to her homophobic, racist parents (Flo and Earl) about her sexual identity. Jesse, likewise, hides her marriage to an Indian doctor, Russell, whom Flo detests for his race and skin color. While racism and homophobia find mention in the film through the characters of Flo and Earl— whose one daughter is married to an Indian and whose other belongs to the

LGBTQIA+ community—these issues are reduced to mindless jokes or incidents and denied the nuanced treatment they deserve. Not surprisingly, Jordan Hoffman calls *Mother's Day* "a goddamn trash masterpiece" for "inelegantly linking many half-baked stories" where neither an ensemble star cast nor a festive theme saves the film from insensitivity and failure (2016).

Mother's Day falls back on a number of clichés trying to drive home its point on same-sex relationships. Flo and Earl are white Texans who drive around in an RV, belong to a generation that apparently struggles with Skype calls, and believes that the greatest ambition in a white woman's life must be to "catch" a successful white man. And much of their homophobia finds its roots in the culture they inhabit. Yes, research does indicate that while gay activism has been as much a reality in Texas as it is in "gay meccas" such as "New York City, San Francisco, and Los Angeles," what is "unique to Texas" is that for a long time, "homosexual conduct" continued to be a crime until *Lawrence v. Texas* in 2003 (Orio 2017, 57). Yes, the political and cultural practices in Texas have produced some subliminal constrains on sexual freedoms of the LGBTQIA+ communities; nonetheless, such practices have also been vocally and strongly critiqued and countered. What Garry Marshall's film does is simply exploit this Texan stereotype and present Flo and Earl as conservative old folk celebrating Eurocentric heteronormativity who, even as they are shocked to meet Gabi's "wife," Max, also almost immediately reconcile with their lesbian daughter as if forcing viewers toward the inevitable happy family reunion that the film ends with. Gabi and Max's relationship is devoid of all layers of complexity, and while it addresses a wider culture of homophobia, it also boasts of melodramatic and almost seamless solutions to this malaise.

Another seemingly disturbing attribute that the LGBTQIA+ community is credited with in *Mother's Day* is appearance. While Max befits the stereotype of a "butch" lesbian and is depicted as a perfectly happy woman comfortable in her own skin, this depiction denies viewers a clear understanding of the covert cultural exclusions that LGBTQIA+ people with nonheteronormative physical appearances have to contend with. Janae Teal and Meredith Conover-Williams, while deconstructing contemporary public discourses on queerness, reveal that "the coming out process, for people with enough privilege to safely do so, now comes with much less risk of being ostracized," but for common people it continues to be a challenge (2016, 13). In fact, "over a quarter of the LGB community," claim Teal and Conover-Williams, "has experienced discrimination" at various levels (2016, 13). The present millennium, according to Teal and Conover-Williams, is "casually homophobic," and members of the LGBTQIA+ community experience as a much a cultural backlash on virtual platforms as in the real world (2016, 13). For turning a blind eye toward the cultural stigma that someone like Max may encounter on a daily basis, *Mother's Day* disappoints viewers looking for a refined treatment of this subject.

For its ill-informed story line, Jen Chaney rightly asks if the makers of *Mother's Day* have "ever observed actual humans" (2016). This is accurate because while it attempts to craft a happy narrative, the film overlooks all nuances that go into making its multihued characters truly happy. And this is especially true for the film's LGBTQIA+ characters, who remain as one-dimensional and as stereotypical as it gets.

See also *No Strings Attached.*

Bibliography

Chaney, Jen. "'Mother's Day' Movie Review: You'll Want to Return This Gift." *Washington Post*, April 28, 2016. Accessed Jan. 24, 2021. https://www.washingtonpost.com/goingoutguide /movies/mothers-day-movie-review-youll-want-to-return-this-gift/2016/04/28/7b37e2ea-0be1 -11e6-8ab8-9ad050f76d7d_story.html.

Hoffman, Jordan. "Mother's Day Review: Almost Transcendentally Terrible." *Guardian*, April 28, 2016. Accessed Jan 24, 2021. https://www.theguardian.com/film/2016/apr/28/mothers-day -review-jennifer-aniston-julia-roberts-jason-sudeikis.

Orio, Scott De. "The Invention of Bad Gay Sex: Texas and the Creation of a Criminal Underclass of Gay People." *Journal of the History of Sexuality* 26, no. 1 (January 2017): 53–87.

Teal, Janae, and Meredith Conover-Williams. "Homophobia without Homophobes: Deconstructing the Public Discourses of 21st Century Queer Sexualities in the United States." *Humboldt Journal of Social Relations* 38 (2016): 12–27.

—Srirupa Chatterjee

MY OWN PRIVATE IDAHO (1991)

DIRECTOR: Gus Van Sant
SCREENPLAY: Gus Van Sant
CAST: River Phoenix (Mike Waters), Keanu Reeves (Scott Favor), William Richert (Bob Pigeon), Udo Kier (Hans), James Russo (Richard Waters), Chiara Caselli (Carmella), Tom Troupe (Jack Favor)
SPECS: 104 minutes; color
AVAILABILITY: Blu-ray/DVD (Criterion Collection)

Mike Waters is a narcoleptic sex worker in Portland, Oregon, who frequently passes out in the middle of a "date." Scott Favor, Mike's best friend, is the privileged son of the mayor and chooses to spend time sleeping on rooftops and charging for sex until he inherits his fortune. Each of them yearns for a parental figure: Mike searches for his missing mother in the faces of strangers, while Scott turns to the colorful Bob Pigeon, a middle-aged man who mentors several other young male street hustlers. Mike and Scott eventually leave Portland to search for Mike's mom, beginning with a visit to Mike's brother in rural Idaho. Mike confesses his love for Scott along the way, which Scott refuses. After a three-way sexual encounter with Hans, a man they first encountered in Portland, their search takes them to Rome, Italy. Mike's mother is missing, but Scott finds Carmella, a beautiful Italian woman he decides to bring back with him to America. Mike and Bob are shunned as Scott inherits his place in society after the mayor's death with Carmella by his side. Bob dies from the rejection, leading to a raucous wake in his honor occurring just nearby the restrained funeral for Scott's father. Mike and Scott glance at each other but do not speak. Later, Mike is back in Idaho. He passes out on the road and is robbed of his belongings before being pulled into an unknown car, which drives away.

My Own Private Idaho is Gus Van Sant's third feature film, following his grainy, low-budget debut *Mala Noche* (1985) and the more commercially viable crime drama *Drugstore Cowboy* (1989). *My Own Private Idaho* fuses the queer rebelliousness of Van Sant's debut and the more visually restrained, character-driven style of his sophomore film with a dizzying array of further influences, including William Shakespeare's *Henriad* and the 1963 novel *City of Night*, written by John Rechy about young male prostitutes. Also woven throughout the film are the sights and sounds of the American West, surreally staged sex montages, and dreamy flashbacks resembling home videos of Mike as a child with his mother. The cumulative effect of these elements is tremendous; *My Own Private Idaho* is considered a signature example of the New Queer Cinema movement of the early 1990s. Film critic B. Ruby Rich referred to the movement's style as "Homo Pomo: there are traces . . . of appropriation and pastiche, irony, as well as a reworking of history with social constructionism very much in mind . . . these works are irreverent, energetic, alternately minimalist and excessive. . . . They're here, they're queer, get hip to them" (2004, 16). That such a bold film stars River Phoenix—famous since his child role in *Stand By Me* (1986)—and Keanu Reeves—then recently made a celebrity by *Bill and Ted's Excellent Adventure* (1989)—perhaps contributes to its endurance as a hallmark of 1990s LGBTQ cinema. Cultural context aside, *My Own Private Idaho*'s narrative and themes stand out for their avant-garde sensibility, queer perspective, and tender emotional story.

The film begins with Mike on an empty road in Idaho: a narrow strip of black pavement, bisected by a dashed yellow line, stretching across the rolling plains toward a distant horizon. He speaks in a voice-over about his affinity for roads and appreciation of both their familiarity and uniqueness: "I always know where I am by the way the road looks. Like, I just know that I've been here before . . . there's not another road anywhere that looks like this road, I mean, exactly like this road. It's one kind of place, one of a kind, like someone's face. Like a fucked-up face" [00:01:55–00:02:55]. Suddenly overcome by a narcolepsy attack, he lays down on the road and sleeps, his eyes rapidly moving behind his closed eyelids. The film moves across a series of disparate images: a mountain with clouds rolling past; a woman with Mike's head in her lap who says, "Don't worry, everything's gonna be all right" [00:03:55]; a small barn in an empty field; a different road undulating over a series of hills; an orange sky pierced by a shooting star; and then, title cards with opening credits intercut with further images. This opening sequence is typical of the avant-garde montage editing used throughout the film. *My Own Private Idaho*'s use of montage aligns with the argument of Soviet filmmaker and theorist Sergei Eisenstein that "montage is not an idea composed of successive shots stuck together but *an idea that derives from the collision between two shots that are independent of one another*" (2009, 27). By mixing images of Mike in the grip of narcolepsy, Mike being comforted by his mother, and rural Idaho, the film creates a thematic association between those seemingly disparate concepts. Narratively, Mike's narcolepsy often marks the transition between geographic space—when Mike "wakes up" from this first episode, he's in Seattle, being fellated by a client—but thematically, his dream-like memories of Idaho and his mother endow his time spent sleeping with the longing for comfort that drives his waking hours. The associative chain is not closed with those themes; Mike's orgasm is visually represented by a barn falling from the sky and smashing on a rural road. Mike's narcoleptic sleep is thus not solely associated with Idaho or with his mother. Rather, all of these themes and others are placed in a constellation of meaning that shifts throughout the film.

The tension and ambiguity inherent to *My Own Private Idaho*'s montage editing is also apparent in the stylization of Scott's narrative. The basic structure of Scott's character progression is informed by that of Prince Hal across Shakespeare's *Henry IV, Part 1*, *Henry IV, Part 2*, and *Henry V*, a series of historically based plays that follow Hal from life as a rambunctious young prince to ruling England as King Henry V. The term "Henriad" here refers to these three plays, although Shakespeare scholars often group between four and eight plays by the term. *My Own Private Idaho* only loosely adapts Hal's trajectory rather than faithfully reproducing Shakespeare's epic story. Shakespearean themes and dialogue primarily surface in the film through Scott's relationship with Bob Pigeon, analogous to Prince Hal's relationship with Sir John Falstaff. While contemporary sexual identity categories have limited value for describing the same-sex relationships that appear throughout Shakespeare's oeuvre, scholar Daniel Juan Gil notes "a sexuality that is structurally distinct from conventionally . . . eroticized male-male camaraderie" in the *Henry IV* plays, which contributes the most material to *My Own Private Idaho* (2011, 117). Bob and Scott's relationship is more explicitly queer than their Renaissance referents, although it is still ambiguous. When Mike asks Scott about Bob by saying, "Didn't you two have . . . a real heavy, uh," Scott finishes the sentence "thing" and then repeats, "We had a real heavy thing going. He was fucking in love with me" [00:22:55–00:23:05]. Scott adds that Bob "taught me more than school did" [00:23:10] and later refers to Bob as "my real father" [00:28:05], suggesting a father-son dynamic. Yet, in the midst of an interaction adapted from Act 1, Scene 2, of *Henry IV, Part 1*, Bob passionately kisses Scott on the mouth. Their relationship thus hews more closely to Shakespeare's Hal and Falstaff than the modern setting would suggest, certainly at least in comparison to Derek Jarman's *Edward II* (1991), another New Queer Cinema film drawing inspiration from Renaissance drama—by Christopher Marlowe, Shakespeare's contemporary—but more deliberately altering the source text's material. Like Hal and Falstaff, Scott eventually rejects his companion and mentor once he comes into his inheritance, leading to the latter's death from heartbreak.

Mike's and Scott's individual character arcs, in which each search for comfort and companionship, also structure their relationship as a pair. Scott often cares for Mike when the latter passes out; an early scene features Mike and Scott being hired by the same client, a middle-aged woman living in a wealthy area. Mike passes out while undressing; Scott and another hustler, Gary, drag him outside to sleep on an empty lawn. Mike begins walking home the next morning and encounters Hans, a German man driving the same car that picked him up the previous night. Hans offers Mikes a ride, but he refuses, only to pass out in the middle of the street. Mike awakens in Scott's arms in Portland. Scott tells him that Hans drove them back to Portland; when Mike says, "I'm forgetting a German guy named Hans," Scott replies, "Well you were sleeping" [00:21:50].

Scott's care for Mike is unseen—and, Mike suspects, involves some sexual exploitation—yet the shot of Scott holding Mike is tenderly composed, their bodies reminiscent of the pietà pose of the Virgin Mary and Jesus depicted throughout Christian art. Mike often rides behind Scott on his motorcycle, placing their faces and bodies in close proximity. Their physical and emotional intimacy is charged by the camera's framing/editing and the star image Phoenix and Reeves bring to their roles. Richard Dyer notes how for many viewers, "The roles and/or the performance of a star in a film were taken as revealing the personality of the star" (1979, 22). Both of *My Own Private Idaho*'s leading men were sex symbols and teen idols at the time of the film's release. When asked by *Interview* magazine if there was concern about taking the roles or negative reactions from it, Reeves scoffed, "Who am I—a politician?," while Phoenix offered a more direct message: "Fuck them. That's all I can say" (Powell and Skyes 1991). Phoenix does admit, though, that if the film had been made ten years prior, only "porno stars . . . maybe one of Warhol's crowd" would've taken the leading roles. The unique production environment of the New Queer Cinema allowed stars such as Phoenix and Reeves to participate in projects such as *My Own Private Idaho*, admittedly one of the higher-budget films from the movement.

The intimacy between Mike and Scott is most directly expressed beside a campfire, a scene rewritten by Phoenix during production. Van Sant remarked that "it was a short, three-page scene that River turned into more like an eight-page scene. . . . It was his explanation of his character" (Fuller 2008). They discuss their families, their faces only illuminated by the flickering fire. After Scott lets slip that he grew up with a maid, Mike says, "If I had a normal family and a good upbringing then I would've been a well-adjusted person" [00:51:20]. Although Scott doesn't see his family as "normal"—"What's a normal dad?" [00:25:05]—Mike pivots the conversation to the two of them. "What do I mean to you?" Mike asks, his voice so soft that it is almost obscured by the fire's noise [00:52:50]. "You're my best friend," Scott responds [00:52:55]. Mike is evasive, quiet, his gaze on the fire rather than his friend. Perhaps sensing Mike's underlying feelings, Scott reiterates that for him sex with men is purely for money: "Two guys can't love each other" [00:53:40]. Mike's wrenching, poetic response makes his feelings clear: "For me, I could love someone, even if I . . . wasn't paid for it. I love you and you don't pay me" [00:53:50]. Although Scott invites Mike to sleep against him and strokes his hair as he falls asleep, an intimate yet romantically ambiguous reaction, Scott either cannot or will not return Mike's affections. Although the two later engage in a three-way sex scene with Hans—presented via quick edits that obscure details but display arrangements of nude bodies—it is clear that the sex is for business not pleasure. Where Mike's yearning for family can be expressed through romantic attraction to men, Scott's inability to requite Mike's love foreshadows his eventual disavowal of same-sex desire and prostitution.

Ostensibly searching for Mike's mother, the pair sell Scott's motorcycle and fly to Rome. The Italian countryside is filmed similarly to Idaho, with the camera capturing wide landscapes emphasizing open space and pastoral nature. Mike's mother is gone and the trail is cold. Scott, however, is more fortunate in Europe. He meets Carmella, a young Italian woman who knew Mike's mother when she was in Italy. Scott and Carmella each profess that they have fallen in love as Mike becomes increasingly depressed. Ultimately, Scott and Carmella return to Portland together while Mike attempts to make money as a sex worker in Rome before also returning to Portland, still working on the streets. The details of their journeys occur off camera, yet the severance of their intimacy is evident.

The film's falling action plays out to Shakespeare's beats as Scott, now sporting a suit and riding in nice cars, assumes his place in bourgeois society with Carmella on his arm. Scott's father apparently died at some point during Scott and Mike's road trip, passing his wealth and prestige to his son. Bob confronts him in a restaurant—Mike is part of the group but remains silent—and is rejected. Prince Hal's disavowal of his former companion and mentor is a significant turning point in Shakespeare's *Henriad*, occurring in the final scene of *Henry IV, Part 2* and marking Hal's transition to King Harry, the eventual war hero against France in *Henry V*. Such events are not represented in the film. Instead, Scott's narrative closes as he sits at his father's solemn funeral, Carmella by his side, as Mike and other street characters gather nearby around Bob's coffin and scream his name. Scott watches them, his face blank. Mike seems to look back, making a face at his onetime friend before joining in a pile of kissing men atop Bob's wooden coffin. The camera pans to the sky, holding for a few seconds before cutting to a clip of salmon swimming upstream and then returning to Idaho: wide skies, open fields, and a road. Mike stands on the road, alone, and remarks that he is "a connoisseur of roads" [01:35:45]. "This road will never end" he says, his words growing unsteady. "It probably goes all the way around the world" [01:35:55]. He falls, caught in a narcoleptic fit. A truck pulls over, but the two men who step from it steal Mike's shoes and bag. The camera moves up and away from his fallen form as a discordant version of "America, the Beautiful" plays. Another car stops: this unknown driver drags Mike into the passenger seat and drives away. The films ends with a title card reading, "Have a nice day" [01:39:25]. There is no answer to Mike and Scott's yearnings at the conclusion of *My Own Private Idaho*, only the vastness of the world and the uncertain motivations of other people.

See also *Nocturnal Animals*; *A Single Man*.

Bibliography

Dyer, Richard. *Stars*. London: British Film Institute, 1979.

Eisenstein, Sergei. "The Dramaturgy of Film Form." In *Film Theory & Criticism*, 7th ed., edited by Leo Braudy and Marshall Cohen, 24–40. New York: Oxford University Press, 2009.

Fuller, Graham. "Gus Van Sant: Swimming against the Current." Focus Features, July 29, 2008. Accessed March 30, 2021. http://www.focusfeatures.com/article/gus_van_sant__swimming_against_the_current.

Gil, Daniel Juan. "The Deep Structure of Sexuality: War and Masochism in *Henry IV, Part 2*." In *Shakesqueer: A Queer Companion to the Complete Works of Shakespeare*, edited by Madhavi Menon, 114–20. Durham, NC: Duke University Press, 2011.

Powell, Paige, and Gini Sykes. "My Own Private Idaho." *Interview*, November 1991. Accessed March 30, 2021. https://www.interviewmagazine.com/film/my-own-private-idaho.

Rich, B. Ruby. "New Queer Cinema." In *New Queer Cinema: A Critical Reader*, edited by Michele Aaron, 15–22. New Brunswick, NJ: Rutgers University Press, 2004.

—Sam Hunter

· N ·

NAZ & MAALIK (2015)

DIRECTOR: Jay Dockendorf
SCREENPLAY: Jay Dockendorf
CAST: Curtiss Cook Jr. (Maalik), Kerwin Johnson Jr. (Naz), Annie Grier (Sarah Mickell), Ashleigh Awusie (Cala), Anderson Footman (Dan)
SPECS: 89 minutes; color
AVAILABILITY: DVD (Wolfe Video)

Naz and Maalik are two high schoolers living in Bedford-Stuyvesant, New York. They are Black, Muslim, and gay, and closeted as well; they keep their relationship hidden from their family and most of their friends. The film follows them as they spend a day hustling cheap trinkets like perfumes, lotto tickets, and candy around the city. Their enterprising ventures are interspersed with conversations about their own romantic situation, the conflict between their sexuality and their faith, ethical concerns often unrelated to their sexuality, and other personal topics. What is presented as an average day of side hustles and hanging out for the two young men is interrupted by an FBI agent named Sarah Mickell, who capitalizes on their hustling and a run-in they had with an undercover cop who tried to sell them a gun. She follows them throughout the day in her attempts to profile them as radical Muslims, adding extra tension to their day as they must now deal with her surveillance on top of their efforts to keep their sexuality hidden from their family. The movie ends with a sense of ambiguity about whether Naz and Maalik will come out to their family and whether their own relationship will continue.

   Naz & Maalik blends the delightful chemistry between its two leads with an overwhelming feeling of surveillance aimed at the pair, who themselves mix their carefree surety as they navigate their home city together with the weight of their complicated situation. The larger themes that the film explores are the conflict between Naz and Maalik's sexual identities and their Muslim faith, the impact this conflict has on their relationship, contemporary Islamophobia in New York City together with racial profiling, and the need for secrecy that inhibits the development of trust between the protagonists. Against this backdrop of surveillance and secrecy are the often humorous, illuminating, and personal conversations that Naz and Maalik have as they spend the day hopping around and selling various items to raise money for college. In the way the film depicts the routine of the two buying and hustling, chatting and arguing, flirting and reflecting, there is the promise and the allure of "what could be" were there not the social, political, and religious pressures they find themselves under. The engaging mundanity of their day on the street is countered by the weight of their assumed terrorism that inflects even the parts of the film that the FBI agent plays no role in; for example, early in the film an Imam welcomes the young men and a small group to their mosque with the line, "If you're here with the NYPD or you're with the FBI, welcome, sincerely. We expect you here" [00:10:30]. Here, too, what should be the mundanity of a prayer service is met with the new mundanity of acknowledging the governmental scrutiny that is assumed to be present; at the very least, it is on everyone's mind. The film, thus, early on, establishes a tone of surveillance that will be doubled by the threat of interpersonal surveillance from Naz's and Maalik's families—in the opening scene of the movie, for example, Naz's sister finds his used condom in the bathroom trashcan, admonishes him that "it's *haraam*," and asks him for twenty-five dollars in return for not telling their parents [00:01:06].

In the film's portrayal of LGBTQIA+ themes, the struggle to be "proper Muslims" and to be true to their sexual identities and their relationship is one that both Naz and Maalik grapple with. Indeed, the story begins the morning after the first night that the two slept together, a night that they keep coming back to during their conversations. When the two first meet up to begin their day, which will include their hustling and buying a chicken to prepare in halal manner for Maalik's mother's birthday, Naz quips, "Like we always do the proper Muslim thing" [00:02:51]. There is a joking tone to his statement, as he says it with a smile that Maalik returns, and the line further establishes the tension between their desire to be "proper Muslims" and their need to be true to their sexual identities in the face of their families' attitude toward sex and sexuality. The line nevertheless establishes a conflict that the movie frequently returns to, which is the tension between being gay and being "proper" Muslims. Together with the previously mentioned scene where they attended a prayer meeting, they refer to the teachings of the Qur'an and the expectations of their faith; at one point, Naz voice-overs a line from the Qur'an about punishing unmarried individuals who have sex. This voice-over is met by Maalik's spoken line, "Only Allah can judge me. I'm sure of that. You know, all these people, what are they? They perfect now? No. We'll see. We'll see when we meet Muhammad. I'll pray for them" [00:19:53–00:20:04]. The two young men take their faith seriously and are shown to have studied the Qur'an—which Maalik pulls from his backpack to quote at one point—as well as pondered the ramifications of its teachings. Maalik's statement offers his own solid faith in Allah as well as the sense that he understands the weight of being observed and judged; this is somewhat ironic considering they spend the whole movie being tailed by the FBI.

What Simone Browne sums up as Naz and Maalik's "acts of loving on each other while moving through public spaces" encapsulates the tension of their private lives and their public, desired displays of affection made more difficult by the behavioral expectations of their religion (2018, 139). In one scene, Maalik rubs Naz's shoulders while they are taking a break from selling, only to be met by Naz's discomfort and a refusal of this affection. When Maalik says, "Why? Nobody's lookin'," Naz responds, "You don't know that" [00:23:13]. This brief exchange mirrors much of their philosophical back and forth that itself reflects their anxiety about being queer in an antagonistic world. Film viewers know, of course, that someone *is* watching thanks to the plotline of the FBI surveillance, but the protagonists also know (despite their initial ignorance about the tailing) that the world, in the form of their family, could be watching too. As the film continues, Naz becomes a little more comfortable with the public affection, and they kiss while in a subway car: Naz's sister, riding in a subway car that passes theirs right as they are kissing, sees them and looks horrified—they do not see her, however. As this scene continues and the two continue to talk and cuddle on the subway, the ramifications of Naz's sister's gaze are doubled by their realization that earlier they each told the FBI agent different alibis about where they were the previous night—Maalik told her the truth, Naz lied and said they were at their friend Dan's house. Two potential outings—one familial, interpersonal, and homophobic, the other state-sanctioned and Islamophobic—collide in this scene where surveillance is literal and implied.

Amid the surveillance and among the tender moments between the protagonists that signal both their love and the hardships on their route to coming of age, *Naz & Maalik* provides hopeful and sometimes humorous instances where the young men's sexual identities are positively acknowledged by people close to them. After the scene on the subway, Naz and Maalik head to Dan's house to warn him that the FBI agent may come by to ask him about Naz's alibi. Naz is about to come out to Dan when the group's conversation is interrupted by the FBI agent, who knocks on the door; Dan does not give her any information and prompts her to leave, but not before she asks, "By any chance, do you think your friends Maalik and Naz might be linked romantically?," to which he replies, "They're good people" [00:57:51]. Moments earlier, the pair and Dan had been discussing being gay and the teachings of the Qur'an (Dan affirms that being gay is *fasiq*, or that it violates Islamic law). When Dan comes back to his living room and confronts Naz and Maalik about their lie (he is understandably worried about having now taken part in their falsehood since the FBI is involved), he asks them if they are gay, and they say yes. A moment later, Maalik asks what gave them away, and Dan responds, "I've known for a long time" [00:59:06]. Here again Naz, Maalik, and Dan are well versed in Islamic teachings that in intertwine with the formers' queer identities, but in this moment there is some clarity; Dan is friends with the young men, has been aware that they are gay, and has continued to be their friend (and further demonstrates his solidarity by not providing any information to the FBI). Like most of the scenes and interactions in the film, there is a level of ambiguity to Dan's solidarity in part because of his statement that being gay is *fasiq* and because after the two young men leave his place, Maalik says, "I don't think he wants to talk about it anymore" [01:02:15]. Indisputable solidarity is presented as hard to come by in Naz and Maalik's world, but conversations and shows of support exist among their Muslim kin, providing a sense that their world of surveillance, anxiety, and possibly even paranoia (which would be understandable after their daylong back-and-forth with the FBI) has room for connection and understanding as well.

At the end of the film, Maalik thinks he is going to come out to his parents, and Naz questions whether he wants to be in a relationship with Maalik anymore; viewers are left without resolution to these plot points, as the two split up for the day and the film ends with Naz getting cited for riding his bike on the subway platform by the same undercover cop who tried to sell them a gun earlier. The cycle of arresting, policing, and profiling continues, and the future of Naz and Maalik (and their relationship) is unknown. Despite the tendency toward ambiguity when it comes to exploring outside support for Naz and Maalik's queer identity, the film's depiction of the joys and trials of two young men broadens the conversation about the need for respect and understanding in the gay community. Its adoption of some of the beats of a coming-of-age story together with the almost picaresque meandering of its protagonists provides a positive view of Naz and Maalik's relationship, while also demonstrating the impact of the larger social forces that would prevent them from being wholly comfortable with a public relationship. The film is ultimately a positive contribution to an archive of films that depict being gay and Muslim in contemporary America.

See also *Moonlight*.

Bibliography

Blizek, William L. "Naz & Maalik." *Journal of Religion & Film* 20, no. 2 (April 2016): article 2.
Browne, Simone. "For Maalik, Naz, Brittany, & Alexis; or, On Loving Black People as a Liberatory Practice." *Cinema Journal* 57, no. 4 (July 2018): 138–42.
Edelstein, David. "Young African-American Muslims Share a Hidden Love in 'Naz & Maalik.'" NPR, January 29, 2016. Accessed March 3, 2021. https://www.npr.org/2016/01/29/464783155/young-african-american-muslims-share-a-hidden-love-in-naz-maalik.

—Nicole Dib

NEIGHBORS 2: SORORITY RISING (2016)

DIRECTOR: Nicholas Stoller
SCREENPLAY: Andrew Jay Cohen, Brendan O'Brien, Nicholas Stoller, Evan Goldberg, and Seth Rogen
CAST: Seth Rogen (Mac Radner), Rose Byrne (Kelly Radner), Zac Efron (Teddy Sanders), Chloë Grace Moretz (Shelby), Dave Franco (Pete)
SPECS: 93 minutes; color
AVAILABILITY: DVD (Universal Pictures Home Entertainment)

This sequel to 2014's *Neighbors* follows the same characters battling a new group of adversaries as the titular nuisance. Instead of frat boys upending their postpartum life, Mac and Kelly Radner's troubles take the form of sorority sisters looking for a safe, affirming, feminist space away from predatory fraternity life and stifling administrative double standards. Big life changes are also in the works for Teddy, the antagonist of the last film, who feels stuck in postcollege not-yet-adulthood while his friends (including the gay and newly engaged Pete) are moving on with their lives. After trying to befriend and support the sisters in the new sorority, Teddy is voted out for his conservative ways and joins Mac and Kelly to force the sisters out of the neighborhood. Each group tries to thwart the other in equally outlandish ways, which ultimately forces the sorority to compromise their values, after which all three parties come to a truce.

Early in the film, viewers are reintroduced to Teddy Sanders. He is at a poker game with his fraternity brothers Scoonie, Garf, and Pete, as well as a new addition to the friend group, Darren. Suddenly, the lights dim. Teddy, Scoonie, and Garf start singing a Jason Mraz song. Surprising Pete (and the viewers who knew him in the first film as heterosexual), Darren makes a heartfelt speech where he asks Pete, revealed to be his boyfriend, to marry him. Pete accepts Darren's proposal, which is greeted by the rest of the men gleefully chanting "USA! USA!" [00:16:06–00:16:10]. This moment of gay romance is both disrupted by an outburst of heterosexual-centered masculinity while at the same time supported and celebrated with sincerity by the straight men in the room. After the proposal, Teddy, Pete, and Darren drink and talk, which gives the audience the chance to acclimate to Pete's life as a gay man. The movie does not hold hands with the audience, catching them up on Pete's coming-out story, but they do reference his previously aggressively heterosexual personality. Pete obliquely mentions that his hypersexuality was part of his process of self-discovery when he tells Teddy, "I was figuring stuff out," but this revelation is undercut for comedic effect when Teddy counters, "Yeah, figuring stuff out knee deep in pussy" [00:16:21–00:16:25].

However, the film makes it clear that Pete's sexuality is not the focus of the story, as the conversation quickly segues into Pete and Darren asking Teddy to move out so that they can begin their lives together. This throws Teddy into a tailspin, and the rest of the film focuses on Teddy's growth from an emotionally stunted frat boy to a grown twentysomething man. Teddy goes from literally running away (which he does after Pete and Darren suggest he find a different place to live) to facing up to and embracing his emotions and his (platonic) love for his close friends, whom he calls his "brothers." While this is another case of a gay character inspiring the emotional growth of a straight one, Pete is no more relegated to the background than he was in the first film. Teddy was always one of the main characters, while Pete had his own, smaller arc, which he does in this movie as well. Additionally (and positively), the movie never wades into the tired "no homo" territory of a straight man proving his masculinity after displaying emotional vulnerability (which the first film was guilty of doing on more than one occasion). If anything, Pete is one of two characters that Teddy gets closest to in the film, the other being Mac. Near the end of the film, Teddy has an epiphany and breaks into Pete and Darren's bedroom in the middle of the night to share his revelation: "When you two got engaged, I was in a bad place, and I thought I was losing my best friend. Then I realized, man, I'm never gonna lose you. Because we're brothers forever" [01:18:36–01:18:49]. He also includes Pete's fiancé in this brotherhood: "I'm not losing a best friend, I'm gaining a best friend's husband" [01:18:52–01:18:56]. And they all embrace, much to the chagrin of Darren, who is startled awake by his de facto "brother-in-law."

Finally, at the end of Teddy's arc, viewers see him ready to walk down the aisle as Pete's best man. Their relationship journey culminates in a heartfelt speech given by Teddy, meant to calm Pete, who is experiencing last-minute doubts before marrying Darren: "Darren loves you more than anyone in the entire world. Darren cherishes his friendship with you. Darren can't imagine his life without you. And Darren is proud to call you his best friend" [01:23:56–01:24:12]. Pete and Teddy embrace after realizing that Teddy was actually talking about himself. Right before Teddy's speech, the audience discovers that he has come into his own in his newfound passion and steady job, gay wedding planning. As a bonus, Teddy mentions that gay men respond positively to him, which Pete posits is because "you are a great guy . . . and they probably want to fuck the shit out of you" [01:24:39–01:24:44]. This does undermine the previous emotional moment between Pete and Teddy using sexual humor, which is a recurring theme in both the first film and the sequel, but not in a way that reasserts Teddy's heterosexuality. He ends the film comfortable in himself, as he feels valued and loved by his clients, friends, and brothers.

Overall, for a raunchy, mainstream comedy, the gay representation embodied by Pete and Darren, and the healthy masculinity championed in the film, is a step in the right direction. However, while Darren is played by John Early, an openly gay comedian, Pete is played by Dave Franco, who is straight in real life. As with trans actors playing trans characters in film, gay actors playing gay characters adds to the sincerity and realism of the characterization because, unlike straight actors, they do not have to "play" gay. The heightened antics of the film may have been grounded more by an actor playing the character without an additional layer of artifice; however, since Franco reprises the same role he played in the first film, this was not necessarily an option.

While LGBTQIA+ representation in mainstream films is not at the level or the quality that it could and should be, it is refreshing to see a summer film with both openly queer characters and openly queer actors portrayed in a positive way instead of being played solely for laughs or shock value.

See also *Big Daddy; Dodgeball: A True Underdog Story; Just Go with It.*

—Genevieve Ruzicka

NIJINSKY (1980)

DIRECTOR: Herbert Ross
SCREENPLAY: Hugh Wheeler, based on the memoir of the same name by Romola Nijinsky
CAST: Alan Bates (Sergei Diaghilev), Leslie Browne (Romola de Pulsky), Jeremy Irons (Mikhail Fokine), George de la Peña (Vaslav Nijinsky)
SPECS: 125 minutes; color
AVAILABILITY: DVD (Olive Films)

Adapted from the memoirs of Vaslav Nijinsky's wife, Romola, Ross's biopic opens with the legendary gay dancer, now in his late twenties, sitting in a padded asylum cell. Wrapped in a straitjacket and staring directly yet emptily into the camera, Nijinsky has suffered his severest mental breakdown, just as World War I has come to an end. The soundtrack bustles with the madcap strains of Igor Stravinsky's *Petrushka*, a ballet Nijinsky premiered in Paris in 1911. To the tune of his earlier triumph, the film flashes back to Budapest, where an adolescent Nijinsky, born to Polish Ukrainian peasants, becomes the lover and disciple of Sergei Diaghilev, the charismatic impresario of the Ballets Russes. Hot-tempered, flagrantly sexual, and startlingly innovative, Nijinsky soon makes a name for himself as both dancer and choreographer. His arrogance inevitably causes strife with fellow artists. He argues with Stravinsky (Ronald Pickup) over the choreography of *The Rite of Spring* and clashes with Mikhail Fokine, the Ballet Russes' principal choreographer, who fears his production of Ravel's *Daphnis and Chloe* will be ruined by the young upstart. After Fokine breaks with the Ballet Russes, Nijinsky becomes principal choreographer and the ballet world's premiere enfant terrible. The tumult of Nijinsky's personal life, however, threatens to sabotage his new success. He is seduced by Romola, a Hungarian aristocrat obsessed with his artistry and who believes she can "liberate" him from his "homosexuality." Their disastrous, neurotic marriage proves her wrong (if not delusional), and Diaghilev, stunned by Nijinsky's heterosexual betrayal, breaks off all relations with him. Nijinsky's personal trials aggravate the mental instabilities from which he has long suffered, and he is condemned to the asylum of the film's opening scene.

Hovering somewhere between soap opera and middlebrow art film, Herbert Ross's *Nijinsky* (following his other ballet-themed film, 1977's *The Turning Point*) was notable in 1980 as an early Hollywood film that took for granted its protagonists' gay identities and desires. Choosing subject matter that allows him to circumvent familiar tropes of the closet and societal persecution, Ross instead focuses on Nijinsky's creative process and eventual mental collapse. Like many biopics, *Nijinsky* hits many of the obligatory "high points" in the life of its famous subject, but it also boasts scenes that insightfully connect Nijinsky's psychic turmoil to his choreographic innovations. By imagining Debussy's ballet *Jeux* as a competitive game of tennis among two men and a woman, Nijinsky's choreography reveals a heart torn between Diaghilev, his patron and lover, and Romola, the woman who tries to "turn him straight." As George de la Peña's Nijinsky says in the film, the three dancers escalate into "stranger and ever more complicated relationships." (The historical Nijinsky's original notion, incidentally, featured an amorous game among three men, an idea then deemed too provocative.) More intense than *Jeux*'s diplomatic love triangle was Nijinsky's choreography for Stravinsky's *Petrushka*, which the film re-creates. In the ballet's final moments, the steps of Stravinsky's doomed puppet-hero become increasingly frantic, and he literally bursts through the stage backdrop, in effect breaking the "fourth wall." In the film's enactment of *Petrushka*'s climax, the schizophrenic Nijinsky clearly expresses a desire to escape his madness as he crashes through the bounds of the stage set. If Nijinsky tried to achieve freedom through his art, he did so in futility. After his institutionalization in 1919, the historical Nijinsky would spend the next three decades in various states of exile or incarceration, never to return to the stage.

Purists may object to the film's simplifications, even if simplifications are needed to turn a mad life into a coherent two-hour narrative. While the real Nijinsky had long suffered mental illness, the film connects his madness to specific, identifiable moments in the story line. The film implies that Nijinsky's neurotic, improbable marriage to the possessive Romola quickly accelerated his slide into schizophrenia. Of course, it is entirely possible his marriage did plunge him into psychotic episodes, but the film's editing suggests a somewhat reductive chain of causality between events. The film's editing also suggests that Nijinsky became more or less debilitated immediately after Diaghilev rebuffed him. In fact, Nijinsky continued to dance intermittently for several years after he and Diaghilev split.

As Nijinsky, George de la Peña projects the required sexuality, egotism, and instability. Director Ross, responsible for *The Sunshine Boys* (1975), *Footloose* (1984), and other commercial fare, emphasizes Nijinsky's sexuality as much as the bounds of mainstream taste would allow. The most provocative moment features Nijinsky and Diaghilev at the beach, the former clad in a swimsuit. From a voyeuristically low angle, the camera, positioned behind Nijinsky, gazes through the gap between his legs, accentuating his enduring sexuality at a moment in the story when he senses his mortality and grows jealous of Diaghilev's wandering eyes. To its credit, the film does link Nijinsky's sexuality to his creative daring, particularly when it visualizes his scandalous 1912 choreography for Debussy's *Prelude to the Afternoon of a Faun*. Sensuously embodying the faun of Mallarmé's source poem, Pena twists and contorts his lithe frame, thirsting for the elusive nymph who enters the stage. In Mallarmé's symbolist poem, the amorous faun drifts into dreams where he can fulfill desires unrequited in life. In Nijinsky's dance, restaged in Ross's film, the faun realizes his passion wide-eyed, in an act of flagrant onanism performed onstage. In the film, the audience gasps in shock, much as it reportedly did at the actual 1912 premiere. The scene ends with a stunned colleague informing Peña's Nijinsky that he has just "masturbated before all of Paris." Possessed by his art, he replies, "It wasn't me—it was the *faun*."

The masses were outraged by Nijinsky's "Faun," but Diaghilev was captivated. The Diaghilev of the film, played imperiously by Alan Bates, indeed sees Nijinsky's "faun" as a seminal moment in ballet history. As openly gay as the era would allow, Diaghilev and his Ballet Russes would continue to foster a queer sensibility onstage—for instance, in the homoerotic choreography for Richard Strauss's 1914 ballet *Josephslegende*, a project begun by Nijinsky but completed by his rivals Fokine and Massine after the jealous Diaghilev cut ties with Nijinsky. One cannot underestimate how Nijinsky's charismatic queerness—as both performer and choreographer—historically transformed the perception and status of male dancers. In the eighteenth and nineteenth centuries, male dancers were ancillary figures, playing second fiddle to prima ballerinas. For the first time, arguably, Nijinsky demanded that male dancers' physicality and dynamism command center stage. The male dancer's intelligence was now seen as integral (not incidental) to the realization of the dance. Unsurprisingly, male audiences were especially threatened by Nijinsky's sexuality, and when he toured New York in 1916, reviewers did nothing to hide their disdain. Critiquing Nijinsky's role in Nikolai Tcherepnin's ballet *Narcisse*, a critic for the *New York Mail* suggested that Nijinsky cut an infantile figure clad in designer Léon Bakst's wool tunic. "With his golden curls, white pinafore, and immaculate nether garments, from which a pair of exceedingly healthy legs protrude," the reviewer said, Nijinsky looked "like a living advertisement for the best food for infants" (cited in McLean 2008, 44). More uncouth was the *New York Tribune*, which opined that "Mr. Nijinsky . . . succeeded in being offensively effeminate, but at most he succeeded in being nothing else" (cited in McLean 2008, 44).

One wishes that Ross's film would have delved more deeply into the public nature of Nijinsky's revolutionary sexuality, but after the crucial *Faun* sequence, the film increasingly focuses on Nijinsky's private life and his futile marriage to Romola. As a generic biopic, the film is unsurprisingly more focused on personalities than on ideas. Apart from Stephen Daldry's *Billy Elliot* (2000) and the gay choreographies of Matthew Bourne, mainstream culture has rarely plumbed the sexuality of male ballet dancers, whose image has been shrouded in homophobia since at least the nineteenth century. Popular culture sees the male dancer's body as antithetical to the athlete's, but the relationship is far more complex. The male dancer obviously shares with the athlete muscularity and physical grace, but he discards the rigidity and stoic bearing that athletes turn into heterosexual posturing. Unlike the athlete, who aims for conquest, the supple dancer—at least in modern dance—assumes more lissome and "open" positions suggestive of vulnerability and even mortality. Perhaps the only athlete who embodies both virile aggression and supine vulnerability is the wrestler, a homoerotic icon since at least Homeric times.

Too mainstream for queer audiences and too arty for the masses, *Nijinsky* received mixed reviews and performed poorly at the box office. The film originally was a project developed by Tony Richardson, who despised Ross's treatment and surely would have mounted something more theatrical and cerebral. Before Ross was chosen as director (after the success of *The Turning Point*), the film was offered to and rejected by Ken Russell, who doubtless would have concocted from Nijinsky's madness a kitschy pageant in the manner of *The Music Lovers* (1971), Russell's feverish biopic of Tchaikovsky. Australian director Paul Cox's *The Diaries of Vaslav Nijinsky* (2001) provides a more impressionistic, less linear account of Nijinsky's life. Employing a voice-over (spoken by Derek Jacobi) cobbled from the more cogent sections of Nijinsky's often impenetrable diaries, Cox's film mixes abstract ballet, archival materials, and fantastic reveries, crafting a collage that transcends the melodrama of Ross's film.

See also *Personal Best*.

Bibliography

McLean, Adrienne L. *Dying Swans and Madmen: Ballet, the Body, and Narrative Cinema.* New Brunswick, NJ: Rutgers University Press, 2008.

—Andrew Grossman

NO STRINGS ATTACHED (2011)

DIRECTOR: Ivan Reitman
SCREENPLAY: Elizabeth Meriwether
CAST: Natalie Portman (Emma), Ashton Kutcher (Adam), Cary Elwis (Dr. Metzner), Guy Branum (Guy), Jake Jackson (Eli), Kevin Kline (Alvin), Greta Gerwig (Patrice), Olivia Thirlby (Katie), Mindy Kaling (Shira), Chris Bridges aka Ludacris (Wallace)
SPECS: 108 minutes; color
AVAILABILITY: DVD (Paramount)

Described by A. O. Scott as "not entirely terrible" but "rougher and randier than" the romcoms released theatrically along with it, Ivan Reitman's *No Strings Attached* is an eminently shallow take on relationships and "commitment phobia" as it delineates the sexual chemistry and emotional attachment between its lead couple, Emma and Adam (2011). Even as the film highlights the complexities of contemporary heteronormative relationships—especially through the character of Emma, who is a busy doctor in Los Angeles and who simply cannot commit despite much going for her, and Adam, who is an emotionally supportive and delightfully handsome television producer—*No Strings Attached* only ends up glorifying heterosexual love in all its normative grandeur to end predictably on a happily-ever-after note. While the plotline, with an eccentric and commitment-phobic female character who sharply contrasts with her charming beau who is always "too happy" leaves much to be questioned about the representation of contemporary womanhood, more problematic is the treatment of nonnormative sexualities in the film, which are not only pushed to the narrative's fringes but also presented merely as farcical asides that produce insensitive frivolity instead of comic humor.

The film begins at a summer camp where an adolescent Emma and Adam meet the first time only to keep meeting through the rest of the narrative. At this moment, viewers hear Color Me Badd's "I Wanna Sex You Up" in the background and realize that the film is both fickle and physical. While it tries to be fun, *No Strings Attached* is an especially problematic film for many reasons. For one, even though its plot is replete with "semi-cynical sexual candor," it does much injustice in authenticating honest same-sex relationships (Scott 2011). In fact, members of the LGBTQIA+ community appear sporadically and as caricatures in this Mills and Boon romance; their representation, if not entirely homophobic, does hint toward a certain marginalization and stigmatization of alternate sexualities. One of the most prominent characters who identifies as gay is Dr. Guy, Emma's colleague, friend, and roommate. Emma constantly and comically draws attention to his sexual identity. He is shown teasing a hungover and naked Adam waking up dazed in Emma's flat with "when we met, you weren't wearing pants" [00:19:22–00:19:32]. Likewise, he also says to his menstruating female room-mates that "[he] love[s] it when [they're] all on the same cycle" since they "all get to be passive-aggressive and fight" and then swooning over Adam's "period mix" for the women with "that's so romantic" [00:42:51–00:44:50]. Viewers, however, barely get to know Guy's real emotions or his relationships until the credits appear in the end and he is shown clandestinely entering a hospital room with Sam, a male staff member, winking at him that "it's okay." Guy's sexual identity therefore is merely a matter of joke and his relationships look mindlessly sexual. Obviously, through Guy, the film offers no substantial narrative on LGBTQIA+ experiences or relationships.

The other two LGBTQIA+ instances in the film are just as frivolous as Guy's case, if not more. Adam's friend, Eli, has two gay fathers, and all references he makes to them are aimed at trivializing same-sex relationships. For instance, when Adam's father begins to date his son's ex-girlfriend, Eli (with a stereotypi-cal air of bromance) tells Adam that "the best part about [his] gay dads" is that "they're never gonna eat out [his] ex-girlfriends" [00:16:00–00:16:15]. Things get more uncomfortable when Patrice, whom Eli likes, remembers him as the man from her college "with two gay dads" who "helped [her] move [her] boxes sopho-more year" and Eli responds saying that while his dads are "the best" and he "love[s] them," he is "super straight" [00:08:03–00:08:12]. Here, if Eli is trying to woo the woman he likes, he is also simultaneously distancing himself from his gay fathers. As if father-son bonds lack depth and hover only around sex jokes resulting in male camaraderie, Eli's references to his fathers, or to most relation-ships for that matter, reek of callousness. The two gay fathers, in turn, make a final appearance in the film as they come to see Eli and his girlfriend while carrying a bouquet of heart-shaped red balloons and childishly chattering how much they "love" Patrice "already" [01:41:27–01:41:30]. The two middle-aged gay men are presented as mere caricatures of same-sex love, and the film implicitly and unapologetically denies them any dignity whatsoever.

A third and most forgettable reference to LGBTQIA+ themes comes from a scene revolving around a Christmas party when two women, Joy and Lisa, sitting next to a heartbroken Adam, suddenly find the "courage" to express their love for each other and, after complimenting one another, end up amorously having sex [00:51:32–00:51:33]. As trite as this forced encounter sounds, what is more offensive is the suggestion that members of the LGBTQIA+ community do not need to connect as people but can simply "hook up" as soon as they recognize that the other person is gay. Not only do such depictions add to the stigma against the LGBTQIA+ community but also suggest that homophobia a is powerful reality even within popular culture.

While *No Strings Attached*, on its face, appears to be located in a fairly liberated world, it underscores several forms of deep-rooted stigma against LGBTQIA+ communities. Research indicates that, in actuality, people within the LGBTQIA+ community can suffer discrimination and even have higher mortality rates in stigmatized communities. In fact, for those who identify as gay, "specific causes of death [have] revealed that suicide . . . and cardiovascular diseases [are] substantially elevated" for "individuals in high-structural-stigma communities, suggesting potential mechanisms linking structural stigma to mortality risk" (Hatzenbuehler 2014, 130). While such severe outcomes may not be true for Reitman's characters, their actions nonetheless highlight the dark underbelly of cultures glorifying normative and heterosexual identities. The film is disturbingly unaware of such realities and belies research that reveals that various forms of abuse, especially "verbal abuse," are often the lot of gay men or other LGBTQIA+ individuals in conservative communities who are "insulted or told that it is better to have sex with an animal than with another man [or a member of the same sex]" (Stahlman et al. 2015, 129). The truth is that even in present-day America and during the Trump years "groups that vilify the LGBTQ community . . . represented the fastest-growing sector among hate groups in 2019" (Southern Poverty Law Center n.d., 12). For ignoring such problematic realities, Reitman's film does much disservice to issues central to lives of individuals within the LGBTQIA+ community.

The problems with *No Strings Attached* are many. If it can be criticized for "ageist humour" for its depiction of Alvin as Adam's lusty old father as someone who compulsively sleeps with his ex-girlfriends, it can be labeled as terribly insensitive for its portrayal of LGBTQIA+ characters (Bradshaw 2011). If the film envisages an honest conversation on sex and relationships without bindings, its vision is rather myopic and tunneled, and by discrediting all nonnormative relationships, the film does anything but create a candid and healthy conversation on human bonds in their various forms and guises.

See also *Little Miss Sunshine; Mean Girls; Mother's Day; Sex and the City; To All the Boys I've Loved Before.*

Bibliography

Bradshaw, Peter. Review of *No Strings Attached* by Ivan Reitman. *Guardian*, February 24, 2011. Accessed February 21, 2021. https://www.theguardian.com/film/2011/feb/24/no-strings -attached-review.

Hatzenbuehler, Mark L. "Structural Stigma and the Health of Lesbian, Gay, and Bisexual Populations." *Current Directions in Psychological Science* 23, no. 2 (April 2014): 127–32.

Scott, A. O. "A Firm Commitment to Casual." *New York Times*, January 20, 2011. Accessed February 21, 2021. https://www.nytimes.com/2011/01/21/movies/21nostringsattached.html.

Southern Poverty Law Center. "The Year in Hate Extremism 2019." N.d. Accessed March 1, 2021. https://www.splcenter.org/sites/default/files/yih_2020_final.pdf.

Stahlman, Shauna, et al. "Sexual Identity Stigma and Social Support among Men Who Have Sex with Men in Lesotho." *Reproductive Health Matters* 23, no. 46 (November 2015): 127–35.

—Srirupa Chatterjee

NOCTURNAL ANIMALS (2016)

DIRECTOR: Tom Ford
SCREENPLAY: Tom Ford, based on the novel *Tony and Susan* by Austin Wright
CAST: Amy Adams (Susan Morrow), Jake Gyllenhaal (Tony Hastings/Edward Sheffield), Michael Shannon (Bobby Andes), Aaron Taylor-Johnson (Ray Marcus), Isla Fisher (Laura Hastings), Ellie Bamber (India Hastings), Armie Hammer (Hutton Morrow), Karl Glusman (Lou), Rob Aramayo (Turk)
SPECS: 116 minutes; color
AVAILABILITY: Blu-ray (Universal Pictures Home Entertainment)

Nocturnal Animals is the second feature film by Tom Ford, the renowned fashion designer. It follows his 2009 adaptation of Christopher Isherwood's *A Single Man*, which features a gay protagonist coping with the death of his boyfriend. *Nocturnal Animals* also focuses on issues of loss, though the context is shifted and the narrative more entangled—viewers are presented with a few days in the life of an upper-class Los Angeles gallerist, Susan, whose actual marriage is crumbling and who receives a package with a draft of her former husband's first novel dedicated to her. While alone in her steel-and-glass mansion on top of a hill, Susan starts to read compulsively, and her imagination weaves the second story in front of the viewers eyes. Here her ex-husband, Edward, is transformed into Tony, a man whose uneventful trip across nocturnal West Texas with his wife and adolescent daughter turns into a nightmare after their car is stopped by a gang of local thugs: the women are abducted and later raped and killed. Tony's quest for justice and revenge resonates strongly with Susan and opens the door to flashes of memories of her relationship with the book's author, especially the conditions of their separation, and triggers menacing doubts about the value of the choices she has made in her life so far.

While *A Single Man*, with its openly gay protagonist, was easily pinpointed as an LGBTQIA+ film, winning among its numerous accolades the Queer Lion for best gay film at the Venice Film Festival, where it premiered in 2009, *Nocturnal Animals* is rather elusive in this respect. To read the film through a queer lens means expanding the concept beyond its home of sexual and gender identity into the realm of narrative and stylistic strategies and a constant play with the audience and their expectations.

Susan, the main character, is married to Hutton, and as their relationship is unraveling, she is beginning to regret leaving her first husband, Edward. Her cravings, as well as those of nearly all the characters, are strictly heterosexual. Interestingly, the Society of LGBTQ Entertainment Critics (GALECA) nominated the film in their Campy Film of the Year category. It did not, however, feature in their LGBT Film of the Year nominations. None of the major reviews published at the time of the film's opening mentions any LGBTQIA+ context or issues, except for a brief note in *Film Comment* where Michael Sragow refers to one of the gay characters as "the lucky one" (2016). This exception rather proves the rule, as the screen time inhabited by gay characters of *Nocturnal Animals* is too fleeting (limited to one sequence) and irrelevant to the main narrative line to leave a deeper imprint on first viewing. It is, however, quite instructive to look at this particular sequence in more detail, as it might help to explain some of the film's inconsistencies mentioned by its critics.

After receiving the manuscript at the beginning of the film, Susan and Hutton go to a party held by Susan's friends Alessia and Carlos. It is in her brief conversation with them that spectators receive most information about Susan's inner turmoil. To her own surprise, she confides to Alessia that, despite appearances, Hutton's business is going downhill and that she feels ungrateful not to be happy while having everything. Alessia tries to comfort her while talking about her marriage to Carlos, who is gay. This fact does not make her sad; on the contrary, it has led her to reevaluate their relationship as based on ultimate love and friendship, which lasts longer than lust. Although this may sound like a cliché and an embodiment of a heterosexist stereotype of gays and their best girlfriends (a trope used in *A Single Man* as well, with the role of the female friend played by Julianne Moore), the contrast with Susan's grim domestic setting makes it sound true and desirable.

Later the same night, Susan talks to Carlos about her fatigue from her own career. Carlos congratulates her exhibition opening the night before, calling it "spectacular . . . incredibly strong, so perfect, with all this junk culture that we live in," yet she dismisses it as "total junk." Carlos then advises her to "enjoy the absurdity" of the superficial and meaningless world of art, as it is "a lot less painful than the real world," but Susan looks unconvinced about adopting this strategy. Very soon, however, she gets a double dose of the "real world," which proves Carlos's advice highly pertinent—first through the book she reads and visualizes, in which violence comes out of the blue, turning everything the characters know and take for granted into ashes, and second through the recollections of her own past, almost two decades ago, yet lurking under the surface of her polished life.

Although both are mental operations—the book visualization cleverly codes Susan's real surroundings and thus connects two seemingly incompatible worlds, that of LA high society and West Texas vast and menacing desert, while recollections of her life with Edward are presented as warm idiosyncratic glimpses of perpetuity—they have profound transformative impact on her current life. In the final sequence of the film, viewers see Susan arranging a meeting with

Edward after finishing reading his novel and dressing for the occasion. She puts on an elegant moss-green velvet dress and her usual mask of heavy makeup. She looks at herself in the mirror and then decides to wipe off the dark red lipstick as if trying to look more like Susan in her flashbacks, where she wore minimal makeup and was enthusiastic about art. She starts to put on her wedding ring but then pauses in the middle of the gesture and takes it off with a gentle smile. Both acts, though slight, speak volumes in Ford's precise visual grammar and indicate Susan's hopes about turning back time and getting together with Edward again. This, however, is an impossible wish. Edward as author has done away with her rather brutally on the pages of his book, and Edward as husband told her explicitly in one of the scenes from their past that she could not get things back once she had disposed of them.

There is no running away from her current life, and as Susan sits as a precious art piece behind the glass of a fancy restaurant, reminiscent of one of Edward Hopper's loners, Carlos's prophetic advice to enjoy the absurdity of their world hovers above her as her only option. This is a rather surprising ending and a shock to the audience, lulled by the last flashback inserted into Susan's getting ready for the dinner with Edward, displaying their intertwined bodies in a loving embrace. Here, just as in the sardonic twist at the finale of *A Single Man*, Ford radically queers the romantic narrative possibilities of the plot and makes the viewers drop their expectations of a happy ending suddenly.

The tension between romantic heterosexual structures and disturbingly queer interventions is, however, present in the film as a whole and is worked out on both the narrative and stylistic levels. One of its most prominent manifestations is located in the film's relish in the surface value of things. As Ford commented in one of the interviews, "a lot of people who work hard on the surface of things—like I do and the characters in my films—are doing it because what's inside isn't so pretty. The surface is armor for me" (Galanes 2016). Ford, his cameraman Seamus McGarvey, and production designer Shane Valentino were very meticulous about their choice and function of costumes, makeup, setting, and framing. Besides the usual categories, the film was nominated for BAFTA awards in 2017 for the best cinematography, production design, and makeup. McGarvey received a prize from the British Society of Cinematographers, among others.

The role of the mise-en-scène in *Nocturnal Animals* cannot be overrated. Pamela Church Gibson argues that "in *Nocturnal Animals*, Ford creates what is arguably a fourth narrative of dress, décor, and lifestyle, spun around Susan and her lavish lifestyle within the overarching narrative" (2017, 634). According to Church Gibson, this fourth narrative disrupts the other three, and thus the narrative trajectory as a whole, as spectators are no longer able to empathize with the characters but get carried away by the lavish details of the mise-en-scène regardless of what actually happens within its contours. This might be read as yet another queering operation, stemming quite organically from Ford's longtime career of a fashion designer.

To illustrate this point about the tension between style and narrative, one particular prop is used in a puzzlingly defamiliarized context yet performs a distinct narrative function—the red sofa. It is presented to the viewers for the first time in the West Texas narrative line, outside in the open, with two naked bodies, of Tony's wife and daughter, both dead, lying on it in an embrace. A cut to the present shows Susan shocked by this macabre installation, calling her own daughter. Another cut frames the daughter's unmoving naked body, embracing her sleeping boyfriend in a very similar pose to the corpses. The uncanny juxtaposition of these two images unwittingly sexualizes the death scene yet lends it a peaceful, almost pleasant tone at the same time. The second scene with the red sofa takes place in Susan's past while she recollects a pivotal moment in her relationship with Edward—a moment when, partially lying on their red sofa, she expressed her doubts about his writing and her budding dissatisfaction with his lack of ambition. The West Texas installation is clearly a product of Susan's mind, as the other scenes demonstrate, and stems equally from her expertise in the exhibition business (Victoria Coren Mitchell noted in her 2017 review that "the whole image could be hung in an art gallery") and from her suppressed guilt. The sofa is thus connecting all three narrative lines while representing the fourth, proposed by Church Gibson.

In his adaptation of the original novel, Ford changes the background of his major protagonist, from the middle-class English professor to successful art dealer, to make the story more personal: "I parody today's world and the superficiality of it—which I helped contribute to" (Gray 2017). The mixed message of this quote is crucial, as it is a guiding principle of the whole film. On the one hand, there is Susan's contempt of the art world, its artificiality and the "junk" it produces, on the other hand, her reliance on surfaces, expressed in the lipstick–wedding ring scene, and her deep involvement in this world, conveyed by the placement of sculptures, paintings, and photographs in her house and gallery office. Ford himself likes to talk about how works of art interspersed in the narrative work on the spectator subliminally and create mini narratives of their own:

> For example, she sees a photo by Richard Misrach [Desert Fire #153 (Man with Rifle), hanging in her mansion], with two guys pointing guns at each other in a grassy field. Later, when she's reading his novel, the characters are in that same grassy field, which we re-created. She might not even know it, and the audience might not be conscious of it. But there are all these little connections, and they hopefully register unconsciously. (Gray 2017)

Ford was very precise about the art used in *Nocturnal Animals*, and many of the pieces came either from his personal collection or were obtained thanks to his interaction with the artists, as Shane Valentino, the production designer, remarks (Rosenthal 2017). There are two artworks created specifically for the film, in Ford's collaboration with the *Nocturnal Animals'* art department, both located in Susan's gallery. One is a painting of bold white letters spelling "REVENGE" on a black background, with droplets of color resembling blood, which speaks directly of Edward's motives in sending Susan his book; the other is a series of videos and an installation opening the very film. The second artwork has caused the biggest controversy among critics and plays a major part in the queer reading of the film.

In the title sequence, viewers see naked bodies of obese women, dressed in nationalistic paraphernalia, reminiscent of the conventional accessories of cheerleaders, with boots, pom-poms and batons, waving flags, and dancing in slow motion. This opening is surprising and presents an array of possible inter-pretations. The link to the main narrative is obscured at this point—only later do viewers learn that this is Susan's installation, with larger-than-life videos of the dancing women and the actual women lying face-down on white gallery cubes, motionless, with nobody from the crowd of visitors actually looking at them. The degree of provocative flamboyance is unmatched elsewhere in the film, which caused the *Guardian* critic Peter Bradshaw to actually dismiss the opening as "a shortcoming that has to be overlooked due to this film's overall bravura brilliance" (2016).

In response to his and other cheering reviews, Victoria Coren Mitchell dis-cusses the use of female bodies in the film, comparing the corpses on the red sofa with the women from the opening sequence:

> The corpses look beautiful. Deliberately beautiful. Titianesque. . . . Director Tom Ford . . . can make anything beautiful—and he really does it with these cadavers. . . . The film opens with an extended sequence of large women . . . dancing naked on podiums. These are not rendered beautiful. They are clearly intended to be grotesque, nightmarish. Because you know what's hideous? Fat women! And you know what's beautiful? Dead women! (Mitchell 2017)

While Mitchell accuses Ford of "fashioning" death and violence in a way bor-dering on the unethical, Jennifer Ruth of *Senses of Cinema* focuses on the class aspect intersecting with gender issues in the film's focus on spectacle:

> We see the casual cruelty of people using other people's bodies for shock value in a way that excludes the humans to whom those bodies belong from the joke. . . . If our queasiness with the scene were to be converted into words, they might form the following questions: why do thin women wear Tom Ford designs and sip white wine while fat women are paraded like circus animals? (2018)

For Susan, the whole installation encapsulates what she means when talking about "junk," despite the fact that she is its mastermind. This is, however, one of the early points when the film may be read as critical of its main protagonist, instead of soliciting empathy from the viewers, asking them to identify with Su-san. The obesity of the models, the framing using sexualized close-ups of pursed made-up lips, and slow motion move the opening sequence definitely toward the spectacular; it is nevertheless important that the women daringly return the spectator's gaze by looking directly into the camera and flaunt their bodies with no trace of shame. Furthermore, the opening is not solely the work of Susan but the result of editorial decisions through which the bodies are intercut in a way inaccessible to the gallery visitors, at times melting into one another.

Ruth argues that obesity is a class issue to a large degree, and from this per-spective, the choice of these naked women appropriating cheerleaders' routines works ironically on more than one level—it touches on the thinness obsession of Western culture, plays with the discomfort of the spectator-voyeur in watching "inappropriate" bodies in sexualized poses (the women are not only overweight but also decidedly older than usual models), and makes the audience ponder these issues for a painfully extended time, due to the slow motion, usually used to highlight something deemed culturally beautiful. On the narrative level, the opening sequence not only anticipates nonconformist treatment of female bodies (the image of the "fashioned" corpses on the red sofa replays this strategy of inverting learned cultural frames of beauty and propriety) but also indicates the closeness of the two diegetic environments, which at first seem impermeable—the West Texas rednecks and Los Angeles art world. As *Nocturnal Animals* demonstrates, they coexist on a fundamental level, despite the geographic and cultural differences on the surface.

These ironies form the queer ripples in the smooth narrative flow and allow *Nocturnal Animals* to be read as a political and critical take on the very world the film creates, as well as its inhabitants. The excessive stylishness and focus on detail serve mainly as a ploy—by foregrounding aesthetic criteria over narrative and moral logic, they bewitch the audience and make them complicit in the crimes committed by the imagination of the film's main protagonist.

See also *A Single Man*.

Bibliography

Bradshaw, Peter. "Nocturnal Animals Review—Tom Ford's Deliciously Toxic Tale of Revenge." *Guardian*, November 3, 2016. Accessed April 9, 2021. https://www.theguardian.com/film/2016/nov/03/nocturnal-animals-review-tom-ford-amy-adams-jake-gyllenhaal.

Church Gibson, Pamela. "The Fashion Narratives of Tom Ford: *Nocturnal Animals* and Contemporary Cinema." *Fashion Theory* 21, no. 6 (2017): 629–46.

Galanes, Philip. "Tom Ford, Ben Mankiewicz and a Fashion-Film Vortex." *New York Times*, November 20, 2016. Accessed April 9, 2021. https://www.nytimes.com/2016/11/20/fashion/tom-ford-ben-mankiewicz-table-for-three.html.

Gray, Tim. "Director Tom Ford Used Two Key Rules for *Nocturnal Animals*." *Variety*, January 6, 2017. Accessed April 9, 2021. https://variety.com/2017/film/spotlight/tome-ford-nocturnal-animals-jake-gyllenhaal-1201954086/.

Mitchell, Victoria Coren. "I'm So Glad to Spoil This Film for You." *Guardian*, January 22, 2017. Accessed April 9, 2021. https://www.theguardian.com/commentisfree/2017/jan/22/nocturnal-animal-film-rape-murder-repulsive.

IMDb. "*Nocturnal Animals*: Awards." Accessed April 9, 2021. https://www.imdb.com/title/tt4550098/awards?ref_=tt_awd.

Rosenthal, Emerson. "Everything We Know about the Art in *Nocturnal Animals*." *Vice*, January 11, 2017. Accessed April 9, 2021. https://www.vice.com/en/article/jpvydk/nocturnal-animals-art-tom-ford-shane-valentino.

Ruth, Jennifer. "What Would Siegfried Kracauer Say about Tom Ford's *Nocturnal Animals*?" *Senses of Cinema* 86 (March 2018). https://www.sensesofcinema.com/2018/feature-articles/nocturnal-animals/.

Sragow, Michael. "Deep Focus: *Nocturnal Animals*." *Film Comment*, November 17, 2016. Accessed April 9, 2021. https://www.filmcomment.com/blog/deep-focus-nocturnal-animals/.

—Veronika Klusakova

• P •

PARIAH (2011)

DIRECTOR: Dee Rees
SCREENPLAY: Dee Rees, based on the short film of the same name by Dee Rees
CAST: Adepero Oduye (Alike), Pernell Walker (Laura), Aasha Davis (Bina), Charles Parnell (Arthur/Father), Kim Wayans (Audrey/Mom), Sahra Mellesse (Sharonda/Sister)
SPECS: 86 minutes; color
AVAILABILITY: DVD (Focus Features)

Recognized as a "cinematic contribution that has made black lesbian coming of age not only visible but universal," the full-length feature *Pariah* originates from the 2007 short film of the same name (Keeling et al. 2015, 425). Main character Alike is seventeen years old and on the cusp of adulthood, discovering who she is amid the pressures of her social world. Sporting masculine clothes, experimenting sexually with women for the first time, seeking out gay clubs, Alike explores her queerness in all its joys and struggles. But her parents, Audrey and Arthur, vacillate between passivity and hostility as Alike rejects their expectations and conventions. After having her first sexual experience with another young woman, Alike comes out to her parents, and Audrey responds aggressively, screaming and hitting Alike until Arthur intervenes. Leaving home, Alike seeks refuge with her best friend Laura, an open lesbian who mentors and nurtures her throughout the film. Together they navigate the demands of growing up as Black, queer, butch women. In the final moments of *Pariah*, it is Laura who sends Alike off at the bus station, where she leaves her childhood home for an uncertain future.

Pariah opens with a quote from Audre Lorde: "Wherever the bird with no feet flew, she found trees with no limbs." A bird with no feet is still a bird that flies. And Lorde provides comfort by explaining that such a queer, wild thing still finds a home. Meaning, before readers even meet Alike, they know she will find her place, her limbless tree, despite the inevitable struggles she will face. Because the film is called *Pariah*, viewers anticipate the central character will be a social outcast, someone on the frayed margins. And while Alike is often on the sidelines, peering into life as it hums through the halls of her high school, Alike is loved and adored. *Pariah* is not about "butch" tragedy. It is not about emotional and sexual repression. It is about liberation, and about how, often, liberation entails a multiplicity of feelings and experiences—both good and bad, hopeful and painful.

Viewers first meet Alike in a dark club. Donning a baggy polo and baseball hat, she gazes wide-eyed and smiling at the women pole dancing. Her face is lit in wonder, even as she passively refrains from throwing them bills, unlike Laura. Instead, she stares up at the women, at turns in awe and overwhelmed. Laura grabs Alike's wrist, cramming bills into her fist, to make her participate.

When she resists, Laura exclaims, "Whatchu come here for?" This film is about that liminal space of queer desire, when the external and interior are painfully incongruent. Alike knows she likes women, but she does not yet know how to express it, often sitting back at clubs while others dance. And she still must hide her desire and who she is from most people, especially her family. Jennifer De-Clue argues that Alike "tests her belonging to a normatively religious, socially conservative, middle-class black family" (Keeling et al. 2015, 424). Belonging, that which defines the pariah by contrast, frames this film. Viewers follow Alike as she moves into and out of moments of belonging—with family, her best friend, and new lovers.

On her way back from the club, Alike changes out of her masculine clothes. This becomes a habit throughout the film. Swapping clothes on her bus route but also in high school bathroom stalls, Alike must shape-shift to preserve the delicate order of her house. When she gets home, her mother, Audrey, confronts her about missing curfew but hedges, saying, "At least you were cute" [00:07:29]. Though subtle, it is crucial to note that Audrey chooses to say, "you *were* cute," as opposed to "you *looked* cute," the implication being that Alike's external appearance must reflect an internal condition or value. Later, her mother coldly says to her, "I know God doesn't make mistakes," tacitly yet firmly rejecting Alike's sexual and gender expressions [00:29:00]. Their relationship stays the same throughout *Pariah*, not because both are locked in obstinacy, but because Audrey refuses to imagine beyond her own expectations and desires. She cuts Alike down and attempts to manage her life by regulating everything from her clothes to her friend group. For example, distrustful of Laura, Audrey introduces Alike to Bina, the daughter of a church friend, hoping this positive influence might interrupt the path Laura represents.

But Bina is misjudged by both Audrey and Alike; taken Bina for a strait-laced (i.e., straight) churchgoing young woman, Alike resists hanging out with her. But after realizing their shared taste in music, the chemistry between them develops. Bina wears bright clothes and actively pursues what she wants. Alike hesitates in dark jackets and brimmed hats. "You play too much," Alike says as Bina flirts with her [00:48:28]. They soon after kiss, attend parties together, and meet one another's friends. Alike believes it to be her first relationship. But after they have a sleepover and are physically intimate for the first time, Bina says, "Last night was just playing around. . . . I'm not 'gay' gay." Alike's first relationship quickly turns into her first heartache.

After her breakup with Bina, Alike arrives home to her parents fighting. Throughout *Pariah*, the house is framed as a dark place. Often moving in and out of shadows, the members of Alike's family are rarely in the same room. The darkened lens and distant bodies express an environment of repression, caution, and secrecy. And it is not only Alike, who informs this environment. Her father seems to be having an affair, speaking in hushed tones on the phone. Audrey maintains a veneer of stability and management, but she is perhaps the most repressed character in the film. When the parents, Alike, and her sister, Sharonda, are all having dinner—a rare scene in which all four appear together—the sisters press Audrey on her own high school experiences. But she refuses to indulge, incredulously asking Arthur if he's "comfortable" with the trajectory of the conversation. She shuts it down. The way Alike's home is shot is important because it illustrates how repression actually operates—it dampens one's spirit across all planes of desire and relationship. Alike resists.

At a pivotal moment in the film, during one of their fights and after Audrey asked Arthur to check in on their daughter to ensure she's on the right path, Audrey screams, "Your daughter is turning into a damn man right before your eyes." To which Arnold yells back, "Shut the fuck up about that Audrey" [01:11:23]. When Alike intervenes and confirms her parents' suspicions, she does it without shame or apology: "There's nothing wrong with me." And it seems like it is her confidence as much as her queerness that ignites her mom's rage. This is the only time in the film viewers see Alike raise her own voice to say, "I'm gay. . . . I'm a lesbian! Yeah, I'm a dyke" [01:12:10]. Audrey responds by slapping Alike across the face and continuing to hit her as she is strewn across the floor. Alike's face endures a substantial cut across the cheekbone—one likely to scar.

Alike immediately leaves home, finding comfort with Laura. Laura lives with her sister, and both are estranged from their parents—a mirror to Alike's own story. Having spent countless hours studying for her GED and working long shifts to pay bills, Laura passes her exam and officially graduates high school. Standing on the bottom steps of her mother's front porch, she attempts to share the celebratory news, but her mother refuses to extend any support or affirmation. Instead, she figuratively and literally peers down at Laura in silence. Laura is also butch, considered more "AG" (i.e., "aggressive") than Alike. But her butch toughness is given dimensions when viewers see her with her own mom, reaching out and vulnerable. The message parallels Alike's story—even though identifiers help us express ourselves, even as being butch or AG externally reflects an internal state, we are also always more than our labels. Language is fluid and complex. It helps us and hinders us. This fluidity is explored through Alike's own writing.

Alike's writing is good—named "descriptive" and "lovely" by her AP English teacher—but her work earlier in the film is distant. Bound up in detailed metaphors, her writing is beautiful but detached. Kathryn Bond Stockton explains that because the queer child "grows toward a question mark" and their "identity is a deferral," they frequently fall back on metaphor as a way to grasp themselves (2009, 3, 11). Not until the end of the film, after the heartache and violence, does Alike risk putting herself into her words. Again, viewers come to understand the outsider in complex ways through Alike. She is a pariah by the world's definitions, but she also finds safety on the fray. In some ways, her reluctance to take risks and jump in reinforces her estrangement. When Alike finally embraces the rewards of risk, her writing breaks open: "Broken to the new light without pushing in / open to the possibilities within, pushing out / See the love shine in through my cracks? / See the light shine out through me?"

Pariah is about being butch, coming out, and being on one's way. Shoniqua Roach argues that *Pariah* "thus exemplifies the black queer liberation plot," but goes on to criticize how this plot hinges on maternal rejection (2019, 219). Alike must leave home, must leave her mother, in order to be free. And it's true: the film ends with Alike again on the bus, but this time she heads toward California for college. The trope is common for a reason, this need to flee. But the film expands beyond such linear trajectories of desire. It is about interiority, as her poems capture: "For even breaking is opening / and I am broken." It is not about escaping the expectations and demands of others, but choosing for ourselves. Alike says it herself, confidently and reflexively as she has always done: "I am not running. I am choosing."

See also *Moonlight*; *Naz & Maalik*.

Bibliography

Keeling, Kara, et al. "Pariah and Black Independent Cinema Today: A Roundtable Discussion." *GLQ* 21, nos. 2–3 (2015): 423–39.

Roach, Shoniqua. "Unpacking *Pariah*: Maternal Figuration, Erotic Articulation, and the Black Queer Liberation Plot." *Signs: Journal of Women in Culture and Society* 42, no. 1 (September 2019): 201–25.

Stockton, Kathryn Bond. *The Queer Child: Or Growing Sideways in the Twentieth Century*. Durham, NC: Duke University Press, 2009.

—CE Mackenzie

THE PERKS OF BEING A WALLFLOWER (2012)

DIRECTOR: Stephen Chbosky
SCREENPLAY: Stephen Chboksy, based on the young adult novel of the same name by Stephen Chbosky
CAST: Logan Lerman (Charlie), Emma Watson (Sam), Ezra Miller (Patrick), Mae Whitman (Mary Elizabeth), Johnny Simmons (Brad)
SPECS: 103 minutes; color
AVAILABILITY: DVD (Lionsgate)

Based on the 1999 novel of the same name, *The Perks of Being a Wallflower* is a coming-of-age story featuring Charlie, a shy and introspective teenager about to start high school. The film follows him throughout his freshman year as he makes friends, attends school dances and football games, gets high at parties, and develops crushes. Throughout the film, Charlie struggles with his mental health, even enduring moments of psychosis. And, in the end, he is admitted to the hospital to receive acute psychological care. It is at the hospital that both his family and the audience learn Charlie has PTSD stemming from sexual abuse he suffered as a child. Though Charlie's mental health is precarious throughout the film, viewers are buoyed by the strong friendships he nurtures with his best friends, seniors Sam and Patrick.

In the opening scene, viewers meet Charlie first through his reflection. He is bent over his desk writing a letter to a "friend." An over-the-shoulder shot shows his face cast across his bedroom window. He reaches out to this unidentified friend because "she said you'd listen and understand" [00:02:06]. Just as in the novel, the epistolary structure of the film allows access to Charlie's interiority—as he reaches out, the audience is brought in. Because the film was written, adapted, and directed by the novel's author, Stephen Chbosky, it follows closely to the original vision for these characters. At the end of this first scene and the initial introduction to Charlie, he writes, "Like, if you met me you wouldn't think I was the weird kid who spent time in the hospital." He hesitates for a moment then continues, "And I wouldn't make you nervous" [00:02:26]. This attention to nerves and anxiety follows Charlie throughout the film, forecasting some future crisis. The audience is told to worry about him, and yet Charlie's vulnerability also fosters a trusting relationship between his character and the audience, meaning they might worry but they are also, simultaneously, excited for and encouraged by him. Just as when viewers first meet Charlie, they get both him and his reflection: multiple possibilities at once.

As Charlie starts high school, he slowly finds a community of other outsiders—Alice the shoplifting goth, Mary Elizabeth the angry vegan Buddhist, and Sam and Patrick (the stepsiblings who become his best friends). With his new crew of friends, Charlie begins experimenting with such adolescent things as drinking, music, and sex. But throughout the film, even in moments marked by joy and excitement, viewers wonder about Charlie—his mental health always precarious, always tipping toward some unknown trigger. Just as Charlie's nerves and aches vibrate through the film so also do his friends move in and out of states of instability, duress, and heartbreak. His best friends, Sam and Patrick, are in their final year of high school, and while they offer Charlie the affection, affirmation, and support he needs, they also ache in their own ways. Sam, with her own history of sexual abuse, navigates an unhealthy relationship with college photography major Craig. And Patrick, who is gay and out, must maintain the secrecy of his relationship with closeted football player Brad. By developing such dimensional characters, characters who exhibit ecstatic joy as much as teen angst, Chbosky allows their identities to be both embedded and fluid. They are always authentically themselves, even as they continue to examine who they are, growing and learning, making mistakes and moving on. Patrick demonstrates this embedded fluidity well.

Charlie and Patrick first meet in shop class, where Patrick unfortunately earns the nickname "Nothing." When his teacher teasingly calls him "Patty-Cakes," he responds with, "Look, my name's Patrick. Either you call me Patrick or call me nothing" [00:04:44]. And so students do. Throughout the film, "Nothing" surfaces in the way nicknames do in the halls of high school—in quotidian but often funny, frustrating, and fraught moments. Take, for example, when two students walk by and say "Hey Nothing" at a football game. Patrick responds with an eye roll and humor, saying, "Oh suck it, virginity pledges" [00:11:13]. But in other moments, the nickname lands hard. Whereas Patrick allows "Nothing" to roll of his back at the game, he is clearly injured by it during the most pivotal scene in the film.

At the apex of the film, Charlie finds himself isolated from friends and struggling to maintain a stable emotional equilibrium. He vacillates between numbing ache and pointed rage and is unable to manage these shifts. Ostracized from his social community because of a messy breakup with his girlfriend, Charlie must watch from a distance as his friends finish out their senior year. He must watch from a distance as Patrick also undergoes a breakup with the school's football quarterback, Brad. Their relationship had been closeted until Brad's father caught them fooling around. And while the school still does not know, Charlie watches Patrick unravel. He watches as, during lunch, Patrick is again called "Nothing." Up until this moment, Patrick's queerness is never a point of insult, mockery, or tension. Walking out of the food line, head low in heartbreak, a classmate says, "Hey Nothing." And all of a sudden, viewers feel the lack that *nothing* is meant to imply—its venom and its vacuum. Moments after, the teasing continues when one of Brad's friends trips Patrick, sending him and his food tray sprawling across the cafeteria floor. The friend sneers, "Oops, sorry Nothing" [01:10:36]. In this moment, *nothing* becomes everything, and Patrick confronts Brad in front of his team. Brad, still wearing bruises from when his father caught him with Patrick, tells him to walk away. He calls him "Nothing" to reinforce the façade of their relationship—that it is no different than any others at the school. And to ensure it lands, Brad says, "Whatever faggot" [01:11:27]. The braiding of the epithet and nickname allows them to inform one another. And though Patrick's queerness is only part of who he is, it implicitly echoes through "Nothing" as lack.

The teasing, the tripping, the denial, and finally the twin violence of being called "Nothing" and "faggot" ignite a fight. At first, just Patrick and Brad fight, but soon Brad's team joins in too. They hold him down and throw punch after punch until Charlie—quiet Charlie, wallflower Charlie—intervenes. This cafeteria scene is pivotal for a number of reasons. It presses the narrative forward, allowing Patrick to move on and bringing Charlie back into the fold of his friends (for protecting and defending Patrick). But it also exposes the deep pain these characters, Charlie and Patrick in particular, face. During the fight, Charlie blacks out. He does not fully remember what happens. The sound cuts from chaos to silence as the camera zeros in on Charlie's face, then his bruised knuckles and shaky hands. Viewers never see Charlie throw a punch. Time jumps forward in those minutes. Instead, the audience witnesses a crowded lunchroom, every student staring at Charlie with mouths agape. This scene removes Charlie from wallflower status and inscribes him with instability—which, to be clear, is neither good nor bad. He moves through and beyond his interiorized ache to protect his friend in a moment of literal blind rage.

Patrick is out and proud. His queerness offers joy, humor, and beauty—for him, his friends, and the audience too. It is not the proverbial source of trouble or the cliché motor of tension. Rather, the homophobia and violence stemming from Brad (as internalized) and Brad's father (as externalized) are what ignite the drama. This is shown in the way Patrick performs during local screenings of *The Rocky Horror Picture Show*. Dressed as Rocky—donning a feather boa and corset and lip-synching along—he leans into the sensuality of his role, exaggerating the words, "Give yourself over to absolute pleasure" [00:32:23]. The framing of this scene honors Patrick. Cameras angles amplify his body and face, marking him beautiful, and they continue to track him as he moves into the audience. Viewers feel part of the *Rocky Horror* audience, sitting next to Charlie while Patrick drapes over him, singing. In this way (and in many ways throughout the film, by both cinematographic and camera work), the viewer is invited into this intimate circle of friends.

This move, from wallflower to participant, happens again and again, sweeping the audience up into its oscillations. At the homecoming dance, Charlie stands against the wall watching Sam and Patrick dance to "Come on Eileen" by Dexys Midnight Runners. As Charlie, hesitant and balking, decides to join his friends on the dance floor, the frame holds close to his face. Viewers stay close by his side. When he enters the floor, Patrick and Sam swirl around him in welcome and everyone starts dancing. Viewers are there too, as viewers, swept up into the magical moment of friendship, spontaneity, and intimacy. Brian Glavely describes the wallflower as one who is in "ambivalent relation to visibility, space, and the social . . . always on the verge of fading into the background, becoming part of the environment, or evading attention entirely" (2015, 134). But Patrick does not let this happen. When Charlie slowly makes his way to the middle of the dance floor, Patrick screams in delight and wraps his scarf around Charlie's neck to signal his embrace. This embrace is of friendship, of course, but Patrick is also affirming Charlie in all of who he is—quiet, awkward, and unsure. This acceptance is an important part of the story, because it allows all the characters to shine in their own fullness, whether that includes mess and ache or joy and humor. Patrick's queerness is an unequivocal and visible part of him; it makes him a good friend—inviting, affirming, and charismatic.

Much of the framing work done in the film underscores quiet intimacy and humming freedom. Even as the characters, Charlie and Patrick especially, are bound up in their pain and struggle, the aches and anxieties are not dire. They signal feeling, that one is alive and living. The most cinematic moment in the film (and book) has Charlie riding in the car with Sam and Patrick. The three share a bench seat in the cab of Patrick's truck as Sam scrolls through radio stations. She serendipitously happens upon a song on the radio and insists on climbing into the truck bed as they speed through a tunnel. As the song blares "and we could be heroes," Charlie turns to Patrick and says, "I feel infinite"

Logan Lerman as Charlie, Ezra Miller as Patrick, and Emma Watson as Sam in *The Perks of Being a Wallflower*. Courtesy of Summit Entertainment/Photofest.

[00:28:16]. David Edelstein describes this moment and the general ethos of the film as "nostalgia with an emphasis on nostos, pain" (2012). Indeed, infinite is not painless even as it is euphoric.

After the cafeteria fight, as the friends sit together on a park bench while Patrick processes his loss, Patrick asks Charlie a pointed question. "Why can't you save anyone?" [01:17:45]. The shot is again intimately framed—darkness surrounds them on the bench. The city lights glow behind them. The question is ambiguous, possibly referring to Brad, but maybe himself. It is an important question because it underwrites the film. This is not the coming-of-age story viewers are used to, where the protagonist overcomes the pain and angst of adolescent turmoil. In fact, viewers never know how each character fares at the end of the film. As Charlie says himself, it is not about having all the answers but about being "both happy and sad," even as one tries to "figure out how that could be" [00:08:05]. Patrick and Charlie clarify these multiplicities of feeling, that one is not either/or, that mental illness does not mean only suffering, that queerness does not mean only tragedy. Even as the audience senses the finitude of a fleeting moment—a song on the radio and the ephemerality of a tunnel—they sense also that they are infinite.

See also *Blockers*; *Love, Simon*; *Mean Girls*; *To All the Boys I've Loved Before*.

Bibliography

Chbosky, Stephen. *The Perks of Being a Wallflower*. New York: MTV Books, 1999.
Edelstein, David. "Freshman Disorientation." *New York*, September 24, 2012. Accessed April 24, 2021. https://nymag.com/movies/reviews/edelstein-perks-of-being-a-wallflower-2012-9/.
Glavey, Brian. *The Wallflower Avant-Garde: Modernism, Sexuality, and Queer Ekphrasis*. New York: Oxford University Press, 2015.

—CE Mackenzie

PERSONAL BEST (1982)

DIRECTOR: Robert Towne
SCREENPLAY: Robert Towne
CAST: Mariel Hemingway (Chris Cahill), Patrice Donnelly (Tory Skinner), Scott Glenn (Terry Tingloff)
SPECS: 124 minutes; color
AVAILABILITY: DVD (Warner Archive)

At the time of its release, *Personal Best* was well regarded for its accurate presentation of women in high-level sports and for its frank depiction of two female athletes who fall in love. Protagonists Chris Cahill and Tory Skinner meet and become romantically involved while training for the Olympics. Set in the four years between qualifying events, the film follows Chris and Tory as they train as friends, teammates, lovers, and competitors. They face some of the more universal obstacles of young love, such as negotiating domestic responsibility and occasional bouts of jealousy; they also navigate the more specific challenges inherent to maintaining athletic careers. Throughout, Chris and Tory's romantic relationship is complicated by their status as competitors while their individual ability to harness the "kill instinct" is challenged by their attachment as lovers.

Their relationship must further incorporate the constant presence of head coach Terry Tingloff, who vacillates between offering gruff support and lecherous understanding. Chris and Tory eventually break up and move out, and Chris begins a romantic relationship with a male Olympic swimmer. Ultimately, Chris and Tory both qualify, seconds apart, for the 1980 Olympics.

It would be a mistake to understate the cultural significance of *Personal Best* to the lesbian community. The relationship between Chris Cahill and Tory Skinner provides a frank, believable love affair. At the time of its debut, the word "homosexual" was favored in mainstream reviews; the word "lesbian" was not spoken in the film. Likewise, bisexuality would have also provided an applicable framework by the end of the film, but remained unarticulated on screen and in print. For lesbians who had been waiting for decades to see themselves on screen, however, representation was long overdue, and *Personal Best* became a kind of shorthand for lesbian sexuality.

The attraction between Chris and Tory reads as authentic long before the question of whether "straights playing gays" had the chance to become culturally relevant. In fact, the relationship reverberated in lesbian consciousness for decades. *Autostraddle* summarizes the established significance of *Personal Best* as a lesbian film mediated across coming-out narratives (*Ellen*), among heterosexuals (*Friends*), as referenced by self-proclaimed "dykes" (the films of Cheryl Dunye), and for trans men (Chaz Bono):

> Upon realizing that she's a lesbian in "The Puppy Episode" in 1996, Ellen wails to her therapist Oprah: "Oh why did I watch *Personal Best*???" In a 1998 episode of *Friends*, when Ross fears that his new girlfriend is becoming gay by hanging out at the gym with his lesbian ex-wife Carol, he whines to Joey: "Two women stretching. You know, they take a steam, things get playful. Didn't you see *Personal Best*?" A customer asks Cheryl about *Personal Best* in 1996's *The Watermelon Woman*. Chaz Bono told Jay Leno that he first realized he was into women when he watched *Personal Best* as a teenager. (Hogan 2020)

Tory's skill, confidence, and defiant charm are all made visible in the opening scene: she releases the shot put, breaks the silence by loudly exclaiming "Alright!" when the steel ball lands, and signals victory by emulating the "jerk-off" gesture at her coach [00:04:56]. Muscled and lean with shaggy dark hair, a determined jawline, and a persistent, playful smirk, hers is "a body we can believe in" (Holland 2011, 94).

Even within the homosocial world of women's track and field, in which womanhood is explicitly scripted as strong, competitive, and self-possessed, Tory presents the unmistakable embodiment and energetic thrust of a woman who loves women. Dismissing all speculation, the undeniably tough and unexpectedly soft-spoken Tory kisses Chris on the first day of their acquaintance. Following decades of erasure, concealment, and the customary killing off of lesbian characters via production codes and institutionalized bias, viewers were finally treated to a sure thing.

Personal Best also broke with the heteronormative, misogynistic demand that girls and women coded as "tomboys" be produced as reassuringly heterosexual. Unlike on-screen contemporaries Amanda Whurlitzer in *Bad News Bears*

(1976), Jo Polinaczek in *Facts of Life* (1979–1988), Watts in *Some Kind of Wonderful* (1987), and either Cagney *or* Lacey (*Cagney and Lacey*, 1982–1988), neither Tory's nor Chris's gender expressions, interests, or professions were excused, rerouted, or justified through reassurances of heterosexuality. This is particularly radical in the world of sports, in which "athletic excellence is submerged under the 'accusation' of lesbianism" and "maintaining one's position depended upon masquerading under these deals of heterosexuality" (Cayleff 2000, 731).

While the richness of the film would undoubtedly have been enhanced by simply acknowledging that Chris and Tory were a couple among friends and teammates, the "open secret" strategy may well have resonated more strongly, and proven more acceptable, across a broad swathe of audiences in 1982. Ambiguity, too, is present throughout the film more generally. Viewers are left with plenty to analyze about the emotional intimacy that Tory shares with their coach, the ways that female friendship can produce multiple forms of attachment, or the ways that lesbian identity and bisexuality are structurally absented throughout the script. In the silences and in what is spoken, *Personal Best* provides plenty of content to appreciate, work with, and contemplate.

In the final scene, Chris and Tory have qualified for the Olympics together. Nonetheless, Chris and Tory remain as they began: athletes striving for their personal best.

See also *Battle of the Sexes*.

Bibliography

Cayleff, Susan E. "Sports, Professional." In *Encyclopedia of Lesbian Histories and Cultures*, edited by Bonnie Zimmerman, 729–32. New York: Routledge, 2000.

Forel, Auguste. *The Sexual Question: A Scientific, Psychological, Hygienic, and Sociological Study*. Translated by C. F. Marshall. New York: Physicians and Surgeons Book Company, 1931.

Hogan, Heather. "Watching 'Personal Best' Was the Main Way to Become a Lesbian in the '80s and '90s." *Autostraddle*, December 22, 2020. Accessed June 6, 2021. https://www.autostraddle.com/personal-best-review/.

Holland, P. Sharon. "The 'Beached Whale.'" *GLQ* 17, no. 1 (2011): 89–95.

—Sasha T. Goldberg

PHILADELPHIA (1993)

DIRECTOR: Jonathan Demme
SCREENPLAY: Ron Nyswaner
CAST: Tom Hanks (Andrew Beckett), Denzel Washington (Joe Miller), Antonio Banderas (Miguel Álvarez), Jason Robards (Charles Wheeler)
SPECS: 126 minutes; color
AVAILABILITY: DVD (Sony Pictures Home Entertainment)

White, well liked, and middle class, Andrew Beckett is a high-flying attorney making his way up the ladder at Wyant Wheeler in Philadelphia. Outside of the office, his private life as a gay man in a long-term relationship with Miguel Álvarez is nobody's business. But after an AIDS-related Kaposi's sarcoma lesion develops on his forehead, Beckett suddenly finds himself dismissed for bad conduct. Convinced he has been framed for discriminatory reasons, Beckett launches a case against his old bosses to fight for legal protection for people living with HIV/AIDS. So begins this landmark film in LGBTQIA+ cinema and American AIDS history. Beckett is unable to find a sympathetic lawyer until he is taken on by a rival, Joe Miller, an African American attorney whose compassion for Beckett is complicated by his ignorance about AIDS and his deep-rooted homophobia. An unlikely pair, Beckett and Miller take on Wyant Wheeler in a courtroom battle that serves to dramatize the moral panic that shaped perceptions of gay men and the AIDS crisis. Beckett's health fails, and he dies shortly after he is vindicated by the jury. Miller, meanwhile, is conveniently cleansed of his ignorance through the experience and ends the film a hero.

Released in 1993, *Philadelphia* was the first Hollywood film to feature a gay protagonist—although arguably shot to prioritize Miller's homophobic gaze. The film remained the highest-grossing film of its kind for more than twenty years, outflanking later classics such as *Brokeback Mountain* (2006) and not out-grossed until *The Imitation Game* in 2014 (Damshenas n.d.). Clearly, *Philadelphia* was—and remains—monumental in how the first decades of the AIDS crisis were understood and are remembered in American popular culture. For this reason, *Philadelphia* was controversial ever since it was announced, for various reasons and for different communities. As Mark Zelinsky notes, the film came "overburdened with demands" to remedy the preexisting representation of AIDS in a violently homophobic and AIDS-phobic discourse; it was edgy for mainstream American audiences but distrusted by LGBTQIA+ people (n.d.). Perhaps Amy Taubin best sums up this furor: *Philadelphia* "has been 13 years in the making and bears the burden of all the films that have not preceded it" (2017). A second controversy was the film's similarity to the real-life case of Geoffrey Bowers, an HIV-positive gay attorney who was dismissed by his bosses in the mid-1980s after developing AIDS-related health complications. Bowers took his employer to court, and his case eventually won. But unlike the Hollywoodized ending of *Philadelphia*, this victory did not happen until six years after Bowers's death. His family later settled with the *Philadelphia* team over alleged uncompensated use of his story for an undisclosed amount.

The unique and profound importance of *Philadelphia* may have set it up for righteous indignation or even failure, but that does not absolve it from critique. Writing after its release, Jeffrey Schmalz argues that it misrepresents the facts of HIV/AIDS to depict "a well-to-do white man with AIDS, when increasingly the face of AIDS is black, female and poor" (1993). He nods to the ways *Philadelphia*—a film that took so long to be made within an entertainment industry that refused to grapple with the impact of the epidemic—regurgitated early and narrow ideas about who was impacted by HIV/AIDS, rather than showing the diversity of people living with the condition.

The film begins with a gentle montage of the multicultural streets of the eponymous city as Bruce Springsteen's Oscar-winning theme song "Streets of Philadelphia" plays in full, before ending with a close-up of the famously cracked Liberty Bell: "This will be a film, the opening credit sequence announces . . . about justice and injustice in America" (Pearl 2003, 63–64). The montage cuts in medias res to Beckett and Miller sparring in court, before viewers follow Beckett to the HIV/AIDS clinic where he awaits results from recent blood work. Surrounded by HIV-positive gay men (played by HIV-positive actors) whose visibly emaciated and effeminate bodies represent different stages of Beckett's future, his identity as a gay man surfaces in the film through his proximity to an AIDS-related death, an important but contentious equivalence. In the following scenes, this identity and his ailing health are juxtaposed with his lifestyle as a powerful attorney; well liked in his office and praised by his bosses, at home he is in and out of hospital as health issues arise, creating a binary between his public life as a closeted attorney and his private life as a HIV-positive gay man living with AIDS. Viewers see his family accepting and cherishing him, overturning the cliché (but all too real) trope of the ostracized HIV-positive gay man. However, the uneasy equilibrium of Beckett's life changes once an AIDS-related lesion on his forehead is clocked by his bosses. His picture-perfect career unravels when he is subsequently dismissed due to crucial paperwork going missing from his desk under suspicious circumstances.

Determined to prove that Wyant Wheeler dismissed him for nefarious, AIDS-phobic reasons, Beckett arrives at Miller's door after being turned away by nine other unsympathetic attorneys. At first, Miller also rejects him, only agreeing to help after witnessing Beckett encounter AIDS-phobic discrimination in the city library in a way that poses parallels between AIDS stigma and the civil rights movement. Focusing on Beckett's choice of a reluctant, homophobic attorney, Larry Kramer argued that the film was "heartbreakingly mediocre . . . often legally, medically and politically inaccurate" (1994). His acerbity is echoed by many AIDS activists who at the time debunked Beckett's inability to find any legal representation other than Miller. Sarah Schulman sees it as "not only absurd but grossly ahistorical" because it overlooks the fact that "gay people built a world of services, advocacy organizations, and personal relationships in response to the epidemic that later became the foundation of support for HIV-infected heterosexuals" (1998, 49–50). While this is true, the tacit juxtaposition of homophobic AIDS stigma and the civil rights movement is intended to bequeath the AIDS crisis enough gravitas to win the spectator's compassion by positing it as a valid comparison.

To Steven Seidman, the dynamic between Miller and Beckett establishes "a hierarchical division" between "'the normal, pure, and powerful heterosexual' and 'the diseased, disgusting, and disenfranchised homosexual'" (2001, 7). The film's premise is hence to chart Miller's journey as he comes to accept gay people as "normal" and people living with AIDS as "innocent." As Miller and Beckett begin to work together on the case as an unlikely duo of bigoted macho man and dying, effete, persecuted gay man, it is easy to understand Kylo-Patrick R. Hart's critique of the film's "kid-glove treatment" of gay male sexuality (2000, 64). Aside from a brief scene at the start of the film, gay male friendship and queer solidarity are virtually absent from Beckett's life, or at least the life that viewers are privy to. Due to anxiety about squeamish mainstream audiences, displays of affection between Beckett and Miguel are so austere that one might mistake them for "very close roommates or best friends" (Hart 2000, 54–55). Moments in which Beckett is shown as engaged in gay culture are few and far between, which is why the party scene midway through the film is so important. Tired of planning his own memorial service as his health declines as the trial goes on, Beckett decides to throw a last-minute party instead. Cut to his condo filled with people in fancy dress. Viewers see the event through Miller's nervous, homophobic eyes: a crowd of flamboyant, effeminate, sometimes gender-nonconforming people, including a cameo from Quentin Crisp.

After the party, Miller sits alone with Beckett as they work on their defense for the case the following day. Beckett congratulates Miller for surviving his "first gay party intact." Miller snaps back that in his childhood, he was raised to believe "that queers dress up like their mother, that they're afraid to fight, that they're a danger to little kids and that all they want to do is get into your pants" [01:16:17]. His invocation of childhood homophobia seems not quite meant as an attack on Beckett, but nor does he refute the words; instead, they hang between the two men, a half threat without resolution. Moving on, Beckett discusses the fact that he might die before the end of the trial and rises from his chair to play an aria sung by Maria Callas, IV drip in his hand like a walking stick. He dances slowly as though the music fills him, translating the opera so that Beckett can understand it: "I am divine! I am oblivion!" [01:21:54]. The composition of the scene warps the film's realism; the room is flooded by an uncanny crimson hue as Beckett—shot from above—lip-synchs and sobs, "so caught up in the aria that he crosses the line from evoking the diva to embodying her" (Taubin 2017). Viewers watch Miller watching Beckett, a soft close-up on his face, before Miller flees the apartment as though to shrug off any identification with Beckett. Standing outside, Miller contemplates returning before laughing at the idea and heading home instead. The opera music continues to play as he lies awake next to his sleeping wife, as though haunted by Beckett's performance of queer abjection.

This evocative, abstract moment in an otherwise realistic and dialogue-centered film has been interpreted by film scholars in different directions. Douglas Crimp declares the scene one of the only authentically queer moments in a film that is focused more on solving Miller's heterosexism than rendering Beckett's subjectivity. Crimp describes his own sense of betrayal at the scene, asking,

> if love is love and it doesn't matter if you're straight or gay, I want to know why Jonathan Demme didn't show Andy getting into bed with his boyfriend as Callas continued to sing. . . . So whose subjectivity is represented here anyway? The answer, of course, is that it's the subjectivity of the spectator, constructed by Demme's film as straight and unaffected by AIDS. (2002, 255)

Unlike Crimp, Taubin applauds the opera scene. She notes that in a more sentimental film, the two men would hug, as though to symbolically eradicate Joe's homophobia. Instead, "Demme lets us understand that what Joe has seen in Andrew and been moved and shaken by, and even envious of, is everything Joe has repressed in order to be a man" and so he flees the apartment to protect his own precarious investment in heterosexual masculinity (2017). Whether or not viewers recognize the scene as an artistic moment of queer pathos that authentically or incompletely speaks to the tragedy of AIDS in some gay men's lives, it is certainly true that Miller's homophobia is less obvious from this moment onward, as though Beckett's sad and strange performance helped him to resolve the childhood homophobia he had described just beforehand.

The moral issues on display in *Philadelphia* come to an apex during the final courtroom scenes as the strain of the trial takes its toll on Beckett. His health rapidly declines as he undergoes questioning from the attorney who is defending his fraudulent, homophobic former employer. The attorney (a woman who privately expresses her own sense of revulsion at her part in the case, as though to verify the moral stakes of the film) asks Beckett to describe his trip to a gay pornographic cinema in the mid-1980s. The film's logic seems to be that he was unfaithful to Álvarez by sleeping with a man he met there, and that he put Álvarez at risk of seroconversion, as though forms of relationships other than enforced monogamy do not exist and as though that risk was deliberately ventured. In this regard, the film blurs normative notions of intimacy with unethical sexual conduct. After the attorney implies that the employers would not have been able to see the lesions across Beckett's face because they are too small, Miller returns to the stand and asks him to undo his shirt to prove otherwise. Visibly deteriorating, Beckett bares his chest to expose the numerous lesions across it, as though a martyr to the trial and to gay men and people living with HIV/AIDS everywhere. A handful of scenes later, he collapses in the court and is last seen "on his deathbed in an oxygen mask" in a hospital room "crowded with children and pregnant women" (Edelman 2004, 18). Edelman argues that the family that surrounds him seems intended to displace the unseen HIV-positive gay men who—the film implies—cost Beckett his life and linger in negative space as specters. Victorious, Beckett "dies happy" (Schulman 1998, 50) that "justice has prevailed" (Grundmann and Sacks 1994, 54). And yet, in so many ways, justice has not prevailed at all.

Writing at the time of the film's release, Roger Ebert calls *Philadelphia* "a ground-breaker" that makes use of "the chemistry of popular stars" and the "reliable genre" of Hollywood courtroom melodrama to expand awareness of HIV/AIDS among otherwise antipathetic audiences (1994). Almost two decades later in 2010, in an improved biopolitical context of HIV/AIDS and white gay men's social standing, Paul Sendziuk argues that the film deserves more nuance than the condemnation it received in queer quarters. He contextualizes the issues with its heteronormative gaze and its choice to foreground affluent white gay experiences of the AIDS epidemic: "Had a Hollywood studio made the film five years earlier, instead of pretending that AIDS did not exist, its focus might have been better warranted" (2010, 445). Although the film was released in 1993 and remains associated with that period, it could well be set several years earlier in 1986, when Bowers was beginning his own case against his employer and gay men were even more directly and unambiguously associated with HIV/AIDS. Although the time between 1986 and 1993 may seem minimal, these years were long when it comes to the cultural and epidemiological politics of AIDS.

The point behind *Philadelphia*, Sendziuk claims, was to offer a film that could be "played in Wichita, Kansas, as well as the East Village" and so to raise "awareness and tolerance outside queer circles" (2010, 446–47). This approach is patronizing and has obvious limitations, positioning certain demographics of HIV-positive and LGBTQIA+ people above others, and so it is unsurprising that the film was considered contentious. Critique of its historically inaccurate, moralized, and whitewashed depiction of people living with HIV/AIDS is substantial and legitimate. As arguably the most famous representation of gay men in the early 1990s, the film's noxious takeaway may well be "that only the homosexual who is a mirror image of the ideal heterosexual citizen is acceptable" (Seidman 2001, 8).

But *Philadelphia* nevertheless still constitutes an important and compassionate—if overburdened and underdelivering—intervention in the homophobia and AIDS-phobia of America in the early 1990s. Even before its release, *Philadelphia* had become a memorial of sorts to the HIV-positive actors who appeared in it as extras and then later died, some before filming had even completed (see Rothman 1995). Today, the enduring popularity and controversy that surrounds the film might show that LGBTQIA+ representation in the mainstream is no simple panacea. Rather, it is steeped in contradiction, in good and bad intentions, in moments of success and failure—even in the same film and at the same time.

See also *Brokeback Mountain*; *Jeffrey*.

Bibliography

Crimp, Douglas. *Melancholia and Moralism: Essays on AIDS and Queer Politics*. Cambridge, MA: MIT Press, 2002.

Damshenas, Sam. "Here Are the 10 Most Financially Successful LGBTQ Films in History." *Gay Times*, n.d. Accessed May 11, 2021. https://www.gaytimes.co.uk/culture/here-are-the-10-most-financially-successful-lgbtq-films-in-history/.

Ebert, Roger. "*Philadelphia*." RogerEbert.com, January 14, 1994. Accessed May 11. 2021. https://www.rogerebert.com/reviews/philadelphia-1994.

Edelman, Lee. *No Future: Queer Theory and the Death Drive*. Durham, NC: Duke University Press, 2004.

Grundmann, Roy, and Peter Sacks. "*Philadelphia*." *Cinéaste* 20, no. 3 (1994): 51–54.

Hart, Kylo-Patrick R. *The AIDS Movie: Representing a Pandemic in Film and Television*. New York: Routledge, 2000.

Kramer, Larry. "Why I Hated *Philadelphia*: A Playwright and Gay Activist Goes to See Hollywood's First Major AIDS Movie and Comes away Bitterly Disappointed." *Los Angeles Times*, January 9, 1994. Accessed May 11, 2021. https://www.latimes.com/archives/la-xpm-1994-01-09-ca-9875-story.html.

Pearl, Monica. "The City of Brotherly Love: Sex, Race, and AIDS in *Philadelphia*." *EnterText* 2, no. 3 (2003): 57–75.

Rothman, Clifford. "*Philadelphia*: Oscar Gives Way to Elegy." *New York Times*, January 1, 1995. Accessed May 12, 2021. https://www.nytimes.com/1995/01/01/movies/film-philadelphia-oscar-gives-way-to-elegy.html.

Schmalz, Jeffrey. "From Visions of Paradise to Hell on Earth." *New York Times*, February 28, 1993. Accessed May 12, 2021. https://www.nytimes.com/1993/02/28/movies/from-visions-of-paradise-to-hell-on-earth.html.

Schulman, Sarah. *Stagestruck: Theater, AIDS, and the Marketing of Gay America*. Durham, NC: Duke University Press, 1998.

Seidman, Steven. "From Identity to Queer Politics: Shifts in the Social Logic of Normative Heterosexuality in Contemporary America." *Social Thought & Research* 24, nos. 1–2 (2001): 1–12.

Sendziuk, Paul. "Philadelphia or Death." *GLQ* 16, no. 3 (2010): 444–49.

Taubin, Amy. "Philadelphia: Un-packaging the Hollywood Aids Drama." BFI, May 9, 2017. Accessed September 12, 2021. https://www2.bfi.org.uk/news-opinion/sight-sound-magazine/features/philadelphia-un-packaging-hollywood-aids-drama-tom-hanks-denzel-washington-jonathan-demme.

Zelinsky, Mark. "The Philadelphia Phenomenon." *Gay & Lesbian Review Worldwide*, n.d. https://glreview.org/article/the-philadelphia-phenomenon/.

—Gabriel Duckels

PINK FLAMINGOS (1972)

DIRECTOR: John Waters
SCREENPLAY: John Waters
CAST: Divine (Divine/Babs Johnson), David Lochary (Raymond Marble), Mink Stole (Connie Marble), Mary Vivian Pearce (Cotton), Edith Massey (Edie), Danny Mills (Crackers)
SPECS: 93 minutes; color
AVAILABILITY: DVD (Warner Archive)

John Waters's *Pink Flamingos* centers on the character of Babs Johnson (aka Divine), who has been hiding away in an off-the-grid pink motor home to escape her fame and notoriety after being declared by national tabloids as "The Filthiest Person Alive." In the trailer and nearby shed live her psychopathic son, Crackers, her egg-obsessed and crib-bound mother Edie, and her traveling companion, Cotton. Her rivals, Connie and Raymond Marbles, run an "adoption clinic," in which they kidnap young women, have them impregnated by their gay manservant, and then sell the babies to lesbian couples. When Divine discovers the Marbles's plan to steal her title as "The Filthiest Person Alive," she goes on a rampage, attempting to get revenge and maintain her "filthy" reputation. The film ends with Divine eating dog feces and grinning at the camera, safe in her filthy habits.

Upon its release, the film was poorly received, both critically and commercially. One critic referred to it as "a human degradation" (Wolff 1975, 17) with scenes of cannibalism, coprophagia, rape, murder, incest, voyeurism, castration, defecation, as well as "a magnificent foot fetish sequence . . . and a party entertainer who has a dancing asshole" (Samuels 1983, 113). Due to this lack of success, *Pink Flamingos* was screened as part of a selection of midnight movies in 1973 at the Elgin Theater in New York City. These midnight screenings, in which audiences would attend repeated screenings of rather unconventional, strange, and transgressive B movies, were a last-ditch attempt by filmmakers and distributors to build a cult film audience.

Audience members who attended frequent screenings of the film would memorize lines of dialogue and recite them as the film played on screen, cheering as the characters engaged in various transgressive acts. It was a social gathering, a place for the youth culture of the community to be outrageous and engage with like-minded people. According to Samuels, watching "the outrage on screen gave you the incentive to be more outrageous in the audience—shouting obscenities, mouthing lines, dressing in drag, issuing forth simulated barfs and real farts" (1983, 123). Screenings of the film were also a place for recreational drug use. John Waters, in a documentary on midnight movies, states: "In the theatres they smoked marijuana, I mean it was a very different time. . . . Everyone was high, one hundred percent of the audience was high every night for *Pink Flamingos*.

I was high when I wrote it. . . . I was not high when I made it" (Samuels 1983, n.p.). The use of drugs during these screenings speaks quite clearly to the film's transgressive nature and the influence of this transgression on the audience.

Transgression involves going against an established code of conduct or to go beyond "the bounds of an aesthetic, ethical or established form of behavior," but it also reinforces the borders of what is considered transgressive in general (Edwards and Grauland 2013, 66). In other words, what is deemed transgressive is only "transgressive" because rules and "conventional" behaviors have been formed against it. According to Chris Jenks, transgression is a conduct that "breaks rules or exceeds boundaries" (2003, 3). However, he is also quick to note that transgressive behavior does not deny these boundaries; "rather it exceeds them and thus completes them" (7). Transgression is not disorder but instead reminds society of "the necessity of order." In a way, *Pink Flamingos* contains such elements of transgression to an extent that viewers are reminded of order and boundaries because it purposefully surpasses them and allows the audience to recognize them. However, this transgression also highlights the film's representation of LGBTQIA+ characters as living in opposition to the heteronormative boundaries of society.

The most openly LGBTQIA+ character in the film is Divine, better known in real life as drag performer Harris Glen Milstead. Before his death in 1988, Milstead performed as a character actor on both stage and screen in mostly female roles under the drag name "Divine." Aside from *Pink Flamingos*, Milstead appeared in numerous other films directed by John Waters, including *Mondo Trasho* (1969), *Multiple Maniacs* (1970), *Female Trouble* (1974), *Polyester* (1981), and *Hairspray* (1988), where he often played various tawdry and "trashy" transgressive characters. Milstead capitalized on this trashy persona by appearing at live venues and other events as Divine, particularly in front of gay audiences. Although Milstead openly embraced his sexual identity as a gay man, he did not consider himself a "drag queen," nor did he consider himself transgender, as often assumed by the public. John Waters often refers to Divine as "he/him," as did Milstead himself. Yet his drag persona allowed him widespread recognition and a type of identification with his LGBTQIA+ audiences.

Jose Esteban Muñoz discusses "queer' performance and its way of "disidentification": "Identification itself can also be manipulated and worked in ways that promise narratives of self that surpass the limits prescribed by the dominant culture" (1999, 96). In other words, queer bodies can manipulate what they see on the screen and situate themselves within and against various discourses through which they are called to identify. Divine acts as an example of an identifier for an LGBTQIA+ cult audience, a figure that can be manipulated, impersonated, or imitated for the audience to situate (or not situate) themselves within a particular cultural discourse.

There are several instances in the film when Divine exhibits this queer identifiability, namely through expressions of transgression. (I use the pronouns "she/her" when discussing Divine as a female character in the film.) In one scene, when interviewed by a group of news reporters, Divine openly expresses her sexual fetishes and "political beliefs":

Mat Hinlin: Divine, are you a lesbian?

Divine: Yes. I have done *everything*.

Ron Vespo: Does blood turn you on?

Divine: It does *more* than turn me on, Mr. Vespo, it makes me *cum*! And more than the sight of it, I love the taste of it, the taste of hot freshly killed blood.

Morey Roberts: Could you give us some of your political beliefs?

Divine: Kill everyone now! Condone first-degree murder! Advocate cannibalism! Eat shit! Filth are my politics, filth is my life! [Posing wildly] Take whatever you like! [She puts hands on crotch and mugs hideously to the cameramen] How's *this* for a center spread? (Waters 1988, 77–78)

This is not to suggest that Divine's politics of condoning murder, cannibalism, and filth are identifiable as part of an LGBTQIA+ identity, but rather as a representation of antiheteronormativity. First, when asked if she is a lesbian, Divine's answer is that she has done "everything," implying sexual openness and fluidity. Her identity is not constructed by boundaries or restrictions in regard to sexual orientation. Second, when asked, "Does blood turn you on?," she expresses her desire and fetish for blood—it does more than turn her on, it makes her "cum." This fetish for blood exhibits a subcultural ideology or transgression that Divine, and most of the main characters of the film, commend and demonstrate throughout.

Gina Marchetti defines the concept of subculture as

Any identifiable and cohesive group which is outside the dominant culture and its ideological norms because of differences of race, age, gender, sexual orientation, lifestyle or outlook. . . . Although subcultures share many common characteristics with the larger cultural formations of which they are a part, they have their own patterns of thought and behavior which are obscure, if not completely incomprehensible, to outsiders. (2008, 406)

Based on Marchetti's definition, subcultures exist outside the ideological norms of dominant culture and, while they share commonalities with this dominant culture, also share distinct, alternative behaviors only understood within their subcultural framework. Dick Hebdige, on the other hand, argues that subculture is a subversion to normalcy, or a common resistance. Through the use of style and the subversion of common objects, subcultures symbolically separate themselves from the dominant societal standard:

Style in subculture is, then, pregnant with significance. Its transformations go "against nature," interrupting the process or "normalization." As such, they are gestures, movements towards a speech which offends the "silent majority," which challenges the principle of unity and cohesion, which contradicts the myth of consensus. Our task becomes . . . to discern the hidden messages inscribed in code on the glossy surfaces of style, to trace them out as "maps of meaning" which obscurely re-present the very contradictions they are designed to resolve or conceal. (Hebdige 1979, 18)

Hebdige's statements on subculture as interrupting a process of normalization, and a challenge to principles of unity in society, is particularly true of Divine's subcultural ideology. In the case of *Pink Flamingos*, the subcultural is defined by differences in normativity as distinguished by the dominant culture in which it exists and this subversion of normalcy. Essentially, Divine being "turned on" by the sight and taste of blood is not an ideological norm of heteropatriarchal culture, but expresses subcultural ideology and a fetish, or inclination, toward subversion, transgression, and the abject.

One of these expressions of subversion in *Pink Flamingos* is coprophagia. In the film's infamous final scene, viewers hear a voice-over from the narrator (Waters himself): "The filthiest people alive? Well, you think you know somebody filthier? Watch as Divine proves that she is not only the filthiest person in the world, she is also the filthiest *actress* in the world. What you are about to see is *the real thing.*" This narration plays as Crackers, Cotton, and Divine walk down the street and spot a dog with its owner. After the dog defecates on the sidewalk, Divine kneels down and eats the dog's feces. She gags twice, grins, and the screen goes to black.

Waters publicly acknowledged that Divine did actually eat dog feces while filming this scene in the Steve Yeager biopic *Divine Trash* (1998). Here, in terms of the abject, the border that signifies the body's separation from death and decay has been broken: "These body fluids, this defilement, this shit are what life withstands, hardly and with difficulty, against death" (Kristeva 1982, 3). Essentially, Divine has ingested the very fluid or defilement that the body rejects. Mary Douglas discusses the external boundaries of filth and bodily fluids as a form of gratification, as well as the power and place of "dirt." External boundaries and internal lines separate fluids within the body, but the danger of bodily fluids exists in the societal idea of "margins," and the orifices of the body symbolize the most vulnerable points of this margin (2002, 120). Therefore, Divine acts as a visual representation of these margins being breached or violated and is disturbing what Kristeva would call "borders, positions [or] rules" (1982, 4). Divine consuming real dog excrement while filming this scene provides a double-layered signification, where any boundaries between artistic representation and reality are also collapsed and violated. The audience, while viewing this real consumption of filth, enters a liminal space at the boundary between genuine transgression and the representation of this transgression in a fictional narrative. It is exactly this liminality, the blurring of boundaries between the normal and the abnormal, that leads to the film's transgressive cult following.

Pink Flamingos exhibits distinct representations of grotesque and transgressive behavior, as well as elements of the abject. These representations give viewers an understanding of why this film has developed a LGBTQIA+ cult following. The film itself contains queer elements (alternative modes of being, nonheteronormative sexuality, a rejection of societal modes of normalcy), and because aspects of queerness already exist in the film, it is appropriated by the queer audience to engage in transgression. In other words, if the queer audience makes a recognizable and deliberate engagement with a film such as *Pink Flamingos*, they are simultaneously constructing a culturally acceptable transgression. The elements of the film that are grotesque, abject, and transgressive represent a rejection of heteronormativity and a mainstream understanding of normality, both of which construct the boundaries of transgression.

Bibliography

Douglas, Mary. *Purity and Danger: An Analysis of Concepts of Pollution and Taboo*. London: Routledge, 2002.

Edwards, Justin D., and Rune Grauland. *Grotesque*. New York: Routledge, 2013.

Hebdige, Dick. *Subculture: The Meaning of Style*. London: Routledge, 1979.

Jenks, Chris. *Transgression*. New York: Routledge, 2003.

Kristeva, Julia. *Powers of Horror: An Essay on Abjection*. Translated by Leon S. Roudiez. New York: Columbia University Press, 1982.

Marchetti, Gina. "Subcultural Studies and the Film Audience: Rethinking the Film Viewing Context." In *The Cult Film Reader*, edited by Ernest Mathijs and Xavier Mendik, 402–18. Maidenhead, UK: McGraw Hill Open University Press, 2008.

Muñoz, José Esteban. *Disidentifications: Queers of Color and the Performance of Politics*. Minneapolis: University of Minnesota Press, 1999.

Samuels, Stuart. *Midnight Movies*. New York: Macmillan, 1983.

———, dir. *Midnight Movies: From the Margin to the Mainstream*. DVD. Artisan/Lionsgate, 2005.

Waters, John. *Trash Trio: Three Screenplays*. London: Forth Estate, 1988.

Wolff, Michael. "So What Do You Do at Midnight? You See a Trashy Movie." *New York Times*, September 7, 1975. Accessed May 29, 2021. https://www.nytimes.com/1975/09/07/archives /so-that-do-you-do-at-midnight-you-see-a-trashy-movie.html.

—John Lynskey

PINK NARCISSUS (1971)

DIRECTOR: James Bidgood
SCREENWRITER: James Bidgood
CAST: Bobby Kendall (Pan/Narcissus), Charles Ludlam (Salesman)
SPECS: 65 minutes; color
AVAILABILITY: DVD (Strand Releasing)

In a mythical world—economically manufactured in a corner of director James Bidgood's New York City apartment—a glowing moon peeks from a sapphire forest. A spider's web dominates the foreground, while the calls of night creatures steal into the soundtrack. The camera dollies toward the artificial moon before the screen fades into an abstract bouquet of psychedelic colors. From these colors emerges a golden, stop-motion butterfly that glides into the chintzy, chiffoned bedroom of a beautiful young man. Alternately representing Pan and Narcissus, he disrobes before a rosy looking glass and gazes at photos of himself in stages of undress. Suddenly, he poses like a bullfighter before a semicircle of six arched mirrors, as the camera's low angles implore viewers to admire him slavishly from below. As if a dream, the scene fades into a public lavatory, where the six arched mirrors become upright, arched urinals. As Kendall readies himself before a urinal, Bidgood's camera readies itself behind Kendall, embracing the span of his buttocks. Injecting a repellent dose of reality, the camera ogles close-ups of bugs and bloody refuse at the bottom of the porcelain. Bidgood eventually fades back into the youth's chintzy bedroom, where he peers into a reflecting pool, sucks on his fingers, and dreams of lazing in a garden—until the extradiegetic sounds of applause recall him to his earlier bullfight. Through crosscutting and the use of stand-ins, Kendall plays both the toreador and a sombrero-topped peasant who proffers a flower—a narcissus—to his heroic alter ego.

This impressionistic wash of images constitutes the main action of *Pink Narcissus*, an 8-mm experiment miraculously filmed over a period of seven years in director Bidgood's Manhattan apartment, on sets he constructed and painted himself. A former clothing designer, drag performer, and male physique photographer, Bidgood intended to film men as straight directors had always filmed women—through a dreamlike lens and with unapologetic objectification. Without any dialogue or a linear narrative, the film constructs an alternative universe in which baroque sets and costumes do the "talking," so to speak. This visual vernacular is enhanced by forced perspectives, physically dyed celluloid, and a palette that, as Bidgood admits, was influenced by the pastel dreamscapes of illustrator and painter Maxfield Parrish (1870–1966).

Bidgood's film—his only one—invites comparison with the kitsch works of contemporaries such as Kenneth Anger and Werner Schroeter, or perhaps with the florid saturnalias of *Fellini: Satyricon* (1969), a film Bidgood greatly admired.

Were *Pink Narcissus* only a private musing on old movies, the film might be little more than exquisitely wrought camp. Yet contrasted with its reveries are moments when "reality" breaks the private spell of Narcissus's bedroom. Halfway through the film, the camera moves toward an open window, allowing the audience to see a fantastically sleazy New York City nightscape, also realized on deliberately artificial, stylized sets. If the bedroom scenes parody Hollywood iconography, the street scenes unashamedly draw on tropes of gay pornography. Amid an urban forest of blinking neon signs, a priest buys kinky toys from a wheeled kiosk. Great neon arrows point everywhere, not only directing the audience's attention to public erotic displays but throbbing phallically themselves. Stalking the street are a panoply of glorious stereotypes ripped from porn magazines and tabooed fantasies: naked, hard-hat-clad construction workers work themselves over; a young man in a Davy Crocket getup strokes himself; altar boys suggestively swing their incense; and a man allows mustard dripping from his hot dog to anoint his member. Into this garish meat market—populated by hustlers from Bidgood's New York neighborhood—wander characters imported from turn-of-the-century vaudeville and German silent films. Part comic expressionism, part Jean Genet, this sequence offers a phantasmagoric vision of a bygone Times Square overrun with hookers, outcasts, and madmen. Bidgood adds to this spectacle an ironic soundtrack: a radio announcer banally opines on healthy breakfasts, stock market reports, and the impotence of Congress, while the bacchanal proceeds unabated.

In its final section, the film returns to the boy's chiffon bedroom, as the sleepy coda from Mussorgsky's *Night on Bald Mountain* slips into the soundtrack. The scene fades into the nocturnal forest of the film's opening, where the young man, naked and wet, makes love to moist leaves. Implicitly, his object of desire tentatively becomes nature, not himself. Sacred choral music rises on the soundtrack, providing a counterpoint to the boy's pagan eros. As the line between sacred and profane dissolves, so does the distinction between Narcissus and his mirror image. The film fades again to the bedroom, now visited by a bowler-hatted gentleman. Played by the gay dramatist Charles Ludlam (who died of AIDS at forty-four), the gentleman had been briefly seen earlier in the Times Square sequence. Presumably, he is the young man's patron, but perhaps he is also Narcissus in another reality, aged a generation or two. Through crosscut gazes, the older gentleman seems to transform into Narcissus. Suddenly, to the sound of shattering glass, a "crack" appears in the film image, as if the film stock itself were fissuring. Initially, Bidgood seems to perpetrate an act of avant-garde self-referentiality, much like the moment in Bergman's *Persona* (1966) when the celluloid image rips apart, revealing clips of primitive silent films and the illusory apparatus of cinema itself. But Bidgood does not expose a hidden cinematic subconscious. As the camera dollies back, what appeared as a metacinematic "crack" in the film turns out to be a strand of the spider's web that foregrounded the film's opening shot. Illusion having looped reality, the film dissolves a final time into the nocturnal forest of dreams.

For decades, *Pink Narcissus* had been something of a myth itself, a cult film originally released without a director identified on screen. The ending credits on extant prints still read "Directed by Anonymous." Though enhancing the film's mystique, this directorial enigma had rather ordinary origins: angry with producers who recut the film without his permission, Bidgood simply disowned the work. Throughout the 1970s and 1980s, *Pink Narcissus* had been "erroneously attributed to both Andy Warhol and Kenneth Anger" and even a closeted Hollywood bigwig (Edgecomb 2006). One could perhaps mistake the film's fetishistic kitsch for the Anger of *Scorpio Rising* (196d), though Bidgood's visual imagination is far more painstaking. Attributing *Pink Narcissus* to Warhol, however, seems entirely unaccountable, for the film's stylization and seven-year production schedule are antithetical to Warhol's habit of artless improvisation. And of course, Warhol abhorred anonymity.

Today, *Pink Narcissus* stands as a masterpiece—perhaps *the* masterpiece—of underground gay kitsch aesthetics, frequently appearing on critics' lists of landmark queer films. Yet the film's ideas extend beyond matters of visual style and erotic excess. Starkly juxtaposing the "interior" bedroom sequences and "exterior" street scenes, the film draws a distinction between the purity of the erotic imagination and the sordid world of commercial exchange. The hermetic visions of Kendall's Narcissus are a world removed from the street scenes, whose prostitutes, hustlers, and exhibitionists engage in crassly materialistic transactions (clearly inspired by Bidgood's own New York environs). Paradoxically, it is the cloistered, hermetic world that sparks freer fantasies, while the streets seem confined and cramped, with pulsing arrows commanding one's gaze. Alternating between a Narcissistic dreamworld and commercial, pulpy images of sex, Bidgood recalls literary critic Frank Kermode's distinction between timeless myth and timely fiction. In *The Sense of an Ending*, Kermode distinguishes mythology from everyday fiction: "Myths are the agents of stability, fictions the agents of change. Myths call for absolute[s], fictions for conditional assent. Myths make sense in terms of a lost order of time . . . fictions, if successful, make sense of the here and now, *hoc tempus*" (Kermode 1967, 39). In Bidgood's film, Narcissistic myth embraces multiple times, spaces, and cultures. Erotic bullfighters become Arabian sultans reincarnated as leathered motorcyclists—yet every metamorphosing vision is only a part of a larger unconscious "stability" that orders desire and is symbolized by the dark, unchanging forest that bookends the film. The urban interludes, meanwhile, are prefabricated "fictions" in Kermode's sense, embedded in the "here and now" of a specific material history: the sleazy, X-rated Times Square of the 1960s and 1970s, now the sanitized home of corporate chain restaurants and the Disney Store.

Importantly, no dialectic emerges between the interior and the exterior, between hermetic myths and meretricious fictions. Each realm remains discrete, never intersecting. Though Bidgood extracts obvious joy from the streets' neon sleaze, he clearly privileges the mythic element, which, like the film itself, is esoteric, anticommercial, and intended for a select audience. On another level, the film's absence of legible narrative elides the difference between myth and fiction altogether, just as the film's abstracted yet explicit sexuality overcomes distinctions between eternal art and transient pornography. The film's own "mythic" anonymity acquires other meanings, too, for it once placed the film outside conventional (and reductive) discourses of auteurism. Though no longer anonymous, *Pink Narcissus* stands as a work of utter self-creation, a lasting testament to a wholly autonomous filmmaker operating outside the world of marketing, promotion, and other commercial trappings of cinematic "fiction."

See also *Beefcake; The Genesis Children; Nijinsky; Score.*

Bibliography

Edgecomb, Sean Fredric. "Camping out with James Bidgood: The Auteur of *Pink Narcissus* Tells All." *Bright Lights Film Journal.* May 1, 2006. Accessed May 16, 2021. https://brightlightsfilm .com/camping-james-bidgood-auteur-pink-narcissus-tells/#.YKDOk6hKgu0.

Hastert, Wolfgang. *The Queer Reveries of James Bidgood.* Documentary film. Germany/USA: Wolfgang Astert Films, Zweites Deutsches Fernsehen, 2000.

Kermode, Frank. *The Sense of an Ending.* New York, NY: Oxford University Press, 1967.

—Andrew Grossman

PORTRAIT OF JASON (1967)

DIRECTOR: Shirley Clarke
SCREEPLAY: n/a
CAST: Jason Holliday/Alan Payne (himself), Shirley Clarke (herself)
SPECS: 105 minutes; black and white
AVAILABILITY: DVD/Blu-ray (Milestone)

"My name is Jason Holliday . . . my name is Jason Holliday . . . my name is Alan Payne." So laughs the impish, inscrutable subject of Shirley Clarke's legendary documentary, a filmed monologue in which Payne, a gay Black hustler (here using the stage name "Jason Holliday") narrates his adventures in the undergrounds of New York and San Francisco, working variously as a prostitute, houseboy, and entertainer. Traversing boundaries of class and ethnicity, he mixes with people from all walks of life, from geriatric johns to staid psychiatrists obsessed with his deviant sexuality. Above all, he dreams of perfecting a cabaret act in which he plays both hipster and "tragic clown," two roles Holliday has already mastered in real life. Clarke begins each section of Holliday's monologue with deliberately blurry shots that come into focus only when he begins speaking, signifying the aspects of his personae that crystallize in particular moments of his on-camera performance. A natural raconteur and joyful exhibitionist, Holliday is charming and articulate, even if his constant, on-camera intake of joints and cocktails often reduces him to giddy laughter. Acting out bits of his prospective show, he dons numerous masks, impersonating Mae West and tossing off lines from *Gone with the Wind*. As a practiced performer, he knows how to self-consciously engage his depression and anger for dramatic effect, and sometimes comedy and subdued rage seamlessly intermingle. "I've suffered expensively . . . I mean *extensively*," he says, in a revealing, tipsy Freudian slip. Beneath his superficial flamboyance, however, lies the defiance of a queer Black man who has retained his humor and humanity in pre-Stonewall America.

Operating on several thematic and theoretical levels simultaneously, *Portrait of Jason* has endured as a watershed in both queer cinema and the American documentary. Most obviously, the film serves as a highly individualized exposé of gay, urban African American experience circa 1967, when Hollywood was unwilling to legitimize even the lives of gay, middle-class white Americans. (William Friedkin's *The Boys in the Band* would appear three years later; in the interim, Hollywood supplied alleged "comedies" like 1969's *The Gay Deceivers*.)

Jason Holliday as himself in *Portrait of Jason*. Courtesy of Milestone/Photofest.

Notably, Clarke's documentary is distinct from much queer underground cinema of the period, removed as it is from the camp ritual of Kenneth Anger and the hip posturing of the Andy Warhol–Paul Morrissey school. The film stands apart, too, from the era's small handful of queer documentaries, such as Frank Simon's *The Queen* (1968), a celebratory view of the contestants at New York's 1967 "Miss All-America Camp" beauty pageant. Clarke is unconcerned with conventional tropes of publicity, pride, or mass approval: the film reveals Holliday unfiltered. The film's framework is so voyeuristic, in fact, that *Portrait of Jason* continues to arouse controversy and elicit accusations against Clarke for manipulative or even unethical filmmaking practices.

Though Clarke, a white filmmaker, has often identified with African American subjects—as in *The Cool World* (1963) and *Ornette: Made in America* (1985)—some have suggested that she exploits Holliday's intoxicated vulnerability. One might believe that Jason's tearful emotional breakdown toward the film's end is not so much the climax of a narrative arc but the foreseeable effects of pot and booze. Director Paul Morrissey found Clarke's technique and overall presentation not only exploitative but inauthentic. "She got him drunk in front of the camera so he'd cry for her," Morrissey argued. "Didn't she realize our people [that is, queers] were acting? It was all artificial, all performance" (Yacowar 1993, 8). Morrissey's criticism is fairly common—and simplistic. That Holliday delivers a performance for the camera—even an inebriated one—does not mean that the performance is the product of directorial manipulation. Nor is there a necessary or even logical connection between inebriation and inauthenticity. By nature, circumstance, and occupation, Holliday is an actor. For him *not* to deliver a performance would be disingenuous, and he performs without censoring or sanitizing his experience. Holliday's stories about sexually servicing wealthy clients reveal that he is no naïf; like the clever, scheming servant of ancient Roman comedy, he knows more than those he ostensibly serves. Holliday realizes his on-camera presence may be loved or reviled, but ultimately, viewers must take him at his own word: "This is a picture that will be saved forever," he says. "No matter how many times I am ridiculous . . . there was one time in my life when I was together, and this [film] is the result."

Implicit in Morrissey's criticism of Clarke and Holliday is the residue of realist ideology, the assumption that the unpracticed presentation of everyday life, marked by inarticulate banality, constitutes cinematic authenticity. But Holliday's performance, at once spontaneous and consciously crafted, goes beyond surface tenets of realism and challenges conventional notions of self-representation. Arguably, the ways Holliday carefully crafts his personae recall the everyday "dramaturgies" that the sociologist Erving Goffman describes in *The Presentation of Self in Everyday Life*. Goffman theorized that daily living entails performative strategies through which social actors present the selves they want others to see—or the selves they believe others expect to see. In public, people present their "frontstage" selves, selecting appearances, gestures, expressions, vocabularies, and social roles appropriate to each interaction. What people choose not to reveal constitutes a "backstage" hidden from public scrutiny. As Goffman says, "there is hardly a legitimate everyday vocation or relationship whose performers do not engage in concealed practices which are incompatible with fostered impressions" (1959, 42). The fact that some people, like Holliday, are more practiced in their performances may alter the quality or framework of a performance but not the basic *fact* of everyday performance. In the case of a queer Black man navigating mid-1960s America, selective self-presentation obviously becomes a defense mechanism. Holliday's front-stage face does not represent a performance given in bad faith, as Morrissey implies; rather, he deploys a face more strategically multilayered than that which an unoppressed interviewee would present.

Most importantly, because all social actors inevitably harbor frontstage and backstage identities, neither the public nor the private sphere has any claim to ethical superiority. Crucial in Goffman's theory is the idea that our interactional, frontstage selves are no less significant and *no less real* than our private selves. Social actors' frontstage dramaturgies could well elicit productive or innovative concepts that remain dormant or unrealized during private moments. Holliday's demonstrative on-camera performance, therefore, could be activating latent yet genuine feelings and perspectives not sensed off camera. In Goffmanian existentialism, furthermore, there exists no unitary place where an authentic self resides. Solitariness has little bearing on the authenticity of the self, and people's private moments do not transpire in an asocial vacuum. One could imagine Holliday alone, performing before a mirror, as tearful and drunk as he is on screen. From a sociopsychological perspective, then, Morrissey's charge of "inauthenticity" seems all the more spurious. Anyone interviewed on camera will be "performing," insofar as we *all* perform in public—and perhaps in private as well. The voyeuristic presence of the camera simply creates a metaperformance, in this case amplifying the self-consciousness with which Holliday chooses his masks and modes of expression.

As it calls to mind Goffman's view of social performance, *Portrait of Jason* undermines the standard truth claims of documentarian vérité. Holliday is not only a trickster but an unreliable narrator, adept at manipulating his audiences. The film thus stands apart from the contemporaneous "direct cinema" documentaries of Frederick Wiseman (*Titicut Follies*), Albert and David Maysles (*Salesman*), and D. A. Pennebaker (*Monterey Pop*), who prided themselves on the supposed objectivity of handheld cameras, minimally edited takes, and the absence of an omniscient narrator. Allowing its subject to monologize at length, *Portrait of Jason* is unapologetically subjective in its focus and presentation. It would be foolish to argue, as Brian Keith Grant does, that the film presents "an unproblematic view of cinematic realism" or that Clarke, like a traditional documentarian, attempts to "apprehend the world directly" (2006, 94). If Clarke's early shorts— such as the abstract *Bridges-Go-Round* (1958) and Oscar-winning *Skyscraper* (on which she collaborated with Pennebaker)—often deal with the dizzying exteriors of urban life, this film probes a complex subject's inner layers, yet without claiming any one layer as more truthful than another. Employing multiple names and identities, Holliday refuses to be pinned down to the stable truths to which vérité aspires, becoming far craftier than the technology that attempts to contain him.

Rather than positing the documentary form's usual distinction between empowered auteurs and objectified interviewees, *Portrait of Jason* represents a work of collective authorship. Through his commanding presence, Holliday becomes as much a filmmaker as Clarke, who allows Holliday to speak without cutaways or gratuitous editorial intrusions. Thomas Waugh has argued that documentarian interviews can be powerful collaborate tools when filmmakers allow their subjects to speak substantively and without interruption. For Waugh, the interview has been unfairly "shunned by the purist inheritors of the non-interventionist American school of verité," whom he characterizes as "macho fetishists of untampered visual surfaces" (1988, 260). In *Portrait of Jason*, visual surfaces mean little. Rather than realist spectacles of cities, landscapes, or mass scenes, the viewer encounters only Holliday's monologue, inflected with emotional layers that deepen and expand as the film progresses. To the degree that Holliday performs directly for Clarke *and* indirectly for an invisible audience, *Portrait of Jason* offers a "flexible and sensitive format for subject-artist interaction" and becomes "a more faithful reflection of the [interactive] circumstances of filmmaking than the pretense of pure observation affected by the [Frederick] Wiseman school" (Waugh 1988, 260–61).

Taken as a collaborative enterprise between Clarke and Holliday, *Portrait of Jason* disrupts the power dynamic of so many documentaries that position an integral, autonomous auteur above editorially fractured interview subjects. Clarke selectively edits Holliday's monologue, of course, but the sheer length of her takes allows Holliday to dominate the screen. It is not at all ironic that Clarke-Holliday's film presents auteur and interviewee as partners in a dialectical adventure that masquerades as a filmed monologue. As a pre-Stonewall queer film, it is vital that an ethic of equality inform the film's creation, even if myopic viewers might misread Holliday's emotionality as the result of directorial manipulation. In light of Morrissey's charges of "exploitation," it is finally worth noting that *Portrait of Jason* is far less commercialistic than Morrissey's *Flesh* (1968) and *Trash* (1970), which rely on copious nudity to spice up the improvisational ramblings of his undertalented casts. Indeed, if Morrissey's films wanted for a nude Joe Dallesandro, it is doubtful that they would have become cult items or attracted much attention at all. Perhaps most remarkably, *Portrait of Jason* is frankly salacious without being conventionally titillating, exposing not the surfaces of skin but the uncomfortable depths of the psyche.

See also *Beefcake; Boys Beware; I Am Michael; The Times of Harvey Milk.*

Bibliography

Grant, Brian Keith. *Schirmer Encyclopedia of Film*. Vol. 2. New York: Schirmer, 2006.

Goffman, Erving. *The Presentation of Self in Everyday Life*. New York: Doubleday, 1959.

Waugh, Thomas. "Lesbian and Gay Documentary: Minority Self-Imaging, Oppositional Film Practice, and the Question of Image Ethics." In *Image Ethics: The Moral Rights of Subjects in Photographs, Film, and Television*, edited by Larry Gross, John Stuart Katz, and Jay Ruby, 248–72. New York: Oxford University Press, 1988.

Yacowar, Maurice. *The Films of Paul Morrissey*. Cambridge: Cambridge University Press, 1993.

—Andrew Grossman

• R •

RAIN MAN (1988)

DIRECTOR: Barry Levinson
SCREENPLAY: Barry Morrow and Ronald Bass
CAST: Dustin Hoffman (Raymond Babbitt), Tom Cruise (Charlie Babbitt), Valeria
  Golino (Susanna), Jerry Molen (Dr. Gerard Bruner)
SPECS: 134 minutes; color
AVAILABILITY: DVD (MGM)

Rain Man is the story of two brothers, Raymond and Charlie Babbitt. Charlie
learns that his father, with whom he never got along well, has died. The father's
three-million-dollar estate, which Charlie was hoping to inherit, will instead go
to a fund overseen by a doctor at a psychiatric hospital. Infuriated by this discovery, Charlie travels to the institution in Cincinnati, Ohio, where he discovers
that he has a brother named Raymond. The remainder of the movie describes
the relationship between the two brothers as they travel across the country back
to California, where Charlie lives. In the course of this adventure, the movie
presents Raymond's behavior as an autistic person and Charlie's frustration with
him as he tries to gain custody of Raymond to get the three-million-dollar estate.
    Patrick McDonagh calls *Rain Man* the "original autism film" (1999, 184).
Rain Man has been considered a prototype of the representation of disability.
When the movie was released in December 1988, it became a critical and commercial success with positive reviews (Ebert 1988). *Rain Man* became the highest-
grossing film of 1988. It also won four Oscars at the 1989 Academy Awards,
including Best Picture, Best Director, Best Original Screenplay, and Best Actor
in a Leading Role. While the film was highly praised for its portrayal of a person
with autism, the representation of disability in connection to asexuality has so
far been neglected. In this film, Raymond functions as a vehicle to further his
brother Charlie's character development. Able-bodied heterosexuality as represented in Charlie and Susanna's relationship can function as a counterpart of
Raymond's supposed disability and asexuality. Raymond's asexuality and its
connection to disability are never questioned in the movie. Any connection of
Raymond to sexuality simply serves as comic relief for the audience.
    Raymond is a high-functioning "autistic savant" (Treffert 2009, 1351). He is,
for example, terrified when his routines are changed. Likewise, he does not have
any understanding of the concept of money. Nonetheless, Raymond is shown
memorizing the phone book up to the letter G in a matter of a few hours. Overall,
Charlie is also annoyed with Raymond's behavior because they have to structure
the road trip according to Raymond's eccentricities: he is terrified of flying, he
has to watch certain TV programs at certain times, he has to be in bed by exactly
11 p.m., he only eats certain foods on certain days, and he does not want to travel
in the rain. All of this causes delays in their trip.

Raymond is shown as a static character who does not change much and is manipulated by others, whereas Charlie goes through various phases in his development from ruthless yuppie to understanding brother. This representation of disability can be read as an example of what Ato Quayson calls "disability as null set and/or moral test" (2007, 37). According to Quayson, this is perhaps the most obvious literary representation of disability. The author defines it as "some form of ethical background to the actions of other characters, or as a means of testing or enhancing their moral standing" (2007, 36). In *Rain Man*, Raymond and his disabilities function as a test for his brother Charlie's moral standing. When Charlie does not understand him at first, criticizes him, and makes fun of him, Raymond is shown as patient. He eventually shows Charlie a way of accepting him and his "eccentricities," so that Charlie, in the end, concludes, "It is not about the money anymore. . . . Why didn't anybody tell me I had a brother, because it would have been nice to know him for more than just these past six days" [01:53:23–01:53:43]. He finally acknowledges Raymond as his brother, and he accepts him because he is more important to him now than the money that he originally pursued. This scene is meant to show Charlie's development. It leaves out any possible development on Raymond's part. In this reading of Raymond's function in the text, Raymond is simply a vehicle through which Charlie, the able-bodied heterosexual character, learns something about the world. The importance of character development is placed on the able body, while the disabled body is a mere sidekick that teaches something but otherwise remains on the margins. According to Quayson, Raymond functions as a test for Charlie's standing (2007). Raymond, as the supposedly disabled character, helps Charlie as the supposedly able character.

Autism is represented in direct connection to asexuality. This does not mean that asexuality constitutes Raymond's disability. Raymond is primarily characterized as a person with autism, but it is this characterization as disabled that goes hand in hand with the automatic assumption that he must be asexual (i.e., not interested in sex). There are several instances in the film that address Raymond in some sexual context, but the characters around him assume that Raymond, in his almost childlike behavior, cannot be sexual or that he does not understand sexuality. In fact, Raymond is seen as confirming these assumptions in his "odd" behavior in situations that relate to sex or sexual behavior. He simply reacts differently from how most people would react in such situations, which the movie uses to further this image of the asexual disabled body. The movie presents a naturalized connection between disability and asexuality.

After Charlie kidnaps Raymond from his home at Wallbrook, Charlie, Susanna, and Raymond share a suite in a hotel on their road trip. Even though there are separate rooms and Raymond occupies his own space, the doors are left open and Raymond can hear noises from the room that Charlie and Susanna occupy. Though the audience understands what the noise means, Raymond carefully makes his way toward it and accidentally discovers Susanna and Charlie having sex in the neighboring room. Raymond imitates Susanna's moans, but he does not understand what he is doing [00:33:35]. He stands in front of Susanna and Charlie's bed and just watches the scene for a few seconds. He loses interest pretty much immediately as he sits down on the bed and turns toward the running TV [00:33:45]. It is clear to the audience that he does not know what he has just witnessed, nor does he seem to care much.

Once Susanna and Charlie notice Raymond, however, their reactions differ. While Susanna just acknowledges his presence and states that Raymond is in the room, Charlie's reaction is anger [00:34:00]. He does not want Raymond there at this intimate moment, and he starts shouting at him, "Get out!" [00:34:05]. Even though the scene is awkward and Charlie is presented as angry, he seems to sense that Raymond does not really understand what has been going on. Charlie follows Raymond into his room to explain the situation: "Well, those noises are none of your business, you understand that, huh?" [00:34:35]. In this scene, Charlie feels his masculinity and intimacy with Susanna threatened as he realizes that Raymond is in the room, watching a scene that he should not witness. But this threat does not last long since Charlie realizes immediately that Raymond does not understand, hence does not pose a "danger." It remains questionable how both Susanna and Charlie assumed instantly that Raymond did not understand the situation. This indicates that they do not take Raymond seriously, especially not when it comes to sexual behavior. They simply assume that he has no sexual interest whatsoever. This scene in the hotel room plays on these assumptions as it represents Raymond turning toward the TV.

When Raymond and Charlie are in Las Vegas, there is another instance that also points toward the assumption that Raymond is asexual and has no real interest in, or understanding of, sex, dating, and relationships. When Raymond takes a break from making money for Charlie by counting cards, he finds himself sitting at a bar—a rare filmic moment of Raymond being on his own. In his expensive new outfit and equipped with a new hairstyle that Charlie imposed on Raymond to make him look "acceptable" in the casino, a woman notices Raymond and keeps smiling at him. She eventually walks over to Raymond to start a conversation with him that is soon interrupted by Charlie, supposedly trying to save Raymond from trouble [01:35:38]. Again, this confirms the assumption that Charlie sees Raymond as an asexual character who cannot possibly be interested in dating, relationships, and sex—while the woman does not know Raymond and assumes none of these things.

The conversation ends abruptly after Raymond asks the woman if she takes any prescription medications [01:36:30]. As she almost runs off, Raymond does not pick up on the fact that the woman has just left him and does not seem likely to want to see him again. Even though he does not read the signs of the situation as most people might understand them, this inquiry reveals, in a surprising twist from the assumptions held so far by Charlie and possibly Susanna, that Raymond does have an understanding of dates and relationships. This scene is followed by a discussion between Raymond and Charlie. Charlie asks Raymond if he liked the woman, and his reply once again implies innocence and a focus on nonsexual attributes: "Yes, she is very sparkly," referring to the jewels and the necklace that the woman was wearing [01:36:57]. Raymond keeps reminding Charlie in the following scenes that he needs to be back at the bar at 10:00 p.m. for his date. Charlie's reactions are a continuation of his assumptions of Raymond being asexual. He brushes Raymond's insistence aside with a laugh, but they nevertheless go to the hotel bar around 10:00 p.m. Their expectations are, however, quite different. While Raymond is convinced that he will meet Iris again for their date, Charlie knows—and viewers are invited to think the same—that Iris will not be there because Charlie supposedly read the signs of the encounter right, while Raymond stubbornly insists on the date.

Susanna arrives at the same conclusion about Raymond's date as Charlie. She exclaims in surprise, "He has a date?" [01:43:41]. This question can be read in a similar way as Charlie's reactions: Susanna assumes he is asexual because he is disabled. His insistence on a date with Iris is at best presented as laughable: it can simply not be true. Susanna and Charlie "know" this since they are part of the able-bodied heterosexual majority, but Raymond does not understand this. This crucial knowledge that Raymond is supposedly missing makes the audience feel pity for him. As soon as a doubt of his asexuality is raised by Raymond's insistence on a date, it is taken away immediately. The audience is reminded of Raymond's disability, and any possibility of a sexual encounter seems impossible by definition.

There is one more attempt in the movie, though, to test this hypothesis. When Susanna and Raymond are by themselves in an elevator in the hotel, she "seduces" him into a kiss [01:47:00]. Previously, Susanna had felt sorry for Raymond for what Charlie has been doing to him. This kiss seems to be her attempt at sympathizing with Raymond, as much as it is a test of his feelings. After the kiss, she asks him how it was, and he replies, "Wet" [01:47:33]. This, in turn, makes Susanna smile and realize that Raymond either does not understand what just happened or that he has a different idea about it. Beyond his comment, Raymond is completely indifferent, which makes Susanna think that her attempt failed.

Some scenes and instances in *Rain Man* potentially disrupt able-bodied heterosexuality, but they are not enough to question the general assumptions of the connection between disability and asexuality. While Raymond's behavior sometimes challenges the assumptions about him as an asexual person with a disability, the movie presents a naturalized link between disability and asexuality. This ultimately reinforces able-bodied heterosexuality as represented in Susanna and Charlie's relationship, whereas Raymond signifies disability and asexuality. The character remains a vehicle through which "the norm" is stabilized. Raymond's disability and asexuality are not questioned by other characters. Raymond helps his Charlie grow as an individual, but he himself remains static. As Raymond returns to Wallbrook and as Susanna and Charlie return to their regular life in California, the assumptions about disability and asexuality remain largely unchallenged. Raymond, as represented through the other characters, continues to be seen as different, disabled, and asexual.

See also *American Beauty; Philadelphia; A Single Man.*

Bibliography

Asexual Visibility and Education Network. https://www.asexuality.org/en/.

Ebert, Roger. "Review of *Rain Man*." RogerEbert.com, December 16, 1988. Accessed May 26, 2021. https://www.rogerebert.com/reviews/rain-man-1988.

McDonagh, Patrick. "Autism and the Modern Identity: Autism Anxiety in Popular Film." *Disability Studies Quarterly* 19, no. 3 (1999): 184–91.

McRuer, Robert. *Crip Theory: Cultural Signs of Queerness and Disability.* New York: New York University Press, 2006.

Quayson, Ato. *Aesthetic Nervousness: Disability and the Crisis of Representation.* New York: Columbia University Press, 2007.

Treffert, Darold A. "The Savant Syndrome: An Extraordinary Condition; A Synopsis: Past, Present, Future." *Philosophical Transactions of the Royal Society B: Biological Sciences* 364, no. 1522 (May 2009): 1351–57. https://www.ncbi.nlm.nih.gov/pmc/articles/PMC2677584/.

—Jana Fedtke

RED RIVER (1948)

DIRECTOR: Howard Hawks

SCREENPLAY: Borden Chase and Charles Schnee, based on the novel *Red River: Blazing Guns on the Chisholm Trail* by Borden Chase

CAST: Walter Brennan (Nadine Groot), Montgomery Clift (Matt Garth), Joanne Dru (Tess Millay), John Ireland (Cherry Valance), John Wayne (Thomas Dunson)

SPECS: 126/133 minutes; black and white

AVAILABILITY: DVD/Blu-ray (Criterion Collection)

Howard Hawks's classic Western begins as young cattle rustler Thomas Dunson, accompanied by grizzled old-timer Groot, dreams of becoming a cattle baron with his own personal brand. He comes across the sole survivor of an Indian raid, adolescent Matt Garth, and soon becomes a father figure to the boy. Imagining his future cattle brand, Dunson draws two parallel lines in the sand, apparently symbolizing the banks of the Red River yet also suggesting the pair's tandem paths. When Matt asks why the prospective brand features Dunson's initial but not an "M" for himself, the elder man responds, "I'll put an 'M' on it when you earn it." Cut to fourteen years later, when Dunson is now a determined yet immoral cattle baron who brands neighboring cattle as his own. Matt is now a young man returned from the Civil War, which has economically ravaged Dunson's empire. As Dunson and Matt plan a cattle drive to Missouri—where a better market presumably awaits—they are joined by freelancing gunhand Cherry Valance. Dunson's men encounter hardship and deprivation on the trail, yet he grows increasingly stern and heartless, putting profits above his men. When a careless hireling causes a deadly stampede, Dunson aims to flog him. The hireling pulls a gun in self-defense, but Matt wounds him in the shoulder, preventing a shootout in which Dunson would surely kill the man. Disillusioned with Dunson's cruel stewardship, the rank and file threaten to mutiny; to maintain order, Dunson, now drinking heavily, plans to hang deserters captured by Cherry, who remains loyal to Dunson. Realizing Dunson is descending into despotism—and perhaps madness—Matt clashes openly with his surrogate father. In a moment that restages the earlier contest between Dunson and the incompetent underling, Cherry wounds Dunson in his shooting hand when Matt pulls his gun. Matt, however, commands the men's loyalty and commandeers the cattle. An enraged, forsaken Dunson swears vengeance, while Matt strikes out on his own, destined to meet Dunson once again in a final showdown.

From silent-era features such as *Hell's Hinges* (1916) and *The Covered Wagon* (1923), to John Ford's genre-defining *Stagecoach* (1939), to cartoonish Hollywood adventures like *Dodge City* (1939) and *The Return of Frank James* (1940), the classical Hollywood Western had reiterated a fairly one-dimensional typology of the cowboy hero. Whether an outlaw (like John Wayne in *Stagecoach* [1939]) or a lawman (like Errol Flynn in *Dodge City* [1940]), the Western gunslinger was not only stoic and stalwart but also sexually repressed. Perhaps no Western epitomized the formula more than George Stevens's elegiac *Shane* (1953), whose titular hero longs for a lovely homesteader but rides off into the sunset alone, obeying esoteric manly codes. The ideology of the traditional Western rested on what might be called a "geography" of heteronormative masculinity: the further West the pioneer traveled, and the greater distance he put between himself and an effete East, the greater his manliness became. Yet because the cowboy hero rarely acted sexually, his performance of straightness was more or less indistinguishable from asexuality. The chaste cowboy hero labored under a paradox: while his inherent heterosexuality is taken for granted, his itinerant lifestyle excludes him from the married, domestic life through which that heterosexuality would come to fruition.

All of this, of course, was the mythology of the *old* Hollywood Western, where sexualities censored by the Hays Code hid behind the cowboy's manly yet prudish swagger. Released in 1948, nine years after John Ford's *Stagecoach* had raised the genre to a genuine art form, Hawks's *Red River* was arguably the first Western to complicate the old model of cowboy masculinity, allowing the hero's buried sexuality—including a latent homosexuality—to rise above the stoic surface. Adapted by Borden Chase from a story originally published in the *Saturday Evening Post*, *Red River* paved the way for the "adult" Westerns of the 1950s, which psychologized the cowboy and absorbed from film noir the notion of a morally ambiguous hero (Chase also cowrote Anthony Mann's tough, noirish 1950 Western *Winchester '73*). As André Bazin had observed, the adult Western's focus on sex and pseudo-Freudian psychology was not so much an addition to a well-worn genre but the belated explication of themes long suppressed.

In *Red River*, Hawks and Chase create images of nuanced, flawed masculinity never before seen in a Western. The film's protagonists are insecure, neurotic, and even susceptible to paranoiac madness (a condition that befalls John Wayne's Dunson). Within this anxious homosocial world arise distinct manifestations of manly love—the implicitly queer attraction between Montgomery Clift's Matt and John Ireland's Cherry and the estranged filial-paternal bond between Matt and Dunson (which *perhaps* harbors an erotic component, if one wishes to see it). Eventually, a heteronormative love story develops between Matt and Tess, a feisty frontierswoman he rescues from marauding Indians. Apart from providing an obligatory love interest, Tess represents a voice of civilized reason within an overridingly masculine wilderness.

Narratively and erotically, the film can be divided into two parts. The first, arranged around the homosocial world of the cattle drive, establishes three sets of dyadic male relationships: Dunson-Matt (as father and adopted son), Matt-Cherry (as rivals or implicit lovers), and Dunson-Cherry (as surrogate father and "alternate" son). The homoerotic tension between Matt and Cherry (whose name alone should raise eyebrows) is hardly veiled, and their initial meeting is laden with double entendres. Eyeing Matt's hip, Cherry remarks, "That's a good-looking gun you were about to use back there . . . can I see it?" Accepting Cherry's weapon, Matt responds, "Maybe you'd like to see mine." As if to defuse the mutually admiring, phallic wordplay, Cherry delivers a line that even the screenwriters must have known was terrible: "There are only two things more beautiful than a good gun: a Swiss watch, or a woman from anywhere." The pair then engage in target practice with airborne tin cans, as gunplay substitutes for erotic discharge. As if to extend the double entendres, Walter Brennan's Groot remarks that Cherry and Matt are "sizing each other up for the future." In later years, Hawks was coy—or feigned coyness—when queried about the film's homoerotic underpinnings. In a 1974 interview, Joseph McBride and Gerald Peary noted that Hawks's Westerns often end with a shot of two men together rather than an image of a heterosexual couple. "Some people have said that the male characters in your films border on homosexuality," they prompt. "What do you think of that?" Hawks replied, "I'd say it's a goddamn silly statement to make. It sounds like a homosexual speaking"—though McBride and Peary's text parenthetically notes that Hawks "smiles" while answering their question (McBride and Peary 2006, 80). Of course, Clift *was* gay, and both he and Ireland milk *Red River*'s subtext to the hilt, whether Hawks intended them to or not.

In the film's second part, when Matt has abandoned Cherry and an increasingly megalomaniacal Dunson, the film's homosocial-cum-homoerotic entanglements are (ostensibly) supplanted by heteronormative romance. Leading the cattle drive, Matt encounters Indians besieging a wagon train he believes is populated by gamblers and loose women. Among the besieged is a "good" woman, Tess, in desperate need of rescue. Tess is a typical Hawks "heroine"—gutsy, strong willed, and loquacious. In a disarming moment, Tess asks Matt why he seems so perturbed as they fend off hordes of Indians. Suddenly, an arrow flies through her shoulder and pins her to a wooden wagon wheel. Without missing a beat, she unblinkingly continues her end of the conversation—an outlandish, curiously funny moment that recalls the screwball Hawks of *Bringing Up Baby* (1938). Belatedly realizing she has been impaled, Tess winces, as if suffering a painful sexual penetration. The scene's (hetero)sexual symbolism is not terribly convincing, however, especially as Joanne Dru's highly stylized acting (in this moment) clashes with the film's otherwise naturalistic performances. Furthermore, heterosexuality is here symbolically inverted, since Matt goes on to *remove* the phallic allow. Matt and Tess nevertheless fall instantly in love, in a manner possible only through the shortcuts of Hollywood screenwriting.

As Matt leaves to finally sell the cattle, Dunson catches up with the cattle drive and encounters Tess, whom Matt has temporarily left alone. In the film's moral turning point, Tess professes to Dunson her love for Matt and begs him to forego his vendetta. When Tess—perhaps disingenuously—says that she'll bear Dunson a biological child if he'll forego revenge, Dunson bitterly reveals that he once thought of Matt as a real son: "He knew someday it would all be his . . . his land, his cattle, the whole thing." Yet Tess's pleadings cannot assuage Dunson. Knowing Matt would not have the heart to kill Dunson in self-defense, Cherry attempts to stop Dunson but is summarily killed himself, though he manages to wound Dunson in the side. Bleeding and incensed, Dunson advances on Matt and goads him into a fight. "Won't anything make a man out of you?" he screams at Matt, firing off rounds that barely miss him. As the two finally fight hand to hand, Tess intervenes, shooting indiscriminately and imploring them to realize what should be obvious: "Anybody with half a mind would know you two love each other!" The two men stare blankly, dumbfounded by her outburst, which not only short-circuits the film's climax but privileges a pacifist, female voice in a masculinist genre. Drained of energy and ire, Dunson turns and deadpans, "You'd better marry that girl, Matt." With paternal love restored through feminine civility, Dunson finally adds an "M" to his trademark, and the two men are figuratively united in branded flesh.

First-time viewers of *Red River* might be disappointed in the script's convenient (re)solutions. After an incredibly tense buildup—Wayne had never been so brutal on screen—Tess's miraculous intercession restores balance to masculine relations in a matter of seconds. The conclusion must also nullify the film's overtures to bisexuality. With Cherry dead and Matt's love for Dunson established as purely filial, the film neatly pairs off Matt and Tess, the film's only significant female character.

Yet the film's ending is as subversive as it is anticlimactic. Violating the bloody rules of the Western genre, *Red River*'s pacifist conclusion allows Wayne's Dunson to be redeemed by love, a resolution obviously unavailable to most Western antagonists, who are either killed or condemned to history's dustbin. (Wayne's equally obsessive Ethan Edwards suffers the latter fate in *The Searchers* [1956] because his *racist* violence is ideologically irredeemable.) *Red River*'s themes of forgiveness and redemption present a more nuanced view of the simplistic dichotomy between savagery and civilization underpinning the Western genre. Here "civilization" is not represented by a burgeoning desert town, the coming of the railroad, or other "exterior" signs of community or technology but by the resolution of characters' ethical struggles. Likewise, savagery is not represented by an outlaw or desperado, for all of the male characters emerge from and operate within the wilderness; even Matt is only *relatively* ethical, for he was complicit in Dunson's horse wrangling from the start. Traditional Westerns extolled the "new" civilization catalyzed by pioneers, but precious few Westerns—at least before the rise of the revisionist, anti-imperialist Westerns of the 1970s—paused to ask what kind of civilization would be built. If American civilization is to progress, it must not only put aside gunslinging violence but learn humility and rebuke the genre-defining quest for vengeance. In this, *Red River* applies a rare Christian solution to the problems of the traditional Western, a genre that often pretended to embrace Christian ethics but seldom turned the other cheek.

The film's pacifistic anticlimax clearly informs the ways *Red River* recasts Western tropes of masculinity. While scholars often have focused on the queer implications of Matt and Cherry's initial meeting, in which they admire one another's "rods," the film is more than a closeted game of spot-the-subtext. The film was remarkable for presenting a new image of Hollywood masculinity in the person of Clift, who gives one of Hollywood's very first method performances. Hawks instructed Clift to underplay, creating a contrast with Wayne's larger-than-life persona (a contrast augmented by the real-life tension between archconservative Wayne and gay, liberal Clift, who reportedly did *not* enjoy one another's company). The tension between the actors is expressed physically. Always gazing downward and seemingly within, Clift enacts a sensitive, brooding masculinity distinct from the genre's typical, rough-hewn hero. Generally framing scenes in medium shots, Hawks allows Clift to express hesitation, shyness, and insecurity with his limbs and the nervous, actorly "business" of his hands. Clift's introspecting performance undermines the Western's gendered assumptions—here the male's stoicism is a sign of neurosis, not of strength, while Tess is the one who is transparent and straight talking.

Though younger audiences might see *Red River* as a relic of the Hollywood closet, late twentieth and early twenty-first-century Hollywood has delivered precious few queer variants on Western mythology. In many ways, allegedly "liberal" Hollywood is still terrified to violate its timeworn and intertwined constructions of genre and gender. Ang Lee's *Brokeback Mountain* (2005) might have garnered mainstream adulation, but few would call it a genuine Western; certainly, it does little to subvert the foundational myths of westward expansion and Manifest Destiny. To find more germane examples, one might have to revisit Maggie Greenwald's gender-bending *The Ballad of Little Jo* (1993), about an outcast young woman who travels west in male guise; to George Englund's psychedelic, homoerotic hippie Western *Zacharia* (1971); or even to Joseph Mankiewicz's *There Was a Crooked Man* (1970), which features John Randolph and Hume Cronyn as bickering gay partners growing grey in an Old West prison, dreaming of settling down in a little cottage after their parole.

See also *Fight Club*.

Bibliography

McBride, Joseph, and Gerald Peary. "Hawks Talks: New Anecdotes from the Old Master." *Film Comment* 10, no. 2 (May–June 1974). Reprinted in Scott Breivold, ed., *Howard Hawks Interviews* (Jackson: University Press of Mississippi, 2006).

—Andrew Grossman

ROPE (1948)

DIRECTOR: Alfred Hitchcock
SCREENPLAY: Arthur Laurents, Hume Cronyn (adaptation), Ben Hecht (uncredited), based on the play of the same name by Anthony Walter Patrick Hamilton
CAST: John Dall (Brandon), Constance Collier (Mrs. Atwater), Edith Evanson (Mrs. Wilson), Farley Granger (Phillip), James Stewart (Rupert Cadell)
SPECS: 78 minutes; color
AVAILABILITY: DVD (Universal Studios Home Entertainment)

Hitchcock's twist on the infamous Leopold-Loeb murder case is ingeniously simple. Rich preppies—and implicit lovers—Brandon and Phillip strangle their friend David on a lark, right before their mutual friends arrive for a dinner party. Claiming the right to kill those he deems "inferior," Brandon sees murder as little more than an intellectual diversion. "The Davids of this world merely occupy space," Brandon tells Phillip. "This is why he was the perfect victim for the perfect murder." To increase the excitement of his deadly game, Brandon conceals David's fresh corpse within a chest he uses as a serving table, as if daring his guests to discover the evidence of his crime. In addition to their close circle of friends—all of whom naturally wonder about David's curious absence—the pair also invite their former prep school headmaster, Rupert, to see if they can stump a rare man they respect. Knowing that Rupert is also an elitist who espouses a pseudo-Nietzschean philosophy, Brandon even suspects that his old headmaster might sympathize with his amoral worldview. As the assembled players sit down to dinner, Brandon muses about murder and Nietzschean amorality, but the provocative banter makes Phillip, Brandon's partner in crime, anxious and unhinged. Sensing Phillip's growing caginess, Rupert begins to catch on. After much excruciating cat and mouse, Rupert finally throws open the chest to discover David's corpse (which remains off camera). To arouse the police, Rupert fires off a gun Brandon previously had hidden in his pocket. Sinking into despair, Rupert realizes the emptiness of what he had once professed, yet he also takes satisfaction in the knowledge that Brandon and Phillip might now face execution themselves.

Like Richard Fleischer's *Compulsion* (1959) and Tom Kalin's *Swoon* (1992), Hitchcock's *Rope* draws on the Leopold-Loeb murder case of the 1920s, and like the director's later *Strangers on a Train* (1951) and *Vertigo* (1958), its plot centers on the conceit of planning a "perfect murder." *Rope* is best remembered, however, for Hitchcock's experimentation with unbroken takes, which allow the film to unfold in real time on a single set, and for a decidedly queer subtext that slipped past the priggish Hays censors. Though *Rope* borrows its scenario from Patrick Hamilton's 1929 stage play—alternately known as *Rope* and *Rope's End*—Hitchcock's stylistic experiment belies the film's theatrical origins. Hitchcock's fluid takes, lasting six to ten minutes each, nimbly roam through the apartment set, intimately drawing the viewer into characters' private moments. (The technique calls attention to itself only when Hitchcock camouflages cuts by dollying the camera toward a character's back or a piece of furniture, creating a momentary "black" space through which two takes can be spliced.) For a director so identified with the excitement of rhythmic montage—from *Psycho*'s shower scene to the attic attack of Tippi Hedrin in *The Birds* (1963)—the long takes might seem uncharacteristic. As Robin Wood has suggested, however, Hitchcock's continuous mise en scène becomes just as cruelly manipulative as the fifty-two slashing cuts that mark Janet Leigh's demise in *Psycho*. Whereas the prolonged *static* takes of many directors—Andrei Tarkovsky, for instance—allow viewers' gazes some freedom to wander, Hitchcock's restless camera constantly prowls around characters, narrowly directing our eyes to certain faces and our ears to eavesdropped conversations. Hitchcock's invasive technique thus becomes, as Wood says, "another means of exerting total control of the gaze and the emotional response of the viewer" (1989, 350).

If Hitchcock manipulates the spectator's gaze, he also forces us to identify with the film's scheming gay protagonists and become complicit in their amorality—quite a bold gesture for the Hollywood of 1948. According to Hollywood historian William Mann, Hitchcock actively sought to make a film that, like *Strangers on a Train*, would link queerness with moral deviance. (Karger 2017). Though today such an equation is embarrassingly passé, it nevertheless flew in the face of Hollywood standards of the day, which expunged any hint of nonheteronormative identity. The film's allusions to queer sexuality are as much a game as its murder plot and possibly even less discreet. Brandon and Phillip's housekeeper, Mrs. Wilson, implies that the two men, both in their twenties, share not only an apartment but a bedroom, remarking that "both must have gotten up on the wrong side of the bed." She later tells Rupert that Brandon and Phillip have been "bickering all day" (like a married couple), and the two men's intimate proximity to one another throughout the film suggests more than criminal conspiracy. Allusions to the men's relationship also reveal Hitchcock's penchant for wry humor. When a young female guest asks if he wants some chicken, Phillip responds, "I don't eat it," only for her to respond, "How queer!" Pressing him to explain his disdain for chicken, she continues, "There must a reason. . . . Freud says there's a reason for everything!" Though an apparently glib response, her suggestion that "everything" has a Freudian explanation implies to the viewer that his sadistic murder of David also has a Freudian—that is, sexual—rationale.

Even without the coy wordplay, Hitchcock creates a palpably sexual tension from the film's very first image: the close-up strangulation of David, a moment nearly as sexualized as the necktie asphyxiation Hitchcock would stage twenty-four years later in *Frenzy* (1972). The historical Leopold and Loeb murdered a fourteen-year-old boy, a crime of (presumably) pederastic sadism beyond the pale of 1940s Hollywood. Yet Hitchcock has his antiheroes commit an even crueler crime, murdering not a passing stranger but a dear friend to prove their "superhumanity." The cruelty is compounded by the visual and moral manipulations Wood ascribes to Hitchcock, who from the outset invests only the audience with the killers' knowledge and perceptions. (Though he represents conventional morality, Jimmy Stewart's Rupert is technically the antagonist.) Hitchcock draws viewers into the killers' confidence and forces the audience to hope—at least partly—that the pair will get away with murder (much as viewers partly want Robert Walker's queer killer to escape capture in *Strangers on a Train*). Of course, the qualifier "partly" is the rub, for the film's overtures to transgression are overwritten by Hollywood's old production code, which not only punishes deviance but makes viewers feel guilty for momentarily siding with evil.

The audience's allegiance to Brandon and Phillip is somewhat weakened by their adolescent understanding of Nietzsche, whose *ubermensch* transcends conventional morality more through Zarathustran magnanimity than through homicidal supper parties. One can ultimately reject Brandon's conceits not because he misunderstands or perverts Nietzsche per se, but because he conforms Nietzschean amorality to his own petty, narcissistic desires. While Brandon sees murder only as sport, not politics, his elitist ideology comes dangerously close to Nazism; under different circumstances, the film suggests, Brandon might have eagerly served the Aryan cause, executing genocide rather than a single murder. Brandon's sense of class hierarchy and privilege is further projected in the film's penthouse set. As his twisted parlor game unfolds, the viewer constantly sees though the set's high windows a cityscape populated with "lowly" mortals Brandon surely holds in contempt.

Brandon reveals his elitist worldview during dinnertime small talk, provocatively suggesting to Rupert that murder need not be immoral and in fact could be an art form reserved for the privileged few. Believing that Brandon is only being irreverent, Rupert responds facetiously: "Think of the problems it would solve, poverty . . . [or] standing in line for theater tickets!" When an older gentleman objects to such tasteless banter, Brandon becomes defensive and attempts—rather clumsily—to distance himself from fascism. "Hitler should be hanged first on account of idiocy," Brandon announces, implying (but never stating) that Hitler's fatal mistake was choosing the wrong people to kill. In the film's denouement, after discovering David's corpse, a stunned Rupert renounces his cavalier opinions about murder. "Something deep inside me would never let me do it!" he cries, asserting a moral compass lacking in the sociopathic Brandon. With conscious irony, Rupert then says to Brandon, "You're going to die." In his final speech, Rupert endorses the death penalty with relish, even fury—not exactly the humanistic sentiment one might expect, given the circumstances. The line carries a particular sting coming from Jimmy Stewart, so often an exemplar of homespun American rectitude. Perhaps only in Anthony Mann's psychological western *The Man from Laramie* (1955) does Stewart summon such wrath—and even then, only after enduring torture. By comparison, Richard Fleischer's *Compulsion*, a thinly veiled depiction of the Leopold and Loeb murder that glosses over their sexual relationship, ends with defense attorney Orson Welles delivering a twenty-minute sermon on the immorality of capital punishment.

True to his *Mr. Smith Goes to Washington* persona, Stewart supposedly was unaware of *Rope*'s rampant queer subtext, but Hitchcock knew that savvy audiences would catch on. As Mann notes, Hitchcock purposefully cast Granger and Dall, two actors known as gay by Hollywood insiders (Karger 2017). Co-screenwriter Arthur Laurents was also "out" in Hollywood circles, as was Adrian, the costumer. In fact, with the husky stage actress Constance Collier playing Mrs. Atwater, one of the dinner guests, Hitchcock feared the film might be *too* queer, thinking that "audiences would perceive Mrs. Atwater as a lesbian, given [Collier's] low voice" (Greven 2017, 129). But all of this gamesmanship adds up to much more than a wink to knowing audiences and a raspberry blown at Hays-era censors. *Rope* might be the first Hollywood film to invite audiences to side—at least tentatively—with ostensibly gay protagonists. In a film suffused with gay undertones and in which murder and "amoral" sexuality are conspicuously conflated, Rupert symbolically yanks Brandon and Phillip from the closet when he throws open the chest to expose David's corpse. One might assume that Brandon and Phillip's quasi-Nietzschean posturing makes them difficult to identify with, but a sympathetic reading of the characters would see beyond their intellectual affectations. In Robin Wood's sensitive analysis, Brandon and Phillip's misanthropy is only the symptom of a self-hatred born of internalized homophobia. The pair's artificial aloofness betrays an attempt to overcompensate for childhood insecurities likely suffered during a homophobic upbringing. Without such a childhood, Brandon's psychosis—and his loss of faith in humanity—would never have been nurtured. Such a reading invests *Rope*, one of Hitchcock's mostly tightly wrought exercises in cruelty, with a bittersweetness that tempers its sadistic veneer.

See also *Basic Instinct*; *Gilda*.

Bibliography

Greven, David. *Intimate Violence: Hitchcock, Sex, and Queer Theory*. New York: Oxford University Press, 2017.

Karger, Dave. "Spotlight on Gay Hollywood." Interview with William J. Mann. Turner Classic Movies. Broadcast, June 9, 2017.

Wood, Robin. *Hitchcock's Films Revisited*. New York: Columbia University Press, 1989.

—Andrew Grossman

• S •

SCORE (1974)

DIRECTOR: Radley Metzger
SCREENPLAY: Jerry Douglas
CAST: Casey Donovan (Eddie), Gerald Grant (Jack), Lynn Lowry (Betsy), Claire Wilbur (Elvira)
SPECS: 84 minutes/92 minutes (uncut); color
AVAILABILITY: DVD (First Run Films)/Blu-ray (Cult Epics)

In the apocryphal City of Leisure, situated on the Idle Sea, lives a sexually liberated community that transcends conventions of monogamy, heterosexuality, jealousy, and egoism. A sunny voice-over tells viewers that the people's "love had nothing to do with the archaic notion of romantic love, which was the subject of many a cautionary tale told by the wary citizens." Two of the community's free spirits are Elvira and her husband, Jack, married swingers who turn their bisexual experimentations into calculated games of scoring "points," apparently a way to assuage potential jealousies. They set their sights on inexperienced, unspoiled newlyweds Betsy and Eddie, who still suffer from bourgeois hang-ups. Eddie—played by Casey Donavan, of *Boys in the Sand* (1971)—has slept with a man only once. Betsy still clings to her Catholic upbringing. Over a weekend featuring partner swapping, catty dialogue, amyl nitrate, and a cannabis-filled phallic peppermill, the men and women repair for therapeutic same-sex encounters, with Jack and Eddie playing sailor and cowboy and Elvira and Betsy retiring to a cozy, mirrored bedroom. By the end of the weekend, Betsy and Eddie have not only entered the erotically liberated classes but have mastered their masters, luring away Elvira and Jack's new male partner for their own playful threesome.

Perhaps more than any other auteur of the late 1960s and early 1970s, Radley Metzger (1929–2017) brought erotica into the middle-class mainstream and made softcore—and eventually hardcore—filmmaking a relatively respectable endeavor. Unlike the innocent "nudie cuties" launched by Russ Meyer's *The Immoral Mr. Teas* (1959) or the so-called roughies of the mid-1960s, Metzger's erotica boasted glossy production values, 35-mm cinematography, and a chic, continental style. Metzger's "European" approach reflects his cinephilic childhood and his early work at Janus Films editing American trailers for Bergman and Antonioni movies. For porn historian Jon Lewis, Metzger qualifies not merely as a sexploitation pioneer but as "an ambitious cineaste with a thing for Antonioni-like composition and ennui" (2002, 255). Perhaps *The Lickerish Quartet* (1970) comes closest to Lewis's description. An arty examination of the sexual neuroses of a decadent couple and their grown son, the film does echo Antonioni in its use of distanced, objectivized framing to signify social and sexual alienation. More acclaimed was Metzger's *Therese and Isabelle* (1968), which employs a complex flashback structure to recall the love between two young women at a repressive

Catholic school. In such films, Metzger's bourgeois sensibility rebuffed the underground ethos of his softcore predecessor Russ Meyer, whose films—such as *Faster, Pussycat, Kill! Kill!* (1965) and *Cherry, Harry, and Raquel!* (1969)—were flamboyant backwoods burlesques made for the grindhouse market.

Though Metzger's early films, like *Therese and Isabelle*, abound with lesbian imagery, they are more or less heteronormative titillations designed for straight male spectators. *Score*, however, is a rare foray into "ecumenical" erotica, affording equal time and explicitness to both lesbian and gay encounters. The film's departure from a heteronormative gaze can be largely credited to screenwriter (and off-Broadway playwright) Jerry Douglas, who adapted his stage play *Score, or No One's Afraid of Virginia Woolf!* Though Douglas's play was set in contemporary New York, the film version moves the action to a mythical seaside setting (actually Yugoslavia), universalizing its themes of erotic liberation and removing the practice of (bi)sexual experimentation from a liberal urban center. This sense of fantasy informs much of Metzger's work. As Metzger has said, "I didn't do pure realism. . . . I never dealt with unintended pregnancy, or herpes or impotence. I presented an idealized enactment of sex—as a unifying force between people" ("A Talk with Radley Metzger" n.d.). Filmed in 1972 but not released until 1974, *Score* might seem more refreshing today than when it was first released. With its playful, gradually intensifying same-sex scenarios, *Score* is unusually aimed at sexually multifarious audiences: bi-curious couples, gays and lesbians, and even unwitting straight men receptive to (or shocked by) unashamed male-male erotica. The film was unfortunately a box-office flop, suggesting that porn's presumed straight male audience was not quite as ready for pansexual liberation as Metzger and Douglas had hoped.

The film nevertheless stands as a reminder that filmmakers fifty years ago attempted to deliver explicit sexuality from the ghetto of porn theaters, bringing not only full nudity but visible signs of arousal into an American film culture obsessed with picayune definitions of "obscenity." (The production of *Score* was contemporaneous with the 1973 Supreme Court decision *Miller v. California*, which concluded that "community standards" should be used to identify what constitutes pornography.) More recently, of course, art films like John Cameron Mitchell's *Shortbus* (2006) or Pascal Arnold and Jean-Marc Barr's *Sexual Chronicles of a French Family* (2012) have embraced unsimulated sex and demolished old taboos. Yet so many of today's porno-art films tend to be self-important "ruminations" on sex or the indulgent, psychoanalytic statements of filmmakers posturing before selective film festival audiences. By contrast, *Score* and its free love rhetoric seem like a modest breath of fresh air. Never dwelling on neurosis, the film presents sexual freedom as a subject in itself, rather than using explicit sex to decorate (or explicate) a dreary art-house tale of nihilistic alienation.

This is not to say that *Score* is an unqualified success. The film's first part suffers terribly from the subscrewball patter of screenwriter Douglas, whose characters turn vapid chatter into a veritable lifestyle. Consider, for instance, an exchange between Eddie and Jack in which the latter attempts to draw parallels between bisexual aptitudes and personality types:

Jack: So, you're a Gemini?

Eddie: Is that bad? I don't know anything about that.

Jack: Gemini men are schizophrenic, split personality . . . double life.

Eddie: I take the Fifth!

Jack: Take whatever you can get!

In the film's second half, the empty repartee of Douglas's script gives way to intense, taciturn scenes of seduction, enlivened with Robert Cornford's deliriously jazzy score (buoyed by electric guitars and wordless vocals). Here, Metzger's direction becomes more stylized and more assured. The director brings the women together by framing them within rebounding mirrors and spotlights the power of cinema itself when Jack projects onto Eddie's open jeans the flickering nudity of an 8-mm stag film, as if the medium were undressing their desires. As each scenario rises to its dramatic and erotic climax, Metzger's crisp parallel editing contrasts, interposes, and melds the male and female couples' mounting ecstasies. As in much porn, however, the seductive psychology of the couples' foreplay and the anticipatory titillation of their gradual undressing are more arousing than the mechanical arrangements of their bared genitalia. Metzger had authorized two versions of the film for exhibition, a softcore eighty-four-minute cut and an X-rated ninety-two-minute version that includes explicit oral copulation but stops just short of full hardcore. The longer version—more consistent with the film's theme of uncensored libidinal freedom—is clearly preferable.

Director Metzger, using the *nom de auteur* "Henry Paris," would venture further into (straight) hardcore in the mid-70s, reaching a commercial and critical peak with *The Opening of Misty Beethoven* (1976), a porn variant of Shaw's *Pygmalion*. In the late 1980s, screenwriter Douglas would turn to cheaper, shot-on-video gay pornography, but his 1975 feature *Both Ways* is worth mentioning. Shot on Super 16 mm, the film reframes the bisexual fantasy of *Score* as a humanistic family drama, as husband Gerald Grant (who plays Jack in *Score*) attempts to juggle a wife and child with his hunky male lover. Though suffering from stilted dialogue and semiprofessional acting, the film realistically illustrates the jealousy and possessiveness absent in *Score*'s swinging utopia.

See also *Boogie Nights; Cruising; The Genesis Children*.

Bibliography

Gorfinkel, Elena. "Radley Metzger's 'Elegant Arousal': Taste, Aesthetic Distinction, and Sexploitation." In *Underground U.S.A.: Filmmaking beyond the Hollywood Canon*, edited by Xavier Mendik and Steven Jay Schneider, 26–39. London: Wallflower Press, 2002.

Lewis, Jon. *Hollywood v. Hard Core*. New York: New York University Press, 2002.

"A Talk with Radley Metzger." *Mondo Digital*, n.d. Accessed March 23, 2021. https://www.mondo-digital.com/radtalk.html.

Weston, Hillary. "Porn Before It Was Chic: An Interview with Radley Metzger on Sex and Cinema." *Blackbookmag.com*, August 19, 2014. Accessed March 23, 2021. https://blackbookmag.com/arts-culture/film/radley-metzger/.

—Andrew Grossman

SEX AND THE CITY (2008)

DIRECTOR: Michael Patrick King
SCREENPLAY: Michael Patrick King, based on characters created by Candace Bushnell
CAST: Sarah Jessica Parker (Carrie Bradshaw), Kim Cattrall (Samantha Jones), Kristin Davis (Charlotte York), Cynthia Nixon (Miranda Hobbes), Chris Noth (Mr. Big), Jennifer Hudson (Louise), Mario Cantone (Anthony Marentino), Willie Garson (Stanford Blatch)
SPECS: 145 minutes (theatrical release), 150 min (extended cut); color
AVAILABILITY: DVD (Warner Bros.)

The first cinematic sequel to the HBO series about the love lives of four New York women, Michael Patrick King's film is a romantic comedy whose central story is that of a happy ending temporarily deferred. *Sex and the City* follows four heterosexual pairs established in the eponymous series, and briefly introduces two new couples, one heterosexual and one gay, but its most significant plotline centers around Carrie's marriage to (Mr.) Big. After a decade-long courtship, Big proposes to Carrie, only to become overwhelmed by the wedding preparations and experience a moment of doubt on the wedding day, resulting in their breakup. The rest of the narrative encompasses Carrie's mourning of the relationship with the help of her friends, who accompany her on what was meant to be her honeymoon, and her eventual realization about her own contribution to Big's doubts about the wedding, as well as stories concerning Miranda's marriage struggles concerning infidelity, Charlotte's longed-for pregnancy, and Samantha's coming to terms with her relationship no longer being sustainable. A tertiary story line follows Louise, a new character, looking for love in New York and finding it back in her home state of Missouri. Ultimately, Carrie and Big reconcile and marry.

Sex and the City is not a film that stands particularly well on its own. Its story is a continuation and a reenactment of the plots of its original TV series, one of HBO's defining productions. The source material comes from semiautobiographical columns published by Candace Bushnell in the *New York Observer* from 1994, then republished as an anthology in 1997. The 1997–2004 TV series follows the lives of Carrie, Samantha, Miranda, and Charlotte as they navigate their thirties or (in Samantha's case) forties, offering a "sharp and iconoclastic" insight into the lives of the four Manhattanites (Nussbaum 2019, 50). The show has since lost much of its acclaim (Nussbaum 2019, 49) and come under criticism for its rampant consumerism as well as the fact that all four characters are white, economically privileged, and "resolutely heterosexual" (Arthurs 2008, 50). Even when Samantha enters a relationship with a woman, this is not acknowledged as evidence of bisexuality but rather presented as an experiment confirming her sexual orientation; the show's use of transphobic and homophobic language has also been a subject of critique. Nonetheless, original versions of *Sex and the City*—book and series—pushed the envelope in "chick lit" and television, respectively, by showcasing women who were far from role models and yet remained unashamed of their sexual desires and behavior, transgressing conservative social mores. In addition, the series, conceived and made by two gay men, Darren Star and Michael Patrick King, features two gay recurring characters—Carrie's friend Stanford Blatch, who appears in twenty-seven episodes, and Charlotte's wedding planner (and later friend) Anthony Marantino, who appears in twelve of the series' ninety-four episodes. Both also make appearances in the cinematic sequels.

The film opens with a recap of the series' conclusion—with all four female protagonists in their long-term relationships. Carrie is a writer whose autobiographical stories secured her relative success. Samantha works as an agent and PR specialist now mostly focusing on the career of her younger partner, Smith Jerrod. Miranda is lawyer and mother, married to Steve, a bartender-turned-publican. And Charlotte is a stay-at-home mother to Lily. Interspersed with flashbacks to the television series, the film offers viewers its first fashion montage as Carrie and her friends walk the streets of New York in a variety of stylish and conspicuous outfits to the accompaniment of Sarah Jessica Parker's traditional Carrie voice-over narration, focusing on "labels" and "love"—the leitmotif of the film. It also features a portrayal of queerness—when Samantha looks lasciviously at a handsome younger man in the street, only for him to meet and kiss his male partner. This first appearance of gayness may be interpreted ambiguously—as a somewhat clumsy way of establishing the film's progressive outlook on love, about which Carrie narrates, or else, less charitably, as situating viewers as heterosexual women, gazing at gay men's casual display of affection for their own voyeuristic pleasure (or, at least, with disappointment at their unavailability).

The plot commences with further displays of consumerism: first, Carrie and Big going apartment shopping and finding what Carrie describes as "real-estate heaven" [00:05:30]: a large, airy penthouse with private roof access, far outside Carrie's price range but well within Big's. This provides an opportunity for pointing out their (lack of) marital status—a real estate agent assumes that they are married, only to be corrected that Big is Carrie's "boyfriend," or "man friend" [00:05:50, 00:06:05]. Big buys the apartment for them and promises to build Carrie a new closet to fit her fashion collection—particularly, her shoe collection. The second display of consumerism takes the form of an auction of jewelry belonging to a jilted former model, who is presented as a cautionary tale to Carrie—like her, the model had failed to secure her future by living with a man without the safety provided by marriage vows and, when their relationship ended, was left with no economic recourse but selling gifts from her former lover. Miranda suggests that Carrie should keep her old apartment despite moving in with Big, to "be . . . smart," but that seems to Carrie to be proof of lack of trust in a shared future, and she rejects the advice [00:07:20]. However, once she presents her plan to Big, saying she means to share in the cost of the penthouse apartment, he offers to marry her to assuage her fears, announcing, nonromantically, that "[he] wouldn't mind being married to [her]" [00:11:30]. Thus, in the context of Carrie and Big's relationship, (heterosexual) marriage is initially represented as a legal and economic institution, one necessary for the protection of the woman's interests but offering little incentive to the man. Carrie, despite her protestations that she is happy with their relationship, longs for marriage, whereas the best Big has to offer is lack of his opposition to that prospect—a conservative, patriarchal portrayal of heterosexuality.

When Carrie informs her friends about the upcoming nuptials, their reactions differ vastly. Charlotte greets the news by announcing it to the entire restaurant (resulting in applause as she emphasizes the impossibility of securing a proposal after such a prolonged courtship) [00:12:40]. Miranda seems indifferent in contrast, whereas Samantha's reaction on the phone is at first nonplussed and only later congratulatory—she explains that she assumed Carrie was, like her, not a person who intended to enter matrimony. With Carrie marrying, Samantha would remain as the only friend without a husband.

Subsequently, wedding preparations commence. At first, the plan is for Carrie to marry Big in a simple city hall ceremony, in a vintage (no-label) outfit, with only closest friends present. This notion is immediately criticized by Anthony Marantino, a wedding planner "given" to Carrie "as a wedding gift" by Charlotte [00:15:10]. While this description, delivered by Carrie in a voice-over, is obviously intended as a joke, and although Anthony's caustic humor allows him to satirize the protagonists, such a statement fits with the earlier portrayal of gay men as objects of female gaze—once again, a gay man is objectified by the narrative and positioned as existing through his relationship to the heterosexual women who employ his talents. Carrie, at first, intends to stick to her plan, but circumstances conspire against that. First, her engagement is announced in the press on "page six" [00:16:40]. Then, her *Vogue* editor asks her to model bridal couture. Finally, after the second fashion montage of the film, with Carrie photographed in a series of dresses from designer labels, Carrie receives a dress by Vivienne Westwood "so special it could bring a wedding tear from even the most disbelieving of women" as a personal gift from the designer [00:19:30–00:19:40]. Carrie is accompanied at the fashion shoot by the second of the film's queer characters, her "old friend . . . Stanford Blatch," a single gay man who shares her interest in fashion and, in this scene, exists primarily to cheer for Carrie's fashion-defined success [00:19:30–00:19:40].

While Samantha and Miranda experience relationship difficulties, and as Carrie sells her apartment and moves out (prompting the film's third fashion montage, involving some of the TV show's iconic outfits), wedding preparations gain momentum, the style of the ceremony is elevated, and the guest lists expands, to Big's chagrin. His discomfort is attributed to it being his "third marriage"—the too-large size of the wedding seems to invite scorn [00:39:20]. His fear is confirmed during rehearsal dinner, when his marital history is mocked by his colleague, and his more general doubts are reaffirmed by Miranda, who is upset after an encounter with her own husband. The two are separated due to Steve's infidelity, and he uses the dinner as an occasion to attempt reconciliation—this causes Miranda to impulsively tell Big that "marriage ruins everything" [00:44:20].

Carrie's wedding, predictably, fails to occur—Big flees, and when he returns to the venue, Carrie is already too angry to forgive him. Instead of marrying, she is whisked off on her nonrefundable honeymoon trip accompanied by her three friends. In Mexico, the women share their doubts about their relationships—only Charlotte is content. The crisis in Miranda's marriage is partly attributed to her not focusing on the relationship's romantic and sexual aspects. She is mocked by Samantha for her unwaxed pubic hair. Her failure to conform to hegemonic heterosexual femininity in its commodified form (i.e., beauty regime) is directly associated with marital unhappiness. However, Samantha's romantic life is also unsatisfactory—while, unlike Miranda, she remains interested in sex, her partner prioritizes his career, and the fact that hers is connected to him makes Samantha feel unhappily dependent.

After the four friends return from Mexico, Carrie repurchases her old apartment and moves forward with her life. She conducts a series of interviews for the position of her personal assistant, with one candidate being a gender-non-conforming person—an Asian man named Paul who is clearly overqualified for the position but wants it due to his fashion interests, exhibited by his wearing stilettos. This scene functions as a brief comedic interlude that once again appropriates male queerness for the amusement of viewers. Carrie does not hire Paul but Louise, who is a young, brokenhearted Black woman, with whose search for love Carrie seems to identify. Louise, much like the film's gay men, performs an auxiliary function in the lives of white characters—she tidies up Carrie's inbox and website, introduces her to rentable fashion, and provides professional companionship while Carrie undertakes renovating her apartment as well as changing her signature hairstyle to avoid recognition once the issue of *Vogue* featuring her is published.

The next part of the film marks the passage of time through a procession of events starting with New Year's Eve, which Carrie and Miranda—currently estranged from their male partners—celebrate together. Another montage occurs. This one is accompanied by "Auld Lang Syne" and features (newly pregnant) Charlotte and (increasingly unhappy) Samantha greeting the new year with their respective partners, Louise reunited with her former boyfriend, lonely Big, and finally, the two gay male characters. While Anthony and Stanford disliked each other in the television series and rejected the notion of dating, on this occasion, they are shown to be relieved to find each other at the party, as the only other person they know. In a moment that seems to be marked by comedic resignation, the two men look around, drink their champagne, and share a kiss at midnight; a meaningful gesture, since *Sex and the City 2* will see them married.

The next events in the film are fashion week, which seems to give Carrie new energy, and Valentine's Day, which Carrie once again spends with Miranda, and the two are mistaken for a lesbian couple. While this is not played as a source of homophobic discomfort, the mistake coincides with the two women reflecting on the failures of their heterosexual relationships: Carrie admits that the wedding became more important to her than Big's feelings, and that she shares the blame for their relationship's end. This prompts Miranda's belated confession—she shares with Carrie that she impulsively warned Big off marriage during the rehearsal dinner. Carrie leaves in anger after telling Miranda that her decision to divorce Steve was a mistake. The two friends reconcile, and Carrie's words about forgiving Steve persuade Miranda to attempt relationship counseling, in the course of which Miranda is given to understand that her rejection of Steve was comparably hurtful as his initial infidelity.

The final part of the film is focused on characters redefining their happiness. For Louise, this means returning to her hometown to marry her old boyfriend. For Miranda, being reunited with Steve, their past mistakes forgotten and

Mario Cantone as Anthony Marentino and Willie Garson as Stanford Blatch in *Sex and the City***. Courtesy of New Line Cinema/Photofest.**

passion rekindled. For Samantha, being single again—she leaves her partner amicably, rejecting monogamy as stifling—a realization prompted by weight gain, as she overeats to avoid cheating. And finally, for Charlotte, expecting her second, long-desired child—and this biological culmination of heterosexual normativity is part of what leads to Carrie's reconciliation with Big. Charlotte's delivery begins during a confrontation with Big, and in the aftermath, her husband appeals to Carrie, explaining that Big still has feelings for her and asking her to consider speaking to him, as he has been leaving her messages to no avail. Only then does Carrie remember that she asked Louise to block his emails—they reappear hidden in a folder whose password turns out to be "love" [02:14:20]. Tellingly, the second factor contributing to the main couple's reunion represents an intermingling of consumerism and fairy tale—it is a pair of stilettos left in the penthouse closet. In a semisubversion of the romantic comedy staple, Carrie races against the clock to recover the Manolo Blahniks before the apartment officially changes owners, only to meet Big there: he also wanted to save her shoes. Spontaneous intercourse is followed by a second proposal, one that embodies a romantic fantasy rather than being "all business," with the Cinderella associations evoked by the shoe and Big kneeling before Carrie as he asks for her hand [02:18:40]. The ensuing civil ceremony is private, and only closest friends are invited to the after-party, including Anthony and Stanford, whose status as a couple remains unconfirmed but can be inferred from their sitting together. The film closes over a montage, scored by Jennifer Hudson's "Dressed in Love," that once again emphasizes the association between clothing and love, here taken to refer also to love of oneself and love of one's friends, as Samantha, again single by choice, celebrates her fiftieth birthday.

The conclusion of the film reinforces much of the status quo of its beginning: only Samantha, who never desired to legalize her relationship, diverges from heterosexual monogamous normativity, whereas the other women's stories largely celebrate adherence to established, conservative social scripts: happiness is found in biological parenthood and marital commitment. Furthermore, the characters who desire a stable relationship are likely to find it with already familiar partners—Carrie and Miranda ultimately reunite with their television series love interests and Louise reunites with her St. Louis boyfriend. The same pattern holds for Stanford and Anthony—while, as previously mentioned, the two characters were explicitly unattracted to each other in the television series, they end up together—as if their being two gay men made their pairing inevitable.

The film has been negatively compared to its television predecessor, with the simplicity of its message and the garish consumerism of its "staggering number of product placements" (Dargis 2008). However, another problem that deserves emphasizing is its conservative message. While the series focuses on a narrow and specific social group, the film's attempts to diversify the cast seem tokenistic: subordinated by that of white straight protagonists and alienating viewers not sharing these characteristics. The sequel film, *Sex and the City 2*, followed in 2010 to an even more negative critical response, and a new season of the show, *And Just Like That . . .*, was set to air in 2021 on the HBO Max platform, prompting the question of whether representation of queer characters will improve—only time will answer that question.

See also *Father of the Bride* Series; *Mean Girls*.

Bibliography

Arthurs, Jane. "*Sex and the City* and Consumer Culture." In *Feminist Television Criticism: A Reader*, edited by Charlotte Brunsdon and Lynn Spigel, 41–56. Maidenhead, UK: Open University Press, 2008.

Dargis, Manohla. "The Girls Are Back in Town." *New York Times*, May 30, 2008. Accessed March 3, 2021. https://www.nytimes.com/2008/05/30/movies/30sex.html.

Nussbaum, Emily. *I Like to Watch: Arguing My Way through the TV Revolution*. New York: Random House, 2019.

—Nelly Strehlau

SHELTER (2007)

DIRECTOR: Jonah Markowitz
SCREENPLAY: Jonah Markowitz
CAST: Trevor Wright (Zach), Brad Rowe (Shaun), Tina Holmes (Jeanne), Jackson Wurth (Cody), Katie Walder (Tori)
SPECS: 97 minutes; color
AVAILABILITY: DVD (Here TV)

Shelter begins with Zach, the leading man, skateboarding along the San Pedro sunset. As he weaves through the rougher parts of town—tagging various buildings in baggy jeans and knockoff Vans—the viewer meets an aspiring artist and

Californian. But this carefree character quickly unravels, weighed down by his dysfunctional home life. Zach's family is dependent on him, and his restaurant job, to make ends meet. In addition to breadwinning, he acts as the surrogate father to his nephew, Cody, whose mother, Jeanne, shows little interest in parenting. In his spare time, Zach finds freedom in surfing and street art. Initially, it seems this is all his life will be, but things get complicated when he reconnects with Shaun, his best friend's brother. An intimacy grows between them but seemingly withers when Zach's family requires more from him. When Jeanne disapproves of Zach's queerness and tries to leave San Pedro without her son, Zach has to choose between a life with Shaun and a life as his family's keeper.

Shelter has sly references to common stereotypes with regard to LGBTQIA+ representation, mainly through Jeanne, who equates "homosexuality" with hypersexualization and pedophilia. When Zach and Shaun's relationship heats up, Jeanne, suspicious of her brother, warns him about Shaun's sexuality. She confronts him through the shower door: "I don't think Shaun is the best guy to be hanging out with half naked, if you know what I mean." She continues, equating "homosexuality" with pedophilia: "and I don't want Cody around that" [0:35:28–0:35:55]. In a clever shot that exemplifies the conflict of same-sex desire spotlighted in the film, Jeanne mentions her disapproval while the camera focuses on Zach's naked body, a grainy silhouette through the shower door. The viewer is invited to desire Zach only to be interrupted by Jeanne's suspicious prodding, showing the constant ill-conceived connection between same-sex attraction and the misconceptions that come with it.

In contrast to Jeanne, Shaun's brother, Gabe, is blithe and supportive, suggesting the film's intent to represent different ways queer people are received and treated by families. Gabe is so tolerant of Shaun's queerness that when he surprises Shaun with a visit, he coyly uses nicknames like "princess" and asks, "You got a guy in there, you slut?" [00:53:04–00:53:08]. Incidentally, Shaun does indeed have someone over, leading to a comical scene of Zach fleeing the house before Gabe notices. While calling gay men "princesses" and "sluts" is not acceptable or commendable in certain spaces, in this film Gabe's treatment of his brother is symbolic of their close bond.

Negative connotations of the LGBTQIA+ community are mostly confined to Jeanne, but the film hints at the surfing community's long history of misogyny and homophobia, being the first to tell a story about queer surfers. It wasn't until 2014—seven years after the film's release—that the plight of LGBTQIA+ surfers would resurface in the documentary *Out in the Line-Up*. And as recently as the fall of 2020, *Surfer* magazine featured a story on the slow progression of LGBTQIA+ acceptance in surfing:

> The ocean may not judge based on sexuality or gender identity, but many surfers do. . . . Just poke around on social media for a bit and you might see Stab's Instagram post about renaming the "sex change" skateboard trick the "Caitlyn Jenner" in surfing. . . . It's not the same as barking slurs in the lineup—which still happens, too—but it has a similar effect in signaling to others who is and isn't welcome in surfing. (Prodanovich 2020, 5)

The film itself gives a lackluster nod to toxic masculinity in the surfing community, but the presence is noted. After Zach and Shaun reconnect, Zach sees Tori, his on-again, off-again girlfriend, and she invites them to hang out. The group ends up at a beach bonfire, chatting and drinking. A man next to Zach asks, "What's the deal? You still seeing Tori, then?" Zach looks over to her, reluctantly shrugs and shakes his head. The man scoffs and responds, "What are you a fag? I mean, she's hot" [00:19:09–00:19:19]. Shaun, who has not yet revealed he is gay, is visibly upset by the term "fag"; he stares blankly into the fire before standing abruptly and walking to the water's edge.

Homophobia's continued presence in surfing makes *Shelter*'s 2007 release a vanguard film in the fight for LGBTQIA+ representation. These characters are not just surfers in name. Surfing is the impetus through which Zach and Shaun spark a relationship and key to Zach's acceptance of his sexuality. In a film that emphasizes Zach's conflict between his burgeoning sexuality and homophobic stereotypes, surfing soothes this conflict. When Zach and Shaun surf together, viewers see two men and their budding intimacy in perfect harmony with nature. The ocean, the beach, and the California cliff sides are in union with these two riding the waves, showing just how natural their love is.

Shelter is certainly unique in its portrayal of a queer surfer love story, but like many queer films, its gay characters have an affinity for creativity. Shaun is a successful writer while Zach explores street art. Besides surfing, art is the pinnacle connection between the two. Creativity is an integral part of their lives as gay men, so much so that after engaging in sex with Shaun for the first time, Zach finds himself inspired to do his biggest and most spotlighted art piece of the film. In his car, after leaving Shaun's house, Zach bites his lip and smiles, ecstatic. An upbeat instrumental follows him to an abandoned building where he paints the outline of a tree. Later, in the montage where Zach and Shaun's relationship grows, the tree expands—twists into red, black, and white branches—overlaid by photographs amid a backdrop of industrial San Pedro. By tying Zach's burgeoning queer relationship with his renewed inspiration to make street art, the film suggests not just that LGBTQIA+ people have an affinity for creativity but that queer love has the power to spur it.

In contrast to Zach and Shaun's creative commonalities, *Shelter* makes a point to enunciate the divergent representations of gay men according to their class, and the clear challenges—and privileges—based on those class positions. Class and money are equal to freedom when it comes to living queerly in *Shelter*. Shaun is from a wealthy family, exemplified in the film by the beachside mansion where he is staying. He is easily accepted by his family (noted above by his brother) and navigates life with relative ease: he lives in LA as a successful writer and has just ended a long-term relationship. Shaun's ability to live openly as a queer man and a successful creative is contrasted with Zach's working-class life. Zach gives up becoming an artist because of his family's socioeconomic status. Later in the film, Zach reveals that he was accepted to CalArts on a full scholarship but turned it down because he felt a responsibility to care for Cody, his sister, and his disabled father. This theme of class and queerness comes to a head in Zach's car. After Jeanne discovers his relationship with Shaun, Zach is visibly upset. When Shaun gets in the car to talk, he and Zach argue, and Zach explicitly brings class into the conversation: "It's not as easy for me as it is for you . . . you just don't get it okay? I can't just take whatever I want. My life is not like that. You know, you and Gabe have been able to point and take, no questions asked. You don't realize that it's not like that for other people" [01:00:34–01:00:57]. Emphasizing their class differences, Shaun cannot understand Zach's confusion. His position of privilege makes him mistake Zach's resentment over his working-class roots for anxiety about coming out. This fight is irreconcilable until the end of the film.

When the two finally do reconcile, Zach has a choice to make. Jeanne has just informed him that she is moving to Portland with her boyfriend, Alan—where Cody is not welcome. This is the climax of the film, when the tension over Cody's upbringing comes to a head. *Shelter* makes clear that family is not about gender, orientation, or biological lineage but about the home it can provide. It concludes this point with an emotional plea from Zach. Faced with the choice of accepting the offer from CalArts or staying in San Pedro to take care of Cody, Zach responds to Jeanne with his own ultimatum: Jeanne can either get over her homophobia, give Cody to him and Shaun, or she can stay in San Pedro and raise Cody alone. With tears in his eyes he tries to reach his sister: "Shaun is really great, Jeannie. He really cares about Cody and me." He gestures at their rundown neighborhood: "Jeannie, take a look around. Every kid should be so lucky. What else could you possibly want for him?" [01:21:34–01:22:13].

Cody's affinity for Shaun and Zach is key for viewers to see which family unit is most suited to raise him. Early in the film, while Zach is watching Cody during Jeanne's shift at the Oceanette, Cody says, "You're my daddy." Zach, taken aback, responds, "No, Cody, I'm your uncle. Your mommy is my sister. That makes me your uncle." But Cody won't hear any of it. He responds, "Nope. You're my Daddy. You're my Daddy. You're my Daddy," over and over [00:10:40–00:10:55]. Later, while Zach and Tori are watching Cody at the beach, they leave him with Shaun to talk about their relationship. When Zach returns, he tries to usher Cody off the beach, but Cody wants to stay, repeating in protest, "Shaun rocks!"

To show its progressive views on family, *Shelter* constantly compares Shaun and Zach's gay relationship to Jeanne and Alan's heterosexual one. Cody's preference for Zach and Shaun is easy to understand. The couple shows a supportive and loving relationship that gives Cody a commendable quality of life. One shot in particular exemplifies this. When Jeanne takes a weekend trip to Oregon with Alan, she gets Zach to watch Cody—again leaning on Zach to care for her child. Zach brings Cody to Shaun's, where the two have a date. In the backyard, Shaun and Zach talk about Zach's sacrifice to care for Cody. Emotional, Shaun takes Zach into his arms to comfort him. The scene cuts to an interior shot with Cody in the foreground, asleep on the couch. To the right of Cody through the window, viewers see Shaun and Zach hugging, swaying side to side. Zach leans into Shaun, safe. The camera slowly zooms out to a yearning instrumental. The shot is a perfect representation of the potential supportive and nurturing family unit that this couple could provide Cody. The montage continues to show them as capable and exceedingly good caregivers. A multitude of scenes show Zach, Shaun, and Cody as a lively family. In contrast, Jeanne and Alan are not conducive to raising Cody. The two are often seen coming home late at night, drunk and boisterous. Their relationship is hectic and borders on abuse.

Representing Zach, Shaun, and Cody as a successful family unit in 2007 is one of the film's most prescient representations of LGBTQIA+ people when understood in the context of the long fight for gay adoptive rights. Ten years prior to the film's release, New Jersey allowed same-sex couples to adopt children—the first state in the United States to do so. But it was not until three years after the film's release that the last state, Florida, lifted its ban on adoption by same-sex couples. In the fight for marriage equality in 2013 and 2015, arguments made before the US Supreme Court included the success of same-sex adoption and played a vital role in securing the right to marry. Presently, in the face of religious freedom laws (such as the Religious Freedoms Restoration Act, passed in Indiana in 2015), the fight for parental rights continues for same-sex couples. In states with these laws, adoption agencies are legally allowed to discriminate against LGBTQIA+ parents. By telling a story built on the quality of care for Cody, rather than Zach and Shaun's sexual orientation, *Shelter* combats the notion that gay men are not suitable parents. The final scene dismisses any doubt about the ability of this gay family unit. Shaun, Zach, and Cody play Frisbee on the beach. A dog runs between their legs, and Shaun's long, shaggy hair signifies the passage of time. They horse around as the camera takes in smiles and laughter, a family that has remained a happy home.

For a 2007 audience pick along the film festival circuit, *Shelter* portrays the LGBTQIA+ community in a myriad of ways: as potential parents, as financially diverse, and even as an integral part of an extremely toxic male–dominated sports culture. These varied representations make the film worth watching. Against a plethora of mainstream queer content that churns out homogenous identities and lifestyles, *Shelter* shows two very different people with two very different stories. In the realm of LGBTQIA+ portrayals, it is one of the only surfer movies, and a tender, earnest story of two people finding—and fighting—for that "shelter" many are looking for.

See also *Brokeback Mountain*; *Dream Boy*.

Bibliography

Prodanovich, Todd. "How LGBTQ+ Surfers Are Creating a More Inclusive Surf Culture." *Surfer*, October 6, 2020. Accessed February 9, 2021. https://www.surfer.com/features/history-lgbtq-surfing/.

Rudolph, Dana. "A Very Brief History of LGBTQ Parenting." Family Equality, October 20, 2017. Accessed February 1, 2021. https://www.familyequality.org/2017/10/20/a-very-brief-history-of-lgbtq-parenting/.

Thomson, Ian. *Out in the Line-Up*. Vimeo, March 2, 2015. February 1, 2021. https://vimeo.com/ondemand/outinthelineupfilm.

—Mark Muster

A SINGLE MAN (2009)

DIRECTOR: Tom Ford
SCREENPLAY: Tom Ford and David Scearce, based on the novel of the same name
  by Christopher Isherwood
CAST: Colin Firth (George), Julianne Moore (Charley), Nicholas Hault (Kenny),
  Matthew Goode (Jim), John Kortajarena (Jim), Paulette Lamori (Alva)
SPECS: 99 minutes; color
AVAILABILITY: DVD (Fade to Black Productions) and streaming (Stan)

Tom Ford's film *A Single Man* is an adaptation of Christopher Isherwood's 1964 novel of the same name. The action takes place on November 30, 1962, the eve of the Cuban Missile Crisis and the last day of life for British academic George Falconer, who works as a professor of English at UCLA. George Falconer is preparing to shoot himself, unable to go on after the death of his lover, Jim, who perished in a car accident. According to Jim's brother-in-law, the funeral service is "just for family." Before he can carry out his plan to commit suicide, George goes to the university to give a lecture, and then hangs out with a male prostitute in the parking lot of a convenience store, sharing cigarettes and a bottle of gin. George politely deflects the offer of company. He then remembers that he has promised to have dinner with his female friend, Charley, an alcoholic who is also a British expat living in Los Angeles. The dinner becomes unpleasant when Charley suggests that the two of them might have had a relationship, save for George turning out to be a "poof." George leaves and heads to the bar where he first met Jim. Here he bumps into Kenny, a handsome student from UCLA. The two of share a drink and then head to the beach, where they skinny-dip. They go back to George's house, where Kenny tends to a cut on George's forehead. Kenny strips naked but George rebuffs him, and Kenny ends up sleeping on the couch. George wakes up in the early morning and discovers that the gun he was planning to use to kill himself is hidden under the covers with Kenny, who is still fast asleep. George takes the gun and locks it in a safe before returning to bed. Asleep again, and dreaming of Jim, he suffers a heart attack and dies.

Colin Firth as George and Jon Kortajarena as Carlos in *A Single Man*. Courtesy of the Weinstein Company/Photofest.

A Single Man plays on the idea that gender and sexuality are performed according to rigid and seemingly immovable scripts (Butler 1990). For George Falconer, the embodiment of an acceptable if not ideal masculinity requires a kind of performance of his life as an expat lecturer at a prestigious university and the sublimination of his love for a recently deceased male partner. Early in the film, viewers hear a voice-over in which he declares, calmy, that "it takes time in the morning for me to become George, time to adjust to what is expected of George and how he should behave." There is an obvious and unbearable tension between his public and private personas. Driving through his neighborhood on the way to work, he witnesses the ordinary, domestic, and heteronormative lives going on around him, and yet his own suburban and domestic life has been shattered by the loss of Jim. Perhaps it is for this reason that he describes his reflection in the bathroom mirror as "not so much a face as the expression of a predicament."

Colin Firth's performance as George earned him a nomination for the Academy Award for Best Actor, and the film received a number of industry accolades, including the Queer Lion Award at the sixty-sixth Venice Film Festival. However, some critics argued that the marketing materials for the film were straight-washed by the omission of direct references to George's identity as a gay man and the focus on his relationship with Charley (Julianne Moore). In an interview with the *Advocate*, Firth described the Weinstein Company's promotional material for the film as "deceptive. . . . It's a beautiful story of love between two men and I see no point in hiding that" (Voss 2009).

For director and writer Tom Ford, *A Single Man* represented a shift from his professional career as a creative director of fashion houses such as Gucci and Yves Saint Laurent. His background in fashion is obvious in the attention to the fine details of the mise-en-scène. Individual scenes such as the car crash, underwater shots of two men swimming, and players on a tennis court have the staged, even serene, quality of fashion photography. These scenes, especially those in slow motion or in flashback, function like postcards that allow the viewer to linger on bodies, surfaces, and visual metaphors, such as the stark contrast of bright red blood on white snow. The meticulously neat and streamlined midcentury style of George's house, car, and clothing match his fastidious attention to the details of his public, "presenting" self, as mentioned above. Moreover, these visual elements underscore the architecture of desire in which George exists: a kind of queer space and time that is marked by the intersection of his life with the zeitgeist of 1960s America (Halberstam 2005). George is literally a man who has run out of time, and yet his final moments herald the movement toward a growing acceptance and recognition of same-sex love and relationships that would form part of the countercultural movement only a few short years after his death.

See also *Nocturnal Animals*.

Bibliography

Butler, Judith. *Gender Trouble: Feminism and the Subversion of Identity*. London: Routledge, 1990.

Halberstam, Jack. *In a Queer Time and Place: Transgender Bodies, Subcultural Lives.* New York: New York University Press, 2005.

Voss, Brian. "Colin Firth: Singled Out." *Advocate*, December 9, 2009. Accessed February 2, 2021. http://www.advocate.com/arts-entertainment/film/2009/12/09/colin-firth-singled-out.

—Paul Venzo and Sabine Planka

SONG OF THE LOON (1970)

DIRECTOR: Andrew Herbert; Scott Hanson (uncredited)
SCREENPLAY: Richard Amory, based on the novel *Song of the Loon: A Gay Pastoral in Five Books and an Interlude* by Richard Amory
CAST: John Iverson (Cyrus Wheelwright), Morgan Royce (Ephraim MacIver), Lancer Ward (John), Brad Fredericks (Mr. Calvin), Jon Evans (Montgomery)
SPECS: 79 minutes; color
AVAILABILITY: VHS (Something Weird Video)

Adapted from Richard Amory's 1966 pulp novel *Song of the Loon: A Gay Pastoral in Five Books and an Interlude*, the film begins as virile mountain man Cyrus Wheelwright encounters a pair of young male lovers in the wilderness of 1870 Oregon. He relates to them the story of his own true love, Ephraim MacIver, a young man who trekked across Native American territories in search of spiritual and sexual fulfillment. The film then flashes back to Ephraim, paddling in a canoe to the sound of epic orchestral music. As he embarks on his quest for eros, Ephraim also flees two villains: Montgomery, his cruel and selfish ex-lover, and Calvin, a closeted Christian missionary who can barely contain his suppressed desires for Montgomery. Ephraim fears retaliation from Calvin, who believes (falsely) that it was Ephraim who had spread rumors of Calvin's "homosexuality." During his wilderness odyssey, Ephraim first encounters a free-spirited Native American, Singing Heron, who has rejected Calvin's attempt to Christianize him. He then meets Cyrus, a white man who has joined the "Loon Society" to which Singing Heron belongs. Members of the society follow a polyamorous ethic, embracing multiple partners and abjuring the jealousy and possessiveness that characterize the relationships of closeted white Christians like Montgomery and Calvin. After forging an erotic, soulful bond with Cyrus, Ephraim sets out to find Bear-Who-Dreams, a Native medicine man who will guide Ephraim on a long-awaited spirit journey. After learning to renounce his lingering, poisonous attachment to Montgomery on his spirit quest, Ephraim rejoins Cyrus at his mountain retreat. Their reunion is only temporary, however, for Ephraim now has adopted the Loon Society's itinerant, polyamorous lifestyle. The expected confrontation with Montgomery and Calvin never occurs; left to their own devices, the two villains become their own worst enemies, left to struggle in the dusty closet of the old American West.

Richard Amory's once-sensational *Song of the Loon* and its semisequels, *Song of Aaron* (1967) and *Listen, the Loon Sings* (1968), were breakthrough pulp novels in their time, pre-Stonewall affirmations of gay love articulated without shame, apology, or self-abnegating stereotypes. In these novels, Amory consciously dispensed with the ironic subtexts of Oscar Wilde, the bourgeois masks of Edward Albee, and other "diversionary" techniques of earlier gay literatures. Advancing a self-consciously lyrical style, Amory (a pseudonym for Richard Love) turned his gaze toward America's founding mythological figure—the ruggedly individualistic, self-sustaining pioneer. His hero, Ephraim, is more or less a gay reincarnation of James Fenimore Cooper's Natty Bumppo, glossed with psychological conflicts symbolic of the gay male experience in mid-twentieth-century America. As a queer underground novelist, however, Amory had no intention of reiterating the racist, imperialist, and patriarchal tropes undergirding standard Western lore. In *Song of the Loon*, Anglo-Christian society is consumed by hypocrisy and gratuitous sexual repression, while Native American life is idyllic, equanimous, and immanently queer. Amory's unapologetically romanticized vision of Native folk life draws on an unexpected source: the Iberian pastoral tradition of the sixteenth century. Amory had, in his own words, "taken certain very European characters from the novels of Jorge De Montemayor and Gaspar Gil Polo, painted them a gay aesthetic red, and transplanted them to the American wilderness" (2005, 10). Those intent on reading "other intentions into these characterizations," he continued, would be "willfully misunderstanding the nature of the pastoral genre" (28). Amory's idealized, pastoral Loon Society is not Rousseauian in the common or reductive sense of the word. The Loon Society's ethos of selfless polyamory and mutually fulfilling partnerships suggests a social structure far more sophisticated than noble savages in a prepolitical state of nature. Here, the Rousseauian fantasy of the uncorrupted savage becomes an ode to uncorrupted sexuality, while the old dichotomy between savagery and civilization is turned on its head, as Native American lifeways represent an aspirational, late-stage civilization that exists beyond white men's perennial values of jealousy and domination.

Released in 1970, the film is, in many ways, a literalistic treatment of its source. Much of the plot follows the novel point for point, and some of the dialogue—such as Singing Heron's speech about jealousy being "the white man's disease"—is taken verbatim from the novel. Nevertheless, Amory was openly critical of the film, and it is easy to see why. The film is unbearably slow, hampered by uniformly wooden acting, and swathed in the kitschy hippie sentimentality that colored so many revisionist Westerns of the early 1970s. Though given an X rating, the film is sexually tame, featuring plentiful nudity but none of Amory's explicit sex (which comprises about a quarter of the novel's word count). In a gambit for respectability, the film replaces the novel's pornographic content with artsy lovemaking montages that emphasize abstracted close-ups of the human form. What elevates Amory's novel are a lyrical prose style and a refined literary self-consciousness, traits that obviously become lost on film. The film's simplifications are especially noticeable in the characterization of Cyrus. In the novel, he is a gentlemanly, erudite outdoorsman given to literary allusions. In the film, he is a stoic stud given to monosyllabic declarations, a representation that particularly irked Amory, who mercilessly criticized what the filmmakers made of his vision.

In all fairness, some of the film's sentimentality is endemic to Amory's narrative and overall framework. Like Elliot Silverstein's *A Man Called Horse* (1970) or even Kevin Costner's bloated *Dances with Wolves* (1990), the story positions Native American spirituality as a romanticized vehicle for a white man's moral and mystical awakening. Here the awakening is represented by Ephraim's consultations with a beefy medicine man and his subsequent spirit quest (which the filmmakers render "psychedelically" with color negatives). It is true that Ephraim is not the typical white adventurer-cum-vicarious-appropriator found in Westerns that poeticize Native American folkways. Unlike Kevin Costner's hero in *Dances with Wolves* or Richard Harris's Anglo colonialist in *A Man Called Horse*, Ephraim exists in a state of self-imposed exile, having already rejected the arrogance and hypocrisies of white Christian society. Indifferent to Manifest Destiny, Amory's heroes are apolitical and agnostic; their conflicts are largely internal and existentialistic, not the stuff of violent conquest. If the Loon Society is unavoidably framed as an Other, it is not one easily (or even possibly) colonized. White society, meanwhile, proposes perpetual alienation rather than moral stability, as Amory's Anglo characters—*all* of them gay men—either internalize Christian homophobia or defect to the egoless Loon Society.

Like Howard Hawks's *Red River* (1948), Amory's novel prepares a narrative of betrayal and vengeance only to switch gears in the final act, offering a climax of forgiveness and redemption rather than gunslinging vengeance. It is precisely in this final act that the novel and film versions radically (and unfortunately) diverge, though it must be noted that the original director, Scott Hanson, was fired late in the production, leaving editor Andrew Herbert to finish the film—a circumstance that perhaps explains the film's unsatisfactory conclusion. In the novel, Cyrus ventures into town and runs into a pathetic, drunken Calvin, who in a moment of moral courage openly expresses his love for Montgomery amid a crowded saloon, much to Montgomery's mortification. Soon after, Ephraim, emboldened by his spirit quest, visits the town finally to confront Montgomery, his nemesis and ex-lover. But the anticipated violence never materializes; Ephraim and Montgomery come to an uneasy truce and implicitly agree to leave the past behind them. Meanwhile, Calvin repudiates his evangelism and approaches Ephraim to atone for his missionary arrogance. Adopting the role of supplicant, he asks Ephraim how he might transform Montgomery into a more selfless and loving partner before wondering if he might one day join the Loon Society himself. The ending of the film version, however, betrays the novel's themes of forgiveness and transformation. Rather than provide Calvin a chance for repentance and queer awakening, Hanson and Herbert's film sees Calvin and Montgomery tussle in the middle of town as a disapproving Cyrus looks on. Denied a narrative mechanism of transformation, the two men are left to take out their aggressions on one another—after which they disappear from the film altogether. The film's reductive ending negates the novel's central premise—that enlightenment is not a finite moral resource but something available to anyone (even Eurocentric missionaries) who seeks it in good faith. By leaving Calvin and Montgomery to their own self-hatred, the film also undoes the intended irony of a missionary named Calvin undergoing a decidedly non-Calvinistic conversion and rejecting his "predestined" existence in the closet.

Though very much a relic of its time, *Song of the Loon* is hardly disposable—it not only reflects a turning point in gay American culture but fundamentally queers the Western genre in ways that mainstream revisionist Westerns never did. Given the film's shortcomings, *Song of the Loon* is that rare specimen that actually could benefit from a remake, yet contemporary audiences probably would balk at Amory's politically incorrect appropriations of indigenous culture, even if he romanticizes Native American societies' "two-spirit" (i.e., nonheteronormative) persons in well-meaning ways. Beyond cultural appropriations, Amory's story provides much that is culturally useful, offering images of unaffected gay masculinity, free from literary stereotypes and fashionable posturing. Imagining an inherently gay universe that positions bittersweet polyamory against possessive monogamy, *Song of the Loon* forces its characters—heroes and villains alike—not to simply declare their sexual identities but to explore how they might queerly live.

See also *Brokeback Mountain; Red River.*

Bibliography

Amory, Richard. *Song of the Loon.* Introduction by Michael Bronski. Vancouver: Arsenal Pulp Press, 2005.

—Andrew Grossman

SPA NIGHT (2016)

DIRECTOR: Andrew Ahn
SCREENPLAY: Andrew Ahn
CAST: Joe Seo (David Cho), Youn Ho Cho (Jin Cho), Haerry Kim (Soyoung Cho)
SPECS: 93 minutes; color
AVAILABILITY: DVD (Strand Releasing)

Spa Night is a deliberate, meditative, slow-paced film set against the backdrop of a contemporary Los Angeles Koreatown. David Cho is the closeted son of immigrant parents, Jin and Soyoung. The film follows timid eighteen-year-old David as he discovers his sexuality through the gay hookup scene in Korean spas and negotiates his role in an immigrant family facing financial hardship.

Despite being shot, produced, and released in the United States, most of the film's dialogue is in Korean, offering a realistic portrayal of the private interactions between characters. In interviews about the film, director Andrew Ahn muses that it could be screened without subtitles for a Korean American audience. Ahn was committed to casting actors of Korean ethnicity in the film rather than have actors from other East Asian countries play Korean American characters. Ahn ran into issues when casting this film, finding few Korean American actors who wanted to be associated with a film with LGBTQIA+ themes. Further, with most of the film's dialogue in Korean, Ahn wanted the lead characters to convincingly sound like immigrants. This eventually led to the decision to cast Haerry Kim and Youn Ho Cho as David's parents.

Although not autobiographical for Ahn, the film was inspired by his efforts to understand his queer and Korean American identities. The Korean bathhouse is the site where both of those identities intersect. The film opens with the Cho family at a spa, engaged in a wholesome, albeit heteronormative, conversation imagining David's own future family. "David, when you get married, I'll come to the spa with my daughter-in-law," Soyoung declares.

David would visit another bathhouse with a group of college students while visiting USC. He would later covertly find employment at this bathhouse. And the bathhouse becomes the space in which he confronts his sexual desires and identity.

The plot of the film is driven by the Cho family's efforts to rebound after they lose the restaurant that they manage and their only source of income. While Jin and Soyoung struggle to recover from their loss and find new employment, they also worry about David and his future.

The Chos are contrasted with the Baek family, who are members of the same church. Mrs. Baek owns another Koreatown restaurant and later employs Soyoung to work as a server for her. Learning of David's interest in attending the University of Southern California, Mrs. Baek arranges for David to shadow her son Eddie, who is a freshman student at USC. She also recommends a tutoring service that Eddie used to help David prepare for the SATs.

At USC, David attends classes with Eddie and joins him for a night out. After a party, Eddie and a group of his friends take David to a karaoke lounge and then to a bathhouse. But as the bathhouse is men only, the women separate from them and go to another one across the street. The three men, David, Eddie, and Peter, remain. They undress and use the sauna and showers.

Having seen a "Help Wanted" sign at the spa, David returns to the spa, where he is hired to clean and help with general operations. He keeps this occupation a secret from his parents, who believe that he should be focused on his SATs. David learns that gay men also use the spa for sexual activity (which is not permitted). After policing this activity, David is later drawn to a Korean man of the same age with whom he has sex in the sauna. The manager observes this behavior, and David resigns.

The yearning gaze figures prominently in the film, including David's examination of his own body. His sexual awakening is foreshadowed as he considers his body in the bathroom mirror—first photographing his torso with his phone, then later capturing an image of his nude body. He later "reflects" on his own sexual identity as he confronts his image in the spa's mirrors. "What are you looking at?" Peter asks sharply, following David's gaze to Eddie's body lounging in the steam room. "Nothing," David responds. While urinating in the spa restroom, Eddie teases David, "Stop looking at my dick."

Joe Seo received the US Dramatic Special Jury Award for Breakthrough Performance at the Sundance Film Festival for his performance in *Spa Night*, indicative of his portrayal of David, depicting a deeply complex character. Awkward and introverted, David's interiority is conveyed in subtle expressions that hint at the yearning and conflict teeming beneath the surface. David's agency is exercised in his observation of his environment, which is steeped in the nuance of his interiority. It is the intensity of his queer gaze through his seemingly complacent demeanor that unsettles its subjects. This same yearning is repeated in the cinematography. Tightly framed close-up shots capture atmospheric details but also exclude action and scenery. The viewers' proximity to David offers physical and emotional intimacy.

Spa Night concludes with David running along an LA sidewalk. A tracking shot accompanied by the sound of his heavy breath suggests that this is an act of escaping—literally running away and taking the viewer along with him. But in a close-up, David pauses, and his breath steadies. He comes into possession of himself, and his head rises. He looks ahead and bolts out of frame. His future is uncertain, but it is his own.

See also *Brokeback Mountain; Star Trek Beyond; The Wedding Banquet.*

Bibliography

Ahn, Andrew, Haisong Li, and Joe Seo. "'Spa Night' Film Director Andrew Ahn Discusses Asian-American Identity." Panel discussion at the Asian American International Film Festival, Asia Society, July 21, 2016. Accessed July 22, 2021. https://asiasociety.org/video/spa-night-film-director-andrew-ahn-discusses-asian-american-identity.

Ahn, Andrew, So Yong Kim, and Lee Isaac Chung. "Korean-American Directors: A Roundtable." Panel discussion, the Korea Society, October 29, 2020. Accessed July 22, 2021. https://www.koreasociety.org/arts-culture/item/1439-korean-american-directors-a-roundtable.

Barber, Laurence. "Coming In." *Metro: Media & Education Magazine*, Summer 2017.

Erbland, Kate. "'Spa Night' Review: Gay Korean Coming-of-Age Drama Finds Resonance in Unlikely Places." *IndieWire*, August 17, 2016. Accessed July 22, 2021. https://www.indiewire.com/2016/08/spa-night-review-andrew-ahn-sundance-1201717645/.

Holden, Stephen. "Review: Wrestling with Gay Identity and Parental Wishes in 'Spa Night.'" *New York Times*, August 18, 2016. Accessed July 22, 2021. https://www.nytimes.com/2016/08/19/movies/spa-night-review.html.

Jung, E. Alex. "In *Spa Night*, the Sauna Plays an Integral Role in the Gay Korean-American Identity." *Vulture*, August 25, 2016. Accessed July 22, 2021. https://www.vulture.com/2016/08/spa-night-and-the-gay-korean-american-identity.html.

Kim, Nelson. "A Conversation with Andrew Ahn (SPA NIGHT)." *Hammer to Nail*, August 19, 2016. Accessed July 22, 2021. https://www.hammertonail.com/interviews/a-conversation-with-andrew-ahn/.

Linden, Sheri. "Review: Director Andrew Ahn and Actor Joe Seo Make Impressive Debuts in Koreatown Drama 'Spa Night.'" *Los Angeles Times*, August 25, 2016. July 22, 2021. https://www.latimes.com/entertainment/movies/la-et-mn-mini-spa-night-review-20160823-snap-story.html.

van Hoeij, Boyd. "'Spa Night': Sundance Review." *Hollywood Reporter*, January 26, 2016. Accessed July 22, 2021. https://www.hollywoodreporter.com/review/spa-night-sundance-review-859659.

—Nick Pozek

STAR TREK BEYOND (2016)

DIRECTOR: Justin Lin
SCREENPLAY: Simon Pegg and Doug Jung, based on characters created by Gene Roddenberry
CAST: John Cho (Sulu), Idris Elba (Krall), Simon Pegg (Montgomery "Scotty" Scott), Chris Pine (Captain James T. Kirk), Zachary Quinto (Commander Spock), Zoe Saldana (Lieutenant Uhura), Karl Urban (Doctor "Bones" McCoy), Anton Yelchin (Checkov)
SPECS: 122 minutes; color
AVAILABILITY: DVD (Paramount)

The third installment of a rebooted *Star Trek* that began with J. J. Abrams's *Star Trek* (2009) and *Star Trek Into Darkness* (2013), *Star Trek Beyond* sees the USS *Enterprise* three years into its five-year mission to "boldly go" and explore the mysteries of the universe. The monotony of space travel is beginning to take a toll on Captain Kirk. He starts to question the point of their mission and, equally, what he wants to achieve with his life. As the crew takes a break on Starbase Yorktown, a distress signal is intercepted. The *Enterprise* embarks on the rescue mission, but as they arrive, the ship is attacked by a swarm of enemy craft controlled by an alien named Krall. The ambush causes extreme damage. Kirk orders the ship be evacuated, and as the *Enterprise* crashes, the crew escape to a nearby planet. As the group attempt to find one another, it is revealed that Krall is actually Captain Balthazar Edison of the USS *Franklin*, who has been stranded and left for dead by the Federation for many years. He has survived by draining people of their life force, which also alters his appearance. Krall intends to unleash a deadly weapon called the Abronath (incidentally, stored aboard the *Enterprise*) on Yorktown as retribution for the Federation's betrayal. It is a race against time for the *Enterprise* crew to prevent Krall from killing the base's unsuspecting population. Kirk and Krall fight, and Kirk manages to push Krall into the path of the lethal substance just as it is released, causing him to disintegrate. The film ends with a new *Enterprise* being built, the crew reunited, and Kirk having rediscovered his love for flying.

According to many critics and viewers, *Star Trek Beyond* represented a serviceable and diverting science-fiction action adventure containing plenty of visual flare, spectacular set pieces, and familiar characters, without breaking any new ground. One might wonder to what the "beyond" of the film's title refers—other than the obvious pushing beyond the known frontier of space—given that there are very few technical, generic, or narrative boundaries that it attempts

Zoe Saldana as Lieutenant Uhura and John Cho as Sulu in *Star Trek Beyond*. Courtesy of Paramount Pictures/Photofest.

to push. Indeed, *Star Trek Beyond*'s plot signals a return to the flavor of the original series with the heroes separately stranded on an alien planet relying on their wit and logic to find each other and best the "baddie." Yet one of the more interesting aspects of this sequel involves the reveal that, in this alternate *Star Trek* universe known as the Kelvin time line, Hikaru Sulu, the *Enterprise*'s long-serving helmsman, is gay.

In the previous two films, this rejuvenated Sulu has appeared calm and capable. Barring a humorous false start in *Star Trek* on the *Enterprise*'s maiden voyage, he is shown as a decisive leader when acting as captain and as a skilled hand-to-hand fighter in confrontations with hostile entities. In other words, Sulu's gay masculinity is in stark contrast to many other Hollywood depictions of gay characters as overly effeminate, ineffectual, and unsympathetic. Up to this point in the film series, little is known of Sulu's backstory. His introduction in *Star Trek Beyond* changes that. Sulu sits in his familiar position on the bridge of the *Enterprise*. Kirk's captain's log is heard as a voice-over, and he describes the rigors of deep-space exploration. The camera tracks around Sulu, who is busily tapping on a screen, and shows he is wearing a wedding ring and has a photograph of a young girl attached to the monitor, presumably his daughter. This occurs at the same time as Kirk describes the sacrifices his crew have made to be away from their loved ones. Kirk's log continues, expounding on some of the effects "prolonged habitation" has had on the crew—namely, an increased libido. Two crew members gaze longingly at one another before stealing a passionate kiss in a secluded area of the ship. Simultaneously, farther down the corridor, a half-naked Checkov is kicked out of a female (alien) crewmate's quarters. In this section, and throughout the three film reboots, the *Enterprise*, Starfleet, the Federation, and, indeed, the entire known universe of *Star Trek* is portrayed as a heteronormative space.

Some leading experts on *Star Trek* criticism have persuasively argued that the franchise is ripe for queer readings. In *Gender and Sexuality in Star Trek*, David Greven challenges the view that *Star Trek* has never represented the LGBTQIA+ community (2014, 1). Through detailed readings of individual television episodes and films, he demonstrates how the attentive viewer can read allegory to discover the queer potential of these stories, some of which do not need that much discovering. Yet the fact remains that, before *Star Trek Beyond*, no openly gay characters were shown to exist within the *Star Trek* universe. At best, queer desire had to be inferred and read onto the texts. At worst, it was completely absent.

As is the case in the original television series *Star Trek* (1966–1969), there is opportunity to read the Kirk–Spock relationship in the Kelvin time line in queer terms. Their relationship begins with competitive hostility, develops into mutual respect, before turning to genuine affection verging on love, be that platonic or sexual. The films show both characters in heterosexual relationships. The Kirk of *Star Trek* and *Star Trek Into Darkness* is shown bedding an array of women, alien and human. And all three films portray the fraught union of Spock and Uhura. However, Kirk and Spock are more often seen together and confiding in one another, with more emphasis placed on *their* relationship than on interactions between them and their female counterparts. This reading takes on a different significance once the viewer learns that Spock is played by openly gay actor Zachary Quinto. Nowhere is this more pronounced than toward the end of *Star Trek Into Darkness*. Effectively a remake of *Star Trek II: The Wrath of Khan* (1982) that reverses Kirk's and Spock's roles, this film sees Kirk sacrifice himself to save the rest of the crew. Spock rushes to the engineering bay to find Kirk sealed behind a glass window and dying of radiation poisoning. Shot like so many film and TV sequences where one member of a heterosexual couple races to the rescue of their other half, the viewer sees Spock dart from the bridge and through the ship's corridors, notably passing Uhura without paying her any attention. Tearfully, Kirk and Spock exchange some final words about their shared friendship and place their hands on the glass that separates them. Regardless of how the film might want a viewer to respond to this scene, it is undeniably a moment of male-male intimacy that is never overtly stated as being anything more than that but certainly allows a queer interpretation.

Unlike the Kirk–Spock interaction, Sulu's sexuality is explicitly stated in *Star Trek Beyond*. The opening montage of humdrum life on the *Enterprise* has established a heterosexual space aboard the ship with male-female couples being formed, sometimes across species distinctions. Unless a viewer had been closely following the promotional campaign ahead of the film's release, where cast and crew confirmed the character's sexuality, the images of Sulu, his wedding ring and daughter's picture, would be subsumed within heteronormativity. However, when the *Enterprise* arrives at Starbase Yorktown for some much-needed downtime, Sulu is shown embracing first his daughter and then another man, who is played by cowriter Doug Jung. In an interview with *Vulture*, John Cho explains the reason behind making Sulu's husband East Asian is to address the culture's attitudes toward the LGBTQIA+ community (Jung 2016). Director Justin Lin chooses to film this moment in an intriguing way. As the crew arrive, they pair off to explore the base's amenities, or rush to meet their loved ones. Kirk is left isolated, but his gaze follows where Sulu has walked out of frame. A sequence of shot-reverse-shots takes place between Sulu reunited with his family and Kirk watching on. One cannot help recalling the captain's earlier log and the loneliness he is feeling. He seems to crave the kind of intimate connection that he describes as happening around him between other crew members. Still observing Sulu, Kirk smiles and there is a fleeting, tantalizing moment where his eyebrows raise ever so slightly. One can read this in various ways. Perhaps Kirk is expressing surprise at discovering Sulu's sexual identity; presumably, he would have noticed the helmsman's ring and photograph on the bridge without necessarily knowing that Sulu had a husband. Or could it be that Kirk, on seeing Sulu and his husband so happy, realizes that he too might desire the same kind of relationship with a woman or a man?

To return to the queer allegory, *Star Trek Beyond* is full of examples where appearances are deceptive. It is evident in the very first sequence. Kirk appears before the elders of an alien race offering an artifact (which turns out to be the Abronath) as a symbol of peace between two warring tribes. The leader becomes angry and prepares to attack, launching itself at Kirk, with others following suit. However, when they reach Kirk, they are no larger than a small dog, camera trickery and manipulation of sound creating the impression that they were hulk-

STAR TREK BEYOND   351

ing beasts. Later, Kirk shares a drink with Bones to celebrate his birthday and commemorate his dead father. Bones has stolen a bottle of scotch from Checkov's quarters to their shared surprise, assuming the Russian would be a vodka drinker. Krall's attack on the *Enterprise* appears to come from one large ship, only for the crew (and viewers) to learn that it is thousands of individual smaller ships arranged in formation. Krall thinks he has the Abronath, but the box is empty, and Kirk has secretly hidden it within the head of another crewmember. Jaylah (Sofia Boutella), whom Scotty meets after escaping the *Enterprise*, seeks shelter in a "house" that is later revealed to be the USS *Franklin* and hidden in plain sight by her holographic reflectors. Finally, Krall is able to physically alter his appearance through a process that drains the life force from his prisoners before the revelation that Krall is actually a former Federation captain. These instances, and many others, provide an allegory for LGBTQIA+ identity where, unless overtly stated, it can be difficult to identify a person based on appearances alone. As Kirk says to the rest of the crew, "there is no such thing as the unknown. Only the temporarily hidden." A prominent theme in the film is community and "finding one's crew" or family. Krall accuses the Federation's ethos of unity as being a weakness, not a strength, which is paralleled by Jaylah's description of his ships as bees being controlled by a hive mind. *Star Trek Beyond* makes its position clear at the end with Krall/Edison disintegrating alone in the isolation of space and the *Enterprise* crew coming together to witness their new ship being built.

Inclusion was part of Simon Pegg's plans for the script when developing Sulu's character. According to Seth Abramovitch of the *Hollywood Reporter*, Pegg and Lin wanted to pay tribute to openly gay actor and LGBTQIA+ rights activist George Takei, who played Sulu in the original series and films. What began as a well-meaning gesture soon soured when Takei expressed his disappointment with the decision, citing that this was not part of *Star Trek* creator Gene Roddenberry's original vision for the character. At the same time as welcoming the inclusion of a gay character, which was long overdue, Takei took exception to that character being Sulu. As indicated in a statement released to the *Guardian*, however, Pegg raised the fact that the later films take place in an alternate time line, meaning that character details from the original series could potentially change. Although the 1960s original series takes place in a future and supposedly more tolerant world, it was still produced at a time when the gay rights movement was only just beginning in America. *Star Trek Beyond* appears in a very different social, cultural, and political American landscape, where LGBTQIA+ identities are more visible if not always necessarily more accepted. Indeed, it is significant that *Star Trek Beyond* was released in the summer of 2016, just months before Donald Trump was elected as president, beginning a four-year term in which he attempted to reverse a number of victories the community had achieved under previous administrations. Later in the same *Guardian* article and echoing the communal spirit of the film he coscripted, Pegg remarks, "Whatever magic ingredient determines our sexuality was different for Sulu in our time line. I like this idea because it suggests that in a hypothetical multiverse, across an infinite matrix of alternate realities, we are all LGBT somewhere."

Despite these positive moves toward equal representation, the Sulu of *Star Trek Beyond* was not given the same treatment as his heterosexual crewmates.

John Cho revealed in an interview with *Vulture* that a shot showing Sulu and his husband sharing a kiss was cut from the final film (Jung 2016), a fate that befell other big-budget science-fiction films released around the same time, like *Jurassic World: Fallen Kingdom* (2017) and *Thor: Ragnarok* (2018). Just like *Star Trek Beyond*'s central theme of appearances being deceptive, the portrayal of a gay *Star Trek* character might look like a bold step forward for the franchise. A closer look reveals queer characters remain subject to the dictates of an industry shaped by heteronormativity. There is still a way to go before the *Star Trek* universe firmly embraces LGBTQIA+ identities, even if this is a necessary first step.

See also *Spa Night*; *The Wedding Banquet*.

Bibliography

Abramovitch, Seth. "George Takei Reacts to Gay Sulu News: 'I Think It's Really Unfortunate.'" *Hollywood Reporter*, July 7, 2016. Accessed 23, 2021. https://www.hollywoodreporter.com /news/george-takei-reacts-gay-sulu-909154.

Greven, David. *Gender and Sexuality in Star Trek: Allegories of Desire in the Television Series and Films*. Jefferson, NC: McFarland, 2014.

Jung, E. Alex. "You Haven't Seen Everything John Cho Can Do." *Vulture*, July 20, 2016. Accessed April 23, 2021. https://www.vulture.com/2016/07/john-cho-star-trek-beyond-c-v-r.html.

Shoard, Catherine. "Simon Pegg: I Respectfully Disagree with George Takei over Gay Sulu." *Guardian*, July 8, 2016. Accessed April 23, 2021. https://www.theguardian.com/film/2016 /jul/08/simon-pegg-defends-gay-sulu-after-george-takei-criticism.

—Adam Vaughan

SUMMER OF SAM (1999)

DIRECTOR: Spike Lee
SCREENPLAY: Victor Colicchio, Michael Imperioli, and Spike Lee
CAST: John Leguizamo (Vinny), Adrien Brody (Ritchie), Mira Sorvino (Dionna), Jennifer Esposito (Ruby)
SPECS: 142 minutes; color
AVAILABILITY: DVD (KL Classics)

New York City, 1977. It is one of the hottest summers on record. At one point, a citywide blackout results in massive looting and vandalism. Reggie Jackson leads the New York Yankees through a winning season and World Series victory. David Berkowtiz, the serial killer known as the ".44 Caliber Killer" and the "Son of Sam," is roaming the streets and targeting young women. This all provides the backdrop for a story about mistrust, paranoia, and fear in an Italian American neighborhood.

Vinny has been unfaithful to his wife, Dionna, multiple times. When his infidelity nearly puts him in the crosshairs of the Son of Sam, Vinny begins to question why he was spared. Vinny's friend Ritchie returns to their neighborhood after being away for some unknown period. While away, Ritchie discovered and embraced the punk music scene. Ritchie now finds himself an outsider among the disco-loving neighborhood locals. As the Son of Sam's victim count continues to rise, the neighborhood locals look for the murderer themselves, with Ritchie becoming their prime suspect.

Summer of Sam was met with controversy on its release. The film faced backlash from family members of the murder victims and even David Berkowitz himself for, arguably, glorifying his crimes (Angulo 1999). *Summer of Sam*, however, is not about Berkowitz. As a character, Berkowitz is only seen or heard in a voice-over for approximately fifteen minutes of the 142-minute run time of the film. *Summer of Sam* is about the effect of Berkowitz's reign of terror on an Italian American community. The film also faced criticism for its portrayal of Italian Americans. One reviewer for the *New York Post* referred to director Spike Lee as racist for the way he portrayed Italian Americans and claimed that "if I were an Italian American, Spike Lee would need several bodyguards" (Dunleavy 1999). Several actors in the film defended Lee, stating that the portrayal of Italian Americans in *Son of Sam* accurately reflects a specific portion of the Italian American population (Angulo 1999). Many of the Italian American characters on display in *Summer of Sam* are depicted as violent and unintelligent. These same characters also regularly spout derogatory statements about a variety of groups, including the LGBTQIA+ community.

Homophobic epithets are used throughout the film to cast Ritchie as an outsider to the neighborhood and eventually a suspect because of his change in fashion and interests. Early in the film, viewers meet several of Vinny's friends and neighborhood locals, including Joey, Brian, Anthony, and Woodstock. Ritchie enters a scene with these characters while wearing a Union Jack T-shirt, a skull necklace, and spiked hair. Ritchie has also adopted a British accent, which draws the ire of the others. Joey finally remarks, "You come back to the neighborhood looking like a fucking freak, sounding like a British fag. We're supposed to be okay with that?" [00:17:41–00:17:46]. In a later scene, Ritchie and Vinny are at a diner when two customers antagonize Ritchie, telling him to "keep looking, you half-a-fag" [01:12:23–01:23-24]. The customers convince the owner of the diner to refuse Ritchie and Vinny service to make them leave.

Viewers eventually learn that Ritchie is a dancer at a gay theater called Male World. Ritchie asks the owner of the theater if he can do a show that night. Viewers then see Ritchie performing a dance routine for a group of men in the audience. Ritchie is also prostituting himself as the audience sees him meet one of the patrons in a private room above the theater after his performance. Later, viewers seem him perform another dance routine and meet another patron in the private room. This is intercut with Ritchie purchasing and playing an expensive guitar.

Ritchie keeps his activities a secret from everyone except Ruby. Ruby is a promiscuous woman who has had sex with several of the neighborhood locals, including Vinny. Ruby and Ritchie begin a relationship, and Ruby begins dressing in punk fashion as well and joins Ritchie's punk band. Ritchie takes Ruby to see him dance at Male World. She is initially shocked, but she supports him, and their relationship grows. Whether Ritchie is bisexual or just performs at the theater and has sex with men for money is not explicitly stated. Ritchie keeps his involvement at the theater a secret from the guys in the neighborhood until Bobby Del Fiore sees him performing there. Ritchie slams Bobby against a wall and threatens him not to tell his secret, but Bobby informs the other neighborhood locals about Ritchie's activities and the threat.

Viewers are also introduced to Bobby, who the neighborhood guys refer to as "Bobby the Fairy" in an earlier scene of the film. Bobby, who has longer hair than the other men, pink sunglasses, and his shirt tied in a knot above his abdomen, approaches Joey to buy drugs. The neighborhood locals use homophobic remarks toward Bobby as attempts at humor. Bobby plays into these remarks and appears not to be offended. When Bobby asks Joey for two bags (of marijuana), Joey replies with "Two what? Two dicks?" [00:44:06–00:44:07]. To which, Bobby replies, "I'll take yours and Ritchie's. Double the pleasure, double the fun" [00:44:08–00:44:11]. When Bobby enters the scene, the locals are discussing the identity of the Son of Sam. Anthony jokingly accuses Bobby by saying, "It said in the *Post* that the killer's a woman hater. That's you, Bobby. You could be the killer" [00:44:22–00:44:25]. Joey interjects, calling Bobby the ".44 caliber queer" [00:44:26–00:44:27], and Anthony adds, "Yeah, a real *homo*-cidal maniac" [00:44:29–00:44:30]. Brian yells out, "He's guilty! Put him through the *penal* system" [00:44:30–00:44:32]. Bobby then approaches Brian and tells him, "Only if I can have you as my cellmate" [00:44:33–00:44:35]. While Brian was happy to make gay jokes toward Bobby, when Bobby directed the joke back toward him, Brian retaliates by putting out his cigarette in Bobby's palm. Angry and in pain, Bobby retreats as Joey chastises Brian, saying, "C'mon, don't burn him. He's a paying customer" [00:44:44-00:44-46]. No longer joking, Brian curtly states, "He's a homo" [00:44:47].

The neighborhood locals clearly view Bobby as being of a lower status than them and worthy of ridicule because he is no longer seen as a "straight" man; however, they still view him as part of the neighborhood. Bobby's sexual orientation makes him different, but being from that neighborhood still makes him "one of them." In one shot of a montage of various characters set to the Who's "Baba O'Riley," the audience sees the neighborhood locals find a battered and bloody Bobby. Bobby was apparently beaten by someone named Rocko. It is not revealed why Bobby was beaten, but one could assume it was because of him being gay. In another shot of the montage, viewers see the neighborhood locals (including Brian, who burned Bobby earlier) beating a group of men and yelling at them not to mess with Bobby.

In one scene, the neighborhood locals are at a pizza parlor discussing who they think the Son of Sam is and compiling a list of possible suspects. Despite their comments earlier, they do not put Bobby on the list that includes Ritchie, "Billy the Jew," and a local priest who they believe is an alcoholic. Their belief that Ritchie is the Son of Sam is cemented when Bobby later reveals that Ritchie is a dancer at the gay theater; if Ritchie has been hiding that, then he must be hiding other things as well. Ritchie possibly being gay pushes their belief that Ritchie could be the killer over the edge. While Bobby is gay, he has always been in the neighborhood. They know him. Ritchie may also be gay, but he is more of an outsider. When the locals eventually decide that Ritchie must be the Son of Sam, even Bobby goes with the group to confront Ritchie and assists them when they attack Ritchie.

While already under suspicion by the locals, once it is discovered that Ritchie is a dancer at Male World, homophobic language is used to convince Vinny that Ritchie is the Son of Sam. Brian begins with, "Tell him about the fag strip joint.

Tell him who the star attraction was" [01:47:47–01:47:50]. Vinny replies with, "What the fuck are you talking about fag joint, come on" [01:47:51–01:47:53]. Bobby chimes in, telling Vinny that Ritchie dances at Male World and makes porn movies. Joey then asks Vinny, "Did you know that about your friend? What else don't you know about this pervert?" [01:48:00–01:48:03]. Vinny tells him that that information does not make Ritchie the Son of Sam. Anthony then says, "Killer, fag, pimp, punk rocker" [01:48:08–01:48:11]. Brian adds, "Queer, pervert, homo, degenerate. Whatever the fuck it is. I mean, come on. Who wants something like that around here anyway?" [01:48:11–01:48:17].

Joey and Brian go looking for Ritchie at the punk club CBGB because they think he is the Son of Sam. Vinny also goes to try to warn Ritchie about Joey and Brian, but then confronts him about what he learned from Bobby. Vinny starts with, "Bobby the fairy tells me you're a nude dancer at a fag club. What am I supposed to do with that?" [01:52:49–01:52:53]. Ritchie reacts in disbelief before Vinny continues with, "Bobby the fairy says you're a fucking fag dancer" [01:52:54–01:52:56]. Ritchie vehemently denies this and attacks Bobby's credibility, saying that "Bobby the fag don't know shit, okay? 'Cause he's a homo, now I'm one?" [01:52:57–01:53:00]. Vinny does not believe Ritchie and says, "I don't know. You tell me. You tell me, are you sucking dick, is that what you're doing?" [01:53:02–01:53:07]. Their argument ends with Ritchie stating, "Hey, first you think I'm the Son of Sam, now I'm a fucking homo. I can't believe this" [01:53:08–01:53:12].

For Ritchie, homophobic epithets are directed toward him by other characters to cast him as an outsider. For Bobby, homophobic epithets are directed toward him by other characters mainly as attempts at humor. The characters in the film also use homophobic epithets to hurt each other. This is exemplified in an argument between Vinny and Dionna. After being denied entry to the disco club Studio 54, Vinny and Dionna accept an invitation to the sex club Plato's Retreat. Dionna is initially uncomfortable with the open sexual activity, but after some drug use, she and Vinny begin to have sex with each other and then other people. While Vinny is having sex with another woman, he watches Dionna have sex with women and other men. Vinny becomes visibly jealous seeing his wife having sex with others despite his persistent infidelity up to that point. During the car ride home, there is awkward silence before they begin to talk about what happened at the club. Dionna, embarrassed, blames the drug use for her involvement. Vinny then tells her, "Don't blame the pills, you fucking lesbian fucking whore" [01:31:59–01:32:01]. Dionna retorts that he was there too and must also be a whore. Vinny responds with, "I can't be a whore because I'm a man. You're the whore, you stupid lesbian fucking whore" [01:32:06–01:32:11]. Upset, Dionna attacks Vinny's masculinity and profession by calling him a "faggot fucking hairdresser" before slapping him [01:32:13]. Vinny stops the car and their argument moves outside the vehicle. Dionna then jumps in the driver's seat and Vinny tells her "You wanna drive? Okay, drive me over there, you fucking dyke" [01:34:20–01:34:22]. Dionna, once again, calls him a "faggot fucking hairdresser" [01:34:25–01:34:26] before driving away and leaving Vinny behind. Vinny is afraid of being left alone because of the Son of Sam, and while he begs

Dionna to let him back in the car, she tells him, "I hope he kills you, you fucking faggot pansy" [01:34:36–01:34:39], as she speeds away.

By the end of the film, Vinny and Dionna's marriage appears to be over as she has moved out of their apartment. Vinny has also lost his job after showing up to work under the influence and accosting his boss (who he was also having an affair with). Lastly, Vinny destroys his relationship with Ritchie by luring Ritchie out of his home so the other neighborhood locals can forcefully turn him over to a local mobster as the Son of Sam. Ritchie is rescued by his stepfather, but not before being severely beaten.

Members of the LGBTQIA+ community may find it difficult to get past the derogatory dialogue in *Summer of Sam* and the way the film portrays its LGBTQIA+ characters. Bobby, an openly gay character, is comfortable associating with characters who freely ridicule his sexuality. He also provides the proverbial "final straw" to make the neighborhood locals act on their suspicions that Ritchie is the Son of Sam by informing them of Ritchie's secret life working at the gay theater. Ritchie, while arguably the most likeable and interesting of the Italian American male characters, is also quick to ridicule Bobby to deflect from accusations that he may be bisexual. Director Spike Lee is a talented filmmaker who has made several thought-provoking films and documentaries dealing with issues of race and urban life (*Do the Right Thing, Malcolm X*, etc.). Despite several strong performances by those in the cast, *Summer of Sam* places in the lower half of Lee's filmography.

See also *The Craft: Legacy*.

Bibliography

Angulo, Sandra P. "Summer of Sam Cast Members Respond to the Media's Criticism." *Entertainment Weekly*, July 2, 1999. Accessed January 29, 2021. https://ew.com/article/1999/07/02/summer-sam-cast-members-respond-medias-criticisms/.

Dunleavy, Steve. "Spike Lee Hits New Low in Racist Moviemaking." *New York Post*, June 25, 1999. Accessed January 29, 2021. https://nypost.com/1999/06/25/spike-lee-hits-new-low-in-racist-moviemaking/.

—Corey Call

• T •

TANGERINE (2015)

DIRECTOR: Sean Baker
SCREENPLAY: Sean Baker and Chris Bergoch
CAST: Kitana Kiki Rodriguez (Sin-Dee), Mya Taylor (Alexandra), Karren Karagulian (Razmik), Mickey O'Hagan (Dinah), James Ransone (Chester), Nash (Ian Edwards) Ashken (Alla Tumanian)
SPECS: 88 minutes; color
AVAILABILITY: DVD (Magnolia Pictures)

Tangerine captures the eventful day of Sin-Dee and Alexandra, two friends and trans sex workers living in downtown Los Angeles. It is Christmas Eve, and Sin-Dee has just been released from jail. The friends are meeting at Donut Time, a popular location for sex workers and their customers. Within the first five minutes of the film, *Tangerine* paints a picture of the social, political, and economic conditions that these characters are entrenched in. As Sin-Dee shares her reflections of jail with Alexandra, it becomes clear that being policed is a common feature of their daily lives. On top of this surveillance, there are financial limitations. This is expressed through Sin-Dee's meager funds to purchase a single

Kitana Kiki Rodriguez as Sin-Dee, James Ransone as Chester, and Mya Taylor as Alexandra in *Tangerine*. Courtesy of Magnolia Pictures/Photofest

donut for the duo to share because her remaining funds went toward the bus to get her there. Despite these social and economic obstacles, the two laugh, joke, share affection, and enjoy one another's presence. As a result, *Tangerine* manages to present the hardships of living on a low income in LA, as trans women of color, without allowing these hardships to totally define the characters. In fact, their ability to undermine and overcome the limitations built into their surroundings makes their loving bonds, commanding personalities, lighthearted humor, and social and emotional resilience all the more accessible to viewers.

The core conflict of *Tangerine* is quickly established when Alexandra accidentally shares news about the cheating habits of Sin-Dee's boyfriend, Chester, while Sin-Dee was in jail. Upon receiving this news, Sin-Dee spirals into a daylong rage, hunting for Chester's "side chick" (named Dinah) in the streets, restaurants, and motels of their neighborhood. This shows that the characters are well versed in their surroundings—they know where they are going and who they will find there—suggesting that they are stable and integral threads in the larger fabric of their community. Amid the chaos, Alexandra attempts—but ultimately fails—to deescalate the situation. In turn, she gives up and decides to work the streets instead. By departing from Sin-Dee, Alexandra adds a second story line to the mix, which consists of her personal encounters with troublesome customers and law enforcement. Alexandra's story line also shows her promoting her vocal performance scheduled for later that evening, handing out flyers to neighborhood associates and friends. Alongside Sin-Dee and Alexandra's adventures, Razmik is introduced as a third story line. Razmik is a cab driver who regularly solicits sex from Alexandra and Sin-Dee. By the end of the film, all three story lines merge back together at Donut Time, where it all began. In this climactic moment, the characters' individual secrets surface, giving rise to conflicts that threaten their own integrity and their interpersonal bonds with one another, ultimately delivering round, developed characters struggling with issues of family, love, lust, and distrust.

Since the release of *Tangerine* in 2015, the film has been regarded as groundbreaking, subversive, and influential in the world of American cinema. The applause that *Tangerine* has received is largely due to the unique and nontraditional methods of filmmaking and a leading cast of transwomen, Kitana Kiki Rodriguez and Mya Taylor. Director Sean Baker met Rodriguez and Taylor at the same Donut Time intersection that serves as the pillar of the film's setting. By casting Rodriguez and Taylor, Baker felt that the most responsible and respectful way to approach the film's subject matter was to submerge himself in their world and let their personal stories shape the film's script. Alongside Taylor and Rodriguez, some of the other cast members featured in *Tangerine* were sourced from popular social media platforms at the time, like Instagram and Vine. The music for the soundtrack was similarly sourced through Vine and SoundCloud, which not only kept the budget of the film low but helped with the recognition of new artists, like the seventeen-year-olds DJ Lightup and DJ Heemie, who produced the trap song "Team Gotti Anthem" that plays early in the film (Watercutter 2015). Casting actors and other personnel by scrolling through social media platforms and allowing Rodriguez's and Taylor's experiences to shape the script causes *Tangerine* to feel like a documentary in many respects, as opposed to a drama-comedy fiction. Other reasons *Tangerine* registers as a documentary is because of the cinematography. *Tangerine* possesses many qualities of cinema verité—a style of filmmaking that avoids extravagant sets, props, and technology. Cinema verité can be identified through stylistic choices, such as handheld cameras and "guerilla-style" recording, which presents characters and settings in their true representational forms. Shot on three iPhones with augmented lenses and the Filmic Pro app, *Tangerine* further flouts Hollywood cinema rules and expectations. By straying from expensive camera equipment and editing software, *Tangerine* succeeds in delivering original styles and mise-en-scènes without losing the vibrant colors, crisp close-ups, and clear depth-of-field shots.

One of the most outstanding features of *Tangerine* is its use of color. While Sin-Dee and Alexandra move throughout their neighborhood, the world is presented through an oversaturation of jewel tones, adding a whimsical aura of fantasy and wonder. Despite making the lived experiences of these characters accessible through realism and documentary styles of filmmaking, Baker's shrouding of these characters in a bit of fantasy—like the jewel-tone colors—cinematically gestures toward the political refusal to fully assimilate to normative reality. McKinley Green suggests that "*Tangerine* disidentifies with conventional cinema by adopting a traditional narrative structure while simultaneously queering both its subject matter and recording method" (2016, 120). This concept of disidentification comes from Josè Esteban Muñoz and is considered a strategic defense mechanism for the LGBTQIA+ community as it allows individuals to submerge themselves in everyday life while maintaining a level of precautionary distance. In this way, *Tangerine* delivers an authentic and accessible glimpse of the lives of its characters while holding it at a safe and incorruptible distance.

This use of color becomes increasingly meaningful in comparison to Razmik's backstory, which reveals that his sexual preferences are incompatible with his home life, which consists of his wife, young child, and extremely conservative, Christian Armenian in-laws. Aside from the bright and colorful lights that embellish the Christmas tree in the corner of Razmik and his family's apartment, the space is otherwise underwhelming. Brown leather and muted paisley prints make up the furniture, while their surrounding walls are a glossy, Dijon-mustard yellow that barely offsets the hardwood floors. This traditional, "normal" setting of Razmik's home resembles a plush cardboard box that he longs to escape from and into the bright and whimsical world of Sin-Dee and Alexandra.

Additional layers of meaning can be pulled from *Tangerine*'s setting: Hollywood during Christmas time. In fact, these themes may serve as passageways toward more complex themes in queer theory. When it comes to social and cultural performativity, the placement of these characters in a Christmas-themed Hollywood manages *not* to exaggerate the queer qualities of the characters but rather to exaggerate the queer qualities embedded in the normative rituals of American society. *Tangerine* exposes the many ways social habits are performed and decorations are used to transform the outward appearance of the world to match the inner beliefs of individuals or groups. For example, one low-angle shot shows a giant inflatable snowman standing in tall contradiction to the California heat. This giant, plastic snowman is perched alongside a lot full of pine trees that grow sparingly in the hot, humid environment of California. Razmik's discriminatory mother-in-law, Ashken, claims that Christmas feels fake without snow before labeling Los Angeles a "beautifully wrapped lie." While Ashken is the most anti-LGBTQIA+ character of the film, her short monologue nonetheless reveals that *all* identities and *all* beliefs (whether normative or marginalized) are socially constructed and maintained through artifice, façades, performances, and learned habits.

By showcasing transgender characters against a Christmas backdrop, *Tangerine* gestures toward foundational arguments in queer theory. Judith Butler approaches gender as a performance in this way. Borrowing from feminist philosopher, Simone de Beauvoir, Butler reminds readers that "one is not born a woman" regardless of their sexual assignment at birth. Rather, one *"becomes a woman."* Essentially, gender is not a stable identity that determines an individual's agency or expressions throughout their life; alternatively, gender is a complex and shifting identity that is shaped and created over time through acts of repetition (Butler 1988, 519). The Hollywood setting of *Tangerine* propels the queer theory debate even further. Hollywood—a space associated with stardom, wealth, and fame since it became the movie capital of the world in the early 1900s—is linked with the production of sexual icons and beauty norms alike. Film theorist Robert C. Allen discusses "star theory" as the phenomenon in which stars and celebrities *become* images, socially structured by a "range of possible meanings"—meanings that are liable to shift and change through the course of history (1985, 173). In queer theory, gender identity and expression are viewed in a similar way: not entirely free from a script but also not limited in possibilities. "Becoming" is an important concept that captures the complex, creative, social, and ever-changing nature of identity.

In one shot, Sin-Dee glides down Hollywood Boulevard. In the background are swarms of tourists and consumers crowding the sidewalk, enamored with the landmark. An eye-line match of Sin-Dee's downward-facing gaze reveals the stars that mark Hollywood's "Walk of Fame"; however, her fast-paced walking paired with her down-turned gaze suggests that she is not infatuated with the ideology that Hollywood Boulevard sells but is a normal person with places to be. This minor example shows how Baker avoids making a spectacle out of Taylor's and Rodriguez's identities. By showcasing the masses of consumers in the background, Baker manages to free Sin-Dee from the gaze of the hyper spectacle-driven culture that she moves through while also showing the invisibility that a character like Sin-Dee can feel when dropped in the center of America's manufacturer of sex iconography and beauty norms.

Part of telling Taylor's and Rodriguez's story meant capturing their environment, which fits the cinema verité style. In doing so, towering palm trees—which have come to represent California as a dreamy Western oasis in the United States—are replaced with telephone poles. Rather than present Hollywood imagery of fame, wealth, and high-end fashion, spectators are shown the outskirts of Hollywood Boulevard, which houses Skid Row, food banks, advertisements for credit loans, drab stretches of concrete, and mini malls housing liquor stores, laundromats, and bail bond agents. Baker avoids reducing the characters to pitiful victims of their environment without shying away from the class conditions that these characters are forced to navigate on a daily basis.

Although the film takes viewers on a comedic and lighthearted ride in the lives of the confident and empowering characters, there are subtle moments of sobering doubt, vulnerability, and safeguarding expressed by them. One of these moments is during the montage of Sin-Dee, when she contemplates the next move in her search for Dinah and Chester at a bus stop. Beethoven's *Coriolanus Overture* plays loudly, and Sin-Dee is shown through abstract angles, giving the scene an epic quality. A deep-focus shot barely captures Sin-Dee's head at the bottom right corner of the frame as she leans forward, smoking a cigarette in deep thought. Sin-Dee then sits up straight, making her person much more visible in the frame, as well as the inner anger and frustration that she exudes. Another abstract shot follows, showing the top half of Sin-Dee's head from behind the bus stop bench. This is intercut with medium shots of her looking over her shoulders and checking her surroundings. Megan Malone (2020) describes the importance of these shots, as they prioritize her thoughts and emotions as opposed to her body, opening up more opportunities for identification between her character and spectators. At the same time, Sin-Dee gives off annoyed and somewhat cautionary gestures, as she looks over her shoulder to gauge the close proximity of a man standing behind her. While spectators are given an outlet for identification with Sin-Dee's emotional output, Sin-Dee's vulnerable position as a transwoman of color living in a big city is an ongoing risk that comes with her visibility.

Another example is during Alexandra's performance of "Toyland." In addition to being disappointed by the lack of support that she received from her community, there is something eerie—even threatening—in the lyrics: "Toyland, Toyland / Little girl and boy land / While you dwell within it / You are ever happy there / Childhood's joy land / Mystic merry toyland / Once you pass its borders / You can ne'er return again." The meaning of these lyrics can be linked to the setting, to innocent exploration and play in childhood, and the more critical and judgmental realm of adulthood. Similar to the previous scene, which placed Sin-Dee's emotions and thought processes in the fore, this scene reveals more about Alexandra's introspection. Both Sin-Dee and Alexandra are presented as extremely strong, independent, and outspoken characters, adding to the value of these thought-provoking moments. And while these more vulnerable and dramatic moments arise, it is interesting how Baker presents them through an expressionistic style—alongside the jewel tones, which add a level of fantasy, the scene of Alexandra's performance is preceded by Alexandra, Sin-Dee, and Dinah "touching up" their makeup in the dimly lit bathroom, in which small beams of ethereal blue light reflect in every direction. Despite being presented with these characters' realities, there are ways the spectator is held at a distance—which again, can be associated with Muñoz's concept of disidentification.

This sobering vulnerability of the characters comes to a head when Sin-Dee is the victim of a transphobic assault after a man in the passenger seat of a car pretends to solicit her before throwing a cup of urine in her face. This event takes place after a fight between Sin-Dee and Alexandra unfolds, in which the former finds out that the latter has been sexually involved with Chester as well. However, the final scene affirms the importance of their loving bond and kinship as Alexandra comforts and cleans the urine from Sin-Dee's body, clothes, and wig. The unconditional love shown between Sin-Dee and Alexandra may simply represent a strong friendship, but their bond is emblematic of "house culture," in which families were created to offset the abandonment experienced by LGBTQIA+ individuals; "house" is the formation of familial bonds for those who have undergone exile from their own unaccepting families. A sense of community is clearly established as Sin-Dee and Alexandra run into other LGBTQIA+ members on the streets, addressing them by name, throughout the film. This community is also sensed in the Donut Time setting, which is recognized—by Chester, Sin-Dee, Alexandra, Razmik, and the cab driver who drives Ashken in her search for Razmik—as a reliable and stable location to convene with one another.

Tangerine opens a unique space for trans characters—and performers—to exist. The positive and playful light through which trans characters are captured in Tangerine is beneficial to the archive of LGBTQIA+ representations in Hollywood cinema, especially since many of these representations of the past consist of harmful and discriminatory stereotypes. According to Green, Tangerine succeeds "as a work of narrative cinema" as well as a film that "constitutes a valuable depiction of queer life and a rich text to examine in relation to queer theory" (2016, 120). All the while, Tangerine reserves themes worth further questioning and critique. For example, in the final scene, in which Alexandra helps Sin-Dee clean herself up in the laundromat, Sin-Dee shows concern about her inability to afford a new wig. Not only does this scene bring the viewer's attention to the reinforcement of beauty "ideals," like donning long, straight hair, but it shows the ways such "ideals" are unaffordable and inaccessible to different races or classes and, therefore, a reinforcement of social stratifications. An abundance of dialogue and considerations can follow a viewing of Tangerine, including intersectional themes of gender, race, and class as they are laid bare without weighing down the spirited development of its characters.

See also Boys Don't Cry; Transamerica.

Bibliography

Allen, Robert C. "Case Study: The Role of the Star in Film History." In Film History Theory and Practice, 172–89. New York: Newbery Award Records, 1985.

Beauvoir, Simone de. The Second Sex. New York: Vintage Books, 2011.

Butler, Judith. "Performative Acts and Gender Constitution: An Essay in Phenomenology and Feminist Theory." Theatre Journal 40, no. 4 (1988): 519–31.

Green, McKinley. "Tangerine." Queer Studies in Media & Pop Culture 1, no. 1 (2016): 119–22.

Malone, Meagan E. "Celebrating Transness: Tangerine and the iPhone." European Journal of English Studies 24, no. 1 (2020): 65–75.

Watercutter, Angela. "Tangerine Is Amazing—but Not Because of How They Shot It." Wired, July 7, 2015. Accessed February 20, 2021. https://www.wired.com/2015/07/tangerine-iphone/.

—Aspen Taylor Ballas

THE TIMES OF HARVEY MILK (1984)

DIRECTOR: Rob Epstein

SCREENPLAY: Rob Epstein, Carter Wilson, and Judith Coburn

CAST: Harvey Fierstein (as the narrator), Harvey Milk (as self), Anne Kronenberg (as self), Tory Hartmann (as self), Tom Ammiano (as self)

Specs: 90 minutes; color/black and white
Availability: DVD (Criterion Collection)

The Times of Harvey Milk begins with a shocked Supervisor Diane Feinstein telling San Franciscans that Mayor George Moscone and Supervisor Harvey Milk, hero to the LGBTQIA+ community, had been shot and killed by Supervisor Dan White. Most memorable are her eyes, widely staring into nothingness. The gasps coming from the reporters give viewers a sense of the shocking nature of this event to a city most accepting of the growing gay rights movement. It also sets the tone for one of the most influential documentaries of the twentieth century. Directed by Rob Epstein and winner of the Academy Award for Best Documentary Feature in 1984, *The Times of Harvey Milk* is "an enormously absorbing film for the light it sheds on a decade in the life of a great American city and on the lives of Milk and Moscone, who made it a better, and certainly a more interesting place to live" (Ebert 1985).

Soon after the video footage of Feinstein, viewers hear the gravelly and uncharacteristically somber voice of actor and gay-rights activist Harvey Fierstein, speaking on the assassinations but focusing his attention primarily on Milk, who considered himself (based on an audio recording of his will presented in the film) a member of a movement greater than himself that moved forward an agenda empowering the 1970s LGBTQIA+ community. Throughout the film, the audience sees footage of Milk filled with life and love, walking the streets of San Francisco, shoulder to shoulder with happy community members and proudly throwing his fist in the air while sitting atop a moving car, a lei around his neck and a wide smile across on his face. He is often depicted as a pleasant man, quick to laugh and connect with those around him. He is shown kissing his lover full on the lips and then guffawing at his forwardness; he exuded an infectious and intimating radiance, at least to some of the filmed interviewees.

Milk, a California camera store owner, was equally beloved and targeted, especially during a time when the Stonewall Uprising in Greenwich Village and the Anita Bryant campaign to repeal gay-rights legislation in Miami were usurping what Rebecca Rosen called "a remarkable period of transformation for gays and lesbians" in that advocacy and alliances were becoming more visible to the general public and in mass media (2014). Epstein's agenda is to chronicle Milk's political influence by using interviews with friends, coworkers, Castro community members, labor unionists, and others—what Dan Krauss calls "a tapestry of testimony" (2015)—and to weave a narrative that would solidify him as a prominent American gay figure. The editing and the camerawork as well as the lack of theatrics and visual acrobatics when filming Epstein's willing subjects makes the film easygoing and educational. Epstein's deceased protagonist lives on because of deft visual storytelling and in the political agendas Milk championed for the diverse peoples of District 5, including his opposition to Proposition 6 ("The Briggs Initiative") "that would have mandated the firing of any gay or lesbian teacher in California public schools, or any teacher who supported gay rights (the term "LGBT" wasn't used back then)" (Ring 2018).

Viewers also learn more about Milk's antagonist, District 8's Dan White, an affable man who firmly spoke about policy and traditional values whom viewers later learn unravels after the Briggs Initiative loss due to job stress and a home life filled with financial issues. White ultimately resigned, then attempted to come back, but was rejected by Mayor Moscone primarily at Milk's behest, which led to the grisly murders. Viewers see video of the covered bodies and frantic police officers, interviews of crying friends, the stunning candlelight vigil, and the equally as stunning "Twinkie Defense" that earned White a mere five and a half years in prison. The verdict led to riots and the destruction of City Hall, but it also provided the United States with a stronger understanding of how the LGBTQIA+ community must continue to fight to gain the rights and freedoms that straight people have. At the end of *The Times of Harvey Milk*, viewers see Milk in slow motion again on the car and hear his distinct voice say that although the gay community cannot live on hope, it has a right to feel hope, and will one day be comfortable enough to come out or fight for the rights they so deserve.

See also *Battle of the Sexes; Behind the Candelabra; Can You Ever Forgive Me?; Kinsey.*

Bibliography

Ebert, Roger. "The Times of Harvey Milk." RogerEbert.com, February 22, 1985. Accessed June 26, 2021. https://www.rogerebert.com/reviews/the-times-of-harvey-milk-1985.

Krauss, Dan. "Rob Epstein's 'The Times of Harvey Milk.'" Documentary.org, July 30, 2015. Accessed June 26, 2021. https://www.documentary.org/column/rob-epsteins-times-harvey-milk.

Ring, Trudy. "The Briggs Initiative: Remembering a Crucial Moment in Gay History." *Advocate*, August 31, 2018. Accessed June 26, 2021. https://www.advocate.com/politics/2018/8/31/briggs-initiative-remembering-crucial-moment-gay-history.

Rosen, Rebecca J. "A Glimpse into 1970s Gay Rights Activism." *Atlantic*, February 26, 2014. Accessed June 26, 2021. https://www.theatlantic.com/politics/archive/2014/02/a-glimpse-into-1970s-gay-activism/284077/.

—Douglas C. Macleod Jr.

TO ALL THE BOYS I'VE LOVED BEFORE (2018)

DIRECTOR: Susan Johnson
SCREENPLAY: Sofia Alvarez, based on the young adult novel of the same name by Jenny Han
CAST: Lana Condor (Lara Jean), Noah Centineo (Peter), Janel Parrish (Margot), Anna Cathcart (Kitty), Trezzo Mahoro (Lucas), Madeleine Arthur (Christine), John Corbett (Dr. Covey)
SPECS: 100 minutes; color
AVAILABILITY: Netflix (Netflix Originals)

Based on Jenny Han's novel of the same name, and the first in a trilogy, *To All the Boys I've Loved Before* focuses on hopeless romantic Lara Jean Covey. As a form of catharsis, she has written five love letters to each of her past crushes only to then store them in her closet, never to be sent or acknowledged. However, this exercise turns to humiliation when her little sister, Kitty, mails the letters in hopes that Lara Jean receives a reciprocated reply. In response to her confessions, Peter, Josh, and Lucas immediately seek out Laura Jean. Nonetheless, in trying to avoid an awkward confrontation with Josh, whom Laura Jean deems an inappropriate match due to his previous romantic relationship with her older sister Margot, she ends up kissing Peter as a diversion tactic. From here, Peter and Lara Jean begin pretending to date in order both to conceal Lara Jean's true feelings from Josh and to make Peter's ex-girlfriend jealous. As they perpetuate this façade, Lara Jean and Peter genuinely fall in love. This causes confusion and uncertainty between the two; however, by the end of the film, they accept their feelings and begin a real relationship.

To All the Boys I've Loved Before includes an LGBTQIA+ character, Lucas Krapf. Laura Jean's good friend Lucas is one of the recipients of her love letters. In private, he responds kindly to the sentiments expressed in her letter but explains, "You know I'm gay, right?" [00:22:45–00:23:00]. While this is a rejection of her romantic feelings, it is also an act of trust. Though Lucas professes to be out, he mentions that his mother knows about his sexuality while his father "kinda knows," insinuating that Lucas is in a liminal space of both being closeted and being out [00:23:05–00:23:15]. That he is not fully comfortable with his sexuality in public or at home depicts a range of experiences to which many in the LGBTQIA+ community may be able to relate. It is a realistic depiction of the apprehension that accompanies coming out, especially to one's family. However, while Lucas explicitly requests that Lara Jean refrain from discussing his sexuality, she fails to do so. When Lara Jean is explaining the nature of her letters to Peter, she mentions that she wrote one to Lucas. Plainly, Peter states, "He's gay," to which Lara Jean unconvincingly replies, "Y-You don't know that," as a weak attempt at hiding Lucas's sexuality, only for Peter to explain, "Everyone knows that" [00:28:00–00:28:30]. In the first conversation Lara Jean has after Lucas entrusts her with his identity as a gay man, she tries to keep his secret but too quickly relents when it is clear that Peter already knows. Lucas's desire for his sexual identity to remain private is not respected here. Yet it is also critical to note that neither Lara Jean nor Peter disparage him for being gay. Both are accepting. Essentially, the depiction of Lucas is complex. He is accepted and loved by his friends, yet they still talk about his sexuality like a dark, exciting secret (failing to respect his explicit wish for their confidentiality).

When considering *To All the Boys I've Loved Before*, the inclusion of Lucas, a gay man of color, is a positive step toward increased intersectional representation in film. However, it is less encouraging that he resides in a liminal space of not feeling comfortable to be fully out as a gay man and not being fully respected by his peer group. Since Lucas's partially closeted status is relatable to many members LGBTQIA+ community, a responsible resolution to this draining position by the film's conclusion would have been most welcome. Moreover, that Lara Jean, Peter, and the others in Lucas's life accept him is heartening; however, that they treat his sexuality as something "Other" than their own, alienating him in the process, is troubling. Overall, the film's portrayal of the LGBTQIA+ community shows promise but leaves great room for improvement.

See also *Love, Simon; The Perks of Being a Wallflower.*

—Randi Hogden

TO WONG FOO, THANKS FOR EVERYTHING! JULIE NEWMAR (1995)

DIRECTOR: Beeban Kidron
SCREENPLAY: Douglas Carter Beane
CAST: Patrick Swayze (Vida Boheme), Wesley Snipes (Noxeema Jackson), John Leguizamo (Chi-Chi Rodriguez), Stockard Channing (Carol Ann), Blythe Danner (Beatrice), Arliss Howard (Virgil), Jason London (Bobby Ray), Chris Penn (Sheriff Dollard)
SPECS: 109 minutes; color
AVAILABILITY: DVD (Universal Pictures Home Entertainment)

To Wong Foo, Thanks for Everything! Julie Newmar follows the narrative of two drag queens, Vida Boheme and Noxeema Jackson, who win an all-expense-paid trip to Hollywood to compete in a national beauty pageant for drag queens. On their way to celebrate, they find Chi-Chi Rodriguez. Vida convinces Noxeema to sell their plane tickets in order to afford a car rental to bring the younger queen with them to Hollywood. In a turn of events, Vida is pulled over and is then sexually assaulted by a police officer during their journey. In an act of self-defense, Vida punches the officer and renders him unconscious. Running from the scene of the assault, the three drive until their car breaks down. Stranded as they are actively pursued by Vida's assailant, the queens are stuck in a midwestern town, and they must wait for their automobile to be repaired. The triad of queens form close bonds with the women of the town and teach them to live to extravagant extremes. After the queens dramatically improve the quality of life in the town, the aforementioned officer arrives to arrest them during the final climax of the film. The townspeople, all of whom have been inspired and touched by the queens, rally to protect Vida, Noxeema, and Chi-Chi. The queens are afforded safe passage by the town's brave act of defiance, and the narrative closes with a sequence depicting a more refined and mature Chi-Chi as she is later crowned with the national title of drag queen of the year.

The character of Vida, the most dominant voice in the narrative and most outright in her activist nature, would appear to be flat and purely performative if her motivations were not otherwise established to have a basis in trauma from her younger years. This trauma is illustrated as Vida drives through her former affluent childhood neighborhood when she is asked by Chi-Chi why she gave up her privileged background, to which she answers, "Vida gave all of this up to be Vida" [00:20:25–00:20:28]. Shortly after, Vida stops by what was her former address. The car pauses as the frame shows an elderly woman opening the door to look out when she catches a glimpse of the three parked outside. Vida reaches out to her before the woman seems to recall a painful memory as she beholds the troop of drag queens. The woman, who may be assumed to be Vida's mother, quickly turns to reenter the house with a troubled look [00:20:33–00:21:00]. This sequence implies that Vida's childhood was rife with struggle and a lack of acceptance derived from her identity. Additionally, it illustrates Vida as an individual who realized an excess of wealth did not provide her the capacity to live a fully self-actualized and authentic life.

Vida's characterization runs as a parallel to Carol Ann, the abused housewife of the town's mechanic. Since Vida is a survivor of domestic abuse, she is motivated to help an active victim recognize her abuse instead of tolerating it. This is evident later in the film when Vida discloses to Carol Ann how she used to explain her father's abuse just as Carol Ann attempts to do with her husband: "I used to tell people that when my father used to call me cruel names, it was just because of his sense of humor" [00:51:42–00:51:43]. The implied abuse from Vida's childhood enables her to relate to Carol Ann. Although Carol Ann's abuse is one of the only points of traumatic conflict that is engaged without a comedic tone during the film, the narrative clearly implies that the motivation for Vida's intervention with the townspeople originates from wanting to help those around her because she has suffered in similar ways. This motivation positions Vida in the role of an unlikely social worker as she takes the time and care to show Carol Ann that, as an individual, she deserves security, acceptance, and authenticity. Vida's relationship to Carol Ann pushes the housewife to see that she deserves much beyond the basic necessities and perceived security that her marriage provides.

In a wider, more communal application of community outreach, Vida and Noxeema show their greatest impact during the planning of the town's "Strawberry Social." As the locals explain more about the social event, Vida asks, "What do strawberries say to anyone here?," and she encourages the local women to create a theme for the year's social event [1:00:10–1:00:12]. The group of women seem confused at the question and are unable to answer beyond a literal capacity. Noxeema answers by combining the literal descriptions of strawberries that the women provide to satisfy the more abstract response that Vida tries to elicit, "Red and wild . . . That's your theme" [1:00:27–1:00:30]. Although comical in setup, this sequence shows that the local culture is based around concrete thoughts and basic needs; they are not accustomed to aesthetic pleasures like Vida and Noxeema. The scene continues with a suggestion and explanation of what "a day with the girls" entails. Paralleling the opening sequences of the movie, which depict Vida and Noxeema getting into drag, the women go through a similar montage of getting into luxurious makeup and clothing. Much like contemporary intervention programs in at-risk communities, the queens of *To Wong Foo* actively teach and promote the skills of mental well-being to the community around them.

After acquiring new clothing from the local store, Noxeema extends this exercise in feminism to a local group of misogynists who frequently stalk the streets. After the group is catcalled by the men, Noxeema confronts the main agitator, Tommy, demanding an apology as she forces him to approach the group of women by painfully gripping his genitals. She continues, explaining to Tommy the proper way to greet women, "Now Tommy, when you encounter such gorgeous ladies, the correct way to greet them is to say, 'Good afternoon, ladies'" [01:03:56–01:04:05]. Noxeema's treatment of the situation reinforces much of what she and Vida taught the women in the previous sequence. Firstly, Noxeema reinforces the self-value they have encouraged the women to realize and cultivate in themselves. Additionally, she teaches them that this value is something that should be used to demand due respect from a community that would otherwise devalue them as solely sexual objects. Lastly, Noxeema extends the lesson to the local men that they should respect women for their innate value. At the core of this moment, Noxeema teaches the community about feminine respect.

However, despite the undeniable aspects of activism that Vida and Noxeema practice, the film as a whole contradicts many of the values it seeks to embody. Although the basis of the plot assumes a pro-LGBTQIA+ and antiracist stance, the comedic style of writing discounts and erases the real danger and persecution that LGBTQIA+ individuals and individuals of color face in American. Sheriff Dollard, one of the main antagonistic forces in the film, is portrayed mostly as humorously incompetent and thusly negates the often fatal nature of police brutality that marginalized individuals face. Kathryn Kane notes that Dollard's unsuccessful and poorly executed motivations lead the audience into a false understanding of the reality of police brutality while discounting the plight of the marginalized:

> With Sheriff Dollard, the film creates a sense of assurance among the audience that such prejudices are no longer tolerated. . . . The film's narrative masks and minimizes the risks one encounters living in a body marked as "other" by sys-

Wesley Snipes as Noxeema, John Leguizamo as Chi-Chi, and Patrick Swayze as Vida in *To Wong Foo, Thanks for Everything! Julie Newmar*. Courtesy of Universal/Photofest.

tems of racial and sexual prejudice. This mockery of racism and heterosexism undermines claims to victimization or demands for protection that members of these groups might request. The movie offers a world where social persecution is erased. (Kane 2005, 30–32)

Aside from the poorly handled subject of race, the film portrays the value of queerness as something primarily to be used for the benefit of the heterosexual characters. The actions and existence of queer characters in this narrative serve and aid the plight of the hetersoexual townspeople. Overall, the film seems to minimize the legitimacy of queerness and racial identity; ironically, this method of storytelling discounts the minorities it attempts to represent and appeals to the comfort of a white heterosexual audience.

To Wong Foo, Thanks for Everything! Julie Newmar is a lighthearted and ambitious attempt to tackle queer representation in a positive light but that sacrifices authenticity to make itself into a more marketable film to the audience of its time. Despite the film's shortcomings, the legitimate intricacies and positive display of community outreach performed by strong queer characters should not be negated by the film's many failures. At the film's core, it focuses on queer characters having the agency and power to improve the world around them. Not only does it embrace traditional norms of femininity and queerness without critical judgment, it also invites viewers to revel in said queerness despite its portrayal being stereotypical and restricting. For contemporary viewers, it also poses a healthy challenge to discern what value can be derived from imperfect narratives as the film ages and transforms into a historic piece of Western cinema.

See also *Cherry Pop*.

Bibliography

Kane, Kathryn. "Passing as Queer and Racing to Whiteness: To Wong Foo, Thanks but No Thanks." Genders 1998–2013, August 10, 2005. Accessed August 15, 2021. https://www.colorado .edu/gendersarchive1998-2013/2005/08/10/passing-queer-and-racing-toward-whiteness-wong -foo-thanks-no-thanks.

—Sean D. Catino

TRANSAMERICA (2005)

DIRECTOR: Duncan Tucker
SCREENPLAY: Duncan Tucker
CAST: Felicity Huffman (Sabrina "Bree" Osbourne/Stanley Schupak), Kevin Zegers (Toby Wilkins), Graham Green (Calvin Many Goats), Fionnula Flanagan (Elizabeth Schupak), Burt Young (Murray Schupak), Carrie Preston (Murray Schupak), Elizabeth Peña (Margaret)
SPECS: 103 minutes; color
AVAILABILITY: DVD (Lisa's Skus)

Transamerica follows the story of Sabrina "Bree" Osbourne, a preoperative transgender woman from Southern California who, while waiting for her male-to-female reassignment surgery, receives a surprise call from Toby, her seventeen-year-old son whom she never knew of until then. Bree's therapist, Margaret, will only approve the surgery when she comes to terms with this new reality in her life. Meanwhile, Toby is being held in a jail in New York and, as such, Bree must meet him there, since he is alone in the world. Posing as a Christian social worker, Bree meets him but does not tell him who she really is, nor does she mention her transgender identity. She bails Toby out of jail and takes him to Los Angeles, where Toby hopes to become a porn star and reconnect with his biological father. Without enough money to fly back to Los Angeles, Bree and Toby take the road instead, and it is during their journey that Toby discovers the truth about Bree's transgender identity. Afterward, they stay at Bree's parents' house in Phoenix, Arizona. There Toby tries to seduce Bree only to find that she is his biological father, which infuriates him. He leaves Bree, who eventually undergoes her vaginoplasty yet feels incomplete without her son. Finally, some months later, Toby—now eighteen and acting in gay pornographic films—visits Bree and they reconcile.

Partly inspired by conversations between director Duncan Tucker and writer Katherine Connella—Tucker's ex-roommate—*Transamerica* was well received by public and critics alike due to the way it addresses the issue of the transgender body (Connella 2006, 50). The film has been compared, in terms of relevance, to works such as *The Adventures of Priscilla: Queen of the Desert* (1994) and *To Wong Foo, Thanks for Everything! Julie Newmar* (1995) as it presents a narrative with a positive view of its LGBTQIA+ character. In spite of the director commenting in several interviews that this is not a film about transsexuality but rather a comedy "about growing up and accepting yourself"—as he asserts in the commentary to the DVD—it is obvious that the transgendered body is at the center of *Transamerica*, particularly the idea of the mobile body (and, consequently, of identity). When Bree is first introduced to the audience, she is wearing clothes that reinforce her as a "hyper-feminine woman," as Amy A. Jensen states, putting her "actions and manner of dressing . . . in line with the stereotypical, heteronormative social expectations of what a woman should look like" (Jensen 2018). In fact, the color pink—predominant in the first and last parts of the film—attests to her need to "constitute herself as a woman" (Jensen 2018) and to be a woman, which initially confirms Bree's need to pursue a "normative existence," as Juett puts it (2010, 76). As the author notes in her analysis of the film, this existence is "simultaneousy [in] play with her connections to family, connections made while embodying a former gender" (2010, 76).

It is also the body or, more specifically, the need for change that makes Bree undertake a journey to meet Toby. Although she wants to ignore the situation and renounce her son, her therapist will only approve her transition if she faces her past. The "road trip" structure of the film plays a key role, not only since it mirrors the need for both physical and emotional change for the protagonist but also because it functions as a way to comment on the stigma of the transgendered body. While the initial conversation between the therapist and Bree is proof of this, with the doctor clearly playing the antagonist to Bree's desire toward gender normalization, there are other key moments in the film that signal Bree's marginal condition, as well as Toby's, as both are presented from the beginning as the "Other."

Forced to go on the road on account of not having enough money to fly back to Los Angeles, they drive back west, stopping in Dallas, Texas, to visit some of Bree's friends, who are having a gender pride party. Curiously, the party scene portrays a noticeably uncomfortable Bree, as opposed to Toby. After leaving the house, she even calls the women in the party "ersatz," meaning phony, "something pretending to be something it's not" [00:45:52]. Nonetheless, Bree is also doing the same as she pretends to be something she is not to Toby by hiding her true identity, while those at the party are actually celebrating their "gender fluid" status (Jensen 2018).

Later, Toby learns that Bree has male genitalia, a discovery that infuriates him mostly because she has been lying to him from the beginning. As the journey advances, the body becomes even more central to the film. Their money and car are stolen, and Toby prostitutes himself to a truck driver as a way of obtaining money, but also lies to Bree by saying that he got money by selling some drugs. They end up getting a ride from a driver—Calvin Many Goats—who, to Toby's dismay, feels attracted to Bree, thus demonstrating that gender "transcends pure biological determination and social construction," as Juett further emphasizes (2010, 92).

Estranged from her family, Bree visits her parents in Phoenix, Arizona, with Toby. In this particular scene, viewers learn why Bree decided to get away from her family as her parents do not approve of her transition, especially Elizabeth, her mother. This is particularly noticeable in the words of her father (and then the mother) when they mention that "your mother and I both love you—[Mother] But we don't respect you" [01:09:30]. Meanwhile, upon knowing the truth about Toby, they welcome him in the family, even inviting him to stay with them, thus proving that both Bree's mother and father are willing to accept the part of Bree's life that symbolizes a heteronormative existence. In spite of this new (pampered) life, Toby does not like the way Bree's parents treat her. Toby eventually learns that Bree is his biological father and, appalled by the news, steals some money and other valuable items and flees during the night, leaving Bree heartbroken. Bree's return to LA (now by plane, with a ticket bought by her parents) signals the end of the journey in many aspects. As in most "road trip" movies, the return to home—wherever that may be—indicates the possibility of change in the main character. She finally undergoes surgery but does not feel complete, as she mentions to the therapist, "I . . . feel like a medieval heretic impaled in a very large and very thick . . . stake . . . with splinters" [01:31:30]. Consequently, after her vaginoplasty, Bree emerges as new but not whole. The two final scenes depict Bree working now as a server (she was formerly a busser) in a Mexican restaurant: dressed in a less formal manner, she now seems looser. This new position suggests a change in status and in life. However, something is missing.

Transamerica foreshadows a "happy ending" by putting Toby and Bree together again in Bree's house. This circular structure—in the sense that both Toby's appearance at the beginning and at the end are disruptive yet life changing—is essential to Bree's path toward understanding herself and her spiritual, physical, and identitary transformation. With Toby back in her life, she feels complete, as the film's trajectory points toward by portraying the reunion of the biological family, now composed of mother and son rather than father and son.

Mobility in *Transamerica* thus functions in terms not only of the body but also of identity. To this extent, Dolly Parton's song "Travelin' Thru," originally written for *Transamerica*, is noteworthy. Indeed, the song announces the power of a film that focuses on a "positive representation of [the] transsexual experience" (Jensen 2018). In this sense, as Juett posits in her analysis of *Transamerica*, the ending scene reveals how Bree cannot be totally free from her past, but she can learn how to understand it, accept it, and, ultimately, find the path toward "reconciliation and redemption" (2010, 78). More than simply pursuing a "normative existence," Bree is ready to strive for an existence according to her own self.

See also *Boys Don't Cry; Tangerine.*

Bibliography

Connella, Katherine. "*Transamerica* and Me." *Advocate*, February 28, 2006, 50.

Cavalcante, André. "Centering Transgender Identity via the Textual Periphery: *Transamerica* and the 'Double Work' of Paratexts." *Critical Studies in Media Communication* 30, no. 2 (2013): 85–101.

Jensen, Amy A. "Gender and the Transsexual Body in *Transamerica.*" *Literator* 39, no. 1 (2018). http://www.scielo.org.za/scielo.php?script=sci_arttext&pid=S2219-82372018000100010&lng=en&nrm=iso.

Juett, JoAnne C. "'Just Travellin' Thru': Transgendered Spaces in *Transamerica.*" In *Coming Out to the Mainstream: New Queer Cinema in the 21st Century*, edited by JoAnne C. Juett and David M. Jones, 60–91. Newcastle upon Tyne: Cambridge Scholars, 2010.

—José Duarte

• U •

THE UNINVITED (1944)

DIRECTOR: Lewis Allen
SCREENPLAY: Dodie Smith, Frank Partos, inspired by the novel of the same name by Dorothy Macardle
CAST: Ray Milland (Roderick), Ruth Hussy (Pamela), Gail Russell (Stella), Donald Crisp (Commander Beech), Cornelia Otis Skinner (Miss Holloway)
SPECS: 99 minutes; black and white
AVAILABILITY: DVD (Criterion Collection)

Roderick "Rick" Fitzgerald and Pamela Fitzgerald are siblings visiting Cornwall on holiday from their shared flat in London. While hiking up a cliff, they discover an empty house and decide to find out if it is for sale. Windward, the former home of the tragically deceased Mary Meredith and her husband, is indeed for sale. However, the dark history of Windward begins to emerge when they meet with the current owner (who is also Mary's father), Commander Beech. Following his daughter's fatal and ostensibly accidental fall from the cliff in front of Windward, Commander Beech raised Mary's infant daughter, Stella. Stella's artist father fled the country following Mary's death and died not long after the death of his wife. When Rick and Pam seek out Commander Beech, they initially meet Stella, who exhibits strange behavior and attempts to dissuade them from buying Windward. Commander Beech sends her away and informs Rick and Pam that he experienced great difficulty renting the house during the twenty years following his daughter's death. He offers to sell Windward to Rick and Pam for a very low price due to nasty rumors surrounding the house. Rick and Pam eagerly agree to the deal but soon find themselves wrapped up in an unresolved mystery surrounding the circumstances of Mary Meredith's life and death. As Rick and Pam dig deeper into the history of the house, a more disturbing tale emerges, and the ghosts of the house begin to stir. While alone at the house, Pam hears a disembodied sobbing that gradually fades at dawn. Rick and Pam notice an oppressive chill in the studio where Stella's father painted both Mary Meredith as well as his Spanish model, Carmel. Rick and Pam contact Miss Holloway, Mary's steadfast companion as well as the director of a psychiatric institution, and realize that the events of the past are much more complicated when Miss Holloway informs them of an affair between Stella's father and Carmel. As Rick develops a romantic relationship with Stella, the hauntings of Windward house increase in intensity and it becomes clear that not one but two ghosts are battling for Stella. One ghost seeks to put Stella in mortal danger and conceal her murderous past; the other seeks to protect Stella and bring to light the truth of Stella's parentage.

A Paramount picture, *The Uninvited* is a loose adaptation of a 1942 novel by Dorothy Macardle, which was originally printed under the title *Uneasy Freehold* and later published in the United States as *The Uninvited*. While some scenes are lifted wholesale from the novel, the plot of the film is vastly different. The novel features a different motivation behind the hauntings, and the underlying sexual themes are mostly absent. *The Uninvited* features two examples of coded lesbian caricatures in the characters of Mary Meredith and her lifelong friend, Miss Holloway. Because the Hays Code prohibited even the mere suggestion or reference to gay characters, the potential relationship between Miss Holloway and Mary, as well as their sexual identity, is incredibly vague. *The Uninvited* is one of many films of this era featuring characters whose sexuality and true identity are all but erased. In her book *Uninvited: Classical Hollywood Cinema and Lesbian Representability*, Patricia White describes the legacy of "homosexuality" in film during the period of 1930 to 1968 as a "legacy of absence." She goes on to explain that "even the play of connotation was forbidden by the Code; the awkward formulation ('inference to,' rather than 'reference to' or 'implication of') implies an attempt to legislate the *viewer's* potential impression of homoerotic content" (White 1999, 1). The effect of this on *The Uninvited* leaves the viewer with few but significant clues as to a potential relationship between Mary Meredith and Miss Holloway.

On the surface, early references to the long-dead Mary Meredith enforce the image of a saintly, devoted, and decidedly heterosexual mother and wife. She is a conventionally feminine beauty, as is apparent in portraits of her hanging in Stella's bedroom as well as in Miss Holloway's office. She is blonde, statuesque, and radiant. This double image of Mary is one of the first clues that she was not what she seemed. White suggests that "the two portraits hint at Mary's duplicity; the façade of proper womanhood hides her lesbian, nonreproductive self" (1999, 71). The film does not feature any flashbacks, and other than her appearance in the portraits, the viewer never sees Mary as a living person (though her ghostly form makes multiple appearances throughout the film). Her life, personality, and the events leading up to her fatal fall from the cliff are revealed in bits and pieces through brief discussions with other characters in the film. The viewer is first introduced to the sinister figure of Miss Holloway when she visits Commander Beech following Stella's paranormal experiences at Windward. Commander Beech implores his daughter's former companion, who now runs her own mental health institute, to "cure" Stella. It is in this conversation that themes of lesbianism become apparent. Miss Holloway begins to reminisce about Mary's beauty as the camera focuses in on Mary's portrait: "Mary was a goddess. Her skin was radiant and that bright, bright hair. How this room brings her back to me. The nights we sat talking in front of that fireplace. Planning our whole lives" [01:07:18]. Miss Holloway even makes a point to "Other" herself and Mary: "It wasn't flirtations and dresses we talked about. We were no silly, giggling girls. We intended to conquer life" [01:07:40]. While not explicitly stated, it can be inferred that this sense of Otherness could arise from an understanding that their feelings toward each other were not heteronormative. After Commander Beech leaves the room, Miss Holloway turns to speak to the portrait of Mary and addresses her as if she is alive: "So they're searching into the past. They shall never find out, my darling. I promise you" [01:08:12]. At this point in the film, the viewer does not know what secret Miss Holloway is keeping, and the vague nature of this statement could be a reference to an illicit relationship between the two women. White explains the significance of this interaction between Miss Holloway and Mary's portrait: "The relationship between the two women takes on its full significance only after one is dead. This reinforces the morbidification of lesbian desire, but also endows it with the romantic and tragic qualities of an impossible love that transcends death" (70).

After Stella is taken away to Miss Holloway's institute, Rick and Pam learn from their neighbor that Miss Holloway was present the night of Mary's death. They also travel to the institute, fully unaware that Stella has been admitted there. While waiting to speak with Miss Holloway, another patient approaches Rick and asks him to give Miss Holloway a nest of stones painted as bird's eggs, a starkly inverted symbol of fertility. Their discussion with Miss Holloway illuminates more details about the night of Mary's death, including an accusation that Mary was murdered by Carmel after trying to prevent her from throwing the infant Stella off the cliff. She continues to speak of Mary with deep love and affection. Miss Holloway's steely command over the false narrative eventually breaks, and she has to correct herself while attempting to conceal the fact that it was Mary and not her husband who ordered Carmel to leave, setting off the fatal chain of events that night. These emotional breaks are interpreted in a sinister light by Rick and Pam following their visit. They leave the meeting unnerved, and both suspect that Miss Holloway is concealing some hidden truth about Mary. In the very next scene, Rick and Pam consult Dr. Scott, Pam's budding love interest and the village doctor who cares for Stella and her grandfather. When they mention that they have spoken with Miss Holloway, he chuckles and asks, "Holy Holloway of Health Through Harmony?," indicating that she has a negative reputation despite being the director of her own hospital [01:20:17]. It is through his predecessor's journals that the viewer finds out that Miss Holloway deliberately murdered Carmel, the woman she felt was responsible for the death of her beloved Mary.

As Rick and Pam uncover conflicting elements of Mary's life, the viewer begins to learn her true nature through her apparitions at Windward. Initially, Rick and Pam believe Carmel to be the malicious ghost and wrongly attribute the blasts of cold air and feelings of oppression to her. However, it is Mary who appears incorporeally in terms of ice and dread and depression. The presence of Mary's ghost "queers" the atmosphere of the spaces she inhabits: the fresh flowers Pam brings into the studio wilt, the music Rick plays veers from a cheerful major key into a haunting minor key. While these changes could be seen through a lens of "queering," the characters in the film interpret these effects as evil and rotten. Following the discovery of her doctor's records, Rick and Pam find out that Mary's icy aura was apparent in her sexual attitudes. This revelation suggests that

> Mary is ultimately revealed to be something other than who everyone thought her to be, and her unnaturalness is finally detected through her rejection of her reproductive role. . . . Mary, far from being the tender mother who brought little Stella a night light, "feared and avoided motherhood," we are told. Mary's lesbianism and sterility are signified by her coldness: the arctic blasts in the studio, her "icy rage" and self-control. (White 1999, 70)

In stark contrast to Mary's frigidity is Carmel—the Spanish model who is eventually revealed to be Stella's biological mother. She gradually emerges from the shadows throughout the film. She is the ghost heralded by the smell of mimosas, who is described as a joyful woman who looks forward to motherhood. Carmel represents heterosexual passion and a normative model of a loving, nurturing, and protective mother—everything that Mary rejects.

Ultimately, it is the discovery that Mary fearfully avoided childbirth while Carmel joyfully embraced the news of her pregnancy that solves the mystery of Stella's parentage. This focus on revealing attitudes concerning motherhood becomes key to understanding the motivations of the hauntings, furthermore suggesting that attitudes toward motherhood provide the ultimate criteria for establishing the moral character of these two ghosts. In her article "Adaptation, Censorship, and Audiences of Questionable Type: Lesbian Sightings in *Rebecca* (1940) and *The Uninvited* (1944)," Rhona J. Berenstein further explores the significance of notions of motherhood within *The Uninvited*:

> In Allen's movie, maternity is sanctified by an orphaned heroine (Stella) whose desire for a mother's care is culturally legible and acceptable, even though it is contextualized in a story about ghosts. In fact, both ghosts are firmly linked to motherhood by either giving birth or adopting, and their transgressive behaviors—Carmel's adultery and the resulting birth of an illegitimate child, and Mary's cruelty and supposedly poor approximation of maternal feelings—were punished by death before the beginning of the movie. (1998, 23)

It is also worth noting that Mary's aversion to heterosexual intercourse and motherhood are treated with almost an equal sense of disgust and shock as her attempt to murder the infant Stella. The more that the viewer learns about Mary and Miss Holloway, the more their queerness becomes tied to and indistinguishable from their murderous wickedness.

Miss Holloway displays an eager curiosity when listening to other characters describe the disturbances at Windward. After speaking with Rick and Pam, she visits with Stella and questions her about her experiences at Windward, appearing to be especially interested in an episode in which Stella, seemingly possessed by the malicious spirit of Mary, sprinted toward the cliff in front of Windward before being saved by Rick. It is clear from her interactions with Stella that she knows that Stella is not Mary Meredith's biological mother and also hates her. She suggests to Stella that she believes her to be mentally ill and that she will not be released from the psychiatric institute anytime soon. However, after finding out that Rick and Pam are on their way to the institute, leaving Windward empty, she soon changes her tune. She calls Stella into her office and asks her if she believes that Mary wishes her to return to Windward and sends her to the house and what she believes will be certain death at the hands of Mary's possessive ghost. Stella leaves just as Rick, Pam, and Dr. Scott arrive to rescue her. They arrive to a scene of madness. Miss Holloway, usually so controlled and composed like Mary, has come unglued and babbles that she has sent Stella to the "cliff and the rocks below the cliff" [01:28:39]. Feeling that she has finally fulfilled her beloved's dying murderous mission, she turns to Mary's portrait and proclaims, "I've done what she wanted at last. Haven't I, Mary? It's all straight now. There are no frayed edges, no loose ends. All straight. All smooth" [01:29:03–01:29:19]. Considering that lesbianism was once considered a mental illness, it is not a very far leap to view Miss Holloway's queerness as being one more clue to her true mental state within the context of the film. *The Uninvited* is certainly not the only film to employ the trope of madness among coded gay characters, and Miss Holloway's downfall into insanity is also echoed in the character of Mrs. Danvers in *Rebecca*. Much in the way that love between two women is only accessed in terms of the supernatural in this film, insanity serves a similar purpose in underscoring the perceived unnaturalness of queer characters.

In Mary's final, spectral appearance in the film, she has been stripped of her physical beauty. Her ghastly appearance results in her father dying of shock, and when Stella turns to face her, still believing her to be her biological mother and protector, she issues a horrified scream. The viewer does not see what Stella and Commander Beech see, but their reactions indicate that Mary's appearance is evil and grotesque. In yet another attempt on Stella's life, Mary compels her to flee the house and sprint toward the cliff. Rick and Pam arrive just in time to save Stella but are too late to give aid to Commander Beech. After Carmel's ghost leads Rick, Pam, Dr. Scott, and Stella to the diary entry that reveals Stella to be Carmel's child, the gentle ghost is satisfied, laughs with joy, and fades away. Mary's ghost remains, and Rick, armed only with a candelabra, goes into the dark stairwell for one final showdown. It is in this scene that Mary's true, ghostly form is revealed. She is recognizable as the same woman in the portraits, but her features are gnarled, shadowed, and quite masculine. This is the Mary that exists without the false façade of motherhood and heterosexuality, and in the context of this film, it is quite ugly. Rick begins to taunt her, and White points out, "Rick's final confrontation with Mary's ghost smacks of queer-bashing: 'What do you want? It's Stella, isn't it? It's too late, we're on to you!' He laughs that the revelations about Carmel have given her 'saintly legend rather a black eye.' This invocation of physical violence underscores the homophobic impulse" (1999, 71). It appears that the combination of shaming and intentional violence are the forces that finally vanquish Mary's malicious spirit. Following his fight on the staircase, Rick goes outside to a beautiful sunrise and is lovingly embraced by Stella. The final frames of *The Uninvited* center on the pairing off of not one but two heterosexual couples. Doctor Scott hints that he, Pam, and their dog will be cohabitating in the near future, indicating that Rick and Stella will live out their married life in Windward. There is a sense of correction and finality, and Rick jokes that his post-ghost-fight jitters are only because "[Mary] could have been [his] mother-in-law" [01:39:05]. At the close of this tale, the house has been cured of its unnaturalness. Mary Meredith and the supernatural queerness she signifies have been violently banished to the shadows, and her lover, Miss Holloway, has descended into madness: two more casualties of Code-era lesbian erasure.

See also *Clue*; *Far from Heaven*; *Gilda*; *Hail, Caesar!*

Bibliography

Berenstein, Rhona J. "Adaptation, Censorship, and Audiences of Questionable Type: Lesbian Sightings in *Rebecca* (1940) and *The Uninvited* (1944)." *Cinema Journal* 37, no. 3 (1998): 16–37.

White, Patricia. *Uninvited: Classical Hollywood Cinema and Lesbian Representability*. Illustrated edition. Bloomington: Indiana University Press, 1999.

—Elizabeth Hays Tussey

. V .

V FOR VENDETTA (2005)

DIRECTOR: James McTeigue, based on the graphic novel of the same name by Alan Moore
SCREENPLAY: Lana Wachowski and Lilly Wachowski
CAST: Natalie Portman (Evey Hammond), Hugo Weaving (V), Stephen Rea (Inspector Eric Finch), Stephen Fry (Gordon Deitrich), John Hurt (Adam Sutler), Tim Pigott-Smith (Peter Creedy)
SPECS: 132 minutes; color
AVAILABILITY: DVD (Warner Bros.)

The near future, Great Britain. The fascist Norsefire Party, led by Chancellor Adam Sutler, runs the country as a police state. Evey Hammond, a young woman who works in the lower rungs of the government's media department, walks alone at night. She is out past curfew and is harassed by a group of Fingermen, the secret police. They intend to rape Evey before a man wearing a Guy Fawkes mask appears and rescues her. V invites Evey to a nearby rooftop where, as Big Ben chimes midnight, announcing November 5, he orchestrates the destruction of London's Old Bailey. The chancellor holds an emergency meeting with the various heads of his state-run departments, including Inspector Finch, ordering them to track down the vigilante and his female accomplice. V hijacks the airwaves and delivers a message to the public encouraging them to remember a time when they were free and to join him one year from now on November 5 in front of the Houses of Parliament. In the months that follow, Evey initially becomes involved in V's cause and is held by V in his underground lair for her safety. However, when she learns that V has a vendetta to kill those who "created" him in Larkhill detention facility two decades earlier, she plans to escape. The residents of Larkhill, detained for being social deviants, are experimented on with drugs. All those but V died during the procedure, which gave him superhuman agility and strength. Evey begins to see the hypocrisy, corruption, and brutality wrought by the government and decides to act. Guy Fawkes Night looms, and V puts his final plans into action. He completes his mission by killing the remaining people on his list, including Chancellor Sutler, but is mortally wounded in a fight with the secret police. Evey finds V, and with his dying words, he urges her to complete his mission by blowing up Parliament. Finch arrives to stop her, but she convinces him that the old world is broken and needs to change. As the government building explodes, thousands of people wearing Fawkes masks gather to watch.

The Britain of *V for Vendetta* is a country in which LGBTQIA+ people do not belong. The film begins with a broadcast by a news anchor, Lewis Prothero, unleashing a diatribe of hate upon various forms of "difference": "I saw it all," he intones, "immigrants, Muslims, homosexuals, terrorists, disease-ridden degenerates." He is using these so-called undesirables as justification for the draconian policies enacted by ruling party Norsefire. Prothero seethes with righteous indignation at the mere thought of these people's existence, the camera cutting in closer with each group on his list until his face fills the screen. He takes a particular delight in saying "homosexuals," pouring over every syllable as if to reinforce its depravity. It is clear, however, that not all his audience agrees with him. As he rages, two viewers in separate households ready themselves in front of mirrors. One of them, Evey Hammond, says, "That's quite enough of that," as she turns off the television. The other is the masked vigilante, V, and he and Evey soon meet for the first time, an encounter that changes the course of both their lives. This is the first of many such coincidences or repeated, mirror images in the film. Yet, unlike so many other superhero films that bring a hero together with a young "damsel in distress," *V for Vendetta* stops short of confirming their heterosexual union at the end. Indeed, the film is a surprisingly queer text for an American studio product.

There are two significant named LGBTQIA+ characters in the film: Gordon Deitrich and Valerie. Deitrich is Evey's manager at the state-run British Television Network (BTN), where he presents a chat show called *Deitrich's Half Hour*. Early on, it is implied that Evey and Gordon have a romantic relationship when another worker teases Evey about seeing "Daddy Deitrich" the previous evening. However, when on the run from the authorities, Evey learns that Deitrich is a closeted gay man and staunchly antigovernment, a fact made clear by his collection of subversive memorabilia hidden in his cellar. His collection includes photographs depicting same-sex BDSM, which Evey sees. Gordon explains, "We're both fugitives in a way," either because he is constantly hiding himself from the authorities or because he is running away from his own sexual identity. Referring to why he kept inviting Evey to his house, Deitrich says, "You see, a man in my position is expected to entertain young and attractive ladies like yourself. Because in this world, if I were to invite who I desired, I would undoubtedly find myself without a home let alone a television show." He concludes his monologue saying, "You wear a mask for so long you forget what was underneath it." Gordon's mask is a metaphorical one rather than the literal mask that V wears. However, these two characters are similar in several respects. They are both tall and speak with deliberate and well-mannered English. They are both interested in the theatrical, V in how he orchestrates his political stunts and attacks on the government (as well as a fondness for classical Hollywood swashbuckler films) and Deitrich through his entertainment show at BTN. V, like Gordon, has a hidden collection of cultural artifacts, which he calls the "Shadow Museum." The film even playfully suggests that Gordon could be the vigilante when he is seen making the same breakfast dish for Evey that V had made earlier and even greets her with the same affected "Bonjour, mademoiselle!" Any truth to the claim is swiftly shut down, however, when Gordon sarcastically points out that his tired old body would not be able to perform such heroics. Nevertheless, as the film constantly reminds viewers, one should not believe in coincidences. At the very least, there is a textual link between Gordon and V, and the potential for a queer reading of the characters' relationship.

This characterization of Deitrich is very different to the original graphic novel, written by Alan Moore and illustrated by David Lloyd. In the source material, Deitrich is Evey's lover and complicit in the government's authoritarian regime rather than a victim of it. It is a change that aligns to the background and politics of the actor who plays Deitrich in the film, Stephen Fry, an openly gay actor/writer and an outspoken critic of the British government. It also reflects the Wachowskis' own affiliation with the LGBTQIA+ community, both having transitioned since the film's release. Gordon ends up being "black-bagged" and carted away by the sinister Fingermen for producing a Benny Hill–style sketch show that pokes fun at the chancellor. This has significant implications for Evey though, as Deitrich's capture is filmed as a mirror image to her mother's arrest from earlier in the film, with her seen terrified and hiding under a bed. Even if Deitrich suffers the same fate as so many other gay characters in popular film, his sacrifice serves a greater purpose. It reveals to Evey the Norsefire regime's cruel disregard for human life.

Evey is grabbed by one of the Fingermen as she tries to escape from Deitrich's house. However, viewers learn later that it is V disguised as a policeman, and he followed Evey that night, worried for her safety. Evey believes that she is being held by Creedy and his henchmen, who interrogate her in the hope she will disclose V's identity and whereabouts. V goes to these extreme lengths because he wants to reveal Norsefire's lies and remove her fear. He also aims to radicalize her to his cause. As with Deitrich, a gay character forms a vital part of V's ploy. Evey lies on the cold, hard floor of her cell, exhausted from another day of torture. She hears a noise coming from a small hole in the wall and finds a sheet of toilet paper on which is written Valerie's story. As Evey reads, Valerie recounts her life in a voice-over and flashback. She tells of her days in secondary school, her adolescent crush on another girl, teachers telling them, "It's a phase," and her parents disowning her after she comes out to them. Her only access to a world beyond the four walls of her cell and the interrogation room, Evey is seen eagerly reading each new note that is left in a continued montage. Valerie becomes an actor (a dream Evey also harbors) and meets her partner Ruth on a movie set. Then the world changes. Norsefire come to power, and they clamp down on so-called social deviants. Flashbacks show two men in bed together before armed police storm their room and violently take them away as Valerie's voice-over asks, "Why do they hate us so much?" Her story ends with both her and Ruth being detained and experimented on as part of the drug trials at Larkhill. In her final note, she urges her unknown reader to know that "whoever you are, I love you." Evey kisses the paper as tears fall down her cheeks. V's plan has the desired effect as Evey resigns herself to death rather than succumb to Norsefire's tyranny. It is at this moment that V reveals himself and that the interrogation was a sham. All but the notes, that is. V explains that Valerie was held in the cell adjacent to his at Larkhill, and she would pass these notes to him—another mirroring between Evey and V. Thus, in both examples—Deitrich's capture by the secret police and Valerie's notes—an LGBTQIA+ character is the catalyst for Evey's transformation from passive bystander to active agent who inherits V's mission to change the world order. As a result, the film suggests that the driving force behind V's anarchist movement is the injustice and intolerance suffered by the LGBTQIA+ community.

See also *Cloud Atlas*.

Bibliography

Keegan, Cáel M. *Lana and Lilly Wachowski*. Urbana: University of Illinois Press, 2018.

Keller, James R. *V for Vendetta as Cultural Pastiche: A Critical Study of the Graphic Novel and Film*. Jefferson, NC: McFarland, 2008.

Ott, Brian L. "The Visceral Politics of *V for Vendetta*: On Political Affect in Cinema." *Critical Studies in Media Communication* 27, no. 1 (2010): 39–54.

Reynolds, James. "KILL ME SENTIMENT: V for Vendetta and Comic-to-Film Adaptation." *Journal of Adaptation in Film & Performance* 2, no. 2 (2009): 121–36.

—Adam Vaughan

VENOM (2018)

DIRECTOR: Ruben Fleischer

SCREENPLAY: Jeff Pinkner, Scott Rosenberg, and Kelly Marcel

CAST: Tom Hardy (Eddie Brock/Venom), Michelle Williams (Anne Weying), Riz Ahmed (Carlton Drake/Riot), Reid Scott (Dan Lewis), Jenny Slate (Dora Skirth)

SPECS: 112 minutes (theatrical release); color

AVAILABILITY: DVD (Columbia Pictures)

Based on the popular Marvel comic series of the same name, 2018's *Venom* follows the bombastic, violent, and darkly comedic story of Eddie Brock and his bonded symbiote, Venom. Eddie Brock's life is destroyed after he initiates an accusatory interview with Life Foundation CEO Carlton Drake. He loses his job, his fiancée, Anne Weying, and any hope of a future in journalism. After a despondent six months, Eddie is dragged back into journalism when Dora Skirth, a Life Foundation scientist, informs Eddie that Drake is fatally testing its latest discovery on the city's homeless population. Eddie breaks into the Life Foundation facility and, while gathering evidence, is attacked by and bonded to the alien symbiote, Venom. Eddie and Venom develop a bond so powerful it causes Venom to rebel against his own species, which wants to completely take over Earth. In the end, Eddie and Venom defeat Drake and his symbiote, Riot, and commit themselves to secretly protecting the city of San Francisco together.

As queerness is deeply tied to gender, the performance of gender, and the presentation of gender, it is important to address the first touchstone of queerness in the film, in particular, *Venom*'s take on masculinity, gender, and power as it is presented in the introduction to Eddie Brock, his behavior, and his costuming in the first twenty minutes. Eddie Brock is a leather-clad, confident, and powerful investigative reporter. Shots of Eddie tearing through the hills of San Francisco on his motorcycle at a breakneck speed are intercut with dramatic scenes of Eddie reporting *The Brock Report* live at several locations, doing everything from calling tech giant Google "our overlords" to accusingly stating, "The city doesn't care about these people" [00:06:50]. Eddie's comments present him as brash and bold, and these shots of him whipping through San Francisco on his motorcycle underscore him as powerful and fearless. As Patrick L. Hamilton notes in *The

Routledge Companion to Gender and Sexuality in Comic Book Studies, superheroes have a "kind of mastery over the space" (Hamilton 2021, 18). These shots of Eddie moving through San Francisco highlight this masculine strength perfectly, showing Eddie easily gliding through the entire city. This is further fleshed out as Eddie parks his bike illegally in front of his company's building, telling the worker present, "There's no such thing as can't!" [00:07:14]. Eddie is a true golden boy. A powerful figure of rugged masculinity, Eddie does what he wants, says what he wants, and truly expects there to be no consequences. While his motivations are presented as good, with Eddie's journalism focusing on social and economic injustice in his news reporting, it is made clear that Eddie's unwillingness to bend has cost him jobs in the past [00:08:15, 00:09:07]. It also, in the first fifteen minutes of *Venom*, costs Eddie and Anne their jobs [00:14:37]. Eddie's masculine bravado vanishes instantly. Instead of being shown standing, powerful and confident, as he is in his first meeting with his boss, Eddie is now sitting, hunched and small, as he is fired. Lacking his leather jacket, Eddie is dressed in soft, layered clothing in cool and neutral colors as Anne ends their relationship. Eddie is visually presented as softer and weaker through his clothing, his masculinity damaged and stripped. And even when Eddie returns to the masculine leather bravado as he attempts to smother his feelings with alcohol six months after his breakup with Anne, the leather is now black and brown, faded, thrown hurriedly over a Filmore College shirt, and quickly shed once Eddie is inside his home and no longer needs to perform his masculinity [00:20:49]. It is highlighted by Anne that it was Eddie, in his masculine bravado, that caused his own downfall: "You did this, Eddie, not Carlton Drake, not the network, you" [00:32:04]. Eddie is a brilliant reporter, and it is not his ideas or his intent that cause his downfall, but his belief that he is too powerful to be touched that causes his life to implode within the first thirty minutes of *Venom*. This is atypical of the superhero genre, where Spiderman and Superman are employed as respectable journalists, and Eddie loses his entire life so quickly through his own actions. Scholars interested in the performance of masculinity, queerness, and the superhero genre will be especially interested in this portion of *Venom*. It is important to note that Eddie ends the film in a comfortable, but masculine, denim-on-denim outfit, his hair and beard trimmed neatly, the various shades of blue on him giving him a relaxed, controlled look. He is confident in himself and his relationship to Anne, and Venom, and does not need to perform his masculinity so aggressively.

Eddie's relationship with Anne has tones of queerness in its nontraditional presentation. Eddie's introduction to the film is him, in bed, being treated to coffee and talking about date night with his girlfriend, Anne. But the scene is not so simple. The first shot of Eddie in the film is Anne's hand sliding over Eddie's pillow, the dramatic music implying a potentially nefarious moment, only for Anne to immediately snatch Eddie's pillow, hit him with it, then dodge Eddie's retaliation and hit him with it again [00:04:55]. Their exchange is playful, and immediately Anne is established as more competent than Eddie due to her already being ready for work, her waking Eddie up, her beating Eddie handily in a quick pillow fight, and her reminding Eddie that he has an important meeting that morning, all in one minute of screen time [00:04:55–00:05:55]. This brief

Tom Hardy as Eddie Brock/Venom in *Venom*. Courtesy of Columbia Pictures/ Photofest.

opening scene demonstrates that Anne is Eddie's equal in this relationship, with Anne having a strongly defined sense of power and control over her part of their bond. After their date night, Eddie and Anne's relationship gains stronger, queerer footing, as Anne takes off her tie, slides it over Eddie's head, tightens it, and proceeds to lead Eddie to the bedroom [00:09:53]. This added layer of female sexual power is not presented as a negative, and Eddie seems happy, stable, and comfortable in this non-hetero-patriarchal form of equality in their relationship.

Additionally, queering Eddie and Anne's relationship is the introduction of Anne's new boyfriend, Dr. Dan Lewis. Dan is warm, unthreatened, and even notes that he admires Eddie [00:30:43]. In another darkly humorous scene, after witnessing Eddie Brock lower himself completely into a lobster tank and then begin to devour a raw lobster, Dan's response is only compassion [00:43:34]. He insists Eddie is his patient and rushes him to his hospital. Under most movie circumstances, Dan's kindness would be presented as weakness, especially when compared to the now superhuman Eddie/Venom. Instead, Dan is presented as a positive figure, not only warmly engaging with but often physically touching Eddie in a comfortable way that presents him as one of few positive forces of masculinity within the film. Dan's continued kindness toward and comfort with Eddie, his girlfriend's ex-fiancé, is abnormal by most movie standards at the very least and creates a blurred line between the emotional "throuple" the group quickly engages in.

The engagement the alien creatures, referred to as symbiotes, must achieve in order to even exist on our planet is queer. The symbiotes can only bond permanently with a "perfect match," with the goal of achieving total symbiosis [00:18:26]. There is a definitively romantic connection to this ideal, the physical manifestation of the "soul mate," two beings whose bodies are made for one another. To put an additional, dark, queer spin onto this idea, however, symbiotes invade the body of their host and remain inside them, resulting in death if they are not a perfect match, taking this idealized, often heteronormative idea of monogamy and giving it a much darker frame.

Symbiotes are genderless, amorphous, and do not reproduce sexually. They are creatures who connect to and potentially bond with the physical form, creating, when not lethal, a unique partnership in which the partners exist and operate as one.

Eddie is Venom's perfect match. In the beginning, when Venom first enters Eddie's body, Venom immediately argues that Eddie is "making *us* look bad" [00:51:02]. Venom immediately sees Eddie as part of himself. This is done with dark humor, with Venom taking control of Eddie's body to fight a number of Drake's guards sent to kill Eddie, but the queer subtext here is apparent. The claiming of this powerful, masculine figure, turned helpless by his own bravado, by a deeply voiced, hugely muscular creature who uses he/him pronouns has overwhelmingly queer overtones. Beyond this, when Venom first bonds with Eddie, Eddie becomes weakened, nervous, and incredibly apologetic. All sense of the masculine bravado that defined his opening character is erased, with Eddie going so far as to apologize for knocking out a guard who tasered him [00:51:35]. Perhaps this less performatively masculine version of Eddie is closer to his true self.

After receiving a call from Anne, Venom asks with something humorously akin to jealousy, "Who is Anne?" After being told it is not his business, Venom responds, "Everything of yours is my business. We have no secrets" [01:02:48]. These lines, given with such sincerity, and responded to by Eddie with such annoyance, invoke the image of a bickering married couple, something Sony and many fans clearly picked up on. An "Official 'Rom-Com' Trailer" was released to YouTube by Sony Pictures Entertainment in November 2018, which reframes the entire film as a romance between Eddie and Venom. The "Symbrock" tag on the internet site Tumblr produces hundreds of pages of fan art and fan fiction dedicated to interpreting the queerness inherent between Eddie and Venom. And the fan-fiction website Archive of Our Own includes more than three thousand Eddie Brock/Venom Symbiote works (2021).

Venom giving his name to Eddie is accompanied by the line, "I am Venom, and you are mine" [01:00:04]. Venom claims to solely be using Eddie as a "ride," but this line holds such intense, queer overtones that it became a core part of the *Venom* romcom trailer. This is especially humorous as, not even five minutes later, Venom notes that he is "starting to like" Eddie [01:05:10]. After meeting Anne, Venom immediately shares with Eddie that he "likes" Anne [01:09:19]. Venom also tries to help repair Eddie's relationship to Anne, adding an additional layer of queerness to Anne's relationship to Eddie, Eddie's relationship with Venom, and Venom's relationship to them both as Venom exists inside of, as a part of, and as a partner to Eddie. There is no normative comparison to the complex relationship that Venom creates between himself and Eddie, and then encourages between himself, Eddie, and Anne.

After being driven by Anne to the hospital, Eddie learns that Venom's presence in his body is killing him. After Venom is forced from Eddie's body by Anne, Eddie delivers an emotional "We're done" to Venom [01:12:40]. Akin to a breakup scene, Eddie storms from the room, his voice tight and eyes watering, veins bulging in his neck as he delivers the line. Anne seeks to comfort him, and Dan worries for Eddie's health, wondering what Venom is, creating an even more complicated foursome of interlocking relationships. Dan cares for Anne and Eddie. Anne loves Eddie and Dan. Venom exists inside of Eddie, "likes" him, and also "likes" Anne, who now has a complicated relationship with both Dan and Eddie. When Dan asks what exactly is going on, Anne gives several explanations as to why Eddie reached out to her, and that "there is nothing going on between me and Eddie" [01:13:09]. The fact that her primary concern is relationship oriented when there is a literal alien involved is played as humorous, especially when Dan's reaction is solely focused on what Venom is, with no jealousy regarding Eddie and Anne's relationship. This precise lack of jealousy and the highlighting of these relationships as the core of this scene is a uniquely positive portrayal of complex, queer relationships. Dan's concerns are for Eddie's well-being.

After being captured by Drake's men and interrogated, Eddie says that he has spent a lot of time with a symbiote "up my ass" [01:15:44]. This is played off as a rude joke, but its framing is remarkably queer. Eddie also states that having a symbiote inside him is "not a lot of fun," but he is also behaving like a man having just gone through a breakup, more betrayed that he thought Venom used him than he is about the potential destruction of Earth. The sexual innuendo also rings far more queer when combined with comments from Tom Hardy, Brock and Venom's actor, during an interview for *IGN*. When responding to the fan question of "Venom vs. Predator vs. Alien," Hardy immediately responds, "Gangbang!," with his costar noting, "Could be" (*IGN* 2018). Venom lives inside Eddie, creating a unique, pseudosexual, if not outright sexual relationship with Eddie. When learning Drake has bonded with the symbiote Riot, Eddie says, "He has one up his ass, too," carrying this theme of the pseudosexual nature of the symbiote's existence within their bonded mate [01:16:19].

It is important to note that Drake and Riot's relationship is much colder. Riot truly views Drake as a means to an end, with his ultimate desire being to invade the planet and devour all human life. Riot notes that the other symbiotes "will follow wherever I lead," and only returns to the use of "we" when reminded to by Drake [01:16:44]. Venom truly cares for Eddie, cementing the queer nature of their relationship in a way that exists beyond this other bonded symbiote.

When Venom returns to rescue Eddie, while possessing Anne's body, he immediately greets Eddie with a kiss [01:17:52]. The kiss lasts several seconds and allows Venom to fuse with Eddie's body again. In this moment, Eddie and the audience can interpret this kiss as one between Anne and Eddie, as Venom is molded to Anne's form, therefore appearing to be a woman and appearing to be Anne. The truth of the kiss's intent is revealed toward the end of the film, when Anne notes, "That was your buddy's idea" [01:28:13]. This clip, and the kiss itself, is used in the so-called romcom trailer to equally great and queer effect. Venom is the one who wants to kiss Eddie, and he is the one who brings it up to

Anne. The symbiotes only need to touch their hosts in order to fuse with their body. Anne could have simply touched Eddie's shoulder, or Venom could have resumed its more slime-like form to slither to Eddie's body, but Venom insists that he kiss Eddie on the mouth to transfer back to his body.

Venom reveals the symbiotes' invasion plan but also notes that "things are different now" [01:19:35]. He states that on Earth, he and Eddie could be more, and that he likes it on Earth. When asked what changed his mind, there is a meaningful pause, and Venom replies, "You. You did, Eddie" [01:20:04]. This entire exchange, viewed through the lens that it was Venom who wanted to kiss Eddie, gives the entire exchange a queer, romantic hue. Venom is willing to go against his entire species in order to stay with Eddie. His feelings for Eddie are what turns him from a monstrous alien set on destroying Earth into an antihero.

As the film closes, Eddie visits Anne, who notes how good it felt to have Venom "inside her," as Eddie describes it, with Venom saying, in Eddie's mind, "You belong with us, Annie" [01:28:46]. Eddie and Venom have fully rebonded and plan to continue to protect San Francisco. In comparison to Venom's introduction of "I am Venom," as the film closes, Eddie and Venom say, in unison, "We are Venom" [01:31:19].

See also *Batman v Superman: Dawn of Justice.*

Bibliography

Archive of Our Own. "Works in: Eddie Brock/Venom Symbiote." 2021. Accessed July 17, 2021. https://archiveofourown.org/tags/Eddie%20Brock*s*Venom%20Symbiote/works.

Hamilton, Patrick L. "Translating Masculinity: The Significance of the Frontier in American Superheroes." In *The Routledge Companion to Gender and Sexuality in Comic Book Studies*, edited by Frederick Luis Aldama, 15–27. London: Routledge, 2021.

IGN. "Tom Hardy and Riz Ahmed Respond to IGN Comments." YouTube.com, October 5, 2018. Accessed July 17, 2021. https://www.youtube.com/watch?v=P_HzLU3sF8I.

Sony Pictures Entertainment. "VENOM—Official 'Rom-Com' Trailer (On Digital 12/11, Blu-ray 12/18)." YouTube.com, November 27, 2018. Accessed July 17. 2021. https://www.youtube.com/watch?v=RuLfubSwbm0.

—Billy Tringali

· W ·

THE WEDDING BANQUET (1993)

DIRECTOR: Ang Lee
SCREENPLAY: Ang Lee, Neil Pang, and James Schamus
CAST: Ah-Lei Gua (Mrs. Gao), Sihung Lung (Mr. Gao), May Chin (Wei-Wei), Winston Chao (Wai-Tung Gao), Mitchell Lichtenstein (Simon)
SPECS: 106 minutes; color
AVAILABILITY: DVD (MGM)

The second film in Ang Lee's "Father Knows Best" Trilogy, *The Wedding Banquet* focuses on a gay couple, Wai-Tung and Simon. The two lead a content, out-and-proud life in New York City, except for the constant pestering of Wai-Tung's parents. Mr. and Mrs. Gao do not know their son is gay and wonder when he will settle down and marry a nice Chinese girl. Wai-Tung himself is an ambitious yet empathetic property manager. While trying to flip buildings for profit, he provides an almost rent-free home for Wei-Wei, a painter from China who is looking to stay in the United States through a green-card marriage. Simon suggests Wai-Tung and Wei-Wei marry, giving her a green card and finally placating

May Chin as Wei-Wei, Ah Lei Gua as Mrs. Gao, Mitchell Lichtenstein as Simon, Sihung Lung as Mr. Gao, and Winston Chao as Wai-Tung Gao in *The Wedding Banquet.* **Courtesy of Samuel Goldwyn Co./Photofest.**

his parent's wishes. But when Wai-Tung's parents surprise him with a trip to America to attend the wedding, Simon, Wei-Wei, and Wai-Tung's charade gets out of hand. The sham couple must now attend a huge wedding banquet in their honor, in the hopes of pleasing Wai-Tung's parents and keeping his secret.

The Wedding Banquet puts its main character at the intersection between American gay culture and patriarchal Chinese tradition. From the beginning, Wai-Tung is pulled between these two opposing identities. In the opening credits, he is at the gym, lifting weights while listening to a cassette of his mother rambling on about domestic life, wishing Wai-Tung would finally get married. She sent the tape from Taiwan to avoid international phone charges. With close-up shots of Wai-Tung's sweating face and body, pushing and pulling various weight machines, viewers hear Mrs. Gao's soothing voice and get a clue into Wai-Tung's internal conflict. Embodying two archetypes: the healthy, gym-going gay, and the dutiful immigrant son, Wai-Tung's identities compete for the same space, questioning how long these opposing selves can coexist.

A film centered on a gay Taiwanese-born Asian American is a notable addition to LGBTQIA+ representation in American film, which—even today—remains predominately white. In her essay "The Cinematic Representation of Asian Homosexuality in *The Wedding Banquet*," Ling-Yen Chua notes, "since psychoanalytic theories of (homo)sexuality were based almost solely on white middle-class (homo)sexuality, it is thus not surprising that contemporary cinematic discourses of homosexuality often exclude nonwhite and working-class subjects." According to Chua, "this led to the contemporary separation of the category of the homosexual from the non-white person" (1999, 100).

The Wedding Banquet spotlights Wai-Tung, an Asian American who performs "white homosexuality" through a middle-class lifestyle. Including his white-collar job and gym habit, Wai-Tung has a white partner, Simon, who is a physical therapist. The two live in a brownstone that they own. Viewers are introduced to their relationship through a fight regarding a vacation to Belize. Wai-Tung has to cancel the trip to attend a zoning hearing about one of his buildings, from which he hopes to make millions. Wai-Tung is impossible to separate from his middle-class characteristics, with even Simon describing him sarcastically as "such a disgusting Yuppie."

The Wedding Banquet has come under fire for the couples' heteronormative dynamic. It even translates, at moments, into a "husband and wife" setup. When Wai-Tung and Wei-Wei stage their relationship for Wai-Tung's parents, Simon is revealed to be the more caring, supportive, even feminine partner—Wei-Wei effectively replaces him as Wai-Tung's wife. In a comical montage where they move Wei-Wei into the apartment before the Gaos' arrival, Simon informs Wei-Wei of Wai-Tung's routine, down to the underwear he wears each day. They tour the apartment, with Wei-Wei writing on a small pad listening to Simon: "He wears Jockey but sleeps in boxer shorts . . . the couch is his own little world. Extra pillows 'cause he likes to drop off to sleep here. Sometimes I have to practically carry him up to bed" [00:20:02–00:20:32]. During the Gaos' stay, Simon helps Wei-Wei perform her wifely duties, including a comical scene where he cooks the Gaos' welcome meal. Wei-Wei sits on the counter drinking while Simon diligently cooks in a wok. Upon hearing Mrs. Gao come downstairs, the two quickly switch places, with Wei-Wei stirring clumsily and Simon sitting on the counter.

These performances led *The Wedding Banquet* to be questioned regarding its label as a "queer film." In his essay "So Queer yet So Straight: Ang Lee's *The Wedding Banquet* and *Brokeback Mountain*," William Leung acknowledges Lee's "*straight*-forward" attitude when directing *The Wedding Banquet* and *Brokeback Mountain* but emphasizes that this attitude gives the film its ability to bring queerness into the mainstream with Western and, importantly, Chinese audiences (2008). LGBTQIA+ portrayals in Chinese and Taiwanese cinema were still rare, even censored, at the time of *The Wedding Banquet*, indicating—partially—Lee's portrayal of a fairly domestic couple, and a film that largely focuses on weddings and Chinese tradition rather than explicitly queer issues.

Other scholars, like Juliette Ledru, argue that the play of gender roles via Wei-Wei and Simon is a way of counteracting racist stereotyping of Asian men and, more broadly, combats the assumed traditional roles of heterosexuality. In her essay "Queer and Asian: Redefining Chinese American Masculinity in *The Wedding Banquet* and *Red Doors*," Ledru argues that Lee uses "observational humor, masquerade and theatricality" to accomplish these goals (2019, 7). By portraying Wai-Tung as a successful businessman (noted previously), she argues the film counteracts the stereotype of Asian men as effeminate and submissive. The doubling of Simon and Wei-Wei, she says, shows how the "authentic" and traditional image of husband and wife is shown to be inauthentic: "Authenticity is thus denounced as something artificial, and heterosexuality and Chinese American masculinity are made to appear as social constructs" (2019, 7). Exposing the artifice of these constructs through masquerade and humor gives credence and credibility to Simon and Wai-Tung's life, making room in cinematic spaces for a gay interracial couple.

Indeed, the film's continued emphasis on the sham of Wei-Wei and Wai-Tung's marriage acts as a useful foil to exemplify a deep and long-term love in a gay male domestic partnership. The performative artifice in Wai-Tung and Wei-Wei's wedding photos contrasts with Simon and Wai-Tung's intimate couple photos, enhancing for viewers the authenticity of Wai-Tung and Simon's relationship. In a comical "de-gaying" of their apartment before the Gaos' arrival, a montage ensues where photos of Simon and Wai-Tung are replaced by Chinese calligraphy (created by Wai-Tung's father) and Wei-Wei's art. Shots of these photos show candid, sweet, even erotic ties between these two men. One photo depicts Wai-Tung, chin up, laughing while Simon shaves him; another is an artsy black-and-white, showing Wai-Tung nude with only a hat covering his genitals; the last photo is a surprise shot of Simon and Wai-Tung in the shower. Contrasting these authentic pictures, Wai-Tung and Wei-Wei's wedding photos are a rigid artifice. Wei-Wei is distorted into various unnatural positions by the photographer: "Turn a little more. White teeth. Smile a little wider. Turn some more" [00:53:43–00:53:53]. These photos are highly staged, enhanced by movie-style lighting.

In "Fake Weddings and the Critique of Marriage," Jeanette Roan interprets their sham marriage as the film's exposure of "the social functions and cultural values of marriage," making it easily translatable to the fight for marriage equality (2014, 748). When Wei-Wei and Wai-Tung enter City Hall, the scene has a Vegas shotgun wedding feel to it. Run by the state of New York, these mass weddings reflect the lack of cultural values behind American marriage. Roan contrasts this scene with our common conception of marriage:

> Boy meets girl. Boy loses girl. Boy gets girl. Fade-in on an outdoor wedding in a beautiful setting on a sunny day. Fade-out on happily ever after. These are not only the conventions of the Hollywood romance, but also the ingredients of popular ideologies of romantic love. Both represent weddings and the marriages they initiate as the logical and ideal endpoint of every good romantic relationship. (2014, 746)

But in *The Wedding Banquet*, love and romance are not the concern of the city officiator. In fact, he seems unconcerned that Wei-Wei does not even understand the vows she makes. During Wai-Tung and Wei-Wei's ceremony, she jumbles "for better, for worse, for richer, for poorer" into "better and richer, no poor" and mistakes "in sickness and in health until death do us part" for "until sickness and death" [00:39:38–00:40:28]. The officiator, a little taken aback, responds, "Groovy," and the two are officially married. Clearly, the cultural value of marriage is not his concern.

But if marriage, in the eyes of law and government, is not part of this ideological form cited by Roan and popularized in the American psyche, then what is it for? When *Obergefell v. Hodges* was before the Supreme Court in 2015, many against same-sex marriage—specifically the Family Research Council (n.d.)—claimed same-sex marriage would cause a breakdown in traditional families. *The Wedding Banquet* shows this belief of "tradition" and "love" that Roan cites to be false far before this landmark legislation. The comical ease with which Wai-Tung and Wei-Wei get "legally" married is acceptable, at the time, because of their heterosexuality. Marriage is shown not to have a traditional or moral value, but to be merely an exclusive right of the relationships between one man and one woman to be used for whatever motivations they see fit.

Wai-Tung's coming out is portrayed by the film in a similar fashion to the wedding. In the same way the film plays on marriage in order to critique it, Wai-Tung's coming out plays on this concept, consequently critiquing the common—American—connection in LGBTQIA+ cinema between coming out and spectacle. When Wai-Tung eventually admits he is gay, Mrs. Gao is shocked and heartbroken. At first, she blames Simon for seducing Wai-Tung, then daydreams about whether his queerness is just a phase. By the end of the film, Mrs. Gao is still ambivalent about her son's queerness. She makes Wai-Tung promise not to tell his father—because of his health, she fears it will literally kill him. But unbeknownst to the family, Mr. Gao already knows Wai-Tung is gay. During a walk with Simon, Mr. Gao reveals that he understands English and has heard everything said in the house between Wai-Tung, Simon, and Wei-Wei. He shares a heartfelt conversation with Simon, saying, "Wai-Tung is my son, and so you are my son also," giving Simon a traditional Chinese gift of money in a red envelope, also given to Wei-Wei to celebrate her wedding. But he has Simon promise not to tell Wai-Tung, Wei-Wei, or Mrs. Gao that he knows, calling it "our secret." When Simon asks Mr. Gao why, he responds, "For family," and switches to Mandarin: "If I didn't let them lie, I'd never have gotten my grandchild" (Wai-Tung and Wei-Wei created this child following the banquet scene) [01:35:45–01:36:42]. He believes this open secret will keep the family intact.

Mr. Gao is right, for the most part. If Wai-Tung had not been so obsessed with keeping his secret from his family, he would not have married Wei-Wei and conceived a child with her, the same child that Mr. Gao cherishes because it will continue the family line, upholding the patriarchal Chinese tradition that he desires from his son. In the end, everyone knows Wai-Tung is gay, and yet everyone is sworn to secrecy, in effect allowing Wai-Tung to be both in and out of the closet. This ambiguous coming out changes the traditional, American coming-out narrative in which coming out is almost always a spectacle. By shying away from spectacle, *The Wedding Banquet* may represent an experience closer to many LGBTQIA+ people's experience, people who may not have had the spectacle of coming out, who may tell one parent and not the other, who may be out to some friends but not to others, who may be out to friends but not to coworkers, who live a life both in and out of the closet.

With a more nuanced coming out experience, the film also shows a unique experience of partners in conservative or traditional family structures. Simon is tolerated but not embraced by the Gaos, exemplified in the wedding album taken back to Taiwan. Before the Gaos board their return flight, everyone looks through the wedding album. They laugh and point at pictures of Wei-Wei and Wai-Tung, until the last few pages show Wai-Tung and Simon, staged almost like a married couple under an arch. Mrs. Gao quickly closes the album. The photographic inclusion of Simon and Wai-Tung's relationship in the wedding album shows Simon is part of this new family and is a tacit—if reluctant—acceptance of Simon by the Gaos.

Against Simon's tacit acceptance, the film portrays him as an essential part of the prolific queer family unit established at the end of the film. After deciding to keep the baby, Wei-Wei asks for Wai-Tung's help, but both agree that Simon should be involved. In the end, the *three* of them decide to raise this baby together, creating a three-parent, queer household. This new family unit is solidified at the end of the film. When the Gaos walk off toward airport security, the camera cuts close to the newly sanctioned family they will leave behind: Wai-Tung, Wei-Wei, and Simon. This scene is mirrored with the Gaos' exit from the wedding banquet. At the end of the party, the Gaos say their goodbyes to the newlywed couple and head back to Simon and Wai-Tung's home. As they leave, the camera cuts close to Wei-Wei in her bridal gown and Wai-Tung in his tuxedo—a newly formed family. These two shots show that this new family unit is made whole by the combination of these three parents.

Simon's participation is what makes this new family unit queer, but it is not the first time he exemplifies a queer idea and issue. He also bears the burden of representing the AIDS crisis. When viewers are introduced to him, he sports an ACT UP "Silence = Death" T-shirt designed by Keith Haring under his lab coat. He also raises awareness about AIDS and safe sex, meeting up with friends to hand out flyers, signifying his participation as an AIDS activist. When he finds out that Wei-Wei is pregnant, he gets infuriated with Wai-Tung—not for having sex with her, but because he had *unsafe* sex with her. Though the film does not dwell on AIDS, the context of the time is felt in these moments, especially during the fight that ensues after Simon finds out Wei-Wei is pregnant. Simon's character is a reminder of the still ongoing fight at this time for proper medical care and grassroots advocacy to stop the epidemic of AIDS in the community at large.

With its heterosexual marriage plot, Taiwanese director, mostly Chinese dialogue, and traditional Chinese patriarchal drama, it is no surprise that *The Wedding Banquet* is often considered not queer enough and not American enough when discussing American LGBTQIA+ films. But the commentary of the film works to highlight the plight of gay immigrants and to expose the social constructs of American marriage, masculinity, and queerness to such a degree that it is as much a film about American gay identity as it is about Chinese tradition. In some ways, the film, like Wai-Tung, is both out and not out for viewers, representing queer characters in a very straight family drama.

See also *The Kids Are All Right; Spa Night; Star Trek Beyond*.

Bibliography

Chua, Ling-Yen. "The Cinematic Representation of Asian Homosexuality in *The Wedding Banquet*." *Journal of Homosexuality* 36, no. 3/4 (1999): 99–112.

Family Research Council. "Ten Arguments from Social Science against Same-Sex Marriage." N.d. Accessed March 24, 2021. www.frc.org/issuebrief/ten-arguments-from-social-science-against-same-sex-marriage.

Ledru, Juliette. "Queer and Asian: Redefining Chinese American Masculinity in *The Wedding Banquet* (Ang Lee, 1993) and *Red Doors* (Georgia Lee, 2006)." *Itinéraires* 2019, nos. 2–3 (2019). https://journals.openedition.org/itineraires/7067.

Leung, William. "So Queer yet So Straight: Ang Lee's *The Wedding Banquet* and *Brokeback Mountain*." *Journal of Film and Video* 60, no. 1 (2008): 23–42.

Lim, Song Hwee. *Celluloid Comrades: Representations of Male Homosexuality in Contemporary Chinese Cinemas*. Honolulu: University of Hawaii Press, 2006.

Roan, Jeanette. "Fake Weddings and the Critique of Marriage: *The Wedding Banquet* (1993), *I Now Pronounce You Chuck and Larry* (2007), and the Marriage Equality Debate." *Quarterly Review of Film and Video* 31, no. 8 (2014): 746–63.

—Mark Muster

WET HOT AMERICAN SUMMER (2001)

DIRECTOR: David Wain
SCREENPLAY: Michael Showalter and David Wain
CAST: Janeane Garofalo (Beth), David Hyde Pierce (Henry), Michael Showalter (Coop), Marguerite Moreau (Katie), Paul Rudd (Andy), Elizabeth Banks (Lindsay), Michael Ian Black (McKinley), Bradley Cooper (Ben), Amy Poehler (Susie), Christopher Meloni (Gene)
SPECS: 97 minutes; color
AVAILABILITY: DVD (Universal Pictures Home Entertainment)

It is August 18, 1981, the last day of the eight-week season at Camp Firewood. There's a talent show in the evening and a range of activities for the young campers, but it's the adult staff's romantic entanglements that drive this satirical take on 1980s movies and culture. Camp director Beth has her eye on the astrophysics professor next door, Henry; among the twentysomething counselors, Coop lusts after Katie, but she can't stay away from Andy, who in turn can't keep his hands off of Lindsay. Victor wants to finally lose his virginity to Abby but can't find the time; J. J. and Gary are determined to hook McKinley up with one of the camp girls, unaware that he's already in a committed relationship with Ben. Hijinks ensue as everyone tries to get what—and who—they want before going home, even as a piece of falling space junk threatens to disrupt the all-important talent show. Also, there's a talking can of mixed vegetables.

It's tough to take any part of *Wet Hot American Summer* seriously given the film's farcical approach to reality. No scene ends without a joke, and, indeed, many scenes exist only as opportunities for the sprawling ensemble cast—stacked with talent who would reappear throughout the next two decades of American film and television—to flex their comedic muscles. An early example has Beth and some counselors heading into town for supplies, where a montage shows them smoking cigarettes, then switching to alcohol and marijuana, before robbing an old woman for cocaine money and passing out in an abandoned house. And then they're back at camp and back to normal, with one remarking that "it's good to get away from camp, even for an hour" [00:32:55]. *Wet Hot American Summer* derives its humor from absurdity, including in the setup and resolution of multiple relationship plots. Ben and McKinley's gay romance is not exempt from this paradigm, yet the film's treatment of their relationship deviates from the typical, often homophobic punch lines assigned to LGBTQIA+ people in mainstream film. Ben and McKinley's relationship is mined for jokes but not

Bradley Cooper as Ben, Janeane Garofalo as Beth, and Michael Ian Black as McKinley in *Wet Hot American Summer*. Courtesy of USA Films/Photofest.

at their expense. Comparing their cinematic relationship with any of the film's other, sometimes ludicrous pairings actually suggests that Ben and McKinley might be the film's most normatively positive representation of love and desire.

Many of *Wet Hot American Summer*'s couples exist as a platform for jokes. The love quadrangle between Coop, Katie, Andy, and Lindsay, for example, sets up a number of quick lines—Coop calling, "I want you inside me," as Katie walks away [00:06:30]—and extended bits, such as Andy letting campers drown while making out with Lindsay. Although Coop is eventually able to attract Katie, the premise of their relationship is mocked from its beginning and Katie's decision at the end of the film to remain with Andy comes as no surprise. Beth and Henry's romance comes closer to being "played straight," with their shared awkwardness reading as charming as well as funny. Whether the jokes are mean-spirited or in good fun, almost everyone at Camp Firewood is invested in finding romance on their last day together. In the words of the camp's juvenile radio DJ, "For those select few of you who went all summer . . . without finding that special someone, today is your day. You don't want to go back home and lie to your friends about a summer romance that didn't even happen, and you don't wanna be the one person who doesn't have anyone to kiss tonight after the talent show" [00:04:45].

When three apparently single male counselors—J. J., Gary, and McKinley—stumble across a group of their female counterparts stripping down to bikinis for a swim, it seems like the setup for a voyeuristic male fantasy. The camera isolates busts and butts as J. J. and Gary quietly yet graphically urge them to "bend over, yes, take 'em off" [00:40:40]. McKinley excuses himself, to the shock of his horny companions. "He gets so uncomfortable whenever we talk openly about sexual issues . . . he's never been with a girl before," J. J. muses [00:40:55]. As McKinley's friends speculate about how to "get McKinley laid," the camera cuts to show him walking into a small shed where Ben is waiting [00:42:10]. The film crosscuts between J. J. and Gary's plotting—and continued spying on the swimming women—and McKinley and Ben. In contrast to J. J. and Gary's voyeurism and vulgar commentary, Ben and McKinley are tender in their movements as they approach each other, touching foreheads and embracing as they undress each other. The two are gently lit by soft gold light, which reflects off their skin, endowing their lovemaking with a romance notably lacking in other couples' scenes. Ben and McKinley are shown having anal sex, the position of their bodies and motions of thrusting explicitly yet tastefully displayed on the screen. The cinematographic treatment of their sex scene—the only sex scene in the film—juxtaposes Ben and McKinley's erotic intimacy with the crassness of their heterosexual coworkers. Anal sex between men, one of the most frequently mocked aspects of gay life, becomes a romantic expression of love in *Wet Hot American Summer* that is not extended to any of the heterosexual couples.

Shortly after this sequence, J. J. and Gary see McKinley and Susie heading into the woods. They pursue, intending to be "eyewitnesses for verification" of their friend having sex with a woman [00:44:10]. Instead, what they see is Ben and McKinley standing in the lake, holding hands with flowers in their hair. Susie plays the flute as Beth officiates a brief ceremony to "consecrate and sanctify the union of McKinley and Ben" [00:44:45]. The two kiss and embrace as a shocked J. J. and Gary each exclaim, "McKinley's a fag!" [00:45:05]. J. J. and Gary's pejorative use of "fag" certainly does not suggest approval. The film moves on to other matters—developing Coop and Katie as well as Beth and Henry's relationship arcs, among other things—and the incident seems forgotten.

Later, as the entire camp is gathered for dinner, J. J. and Gary throw open the cafeteria doors. "McKinley and Ben!" they yell in harsh voices. "This is for you!" [00:58:35]. The brief tension is quickly resolved, though, when they carry in a large box and say, "It's a chaise lounge, we didn't know if maybe you guys already had one, we have the receipt if you do" [00:58:50]. The whiplash created by this moment is clearly comedic as all four men embrace, Ben enthusing that "it goes with the chenille throw cloth Beth's sister gave us" [00:58:55]. The joke, then, is not that two men could be in love or have sex with each other. Instead, the scene's humor comes from the audience's expectations of what typically happens in mainstream American film when a gay character is outed: violence. The happy resolution to their drama differs from the other couples of the film, most of whom break up. Although jokes abound in *Wet Hot American Summer*, LGBTQIA+ people are not targeted by any mean-spirited digs.

See also *Kissing Jessica Stein*.

—Sam Hunter

• Y •

YES, GOD, YES (2019)

DIRECTOR: Karen Maine

SCREENPLAY: Karen Maine, based on the short film of the same name by Karen Maine

CAST: Natalia Dyer (Alice), Timothy Simons (Father Murphy), Wolfgang Novogratz (Chris), Francesca Weal (Laura), Susan Blackwell (Gina), Parker Wierling (Wade)

SPECS: 78 minutes; color

AVAILABILITY: DVD (Artisan/Lionsgate)

Yes, God, Yes is a full-feature version of Karen Maine's short film of the same name (2017). Natalia Dyer stars as Alice, a high school junior attending a strict midwestern Catholic school in the early 2000s. The film opens with a quote from the Book of Revelation denouncing "sexually immoral" acts, followed by a series of establishing shots that reinforce the conservatism of this setting—a pro-life poster and admonitions about young women's skirts being the wrong length. Coming of age in the early days of the Internet (the film makes extensive reference to dial-up internet and chat rooms), Alice uses her computer to afford her an escapist window on the world beyond school, church, and the stifling conformity of life in small-town middle America. It also allows Alice to sate her sexual curiosity and seek answers to her questions she knows she will not find in school, where sex education classes are taught by the fire-and-brimstone priest, Father Murphy. His classes are moralizing diatribes focused on instilling an oppressive sense of religious doctrine and fear of any form of deviance in his students. Falling victim to an unsubstantiated rumor concerning her behavior with a fellow student at a party, Alice's moral integrity is called into question. Disappointed at her subsequent dismissal from her serving role in mass, she decides to attend the school's "Kirkos Retreat" program (a four-day-long camp for Catholic teenagers) in an attempt at atonement. During the retreat, however, she develops a romantic attraction to one of the group leaders, to whom she later makes an unsuccessful pass. A number of other misdemeanors further compromise her standing among the retreat staff, as well as in the eyes of Father Murphy (whom she later witnesses in a compromising position watching pornography on his office computer), and she abandons the retreat. Slipping away one night, Alice stumbles across a backwoods gay bar where she unexpectedly finds sanctuary and receives counsel from the bar's owner, Gina, who helps in revealing to her the innate hypocrisy and contradictions of people (even those who may appear to be beyond reproach such as Father Murphy) and suggests she consider applying to college further afield to give her a fresh perspective on the world. Liberated by this new idea, the film ends as Alice returns to school with a more robust and less scrupulous attitude to her own life and imperfections. She confronts Father

Murphy in confession, making a veiled reference to his own indiscretion, and finally researches colleges on the East and West Coasts, evidently intending to follow Gina's advice.

This film, although milder in tone and, in some ways, not as sophisticatedly achieved, is most obviously comparable to *The Miseducation of Cameron Post* (2018) and is one of an increasing number of films centering on young peoples' experiences of Christian camps and "conversion centers" (other examples include *Jesus Camp* [2006], *Boy Erased* [2018], and *Pray Away* [2020]). Unlike *Cameron Post*, however, *Yes, God, Yes* is not specifically LGBTQIA+ themed and instead focuses on the sexual confusion experienced by a heterosexual protagonist. That said, it is worth mentioning that this distinction is not made so overtly in the director's original short film, which features a scene interesting because it remains the only aspect of the original film not subsequently reprised in the full feature. Here Alice walks down a busy high school hallway in slow motion, struggling to contend with the various temptations that meet her gaze. The camera initially falls on a passing male student's open trouser fly before panning briefly to a young woman's transparent top with clearly visible breasts beneath, finally coming to rest on an icon of Christ hung above the hallway. In addition to the way this scene (as it appears in the short film at least) encourages the viewer to consider how Alice's experience of her burgeoning sexuality may *not* be allied to a specific gender, it also indicates how Alice's "flesh struggle," or what Daniel Cutrara calls in *Wicked Cinema* (2014) the "spirit/flesh dichotomy," results in an "undermining of the divine" (the scene described happening literally below the hanging icon).

Alice's experiences with Catholicism shift throughout the film, starting as something she perceives as laughably puzzling but fairly benign (in one of the film's many comedic notes, her friend reminds Alice that her request to rewind the sex scene in *Titanic* is likely to be considered sinful) but becoming something more abject because of the way it attempts to censor and oppress an aspect of her identity—her sexuality—that is becoming an increasingly important and prominent part of her life. In this way, the primary question the film asks is, to what extent can you truly belong to a place or group that attempts to negate or cast aspersions over the person you are? It is for this reason that Alice's meeting with Gina in the penultimate act of the film is such a pivotal part of the narrative, and it is this (albeit brief) section of the movie, wherein Alice comes into contact with and experiences a crucial moment of growth through her association with a queer character, that could be said to make this film a key example of queer-positive cinema.

In their 2017 study of lesbians in film, Millward, Dodd, and Fubara-Manuel consider how "positive role models such as out lesbians, are sources of strength and influences to help women feel that their own identities are acceptable and to feel pride in their resilience" (103). This, ostensibly, is the situation depicted in Alice's meeting with Gina in the bar. Despite the fact that she is clearly underage and has run away from the retreat (Alice still has on her Kirkos T-shirt, making this doubly obvious), Gina serves her a drink and treats her as an adult. Refreshed by this attitude, Alice confides in her about her fears and struggles at school, and Gina responds, giving her some key advice. Initially explaining to

Alice that, like her, she "used to be Catholic and went to Catholic school," Gina goes on to consider the things that changed her and resulted in her questioning the worldview she had grown up with:

> San Francisco. The seventies. Sex. Women. Lots of reasons. But I remember being your age and just being scared shitless that I was going to wind up in hell. . . . You know, the truth is, nobody knows what they're doing any more than the rest of us. We're all just trying to figure out our shit. . . . Have you thought about where you might go to college? Why don't you check out some schools on the East and West Coasts? You might like getting out of this town for a bit.

For Gina, then, salvation came, not through her engagement with Catholicism, but instead through experiences that reassured her that binary moral codes were fundamentally hypocritical because ultimately, religious or not, individuals have in common the fact that "we're all just trying to figure out our shit." Added to this is the point that a young person hungry for a less judgmental and more liberated lifestyle may be well advised to spread her wings. It is also notable that Alice's meeting with Gina is presented as confessional in tone, echoing the previous experiences of confession that Alice has shared with Father Murphy, albeit this time resulting in genuine understanding, empathy, and growth (rather than the rote rituals and arbitrary penance that are the typical outcome of the latter's approach to the sacrament). Through the character of Gina, the film attests to how, as David Alderson considers in his work *Sex, Needs and Queer Culture*, queerness is inexorably equated with liberation—with learning how to become true to who you are and also understanding that freedom necessitates adopting a questioning stance against those who claim to represent "ideal" morals or virtues (2016). Crucial, too, is the point the film implies that although this lesson may be borne out by a queer character, it nevertheless applies to anyone experiencing any form of oppression. This includes, in the context of this film, the experience of a heterosexual adolescent learning to come to terms with and explore one of the facets that all humans share, sexuality, against an atmosphere of judgment. Such a questioning and, at times, angry stance on oppressive religious and moral doctrine, as well as the use of a queer character to expose the inevitable hypocrisies and contradictions all of us (even Father Murphy) contain, particularly in terms of the effect of this on individuals like Alice who are negotiating the formative terrain of adolescence, is this film's significant strength.

See also *But I'm a Cheerleader*; *Dream Boy*; *I Am Michael*.

Bibliography

Alderson, David. *Sex, Needs and Queer Culture: From Liberation to the Postgay.* London: ZED, 2016.

Cutrara, Daniel. *Wicked Cinema: Sex and Religion on Screen.* Austin: University of Texas Press, 2014.

Millward, Liz, Janice G. Dodd, and Irene Fubara-Manuel. *Killing Off the Lesbians: A Symbolic Annihilation on Film and Television.* Jefferson, NC: McFarland, 2017.

—Ben Screech

Index

Page references for figures are italicized.

About the Editors and Contributors

Erica Joan Dymond, PhD, is an assistant professor at East Stroudsburg University. Her research has been published in peer-reviewed journals such as the *Journal of Popular Culture* as well as the *Explicator*. Her work also appears in numerous academic volumes, such as *The Encyclopedia of Japanese Horror Films*, *The Encyclopedia of Racism in American Films*, and *A Cuban Cinema Companion*, all published by Rowman & Littlefield. Dr. Dymond is also the coeditor of *The Encyclopedia of Sexism in American Film* (Rowman & Littlefield, 2019). She has been a consulting editor for the peer-reviewed academic journal the *Explicator* since 2011 and has been a manuscript reviewer for the Amazon Breakthrough Novel Award and a peer reviewer for Focal Press, Columbia University Press, and Routledge.

Salvador Jimenéz Murguía, PhD, is an associate professor of sociology. He is the coeditor of *The Encyclopedia of Spanish Cinema* (2018) and the editor of *The Encyclopedia of Japanese Horror Films* (2016) and *The Encyclopedia of Racism in American Films* (2018), all published by Rowman & Littlefield.

* * *

Aspen Taylor Ballas holds a master's in the humanities with a concentration in visual studies from the University of Colorado at Denver. She is an instructor in the humanities and social sciences at Northern New Mexico College. While cinema is her primary area of research, her work in visual studies extends to fine art and popular media. Her work is largely influenced by critical theory, decolonial thought, race studies, Marxism, and existentialism.

Angela Beauchamp is an administrator for the Film and Digital Arts Department and a lecturer in film history at the University of New Mexico. Recent publications include an article on representations of Eleanor Roosevelt in film and television in *Americana: The Journal of American Popular Culture, 1900 to Present* (2020). Beauchamp was coeditor of the 2019 Basement Films book *Black Material* and holds an MA in film theory and gender studies from Skidmore College.

Angelos Bollas, PhD, is an early career researcher of sexuality and cultural studies. He is interested in practices of Othering in representations of sexuality in corporate and mainstream media.

Corey Call received his PhD in public policy and administration from Virginia Commonwealth University. He is an assistant professor in the Department of Sociology, Anthropology, and Criminal Justice Studies at Longwood University in Farmville, Virginia. His primary research interests concern sex offending, sex offender management policies, serial murder, and media portrayals of criminal justice. His research has been featured in a variety of academic journals, including *Homicide Studies, Journal of Criminal Justice and Popular Culture, American Journal of Criminal Justice, Sexual Abuse: A Journal of Research and Treatment,* and *Criminal Justice Studies.*

Sean D. Catino (they/them) is a 2020 graduate of East Stroudsburg University. They hold a BA in writing and an AS in theater. Catino has previously been featured in the *Rising Phoenix Review* and *Heirlock Literary Magazine.* They are a digital content and SEO specialist and plan to continue their studies in fiction and narrative at the graduate level.

Srirupa Chatterjee is an associate professor of English in the Department of Liberal Arts, Indian Institute of Technology Hyderabad, India. She specializes in gender and body studies, contemporary and multiethnic American fiction, and literary theory. Her forthcoming books include *Body Image in Contemporary American Young Adult Literature* and *Body Studies in Literature, Culture and Theory,* along with two coedited books, *Female Body Image in Contemporary Indian Literature and Culture* and *Gendered Violence in Public Spaces: Women's Narratives of Travel in Neoliberal India.*

April Taylor Clark is a PhD student in the Women's, Gender, and Sexuality Studies Department at SUNY Stony Brook.

Anya Crittenton (they/them) is a Los Angeles–based journalist advocating for queer voices and social justice. They are currently the editorial associate for the nonprofit Green America, with bylines at *Gay Star News,* the *Mary Sue,* and /*Film.* In 2019, they received their MA in journalism from CSU Northridge, where they won first place at the annual CSUNposium for their thesis on *Teen Vogue,* intersectionality, and social media.

Amy Cummins, PhD, is professor of English in the Department of Literatures and Cultural Studies, College of Liberal Arts, at the University of Texas Rio Grande Valley. She works in the English education area.

Jacob DeBrock is currently an English PhD student at the University of Mississippi. He received his bachelor's from the University of Toledo and his master's from the University of Louisville. His academic interests include African American literature and culture, film studies, queer studies, and disability studies.

Michael Diambri is a scholar of the history of gender and sexuality at USC.

Nicole Dib is an assistant professor in the English Department at Southern Utah University. She specializes in contemporary American literature, comparative ethnic approaches to literary studies, critical race studies, and road-trip narratives. Her teaching and research intersect several fields in the humanities, drawing from literary studies, cultural studies, mobility studies, and ethnic studies. Her scholarly work appears or is forthcoming in venues including *MELUS:*

Multiethnic Literature of the United States, Studies in the Novel, Feminism and Comics: New Essays on Interpretation, and *Teaching the Classics in the U.S. Prison System.*

José Duarte teaches cinema at the School of Arts and Humanities, Universidade de Lisboa. He is a researcher at ULICES (University Lisbon Centre for English Studies) and the coeditor of *The Global Road Movie: Alternative Journeys around the World* (2018) and *The Films of João Pedro Rodrigues and João Rui Guerra da Mata* (2022). His main research interests include film history, North American cinema, Portuguese cinema, television, and popular culture.

Gabriel Duckels is a Harding Distinguished Postgraduate Scholar at the University of Cambridge, completing a doctoral thesis on the relationship between HIV/AIDS and melodramatic expression in young adult literature and popular culture. His research can be found in the *Children's Literature Association Quarterly* and the *European Journal of Cultural Studies,* among other places.

Sandra Eckard, PhD, is a professor of English at East Stroudsburg University, where she teaches writing, education, and literature courses. In addition, Dr. Eckard is the director of the Writing Studio, a tutoring space for student writers. Her research focuses are writing center theory, writing pedagogy, reading theory, and teaching with popular culture. Her publications include *The Ties That Bind: Storytelling as a Teaching Technique in Composition Classrooms and Writing Centers, Yin and Yang in the English Classroom: Teaching with Popular Culture Texts,* and the Comic Connections series from Rowman & Littlefield.

Rebecca Feasey, PhD, is senior lecturer in Film and Media Communications at Bath Spa University. She has published a range of work on the representation of gender in popular media culture. She has published in journals such as *Feminist Media Studies* and the *Journal of Gender Studies.* She has written book-length studies on masculinity and popular television (2008), motherhood on the small screen (2012), maternal audiences (2016), and infertility and nontraditional family building in the media (2019).

Jana Fedtke, PhD, is assistant professor of English at the American University of Sharjah (United Arab Emirates). Her research and teaching interests include transnational literatures with a focus on South Asia, gender studies, and postcolonial literatures. Dr. Fedtke's work has been published in *Online Information Review, Journalism Practice, Journal of Further and Higher Education, South Asian History and Culture, Asexualities: Feminist and Queer Perspectives, The Communication Review, South Asian Review,* and *MAI: Feminism and Visual Culture.*

Caryn S. Fogel is the communications specialist at a water resources consulting firm in Tucson, Arizona. She oversees the production of technical reports and proposals and is developing workshops to help the scientific staff improve their writing skills. Prior to moving to the Southwest in 2018, Caryn was the editorial project manager at East Stroudsburg University of Pennsylvania, where she earned a bachelor of arts in English and master of arts in professional and digital media writing. Caryn has studied a variety of writing styles, including fiction, creative nonfiction, poetry, technical writing, and reviewing the arts.

Sasha T. Goldberg is a professor, researcher, and author who holds a PhD in gender studies from Indiana University and a master's degree in Judaism from the Graduate Theological Union. Her work centers on butch women, female masculinities, and lesbian specificity; she also specializes in grief, loss, and pastoral care. In her previous life, she ran intergenerational LGBTQ and Jewish nonprofits. Her scholarship is therefore interdisciplinary by design, intersectional by dedication, and fueled by the pursuit of access, justice, and equity. Dr. Goldberg has lectured internationally on gender, sex, and sexuality.

Amanda S. Grieme, mental health awareness advocate and educator, is the author of *Paging Dr. Freedman* (2019) and *H.O.L.D. F.A.S.T.: Ride Out Life with Bipolar Disorder* (2020) and innovator of the H.O.L.D. F.A.S.T. Method. She uses writing and radio to share her message of hope in this ever-cycling existence.

Andrew Grossman is the editor of the anthology *Queer Asian Cinema: Shadows in the Shade*, an associate editor of and contributor to *Bright Lights Film Journal*, and a columnist for Popmatters.com. He has contributed book chapters to numerous anthologies, including *24 Frames: Korea and Japan*; *New Korean Cinema*; *Chinese Connections: Critical Perspectives on Film, Identity, and Diaspora*; *Asexualities: Queer and Feminist Perspectives*; *Movies in the Age of Obama*; *Hong Kong Horror Cinema*; and *The Routledge Handbook of Male Sex Work*. He also produced and directed a feature documentary, *Not That Kind of Christian!!*, which was featured at the 2007 Montreal World Film Festival.

Dyuti Gupta is currently pursuing her PhD in English and American studies from the University of Manchester. She graduated from the University of Delhi (India) with a bachelor's degree in English literature and went on to complete her master's degree in the same from Ambedkar University Delhi (India). Her research specializations are postcolonial studies, war writing, gender theory, and family sociology. She has participated in and presented research papers at many prestigious national and international conferences. Having worked with media houses and nonprofit organizations in the past, she aims to build a future for herself in academia.

Greggory S. Hanson is a graduate student at East Stroudsburg University working on MAs in professional and digital media writing as well as history.

Jon Heggestad is a lecturer in the English Department at the University of Wisconsin–Eau Claire, where he teaches courses on film, new media, and writing. His research focuses on queer representation and queer family making across media. His other recent publications have appeared in journals like the *Lion and the Unicorn* and *Queer Studies in Media & Popular Culture*.

Randi Hogden is a senior English literature and history student at East Strouds-burg University in northeastern Pennsylvania. She is the recipient of the Joan Brimer-Cramer '41 Endowed Scholarship.

Sam Hunter is a PhD student in cinema and media studies at UCLA. His research interests include queer screen culture, new media and Internet history, and Marxist media theory and praxis. His writing has been published in *Film & History* and *New Media & Society*.

Tuğba Karaca was born and raised in Germany. She received her bachelor of arts degree at the University of Wuppertal (BUW) and is currently working on her master's of education studies. In 2019, she successfully attended the University of East Stroudsburg in Pennsylvania in a student exchange program. In addition to her occupation as a student assistant in BUW's English Department, she teaches German and math classes at a primary school.

Kel R. Karpinski is a librarian and assistant professor at CUNY–NYC College of Technology. Kel does research focusing on queer films and novels from World War II to early gay liberation, especially as it relates to sailors and hustlers in Times Square and how these texts map queer desire onto the city. Kel also makes zines about queer sailors and is an organizer for the NY Queer Zine Fair.

Veronika Klusakova graduated from the Department of Theatre and Film Studies and the Department of English and American studies at the Faculty of Arts, Palacky University, in Olomouc, Czech Republic. She holds a PhD in American studies. She is currently teaching film history in connection with selected interdisciplinary concepts (the cinema and literature of the American South in a social-political frame, the politics of childhood in cinema, the cinema of attractions, and contemporary film) at FAMU, Prague. In her research, she focuses on the issues of gender, class and race, the gothic, and the American South in US visual culture.

Karen Kohoutek is an independent scholar who has published about weird fiction and cult films in various journals, literary websites, and critical anthologies. Her essays have recently appeared in the 2021 books *ReFocus: The Films of Doris Wishman* and *Robert E. Howard Changed My Life*, and will appear in the forthcoming *Black Panther and Philosophy*. She lives in Fargo, North Dakota.

Curt Lund (he/him) is a designer, historian, and multimedia artist whose work centers around collecting and identity. Lund is assistant professor in the Department of Digital Media Arts at Hamline University in St. Paul, Minnesota.

John Lynskey received his PhD in film studies from the University of Edinburgh and a master's in literatures of the Americas from Trinity College Dublin. He has presented his work at numerous conferences, including Cine-Excess and Film-Philosophy, and acted as the co-organizer of Don't Look: Representations of Horror in the 21st Century conference in 2018. His work has been published in several publications, including *New Queer Horror Film and Television* (2020) and *BAFTSS Open Screens Journal*. He currently holds the position of adjunct professor at Holy Family University in Philadelphia, where he teaches courses in English, rhetoric, and public speaking.

CE Mackenzie is a PhD candidate at the University of Pittsburgh, where they study at the intersections of health rhetoric, trans and affect studies, and theories of epistemology. Their work can be found in a range of places, including *Prose Studies, Rhetoric of Health and Medicine*, and *QED: A Journal of GLBTQ Worldmaking*.

Douglas C. MacLeod Jr. is an associate professor and chair of liberal studies and teaches composition and communication at SUNY Cobleskill. He has presented on various subjects at conferences, including *The Twilight Zone*, Alfred Hitchcock, *Marathon Man*, empathy in the digital age, stand-up comedy as a tool for composition writers, and Oliver Stone. He is also widely published, having produced book chapters (on such topics as religion and cinema and Bonnie and Clyde), encyclopedia entries, and book reviews for various print and online academic journals, including *Film and History, Scope, Warscapes*, and the *Journal of American Studies of Turkey*.

Banibrata Mahanta is professor of English literature at Banaras Hindu University, India. His areas of interest are the changing contours of Indian nationalist thought in Indian English literature and culture and literary theory, especially disability theory. He is a theater enthusiast and has been associated with a few amateur theatrical productions. His recent works include a monograph titled *Disability Studies: An Introduction* (2016), the edited volume *English Studies in India: Contemporary and Evolving Paradigms* (2018), and an English translation of the Hindi novel *Lavanyadevi* (forthcoming), for which he was awarded the PEN America Translation Grant in 2021.

Meredith M. Malburne-Wade, PhD, serves as the director of fellowships and awards at James Madison University (JMU), where she mentors students applying for competitive awards, such as the Fulbright US Student Program and Rhodes Scholarship. The author of *Revision as Resistance in Twentieth-Century American Drama*, she holds a BA in English and French from Wellesley College, an MA in English from Georgetown University, and a PhD in twentieth-century American literature from UNC–Chapel Hill. She teaches interdisciplinary courses for the JMU Honors College on a wide range of topics, from monsters in American literature and film to portrayals of female sexuality.

Cara McClintock-Walsh, PhD, is a professor of English at Northampton Community College, where she teaches courses in women and gender studies and Irish literature. She is also the coordinator of the Honors Program and currently holds the Robert J. Kopecek Endowed Chair in the Humanities. She has published articles on Irish literature (in the collection *W.B. Yeats and Postcolonialism*), modern American literature, and topics involving gender and representation in film. Her current scholarship involves unearthing the connections between African American and Irish theater in the early twentieth century.

Layla Ferrández Melero graduated with a degree in English philology from Universidad de Zaragoza in 2012. She obtained her master's degree in English linguistics in 2013 at Universidad Complutense de Madrid. Currently, she is a PhD candidate at Universidad Autónoma de Madrid and is writing a thesis on Elizabeth Bowen. Her research focuses on identity formation and the relation between Bowen's female characters and the places they inhabit.

Mark Muster is a 2019 graduate of the English MA program at Syracuse University. His work primarily covers queer studies in media and film with writing published in *Broadly Textual* and a podcast on B-list queer movies titled *Queens of the B's*. He is a recipient of the Mary Hatch Marshall Award and the Best Paper Prize at Stony Brook University's Literature as Activism Conference and is a former scholar at the Cornell School of Criticism and Theory. He is currently a content strategist and writer living in New York City.

Peter Piatkowski is a writer, teacher, and a higher education professional. After earning his MFA in creative writing from Roosevelt University and his MA in English literature from DePaul University, he taught with the City Colleges of Chicago for a number of years. He has had work published in anthologies, journals, and books, including *Beyond Binaries*, *Off the Rocks*, *Tim Burton's Bodies*, and *The View from Here*. He is currently working on research on the cinema of Nora Ephron and its intersection with foodie culture.

Sabine Planka, PhD, is a literary scholar working in the field of literature/media for children and young adults from the nineteenth to the twenty-first century, considering its art historical and filmic aspects. She has published various articles, has (co)edited essay collections, and has presented lectures in the above named fields. She works as a subject librarian for the humanities at the university library of Fern Universität Hagen (Germany) and as a visiting lecturer at Bielefeld University (Germany) in the field of children's literature. Additionally, she works as a reviewer for various magazines and published her first children's novel in October 2020.

Todd K. Platts is professor of sociology at Piedmont Virginia Community College, Charlottesville. He has authored many articles and chapters on horror cinema. He is coeditor of *Blumhouse Productions: The New House of Horror* (2022). He is currently editing a collection on *The Conjuring*.

Nick Pozek is an educator, theorist, and mediator whose work focuses on the intersection of power, philanthropy, institutions, and globalization. He serves as the assistant director of Asian Law Programs at Columbia University and is a trustee of Global Community Charter School. He has also held leadership roles at the League of American Orchestras, Asia Society, and Carnegie Museum of Art.

Genevieve Ruzicka is a second-year PhD student in the Women's, Gender, and Sexuality Studies Department at Stony Brook University. Her work deals with representations of gender, sexualities, and race in television and film. She has presented at popular culture conferences across the country and is currently working on a dissertation that engages with science-fiction television centered around time travel.

Ben Screech is a lecturer in English and education at the University of Gloucestershire in Cheltenham, United Kingdom. The majority of his research centers on children's and young adult writing, but he also publishes on various aspects of wider contemporary culture. He is currently working on an extended project exploring the relationship between young peoples' disciplinary literacy skills and their social and emotional development. In summer 2022, he will be a visiting fellow at the International Youth Library in Munich.

Nelly Strehlau is assistant professor in the Department of Anglophone Literature, Culture and Comparative Studies at the Institute of Literature, Faculty of Humanities, of Nicolaus Copernicus University in Toruń. Her PhD (defended in 2018) analyzed feminist and postfeminist hauntings in American television series about female lawyers. She is the author of multiple articles dedicated to American and British television, published in English and Polish. Her current research encompasses interrogation of popular culture from the perspective of affect studies and hauntology, with a special interest in women's authorship and (post)feminism.

Billy Tringali holds a master's of science in library and information science from the University of Illinois at Urbana-Champaign. He currently serves as a research and instruction librarian at Babson College. He is the founder and editor-in-chief of the *Journal of Anime and Manga Studies*, the only open-access journal dedicated to the study of anime, manga, cosplay, and their fandoms. He is a lifetime member of the Popular Culture Association. His research interests include fan participation, queer studies, the figure of the vampire in media and culture, and anime and manga studies.

Elizabeth Hays Tussey has an MFA from Northeast Ohio MFA Consortium.

Adam Vaughan, PhD, is associate lecturer in the Southampton Film School at Solent University in the United Kingdom. His research interests include the performance of identity in documentary film, queer cinema, and the political implications of personal identity in LGBTQ+ cinema. His first monograph, *Doing Documentary, Becoming Subjects: Performance and Performativity in Documentary Cinema*, is due to be published in 2022. He has contributed chapters to edited collections on twenty-first-century European documentary and the historical biopics of Derek Jarman. He is also reviews editor for the Screening Sex network.

Paul Venzo is a senior lecturer in writing and literature at Deakin University, Australia. Taking a multidisciplinary approach to questions of identity, his research covers topics such as poetry and poetics, translation, sexuality and gender, and children's literature. His writing on queer approaches to understanding subjectivity has been published widely in national and international journals and books, and he is the coeditor of the recent collection *Sexuality in Literature for Children and Young Adults*. His first children's book, on Australia's Great Southern Reef, is due for publication in 2022.

Jamie Wagman is an associate professor of gender and women's studies and history at Saint Mary's College in Indiana. She teaches courses on US histories of sexuality and feminist theory and has a PhD in American atudies. She has been a Fulbright Specialist, a NEH Summer Scholar, and an Indiana Humanities Suffrage Speakers Bureau historian.

Katherine Walker earned a PhD in sociology from UMass Amherst, an MS in sociology from Virginia Commonwealth University, and a BA in art history from the University of Virginia. Currently the director of institutional effectiveness and research at Randolph-Macon College, she previously was an associate professor at Virginia Commonwealth University and has held visiting positions at the College of William and Mary and the University of Richmond. Her published works explore incipient cultural changes, from the Internet's effect on identity to controversies over Confederate commemoration.

Printed in the USA
CPSIA information can be obtained
at www.ICGtesting.com
LVHW011941021123
762360LV00096B/632

9 781538 153901